CHURCH AND STATE IN THE MODERN AGE

Church and State
in the Modern Age

A Documentary History

Edited by
J. F. MACLEAR

New York   Oxford
OXFORD UNIVERSITY PRESS
1995

Oxford University Press

Oxford   New York
Athens   Auckland   Bangkok   Bombay
Calcutta   Cape Town   Dar es Salaam   Delhi
Florence   Hong Kong   Istanbul   Karachi
Kuala Lumpur   Madras   Madrid   Melbourne
Mexico City   Nairobi   Paris   Singapore
Taipei   Tokyo   Toronto

and associated companies in
Berlin   Ibadan

Copyright © 1995 by Oxford University Press, Inc.

Published by Oxford University Press, Inc.,
198 Madison Avenue, New York, New York 10016

Oxford is a registered trademark of Oxford University Press

Library of Congress Cataloging-in-Publication Data
Church and state in the modern age : a documentary history /
edited by J. F. Maclear.
p.   cm.   Includes bibliographical references.
ISBN 0-19-508681-3
1. Church and state—History—17th century—Sources.   2. Church
and state—History—18th century—Sources.   3. Church and state—History—
19th century—Sources.   4. Church and state—History—20th century—Sources.
5. Church and state—Europe—History—Sources.   6. Church and state—
America—History—Sources.   I. Maclear, J. F.
BR450.C48   1995
322'.1'0903—dc20   94-30051

9 8 7 6 5 4 3 2 1

Printed in the United States of America
on acid-free paper

For D. G. M. *and* A. G. M.

Preface

The aim of this book has been to present some fundamental documents in the history of church and state relations, primarily in Europe and America and chiefly since the eighteenth century. Despite the past and continuing importance of this theme, there has been a surprising lack of any collection making available the basic documents in the field. It is true, of course, that source collections for European and American history are numerous, and these commonly touch on areas of church-state conflict, though generally the subject has been a tangential one and the treatment cursory. It is also true that several collections of documents on church history exist. But these tend to concentrate on earlier periods—ancient, medieval, and the Reformation. When they have dealt with the modern age, they have seldom focused on church and state problems and they have often had a denominational orientation. This collection has an end in view different from these earlier publications. It seeks to document, as comprehensively as possible, the evolution of the post-Reformation churches—Catholic, Protestant, and Orthodox—in their relation to the simultaneously evolving modern state in areas where Christian culture has historically predominated.

I am aware that by various definitions the "modern age" may be thought to commence at any time from Renaissance to post-Napoleonic nineteenth century. But for the purposes of this collection the term (primarily) describes developments beginning toward the end of the seventeenth century. This definition may be somewhat arbitrary, but it is not entirely so. Events of the earlier seventeenth century—Huguenot commotions in France, the Thirty Years War in the Empire, the Puritan role in the English Revolution—certainly foreshadowed in significant ways the shaping of modern politics, but the problems that provoked them were essentially problems of the age of the Reformation and Counter-Reformation. By the century's end, in contrast, the secular-oriented and centralized nation-state was beginning to assume some definition, and at the same time the dogmatic relaxation associated with the approaching Enlightenment was already in evidence. I confess that somewhat inconsistently I have violated this scheme in including very early American documents. But since the "American experiment" proved to be an important and critical turn in church-state history, it seemed useful to provide the documentary bases from which the American tradition of "separation" evolved.

To the task of assembling documents I have tried to bring some limiting principles of selection. I have adhered to a preciser meaning of "document." This collection is not a book of "readings." It seeks to draw only on the official or nearly official record—public acts, declarations, or decisions of states, churches, parties, movements, and so forth. Temptations to use correspondence, memoirs, biography and autobiography, historical narrative, essays, treatises, and the like have been resisted, though often with regret. There have been a few marginal inclusions such as Gladstone's *Vatican Decrees* or Dupanloup's *September Convention,* but these were received by contemporaries as political documents or party manifestos rather than mere personal testaments. I readily agree that this criterion does not permit the assembling of the whole record, and even that possibly it may distort the real record, but to have opened the work to other literature would have broadened the task beyond all manageable limits.

I have had to eliminate some possibilities because they were either too long or, more rarely, so brief as to be of little help. Lengthy documents can sometimes be safely condensed, and I have occasionally tried to do so, but generally I discarded the document of which only a small portion could be included. Similarly, in the interests of balance, I excluded writings if issues with which they were associated were already adequately served by other selections.

Of the documents that presented legitimate claims to inclusion on these bases, I have tried to give space to those central and essential pieces to which scholarly reference is most frequently made. Generally, this has meant the inclusion of documents produced by notable conflicts and crises, of those that initiated or re-flected some new stage in church-state relations, or of those with broad and lasting historical consequences. Occasionally, I have provided a typical representative of a class of documents, such as the Württemberg Religious Edict of 1806 or the Mexi-can Constitution of 1917, but usually I have disapproved of inclusions that have seemed merely illustrative. Yet even with these criteria, I am aware of the subjec-tive character of any collection. To some there will seem to be glaring omissions and dubious inclusions. There are but few documents from Latin America and from the historic British Empire. Orthodoxy and eastern Europe have probably been slighted. Conflicts growing out of the missionary movement have been touched on only in the most obvious case of China. Conversely, the book may seem overloaded with revolutionary documents, Roman curial pronouncements, or United States Supreme Court decisions. Developments in France may seem to receive dispropor-tionate emphasis. Social Christianity or Jewish emancipation may be challenged on the ground of relevance, though I think both may be defended as essential elements of changing political orientations in the church and changing religious orientations in the state. To such objections I enter various pleas. Considerations of interest, variety, and space were all given some hearing. Two other influences helped mold the collection in a fundamental way. First, I have dwelt on, say, the American colonial experience or the French Revolution, because I judge them to be of deci-sive importance in the unfolding pattern of the relationship between religion and the state. Interpretation is unavoidable in the selection of texts, and though I have aimed generally at the detachment especially appropriate to a work of reference, this much perspective must be freely acknowledged. And second, I have assumed that inclu-sions should meet the needs of English-speaking scholars generally and should also serve the work of teachers and students of history, government, and religion in American colleges, universities, and seminaries. Hence the rather American flavor to the collection. Doubtless another editor (and certainly another editor in Europe, Latin America, or the "third world") might have produced a different selection.

Documents have been organized in general but not perfect chronological order. My preference for a source book concerned with a single nation or a limited subject or period would be an undeviating chronological arrangement. But the theme of this book, ranging as it does over a wide variety of nations, communions, and traditions, seemed to require some compromise with a more topical approach. Groupings have not always rested on the same basis. Sometimes topics have centered on a particular church, sometimes on a single nation, sometimes on a broad crisis affecting several churches and nations at the same time (as in 1848). This compromise contributes its own problems, but I believe that it may be useful in helping those less familiar with the subject to approach the material, while the specialist should not be greatly inconvenienced.

I have provided the documents with only a minimum of editorial comment. The statement preceding each selection is intended to present only what is indispensable to the understanding of the following text. Very rarely have I appended explanatory notes. Generally I have done so only where the unabridged Webster-Merriam dictionary has supplied no assistance in identification or definition. The documents themselves have been taken from available English translations whenever they could be discovered. In the case of some but not all translations the original source has also been given. Where necessary, foreign texts have been newly translated. The suggestions for reference following the document are in no sense to be viewed as a proper bibliography. For the most part, I have tried merely to suggest several readings, preferably in English, where the background to the document might be more fully explored. For the sake of more specialized scholars I have also sometimes included more focused or detailed treatments (occasionally in foreign languages), a practice most often followed in connection with less familiar documents from outside the Anglo-American tradition. The recommended readings themselves often contain extensive bibliography. A brief list of more general readings on church and state will be found at the end of the book.

In reproducing the documents I have tried to follow these rules:

1. Texts originally in English have been presented exactly as in the source, with two exceptions (a) Some practices of seventeenth- and eighteenth-century calligraphy, spelling, and printing are difficult to reproduce, and slight adjustments to more modern forms have been made. (b) Punctuation, capitalization, and excessive use of italics and commas, have sometimes been modified in some older documents to make for easier reading.

2. Translations, especially the older translations, have not been treated with the same reverence. Accordingly, capitalization, punctuation, and spelling have sometimes been slightly altered, though no effort has been made to standardize style in the various translations. Usually such change has been made only where clarity and consistency seemed to require it.

3. Where less than three-quarters of the document has been reproduced, it has been identified as "extract" or "extracts." Otherwise it is complete or substantially complete. However, conventional greetings and conclusions have been omitted in all cases. Structural repetitions such as "article" or "paragraph" have sometimes

been eliminated without indication. Footnotes, marginal notes, biblical references, and legal citations in judicial decisions have been omitted except where they seemed essential.

4. All other omissions in the reproduced text have been indicated by the ellipsis (. . .). I realize that readers are dependent on the editor's judgment in such cases, but I have tried to permit no omission that might seriously alter the sense or flavor of a sentence. Where a substantial paragraph or several paragraphs or more than twenty-five lines within a single paragraph have been dropped, a separate line of ellipsis has been used; however, no such indication appears at the beginning or end of the reproduced selection.

5. The date indicated is the date carried on the document unless another significance is stated. Dates of parliamentary acts are those of the royal assent.

For assistance in this work my debts to others are many. While I must take responsibility for translations, I have received valued assistance from faculty colleagues and other members of the university community and from Wilhelmina Richter and Allan Maclear. The courtesy of the authors, translators, and publishers who have permitted reproduction of their works has been noted in the proper places. Of the many librarians who have been helpful, I should like especially to mention those at Williams College, Harvard University, the Library of Congress, the University of Minnesota, the University of Chicago, and the Newberry Library.

Woodford, Vermont   J. F. M.
September 1994

Contents

I

CHURCH AND STATE BEFORE THE FRENCH REVOLUTION

✦ ✦ ✦ The Gallican Church in the Ancien Régime

1   Gallican Articles

March 19, 1682

Gallicanism, stressing the traditions and freedoms of the French Catholic Church at the expense of papal authority, often drew support from crown, lawyers, and many clergy. In 1682 Louis XIV (1643–1715), in controversy with Rome and encouraged by an assemblage of clergy, had Bishop Bossuet (1627–1704) draw up the Gallican Articles. They joined several strands: the Catholic particularism common in eighteenth-century Europe, the late medieval conciliar tradition, and the claims of divine-right monarchy. The articles were condemned by Alexander VIII in 1690 and withdrawn by Louis in 1693, but continued to command significant support throughout the eighteenth century.

There are many who labour to subvert the Gallican decrees and liberties which our ancestors defended with so much zeal, and their foundations which rest upon the sacred canons and the tradition of the Fathers. Nor are there wanting those who, under the pretext of these liberties, seek to derogate from the primacy of St. Peter and of the Roman Pontiffs his successors; from the obedience which all Christians owe to them, and from the majesty of the Apostolic See, in which the faith is taught and the unity of the Church is preserved. The heretics, on the other hand, omit nothing in order to represent that power by which the peace of the Church is maintained, as intolerable both to kings and to their subjects; and by such artifices estrange the souls of the simple from the communion of the Church, and therefore from Christ. With a view to remedy such evils, we, the archbishops and bishops assembled at Paris by the king's orders, representing, together with the other deputies, the Gallican Church . . . declare as follows:

1. St. Peter and his successors, vicars of Christ, and likewise the Church itself, have received from God power in things spiritual and pertaining to salvation, but not in things temporal and civil; inasmuch as the Lord says, My kingdom is not of this world; and again, Render unto Caesar the things which be Caesar's, and unto God the things which be God's. The Apostolic precept also holds, Let every soul be subject unto the higher powers, for there is no power but of God; the powers that be are ordained of God; whosoever therefore resisteth the power resisteth the ordinance of God. Consequently kings and princes are not by the law of God subject to any

ecclesiastical power, nor to the keys of the Church, with respect to their temporal government. Their subjects cannot be released from the duty of obeying them, nor absolved from the oath of allegiance; and this maxim, necessary to public tranquillity, and not less advantageous to the Church than to the State, is to be strictly maintained, as conformable to the word of God, the tradition of the Fathers, and the example of the Saints.

2. The plenitude of power in things spiritual, which resides in the Apostolic See and the successors of St. Peter, is such that at the same time the decrees of the OEcumenical Council of Constance, in its fourth and fifth sessions, approved as they are by the Holy See and the practice of the whole Church, remain in full force and perpetual obligation; and the Gallican Church does not approve the opinion of those who would depreciate the said decrees as being of doubtful authority, insufficiently approved, or restricted in their application to a time of schism.[1]

3. Hence the exercise of the Apostolic authority must be regulated by the canons enacted by the Spirit of God and consecrated by the reverence of the whole world. The ancient rules, customs, and institutions received by the realm and Church of France remain likewise inviolable; and it is for the honour and glory of the Apostolic See that such enactments, confirmed by the consent of the said See and of the churches, should be observed without deviation.

4. The Pope has the principal place in deciding questions of faith, and his decrees extend to every church and all churches; but nevertheless his judgment is not irreversible until confirmed by the consent of the Church.

These articles, expressing truths which we have received from our fathers, we have determined to transmit to all the churches of France, and to the bishops appointed by the Holy Ghost to preside over them, in order that we may all speak the same thing, and concur in the same doctrine.

Source: W. Henley Jervis, *The Gallican Church. A History of the Church of France, from the Concordat of Bologna,* A.D. *1516, to the Revolution* (London, 1872), II, 49–51. Latin text in Léon Mention, *Documents relatifs aux rapports du clergé avec la royauté de 1682 à 1705* (Paris, 1893–1903), p. 26.

SUGGESTIONS FOR BACKGROUND AND REFERENCE

G. R. Cragg, *The Church and the Age of Reason, 1648–1789* (London, 1961), pp. 17–36.
A. G. Martimort, *Le gallicanisme de Bossuet* (Paris, 1953), pp. 361–523.
W. Müller et al., *The Church in the Age of Absolutism and Enlightenment* (New York, 1981), pp. 57–70.
New Cambridge Modern History (Cambridge, 1957–1970), V, 135–39.
Source for this document, II, 23–59.

1. The decree *Sacrosancta* (April 1415), the most important legislation of the council, asserted: "This holy Council of Constance . . . declares, first that it is lawfully assembled in the Holy Spirit, that it constitutes a General Council, representing the Catholic Church, and that therefore it has its authority immediately from Christ; and that all men, of every rank and condition, including the Pope himself, is [*sic*] bound to obey it in matters concerning the Faith, the abolition of the schism, and the reformation of the Church of God in its head and its members. . . ." See Henry Bettenson (ed.), *Documents of the Christian Church* (New York, 1963), p. 135.

2 Revocation of the Edict of Nantes

October 1685[1]

Henry IV's great toleration settlement of 1598, modified in 1629, endured eighty-seven years before it was destroyed by his grandson. Before revocation government pressure and rewards produced some conversions, but the allegation in the edict that most Huguenots had become Catholic was untrue. Responsibility for the policy has been variously assigned to Mme. de Maintenon (Louis's morganatic wife), the Marquis de Louvois (war minister), and the bishops, but Louis himself welcomed the chance to demonstrate orthodoxy and achieve religious uniformity. The act does not seem to have been unpopular with Frenchmen, but the resultant persecution and Huguenot emigration adversely affected the French economy and international position.

The King Henry the Great, our grandfather of glorious memory, wishing that the peace he had procured for his subjects after the great losses they had suffered by the civil and foreign wars, should not be disturbed on account of the said R. P. R.,[2] . . . did, by his edict given at Nantes, . . . regulate the conduct to be pursued towards those of the said Religion, the places where they could exercise it, established extraordinary judges to administer justice to them, and in fine, provided by private articles for all which might be deemed necessary to maintain tranquillity in his kingdom, and to diminish the aversion between persons of both religions; in fine, that he might be in a better state to work, as he had resolved to do, to reunite to the church those who had so easily withdrawn from it. And as the intention of the King . . . was not effected on account of his sudden death and . . . from 1635 till the truce concluded in the year 1684 with the Princes of Europe, the kingdom being scarcely a moment free from agitation, it was impossible to do any thing for the advantage of religion except to diminish the number of exercises of the R.P.R. by the interdiction of such as were found to be prejudicial to the provisions of the edicts and by the suppression of the mixed Chambers, whose erection had been made only provisionally. . . .[3] We see now . . . that our pains have the end which we proposed, since the better and larger portion of our subjects of the said R.P.R. have embraced the Catholic Religion: and inasmuch as the execution of the said edict, and of all that has been ordered in favor of the said R.P.R. has been useless, we have judged that we could do nothing better to efface entirely the memory of the troubles . . . that the progress of this false religion has caused in our kingdom . . . than to revoke entirely the Edict of Nantes, and the special articles granted in consequence of it and all that has been done in favor of the said Religion.

    I. Be it known, that we . . . have by this present perpetual and irrevocable Edict

---

    1. October 17 was the probable date of the king's signature.

    2. R. P. R.: *Religion Prétendue Reformée* = the so-called Reformed religion.

    3. The Edict of Nantes had provided for "mixed chambers" of Protestant and Catholic judges, to be attached to the Parlement of Paris and provincial parlements to render decision on disputes arising from the edict.

suppressed and revoked . . . the Edict of the King our said grandfather, given at Nantes . . . and the edict given at Nismes in the month of July, 1629, declaring them null and void . . . ; and in consequence, we will . . . that all the temples of those of the said R.P.R. situated within our kingdom, countries, lands, and seigneuries, under our authority, shall be immediately destroyed.

II. We forbid our subjects of the R.P.R. from assembling again for the exercise of said Religion in any other place or private house, under any pretext whatever, even if the said exercises have been allowed by decrees of our council.

III. We forbid in like manner all lords of whatever quality from the exercise thereof in their houses and fiefs, . . . under pain, against all our subjects who shall take part in the said exercise, of confiscation of body and goods.

IV. We command all ministers of said R.P.R., who will not be converted to, and embrace the Catholic, Apostolic and Roman Religion, to leave our kingdom and lands . . . within fifteen days after the publication of our present Edict, without making any delay, nor, during the said time of fifteen days, shall they preach, exhort, or have any other exercise thereof, under penalty of the galleys.

V. We will that those said ministers, who shall be converted, shall continue to have, during their lives, and their widows after their decease, the same exemptions from taxes, and from the lodging of soldiers, which they have enjoyed whilst they were ministers, and further, we will pay to the said ministers, during their lifetime, a pension one third larger than their salaries as ministers, a moiety of which shall be allowed to their widows after their decease, as long as they remain in a state of widowhood.

VI. If any of the said ministers shall desire to become lawyers, or to take the degree of Doctor of Law, we will and intend that they shall dispense with the three years of study prescribed by our declarations; and having passed the usual examinations, and by them shown to be capable, they shall be received as doctors by paying only a half of the fees usually paid for that end at each university.

VII. We forbid private schools for the instruction of the children of the said R.P.R., and, generally, all things whatever, which can be considered a concession, whatever it may be, in favor of said Religion.

VIII. With regard to the children of persons of the said R.P.R., born hereafter, we order that they shall for the future be baptized by the parish priest. We enjoin on fathers and mothers to send them to church for that purpose, under pain of a penalty of five hundred livres; and the children afterwards shall be educated in the principles of the Catholic, Apostolic and Roman Religion of which we expressly order our judges to see to the execution.

IX. And, as a mark of our clemency towards our subjects of the said R.P.R., who may have withdrawn from our kingdom, countries and possessions, previous to the publication of our present Edict, We will and command that, in case they shall return within four months from the day of said publication, they can, and shall be allowed to enter on the possession of their property, and to enjoy the same as fully as though they had always remained here; on the contrary, the properties of those who shall not return within the said four months, . . . shall remain and be confiscated in consequence of our declaration of the 20th of August last.

X. We make very express and repeated prohibitions to all our subjects of the said R.P.R. from departing, them, their wives and children, from our said kingdom, . . . or from carrying away their properties and effects, under pain, for the men, of the galleys, and of confiscation of body and goods for the women.

IX. We will and understand that the declarations made against relapses shall be executed according to their form and tenor.

With regard to the remainder of the said R.P.R., until it shall please God to enlighten them, as he has the rest, they shall continue to dwell in the cities and places of our kingdom, . . . and may continue their business, and enjoy the possession of their property without being troubled or disturbed under pretext of the said R.P.R., on condition . . . of having no exercise, nor assembling under pretext of prayer, or of worship of said Religion, of any nature whatever, under the abovementioned penalties of body and goods.

Source: Philip Schaff, *The Progress of Religious Freedom as Shown in the History of Toleration Acts* (New York, 1889), pp. 113–115; French text in [A. J. L.] Jourdan, [F. A.] Isambert, Decrusy (eds.), *Recueil général des anciennes lois françaises, depuis l'an 420 jusqu'à la révolution de 1789* (Paris, 1822–1833), XIX, 530–534.

SUGGESTIONS FOR BACKGROUND AND REFERENCE

Cambridge Modern History (New York, 1903–1912), V, 19–26.
E. G. Leonard, *A History of Protestantism* (London, 1961), II, 414–448.
J. Queniart, *La révocation de l'Édit de Nantes: Protestants et catholiques en France de 1598 à 1685* (Paris, 1985).
W. J. Stankievicz, *Politics and Religion in Seventeenth-Century France* (Berkeley, 1960).

3   Toleration Edict (Extracts)

November 19, 1787

This edict represents the final testament of the ancien régime on religious policy. In the eighteenth century French Protestantism had revived, the laws were less rigorously applied, and the reforming minister, Turgot, accorded de facto recognition to Reformed pastors. The change in French opinion, represented and fostered by the *philosophes,* prepared the way for this cautious restoration of Huguenot civil rights, petitioned for by the Assembly of Notables, despite some determined clerical opposition. Louis XVI (1774–1793) announced the edict in November, but it was not registered by the Parlement of Paris until January 29, 1788).

Imitating our august predecessors, we shall always favor with all our power the means of instruction and persuasion which tend to bind all our subjects to the common profession of the ancient faith of our kingdom, excluding . . . all those ways of violence which are as contrary to the principles of reason and humanity as to the true spirit of Christianity. But until divine Providence . . . effects this happy revolution, our justice and our kingdom's interest do not permit us any longer to exclude from the rights of civil status those of our subjects or foreigners domiciled in our empire who do not profess the Catholic religion. . . . No longer, therefore, should we allow our laws to punish them pointlessly for the misfortune of their birth by depriving them of rights which nature continuously demands for them.

* * *

The Catholic religion . . . shall alone enjoy the rights and honors of public worship in our kingdom, while our other non-Catholic subjects . . . shall have from the law only what natural right does not permit us to refuse them, record of their births, marriages, and deaths, in order that they may enjoy, as all our other subjects, the civil benefits which result from them. For these purposes, etc.

1. In our kingdom the Catholic, Apostolic, and Roman religion alone shall enjoy public worship, and the births, marriages, and deaths of those of our subjects who profess it may in no case be recorded except by following the rites and usages of the said religion authorized by our ordinances.

Nonetheless, we permit those of our subjects who profess another religion . . . to enjoy all properties and rights which may . . . belong to them by . . . ownership or succession, and to practice their commerce, arts, crafts, and professions without their being troubled or molested under pretext of religion.

However, we except from the said professions all posts of judicature, having provision from us or our lords, municipal offices having duties of judicature, and all posts which confer the right of public instruction.

2. Accordingly, those of our subjects or foreigners domiciled in our kingdom who are not of the Catholic religion may contract marriages in the form which shall be prescribed below; we will that the said marriages may have in the civil order . . . the same effect as those contracted and celebrated in the ordinary form for our Catholic subjects.

3. Nevertheless, we do not mean that those who profess a religion different from the Catholic religion may regard themselves as forming a body, a community, or a particular society in our kingdom. Neither may they collectively frame any request, delegate any authority, take any resolution, make any purchase or perform any other act whatsoever. We strictly forbid . . . all judges, clerks, notaries, attorneys, and other public officers to answer, receive, or sign said requests, proxies, resolutions, or other documents on pain of deprivation; we forbid all our subjects to appear as agents of the said pretended communities or societies, on pain of being considered favorers and protectors of illicit assemblies and associations, and as such punished according to the rigor of the laws.

4. Nor may those who call themselves ministers or pastors of another religion than the Catholic religion take the said title in any document, wear in public attire different from that of others of the said religion, or assume any prerogative or distinction; we forbid them especially to presume to issue any marriage, birth, or death certificates, which we declare from this moment void and of no effect. . . .

5. We similarly forbid all our subjects or foreigners living or traveling in our states, of whatever religion they are, to depart from the respect owed to the Catholic religion and its holy ceremonies . . . .

6. We command them to conform to police regulations with respect to the

observation of Sunday and authorized holidays, to the end that they may neither sell nor keep open shop on the said days.

7. Moreover, we will that all persons settled in our kingdom and not professing the Catholic religion . . . be required to contribute as our other subjects and in proportion to their property and ability to the maintenance, repair, and reconstruction of parish churches, chapels, presbyteries, dwellings of secular priests or of religious employed in the celebration of divine service, and generally to all charges of this nature . . . .

8. Those of our subjects or foreigners . . . not of the Catholic religion who wish to be joined in the bond of marriage shall be required to have their bans published in the present place of domicile of each of the contracting parties . . . .

* * *

16. [The parties] shall have the right . . . to declare the said marriage before the said curés or vicars or before the first officer of justice, . . . submitting certificates of the said publishing without objection, the withdrawal of objection, if any, the copy of licenses . . . , with the consent of their fathers, mothers, guardians, or trustees . . . .

* * *

18. The said curé or vicar or said judge shall declare to the parties in the name of the law that they are joined in legitimate and indissoluble marriage and shall inscribe the said declarations on the two duplicates of the register intended for that purpose . . . .

* * *

25. The birth of children to our non-Catholic subjects married according to the forms prescribed in our present edict shall be recorded either by the certificate of baptism . . . or by the declaration that the father and two domiciled witnesses shall make before the judge of the place . . . .

* * *

27. In case of death of one of our subjects or foreigners living or traveling in our kingdom, to whom ecclesiastical burial cannot be granted, the *prévôts des marchands,*[1] mayors, aldermen, councillors, syndics, or other administrators of towns, boroughs, and villages, shall set aside in each of the said places a suitable and decent ground for interment . . . .

28. The death declaration shall be made by the two nearest relatives or neighbors of the deceased, and in their default, by our attorney . . . .

* * *

37. By our present edict, moreover, we do not mean to detract from the concessions made by us or the kings our predecessors to the Lutherans settled in Alsace, nor from those made to those of our other subjects to whom the practice of a religion

1. The mayors of Paris and Lyons bore this designation.

different from the Catholic religion may have been permitted in some provinces or towns of our kingdom, with respect to which regulations shall continue to be carried out.

Source: [A. J. L.] Jourdan, [F. A.] Isambert, Decrusy (eds.), *Recueil général des anciennes lois françaises, depuis l'an 420 jusqu'à la révolution de 1789* (Paris, 1822–1833), XXVIII, 472–482.

SUGGESTIONS FOR BACKGROUND AND REFERENCE

G. Adams, *The Huguenots and French Opinion, 1685–1787: the Enlightenment Debate on Toleration* (Waterloo, Ont., 1991), pp. 295–306.

G. Bonet-Maury, *Histoire de la liberté de conscience en France depuis l'Édit de Nantes jusqu'à juillet 1870* (Paris, 1900), pp. 36–87.

R. C. Poland, *French Protestantism, and the French Revolution, 1684–1815* (Princeton, 1957), pp. 27–82.

✦✦✦ The English Church

4 Toleration Act (Extracts)

April 18, 1689

After the Glorious Revolution in 1688, statutory relief for Dissenters, most of whom had sympathized with the movement against James II, could not be denied. The major issue in revising the Restoration religious settlement was whether to enact toleration or "comprehension," the latter being the inclusion of moderate Dissenters—practically, Presbyterians—within an enlarged state church. A Comprehension Bill failed in the Commons in 1689, but the Toleration Bill, granting limited privileges to non-Anglican but Trinitarian Protestants, passed.

FORASMUCH as some Ease to scrupulous Consciences in the Exercise of Religion may be an effectual Means to unite Their Majesties Protestant Subjects in Interest and Affection:

II. Be it enacted . . . That neither the Statute made in the three and twentieth Year of . . . Elizabeth, intituled, *An Act to retain the Queen's Majesty's Subjects in their due Obedience;* nor the Statute made in the twenty-ninth Year of the said Queen, intituled, *An Act for the more speedy and due Execution of certain Branches of the Statute made in the three and twentieth Year of the Queen's Majesty's Reign,* viz. the aforesaid Act; nor that Branch or Clause of a Statute made in the first Year of . . . the said Queen, intituled, *An Act for the Uniformity of Common Prayer* . . . ; whereby all Persons, having no lawful or reasonable Excuse to be absent, are required to resort to their Parish Church . . . ; nor the Statute made in the third

Year of . . . James the First, intituled, *An Act for the better discovering and repressing Popish Recusants;* nor that other Statute made in the same Year, intituled, *An Act to prevent and avoid Dangers which may grow by Popish Recusants;* nor any other Law . . . made against Papists or Popish Recusants, except the Statute made in the five and twentieth Year of King Charles the Second, intituled, *An Act for preventing Dangers which may happen from Popish Recusants;* and except also the Statute made in the thirtieth Year of the said King . . . intituled, *An Act for the more effectual preserving of the King's Person and Government . . . ;* shall be construed to extend to any Person . . . dissenting from the Church of England, that shall take the Oaths mentioned in a Statute made this present Parliament, intituled, *An Act for removing and preventing all Questions and Disputes concerning the assembling and sitting of this Present Parliament;* and shall make and subscribe the Declaration mentioned in a Statute made in the thirtieth Year of . . . Charles the Second, intituled, *An Act to prevent Papists from sitting in either House of Parliament;* which Oaths and Declaration the Justices of Peace at the General Sessions . . . are hereby required to tender and administer to such Persons as shall offer themselves to take, make, and subscribe the same, and thereof to keep a Register . . . .

* * *

IV. . . . all . . . Persons that shall . . . take the said Oaths, and make and subscribe the Declaration aforesaid, shall not be liable to any Pains, Penalties, or Forfeitures, mentioned in an Act made in the five and thirtieth Year of . . . Elizabeth, intituled, *An Act to retain the Queen's Majesty's Subjects in their due Obedience;* nor in an Act made in the two and twentieth Year of . . . Charles the Second, intituled, *An Act to prevent and suppress seditious Conventicles;* nor shall any of the said Persons be prosecuted in any Ecclesiastical Court, for or by reason of their non-conforming to the Church of England.

V. Provided always, . . . That if any Assembly of Persons dissenting from the Church of England shall be had in any Place for religious Worship with the Doors locked, barred, or bolted, during any Time of such meeting together, all . . . Persons, that shall come to and be at such Meeting, shall not receive any Benefit from this Law . . . .

VI. Provided always, That nothing herein contained shall be construed to exempt any of the Persons aforesaid from paying of Tythes or other parochial Duties. . . .

VII. . . . if any Person dissenting . . . shall hereafter be chosen or otherwise appointed to bear the office of High-constable, or Petit-constable, Churchwarden, Overseer of the Poor, or any other parochial or Ward Office, and such Person shall scruple to take upon him any of the said Offices in regard of the Oaths . . . , every such Person shall and may execute such Office or Employment by a sufficient Deputy . . . .

VIII. . . . no Person dissenting from the Church of England in holy Orders, or pretended holy Orders, . . . nor any Preacher or Teacher of any Congregation of Dissenting Protestants, that shall make and subscribe the Declaration aforesaid, and take the said Oaths at the General or Quarter Sessions . . . and shall . . . subscribe the Articles of Religion . . . except the thirty-fourth, thirty-fifth, and thirty-sixth and these Words of the twentieth Article, viz. "the Church hath Power to decree Rites or Ceremonies, and Authority in Controversies of Faith, and yet," shall be liable to any of the Pains or Penalties mentioned in an Act made in the seventeenth Year of . . . Charles the Second, intituled, *An Act for restraining Non-conformists from inhabiting in Corporations:* nor the Penalties mentioned in the aforesaid Act made in the two and twentieth Year of His said late Majesty's Reign, for or by reason of such Persons preaching at any Meeting for the Exercise of Religion; nor to the Penalty of one hundred Pounds mentioned in an Act made in the thirteenth and fourteenth of King Charles the Second, intituled, *An Act for the Uniformity of publick Prayers* . . . for officiating in any Congregation for the Exercise of Religion permitted and allowed by this Act.

* * *

X. And whereas some Dissenting Protestants scruple the baptizing of Infants; Be it enacted . . . That every Person in pretended holy Orders . . . or Preacher, or Teacher, that shall subscribe the aforesaid Articles of Religion, except before excepted, and also except Part of the seven and twentieth Article touching Infant Baptism, and shall take the said Oaths, and make . . . the Declaration . . . shall enjoy all the Privileges, Benefits, and Advantages, which any other Dissenting Minister . . . might have or enjoy by virtue of this Act.

* * *

XIII. And whereas there are certain other Persons, Dissenters . . . who scruple the taking of any Oath; Be it enacted . . . That every such Person shall make . . . the aforesaid Declaration, and also this Declaration of Fidelity following, viz.

"I, *A.B.,* do sincerely promise and solemnly declare before God and the World, that I will be true and faithful to King William and Queen Mary; and I do . . . detest, and renounce . . . that damnable Doctrine and Position, *That Princes excommunicated or deprived by the Pope, or any Authority of the See of Rome, may be deposed or murthered by their Subjects, or any other whatsoever.* And I do declare, that no foreign Prince . . . hath . . . any Power . . . within this realm."

And shall subscribe a Profession of their Christian Belief in these Words:

"I, *A.B.,* profess Faith in God the Father, and in Jesus Christ his Eternal Son, the true God, and in the Holy Spirit, one God blessed for evermore; and do acknowledge the Holy Scriptures of the Old and New Testament to be given by Divine Inspiration."

Which Declarations and Subscription shall be made and entered of Record at the General Quarter-Sessions . . . . And every such Person . . . shall be exempted from all the Pains and Penalties . . . .

* * *

XVI. Provided always . . . That all the Laws made . . . for the frequenting of divine Service on the Lord's Day, commonly called Sunday, shall be still in Force, and executed against all Persons that offend . . . except such Persons come to some

Congregation or Assembly of religious Worship, allowed or permitted by this Act.

XVII. Provided always . . . That neither this Act, nor any Clause, Article, or Thing herein contained, shall extend . . . to any Papist or Popish Recusant whatsoever, or any Person that shall deny in his preaching or writing the Doctrine of the Blessed Trinity, as it is declared in the aforesaid Articles of Religion.

* * *

XIX. Provided always, That no Congregation or Assembly for Religious Worship shall be permitted or allowed by this Act, until the Place of such Meeting shall be certified to the Bishop of the Diocese, or to the Archdeacon of that Archdeaconry, or to the Justices of the Peace . . . .

Source: 1 Gul. & Mar., c. 18; *The Statutes at Large, of England and of Great-Britain* (London, 1811), V, 513–519.

SUGGESTIONS FOR BACKGROUND AND REFERENCE

Cambridge Modern History (New York, 1903–1912), V, 324–337.

G. R. Cragg, *Puritanism in the Period of the Great Persecution, 1662–1688* (Cambridge, 1957).

J. Israel, N. Tyacke, O. P. Grell, *From Persecution to Toleration: the Glorious Revolution and Religion in England* (Oxford, 1991).

D. Ogg, *England in the Reigns of James II and William III* (Oxford, 1955), pp. 222–245.

A. A. Seaton, *The Theory of Toleration under the Later Stuarts* (Cambridge, 1911).

5   Lord Mansfield's Judgment (Extract)

February 4, 1767

This House of Lords decision, confirming the legality and security of Dissent, arose from a lucrative but perverted interpretation of the Corporation Act of 1661 by the City of London. Dissenters were elected as sheriffs and then fined for failing to qualify by taking the required oaths and communion in an Anglican church. Appeal from the city magistrates to the Court of Delegates and finally to the Lords elicited the speech of Lord Chief Justice Mansfield (1705–1793). (The case was Chamberlain of London against Allen Evans, Esq.)

But the case is quite altered since the Act of Toleration: it is now no crime for a man, who is within the description of that act, to say he is a dissenter; nor is it any crime for him not to take the sacrament according to the rites of the church of England: nay, the crime is, if he does it contrary to the dictates of his conscience.

If it is a crime not to take the sacrament at church, it must be a crime by some law; which must be either common or statute law, the canon law inforcing it depending wholly upon the statute law. Now the statute law is repealed as to persons capable of pleading that they are so and so qualified; and therefore the canon law is repealed with regard to those persons. If it is a crime by common law, it must be so either by usage or principle. There is no usage or custom, independent of positive law, which makes nonconformity a crime. The eternal principles of natural religion are part of the common law; the essential principles of revealed religion are part of the common law: so that any person reviling, subverting, or ridiculing them, may be prosecuted at common law. But it cannot be shewn from the principles of natural or revealed religion, that, independent of positive law, temporal punishments ought to be inflicted for mere opinions with respect to particular modes of worship.

Persecution for a sincere, though erroneous, conscience, is not to be deduced from reason or the fitness of things; it can only stand upon positive law.

It hath been said that "the Toleration Act only amounts to an exemption of Protestant Dissenters from the penalties of certain laws therein particularly mentioned, and to nothing more; that if it had been intended to bear, and to have any operation upon the Corporation Act, the Corporation Act ought to have been mentioned therein . . . ."[1] But this is much too limited and narrow a conception of the Toleration Act; which amounts consequentially to a great deal more than this; and it hath consequentially an influence and operation upon the Corporation Act in particular. The Toleration Act renders that which was illegal before, now legal; the Dissenters' way of worship is permitted and allowed by this act; it is not only exempted from punishment, but rendered innocent and lawful; it is established: it is put under the protection, and is not merely under the connivance, of the law. In case those who are appointed by law to register dissenting places of worship, refuse on any pretence to do it, we must, upon application, send a mandamus to compel them.

Now there cannot be a plainer position, than that the law protects nothing, in that very respect in which it is in the eye of the law, at the same time, a crime. Dissenters, within the description of the Toleration Act, are restored to a legal consideration and capacity; and an hundred consequences will from thence follow, which are not mentioned in the Act. For instance, previous to the Toleration Act, it was unlawful to devise any legacy for the support of dissenting congregations, or for the benefit of dissenting ministers; for the law knew no such assemblies, and no such persons; and such a devise was absolutely void, being left to what the law called superstitious purposes. But will it be said in any court in England, that such a device is not a good and valid one now? And yet there is nothing said of this in the Toleration Act. By that act the Dissenters are freed, not only from the pains and penalties of the laws therein particularly specified, but from all ecclesiastical censures, and from all penalty and punishment whatsoever on account of their nonconformity; which is allowed and protected by this act, and is therefore in the eye of the law no longer a crime. Now if the defendant may say he is a Dissenter; if the law doth not stop his mouth; if he may declare, that he hath not taken the sacrament according to the rites of the Church of England without being considered as criminal; if, I say, his mouth is not stopped by the law, he may then plead, his not having

---

1. By Exchequer Baron George Perrot, the only judge to speak against a decision in favor of the Dissenters. The Corporation Act (1661) required mayors, aldermen, and other municipal magistrates to take the oaths of allegiance and supremacy, to swear that it was unlawful to resist the king, and to take communion in the Church of England.

taken the sacrament according to the rites of the Church of England, in bar of this action. It is such a disability as doth not leave him liable to any action, or to any penalty or punishment whatsoever.

Source: The Parliamentary History of England, from the Earliest Period to the Year 1803 (London, 1813), XVI, 319–320.

SUGGESTIONS FOR BACKGROUND AND REFERENCE

R. B. Barlow, *Citizenship and Conscience: A Study of the Theory and Practice of Religious Toleration in England during the Eighteenth Century* (Philadelphia, 1963).

E. Heward, *Lord Mansfield* (Chichester, 1979).

6   Catholic Relief Act (Extracts)

June 3, 1778

Tudor-Stuart legislation against Roman Catholics, though rarely enforced in the later eighteenth century, remained law and could be exploited by unscrupulous blackmailers. This act, introduced by the Whig statesman, Sir George Savile (1726–1784), swept away some disabilities for those Catholics who repudiated the Stuarts and certain political teachings ascribed to the Catholic Church. Further disabilities were to be removed by an act of 1791.

WHEREAS it is expedient to repeal certain Provisions in an Act of the Eleventh and Twelfth Years of . . . William the Third, intituled, *An Act for the further preventing the Growth of Popery,* whereby certain Penalties and Disabilities are imposed on Persons professing the Popish Religion: . . . be it enacted . . . That so much of the said Act as relates to the apprehending, taking or prosecuting of Popish Bishops, Priests or Jesuits; and also so much of the said Act as subjects Popish Bishops, Priests or Jesuits, and Papists, or Persons professing the Popish Religion, and keeping School, or taking upon themselves the Education or Government or Boarding of Youth . . . to perpetual Imprisonment; and also so much of the said Act as disables Persons educated in the Popish Religion, or professing the same, under the Circumstances therein mentioned, to inherit or take by Descent, Devise or Limitation, in Possession, Reversion or Remainder, any Lands, Tenements or Hereditaments . . . and gives to the next of Kin, being a Protestant, a Right to have and enjoy such Lands, Tenements, and Hereditaments; and also so much of the said Act as disables Papists . . . to purchase any Manors, Lands, Profits out of Lands, Tenements, Rents, Terms or Hereditaments . . . and makes void all and singular Estates, Terms and other Interests or Profits whatsoever out of Lands . . . to or for the Use or Behoof of any such . . . Persons . . . are hereby repealed.

* * *

IV. Provided also, That nothing herein contained shall extend . . . to any Person . . . but such who shall, within . . . Six Calendar Months after the passing of this Act, or of accruing of his, her or their Title, being of the Age of Twenty one Years, or who, being under . . . Twenty one Years, shall, within Six Months after he or she shall attain the Age of Twenty one Years, or being of unsound Mind, or in Prison, or beyond the Seas, then within Six Months after such Disability removed, take and subscribe an Oath in the Words following:

"I, A.B., do sincerely promise and swear, That I will be faithful and bear true Allegiance to His Majesty King George the Third, and him will defend, to the utmost of my Power, against all Conspiracies and Attempts whatever that shall be made against his Person, Crown, or Dignity; and I will do my utmost Endeavor to disclose and make known . . . all Treasons and traiterous Conspiracies . . . ; and I do faithfully promise to maintain, support and defend . . . the Succession of the Crown in His Majesty's Family against any Person or Persons whatsoever; hereby utterly renouncing and abjuring any Obedience or Allegiance unto the Person taking upon himself the Stile and Title of Prince of Wales in the Lifetime of his Father, and who, since his Death, is said to have assumed the Stile and Title of King of Great Britain, by the Name of Charles the Third, and to any other Person claiming or pretending a Right to the Crown . . . ; and I do swear, that I do reject and detest as an unchristian and impious Position, That it is lawful to murder . . . Persons . . . under Pretence of their being Heretics; and also . . . That no Faith is to be kept with Heretics: I further . . . reject and abjure the Opinion, That Princes excommunicated by the Pope and Council, or by any Authority of the See of Rome, or by any Authority whatsoever, may be deposed or murdered by their Subjects, or any Person whatsoever; And I do declare, that I do not believe that the Pope of Rome, or any other foreign Prince, Prelate, State or Potentate hath or ought to have any temporal or civil Jurisdiction, Power, Superiority or Pre-eminence, directly or indirectly, within this Realm. And I do solemnly . . . declare, That I do make this Declaration, and every Part thereof, in the plain and ordinary Sense of the Words . . . without any Evasion, Equivocation or mental Reservation whatever, and without any Dispensation already granted by the Pope . . . ; and without thinking that I . . . can be acquitted before God or Man, or absolved of this Declaration . . . although the Pope . . . shall dispense with or annul the same, or declare that it was null or void."

Source: 18 Geo. III, c. 60; *The Statutes at Large, of England and of Great-Britain* (London, 1811), XIV, 389–391.

SUGGESTIONS FOR BACKGROUND AND REFERENCE

R. B. Barlow, *Citizenship and Conscience: A Study of the Theory and Practice of Religious Toleration in England during the Eighteenth Century* (Philadelphia, 1963), pp. 203–213.

D. Gwynn, *The Struggle for Catholic Emancipation (1750–1829)* (London, 1928), pp. 31–40.

P. Hughes, *The Catholic Question 1688–1829* (New York, 1929), pp. 142–150.

E. I. Watkin, *Roman Catholicism in England from the Reformation to 1950* (Oxford, 1957), pp. 103–151.

❖ ❖ ❖

7   Russian Imperial Decree and Religious Regulation (Extracts)

January 25, 1721, and September 16, 1721

Byzantine Caesaropapism, naturalized in Russia with Orthodoxy, was temporarily challenged by two great patriarchs of the seventeenth century, Philaret and Nikon. (For English texts of Nikon's political thought, see William Palmer, *The Patriarch and the Tsar* [London, 1871].) Peter the Great (1682–1725) decisively reasserted state control over the church, partly prompted in this by concern over clerical hostility to his reforms and Westernization. At the death of Patriarch Adrian in 1700, Peter prevented the naming of a successor, and in 1721 patriarchal powers were vested in a Holy Synod appointed by the tsar. The plan, originally drawn up by Peter's ecclesiastical adviser, Theophan Prokopovich (1681–1736), paralleled Peter's experiments with collegiate organization of secular administration. The oath for Synod members was the same as that for members of the Senate. The decree of January 25, 1721, was followed by the publication of the regulations on September 16, 1721, (earlier approved in February 1720) defining the jurisdiction of the Synod in detail. A later appendix (April 1722) dealt with monasticism, and a decree of May 1722 provided for a procurator to be attached to the Synod. This system, controlled largely by the procurator, continued to rule the Russian church in the tsar's interest until the 1917 revolution.

Decree of January 25, 1721:

[1]WE therefore, after the Example of former religious Kings, recited in the Old and New Testaments, having taken upon Us the Care of the Regulation of the Clergy, and Spiritual Order, and not seeing any better way for it than a REGULATION by a Synod, . . . appoint a Spiritual College, i.e. a Spiritual Synodical Administration, which is authoriz'd to rectify according to the Regulation here following, all Spiritual Affairs throughout the *Russian* Church. And We require all our faithful Subjects of every Rank and Condition, Spiritual and Temporal, to account this Administration powerful and authoritative, and to have recourse to it for the Direction,

---

1. This contemporary English version is the work of Thomas Consett, "Chaplain to the British Factory in Russia." The translation, though somewhat archaic in language, is literal and carefully done. (For Consett, see J. Cracraft, *For God and Peter the Great: The Works of Thomas Consett 1723–1729* [Boulder, Colo., 1982].) It may be compared to a modern translation in A. V. Muller, *The Spiritual Regulation of Peter the Great* (Seattle, 1972).

Resolution, and Determination of their most private Spiritual Affairs, and to acquiesce in its definitive Sentence, to obey its Decrees and Orders in every thing, under the Pain of a severe Punishment, for Disobedience and Contumacy, as in the other Colleges.

This College must also perfect hereafter their REGULATION with more Rules, such as the different Occasions of various Affairs shall require; but the Spiritual College must not do This without Our Consent.

WE constitute Members in this Spiritual College, as is here specify'd, one President, two Vice-Presidents, four Counsellors, four Assessors.

And because it is mention'd in the first Part of this Regulation, in the 7th and 8th Sections, That the President is liable to be try'd by his Brethren, to wit, in the same College, in Case he does any thing amiss; We therefore allow him one Vote, as the rest have.

All the Members of this College, at their entring on their Office, must take Oath, and Promise on the Holy Gospel, in the Form of Oath hereto annex'd.

* * *

The OATH *taken by the Members of the* Spiritual College.
I, undernamed, promise and swear by Almighty God, on his Holy Gospel,

THAT I . . . shall every way endeavour, in the Counsels, Judgments, and in all the Proceedings of this Spiritual, Legislative Synod, at all Times to search out the very Truth and Right, and to act in all Things conformably to the Rules or Canons prescrib'd in the *Spiritual Regulation.* And if any Canons shall hereafter be decreed by the Suffrage and Concurrence of the *Spiritual Administrators,* and the Consent of his Imperial Majesty. These I will act by, according to my Conscience, without Respect of Persons free from Enmity, Emulation, and Strife. And plainly, to be influenc'd by no kind of Fears, but that of God . . . .

I swear also, . . . That, always . . . I will apply myself to every Affair of this Legislative Synod, as to a Work of God, industriously, and with all diligence, to the utmost of my power, wholly disregarding my own Pleasure and Ease. And I will not pretend Ignorance, but if I am doubtful in any Case, I will labour diligently to come at the right Understanding and Knowledge of it, by searching into the Holy Scriptures, examining the Canons and Decrees of Councils, and taking into Consideration the unanimous Consent of the Great and Primitive Doctors.

I again swear by Almighty God, That I will . . . continue a faithful, good, and obedient Servant, and subject to my natural and true Sovereign PETER, the Great, Emperor and Sovereign of all Russia, &c. And after him, to his Imperial Majesty's august lawful Successors, who by the will and uncontroulable Power of his Imperial Majesty are appointed, or shall hereafter be appointed, and qualify'd to ascend the Throne; and to her Sovereign Majesty the Empress Catharina Alexierna. And every Right, Prerogative, or Preheminence belonging to the Supreme Sovereignty, Power and Dominion of his Imperial Majesty, which is legal, or shall hereafter be legally establish'd; to guard and defend with the best of my Skill, Power, and Ability; and, if need be, with my Life and Fortune. . . . As to any Diminution of, or Detriment and Damage to His Majesty's Interests, as soon as I am acquainted with it, I will endeavour not only to Discover it in due time, but by all Means to remedy, or put a stop to it. And when for the Service and Interest of His Majesty, or the Church, I am Privy to any Secret Affair, of whatever Kind it is which I am commanded to keep a Secret, I will keep it with perfect secresy . . . .

I acknowledge upon Oath, that the Monarch of all *Russia* himself . . . is the Supreme Judge of this Spiritual College.

I further swear by the All-seeing God, that all the Particulars I have now sworn to, I do not only explain and understand in my Mind, as I have utter'd them with my Mouth, but in the Force and Sense, whatever Force and Sense it is, which the Words here written do express to those that hear and read them.

I assert upon Oath, God . . . being Witness of my Oath, that it is no Lye. If it is a Lye, and not from my Conscience, let the same Righteous Judge be my Avenger.

In Confirmation of this my Oath, I kiss the Words and Cross of my Saviour. *Amen.*

From the First Part of the Regulation:

And lest any one should imagine this Method of Regulation improper and unnecessary, and that the Spiritual Affairs of any Community are better administer'd by a single Person, as every Bishop alone directs the Affairs of his particular District or Diocese: Here are added divers weighty Reasons, which shew, that this Synodical, perpetual Regulation, by way of a perpetual Synod or Assembly, is most perfect, and much preferable to any single Administration, especially in a Monarchical Government, such as Ours of *Russia* is.

1st, In the first Place, Truth is more clearly discover'd by the mutual Conference of an Assembly, than by a single Person. It is an old *Greek* Proverb, *Second Thoughts are wiser than the First;* How much more wisely then will the concurring Opinions of many determine, concerning any Business, than the Opinion of one Man. . . .

* * *

2dly, And as the Certainty of knowing any thing, so the Power of executing it is here greater; because the Decree of an Assembly inclines Men more to Belief and Submission, than the Authority and Command of one single Person.. . .

* * *

3dly, . . . where a College for Regulation is constituted by the Grand Monarch, and under his Direction; it is there manifest that their College is no Faction united in a secret Confederacy for their own Interest, but are Persons come together, for the common Good, by the Will of the Prince, and Consent of the rest of his Subjects.

4thly, . . . in a single Administration, Affairs are often delay'd or neglected, by reason of insuperable Difficulties attending the Administrator, or through Sickness and Indisposition; and when he dies, there is a full Stop to Business. But in an Administration by an Assemmbly; tho' one is absent, suppose the chief Person of that Body, yet others remain to act, and Business goes forward in an uninterrupted Course.

5thly, . . . in such a College there is no room for Partiality, Fraud, or Bribery, so as to join in Defence of the guilty, or in Condemnation of the innocent Party: Where should one of them favour, or be prejudic'd against the Person upon Tryal; yet a second or a third, or all the Rest are free from such Prejudice and Partiality; and there is no danger of Bribes, where Matters are not transacted arbitrarily, but upon just and weighty Reasons, and one is afraid of another, lest if he gives not good Reasons for his Opinion, he should be suspected or detected of Bribery; especially if the College consists of such Members as cannot possibly all of them enter into a secret Combination, that is, if the Persons are of a different Order and Vocation, Bishops, Archimandrites, Egumens and Protopopes. In truth, 'tis inconceiveable how such a Body should together dare to conceal a fraudulent Design, much less conspire in carrying on an act of Injustice.

6thly, . . . a College, entirely free has in itself the Spirit to pass righteous Judgement, and fears not the Resentment of the Great and Powerful, as a single Ruler usually does; because it is not so easy to form Accusations against a Number, especially against Persons of different Ranks, as against one Man.

7thly, This is an Argument of great Weight . . . , That a Nation has no Suspicion or Apprehension of Tumults and Sedition, from a Synodical Administration, which yet it has too just Cause to fear from a single Spiritual Ruler. For the ignorant Vulgar People do not consider how far the Spiritual Power is removed from, and inferior to the Regal, but in Admiration of the Splendor and Dignity of an High-Priest consider such a Ruler as a second Sovereign, equal in Power to the King himself, or above him, and imagine the Spiritual Order to be another, and better Sovereignty; . . . and if seditious Disputes of some aspiring Ecclesiasticks are set on foot, they take fire like dry stubble; their silly Minds are so biass'd with these Conceits, that in every Affair they regard not so much the Prince, as the High-Priest; and on the Report of a Quarrel between them, they blindly and distractedly adhere to, and take part with the Spiritual rather than their Civil Ruler, and impudently gather together, and raise a Tumult in his Defence, and poor miserable Men flatter themselves, that they come together for God's Service, and do not pollute their Hands, but sanctify them, when they proceed even to shedding of Blood.

They are no simple, but a crafty part of a Kingdom, that greatly rejoice in this Disposition of the People; and being disaffected to their Sovereign, and observing a Misunderstanding between him and the Priests embrace this Opportunity as most favourable to the Execution of their Malice, and under a pretence of Zeal for the Church, make no scruple to lift up their Hands against the Lords's anointed. The Commonalty are excited to this Impiety as to a Work of God, especially when the chief Pastor is puff'd up with a great Opinion of himself, and will not rest quiet; 'tis miserable to reflect what Calamities will hence ensue.

And we are not only capable of making this Conjecture in our Thoughts, . . . but it has very often been demonstrated in fact in many Countries, and is particularly manifested in the History of *Constantinople* down from the Reign of *Justinian* to this time. And the Pope effected so great things by this Means, he did not only overthrow the *Roman* Empire, and grasp a great part of it himself, but more than once has almost shaken the Power of other Dominions, and threaten'd them with the last Destruction. To say nothing of the like Contentions that have been amongst us.

In a Synodical Spiritual Administration there is no place for such a Mischief; to wit, on the President himself, the great and extravagant Applauses of the People are not therein bestow'd; nothing more than the Titles of Eminence and Respect: there are no high Opinions of him, nor can Flatterers exalt him with immoderate Commendations; for what is well done in such an Administration cannot be ascrib'd to the President alone: The Appellation itself of president is not an arrogant one, for it denotes nothing more than one that presides; for which reason he cannot think highly of himself, or others think so of him. And when the nation is farther convinc'd that this Synodical Power is establish'd by a Law of the Monarch, with the advice of his Senate, they will entirely acquiesce under it, and lay aside all hopes of having their Seditions supported by the assistance of the Spiritual Order.

8thly, This good will farther accrue to Church and State from such a Synodical Administration, that therein not only every one of the Assessors, but the President himself, . . . is subject to the Judgment of his Brethren, that is, to his College, if he is in any respect a notorious Transgressor; not as is done where one Ecclesiastick governs, for he is unwilling to be try'd by his Peers, the Bishops, and should he be compell'd hereto, the common People who consider not, and but ill distinguish what is righteous Judgment, wou'd contemn or censure such a Tryal. Hence it becomes necessary to summon a General Council against such an impious Single-Ruler; which yet cannot be done in any Country without great trouble and expence, and at this time (whilst the *Eastern* Patriarchs live under the Yoke of the Turk, and the Turks are more jealous of our Sovereign than formerly) it seems altogether impracticable.

9thly, Finally, such a Synodical Administration will be as a School of Spiritual Improvement; for each Assessor, by the Communication of many and different Decisions, Counsels and regular Reasonings (such as various Cases require) will readily be instructed in Spiritual Polity, and by daily Exercise be so well practic'd in it, as to be perfectly qualify'd to minister in the House of God, and afterward by an easy step, from being of the Number of the Collegues or Assessors, be deservedly themselves advanc'd to the Dignity of the High Priesthood. And thus, by God's assistance, Barbarism will speedily be banish'd from the Spiritual Order in Russia, and we have good reason to hope for a thorough Reformation.

From the Third Part of the Regulation:

It is now high Time to treat of Rulers that constitute the Spiritual College.

1st, THE Number of the Rulers is twelve in all, and is made up of Persons of different Ranks, as Bishops, Archimandrites, Egumens,[2] Protopopes.

Of which Number are three Bishops, and of the rest as many of each Order as are thought requisite.

2dly, Care must be had, that no Archimandrites or Protopopes be chosen into this Number that are under any Bishop who is a Member of this College; for such Archimandrite or Protopope will always observe on what Side of the Question his

---

2. Egumen = Higumenos, a title of honor for a priest-monk of distinction.

Bishop inclines, and be biass'd the same way; and so two or three Persons will become, as it were, one Man.

It ought also to be well understood, what the Spiritual College is oblig'd to do, how to act and proceed in Affairs brought before them, and what Power it has to put them in Execution.

* * *

1st, The first and principal Duty of the Spiritual College, is to examin and state the Duties of all Christians in general, and in particular of Bishops, Presbyters, and of the other Ecclesiasticks, of Monks, and of Masters and Scholars, and also of Laymen, so far as they are partakers of the Spiritual Institution, and therefore some few Duties of each of these Orders are here set down.

The Spiritual College is to take Notice, whether every one continues in his Vocation, and to admonish and punish Offenders.

Some Duties are also special, as are here subjoin'd.

2dly, To manifest and publish to all Christians of what Rank soever, that whoever makes any useful Discoveries, or finds out any thing for the better Regulation of the Church, that he be permitted to acquaint the Spiritual College herewith . . . .

3dly, If any one composes a Theological Treatise on any Subject, and does not print it till he has first presented it to the College, it is the Duty of the College to examin whether there is any thing in it contrary to orthodox Doctrine.

4thly, If a dead Body is any where shewn to be uncorrupted, or there goes a Report of an Apparition or a Miracle, the College is to enquire into the Truth of it . . . .

5thly, If any one accuses another, that he is a Schismatick or a Broacher of some new Doctrine, he must evidence this, and convict him in the Spiritual College.

6thly, Some doubtful Cases of Conscience now and then come up . . . . These and other difficult Cases are to be referr'd to the Spiritual College to be carefully examin'd and resolv'd.

7thly, As for those that are promoted to be Bishops, this Testimony must first be given of them that they are not Superstitious nor Vagrants, nor Hucksters of Saints; and Enquiry made where and how they have liv'd. Witnesses to be interrogated, whence the Man has got his Wealth, who is observ'd to be rich.

8thly, To the Judicature of the Spiritual College are referr'd the Tryals of Bishops, if there are Complaints against them. But these Things especially come under the Cognizance of this Court, viz. controverted Marriages, Cases of Divorce, Grievances laid on the Clergy, or a Monastery, by their Bishop, or Injuries done by one Bishop to another. In a word, all the Affairs which the Patriarchs had heretofore the Direction of.

9thly, The College is to enquire, who has the Care of the Church-Lands, and how he manages them; where for the Purpose, the Granaries are kept, and where the pecuniary Profits, if there are any, are reposited? Whether he thievishly embezzles and wastes the Church-Provisions? The College is then to prosecute and bring such Purloiner to condign Punishment.

10thly, When a Bishop or inferiour Clergyman suffers an Injury from some

Potent or Great Man, he is not to seek his Remedy in the Spiritual College, but in the College of Justice, or afterward, in the Senate. Only the injur'd Person must open his Case to the Spiritual College, and then the President and the whole College shall join in Succouring their suffering Brother, and detach some worthy Men out of their Body to sollicit his Cause and to ask for Justice, where it is requir'd.

11thly, Confessors or the Spiritual Fathers of Persons of Distinction, if they apprehend Difficulty in any Case, are to represent it to the Spiritual College, and the College of Justice; and both these Colleges shall judge and decide the Question.

12thly, The Spiritual College shall appoint Laws for the Distribution of Alms, because herein are great Abuses. Many base People in perfect Health, because they will not labour, are dismiss'd to go a begging, and they ramble every where without any Shame. . . .

* * *

But to sum up in brief the Mischiefs that are done by these Villains. In the publick Roads as they find their Opportunity, they break open Carriages; they are Incendiaries, and hire themselves out for Spies to Rebels and Traitors; they rail at Government, and wickedly traduce the Sovereign himself, and incline and excite the People to vilify and despise Dignities. Some pervert even the most Christian Duties, they go not to Church out of a Principle of Duty, but only to howl incessantly in the Church. And what is a Barbarity and Inhumanity that exceeds Belief; some put out the Eyes of their Children, disjoint their Hands and Arms, and dismember them, to make them really necessitous, and the greater Objects of Charity. O, a wicked Race of Men indeed! It is therefore the great Duty of the Spiritual College to consider well hereof, and to consult the best way of extirpating this Evil, to prescribe Rules for Alms-deeds; and after they have drawn up those Rules, to entreat his Imperial Majesty, that he will please to ratify and enforce them with his Royal Edict.

13thly, And it is not the least Part of their Duty to restrain Priests from Simony, and to prevent their impudent Exactions. For this Purpose it is requisite that they advise with the Senators, what Number of Houses shall be allotted to each Parish, out of the Rents of which so much is to be given to the Priest, and to the lesser Orders of the Church, as may be a Competency, according to their Ranks, and that they may not hereafter exact unreasonable Dues for Christenings, Burials, Marriages, &c.

But this our Appointment does not debar good Men from giving to the Priest what they are dispos'd to bestow upon him out of Charity and Good-Will.

Source: Tho. Consett (ed.), *The Present State and Regulations of the Church of Russia* (London, 1729), pp. 3–10, 15–22, 104–112. Russian and Latin texts in C. Tondini, *Règlement ecclésiastique de Pierre le grand* (Paris, 1874).

SUGGESTIONS FOR BACKGROUND AND REFERENCE

J. Cracraft, *The Church Reform of Peter the Great* (Stanford, 1971).

W. K. Medlin, *Moscow and East Rome. A Political Study of the Relations of Church and State in Muscovite Russia* (Geneva, 1952).

P. N. Miliukov, *Outlines of Russian Culture* (Philadelphia, 1942), I, 122–150.
W. Müller et al., *The Church in the Age of Absolutism and Enlightenment* (New York, 1981), pp. 183–213.
R. Stupperich, *Staatsgedanke und Religionspolitik Peters des Grossen* (Königsberg, 1936).
N. Zernov, "Peter the Great and the Establishment of the Russian Church," *Church Quarterly Review*, Vol. CXXV (January–March 1938), pp. 265–293.

8   *Dominus ac Redemptor* (Extracts)

July 21, 1773

Hostility to the Jesuits, upholders of the authority of Rome, was characteristic of the Catholic nationalism of the eighteenth century. It was a sentiment also shared by centralizing states and exponents of the Enlightenment. The resulting anti-Jesuit movement won its first significant victory in 1759 when the regalist minister, Pombal, expelled the order from Portugal. In France, where the attack was strengthened by Jansenist antagonism, the Jesuits were suppressed in 1764. Spain and Naples followed suit in 1767. These states then exacted suppression of the order from Clement XIV (1769–1774). Some members sought asylum in Russia and Prussia until the order was restored in the next century.

. . . almost at the very moment of its institution, there arose in the bosom of this [Jesuit] Society divers seeds of discord and dissension, not only among the companions themselves, but with other regular orders, the secular clergy, the academies, the universities, the public schools, and lastly, even with the princes of the states in which the Society was received. These dissensions . . . arose sometimes concerning the nature of their vows, the time of admission to them, the power of expulsion . . . . Sometimes concerning the absolute authority assumed by the general . . . and on matters relating to the good government and discipline of the order. Sometimes concerning different points of doctrine, concerning their schools, or such of their exemptions and privileges as the ordinaries, and other civil or ecclesiastical officers, declared to be contrary to their rights and jurisdiction. In short, accusations of the heaviest nature, and very detrimental to the peace and tranquillity of the christian republic, have been continually received against the order. Hence the origin of that infinity of appeals and protests against this society, which so many sovereigns have laid at the foot of the throne of our predecessors, Paul IV, Pius V, and Sixtus V.

* * *

. . . In vain did [the popes] endeavour, by salutary constitutions, to restore peace to the church; as well with respect to secular affairs with which the company ought not to have interfered, as with regard to the missions; which gave rise to great disputes . . . of the Company with the ordinaries, with other religious orders, about the holy places, and communities of all sorts in Europe, Africa, and America,

. . . as likewise concerning the meaning and practice of certain idolatrous ceremonies, adopted in certain places in contempt of those rites which are justly approved by the universal catholic church; and, further concerning the use and explication of certain maxims, which the Holy See has, with reason, proscribed as scandalous, and manifestly contrary to good morals . . . .[1]

* * *

Actuated by so many and important considerations, . . . we do . . . SUPPRESS AND ABOLISH THE SAID COMPANY: we deprive it of all activity whatever, of its houses, schools, colleges, hospitals, lands, and in short of every other place whatever, . . . in whatever kingdom or province they may be situated. We abrogate and annul its statutes, rules, customs, decrees, and constitutions . . . . In like manner we annul all and every its privileges . . . . We declare all, and all kind of authority of the general, the provincials, the visitors, and other superiors of the said society, to be for ever annulled and extinguished . . . . We do likewise order that the said jurisdiction and authority be transferred to the respective ordinaries . . . . [We] do hereby forbid the reception of any person to the said Society, the novitiate or habit thereof. And with regard to those who have already been admitted, our will is, that they be not permitted to make profession of the simple solemn absolute vows . . . . Farther we do will . . . that those who are now performing their novitiate, be speedily . . . sent back to their own homes.

* * *

As to such of the companions as are already promoted to holy orders, we grant them permission to quit the houses and colleges of the company, and to enter into any other regular order, already approved by the Holy See. Or otherwise we do permit them to live at large, as secular priests and clerks, always under a perfect and absolute obedience to the jurisdiction of the ordinary of the diocese, where they shall establish themselves. . . . With regard to those who have made the last vows, . . . and who, either through fear of not being able to subsist for want of a pension, or from the smallness thereof, or because they know not where to fix themselves, or on account of age, infirmities, or other grave and lawful causes, do not choose to quit the said colleges or houses, they shall be permitted to dwell therein, provided always that they exercise no ministry whatsoever in the said houses or colleges, and be entirely subject to the ordinary of the diocese . . . . And to this end a member of the regular clergy, recommendable for his prudence and sound morals, shall be chosen to preside over and govern the said houses; so that the name of the Company shall be, and is, for ever extinguished and suppressed.

Source: [House of Commons], *Report from the Select Committee Appointed to report the nature and substance of the Laws and Ordinances existing in Foreign States, respecting the Regulation of their Roman Catholic Subjects* . . . . (1816), pp. 411–412, 414, 416–418. Latin text, ibid.

1. Jesuits, whose Oriental missions policy permitted some accommodation to native culture, had been attacked for allegedly sanctioning superstitious and idolatrous customs. See *New Catholic Encyclopedia* (New York, 1967), Vol. IX, "Malabar Rites Controversy."

SUGGESTIONS FOR BACKGROUND AND REFERENCE

C. Hollis, *The Jesuits: A History* (New York, 1968), pp. 135–156.
New Cambridge Modern History (Cambridge, 1957–1970), VII, 122–126.
F. Nielsen, *The History of the Papacy in the Nineteenth Century* (London, 1908), I, 56–87.
R. R. Palmer, *Catholics and Unbelievers in Eighteenth Century France* (Princeton, 1939).
L. von Pastor, *The History of the Popes from the Close of the Middle Ages* (London, 1899–
1953), XXXVIII, 216–345.

9 Austrian Edict of Toleration (Extracts)

October 13, 1781

Probably the most earnest—and incautious—of the reforming rulers of
the Enlightenment, Emperor Joseph II (1780–1790), attempted sweeping alterations in Austrian Catholicism. Despite objections from some
Catholics at home and from Rome, "Josephinism" eventually embraced
bureaucratic control of seminaries and religious orders, secularization of
some church property, attenuation of the connection between bishops
and papacy, manipulation of bishoprics and parishes, and generally centralization of church administration under imperial control. The Toleration Edict, a product of the same rationalist perspective, granted limited
rights to Lutherans, Reformed, and Orthodox in the Hapsburg dominions. (It did not apply to non-Hapsburg parts of the Holy Roman Empire.) Full toleration had to await the Protestant Patent of 1861.

Convinced, on the one hand, of the perniciousness of all constraint of conscience
and, on the other hand, of the great profit to religion and the state which arises from
a truly Christian tolerance, We have come to the decision to permit the followers of
the Augsburg and Helvetic religions and the non-Uniate Greeks to worship privately
everywhere according to their religion . . . . The privilege of public religious worship shall be preserved to the Catholic religion alone. . . .

First: Where there are 100 families of non-Catholic subjects, they may erect a
prayer house of their own as well as a school, even if they do not all live in the
vicinity of the prayer house or of their minister, but a part of them live a few hours
distant. Those from a greater distance may go to the nearest prayer house as often as
they please, so long as it is located within the imperial-royal domains. Also ministers from these domains may visit coreligionists and assist them, as well as the sick,
with necessary instruction and comfort of body and soul. However, under strictest
accountability, they must never hinder a Catholic priest, asked for by any of the
sick, from being called in.

Unless it has already been done in another manner, We expressly order concerning the prayer house that it have no chimes, bells, steeples, or public entrance from
the street so as to simulate a church. However, in other respects they may build it of
whatever material they please. Also they are entirely free to administer their sacra-

ments . . . , to bring them to the sick in the affiliated area, and to have public funerals accompanied by their clergy.

Second: They are free to appoint their own schoolmasters, who shall be maintained by their congregations. Nonetheless, Our provincial school authority shall supervise schoolmasters concerning educational method and organization . . . .

Third: The non-Catholic inhabitants of a locality who endow and support their pastors may choose the same. But if the authorities are willing to provide support, they should then enjoy the *jus praesentandi*.[1] However, We reserve to Ourselves the confirmation in such manner that where Protestant consistoriers exist, confirmation shall be by them . . . .

* * *

Fifth: We graciously grant that jurisdiction in matters touching the religious life of non-Catholics be laid upon Our provincial political authorities who, with the assistance of some of their [the non-Catholics'] pastors and theologians, shall declare and determine according to their religious principles, without prejudice to further recourse to Our political Court Chancery.

Sixth: The issuing of declarations at marriages, which has become usual on the part of non-Catholics, concerning the education of their children in the Roman Catholic religion is to be wholly discarded in the future, because children of both sexes of a Catholic father are to be reared in the Catholic religion without question. This is to be regarded as a prerogative of the dominant religion. On the other hand, children of a Protestant father and Catholic mother shall follow them according to their sex.

Seventh: In the future non-Catholics may be admitted to the purchase of houses and property, to the freedom of towns and companies [*Bürger- und Meister-Rechte*], to academic degrees and the civil service by dispensation. They are to be held to no form of oath other than that which is agreeable to their religious principles, nor to attendance at processions or functions of the dominant religion, if they themselves do not desire it. In all selections and bestowal of employment the integrity and capability and then the Christian and moral behavior of the candidate are alone to receive consideration, without regard to any difference in religion . . . .

Source: Gustav Frank, *Das Toleranz-patent Kaiser Joseph II* (Vienna, 1882), pp. 37–40.

SUGGESTIONS FOR BACKGROUND AND REFERENCE

M. C. Goodwin, *Papal Conflict with Josephism* (New York, 1938).
New Cambridge Modern History (Cambridge, 1957–1970), VI, 290–293.
F. Nielsen, *The History of the Papacy in the Nineteenth Century* (London, 1906), I, 109–136.
C. H. O'Brien, *Ideas of Religious Toleration at the Time of Joseph II* (Philadelphia, 1969).

1. Patronage right empowering possessor to nominate qualified clergyman to ecclesiastical vacancy.

S. K. Padover, *The Revolutionary Emperor: Joseph the Second, 1741–1790* (New York, 1934).

L. von Pastor, *The History of the Popes from the Close of the Middle Ages* (London, 1899–1953), XXXIX, 421–479. Source for this document.

10   Punctation of Ems (Extracts)

August 25, 1786

Though not identical with French Gallicanism and Austrian Josephinism, German Febronianism similarly sought to loosen an area of the Catholic church from effective papal authority. In 1763 "Febronius," actually Johann Nikolaus von Hontheim, coadjutor bishop of Trier, published *The State of the Church and of the Legitimate Power of the Roman Pontiff,* in which he stressed the authority of bishops and the superiority of a general council to the pope. Though condemned by Clement XIII in 1764, Febronianism was widely adopted in Germany. Its chief political expression was the joint declaration of the three archbishops-electors of the Holy Roman Empire and the archbishop of Salzburg, signed by their deputies at Ems, and occasioned by the establishment of a papal nunciature at Munich.

Although the Pope at Rome is, and continues to be, the Head and Primate of the whole Church, and the centre of unity, holding from God the jurisdiction required for that purpose, insomuch that every Catholic is bound ever, and most respectfully, to yield to him canonical obedience, yet all other privileges and reservations, not connected with this primacy in the earlier centuries of the Christian era, but which have emanated from the later Decretals of Isidore, to the manifest prejudice of the Bishops, cannot, now that the forgery and fallacy of them is sufficiently proved, and generally acknowledged, be drawn within the limits of that jurisdiction, as they must be classed with the encroachments of the Roman Court. The Bishops are then justified in reassuming, under the powerful protection of his Imperial Majesty, the exercise of the authority granted to them by God, more particularly, as no remonstrances, addressed to the Papal See, relative to this subject, have been of any avail.

The leading points of this question are exhibited in the following propositions, and in the direct inferences deduced from them:—

I. CHRIST, the founder of our Holy Church, has granted to the Apostles, and to their successors the Bishops, an unlimited power to "bind and to loose," in all cases, where either the necessity, or the good of their Churches, or of the faithful belonging to them, may require it.

(a) Wherefore, agreeably to the nature of the original constitution of the Church, . . . all persons, without distinction, living within the dioceses of the Bishops, are placed under their orders, as to matters of religion, both internal and external.

(b) Hence diocesans, in cases of appeal, shall not be permitted to pass over their immediate ecclesiastical superiors with a view of applying to the Court of Rome. However, in such cases as are specified by the Canon Law, they are not prevented from appealing to the higher Ecclesiastical Authorities, according to the degrees of the Hierarchical Constitution.

(c) Exemptions being at variance with the discharge of the episcopal office, shall be no more allowed; yet this prohibition does not apply to those bodies and individuals, whose exemption has been confirmed by Imperial Charter . . . .

(d) No Members of Religious Orders shall be allowed to receive of their Generals . . . or Chapters-General, or of other superiors residing out of Germany, (from every connection with whom they are hereby entirely absolved,) any orders or replies, or to attend the general assemblies, or to send thither any pecuniary contributions, under any pretext whatever.

II. It is lawful for every Bishop, in virtue of the power "of binding and loosing," which he holds from God, to enact laws, and to dispense with them upon sufficient grounds. He alone is acquainted with the wants of his flock, and with the proper means for relieving them, and ought, therefore, to possess the power of granting to the faithful, for a time specified, or as long as it may appear expedient, some indulgence, both as to the particular, and the general Church Laws.

(a) Wherefore he is competent to grant dispensations . . . with respect to the general prescriptions relating to abstinence . . . .

(b) As also, to remove those obstacles to marriages, for which the Holy See hitherto used to grant general powers of dispensation . . . .

* * *

(e) They shall also absolve the conventual clergy from their solemn vows, where sufficient canonical reasons shall appear for it . . . .

* * *

IV. Accordingly,

(a) No further application shall be made to the Court of Rome for what are termed *facultates quinquennales,*[1] but it shall be competent to Bishops to grant dispensations, whenever any canonical grounds appear for it . . . . All dispensations obtained abroad, shall be null and void.

(b) No bulls, briefs, or other ordinances of the Pope, shall be binding on Bishops, unless the latter signify their formal assent.

(c) Without such assent, no declarations, replies, or orders from Rome whatsoever, shall be valid in Germany.

(d) All Nunciatures to cease totally. Nuncios can be received only in the character of Envoys from the Pope . . . .

* * *

VIII. To do away entirely [with] the transmission of ecclesiastical benefices by inheritance, it is ordered, that

1. Powers to perform certain canonical functions, granted by the Holy See to bishops for a term of five years.

(a) The *resignationes in favorem*,[2] whether real or fictitious, shall be inadmissible every where throughout Germany, . . . whether given in to the Court of Rome, or to the Bishops. They must be made without any reservation of the party resigning, so as to enable the Bishop, or whoever has the gift of it, freely to bestow the benefice on whom he pleases.

* * *

XIII. Finally, in order to exclude from the German Churches all foreign candidates, . . . all who are not natives of Germany are incapable of obtaining a benefice, unless they have previously been naturalized; still, however, this latter exception cannot derogate from any statutes that may have been enacted by some Chapters on this subject.

XIV. The dispensations of the Court of Rome can never affect any statutes of German Churches.

* * *

XX. The oath required from Bishops, devised by Pope Gregory VII, . . . which enforces the duties belonging to a vassal, rather than canonical obedience, ought no longer to be taken . . . . Another oath is, therefore, to be substituted in its stead, so worded as not to trench either on the Pope's primacy, or on the rights of the Bishops.

XXI. The hardships which the Bishopricks of Germany suffer through the Annates and the Pall-money, may be inferred not only from the incredible sums of money hitherto sent . . . to Rome, but from the debts thereby contracted and accumulated in many Bishoprics. . . . Now, though the German Nation will have no objection to pay a compensation for the Annates and *Pallium*-money, . . . yet it cannot but wish . . . that the said compensation may be . . . fixed, according to the estimated revenues of the Archbishopricks and Bishopricks, within two years, either at a National Council, or . . . by His Imperial Majesty and the whole Empire. If . . . the Court of Rome should refuse either the confirmation . . . or the *Pallium,* the German Archbishops and Bishops will be sure of finding in the ancient discipline of the Church such remedies as shall preserve them, on the one hand, from trespassing on the reverence and subordination due to the See of Rome, and, on the other, enable them tranquilly to discharge their . . . offices . . . .

XXII. All matters which . . . are referrible to the Ecclesiastical Jurisdiction, must

(a) Be tried, in the first place, in the Ecclesiastical Court of each particular Diocese; and if the cause is to be removed to a higher tribunal, an appeal shall lie from the Bishop to the Metropolitan Court.

(b) The Papal Nuncios must not interfere in any cause . . . .

* * *

2. Resignation with the stipulation that the relinquished benefice be conferred on another specified person.

(d) Should any appeal be brought . . . to . . . Rome, the latter shall appoint *Judices in partibus,*[3] and those [shall be] natives . . . .

(e) This object will be accomplished yet more effectually, if every Archbishop, with the concurrence of his Suffragans, establish in his respective diocese, a Synodal Court of Justice, and remove thither all causes of appeal. . . .

XXIII. If the Archbishops and Bishops . . . should . . . be again reinstated in those rights which belong to them . . . they will then . . . be capable . . . to proceed speedily to the amendment of the Church discipline . . . .

For the rest, as the *Concordatum Aschaffenburgense* has . . . been considered as one of the greatest grievances of the German Nation; . . . the German Nation most earnestly . . . express an expectation, that His Imperial Majesty . . . will be pleased to apply to . . . Rome, in order . . . to bring about, within two years at farthest, a National Council . . . .[4]

Source: [House of Commons], *Report from the Select Committee Appointed to report the nature and substance of the Laws and Ordinances existing in Foreign States, respecting the Regulation of their Roman Catholic Subjects* . . . . (1818), pp. 150–154. German text (summary) in C. Mirbt, *Quellen zur Geschichte des Papsttums und des römischen Katholizismus* (Tübingen, 1901), pp. 326–328.

SUGGESTIONS FOR BACKGROUND AND REFERENCE

J. Kuntziger, *Fébronius et le fébronianisme* (Brussels, 1889).

W. Müller et al., *The Church in the Age of Absolutism and Enlightenment* (New York, 1981), pp. 453–469.

New Catholic Encyclopedia (New York, 1967), Vol. V, "Febronianism."

New Schaff-Herzog Encyclopedia of Religious Knowledge (Grand Rapids, Mich., 1952), Vol. IV, "Congress of Ems."

F. Nielsen, *The History of the Papacy in the Nineteenth Century* (London, 1906), I, 109–136.

L. von Pastor, *The History of the Popes from the Close of the Middle Ages* (London, 1899–1953), XL, 43–65.

11   Prussian Religious Edict of 1788 (Extracts)

July 19, 1788

Though his scepticism inspired religious toleration in Prussia, Frederick II (1740–1786) maintained and clarified state control over most external

---

3. Appeals to the Holy See, if not decided in Rome itself, were heard by authorized judges in the country of origin.

4. At Aschaffenburg, 1447, Frederick III and a party of the German princes rendered formal recognition to Pope Nicholas V during the struggle between the papacy and the Council of Basel (1431–1449). The agreement, confirmed in Vienna, 1448, marked the victory of the papacy over the conciliar movement in Germany. An earlier section of this Punctation (VII) enlarged on this conciliar contest.

acts of religion. (The details were codified in the *Landrecht*, II, xi, published in 1794 but earlier compiled by Frederick's jurists.) His successor, Frederick William II (1786–1797), distrusted the rationalism appearing in the church and universities. Consequently, the royal favorite, Johann Christoph von Wöllner (1732–1800), without consulting the church, drew up this decree providing for strict inquisition, discipline, and censorship. The purge was not efficiently conducted, but the edict demonstrated the Erastianism of the Prussian system.

1. We order, enjoin, and command, that all the three principal persuasions of the Christian Religion, namely the Reformed, the Lutheran, and the Roman Catholic, be preserved, maintained, and protected in all the Provinces of our dominions, according to the Constitution which they have till now had . . . .

2. But on the other hand, we will that the ancient toleration which has long distinguished the Prussian dominions, in respect of other religious sects and parties, be preserved as before; and that at no time shall it be suffered to constrain, in any manner, the consciences of our subjects, whilst each of them peaceably fulfils, as a good citizen, his duties to the State, keeps to himself his private opinions, and takes strict care not to disseminate them, to persuade others of them, and to inspire them with errors or uncertainties relative to their faith; for, as to every man belongs the care of his own salvation, it is necessary that in this matter he exercises entire liberty; and, the cares of a Christian Prince . . . ought to be confined to causing the people to be instructed by the teachers and preachers in the purity and incorruptibility of true Christianity . . . .

. . . But our Ecclesiastical Department must hereafter take care, that there be not held under the name of a religious assembly other meetings hurtful to the Christian Religion and to the State; means which might be adopted by new teachers and other dangerous men to gain adherents and make proselytes, which would be a great abuse of toleration.

3. We expressly forbid . . . every species of proselytism; and we desire that no Ecclesiastics or other persons of different religious sects shall . . . force, engage, or persuade, in any manner whatsoever, those of a different persuasion to adopt and receive their particular principles or opinions on Religion . . . .

* * *

6. We order . . . that, in the Reformed as well as in the Lutheran Church, the old liturgies and ecclesiastical ordinances shall be preserved; only we consent . . . that . . . the language be changed of those ordinances made at the time when the German language was not yet formed . . . . We are also desirous that some ancient usages and inessential ceremonies be abolished; which we leave to the disposition of our Ecclesiastical Department . . . .

7. . . . we have observed with regret that several Clergy of the Protestant Communion permit themselves a liberty altogether unbounded . . . ; that they deny several fundamental points and truths of the Christian Religion in general, and in their exhortations adopt a new fangled stile, entirely different from the spirit of true

Christianity . . . . They blush not to renew the miserable errors of Socinians, Deists, and Naturalists, long ago refuted, and to diffuse them among the people with as much boldness as imprudence under the name of Philosophy . . . . They blush not to diminish daily the authority of the Bible as the revealed Word of God . . . ; to give forced explanations of it, or even to reject it entirely . . . . [We] consider it one of the first duties of a Christian Prince to protect in his dominions the Christian Religion . . . ; to maintain it there in all its ancient and primitive dignity . . . ; and in order that the poor people may not be made the sport of the illusions of new-fangled teachers, and that millions of our good subjects may not be deprived of the tranquillity of their life and their consolation on a death-bed . . . .

8. We therefore order . . . all Ecclesiasticks, Preachers, and Schoolmasters of the Protestant Religion, under pain of deprivation, or even a more severe punishment . . . , that in future they be not guilty of the errors indicated in the 7th article, or others of the same species, by disseminating them in the exercise of their functions, or in any other manner public or private. . . . [Still] less shall we suffer that . . . each Ecclesiastic shall act according to his own ideas and pleasure, and that he shall be at liberty to instruct the people in such or such a manner in the fundamental truths of Christianity; to adopt or reject them at their discretion. . . . On the contrary, it is necessary that there should be a model, a rule, and a regulation [*Richtschnur, norma und regel*] firmly established, according to which the people may be faithfully . . . instructed by the Teachers in matters of faith; and this rule has been till now . . . the Christian Religion, according to the three principal persuasions . . . ; and this general rule . . . we are not disposed to allow to be changed in the minutest article by these pretended apostles of Philosophy [*Aufklärer*], after their disordered ideas. Every man who teaches Christianity . . . ought . . . to teach that which bears the fixed and positive doctrine of the sect of his religion . . . . If he teach any other thing, he is already punishable by the civil laws, and he cannot properly longer hold his office. [. . . In] other respects we freely grant to the Ecclesiastics . . . a liberty of conscience equal to that of our other subjects, and are very far from constraining them in the smallest degree with regard to their internal conviction. Thus the Minister of the Christian Religion who . . . . is convinced of things contrary to those prescribed . . . ought to take care lest this conviction lead him into risks and dangers. . . . [He] ought to resign a charge which . . . he feels himself incapable of fulfilling . . . . However, . . . we are willing even to suffer the Ecclesiastics who may be known to be unfortunately more or less infected by the errors expressed in article 7 to remain quiet in their charges; only in the instructions they give their flock, the rules of doctrine must always be kept sacred and inviolable. . . .

9. In consequence we order . . . our Ecclesiastical Department . . . to have constantly an attentive eye over all the Ecclesiastics . . . in order that all those who teach in the churches and schools do their duty . . . .

10. . . . we order . . . that the Livings and the Chairs of Theology in our Universities, as well as the places in the Schools, be filled by persons who have given no reason to doubt of their being perfectly convinced of what they ought to teach publicly; but all the other candidates, who manifest other principles, ought to

be excluded without delay, an exclusion of which we give the liberty and power
to the said Ministers.

* * *

13. . . . . We shall . . . pay particular attention . . . to the well-being of the
Ministers and Preachers who have fulfilled their duties; and . . . we hereby renew
the edict . . . exempting their sons from military service; and we ordain
that . . . all the sons of Ecclesiastics . . . as well as the sons of the Public Instructors of Youth . . . be comprised in this exemption, if they are devoted to the
sciences, the arts, drawing, or commerce; but those who prefer a trade, or any other
profession, or who have studied without success shall be excluded from the privilege; and in that respect we shall give the necessary orders to our regiments for their
service . . . .

Source: L. P. Ségur, *History of the Principal Events of the Reign of Frederic William II*
(London, 1801), I, 437–450. German text in *Publicationen aus den königlichen Preussischen Staatsarchiven,* LIII, 250–257.

SUGGESTIONS FOR BACKGROUND AND REFERENCE

Cambridge Modern History (New York, 1903–1912), VI, 702–728.
G. S. Ford, "Wöllner and the Prussian Religious Edict of 1788," *American Historical
Review,* Vol. XV, No. 2 (January 1910), pp. 264–280, and No. 3 (April 1910),
pp. 509–525.
F. H. Geffcken, *Church and State* (London, 1877), II, 23–33.
K. D. Macmillan, *Protestantism in Germany* (Princeton, 1917), pp. 148–163.
L. Tümpel, *Die Entstehung des brandenburgisch-preussischen Einheitsstaates im Zeitalter
des Absolutismus, 1609–1806* (Berlin, 1915), pp. 223–239.

✦ ✦ ✦ The American Experiment

12 Early Virginia Legislation

1606–1643

Until the Revolution, the colonies of the South were all to maintain
Anglicanism as a state religion. The Virginia church, earliest and strongest of these southern Establishments, was organized as a matter of course
by the first authorities, who, unlike some later English settlers, had
conventional English views of church-state relations. Religion did not
dominate the Virginia enterprise as it did the New England colonies and
Pennsylvania, but a religious concern was evident in the decrees of the
London Company, led by the Puritan sympathizer, Sir Edwin Sandys,

and in the piety of the early settlers. The Puritan note was striking in "Dale's Laws." These were brought to Virginia by Lieutenant Governor Sir Thomas Gates in 1610 and subsequently confirmed by Sir Thomas Dale (d. 1619), who ruled in the summer of 1611 and again from 1614 to 1616. Yet express statutory foundation for the Establishment was enacted only after the colony passed from the London Company to the crown in 1624, with an accompanying eclipse of the Puritan element and a growing stress on Anglican conformity. The vestry, destined to have a large place in southern Anglicanism, was legally provided for in 1643, and perhaps earlier. Five pieces of this early Virginia legislation are reproduced below.

A. James I's Articles, Instructions and Orders, November 20, 1606:

. . . wee doe specially ordaine, charge, and require, the said presidents and councells, and the ministers of the said several colonies respectively, . . . that they, with all diligence, care, and respect, doe provide, that the true word, and service of God and Christian faith be preached, planted, and used, not only within every of the said several colonies, and plantations, but alsoe as much as they may amongst the salvage people which doe or shall adjoine unto them, or border upon them, according to the doctrine, rights, and religion now professed and established within our realme of England, and that they shall not suffer any person . . . to withdrawe any of the subjects or people inhabiting . . . any of the said several colonies and plantations from the same, or from their due allegiance, unto us, . . . as their immediate soveraigne under God . . . .

* * *

. . . Furthermore, . . . wee doe hereby . . . ordaine, that every person . . . shall from time to time well entreate those salvages in those parts, and use all good meanes to draw the salvages and heathen people . . . to the true service and knowledge of God, and that all just, kind and charitable courses, shall be holden with such of them as shall conforme themselves to any good and sociable traffique and dealing with the subjects of us, . . . whereby they may be the sooner drawne to the true knowledge of God . . . .

B. Dale's Laws, May 24, 1610:

1. First since we owe our highest and supreme duty . . . to him, from whom all power and authoritie is derived, . . . the King of Kings, the commaunder of commaunders, and Lord of Hostes, I do strictly commaund . . . all Captaines and Officers, of what qualitie or nature soever, whether commanders in the field, or in . . . townes, . . . or fortresses, to have a care that the Almighty God bee duly and daily served, and that they call upon their people to heare Sermons, as that also they diligently frequent Morning and Evening praier themselves by their owne

examplar and daily life, and dutie herein, encouraging others thereunto, and that such, who shall often and wilfully absent themselves, be duly punished according to the martiall law in that case provided.

2. That no man speak impiously or maliciously, against the holy and blessed Trinitie, or any of the three persons, that is to say, against God the Father, God the Son, and God the holy Ghost, or against the knowne Articles of the Christian faith, upon paine of death.

3. That no man blaspheme Gods holy name upon paine of death, or use unlawful oathes, taking the name of God in vaine, curse, or banne, upon paine of severe punishment for the first offense so committed, and for the second, to have a bodkin thrust through his tongue, and . . . for the third time so offending, he shall be brought to a martiall court, and there receive censure of death . . . .

* * *

5. No man shall speake any word, or do any act, which may tend to the derision, or despight of Gods holy word upon paine of death: Nor shall any man unworthily demeane himselfe unto any Preacher, or Minister of the same, but generally hold them in all reverent regard, and dutiful intreatie, otherwise he the offender shall openly be whipt three times, and ask publike forgivenesse in the assembly of the congregation three several Saboth daies.

6. Everie man and woman duly twice a day upon the first towling of the Bell shall upon the working daies repaire unto the Church, to hear divine Service upon pain of losing his or her dayes allowance for the first omission, for the second to be whipt, and for the third to be condemned to the Gallies for six Moneths. Likewise no man or woman shall dare to violate or breake the Sabboth by any gaming, publique or private abroad, or at home, but duly sanctifie and observe the same, both himselfe and his familie, by preparing themselves at home with private prayer, that they may be the better fitted for the publique, according to the commandementes of God, and the orders of our Church, as also every man and woman shall repaire in the morning to the divine service, and Sermons preached upon the Saboth day, and in the afternoon to divine service, and Catechising, upon paine for the first fault to lose their provision, and allowance for the whole weeke following, for the second to lose the said allowance, and also to be whipt, and for the third to suffer death.

7. All Preachers or Ministers within this our Colonie, or Colonies, shall in the Forts, where they are resident, after divine Service, duly preach every Sabbath day in the forenoone, and Catechise in the afternoone, and weekely say the divine service, twice every day, and preach every Wednesday, likewise every Minister where he is resident . . . shall chuse unto him, foure of the most religious and better disposed as well to informe of the abuses and neglects of the people in their duties, and service to God, as also to the due reparation, and keeping of the Church handsome, and fitted with all reverent observances thereunto belonging: likewise every Minister shall keepe a faithful and true Record, or Church Booke, of all Christnings, Marriages, and deaths . . . .

* * *

10. No man shall bee found guilty of Sacriledge, which is a Trespasse as well committed in violating and abusing any sacred ministry, duty or office of the Church, irreverently, or prophanely, as by beeing a Church robber, to filch, steale or carry away any thing out of the Church appertaining thereunto, or unto any holy, and consecrated place, to the divine Service of God, which no man should doe upon paine of death . . . .

* * *

33. There is not one man nor woman in this Colonie now present, or hereafter to arrive, but shall give up an account of his and their faith, and religion, and repair unto the Minister, that by his conference with them, hee may understand, and gather, whether heretofore they have beene sufficiently instructed, and catechised in the principles and grounds of Religion, whose weaknesse and ignorance herein, the Minister finding, and advising them in all love and charitie, to repaire often unto him, to receive therein a greater measure of knowledge, if they shal refuse so to repaire unto him, and he the Minister give notice thereof unto the Governour, . . . the Governour shall cause the offender for this first time of refusall to be whipt, for the second time to be whipt twice, and to acknowledge his fault upon the Saboth day, in the assembly of the congregation, and for the third time to be whipt every day until he hath made the same acknowledgement, and asked forgiveness for the same, and shall repaire unto the Minister, to be further instructed . . . .

C. An Act of March 1624:

1. THAT there shall be in every plantation, where the people use to meete for the worship of God, a house or roome sequestred for that purpose, and not to be for any temporal use whatsoever, and a place empaled in, sequestered only to the buryal of the dead.

2. That whosoever shall absent himselfe from divine service any Sunday without an allowable excuse shall forfeite a pound of tobacco, and he that absenteth himselfe a month shall forfeit 50lb. of tobacco.

3. That there be an uniformity in our church as neere as may be to the canons in England; both in substance and circumstance, and that all persons yeild readie obedience unto them under paine of censure.

4. That the 22d of March be yeerly solemnized as holliday,[1] and all other hollidays (except when they fall two together) betwixt the feast of the annuntiation of the blessed virgin and St. Michael the archangell, then only the first to be observed by reason of our necessities.

5. That no minister be absent from his church above two months in all the yeare upon penalty of forfeiting halfe his means, and whosoever shall absent above fowre months in the year shall forfeit his whole means and cure.

6. That whosoever shall disparage a minister without bringing sufficient proofe to justify his reports whereby the mindes of his parishioners may be alienated from

---

1. Commemorating the colony's escape from total extirpation by the Indians, March 22, 1622.

him, and his ministry prove the less effectual by their prejudication, shall not only pay 500lb. waight of tobacco but also aske the minister so wronged forgiveness publickly in the congregation.

7. That no man dispose of any of his tobacco before the minister be satisfied, upon pain of forfeiture double his part of the minister's means, and one man of every plantation to collect his means out of the first and best tobacco and corn.

D. An Act of March 1630:

IT is ordered, That all ministers residing and beeing, or who hereafter shall reside and bee within this colony, shall conforme themselves in all thinges according to the cannons of the church of England. And if there shall bee any that, after notice given, shall refuse for to conforme himselfe, hee shall undergoe such censure, as by the said cannons in such cases is provided for such delinquent. And that all acts formerly made concerning ministers shall stand in force, and bee duly observed and kept.

E. An Act of March 2, 1643:

That there be a vestrie held in each parish, for the makeing of the leavies and assessments for such uses as are requisite & necessary for the repairing of the churches, &c. and that there be yearly chosen two or more churchwardens in every parish.

Itt: That the most sufficient and selected men be chosen and joyned to the minister and churchwardens to be of that Vestrie.

Itt: That there be a yearly meeting of the ministers & churchwardens before the comander & com'rs. of every county court in nature of a visitation according to the orders & constitutions of the church of England, which is there usually held every yeare after Christma's.

Itt: That there be an oath administered to the churchwardens that they deliver in a true presentment in writing of such misdemeanors as to their knowledge have been comitted the year before, whilst they have been churchwardens, namely, swearing, prophaning God's name, and his holy Sabboths, abuseing his holy word and commandments, contemning his holy sacraments . . . .

* * *

It is also enacted & confirmed, by the authority aforesaid that the vestrie of evrie parish with the allowance of the commander & com'rs. of the county living & resideing within the said parish, or the vestrie alone in case of their non residence shall from henceforward have power, to elect and make choyce of their ministers, And he or they so elected by the commander and comr's. or by the vestrie in case of non residence as aforesaid to be recommended and presented to the said comander and com'rs. or vestrie alone, to the Governour & so by him admitted, Provided that it shall be lawfull for the Gov'r. for the time being to elect and admit such a minister as he shall allow of in James-Citty parish, And in any parish where the Governour & his successors shall have a plantation provided he or they enjoy not that priviledge but in one parish where he or they have such a plantation, And upon the neglect or misbecomeing behaviour of the ministers or any of them, compl't. thereof being made by the vestrie, The Governour & Council are requested so to proceed against such minister or ministers by suspension or other punishment as they shall think fitt & the offence require. Removeall of such ministers to be left to the Grand Assembly.

Source: A. William W. Hening, *The Statutes at Large; Being a Collection of All the Laws of Virginia from the First Session of the Legislature in the Year 1619* (New York, 1823), I, 68–69; B. Peter Force (ed.), *Tracts and Other Papers* (Washington, D.C., 1844), III, No. 2, 9–19; C. Hening, *Statutes,* I, 122–124; D. ibid., 149; E. ibid., 240–242.

SUGGESTIONS FOR BACKGROUND AND REFERENCE

G. M. Brydon, *Virginia's Mother Church* (Richmond, Va., 1947–1952), Vol. I.

E. C. Chorley, "The Planting of the Church in Virginia," *William and Mary Quarterly,* 2d Ser., Vol. X, No. 3 (July 1930), pp. 191–213.

P. Miller, "The Religious Impulse in the Founding of Virginia," *William and Mary Quarterly,* 3d Ser., Vol. V, No. 4 (October 1948), pp. 492–522.

W. H. Seiler, "Church of England as the Established Church in Seventeenth-Century Virginia," *Journal of Southern History,* Vol. XV, No. 4 (November 1949), pp. 478–508.

13   Early Massachusetts Legislation

1629–1647

The three New England colonies of Massachusetts, Connecticut, and New Hampshire maintained Congregational Establishments, lasting in the case of Massachusetts until 1833, but these were different in kind from the southern state churches. The original settlers of Massachusetts arrived with a complex but well-developed theory of proper church-state relations that differed from prevailing conceptions, both Anglican and Reformed. Like all Puritans, they decried the existing English territorial Establishment as Erastian and unscriptural. As Congregationalists, they also rejected a Presbyterian state church, which, they feared, gave spiritual powers to the unconverted. In New England itself they vigorously condemned radical separation of church and state when Roger Williams attempted to promote it. Rather, they taught that the church, which was limited to professing and practicing saints, and the state were equal and separate administrations of the same Christian community, each with its own proper authority and directed toward mutual support rather than competition. Accordingly, they expected government to uphold true and suppress false religion. In practice they provided for compulsory attendance at worship (even for the unregenerate), financial support of churches, official intolerance, and general government watchfulness over and regulation of the entire ecclesiastical system. Since the reprobate might not be entrusted with political power, government was placed in the hands of church members, though there might be popular choice within that limitation. Magistracy, founded to promote obedience to the divine will, sought guidance from scripture. Yet ministers and magistrates, while generally in harmony, jealously maintained the distinction between the civil and ecclesiastical spheres and the rights of each. No comprehensive statute established the Massachusetts system. Following are seven short but basic pieces of legislation.

A. Massachusetts Bay Company Provision for Ministry and Churches, October 15, 1629:

That the charge of the ministers now there [New England], or that shall hereafter goe to resyde there, as also the charge of building convenyent churches, and all other publique works vpon the plantacion, bee, in like mann[er] indifferently borne, the one halfe by the Companyes ioynt stock for the said tearme of 7 yeares, and the other halfe by the planters.

B. An Act of May 18, 1631:

. . . & to the end the body of the commons may be preserued of honest & good men, it was likewise ordered and agreed that for time to come noe man shalbe admitted to the freedome of this body polliticke, but such as are members of some of the churches within the lymitts of the same.

C. An Act of March 4, 1635:[1]

Whereas complainte hath bene made to this Court that dyvers persons within this jurisdiccion doe vsually absent themselues from church meeteings vpon the Lords day, power is therefore giuen to any two Assistants to heare & sensure, either by ffyne or imprisonment, (att their discrecion) all misdemeanors of that kinde committed by any inhabitant within this jurisdiccion, provided they exceede not the ffine of v s[hillings] for one offence.

D. An Act of March 3, 1636:

Forasmuch as it hath bene found by sad experience, that much trouble and disturbance hath happened both to the church & civill state by the officers & members of some churches, which have bene gathered within the limitts of this jurisdiccion in a vndue manner, & not with such publique approbacion as were meete, it is therefore ordered that all persons are to take notice that this Court doeth not, nor will hereafter, approue of any such companyes of men as shall henceforthe ioyne in any pretended way of church fellowshipp, without they shall first acquainte the magis-

---

1. To permit easier reading, the superscript abbreviations in the documents, common in seventeenth-century calligraphy, have been spelled out and absorbed in the text.

trates, & the elders of the greater parte of the churches in this jurisdiccion, with their intencions, & have their approbacion herein. And ffurther, it is ordered, that noe person, being a member of any churche which shall hereafter be gathered without the approbacion of the magistrates, & the greater parte of the said churches, shalbe admitted to the ffreedome of this commonwealthe.

E. An Act of September 6, 1638:

This Court takeing into consideration the necessity of an equall contribution to all common charges in townes, & observing that the cheife occation of the defect hearin ariseth from hence, that many of those who are not freemen, nor members of any church, do take advantage thereby to withdraw their helpe in such voluntary contributions as are in vse,—

It is therefore hearby declared, that every inhabitant in any towne is lyable to contribute to all charges, both in church & common welth, whereof hee doth or may receive benefit; & withall it is also ordered, that every such inhabitant who shall not volentarily contribute, proportionably to his ability, with other freemen of the same towne, to all common charges, as well for vpholding the ordinances in the churches as otherwise, shalbee compelled thereto by assessment & distres to bee levied by the cunstable, or other officer of the towne, as in other cases.

F. An Act of November 4, 1646:

Albeit faith be not wrought by the sword, but by the word, & therefore such pagan Indians as have submited themselues to our government, though we would not neglect any due helps to bring them on to grace, & to the meanes of it, yet we compell them not to the Christian faith . . . ; nevertheles, seing the blaspheming of the true God cannot be excused by any ignorance or infirmity of humane nature, the eternall power & Godhead being knowne by the light of nature & the creation of the world . . . , it is therefore ordered & decreed, by the Corte . . . that no person within this iurisdiction, whether Christian or pagan shall wittingly & willingly presume to blaspheme his holy name, either by wilfull or obstinate deniing the true God, or his creation or government of the world, or shall curse God, or reproach the holy religion of God . . . ; if any person or persons whatsoever . . . shall break this lawe they shalbe put to death.

* * *

Though no humane power be Lord over the faith & consciences of men, & therefore may not constraine them to beleeve . . . , yet because such as bring in damnable heresies, tending to the subversion of the Christian faith, & destruction of the soules of men, ought duely to be restrained . . . , it is therefore ordered . . . if any Christian . . . shall go about to subvert & destroy the Christian faith & religion, by broaching or maintaining any damnable heresy, as deniing the immortality of the soule, or the resurrection of the body, or any sinn to be repented of in the regenerate, or any evill done by the outward man to be accounted sinn, or deniing that Christ gave himselfe a ransome for our sinns, or that we are iustified by his death & righteousnes, but by the perfection of our owne works, or deniing the morallity of the 4th commandement, or any other heresy of such nature & degree, every such person continuing obstinate therein, after due meanes of conviction, shall pay to the common treasury during the first six months 20 s[hillings] a month, & for the next six months 40 s[hillings] per m[onth], & so to continue dureing his obstinacy; & if any such person shall endeavor to seduce others . . . , he shall forfeit . . . for every severall offence therein, five pounds.

G. Massachusetts School Law of 1647, November 11, 1647:

It being one cheife proiect of that ould deluder, Satan, to keepe men from the knowledge of the Scriptures, as in former times by keeping them in an unknowne tongue, so in these latter times by perswading from the use of tongues, that so at least the true sense & meaning of the originall might be clouded by false glosses of saint seeming deceivers, that learning may not be buried in the grave of our fathers in the church and commonwealth, the Lord assisting our endeavors,—

It is therefore ordered, that every towneship in this iurisdiction, after the Lord hath increased them to the number of 50 housholders, shall then forthwith appoint one within their towne to teach all such children as shall resort to him to write & reade, whose wages shall be paid either by the parents or masters of such children, or by the inhabitants in generall, by way of supply, as the maior part of those that order the prudentials of the towne shall appoint; provided, those that send their children be not oppressed by paying much more than they can have them taught for in other townes; & it is further ordered, that where any towne shall increase to the number of 100 families or householders they shall set up a grammer schoole, the master thereof being able to instruct youth so farr as they may be fited for the university, provided, that if any towne neglect the performance hereof above one yeare, that every such towne shall pay 5 [pounds] to the next schoole till they shall performe this order.

Source: A. *Records of the Governor and Company of the Massachusetts Bay* (ed. Nathaniel B. Shurtleff) (Boston, 1853), I, 55; B. ibid., 87; C. ibid., 140; D. ibid., 168; E. ibid., 240–241; F. ibid., II, 176–177; G. ibid., 203.

SUGGESTIONS FOR BACKGROUND AND REFERENCE

S. Foster, *Their Solitary Way: The Puritan Social Ethic in the First Century of Settlement in New England* (New Haven, 1971).

D. D. Hall, *Puritanism in Seventeenth-Century Massachusetts* (New York, 1968).

G. L. Haskins, *Law and Authority in Early Massachusetts* (New York, 1960).

P. Miller, *The New England Mind: The Seventeenth Century* (New York, 1939).

E. S. Morgan, *Visible Saints: The History of a Puritan Idea* (New York, 1963).

D. B. Rutman, *American Puritanism. Faith and Practice* (Philadelphia, 1970).

14   Cambridge Platform (Extracts)

August 1648

The Cambridge Platform was the fundamental authoritative statement of Congregational church government in early New England history. It was produced by the synod that met intermittently from 1646 to 1648 at the request of the Massachusetts General Court to draw up an exposition of the New England way. In England in the 1640s Puritanism was fragmenting into various parties—Presbyterian, Independent, Baptist, and others—and in the Westminster Assembly, summoned to reform the national church, the Presbyterian majority was defining its interpretation of Puritan faith and discipline. Against this background the Cambridge theologians met to express their "hearty assent" to the Westminster Confession of Faith but also to draw up a different polity based on a model of Richard Mather (1596–1669). Both steps were unanimously voted by the synod "the last of the sixth month, 1648," and after reference to the churches, the platform was officially accepted by the court in 1651. It remained the standard for both Massachusetts and Connecticut throughout the seventeenth century. Although the entire document is helpful to an understanding of the New England way in church and state, only sections dealing expressly with magistracy are reproduced here.

From Chapter XI:
Of the Maintenance of Church Officers

The Apostle concludes, that necessary & sufficient maintenance is due unto the ministers of the word: from the law of nature & nations, from the law of Moses, the equity thereof, as also the rule of common reason. . . .

* * *

4. Not only members of Churches, but all that are taught in the word, are to contribute unto him that teacheth, in all good things. In case that Congregations are defective in their contributions, the Deacons are to call upon them to doe their duty: if their call sufficeth not, the church by her powr is to require it of their members, & where church-powr through the corruption of men, doth not, or cannot attaine the end, the Magistrate is to see ministry be duely provided for, as appears from the commended example of Nehemiah. . . .

From Chapter XIV:
Of Excommunication & Other Censures

5. While the offender remayns excommunicate, the Church is to *refrayn from all member-like communion* with him in spirituall things, & also from all familiar

communion with him in civil things, farther then the necessity of natural, or domestical, or civil relations doe require . . . .

6. Excommunication being a spirituall punishment, it doth not prejudice the excommunicate in, nor deprive him of his *civil rights,* & therefore toucheth not princes, or other magistrates, in point of their civil dignity or authority. And, the excommunicate being but as a publican & a heathen, heathens being lawfully permitted to come to hear the word in church assemblyes; wee acknowledg therefore the like liberty of hearing the word, may be permitted to parsons excommunicate, that is permitted unto heathen. . . .

From Chapter XVI:
Of Synods

3. Magistrates have powr to call a Synod, by calling to the Churches to send forth their Elders & other messengers, to counsel & assist them in matters of religion; but yett the constituting of a Synod, is a church act, & may be transacted by the churches, even when civil magistrates may be enemyes to churches and to church assemblyes.

From Chapter XVII:
Of the Civil Magistrates Powr in Matters Ecclesiastical

It is lawfull, profitable & necessary for christians to gather themselves into Church estate, and therein to exercise all the ordinances of christ according unto the word, although the consent of Magistrate could not be had therunto, because the Apostles & christians in their time did frequently thus practise, when the Magistrates being all of them Jewish or pagan, & mostly persecuting enemies, would give no countenance or consent to such matters.

2. Church-government stands in no opposition to civil government of commonwelths, nor any intrencheth upon the authority of Civil Magistrates in their jurisdictions; nor any whit weakneth their hands in governing; but rather strengthneth them, & furthereth the people in yielding more hearty & conscionable obedience unto them . . . .

The powr & authority of Magistrates is not for the restraining of churches, or any other good workes, but for helping in & furthering therof; & therfore the consent & countenance of Magistrates when it may be had, is not to be sleighted, or lightly esteemed; but on the contrary; it is part of that honour due to christian Magistrates to desire & crave their consent & approbation therin: which being obtayned, the churches may then proceed in their way with much more encouragement & comfort.

4. It is not in the powr of Magistrates to compell their subjects to become church-members, & to partake at the Lords table . . . .

5. As it is unlawfull for church-officers to meddle with the sword of the Magistrate, so it is unlawfull for the Magistrate to meddle with the work proper to church-officers. . . .

6. It is the duty of the Magistrate to take care of matters of religion, & to

improve his civil authority for the observing of the duties commanded in the first, as well as for observing of the duties commanded in the second table. They are called Gods. The end of the Magistrates office, is not only the quiet & peaceable life of the subject, in matters of righteousness & honesty, but also in matters of godliness, yea of all godliness. . . .

7. The object of the powr of the Magistrate, are not things meerly inward, & so not subject to his cognisance & view, as unbeleife hardness of heart, erronious opinions not vented; but only such things as are acted by the outward man; neither is their powr to be exercised, in commanding such acts of the outward man, & punishing the neglect therof, as are but meer inventions, & devices of men; but about such acts, as are commanded & forbidden in the word; yea such as the word doth clearly determine . . . .

8. Idolatry, Blasphemy, Heresy, venting corrupt & pernicious opinions, that destroy the foundation, open contempt of the word preached, prophanation of the Lords day, disturbing the peaceable administration & exercise of the worship & holy things of God, & the like, are to be restrayned, & punished by civil authority.

9. If any church one or more shall grow schismaticall, rending it self from the communion of other churches, or shall walke incorrigibly or obstinately in any corrupt way of their own, contrary to the rule of the word; in such case, the Magistrate is to put forth his coercive powr, as the matter shall require. . . .

Source: Williston Walker, *The Creeds and Platforms of Congregationalism* (New York, 1893), pp. 220, 221, 228, 233, 234–237.

SUGGESTIONS FOR BACKGROUND AND REFERENCE

Source for this document, pp. 157–188.
References for Document 13.

15   Maryland Toleration Act (Extracts)

April 21, 1649

English Catholicism secured an American foothold through the efforts of the Stuart courtier and secretary, George Calvert (d. 1632), and his son, Cecilius (1605–1675). Under the latter the settling of the Chesapeake colony began in 1634. In addition to the charter requirement, various factors combined to influence the Maryland experiment in religious equality. Religious contention was personally distasteful to the proprietors. English government, Anglican and—after 1640—increasingly Puritan, was watchful over the proprietorship. Maryland itself was settled primarily by Protestants; English Catholicism was too small, conservative, and aristocratic to send emigrants in significant numbers. The policy of mutual religious forbearance was practiced from the beginning, but given statutory basis by this act of the Maryland Assembly in 1649 when English events—the triumph of Puritanism and the New Model Army—threatened the collapse of the entire Calvert and Catholic enterprise. The act commanded mutual toleration and condemned forcing of conscience, but preserved the death penalty for blasphemy. For a few years in the 1650s the proprietorship was lost and Catholicism proscribed, but the former policy of religious freedom continued dominant in practice throughout the colonial period, though modified by the legal Establishment of Anglicanism in 1702.

[1]Be it . . . enacted . . . That whatsoever p[er]son . . . within this Province . . . shall . . . blaspheme God, that is Curse him, or deny our Saviour Jesus Christ to bee the sonne of God, or shall deny the holy Trinity the ffather sonne and holy Ghost, or the Godhead of any of the said Three p[er]sons of the Trinity or the Unity of the Godhead . . . shalbe punished with death and confiscation . . . of all his or her lands and goods . . . .

And bee it also Enacted . . . That whatsoever p[er]son . . . shall . . . utter any reproachfull words or Speeches concerning the blessed Virgin Mary . . . or the holy Apostles or Evangelists . . . shall . . . for the first offence forfeit . . . ffive pound Sterling or the value thereof to be Levyed on the goods and chattells of every such p[er]son soe offending, but in case such Offender . . . shall not then have goods . . . sufficient for the statisfyeing of such forfeiture, . . . such Offender . . . shalbe publiquely whipt and bee ymprisoned during the pleasure of the Lord Proprietary . . . . And that every such Offender . . . for every second offence shall forfeit tenne pound sterling . . . or [if lacking sufficient goods] bee . . . whipt and imprisoned as before is expressed. And that every p[er]son . . . shall for such third Offence forfeit all his lands and Goods and bee for ever banished . . . out of this Province.

And be it also further Enacted . . . that whatsoever p[er]son . . . shall . . . in a reproachful manner . . . declare . . . any p[er]son . . . inhabiting residing traffiqueing trading or comerceing within this Province or within any the Ports, Harbors, Creeks or Havens to the same belonging an heritick, Scismatick, Idolator, puritan, Independant, Prespiterian, popish prest, Jesuite, Jesuited papist, Lutheran, Calvenist, Anabaptist, Brownist, Antinomian, Barrowist, Roundhead, Sepatist, or any other name or terme . . . relating to matter of Religion shall for every such Offence forfeit . . . tenne shillings sterling . . . , the one half thereof to be . . . paid unto the person . . . of whom such reproachfull words are . . . spoken . . . , and the other half thereof to the Lord Proprietary . . . . But if such p[er]son . . . shall not have Goods sufficient . . . to satisfie the penalty . . . then the p[er]son . . . shalbe publickly whipt, and shall suffer imprisonment without baile or maineprise[2] untill hee shee or they respectively shall satisfy the party soe

---

1. Paragraphing altered for easier reading, and superscript abbreviations spelled out and absorbed in text.

2. Mainprise: An order freeing a prisoner as soon as sureties agreed to be bound for his appearance in court. Mainprise became like bail, though originally it implied a laxer degree of responsibility than bail.

offended . . . by asking him or her . . . forgivenes publiquely . . . before the Magistrate . . . .

And be it further likewise Enacted . . . That every person . . . that shall . . . prophane the Sabbath or Lords day called Sunday by frequent swearing, drunkennes or by any uncivill or disorderly recreacion, or by working on that day when absolute necessity doth not require it shall for every such first offence forfeit 2 s[hillings] 6 [pence] sterling . . . and for the second offence 5 s[hillings] . . . and for the third offence and soe for every time . . . afterwards 10 s[hillings] . . . .

And whereas the inforceing of the conscience in matters of Religion hath frequently fallen out to be of dangerous Consequence in those commonwealthes where it hath been practised, And for the more quiett and peaceable government of this Province, and the better to preserve mutual Love and amity amongst the Inhabitants thereof. Be it Therefore . . . enacted (except as in this Present Act is before Declared and sett forth) that noe person . . . whatsoever within this Province . . . professing to beleive in Jesus Christ, shall . . . bee any waies troubled, Molested or discountenanced for or in respect of his or her religion nor in the free exercise thereof . . . nor any way compelled to the beleife or exercise of any other Religion against his or her consent, soe as they be not unfaithfull to the Lord Proprietary, or molest or conspire against the civill Government . . . . And that all & every p[er]son . . . that shall presume Contrary to this Act . . . willfully to wrong disturbe trouble or molest any person . . . professing to beleive in Jesus Christ for or in respect of his or her religion or the free exercise thereof . . . shalbe compelled to pay trebble damages to the party soe wronged or molested, and for every such offence shall also forfeit 20 s[hillings] sterling in money or the value thereof, half therof for the use of the Lord Proprietary . . . and the other half for the use of the party soe wronged . . . Or if the partie soe offending . . . shall refuse or bee unable to recompense the party soe wronged, or to satisfy such ffyne or forfeiture, then such Offender shalbe severely punished by publick whipping & imprisonment during the pleasure of the Lord Proprietary . . . without baile or maineprise . . . .

Source: William H. Browne (ed.), *Archives of Maryland* (Baltimore, 1883), I, 244–247.

SUGGESTIONS FOR BACKGROUND AND REFERENCE

M. P. Andrews, *The Founding of Maryland* (New York, 1933), pp. 143–172.

T. O. Hanley, *Their Rights and Liberties* (Westminster, Md., 1959).

J. D. Krugler, "Lord Baltimore, Roman Catholics, and Toleration: Religious Policy in Maryland during the Early Catholic Years, 1634–1649," *Catholic Historical Review,* Vol. 65, No. 1 (Jan. 1979), pp. 49–75.

B. C. Steiner, *Maryland during the English Civil Wars* (Baltimore, 1906–1907).

16   Flushing Remonstrance (1657) and Dutch West India Company Instructions (1663)

December 27, 1657; April 16, 1663

Though seventeenth-century Holland had a reputation for liberty and tolerance, the Dutch West India Company made an effort to maintain religious uniformity for the Reformed Church in New Netherlands. Though generally successful among the Dutch, this policy, vulnerable in any case because of the Company directors' preoccupation with commerce, broke down when applied to the Lutherans of conquered New Sweden and the Long Island Congregationalists from New England. Free exercise of religion was granted to the New Englanders in 1641 and confirmed by the States-General in 1661, but this liberty did not extend to the radical Quakers, considered to be intolerably subversive both religiously and politically. Governor Peter Stuyvesant's attempt to enforce the ban elicited protest from the Long Island village of Flushing in 1657. Stuyvesant continued his efforts until 1663 when the Company, pleading economic necessity, intervened.

Flushing Remonstrance, 1657:

[1]Right Honnorable.

You have beene pleased to send vp vnto vs a certain Prohibition or Command that wee shoulde not receive or entertaine any of those people called *Quakers* because they are supposed to bee by some seducers of the people. For our parte wee cannot condem them in this case, neither can wee stretch out our hands against them to punish, bannish, or persecute them. For out of Christ God is a Consuming fire, and it is a feareful [thing] to fall into the handes of the liveing God. Wee desire therefore in this case not to iudge, least wee be iudged, neither to Condem, least wee bee Condemed, but rather let every man stand and fall to his own.

Maister, wee are bounde by the Law to doe good vnto all men, especially to those of the Household of faith, and though for the present wee seeme to bee vnsensible of the law and the Lawgiver: yet when death and the Law assault vs, if we haue our advocate to seeke who shall pleade for vs in this case of Conscience betwixt god and our owne soules, the powers of this world can neither attack vs, neither excuse vs. For if god iustifye, who can Condem, and if god Condem, there is none can justifye.

And for those Jealowsies and suspitions which some haue of them, that they are destructiue vnto Magistracy and Ministery, that cannot bee: for the Magistrate hath the Sword in his hand and the Minister hath the Sword in his hand, as witnesse those tow great examples which all Maiestrates and Ministers are to follow, M[oses] and

---

1. Document has been slightly altered to make for easier reading. Text has been broken into sentences, punctuation added, and paragraphing introduced.

Christ, whom god raised vp, Maintained, and defended against all the Enemies both of flesh and spirit. And therefore that which is of god will stand, and that which is of man will [come] to noething: And as the Lord hath taught Moses, or the Civill power, to giue an outward libertie in the State by the Law written in his heart, designed [for] the good of all, and can truely iudge who is good and who is evill, who is true and who is false, and can pass definitiue sentence of life or [death] against that man which rises vp against the fundamental law of the States Generall, soe [he] hath made his Ministers a savor of life vnto [life?] and a savor of death vnto death.

The law of loue, peace, and libertie in the states extending to *Jewes, Turkes,* and *Egiptians,* as they are Considered the sonnes of Adam, which is the glory of the outward State of *Holland,* soe loue, peace, and libertie extending to all in Christ Jesus, Condems hatred, warre, and bondage. And becawse our Saviour saith it is Impossible but that offences will come, but woe bee vnto him by whom they Commeth, our desire is not to offend one of his little ones in what soever forme, name, or title hee appeares in, whether presbiterian, independant, Baptist, or Quaker, but shall bee glad to see any thing of god in any of them: desireing to doe vnto all men as wee desire all men shoulde doe vnto vs, which is the true law both of Church and State. For our Saviour saith this is the Law and the Prophets.

Therefore if any of these said persons come in loue vnto vs, wee cannot in Conscience lay violent hands vpon them, but giue them free Egress and Regresse into our Towne and howses, as god shall perswade our Consciences. And in this wee are true subiects both of Church and State, for wee are bounde by the law of god and man to doe good vnto all men and evill to noe man, and this is according to the Pattent and Charter of our Towne, giuen vnto vs in the name of the States Generall, which wee are not willing to infringe and violate, but shall houlde to our pattent and shall remaine your Humble Subiects, the inhabitants of Vlishing . . . .

Company Directors' Instructions to Stuyvesant, 1663:

Your last letter informed us that you had banished from the province and sent hither by ship a certain Quaker, *John Bowne* by name: although we heartily desire, that these and other sectarians remained away from there, yet as they do not, we doubt very much, whether we can proceed against them rigorously without diminishing the population and stopping immigration, which must be favored at a so tender stage of the country's existence. You may therefore shut your eyes, at least not force people's consciences, but allow every one to have his own belief, as long as he behaves quietly and legally, gives no offence to his neighbors and does not oppose the government. As the government of this city has always practised this maxim of moderation and consequently has often had a considerable influx of people, we do not doubt, that your Province too would be benefitted by it.

Source: B. Fernow (ed.), *Documents Relating to the Colonial History of the State of New York* (Albany, 1883), XIV, 402–403, 526.

SUGGESTIONS FOR BACKGROUND AND REFERENCE

R. M. Jones, *The Quakers in the American Colonies* (New York, 1911), pp. 215–241.
A. P. Stokes, *Church and State in the United States* (New York, 1950), I, 166–167.
F. J. Zwierlein, *Religion in New Netherlands* (Rochester, N.Y., 1910), pp. 213–246.

17 Rhode Island Charter (Extract)

July 8, 1663

Puritan radicals, many of them outcasts from Massachusetts Bay, settled the Narragansett region. Some of them, like Roger Williams and some Baptists, were prompted by the dichotomy of nature and grace in Puritan thought to embrace a radical disjunction of the two realms in practice. Others, extreme Spiritists such as Anne Hutchinson's Antinomians and the followers of Samuel Gorton, disbelieved in the relevance of earthly helps to the Spirit's work in the world. In either case the result was a separation of church and state. Furthermore, this course was a practical necessity in view of the wide religious diversity of Rhode Island. Because of the irregular origin and settlement of the Narragansett country, none of the four towns that later joined to form the colony—Providence, Portsmouth, Newport, or Warwick—had any legal foundation for itself or security for its institutions. When neighboring colonies, distrustful of Rhode Island's religious experimentation and political disorder, threatened conquest, some colonial leaders, notably Williams, sought to reduce vulnerability by securing an English charter. Williams obtained a parliamentary charter in 1644, confirmed by Cromwell in 1655. Another charter, which explicitly preserved religious liberty, was secured by John Clarke from Charles II (1660–1685) in 1663. It served the colony for 180 years.

Whereas wee have been informed, by the humble petition of our trustie and well beloved subject, John Clarke, on the behalf of Benjamine Arnold, William Brenton, William Coddington, . . . and the rest of the purchasers and ffree inhabitants of our island, called *Rhode-Island,* and the rest of the colonie of Providence Plantations . . . that they, pursueing, with peaceable and loyall mindes, their sober, serious and religious intentions, of godlie edifieing themselves, and one another, in the holie Christian ffaith and worshipp as they were perswaded; together with the gaineing over and conversione of the poore ignorant Indian natives . . . to the sincere professione and obedienc of the same ffaith and worship, did, not onlie . . . transport themselves out of this kingdome of England into America, but alsoe, since their arrivall there, after their first settlement amongst other our subjects in those parts, ffor the avoideing of discorde, and those manie evills which were likely to ensue upon some of those oure subjects not beinge able to beare . . . theire different apprehensiones in religious concernements . . . did once againe leave theire desireable stationes and habitationes, and with excessive labour and travell, hazard and charge, did transplant themselves into the middest of the Indian natives . . . ; where, by the good Providence of God . . . they have not onlie byn preserved to admiration, but have increased and prospered . . . .

And whereas, in theire humble addresse, they have ffreely declared, that it is much on their hearts (if they may be permitted), to hold forth a livlie experiment, that a most flourishing civill state may stand and best bee maintained, and that among our English subjects, with a full libertie in religious concernements; and that true pietye rightly grounded upon gospell principles, will give the best and greatest security to sovereignetye, and will lay in the hearts of men the strongest obligations to true loyaltye: *Now know yee,* that wee beinge willinge to encourage the hopefull undertakeinge of oure sayd loyall and loveinge subjects, and to secure them in the free exercise and enjoyment of all theire civill and religious rights . . . ; and to preserve unto them that libertye, in the true Christian ffaith and worshipp of God, which they have sought with soe much travaill . . . to enjoye; and because some of the people and inhabitants of the same colonie cannot, in theire private opinions, conforme to the publique exercise of religion, according to the litturgy, formes and ceremonyes of the Church of England, or take or subscribe the oaths and articles made and established in that behalfe; and for that the same, by reason of the remote distances of those places, will (as wee hope) bee noe breach of the unitie and unifformitie established in this nation: Have therefore thought ffit, and doe hereby . . . declare . . . that noe person within the sayd colonye, at any tyme hereafter, shall bee any wise molested, punished, disquieted, or called in question, for any differences in opnione in matters of religion, and doe not actually disturb the civill peace of our sayd colony; but that all and everye person and persons may . . . have and enjoye his and theire owne judgments and consciences, in matters of religious concernments . . . ; they behaving themselves peaceablie and quietlie, and not useing this libertie to lycentiousnesse and profanenesse, nor to the civill injurye or outward disturbeance of others; any lawe, . . . usage or custome of this realme, to the contrary hereof, in any wise, notwithstanding. . . .

Source: Francis Newton Thorpe (ed.), *The Federal and State Constitutions* (Washington, D.C., 1909), VI, 3211–3213.

SUGGESTIONS FOR BACKGROUND AND REFERENCE

S. H. Brockunier, *The Irrepressible Democrat: Roger Williams* (New York, 1940).
R. M. Jones, *The Quakers in the American Colonies* (New York, 1911), pp. 45–62.
W. G. McLoughlin, *Rhode Island, A History* (New York, 1986), pp. 3–49.
E. S. Morgan, *Roger Williams: the Church and the State* (New York, 1987).

18 Great Law of Pennsylvania (Extract)

December 7, 1682

The most mystical of the groups that emerged from radical Puritanism, Quakers fostered an extreme spiritual piety, divorced from any reliance on worldly institutions or powers. Hence they believed strongly that the ideal political society was one that confined the magistrate to civil things and left the Spirit free to strive and conquer in men's hearts without human interference. Persecuted in England, Quakers won the opportunity to make their "holy experiment" in Pennsylvania, obtained by Charles II's charter of 1681 to William Penn (1644–1718). Penn determined to make the grant a refuge, not only for his coreligionists, but for the oppressed in conscience from every land. Among the "Laws agreed upon in England," included in his first Frame of Government (1682), was Article XXXV, guaranteeing "That all persons living in this province, who confess and acknowledge the one Almighty and eternal God, to be the Creator, Upholder and Ruler of the world; and that hold themselves obliged in conscience to live peaceably and justly in civil society, shall, in no ways, be molested or prejudiced for their religious persuasion, or practice, in matters of faith and worship, nor shall they be compelled, at any time, to frequent or maintain any religious worship, place or ministry whatever" (Francis Newton Thorpe [ed.], *The Federal and State Constitutions* [Washington, D.C., 1909], V, 3063). Shortly after he arrived in the province, Penn met the freemen at Upland (Chester) and there enacted the Great Law, amplifying this concern for religious freedom.

Whereas the glory of Almighty God, and the good of mankind, is the reason and end of government, and therefore government, in itself, is a venerable ordinance of God; and forasmuch as it is principally desired and intended by the proprietary and governor, and the freemen of the province of Pennsylvania . . . to make and establish such laws as shall best preserve true Christians and civil liberty, in opposition to all unchristian, licentious, and unjust practices, whereby God may have his due, Caesar his due, and the people their due, from tyranny and oppression of the one side, and insolency and licentiousness of the other, so that the best and firmest foundation may be laid for the present and future happiness of both the governor and people of this province . . . and their posterity.—Be it therefore enacted, by William Penn, proprietary and governor, by and with the advice and consent of the deputies of the freemen of this province . . . .

1. Almighty God being only Lord of conscience, father of lights and spirits, and the author as well as object of all divine knowledge, faith, and worship, who only can enlighten the mind, and persuade and convince the understanding of people, in due reverence to his sovereignty over the souls of mankind. It is enacted by the authority aforesaid, that no person . . . who shall confess and acknowledge one Almighty God to be the creator, upholder, and ruler of the world and that professeth him or herself obliged in conscience to live peaceably and justly under the civil government, shall in anywise be molested or prejudiced for his or her conscientious persuasion or practice, nor shall he or she at any time be compelled to frequent or maintain any religious worship, place, or ministry whatever, contrary to his or her mind, but shall freely and fully enjoy his or her Christian liberty in that respect, without any interruption or reflection; and if any person shall abuse or deride any

other for his or her different persuasion and practice in matter of religion, such shall be looked upon as a disturber of the peace, and be punished accordingly. But to the end that looseness, irreligion, and atheism may not creep in under pretence of conscience, . . . be it further enacted . . . that according to the good example of the primitive Christians, and for the ease of the creation, every first day of the week, called the Lord's Day, people shall abstain from their common toil and labour, that whether masters, parents, children, or servants, they may the better dispose themselves to read the Scriptures of truth at home, or to frequent such meetings of religious worship abroad as may best suit their respective persuasions.

    2. . . . all officers and persons commissionated and employed in the service of the government of this province, and all members and deputies elected to serve in assembly thereof, and all that have right to elect such deputies, shall be such as profess and declare they believe in Jesus Christ to be the Son of God, and Saviour of the world, and that are not convicted of ill-fame, or unsober and dishonest conversation, and that are of one and twenty years of age at least. And . . . whosoever shall swear, in their conversation, by the name of God, or Christ, or Jesus, being legally convicted thereof, shall pay for every such offence five shillings, or suffer five days' imprisonment in the house of correction, at hard labour, to the behoof of the public, and be fed with bread and water only, during that time.

    3. . . . whosoever shall swear by any other thing or name . . . shall, for every such offence, pay half a crown, or suffer three days' imprisonment . . . at hard labour, having only bread and water for their sustenance.

    4. And . . . whosoever shall speak loosely and profanely of Almighty God, Christ Jesus, the Holy Spirit, or the Scriptures of truth . . . shall, for every such offence, pay five shillings, or suffer five days' imprisonment . . . at hard labour, . . . and be fed with bread and water only, during that time.

Source: Samuel Hazard, *Annals of Pennsylvania, from the Discovery of the Delaware* (Philadelphia, 1850), pp. 619–620.

SUGGESTIONS FOR BACKGROUND AND REFERENCE

E. Beatty, *William Penn as Social Philosopher* (New York, 1939).
E. B. Bronner, *William Penn's Holy Experiment* (New York, 1962).
R. M. Jones, *The Quakers in the American Colonies* (New York, 1911), pp. 417–494.

19   Pennsylvania Constitution (Extract)

September 28, 1776

With independence most of the states produced new constitutions, more or less influenced by the prevailing natural rights philosophy of the revolutionary era. The Pennsylvania document was typical of several that excluded Establishments and proclaimed freedom of religion, but officially retained some Christian or Protestant confessional basis. In the case of Pennsylvania this appeared in the religious test for office, adopted despite the misgivings of Benjamin Franklin (who presided at the convention). The Philadelphia Jews petitioned against the clause in 1783, which was dropped in 1790 with the added provision "That no person, who acknowledges the being of a God and a future state of rewards and punishments, shall, on account of his religious sentiments, be disqualified to hold any office or place of trust or profit under this commonwealth."

From the Declaration of Rights:

II. That all men have a natural and unalienable right to worship Almighty God according to the dictates of their own consciences and understandings: And that no man ought or of right can be compelled to attend any religious worship, or erect or support any place of worship, or maintain any ministry, contrary to, or against, his own free will and consent: Nor can any man, who acknowledges the being of a God, be justly deprived or abridged of any civil right as a citizen, on account of his religious sentiments or peculiar mode of religious worship: And that no authority can or ought to be vested in, or assumed by any power whatever, that shall in any case interfere with, or in any manner controul, the right of conscience in the free exercise of religious worship.

From Section 10 of the Plan or Frame of Government:

And each member, before he takes his seat, shall make and subscribe the following declaration, viz:

I do believe in one God, the creator and governor of the universe, the rewarder of the good and the punisher of the wicked. And I do acknowledge the Scriptures of the Old and New Testament to be given by Divine inspiration.

And no further or other religious test shall ever hereafter be required of any civil officer or magistrate in this State.

Source: Francis Newton Thorpe (ed.), *The Federal and State Constitutions* (Washington, D.C., 1909), V, 3100, 3082, 3085.

SUGGESTIONS FOR BACKGROUND AND REFERENCE

A. Nevins, *The American States during and after the Revolution, 1775–1789* (New York, 1924), pp. 117–170.
D. Rothermund, *Layman's Progress: Denominations and Political Behavior in Colonial Pennsylvania* (Philadelphia, 1962).
J. P. Selsam, *Pennsylvania Constitution of 1776* (Philadelphia, 1936).
T. Thayer, *Pennsylvania Politics and the Growth of Democracy, 1740–1776* (Philadelphia, 1953).

20   Hanover Presbytery Memorial

October 24, 1776

The Revolution prompted a sweeping revision in the legal position of the Church of England in several of the states of the new nation. The weak popular basis of Anglicanism, its Tory taint, the political and social upheaval, the eighteenth-century natural rights philosophy, and the hostility of other denominations all conspired to undermine the precarious Anglican Establishments of the colonies. Southern Anglicanism was probably strongest in Virginia (though even there it was a minority church), but the first Virginia Assembly under the new state constitution in 1776 was assailed with demands for complete religious freedom. This memorial, probably written by Caleb Wallace (1742–1814), clerk of the Hanover Presbytery, and considered by the legislature on October 24, signalized Presbyterian adherence to the campaign and powerfully promoted the alliance of Enlightenment and Dissent, which ultimately succeeded in the religious liberty statute of 1786.

The Memorial of the Presbytery of Hanover humbly represents,—That your memorialists are governed by the same sentiments which have inspired the United States of America; and are determined that nothing in our power and influence shall be wanting to give success to their common cause. We would also represent, that dissenters from the church of England, in this country, have ever been desirous to conduct themselves as peaceable members of the civil government, for which reason they have hitherto submitted to several ecclesiastical burdens, and restrictions, that are inconsistent with equal liberty. But now when the many and grievous oppressions of our mother country, have laid this continent under the necessity of casting off the yoke of tyranny, and of forming independent governments upon equitable and liberal foundations, we flatter ourselves that we shall be freed from all the incumbrances which a spirit of domination, prejudice, or bigotry, hath interwoven with most other political systems. This we are the more strongly encouraged to expect, by the Declaration of Rights, so universally applauded for that dignity, firmness and precision with which it delineates and asserts the privileges of society, and the prerogatives of human nature; and which we embrace as the *magna charta* of our commonwealth, that can never be violated without endangering the grand superstructure, it was destined to sustain.[1] Therefore we rely upon this *Declaration*, as well as the justice of our honourable Legislature, to secure us the *free exercise of religion according to the dictates of our consciences:* and we should fall short in our

1. The Declaration of Rights, drawn up by George Mason, was adopted by the Virginia Convention on June 12, 1776. Article 16, the work of Patrick Henry, declared: "That religion, or the duty which we owe to our Creator, and the manner of discharging it, can be directed only by reason and conviction, not by force or violence; and therefore all men are equally entitled to the free exercise of religion, according to the dictates of conscience; and that it is the mutual duty of all to practise Christian forbearance, love, and charity towards each other." For entire Declaration, see Francis Newton Thorpe (ed.), *The Federal and State Constitutions* (Washington, D.C., 1909), VII, 3813–3814.

duty to ourselves, and the many and numerous congregations under our care, were we, upon this occasion, to neglect laying before you a state of the religious grievances under which we have hitherto laboured; that they no longer may be continued in our present form of government.

It is well known, that in the frontier counties, which are justly supposed to contain a fifth part of the inhabitants of Virginia, the dissenters have borne the heavy burdens of purchasing glebes, building churches, and supporting the established clergy, where there are very few Episcopalians, either to assist in bearing the expense, or to reap the advantage; and that throughout the other parts of the country, there are also many thousands of zealous friends and defenders of our State, who, besides the invidious, and disadvantageous restrictions to which they have been subjected, annually pay large taxes to support an establishment, from which their consciences and principles oblige them to dissent: all which are confessedly so many violations of their natural rights; and in their consequences, a restraint upon freedom of inquiry, and private judgment.

In this enlightened age, and in a land where all, of every denomination are united in the most strenuous efforts to be free, we hope and expect that our representatives will cheerfully concur in removing every species of religious, as well as civil bondage. Certain it is, that every argument for civil liberty, gains additional strength when applied to liberty in the concerns of religion; and there is no argument in favour of establishing the Christian religion, but what may be pleaded, with equal propriety, for establishing the tenets of Mahomed by those who believe the Alcoran: or if this be not true, it is at least impossible for the magistrate to adjudge the right of preference among the various sects that profess the Christian faith, without erecting a chair of infallibility, which would lead us back to the church of Rome.

We beg leave farther to represent, that religious establishments are highly injurious to the temporal interests of any community. Without insisting upon the ambition, and the arbitrary practices of those who are favoured by government; or the intriguing seditious spirit, which is commonly excited by this, as well as every other kind of oppression; such establishments greatly retard population, and consequently the progress of arts, sciences, and manufactories: witness the rapid growth and improvements of the northern provinces, compared with this. No one can deny that the more early settlement, and the many superior advantages of our country, would have invited multitudes of artificers, mechanics, and other useful members of society, to fix their habitation among us, who have either remained in their place of nativity, or preferred worse civil governments, and a more barren soil, where they might enjoy the rights of conscience more fully than they had a prospect of doing it, in this. From which we infer, that Virginia might have now been the capital of America, and a match for the British arms, without depending on others for the necessaries of war, had it not been prevented by her religious establishment.

Neither can it be made to appear that the gospel needs any such civil aid. We rather conceive that when our blessed Saviour declares his *kingdom is not of this world,* he renounces all dependence upon state power, and as his *weapons are spiritual,* and were only designed to have influence on the judgment, and heart of man, we are persuaded that if mankind were left in the quiet possession of their unalienable rights and privileges, Christianity, as in the days of the Apostles, would continue to prevail and flourish in the greatest purity, by its own native excellence, and under the all disposing providence of God.

We would humbly represent, that the only proper objects of civil government, are the happiness and protection of men in the present state of existence; the security of the life, liberty and property of the citizens; and to restrain the vicious and encourage the virtuous by wholesome laws, equally extending to every individual. But that *the duty which we owe our Creator, and the manner of discharging it, can only be directed by reason and conviction;* and is nowhere cognizable but at the tribunal of the universal Judge.

Therefore we *ask no ecclesiastical establishments for ourselves;* neither can we approve of them when granted to others. This indeed would be giving exclusive or separate emoluments or privileges to one set (or sect) of men, without any special public services to the common reproach and injury of every other denomination. And for the reasons recited we are induced earnestly to entrust, that all laws now in force in this commonwealth, which countenance religious domination, may be speedily repealed—that all, of every religious sect, may be protected in the full exercise of their several modes of worship; and exempted from all taxes for the support of any church whatsoever, further than what may be agreeable to their own private choice, or voluntary obligation. This being done, all partial and invidious distinctions will be abolished, to the great honour and interest of the State; and every one be left to stand or fall according to merit, which can never be the case, so long as any one denomination is established in preference to others.

Source: William Henry Foote, *Sketches of Virginia* (Philadelphia, 1850), I, 323–324.

SUGGESTIONS FOR BACKGROUND AND REFERENCE

T. Buckley, *Church and State in Revolutionary Virginia, 1776–1787* (Charlottesville, Va., 1977).

H. J. Eckenrode, *Separation of Church and State in Virginia* (Richmond, Va., 1910).

E. F. Humphrey, *Nationalism and Religion in America, 1774–1789* (Boston, 1924), pp. 66–104, 359–406.

R. Isaac, *The Transformation of Virginia: Community, Religion, and Authority, 1740–1790* (Chapel Hill, N.C., 1982).

A. P. Stokes, *Church and State in the United States* (New York, 1950), I, 366–397.

21   Massachusetts Constitution (Extract)

March 2, 1780

Unlike the Anglican Establishments in the South, New England Congregationalism commanded substantial popular approval for its state support, despite efforts of Baptists, Quakers, Episcopalians, and political liberals to challenge the Congregational position. In Massachusetts and Connecticut there was no sudden overturning of the religious system, but rather a gradual relaxation of Congregational privilege with extension of some of the benefits of public support to other Protestant denominations. Efforts, chiefly by Baptists, to secure a definite separation of church and state failed at the 1780 constitutional convention, which instead adopted a declaration of rights written largely by John Adams (1735–1826). (Chapter VI of the constitution required elected state officials to swear "I believe the Christian religion, and have a firm persuasion of its truth.") Another half century was to pass before complete disestablishement was achieved.

II. It is the right as well as the duty of all men in society, publicly, and at stated seasons, to worship the SUPREME BEING, the great Creator and Preserver of the universe. And no subject shall be hurt, molested, or restrained, in his person, liberty, or estate, for worshipping GOD in the manner and season most agreeable to the dictates of his own conscience; or for his religious profession of sentiments; provided he doth not disturb the public peace, or obstruct others in their religious worship.

III. As the happiness of a people, and the good order and preservation of civil government, essentially depend upon piety, religion, and morality; and as these cannot be generally diffused through a community but by the institution of the public worship of GOD, and of public instructions in piety, religion, and morality: Therefore, to promote their happiness, and to secure the good order and preservation of their government, the people of this commonwealth have a right to invest their legislature with power to authorize and require, and the legislature shall, from time to time, authorize and require, the several towns, parishes, precincts, and other bodies politic, or religious societies, to make suitable provision, at their own expense, for the institution of the public worship of GOD, and for the support and maintenance of public Protestant teachers of piety, religion, and morality, in all cases where such provision shall not be made voluntarily.

And the people of this commonwealth have also a right to, and do, invest their legislature with authority to enjoin upon all the subjects an attendance upon the instructions of the public teachers aforesaid, at stated times and seasons, if there be any on whose instructions they can conscientiously and conveniently attend.

Provided, notwithstanding, that the several towns, parishes, precincts, and other bodies politic, or religious societies, shall, at all times, have the exclusive right of electing their public teachers, and of contracting with them for their support and maintenance.

And all moneys paid by the subject to the support of public worship, and of the public teachers aforesaid, shall, if he require it, be uniformly applied to the support of the public teacher or teachers of his own religious sect or denomination, provided there be any on whose instructions he attends; otherwise it may be paid towards the support of the teacher or teachers of the parish or precinct in which the said moneys are raised.

And every denomination of Christians, demeaning themselves peaceably, and as good subjects of the commonwealth, shall be equally under the protection of the law: and no subordination of any one sect or denomination to another shall ever be established by law.

Source: Francis Newton Thorpe (ed.), *The Federal and State Constitutions* (Washington, D.C., 1909), III, 1889–1890.

SUGGESTIONS FOR BACKGROUND AND REFERENCE

J. C. Meyer, *Church and State in Massachusetts from 1740 to 1833* (Cleveland, 1930), pp. 90–132.

S. E. Morison, "The Struggle over the Adoption of the Constitution of Massachusetts, 1780," *Massachusetts Historical Society, Proceedings*, Vol. L (1917), pp. 353–412.

A. Nevins, *The American States during and after the Revolution, 1775–1789* (New York, 1924), pp. 172–184.

22   Memorial and Remonstrance Against Religious Assessments [Virginia]

1785

The revolutionary assault on the privileged position of Virginia Anglicanism, though successful in winning concessions, began a long battle in state politics. Though a minority in the state, Anglicans enjoyed social and economic prominence and constituted a majority in the General Assembly. Many prominent Virginians, though opponents of religious injustice, were reluctant to sever entirely the church-state connection. In the 1780s this sentiment focused on plans for indiscriminative governmental support to all Christian denominations. General assessment bills, differing in detail, provided that sheriffs should collect taxes for the support of the denomination designated by the taxpayer. The bill before the legislature in 1784 stipulated that where the citizen failed to designate, the assessment would be used for education. Promoted by Patrick Henry, the measure also won favor with John Marshall and Washington. It passed preliminary votes in the Assembly, but James Madison (1751–1836), a determined opponent, prevented final consideration until autumn 1785. His memorial and remonstrance, distributed widely during the summer of 1785, contributed to the defeat of the bill, leaving the way open for Jefferson's statute for religious freedom. (The memorial has figured prominently in modern discussion of the constitutionality of nonpreferential government aid to religion. See especially *Everson* v. *Board of Education of Ewing Tp. et al.*, 330 U.S. 1.) The memorial is addressed to the General Assembly of the Commonwealth of Virginia.

We, the subscribers, citizens of the said Commonwealth, having taken into serious consideration, a Bill . . . entitled "A Bill establishing a provision for Teachers of the Christian Religion," and conceiving that the same . . . will be a dangerous abuse of power, are bound . . . to remonstrate against it, and to declare the reasons by which we are determined. We remonstrate against the said Bill,

1. Because we hold it for a fundamental and undeniable truth, "that Religion or the duty which we owe to our Creator, and the Manner of discharging it, can be directed only by reason and conviction, not by force or violence."[1] The Religion then of every man must be left to the conviction and conscience of every man; and it is the right of every man to exercise it as these may dictate. This right is in its nature an unalienable right. It is unalienable; because the opinions of men, depending only on the evidence contemplated by their own minds, cannot follow the dictates of other men: It is unalienable also; because what is here a right towards men, is a duty towards the Creator. It is the duty of every man to render to the Creator such homage, and such only, as he believes to be acceptable to him. This duty is precedent both in order of time and degree of obligation, to the claims of Civil Society. Before any man can be considered as a member of Civil Society, he must be considered as a subject of the Governor of the Universe: And if a member of Civil Society, who enters into any subordinate Association, must always do it with a reservation of his duty to the general authority; much more must every man who becomes a member of any particular Civil Society, do it with a saving of his allegiance to the Universal Sovereign. We maintain therefore that in matters of Religion, no man's right is abridged by the institution of Civil Society, and that Religion is wholly exempt from its cognizance. True it is, that no other rule exists, by which any question which may divide a Society, can be ultimately determined, but the will of the majority; but it is also true, that the majority may trespass on the rights of the minority.

2. Because if religion be exempt from the authority of the Society at large, still less can it be subject to that of the Legislative Body. The latter are but the creatures and vicegerents of the former. Their jurisdiction is both derivative and limited: it is limited with regard to the co-ordinate departments, more necessarily is it limited with regard to the constituents. The preservation of a free government requires not merely, that the metes and bounds which separate each department of power may be invariably maintained; but more especially, that neither of them be suffered to overleap the great Barrier which defends the rights of the people. . . .

3. Because, it is proper to take alarm at the first experiment on our liberties. . . . Who does not see that the same authority which can establish Christianity, in exclusion of all other Religions, may establish with the same ease any particular sect of Christians, in exclusion of all other Sects? That the same authority which can force a citizen to contribute three pence only of his property for the support of any one establishment, may force him to conform to any other establishment in all cases whatsoever?

4. Because, the bill violates that equality which ought to be the basis of every law . . . . If "all men are by nature equally free and independent,"[2] all men are to be considered as entering into Society on equal conditions; as relinquishing no more, and therefore retaining no less, one than another, of their natural rights. Above all are they to be considered as retaining an "equal title to the free exercise of

1. Decl. Rights, Art. 16. [This article was drafted by Patrick Henry.]
2. Decl. Rights, Art. 1.

Religion according to the dictates of conscience."[3] Whilst we assert for ourselves a freedom to embrace, to profess and to observe the Religion which we believe to be of divine origin, we cannot deny an equal freedom to those whose minds have not yet yielded to the evidence which has convinced us. If this freedom be abused, it is an offence against God, not against man: To God, therefore, not to men, must an account of it be rendered. As the Bill violates equality by subjecting some to peculiar burdens; so it violates the same principle, by granting to others peculiar exemptions. Are the Quakers and Menonists the only sects who think a compulsive support of their religions unnecessary and unwarrantable? Can their piety alone be intrusted with the care of public worship? Ought their Religions to be endowed above all others, with extraordinary privileges, by which proselytes may be enticed from all others? We think too favorably of the justice and good sense of these denominations, to believe that they either covet pre-eminencies over their fellow citizens, or that they will be seduced by them, from the common opposition to the measure.

5. Because the bill implies either that the Civil Magistrate is a competent Judge of Religious truth; or that he may employ Religion as an engine of Civil policy. The first is an arrogant pretension falsified by the contradictory opinions of Rulers in all ages, and throughout the world: The second an unhallowed perversion of the means of salvation.

6. Because the establishment proposed by the Bill is not requisite for the support of the Christian Religion. To say that it is, is a contradiction to the Christian Religion itself; for every page of it disavows a dependence on the powers of this world: it is a contradiction to fact; for it is known that this Religion both existed and flourished, not only without the support of human laws, but in spite of every opposition from them; . . . Nay, it is a contradiction in terms; for a Religion not invented by human policy, must have pre-existed and been supported, before it was established by human policy. It is moreover to weaken in those who profess this Religion a pious confidence in its innate excellence, and the patronage of its Author; and to foster in those who still reject it, a suspicion that its friends are too conscious of its fallacies, to trust it to its own merits.

7. Because experience witnesseth that ecclesiastical establishments, instead of maintaining the purity and efficacy of Religion, have had a contrary operation. During almost fifteen centuries, has the legal establishment of Christianity been on trial. What have been its fruits? More or less in all places, pride and indolence in the Clergy; ignorance and servility in the laity; in both, superstition, bigotry and persecution. Enquire of the Teachers of Christianity for the ages in which it appeared in its greatest lustre; those of every sect, point to the ages prior to its incorporation with Civil policy. Propose a restoration of this primitive state in which its Teachers depended on the voluntary rewards of their flocks; many of them predict its downfall. On which side ought their testimony to have greatest weight, when for or when against their interest?

8. Because the establishment in question is not necessary for the support of Civil

3. Art. 16.

Government. If it be urged as necessary for the support of Civil Government only as it is a means of supporting Religion, and it be not necessary for the latter purpose, it cannot be necessary for the former. If Religion be not within [the] cognizance of Civil Government, how can its legal establishment be said to be necessary to Civil Government? What influence in fact have ecclesiastical establishments had on Civil Society? In some instances they have been seen to erect a spiritual tyranny on the ruins of Civil authority; in many instances they have been seen upholding the thrones of political tyranny; in no instance have they been seen the guardians of the liberties of the people. Rulers who wished to subvert the public liberty, may have found an established clergy convenient auxiliaries. A just government, instituted to secure & perpetuate it, needs them not. Such a government will be best supported by protecting every citizen in the enjoyment of his Religion with the same equal hand which protects his person and his property; by neither invading the equal rights of any Sect, nor suffering any Sect to invade those of another.

9. Because the proposed establishment is a departure from that generous policy, which, offering an asylum to the persecuted and oppressed of every Nation and Religion, promised a lustre to our country, and an accession to the number of its citizens. What a melancholy mark is the Bill of sudden degeneracy? Instead of holding forth an asylum to the persecuted, it is itself a signal of persecution. It degrades from the equal rank of Citizens all those whose opinions in Religion do not bend to those of the Legislative authority. Distant as it may be, in its present form, from the Inquisition it differs from it only in degree. The one is the first step, the other the last in the career of intolerance. . . .

10. Because, it will have a like tendency to banish our Citizens. The allurements presented by other situations are every day thinning their number. To superadd a fresh motive to emigration . . . would be the same species of folly which has . . . depopulated flourishing kingdoms.

11. Because, it will destroy that moderation and harmony which the forbearance of our laws to intermeddle with Religion, has produced amongst its several sects. Torrents of blood have been spilt in the old world, by vain attempts of the secular arm to extinguish Religious discord, by proscribing all difference in Religious opinions. Time has at length revealed the true remedy. Every relaxation of narrow and rigorous policy . . . has been found to assuage the disease. The American Theatre has exhibited proofs, that equal and compleat liberty, if it does not wholly eradicate it, sufficiently destroys its malignant influence on the health and prosperity of the State. If with the salutary effects of this system under our own eyes, we begin to contract the bonds of Religious freedom, we know no name that will too severely reproach our folly. At least let warning be taken at the first fruits of the threatened innovation. The very appearance of the Bill has transformed that "Christian forbearance,[4] love and charity," which of late mutually prevailed, into animosities and jealousies, which may not soon be appeased. What mischiefs may not be dreaded should this enemy to the public quiet be armed with the force of a law?

12. Because, the policy of the bill is adverse to the diffusion of the light of Christianity. . . . it at once discourages those who are strangers to the light of

4. Art. 16.

[revelation] from coming into the Region of it; and countenances, by example the nations who continue in darkness, in shutting out those who might convey it to them. Instead of levelling as far as possible, every obstacle to the victorious progress of truth, the Bill with an ignoble and unchristian timidity would circumscribe it, with a wall of defence, against the encroachments of error.

13. Because attempts to enforce by legal sanctions, acts obnoxious to so great a proportion of Citizens, tend to enervate the laws in general, and to slacken the bands of Society. . . .

14. Because a measure of such singular magnitude and delicacy ought not to be imposed, without the clearest evidence that it is called for by a majority of citizens: and no satisfactory method is yet proposed by which the voice of the majority . . . may be determined . . . . "The people of the respective counties are indeed requested to signify their opinion . . . " But the representation must be made equal, before the voice either of the Representatives or of the Counties, will be that of the people. . . .

15. Because, finally, "the equal right of every citizen to the free exercise of his Religion according to the dictates of conscience" is held by the same tenure with all our other rights. If we recur to its origin, it is equally the gift of nature; if we weigh its importance, it cannot be less dear to us; if we consult the Declaration of those rights which pertain to the good people of Virginia, as the "basis and foundation of Government,"[5] it is enumerated with equal solemnity, or rather studied emphasis. . . .

Source: Gaillard Hunt (ed.), *The Writings of James Madison* (New York, 1901), II, 183–190.

SUGGESTIONS FOR BACKGROUND AND REFERENCE

I. Brant, *James Madison* (Indianapolis and New York, 1941–1961), II, 343–355.
E. S. Gaustad, *Faith of Our Fathers. Religion and the New Nation* (San Francisco, 1987), pp. 39–52.
D. Malone, *Jefferson and His Time* (Boston, 1948–1962), I, 274–280.
References for Document 20.

23   Virginia Act for Religious Freedom

January 16, 1786

In opposition to the project for state support to all Christian denominations, Jefferson (1743–1826) and Madison championed complete religious freedom and were vigorously supported in this by Dissenters, notably Baptists and Presbyterians. Jefferson's bill for religious freedom, drawn up in 1777, was presented to the legislature during his governorship in 1779, but determined opposition delayed approval until

5. Decl. Rights-title.

1786. Jefferson considered the act one of his major achievements, second in importance only to the Declaration of Independence.

I. WHEREAS Almighty God hath created the mind free; that all attempts to influence it by temporal punishments or burthens, or by civil incapacitations, tend only to beget habits of hypocrisy and meanness, and are a departure from the plan of the Holy author of our religion, who being Lord both of body and mind, yet chose not to propagate it by coercions on either, as was in his Almighty power to do; that the impious presumption of legislators and rulers, civil as well as ecclesiastical, who being themselves but fallible and uninspired men, have assumed dominion over the faith of others, setting up their own opinions and modes of thinking as the only true and infallible, and as such endeavouring to impose them on others, hath established and maintained false religions over the greatest part of the world, and through all time; that to compel a man to furnish contributions of money for the propagation of opinions which he disbelieves, is sinful and tyrannical; that even the forcing him to support this or that teacher of his own religious persuasion, is depriving him of the comfortable liberty of giving his contributions to the particular pastor, whose morals he would make his pattern, and whose powers he feels most persuasive to righteousness, and is withdrawing from the ministry those temporary rewards, which proceeding from an approbation of their personal conduct, are an additional incitement to earnest and unremitting labours for the instruction of mankind; that our civil rights have no dependence on our religious opinions, any more than our opinions in physics or geometry; that therefore the proscribing any citizen as unworthy the public confidence by laying upon him an incapacity of being called to offices of trust and emolument, unless he profess or renounce this or that religious opinion, is depriving him injuriously of those privileges and advantages to which in common with his fellow-citizens he has a natural right; that it tends only to corrupt the principles of that religion it is meant to encourage, by bribing with a monopoly of worldly honours and emoluments, those who will externally profess and conform to it; that though indeed these are criminal who do not withstand such temptation, yet neither are those innocent who lay the bait in their way; that to suffer the civil magistrate to intrude his powers into the field of opinion, and to restrain the profession or propagation of principles on supposition of their ill tendency, is a dangerous fallacy, which at once destroys all religious liberty, because he being of course judge of that tendency will make his opinions the rule of judgment, and approve or condemn the sentiments of others only as they shall square with or differ from his own; that it is time enough for the rightful purposes of civil government, for its officers to interfere when principles break out into overt acts against peace and good order; and finally, that truth is great and will prevail if left to herself, that she is the proper and sufficient antagonist to error, and has nothing to fear from the conflict, unless by human interposition disarmed of her natural weapons, free argument and debate, errors ceasing to be dangerous when it is permitted freely to contradict them:

II. *Be it enacted by the General Assembly,* That no man shall be compelled to frequent or support any religious worship, place, or ministry whatsoever, nor shall be enforced, restrained, molested, or burthened in his body or goods, nor shall otherwise suffer on account of his religious opinions or belief; but that all men shall be free to profess, and by argument to maintain, their opinion in matters of religion, and that the same shall in no wise diminish, enlarge, or affect their civil capacities.

III. And though we well know that this assembly elected by the people for the ordinary purposes of legislation only, have no power to restrain the acts of succeeding assemblies, constituted with powers equal to our own, and that therefore to declare this act to be irrevocable would be of no effect in law; yet we are free to declare, and do declare, that the rights hereby asserted are of the natural rights of mankind, and that if any act shall be hereafter passed to repeal the present, or to narrow its operation, such act will be an infringement of natural right.

Source: William W. Hening (ed.), *The Statutes at Large, Being a Collection of All the Laws of Virginia* (New York, 1823), XII, 84–86.

SUGGESTIONS FOR BACKGROUND AND REFERENCE

R. C. Vaughan and M. D. Peterson, *The Virginia Statute for Religious Freedom: its Evolution and Consequences in American History* (New York, 1988).
References for Documents 20 and 22.

24   United States Constitution (Extracts)

September 17, 1787 [adopted in Convention]

Though a Bill of Rights was proposed at the Philadelphia Convention, the original document dealt with religion only in Article VI. (The omission of reference to God was unfavorably noted by some contemporaries.) In June 1789 Madison proposed to Congress a Bill of Rights, duly adopted and ratified as the first ten amendments, of which the first contained the fundamental statute on church-state relations in America. The prohibition at first applied to the federal government only and was not made applicable to the states until after judicial interpretation of the Fourteenth Amendment, adopted in 1868. (Despite its much later origin, the relevant section of the Fourteenth Amendment is here included for completeness.)

From Article VI:

The Senators and Representatives before mentioned, and the Members of the several State Legislatures, and all executive and judicial Officers, both of the United States and of the several States, shall be bound by Oath or Affirmation, to support this Constitution; but no religious Test shall ever be required as a Qualification to any Office or public Trust under the United States.

The First Amendment, Declared in Force December 15, 1791:

Congress shall make no law respecting an establishment of religion, or prohibiting the free exercise thereof; or abridging the freedom of speech, or of the press; or the right of the people peaceably to assemble, and to petition the Government for a redress of grievances.

The Fourteenth Amendment, Section 1, Declared Ratified July 28, 1868:

All persons born or naturalized in the United States, and subject to the jurisdiction thereof, are citizens of the United States and of the State wherein they reside. No State shall make or enforce any law which shall abridge the privileges or immunities of citizens of the United States; nor shall any State deprive any person of life, liberty, or property, without due process of law; nor deny to any person within its jurisdiction the equal protection of the laws.

Source: Francis Newton Thorpe (ed.), *The Federal and State Constitutions* (Washington, D.C., 1909), I, 27, 29, 31.

SUGGESTIONS FOR BACKGROUND AND REFERENCE

I. Brant, *James Madison* (Indianapolis and New York, 1941–1961), Vol. III.

E. F. Humphrey, *Nationalism and Religion in America, 1774–1789* (Boston, 1924).

J. James, *The Framing of the Fourteenth Amendment* (Urbana, Ill., 1956).

R. A. Rutland, *Birth of the Bill of Rights: 1776–1791* (Chapel Hill, N.C., 1955).

A. P. Stokes, *Church and State in the United States* (New York, 1950), I, 518–599.

R. A. Wells and T. A. Askew (eds.), *Liberty and Law: Reflections on the Constitution in American Life and Thought* (Grand Rapids, Mich., 1987).

25   Ohio Constitution (Extract)

November 29, 1802

Ohio was the first state to be formed from the Northwest Territory, and its constitutional provision for religious freedom was foreshadowed by language in the Northwest Ordinance, passed by the Continental Congress in 1787 (reenacted 1789). Article I had stated that "no person, demeaning himself in a peaceable and orderly manner, shall ever be molested on account of his mode of worship, or religious sentiments," and Article III had added that "religion, morality, and knowledge being necessary to good government and the happiness of mankind, schools and the means of education shall forever be encouraged." Article V had then required states formed from the territory to enact constitutions "in conformity to the principles contained in these articles."

Ohio's constitution restated and expanded these principles, joining traditions of separation and state benevolence toward religion. Several other Western states repeated or approximated this terminology at the time of their admission.

From Article VIII, Section 3:

That all men have a natural and indefeasible right to worship Almighty God according to the dictates of their conscience; that no human authority can, in any case whatever, control or interfere with the rights of conscience; that no man shall be compelled to attend, erect, or support any place of worship, or to maintain any ministry, against his consent; and that no preference shall ever be given by law to any religious society or mode of worship, and no religious test shall be required, as a qualification to any office of trust or profit. But religion, morality, and knowledge being essentially necessary to the good government and the happiness of mankind, schools and the means of instruction shall forever be encouraged by legislative provision, not inconsistent with the rights of conscience.

Source: Francis Newton Thorpe (ed.), *The Federal and State Constitutions* (Washington, D.C., 1909), V, 2910.

SUGGESTIONS FOR BACKGROUND AND REFERENCE

E. S. Gaustad, *Faith of Our Fathers. Religion and the New Nation* (San Francisco, 1987), pp. 151 ff.

A. P. Stokes, *Church and State in the United States* (New York, 1950), I, 480–482, 613–614.

C. Wittke (ed.), *The History of the State of Ohio* (Columbus, Ohio, 1941–1944), II, 3–31.

✦ ✦ ✦ Diversity and Establishment in the Canadas

26 The Quebec Act (Extracts)

June 22, 1774

Unlike the United States, Canada's historical evolution produced no constitutional tradition of church-state separation, although British North America exhibited growing religious diversity by the end of the eighteenth century. The Church of England was officially (though weakly) established in the maritime colonies (Nova Scotia 1758, New Brunswick 1786, Prince Edward Island 1803), and after the American Revolution an influx of colonial Loyalists and British immigrants laid the foundations of a predominantly Protestant Upper Canada. Protestants were divided among several denominations, but French-speaking Lower Canada was overwhelmingly Roman Catholic. Although the British government had originally given consideration to Anglicizing the French province after conquest (1759–1760), ethnic and religious realities eventually conduced to the grant of guarantees for Catholicism in the Quebec Act of 1774.

This famous legislation was fundamental to future church-state relations in British North America. The statute was intended by Lord North's ministry to serve as a comprehensive settlement for the vast area ceded by France at the close of the Seven Years War, though it also included trans-Appalachia north of the Ohio River in its terms. Instead of introducing British law and parliamentary institutions, it largely reestablished the social and political structure of New France, confirmed seigneurial rights, and protected the traditional privileges of the Catholic church, including the tithe. Promise was also made for future support for "a Protestant Clergy within the said Province." The act was vilified by parliamentary Whigs and leaders of the English colonies as a design for arbitrary government and a threat to Protestantism. As such, it contributed to the coming of the American Revolution, but it also attracted the loyalty of French Catholics in the province.

V. And, for the more perfect Security and Ease of the Minds of the Inhabitants of the said Province, it is hereby declared, That His Majesty's Subjects professing the Religion of the Church of *Rome* of and in the said Province of *Quebec*, may have, hold, and enjoy the free Exersice of the Religion of the Church of *Rome*, subject to the King's Supremacy, declared and established by an Act made in the First Year of the Reign of Queen *Elizabeth* . . . ; and that the Clergy of the said Church may hold, receive, and enjoy their accustomed Dues and Rights, with respect to such Persons only as shall profess the said Religion.

VI. Provided nevertheless, That it shall be lawful for His Majesty, his Heirs or Successors, to make such Provision out of the rest of the said accustomed Dues and Rights for the Encouragement of the Protestant Religion, and for the Maintenance and Support of a Protestant Clergy within the said Province, as he or they shall from time to time think necessary and expedient.

VII. Provided always, . . . That no Person, professing the Religion of the Church of *Rome*, and residing in the said Province, shall be obliged to take the Oath required by the said Statute passed in the First Year of the Reign of Queen *Elizabeth*, or any other Oaths substituted by any other Act in the Place thereof; but that every such Person who, by the said Statute, is required to take the Oath therein mentioned, shall be obliged . . . to take and subscribe the following Oath before the Governor or such other Person in such Court of Record as His Majesty shall appoint, who are hereby authorized to administer the same; *videlicet*,

"I A.B. do sincerely promise and swear, That I will be faithful, and bear true Allegiance to His Majesty King George, and him will defend to the utmost of my Power, against all traiterous Conspiracies and Attempts whatsoever, which shall be made against his Person, Crown, and Dignity; and I will do my utmost Endeavour to disclose and make known to His Majesty, his Heirs and Successors, all Treasons and traiterous Conspiracies and Attempts which I shall know to be against him, or any of them; and all this I do swear without any Equivocation, mental Evasion or secret Reservation, and renouncing all Pardons and Dispensations from any Power or Person whomsoever to the contrary.

So help me GOD.

* * *

VIII. . . . all His Majesty's *Canadian* Subjects, within the Province of *Quebec,* the religious Orders and Communities only excepted, may also hold and enjoy their Property and Possessions, together with all Customs and Usages relative thereto, and all other their Civil Rights, in as large, ample and beneficial manner as if the said Proclamation, Commissions, Ordinances, and other Acts and Instruments had not been made, and as may consist with their Allegiance to His Majesty and Subjection to the Crown and Parliament of *Great Britain;* and that in all Matters of Controversy relative to Property and Civil Rights, Resort shall be had to the Laws of *Canada,* as the Rule for the Decision of the same; and all Causes that shall hereafter be instituted in any of the Courts of Justice . . . shall, with respect to such Property and Rights, be determined agreeably to the said Laws and Customs of *Canada,* until they shall be varied or altered by any Ordinances that shall, from time to time, be passed in the said Province by the Governor, Lieutenant Governor or Commander in Chief for the time being, by and with the Advice and Consent of the Legislative Council of the same . . . .

Source: 14 Geo. III, c. 83; *The Statutes at Large, of England and of Great-Britain* (London, 1811), XIII, 791–792.

SUGGESTIONS FOR BACKGROUND AND REFERENCE

R. Coupland, *The Quebec Act. A Study in Statesmanship* (Oxford, 1925).
J. S. Moir, *The Church in the British Era. From the British Conquest to Confederation* (Toronto, 1972), pp. 35–47.
H. Neatby, *Quebec. The Revolutionary Age 1760–1791* (Toronto, 1966), pp. 125–141.

27 Canadian Constitutional Act (Extracts)

June 10, 1791

After the American Revolution many discontented Loyalists emigrated to the British maritime colonies, to British territories adjacent to the Great Lakes (Upper Canada), and even to the predominantly French-language Lower Canada. In recognition of this new pattern of settlement, Parliament amended the Quebec Act, dividing the Province into Upper and Lower Canada and granting demands for common law, free-hold tenure, and legislative assembly. At the same time it also explicitly established and endowed "the Protestant Clergy", that is, the Church of

England, with tracts of crown lands as settlement progressed. The act, unchallenged at the time, became the basis for much of a prolonged controversy over the "clergy reserves" in the nineteenth century.

XXXVI. . . . it shall . . . be lawful for His Majesty, his Heirs or Successors, to authorize the Governor or Lieutenant Governor of each of the said Provinces respectively, . . . to make, from and out of the Lands of the Crown within such Provinces, such Allotment and Appropriation of Lands, for the Support and Maintenance of a Protestant Clergy within the same, as may bear a due proportion to the Amount of such Lands within the same as have at any time been granted by or under the Authority of His Majesty; and that whenever any Grant of Lands within either of the said Provinces shall hereafter be made, . . . there shall at the same time be made . . . a proportionable Allotment and Appropriation of Lands for the above-mentioned Purpose, within the Township or Parish to which such Lands so to be granted shall appertain or be annexed, or as nearly adjacent thereto as Circumstances will admit; . . . and that such Lands . . . shall be, as nearly as the Circumstances and Nature of the case will admit, of the like Quality as the Lands in respect of which the same are so alloted and appropriated, and shall be, as nearly as the same can be estimated at the time of making such Grant equal in Value to the seventh Part of the Lands so granted.

XXXVII. . . . all and every the Rents, Profits or Emoluments, which may at any time arise from such Lands so allotted and appropriated as aforesaid, shall be applicable solely to the Maintenance and Support of a Protestant Clergy within the Province in which the same shall be situated, and to no other Use or Purpose whatever.

XXXVIII. . . . it shall . . . be lawful for His Majesty, his Heirs or Successors, to authorize the Governor or Lieutenant Governor of each of the said Provinces respectively, . . . with the advice of such Executive Council as shall have been appointed by His Majesty, . . . to constitute and erect, within every Township or Parish which now is or thereafter may be formed, constituted, or erected within such Province, one or more Parsonage or Rectory, . . . according to the Establishment of the Church of *England;* and from time to time, by an Instrument under the Great Seal of such Province, to endow every such Parsonage or Rectory with so much or such Part of the Lands so allotted and appropriated as aforesaid, in respect of any Lands within such Township or Parish, which shall have been granted subsequent to the Commencement of this Act, or of such Lands as may have been allotted and appropriated for the same Purpose, by or in virtue of any Instruction which may be given by His Majesty, in respect of any Lands granted by His Majesty before the Commencement of this Act, as such Governor, Lieutenant Governor, or Person administering the Government, shall, with the Advice of the said Executive Council, judge to be expedient under the then existing Circumstances of such Township or Parish.

XXXIX. . . . it shall . . . be lawful for His Majesty, his Heirs or Successors, to authorize the Governor, Lieutenant Governor, or Person administering the Government of each of the said Provinces respectively, to present to every such Parsonage or Rectory an Incumbent or Minister of the Church of *England,* who shall have been duly ordained according to the Rites of the said Church, and to supply from time to time such Vacancies as may happen therein; and that every Person so presented to any such Parsonage or Rectory, shall hold and enjoy the same, and all Rights, Profits, and Emoluments thereunto belonging or granted, as fully and amply, and in the same manner, and on the same Terms and Conditions, and liable to the Performance of the same Duties, as the Incumbent of a Parsonage or Rectory in *England*.

Source: 31 Geo. III, c. 31; *The Statutes at Large, of England and of Great-Britain* (London, 1811), XVII, 563–565.

SUGGESTIONS FOR BACKGROUND AND REFERENCE

A. Craig, *Upper Canada. The Formative Years 1784–1841* (Toronto, 1963), pp. 1–19.

J. S. Moir, *The Church in the British Era. From the British Conquest to Confederation* (Toronto, 1972), pp. 58–62.

A. Wilson, *The Clergy Reserves of Upper Canada. A Canadian Mortmain* (Toronto, 1968), pp. 3–17.

II

THE FRENCH REVOLUTIONARY ERA, 1789 – 1815

✦ ✦ ✦

28   Decree on the Confiscation of Church Property

November 2, 1789

The French Revolution began against the background of a bankrupt state. Financial necessity thus combined with *philosophe* anticlericalism and radical Gallicanism to secure passage of this measure by a vote of 568 to 346. (The tithe had earlier been confiscated in the August decrees.) Yet opposition was strong. Some of the *cahiers* had proposed reorganization of church wealth, but not confiscation. Opponents argued that the church held land in trust for the performance of educational and charitable work and that confiscation would jeopardize all security of property. The National Assembly was unwilling to implement the decree at once, but eventually it led to the thorough reform of the maintenance of religion embodied in the Civil Constitution of the Clergy.

The National Assembly decrees,

1st, That all ecclesiastical properties are at the disposal of the nation, on condition that suitable provision be made for the expenses of worship, the support of ministers, and poor relief under the supervision and according to the instructions of the provinces;

2nd, That in the provision to be made for the support of ministers of religion *not less than twelve hundred livres per annum* be assured for the endowment of each living, exclusive of dwelling and gardens attached thereto.

Source: Jean B. Duvergier (ed.), *Collection complète des lois, décrets, ordonnances, règlements, avis du conseil d'état* (Paris, 1834–1906), I, 54–55.

SUGGESTIONS FOR BACKGROUND AND REFERENCE

R. Aubert et al., *The Church between Revolution and Restoration* (New York, 1981), pp. 11–50.

A. Aulard, *Christianity and the French Revolution* (London, 1927).

A. Dansette, *Religious History of Modern France* (Freiburg, Germany, 1961), I, 1–157.

A. Debidour, *Histoire des rapports de l'église et de l'état en France de 1789 à 1870* (Paris, 1898), pp. 1–323.

P. de la Gorce, *Histoire religieuse de la Révolution française* (Paris, 1909–1923).

J. P. Joshua and C. Geffre, *1789: the French Revolution and the Church* (Edinburgh, 1989).

A. Latreille, *L'Église catholique et la Révolution française* (Paris, 1946).

C. Ledré, *L'Église de France sous la Révolution* (Paris, 1949).

J. Leflon, *La crise révolutionnaire, 1789–1846* (Paris, 1949), pp. 17–273.

J. McManners, *The French Revolution and the Church* (New York, 1969).

C. S. Phillips, *The Church in France 1789–1848: A Study in Revival* (London, 1929), pp. 1–149.

29   Decree on Protestant Liberty

December 24, 1789

In one of its early acts the National Assembly gave application to the royal edict of 1787 and to the promises contained in its own Declaration of the Rights of Man and of the Citizen that "all citizens, being equal before (the law), are equally eligible to all public positions" (article 6), and that "no one shall be molested because of his opinions, even religious opinions, provided their expression does not disturb the public order established by law" (article 10). Jews, however, were not covered by the act, probably because of cautions arising from reports of the unpopularity of Alsatian Jews.

The National Assembly, without intending anything prejudicial to Jews, on whose position it reserves the right to declare, and in order that no reasons for exclusion, other than those resulting from constitutional decrees, may be opposed to the eligibility of any citizen, has decreed as follows:

1st, Non-Catholics who have completed all the conditions prescribed in the preceding decrees of the National Assembly for electors and eligibility may be elected to all government offices without exception; 2nd, Non-Catholics, like other citizens, are capable of all civil and military employment.

Source: Jean B. Duvergier (ed.), *Collection complète des lois, décrets, ordonnances, règlements, avis du conseil d'état* (Paris, 1834–1906), I, 89.

SUGGESTIONS FOR BACKGROUND AND REFERENCE

H. M. Baird, *The Huguenots and the Revocation of the Edict of Nantes* (New York, 1895), II, 550–570.

G. Bonet-Maury, *Histoire de la liberté de conscience en France depuis l'Édit de Nantes jusqu'à juillet 1870* (Paris, 1900), pp. 88–96.

J. Dedieu, *Histoire politique des protestants français (1715–1794)* (Paris, 1925).

B. C. Poland, *French Protestantism and the French Revolution, 1685–1815* (Princeton, 1957).

30   Decree Suppressing Monastic Vows

February 13, 1790

French monasticism was in decline before the Revolution, and some congregations had already been dissolved. This decree occasioned little protest, and many monks reentered civil life.

1. The constitutional law of the kingdom shall no longer recognize solemn monastic vows of persons of either sex. Consequently, the regular orders and congregations in which such vows have been made are and shall remain suppressed in France, and no similar ones may be established in the future.

2. All individuals of either sex living in monasteries and religious houses may leave them by making a declaration before the local municipality, and a suitable pension shall immediately be provided for them. Also, houses shall be set aside to which the religious who do not wish to profit by the provision of the present article shall be required to withdraw. Moreover, for the present no change shall be made with regard to houses charged with public education nor with charitable establishments until a decision shall be taken in these matters.

3. Nuns may remain in the houses where they are at present, and they are expressly excepted from the article which obliges monks to consolidate several houses into one.

Source: Jean B. Duvergier (ed.), *Collection complète des lois, décrets, ordonnances, règlements, avis du conseil d'état* (Paris, 1834–1906), I, 100.

SUGGESTIONS FOR BACKGROUND AND REFERENCE

P. Nourrisson, *Histoire légale des congrégations religieuses en France depuis 1789* (Paris, 1928), I, 1–79.
References for Document 28.

31   Civil Constitution of the Clergy (Extracts)

July 12, 1790

The ecclesiastical committee of the National Assembly made its report in May 1790, and the Constitution was passed on July 12. The term "civil" suggested the state's concern with external rather than doctrinal aspects of the church and also the clergy's new position as salaried functionaries of the state. The king was reluctant to assent to the measure but eventually did so. The pope did not openly disclose his opposition until the following year. The French clergy divided, a majority of lower clergy and a small minority of bishops at first accepting the new arrangements. The opposition, which grew after the imposition of the oath and the papal condemnation, challenged the right of the civil power unilaterally to alter the constitution of the church. Apostolic succession was barely preserved by the willingness of a few bishops, notably Talleyrand, to serve the Constitutional Church. Yet the schism grew rapidly and involved the laity.

The Constitution reflected Gallicanism in the scant regard paid to papal authority. The Enlightenment was evident in the concern for a reasoned and balanced simplification of the entire ecclesiastical structure, which, in fact, exactly paralleled the provisions in the making for civil administration. The elective principle, permitting non-Catholics to participate in the choice of clergy, raised special difficulties for many Catholics.

Title I. Ecclesiastical Offices

1. Each department shall form a single diocese, and each diocese shall have the same extent and limits as the department.

2. The episcopal sees of the eighty-three departments of the kingdom shall be established as follows:

That of the department of Seine-Inférieur at Rouen; that of the department of Calvados at Bayeux . . . . [The names of the remaining episcopal sees are here omitted.]

All other bishoprics in the eighty-three departments of the kingdom, which are not included by name in the present article, are and forever shall be suppressed.

The kingdom shall be divided into ten metropolitan districts, the seats of which shall be Rouen, Rheims, Besançon, Rennes, Paris, Bourges, Bordeaux, Toulouse, Aix, and Lyons. The archbishoprics shall have the following designations:

That of Rouen shall be called the archbishopric of the Channel Coasts; that of Rheims, the archbishopric of the Northeast . . . . [The names of the remaining archbishoprics are here omitted.]

3. [This article enumerates the departments included in each archbishopric.]

4. No church or parish of France nor any French citizen may recognize, upon any occasion or upon any pretext whatsoever, the authority of an ordinary bishop or of an archbishop whose see shall be under the supremacy of a foreign power, nor that of his representatives residing in France or elsewhere; without prejudice, however, to the unity of the faith and the communion which shall be maintained with the visible head of the universal church, as hereinafter provided.

5. After the bishop of a diocese has given his decision in his synod about matters within his competence, an appeal may be taken to the archbishop, who shall give his decision in the metropolitan synod.

6. A new organization and division of the parishes of the kingdom shall be undertaken immediately in concert with the diocesan bishops and the district administrations. The number and extent of the parishes shall be determined according to regulations which shall be established.

7. The cathedral church of each diocese shall be restored to its ancient condition by the suppression of parishes and the redistribution of dwellings which it may be deemed appropriate to unite thereto, and it shall be at the same time the church of the parish and of the diocese.

8. The episcopal parish shall have no other immediate pastor than the bishop. All priests established there shall be his vicars . . . .

9. There shall be sixteen vicars of the cathedral church in cities of more than ten thousand residents, but only twelve where the population is smaller than ten thousand residents.

10. A single seminary shall be preserved or established in each diocese to prepare men for [holy] orders, without intending any prejudice for the present to other houses of instruction and education.

11. The seminary shall be established, whenever possible, near the cathedral church, and even within the precincts of the buildings intended for the bishop's lodging.

12. For the guidance and instruction of young students received into the seminary there shall be a superior vicar and three directing vicars subordinate to the bishop.

* * *

14. The vicars of the cathedral churches and the superior vicars and directing vicars of the seminary shall form the regular and permanent council of the bishop, who shall perform no act of jurisdiction which concerns the government of the diocese or of the seminary until he has consulted them. The bishop may, however, in the course of his visits issue such provisional ordinances as may be necessary.

15. In all cities and towns of not more than six thousand residents there shall be only one parish. Other parishes shall be suppressed and united with the principal church.

16. In cities of more than six thousand residents each parish may include a greater number of parishioners, and as many parishes shall be preserved or established as the needs of the people and localities require.

17. The administrative assemblies, in concert with the diocesan bishop, shall indicate to the next legislature the parishes and annexes or chapels of ease in town and country which it is proper to preserve or enlarge, establish or suppress; and they shall define these districts according to what the needs of the people, the dignity of religion, and the different localities require.

* * *

20. All titles and offices other than those mentioned in the present constitution, dignities, canonries, prebends, demi-prebends, chapels, chaplaincies, both in cathedral and collegiate churches, all regular and secular chapters for either sex, abbacies and priorships, both regular and *in commendam,* for either sex, as well as all other benefices and prestimonies[1] in general, of whatever kind or denomination, are from the day of this decree extinguished and suppressed and shall never be reestablished in any form.

* * *

Title II. Appointments to Benefices

1. Beginning with the day of publication of the present decree there shall be but one mode of choosing bishops and parish priests, namely that of election.

2. All elections shall be by ballot and shall be decided by the absolute majority of the votes.

3. The election of bishops shall take place according to the prescribed form and by the electoral body designated in the decree of December 22, 1789, for the appointment of members of the departmental assembly.

---

1. Funds or revenues established in support of unbeneficed priests.

4. On receiving news of a vacancy in an episcopal see, through death, resignation, or other cause, the departmental *procureur-général-syndic* shall give notice to the district *procureurs-syndics* to convene the electors who determined the last election of members of the administrative assembly; and at the same time, he shall indicate the day when the bishop's election shall take place, which shall be at latest the third Sunday after his letter of notification.[2]

* * *

6. A bishop's election may take place or be initiated only upon a Sunday in the principal church of the chief town of the department, at the close of the parish mass, at which all the electors are required to be present.

7. To be eligible for a bishopric, one must have fulfilled for at least fifteen years the duties of ecclesiastical ministry in the diocese as a parish priest, officiating minister or vicar, or as superior or directing vicar of the seminary.

* * *

17. The archbishop or senior bishop of the province shall have the right to examine the bishop-elect in the presence of his council upon his doctrine and character. If he deems him qualified, he shall give him canonical institution. If he believes it is his duty to refuse this, the reasons for his refusal shall be recorded in writing and signed by the archbishop and his council, reserving to the parties concerned the right to appeal by writ of error as hereinafter provided.

18. The bishop applied to for confirmation may not require from the bishop-elect any oath other than profession of the Catholic, Apostolic, and Roman religion.

19. The new bishop shall not apply to the pope for any confirmation, but shall write to him as the visible head of the universal church, in testimony to the unity of faith and communion maintained with him.

* * *

21. Before the ceremony of consecration begins, the bishop-elect shall take a solemn oath in the presence of the municipal officers, the people, and the clergy, to guard with care the faithful of his diocese who are entrusted to him, to be faithful to the nation, the law, and the king, and to support with all his power the constitution decreed by the National Assembly and accepted by the king.

* * *

25. The election of parish priests shall take place according to the prescribed forms and by the electors designated in the decree of December 22, 1789, for the election of members of the administrative assembly of the district.

26. The assembly of electors for appointment to livings shall form each year at the time of the formation of the district assemblies, even though there is only one vacant living in the district; for which purpose the municipalities shall be required to

---

2. A decree of December 22, 1789, had provided for these legal officials of departments and districts and charged them with oversight of the execution of the laws.

give notice to the district *procureur-syndic* of all vacancies of livings occurring in their *arrondissement* through death, resignation, or other cause.

* * *

29. Each elector, before depositing his ballot in the ballot box, shall swear to vote only for that person whom he has conscientiously chosen in his heart as the most worthy, without having been influenced by any gifts, promises, solicitations or threats. The same oath shall be required at the election of the bishops as in the case of parish priests.

30. The election of parish priests may be held or begun only on a Sunday in the principal church of the chief town of the district, at the close of the parish mass, at which all electors are required to be present.

* * *

32. To be eligible for a living it shall be necessary to have fulfilled the duties of vicar in a parish or hospital or other institution of charity of the diocese for at least five years.

* * *

38. The parish priests elected and installed shall take the same oath as the bishops on a Sunday in their church before the parish mass, in the presence of the municipal officers of the place, the people and the clergy. Until then they may not perform any pastoral function.

* * *

40. Bishoprics and livings shall be regarded as vacant until those elected to fill them have taken the oath above mentioned.

* * *

Title III. Salaries of Ministers of Religion

1. Ministers of religion, performing as they do the first and most important functions of society, and forced to live continuously in the place of service to which they have been called by the confidence of the people, shall be maintained by the nation.

2. Every bishop, parish priest, and officiating clergyman in an annex or chapel of ease shall be furnished with a suitable dwelling, on condition, however, that the occupant shall make all the necessary current repairs. At present this shall not affect in any way those parishes where the priest now receives a money equivalent instead of his dwelling. The departments shall, moreover, have cognizance of requests made by the parishes and by the priests. Salaries shall be assigned to each, as indicated below.

3. The stipend of bishops shall be as follows: for the bishop of Paris 50,000 *livres;* the bishops of cities having a population of 50,000 or more, 20,000 *livres;* other bishops, 12,000 *livres.*

* * *

5. The stipend of parish priests shall be as follows: In Paris, 6,000 *livres*.
In cities with a population of 50,000 or more, 4,000 *livres*.
In those with a population of fewer than 50,000 but more than 10,000, 3,000 *livres*.
In cities and towns with a population below 10,000 but more than 3,000, 2,400 *livres*.
In all other cities, towns, and villages where the parish has a population between 2,500 and 3,000, 2,000 *livres;* in those between 2,000 and 2,500, 1,800 *livres;* in those with a population of fewer than 2,000 but more than 1,000, the salary shall be 1,500 *livres;* in those with 1,000 inhabitants and fewer, 1,200 *livres*.

* * *

7. Monetary stipends of ministers of religion shall be paid every three months, in advance, by the treasurer of the district . . . .

* * *

11. The rate fixed above for the payment of ministers of religion shall go into effect upon the day of publication of this decree, but only in the case of those who shall be afterward provided with ecclesiastical offices. The remuneration of the present titularies, both those whose offices or functions are suppressed and those whose titles are retained, shall be fixed by special decree.

12. In view of the salary assured to them by the present constitution, bishops, parish priests, and vicars shall perform the episcopal and priestly functions gratis.

Title IV. The Law of Residence

1. The law of residence shall be strictly observed, and all vested with an ecclesiastical office or function shall be subject thereto without any distinction or exception.

2. No bishop shall absent himself from his diocese more than fifteen consecutive days during the year, except in case of genuine necessity and with the consent of the directory of the department in which his see is located.

3. Similarly, parish priests and vicars may not absent themselves from the place of their duties beyond the term fixed above, except for grave reasons, and even in such cases priests must obtain the consent of both their bishop and the directory of their district, and the vicars that of the parish priest.

4. In case a bishop or a priest violates this law of residence, the municipal government shall inform the departmental *procureur-général-syndic,* who shall summon him in writing to return to his duties, and after a second monition, shall take steps to have his salary declared forfeited for the entire time of his absence.

* * *

6. Bishops, parish priests, and vicars may, as active citizens, be present at the primary and electoral assemblies. They may be named electors or deputies to the legislative bodies, or elected members of the general council of their commune and of the administrative councils of their district and department; but their duties are declared incompatible with those of mayor and other municipal officials and of

members of the directories of the district and of the department; and if elected thereto, they must make a choice.

Source: Jean B. Duvergier (ed.), *Collection complète des lois, décrets, ordonnances, règlements, avis du conseil d'état* (Paris, 1834–1906), I, 242–248.

SUGGESTIONS FOR BACKGROUND AND REFERENCE

E. Préclin, *Les Jansénistes du XVIIIe siècle et la constitution civile du clergé* (Paris, 1929).
L. Sciout, *Histoire de la constitution civile du clergé (1790–1801)* (Paris, 1872–1881).
References for Document 28.

32   Decree on the Clerical Oath

November 27, 1790

Opponents of the Civil Constitution attempted to ignore it and retain their posts under the old arrangements. The Assembly thereupon imposed the oath provided for in the Constitution, a promise to watch over the faithful and to be loyal to nation, law, crown, and the constitution decreed by the National Assembly. Acceptance of the ecclesiastical reorganization was implied. The requirement of the oath precipitated the bitter split between Jurors and Nonjurors which lasted until the Napoleonic settlement. The difficulty of decision for many curés who had at first accepted the Civil Constitution was very great. Popular opinion and local officials in many places harassed Nonjurors, especially as they tended to become active in counterrevolution.

1. Bishops and former archbishops and curés maintained in office shall be required, if they have not already done so, to take the oath for which they are liable by article 39 of the decree of July 13 last, and regulated by articles 21 and 38 of that of the 12th of the same month concerning the Civil Constitution of the Clergy.

In consequence, they shall swear . . . to watch carefully over the faithful of the diocese or parish entrusted to them, to be faithful to the nation, to the law, and to the king, and to maintain with all their power the Constitution decreed by the National Assembly and accepted by the king; to wit, those who are presently in their dioceses or livings, within a week; those who are absent but are in France, within a month; and those who are outside France, within two months; all dating from the publication of the present decree.

2. Vicars of bishops, superiors and directors of seminaries, vicars of curés, teachers of seminaries and colleges and all other public ecclesiastical functionaries shall, within the same periods, take the [same] oath . . . .

3. The oath shall be taken on a Sunday at the conclusion of the mass; to wit, by bishops, former archbishops, their vicars, superiors and directors of seminaries, in the episcopal church; and by the curés, their vicars, and all other public ecclesiastical functionaries, in their parish church; all in the presence of the general council of

the commune and the faithful. To this end, at least two days in advance they shall declare in writing to the clerk of the municipality their intention to take the oath and shall consult with the mayor to decide upon the day.

4. Those of the said bishops, former archbishops, curés and other public ecclesiastical functionaries who are members of the National Assembly and who now exercise their duties as deputies, shall take the oath which concerns them respectively at the National Assembly, within a week of the day on which the sanction of the present decree will have been announced; and within the week following they shall send a certificate of their oath to their municipality.

5. Those of the said bishops, former archbishops, curés and other public ecclesiastical functionaries who have not taken, within the determined periods, the oath prescribed for them respectively, shall be deemed to have renounced their office, and provision for their replacement shall be made, as in the case of vacancy by resignation, according to Title II of . . . the Civil Constitution of the Clergy. To which end the mayor shall be required to report a failure to take the oath a week after the expiration of the said periods . . . .

6. In case the said bishops, former archbishops, curés, and other public ecclesiastical functionaries, after having taken their respective oaths, fail therein, either by refusing to obey the decrees of the National Assembly, accepted or sanctioned by the king, or by forming or inciting opposition to their execution, they shall be prosecuted in the district courts as rebels to the law, and punished by loss of their stipend, and moreover, declared deprived of the rights of active citizenship and incapable of any public function. Accordingly, provision shall be made for their replacement . . . .

7. Those of the said bishops, former archbishops, curés, and other public ecclesiastical functionaries maintained in office and refusing to take their respective oaths, as well as those who have been suppressed, together with members of secular ecclesiastical bodies likewise suppressed, who take up any of their public duties or those which they perform in a body, shall be prosecuted as disturbers of public order and punished with the same penalties as above.

8. All ecclesiastical or lay persons who combine to plan disobedience to the decrees of the National Assembly accepted or sanctioned by the king, or to form or incite opposition to their execution, shall be likewise prosecuted as disturbers of public order and punished according to the rigor of the laws.

Source: Jean B. Duvergier (ed.), *Collection complète des lois, décrets, ordonnances, règlements, avis du conseil d'état* (Paris, 1834–1906), II, 59–60.

SUGGESTIONS FOR BACKGROUND AND REFERENCE

References for Document 28.

33 *Charitas* (Extracts)

April 13, 1791

Pius VI (1775–1799) had privately indicated his opposition to the Civil Constitution to the king and the bishops and issued an earlier bull in March 1791. The revolt of papal subjects in Avignon and their demand for annexation to France added further irritation. *Charitas,* issued in April, condemned the loss of tithes, annates, and church lands; invoked Catholic resistance to the Civil Constitution; and encouraged Nonjurors. In the next month the papal nuncio left Paris.

. . . We have just learned of the war against the Catholic religion which has been started by the revolutionary thinkers who as a group form a majority in the National Assembly of France. We have wept in God's presence, shared Our sorrow with the cardinals, and proclaimed public and private prayers. Then We wrote to King Louis, on July 9, 1790, and repeatedly encouraged him not to confirm the Civil Constitution of the Clergy which would lead his people into error and schism. For it was intolerable that a political assembly should change the universal practice of the Church, disregard the opinions of the holy Fathers and the decrees of the councils, overturn the order of the hierarchy and control the election of bishops, destroy episcopal sees, and introduce a worse form into the Church after removing the better.

* * *

We Ourselves immediately engaged in the task of examining all the articles of the Constitution. The Assembly, although it heard the unanimous views of the French Church, did not abandon its design, but tried all the more to destroy the firmness of the bishops. But it knew well that none of the metropolitans or the senior bishops would agree to ordain new bishops who were elected in the municipal districts by laity, heretics, unbelievers, and Jews as the published decrees commanded. It also understood that this foolish form of Church government could nowhere survive, for without the bishops the entire appearance of the church would vanish. As a result the Assembly considered publishing other even more foolish decrees . . . . These decrees, with the king's approval, provided that any bishop from a different district could consecrate the elected persons if the metropolitan or senior bishop refused to do so.

Furthermore, to instantly disperse all faithful bishops and parish priests, the decrees provided that all pastors should swear unequivocally that they would observe the Constitution . . . . Those who refused were to be considered expelled from their office . . . . When the lawful pastors and ministers were driven out, by force if necessary, the municipal districts would set about electing new bishops and parish priests. Upon election these men were to disregard the metropolitans and

From *The Papal Encyclicals,* ed. Claudia Carlen, I.H.M., 5 vols. (1981; reprint, Ann Arbor, Mich.: Pierian Press, 1990), © Claudia Carlen, used with permission.

senior bishops who had refused the oath, and to go to the Assembly Executive which would appoint some bishops to ordain them. . . .

New pastoral letters to their flocks were published by the French bishops . . . . They agreed that these civil oaths should be regarded as perjury and sacrilege, unbefitting not merely the clergy but any Catholic; all actions which are based on these oaths should be seen as schismatic, null, void, and liable to severe censures.

* * *

Therefore to hinder the spread of schism from the start, to recall to their duty those who have strayed, to fortify the good in their purpose, and to preserve religion . . . , We . . . answer the prayers of the entire group of bishops of the French church. . . . We proclaim that each and every cardinal, archbishop, bishop, abbot, vicar, canon, parish priest, curate and member of the clergy, whether secular or regular, who has purely and simply taken the Civil Oath . . . is suspended from the exercise of his office and will act irregularly if he exercises his office unless he abjures his oath within forty days from this date. . . .

Furthermore, We declare specifically that the elections of the said Expilly, Marolles, Saurine, Massieu, Lindet, Laurent, Heraudin, and Gobel . . . are unlawful, sacrilegious, and utterly void. . . .[1]

We similarly declare . . . that their consecrations were sinful and are illicit, unlawful, sacrilegious . . . and they have been suspended from all exercise of the episcopal office.

We declare likewise that Charles, bishop of Autun; Jean-Baptiste, bishop of Babylon; and Jean-Joseph, bishop of Lidda have been suspended from all exercise of their episcopal office as sacrilegious consecrators or assistants; all who gave them help, consent, or counsel at those accursed consecrations have been suspended from the exercise of their priestly, or other, office.[2]

* * *

However to prevent greater evils, We decree . . . that all other elections by the electors of municipal districts to French cathedral and parochial churches . . . have been, are, and will be void, unlawful, sacrilegious, and utterly null, and We hereby rescind, efface, and revoke them. We therefore declare that men who have been or will be elected wickedly and wrongfully, whether to cathedral or parochial churches, lack all ecclesiastical and spiritual jurisdiction . . . and that bishops who have been or will be illicitly consecrated are suspended from all exercise of their episcopal office; parish priests who have been or are to be invalidly appointed are suspended from their priestly ministry.

* * *

1. Expilly, named to the department of the Aisne, was first of the new constitutional bishops to be consecrated. Gobel became metropolitan of Paris in 1791.

2. These three bishops, Talleyrand, Du Bourg-Miroudot, and Gobel, participated in the first constitutional consecration. Gobel alone subsequently consecrated forty-eight of the new bishops.

With the greatest possible kindness, We have declared the canonical penalties imposed until the present in order that the evil deeds already accomplished may be corrected and prevented from spreading abroad. . . .

. . . However, if Our mild manner of action and paternal warnings come to nothing—may God prevent this!—they should be aware that We do not intend to spare them those heavier penalties to which they are liable under the canons. They may be quite certain that We will anathematize them and proclaim them as such to the whole Church, since they are schismatic and cut off from communion with the Church and with Us.

Source: Claudia Carlen (ed.), *The Papal Encyclicals 1740–1878* (Ann Arbor, Mich., 1990), pp. 177–183. Latin text in *Bullarium Romanorum (Magnum): Continuatio* (Graz, 1963–1964), VI, 2324–2333.

SUGGESTIONS FOR BACKGROUND AND REFERENCE

E. E. Y. Hales, *Revolution and Papacy 1789–1846* (Garden City, N.Y., 1961), pp. 83–88.
L. von Pastor, *The History of the Popes from the Close of the Middle Ages* (London, 1899–1953), II, 165–186.

34   Decree on Publication of Papal Communications

June 9, 1791

This decree was the legislature's reply to *Charitas,* but it was not without some precedent in French tradition. Former governments of France and other European states had often prohibited publication of papal dispatches lacking authorization from the crown. In the National Assembly the measure was defended in traditional Gallican terms. Yet it sealed the break with Rome and sharpened religious conflict in France.

The National Assembly, having heard its united constitutional and ecclesiastical committees; considering that it is important to national sovereignty and to the preservation of public order in the kingdom to fix constitutionally the forms which safeguard the ancient and wholesome maxims by which the French nation has always protected itself against the encroachments of the court of Rome, without slighting the respect owed to the head of the Catholic church, decrees as follows:

1. No briefs, bulls, rescripts, constitutions, decrees, or other communications of the court of Rome, under whatsoever designation, may be recognized as such, received, published, printed, posted, or otherwise put into execution in the kingdom; but they shall be void and of no effect unless they have been presented to the legislative body, considered and verified by it, and unless their publication or execution has been authorized by a decree sanctioned by the king, and promulgated in the forms established for the publication of laws.

2. Bishops, curés, and all other public functionaries, whether clerical or lay,

who in contravention of the preceding article shall read, distribute, have read, distributed, printed, posted, or shall otherwise give publicity or execution to briefs, bulls, rescripts, constitutions, decrees, or other communications of the court of Rome, not authorized by a decree of the legislative body sanctioned by the king, shall be criminally prosecuted as disturbers of public order, and punished with the penalty of civic degradation, without prejudice to the execution of article 2 of the decree of May 7 last.[1]

Source: Jean B. Duvergier (ed.), *Collection complète des lois, décrets, ordonnances, règlements, avis du conseil d'état* (Paris, 1834–1906), III, 10.

SUGGESTIONS FOR BACKGROUND AND REFERENCE

References for Document 28.

35   Decree on Worship of the Supreme Being

May 7, 1794 [18 Floréal, Year II]

War, counterrevolution, the fall of the monarchy, and the Terror drove religion underground by 1793. Officially Catholicism was not disestablished and the Constitution of 1793 provided for freedom of worship, but dechristianization was evident in persecution, civil festivals to *la patrie,* and the new republican calendar. Some clergy, both Protestant and Catholic, openly renounced their faith and functions. In 1793 many churches were turned into Temples of Reason, while many Frenchmen remained apparently indifferent to the break in religious continuity. Some Jacobins, especially Robespierre, disliked this extremism that seized the initiative from the Convention, scandalized some republicans, and violated the theism of Rousseau. Hence Robespierre secured the decree establishing the cult of the Supreme Being, but only he seems to have taken it seriously; whatever vitality the cult possessed was drawn from nationalism.

1. The French people recognize the existence of the Supreme Being and the immortality of the soul.

2. They recognize that the worship worthy of the Supreme Being is the practice of the duties of man.

3. They place in the first rank of these duties [the obligation] to detest bad faith and tyranny, to punish tyrants and traitors, to rescue the unfortunate, to respect the weak, to defend the oppressed, [and] to do to others all the good that one can and not to be unjust toward anyone.

1. This article defined speeches against the Constitution or Civil Constitution of the Clergy as criminal offenses.

4. Festivals shall be established to remind man of the thought of the Divinity and of the dignity of his being.

5. They shall take their names from the glorious events of our revolution, from the virtues most dear and most useful to man and from the great benefactions of nature.

6. The French Republic shall celebrate every year the festivals of July 14, 1789, August 10, 1792, January 21, 1793, and May 31, 1793.[1]

7. It shall celebrate on the days of *décadi* the festivals which follow: to the Supreme Being and to nature; to the human race; to the French people; to the benefactors of humanity; to the martyrs of liberty; to liberty and equality; to the Republic; to the liberty of the world; to the love of country; to the hatred of tyrants and traitors; to truth; to justice; to modesty; to glory and immortality; to friendship; to frugality; to courage; to good faith; to heroism; to disinterestedness; to stoicism; to love; to conjugal love; to paternal love; to maternal tenderness; to filial piety; to childhood; to youth; to manhood; to old age; to misfortune; to agriculture; to industry; to our forefathers; to posterity; to happiness.[2]

8. The Committees of Public Safety and Public Instruction are charged to present a plan of organization for these festivals.

9. The National Convention summons all talents worthy to serve the cause of humanity to the honor of contributing to their establishment by hymns and patriotic songs and by all means which can further their beauty and utility.

10. The Committee of Public Safety shall confer distinction upon those works which seem most suited to fulfill these purposes and shall reward their authors.

11. Liberty of worship is maintained, in conformity with the decree of 18 Frimaire.[3]

12. Every gathering that is aristocratic and contrary to public order shall be suppressed.

13. In case of disturbances of which any worship whatsoever may be the

---

1. Anniversaries of the capture of the Bastille, the insurrection overthrowing the constitutional monarchy, the king's execution, and the fall of the Girondins.

2. The new calendar, adopted October–November 1793, divided each month into three parts of ten days each (*décades*), of which the tenth was *décadi*.

3. This decree of December 8, 1793, provided for a qualified religious liberty. The text is published in Jean B. Duvergier (ed.), *Collection complète des lois, décrets, ordonnances, règlements, avis du conseil d'état* (Paris, 1834–1906), VI, 333. Its principal provisions were as follows:

"1. Violence or intimidations contrary to liberty of worship are forbidden.

"2. The surveillance of the constituted authorities and the activity of the state shall be restricted in this respect to matters which concern them in measures of police and public security.

"3. By the preceding provisions the Convention does not intend to derogate in any manner from the laws or precautions of public safety against refractory or turbulent priests, or against all those who have attempted to use religion as a pretext for compromising the cause of liberty, . . . [nor] to furnish anyone whomsoever with any pretext for disturbing patriotism and relaxing the vigor of the public spirit.

"The Convention invites all good citizens, in the name of the nation, to abstain from all disputes which are theological or foreign to the great interests of the French people, in order to cooperate by every means in the triumph of the Republic and the ruin of its enemies."

occasion or motive, those who may excite them by fanatical preaching or by counterrevolutionary insinuations, [or] those who may provoke them by unjust and gratuitous violence, shall likewise be punished with the severity of the law.

14. A special report upon the provisions of detail relative to the present decree shall be made.

15. A festival in honor of the Supreme Being shall be celebrated upon 20 Prairial next.

David is charged to present the plan thereof to the National Convention.[4]

Source: Gazette Nationale ou Le Moniteur Universel, Nonidi 19 Floréal, l'an 2 (Jeudi 8 Mai 1794, vieux style).

SUGGESTIONS FOR BACKGROUND AND REFERENCE

A. Aulard, Le culte de la raison et le culte de l'Être suprême (1793–1794) (Paris, 1904).
A. Mathiez, Les origines des cultes révolutionnaires (Paris, 1904).
References for Document 28.

36   Thermidorean Settlement: Separation Decree and Constitution of the Year III (Extracts)

February 21, 1795 (3 Ventôse, Year III); August 22, 1795 (5 Fructidor, Year III)

In the Thermidorean reaction following the fall of Robespierre and the dismantling of the Terror, the Convention adopted a policy of cautious toleration of religion accompanied by suspicious surveillance and regulation. The approach was tersely stated in two brief documents. The Decree of February 21, 1795, at last ended the pretense of a state church; it ostensibly granted religious liberty but was primarily concerned with restrictions and limitations to be imposed upon it. (A later decree of May 30, 1795 [11 Prairial, Year III], permitted provisional free use [under communal control] of those nonalienated church buildings that had been used for worship in September 1793.) Six months later the Constitution of the Year III established the Directory. Though the longest of the three revolutionary constitutions, this document treated religion only briefly in Article 354.

The measure of freedom granted by this policy was accompanied by some revival of both Constitutional and Nonjuring churches, though some local persecutions continued and official harassment intensified again in 1797.

---

4. Jacques-Louis David (1748–1825), artist and revolutionary.

Decree of February 21, 1795 (3 Ventôse, Year III):

1. In conformity with article 7 of the *Declaration of the Rights of Man* and with article 122 of the constitution [of the Year I], the practice of any cult may not be disturbed.

2. The Republic funds none of them.

3. It does not provide any premises, either for the practice of worship or the lodging of ministers.

4. The ceremonies of every worship are forbidden outside of the precincts chosen for their practice.

5. The law does not recognize any minister of religion; no one may appear in public with garments, ornaments or costumes set apart for religious ceremonies.

6. Every gathering of citizens for the practice of any worship whatsoever is subject to the surveillance of the constituted authorities. That surveillance is confined to measures of police and public security.

7. No symbol peculiar to a religion of any kind may be placed in or on the outside of a public place. No inscription may identify the place which is dedicated to [religion]. No proclamation or public summons may be made in order to call the citizens there.

8. The communes or communal sections in collective name shall not acquire nor lease buildings for the practice of religions.

9. No perpetual or life annuity may be formed nor any tax established to discharge their expenses.

10. Whosoever shall violently disturb ceremonies of any religion whatsoever or abuse the objects of it shall be punished according to the law of 19–22 July, 1791 . . . .

From the Constitution of the Year III:

354. No one, while conforming to the law, may be prevented from practicing his chosen religion.

No one may be forced to contribute to the expenses of a sect. The Republic pays none of them.

Source: Jean B. Duvergier (ed.), *Collection complète des lois, décrets, ordonnances, règlements, avis du conseil d'état* (Paris, 1834–1906), VIII, 25–26; ibid., 240–241.

SUGGESTIONS FOR BACKGROUND AND REFERENCE

A. Mathiez, *After Robespierre. The Thermidorian Reaction* (New York, 1931), pp. 137–155.
References for Documents 28 and 35.

37   Decree on Regulation of Religious Bodies

September 29, 1795 [7 Vendémiaire, Year IV]

A month after the 1795 Constitution with its guarantee of religious freedom was proclaimed, this apparatus of state regulation was officially enacted. The change had been forecast in the withdrawal of clerical salaries in September 1794 and in the Decree of February 21, 1795. The system of church-state separation only superficially resembled the American solution. Restrictions on religion were explicit, and the "neutral" state was more suspicious than benevolent. But for a time, France, like America, was a nation of religious diversity—diversity comprised in this case of Constitutionals, Nonjurors, Lutherans, Calvinists, Jews, agnostics, and various cults. The system outlined in this law was officially retained until the Napoleonic settlement of 1801.

Title I. Surveillance of the Practice of Worship

Preliminary and General Provision

1. Every gathering of citizens for the practice of any worship whatsoever is subject to the surveillance of the constituted authorities.

Such surveillance is confined to measures of police and public security.

Title II. Guarantee of the Free Practice of All Worship

2. Those who insult the objects of any worship whatsoever in places designated for the practice thereof, or its ministers in their duties, or who interrupt the religious ceremonies of any other worship whatsoever with a public disturbance shall be fined not more than five hundred nor less than fifty *livres* per person, and imprisoned for not more than two years nor less than one month, without prejudice to the penalties provided by the Penal Code if the nature of the act gives occasion for them.

3. Under the penalties provided in the preceding article, all judges and administrators are forbidden to use their authority, and all persons are forbidden to use violence, abuse, or threats, to restrain one or more persons from celebrating certain religious festivals or from observing any day of rest, . . . either by forcing them to open or close their workshops, shops, or warehouses, or by hindering agricultural labor, or in any other manner whatsoever.

* * *

Title III. Civic Guarantee Required of All Ministers of Religion

5. No one may discharge the ministerial duties of any religion in any place whatsoever unless he previously makes, before the municipal administration or the municipal deputy . . . , a declaration . . . .

6. The formula of the declaration required above is as follows: "The _____ before us _____ has appeared N. (*the name and given names only*) resident of _____ who has made the following declaration:

"I recognize that the universality of French citizens is the sovereign, and I promise submission and obedience to the laws of the Republic.

"We have given him an acknowledgment of such declaration and he has signed with us."

A declaration containing anything more or less shall be null and void. Those who receive it shall each be punished with a fine of five hundred *livres,* and with imprisonment for not more than one year nor less than three months.

7. Every person who, a *décade* after the publication of the present decree, practices the ministry of a religion without having satisfied [requirements] of the two preceding articles, shall suffer the punishment provided in article 6; and for a second offense, he shall be condemned to ten years' imprisonment.

8. Every minister of religion who, after having made the declaration, . . . retracts or modifies it, or makes contrary professions or reservations, shall be forever banished from the territory of the Republic.

If he returns, he shall be condemned to imprisonment, also for life.

Title IV. Guarantee Against Any Religion Which May Attempt To Become Exclusive or Dominant

Section 1. Expenses of Religious Bodies

9. Communes or communal sections may neither acquire nor lease in collective name premises for the practice of worship.

10. No perpetual or life annuity may be formed, nor any tax established, to pay the expenses of any religion, or for the lodging of its ministers.

* * *

12. Those who attempt, by injuries or threats, to force one or more persons to contribute to the expenses of a religion, or who instigate such injuries or threats, shall be punished with a fine of not less than fifty nor more than five hundred *livres.*

* * *

Section 2. Places Where Display of Special Symbols of a Religion Is Prohibited

13. No special symbol of a religion may be raised, fixed, or attached in any place whatsoever in such manner as to be exhibited to the view of citizens, except within the premises set apart for the worship of the same religion, or inside private houses, workshops or warehouses of artists and merchants, or public buildings intended for the reception of works of art.

* * *

Section 3. Places Where Religious Ceremonies Are Forbidden

16. The ceremonies of every religion are prohibited outside the precincts of the building selected for worship.

This prohibition does not apply to ceremonies which occur within the precincts of private houses, provided that, besides the persons living there, the gathering . . . does not number more than ten persons.

17. The premises selected for the exercise of worship shall be . . . declared to the municipal deputy in communes of fewer than five thousand inhabitants, and to the municipal administrations of the canton or *arrondissement* in others . . . .

18. Violation of articles 16 or 17 shall be punished with a fine of not more than five hundred nor less than one hundred *livres,* and with imprisonment for not more than two years nor less than one month.

For a second offense the minister of religion shall be condemned to ten years' imprisonment.

19. Under the penalties provided in the preceding article, no one may appear in public wearing garments, ornaments, or costumes set apart for religious ceremonies or for a minister of religion.

Section 4. Documents of Civil Status

20. All judges, administrators, and public functionaries whosoever are forbidden to give any regard to testimonials from ministers or alleged ministers of religion about the civil status of citizens . . . .

* * *

Title V. Certain Offenses Which May Be Committed Because of or by the Abuse of the Practice of Worship

22. Every minister of religion who, outside the premises . . . set apart for the ceremonies or practices of a religion, reads or has read in an assembly of persons, or who posts or has posted, distributes or has distributed, a writing emanating from or announced as emanating from a minister of religion not resident in the French Republic, or even from a minister of religion resident in France who declares himself the delegate of another not resident there, shall be . . . condemned to six months of imprisonment. . . .

23. Every minister of religion who commits any of the following offenses, either in his discourses, exhortations, sermons, invocations, or prayers, in any language whatsoever, either by reading, publishing, posting, distributing . . . a writing of which he or any other is the author, shall be condemned to life imprisonment;

To wit: if, by the said writing or discourse, he has urged the reestablishment of monarchy in France, or the overthrow of the Republic, or the dissolution of the national representation;

Or if he has incited murder, or prompted the defenders of the fatherland to desert their banners, or their fathers and mothers to recall them;

Or if he has reproached those who wished to take up arms for the support of the republican constitution and the defense of liberty;

Or if he has called on persons to cut down the trees dedicated to liberty, or to take down or debase its symbols or colors;

Or finally, if he has exhorted or encouraged any persons whomsoever to treason or rebellion against the government.

24. If by writings, placards, or discourses a minister of religion seeks to mislead citizens by representing as unjust or criminal the sales or acquisitions of national

property formerly possessed by clergy or *émigrés* he shall be condemned to a fine of one thousand *livres* and imprisonment for two years.

Moreover, he shall be forbidden to continue his duties as a minister . . . .

Source: Jean B. Duvergier (ed.), *Collection complète des lois, décrets, ordonnances, règlements, avis du conseil d'état* (Paris, 1834–1906), VIII, 294–296.

SUGGESTIONS FOR BACKGROUND AND REFERENCE

References for Document 28.

✦ ✦ ✦ The Napoleonic Settlement

38   Concordat of 1801

July 15, 1801 [26 Messidor, Year IX][1]

Bonaparte was probably an agnostic, but he nourished no doctrinaire hatred for *émigrés* and Catholics, and he was ready to exploit religion for political advantage. He apparently believed that reconciliation with Rome would heal the schism in French Catholicism, advance internal stability, and subvert royalism. Negotiations, begun in 1800, were successfully concluded in 1801 with Ercole Consalvi (1757–1824), papal secretary of state. This concordat differed from previous concordats not only in the state's abandonment of any genuine confessional position but also in the new means for securing the political usefulness of the clergy. The concordat seems to have fulfilled expected propaganda aims. However, some of the Nonjuring bishops declined to resign their posts to convenience Bonaparte in making new appointments. They were deposed by Rome, but continued to lead a small Nonjuring church (*la petite église*), which lasted until 1893. From this, as from the failure to restore separate financial resources to the French church, Gallicanism suffered. Despite an unsuccessful attempt to replace it at the Restoration, the concordat served various French governments until 1905.

The government of the French Republic recognizes that the Catholic, Apostolic, and Roman religion is the religion of the great majority of French citizens.

His Holiness likewise recognizes that this same religion has derived and at this time again expects the greatest benefit and renown [*éclat*] from the establishment of Catholic worship in France and from the personal profession of it made by the Consuls of the Republic.

1. Ratifications exchanged September 10, 1801 (23 Fructidor, Year IX); promulgated April 8, 1802 (18 Germinal, Year X).

Consequently, after this mutual recognition, as much for the benefit of religion as for the maintenance of internal tranquillity, they have agreed as follows:

1. The Catholic, Apostolic, and Roman religion shall be practiced freely in France. Its worship shall be public, and in conformity with the police regulations which the government deems necessary for public tranquillity.

2. A new delimitation of the French dioceses shall be made by the Holy See in concert with the government.

3. His Holiness shall declare to the titular holders of French bishoprics that with firm confidence he expects from them, for the benefit of peace and unity, every sort of sacrifice, even that of their sees.

If, after this exhortation, they should refuse this sacrifice required for the welfare of the Church (a refusal which His Holiness, nevertheless, does not expect), provision shall be made for the government of the bishoprics of the new delimitation by new nominees in the following manner:

4. Within three months following the publication of the bull of His Holiness, the First Consul of the Republic shall nominate to the archbishoprics and bishoprics according to the new delimitation. His Holiness shall confer canonical institution, following the forms established in regard to France before the change of government.

5. Nominations to bishoprics which shall become vacant in the future shall likewise be made by the First Consul, and canonical institution shall be given by the Holy See, in conformity with the preceding article.

6. Before entering upon their functions, the bishops shall take directly at the hands of the First Consul the oath of fidelity which was in use before the change of government, expressed in the following terms:

"I swear and promise to God, upon the Holy Gospels, to remain in obedience and fidelity to the government established by the Constitution of the French Republic. I also promise not to have any correspondence, nor to participate in any council, nor to support any conspiracy, whether internal or external, which may be opposed to public tranquillity; and if, within my diocese or elsewhere, I learn that anything to the prejudice of the state is being contrived, I will make it known to the government."

7. Ecclesiastics of the second rank shall take the same oath at the hands of the civil authorities designated by the government.

8. The following form of prayer shall be repeated at the end of divine services in all Catholic churches of France: *Domine, salvam fac Republicam; Domine, salvos fac Consules.*

9. The bishops shall make a new division of the parishes of their dioceses, which shall have effect only after the consent of the government.

10. Bishops shall appoint parish priests. Their choice may fall only on persons acceptable to the government.

11. Bishops may have a chapter in their cathedrals and a seminary for their dioceses, but the government is under no obligation to endow them.

12. All metropolitan, cathedral, parochial and other nonalienated churches needed for worship shall again be placed at the disposal of the bishops.

13. His Holiness, in the interest of peace and the happy reestablishment of the Catholic religion, declares that neither he nor his successors will trouble in any manner the purchasers of alienated ecclesiastical property, and that, in consequence, the ownership of these same properties, and the rights and revenues attached to them, shall rest unchallenged in their hands or in those of their assigns.

14. The government shall assure a suitable stipend to the bishops and parish priests whose dioceses and parishes are affected by the new delimitation.

15. The government shall likewise take measures so that French Catholics, if they desire, may make grants in favor of the churches.

16. His Holiness recognizes in the First Consul of the French Republic the same rights and prerogatives which the former government enjoyed respecting the Holy See.

17. It is agreed between the contracting parties that if any of the successors of the present First Consul shall not be Catholic, the rights and prerogatives mentioned in the article above and the nomination to bishoprics shall be regulated, as regards him, by a new convention.

Source: Jean B. Duvergier (ed.), *Collection complète des lois, décrets, ordonnances, règlements, avis du conseil d'état* (Paris, 1834–1906), XIII, 90–91.

SUGGESTIONS FOR BACKGROUND AND REFERENCE

R. Aubert et al., *The Church between Revolution and Restoration* (New York, 1981), pp. 50–82.

Cambridge Modern History (New York, 1903–1912), II, 180–207.

G. L. M. J. Constant, *L'Église de France sous le Consulat et l'Empire, 1800–1814* (Paris, 1928).

S. Delacroix, *La réorganisation de l'église de France après la Révolution (1801–1809)* (Paris, 1962).

E. E. Y. Hales, *The Emperor and the Pope* (London, 1962).

F. Nielsen, *The History of the Papacy in the Nineteenth Century* (London, 1906), I, 219–259.

M. O'Dwyer, *The Papacy in the Age of Napoleon and the Restoration: Pius VII, 1800–1823* (Lanham, Md., 1985), pp. 49–63.

J. M. Robinson, *Cardinal Consalvi, 1757–1824* (New York, 1987).

References for Document 28.

39 Organic Articles (Extracts)

April 8, 1802 [18 Germinal, Year X]

Not negotiated and not mentioned in the Concordat of 1801, these stringent regulations were nonetheless published by Napoleon as a unilateral addendum to the agreement. Their purpose was to strengthen the position of the state and mollify doctrinaire republican opposition to a Catholic reconciliation. The papacy was outraged, but its protests were ignored.

Title I. The Administration of the Catholic Church in Its General Relations with the Rights and Police Power of the State

1. No bull, brief, rescript, decree, commission, provision, signature serving as a provision, nor other dispatches from the court of Rome, even concerning individuals only, may be received, published, printed, or otherwise put into execution without government authorization.

2. No person styling himself nuncio, legate, vicar or apostolic commissioner, or availing himself of any other designation, may, without the same authorization, exercise on French soil or elsewhere any function pertaining to the affairs of the Gallican church.

3. Decrees of foreign synods, even those of general councils, may not be published in France before the government has examined their form, their conformity with the laws, rights and liberties of the French Republic, and everything which in their publication may alter or affect public tranquillity.

4. No national or metropolitan council, no diocesan synod, no deliberative assembly shall take place without the express permission of the government.

5. All ecclesiastical functions shall be gratuitous, except for offerings which shall be authorized and determined by regulations.

6. There shall be recourse to the Council of State in all cases of abuse on the part of superiors and other ecclesiastical persons.

Cases of abuse are usurpation or excess of power, violation of laws and regulations of the Republic, infraction of rules sanctioned by the canons received in France, assault upon the liberties, freedoms, and customs of the Gallican church, and every undertaking or proceeding which, in the exercise of worship, may compromise the honor of citizens, arbitrarily disturb their consciences, or degenerate into oppression or injury against them, or into public scandal.

* * *

Title II. Ministers

Section I. General Provisions

9. Catholic worship shall be carried on under the direction of archbishops and bishops in their dioceses, and under that of priests in their parishes.

10. Every privilege involving exemption from or grant of episcopal jurisdiction is abolished.

11. With government authorization archbishops and bishops may establish cathedral chapters and seminaries in their dioceses. All other ecclesiastical establishments are suppressed.

12. Archbishops and bishops shall be free to add to their name the title of *Citizen* or *Monsieur*. All other titles are forbidden.

Section II. Archbishops or Metropolitans

13. Archbishops shall consecrate and install their suffragans. In case of hindrance or refusal on their part, the senior bishop of the metropolitan district shall act for them.

* * *

Section III. Bishops, Vicars General, and Seminaries

16. No one may be appointed bishop unless he is thirty years of age and a French native.

* * *

18. The priest appointed by the First Consul shall promptly seek investiture from the pope.

He may not exercise any function until the bull conveying his investiture has received the approval of the government and until he has personally taken the oath prescribed by the convention concluded between the French government and the Holy See.

This oath shall be taken to the First Consul. A report of it shall be drawn up by the secretary of state.

19. Bishops shall appoint and install the parish priests. But they shall not announce appointments nor give canonical investiture until this appointment has been approved by the First Consul.

20. They shall be required to reside in their dioceses. They may leave them only with the permission of the First Consul.

* * *

23. Bishops shall be charged with the organization of their seminaries, and regulations for this organization shall be submitted for the First Consul's approval.

24. Those chosen to teach in seminaries shall subscribe the declaration [Gallican Articles] made by the clergy of France in 1682 and published in an edict of the same year. They shall consent to teach the doctrine contained therein, and the bishops shall address a copy in due form of this submission to the councillor of state responsible for all matters relating to religion.

25. Each year the bishops shall send to this councillor of state the names of persons who will study in seminaries and who plan to enter the clerical order.

26. They shall not ordain any ecclesiastic unless he proves that he has property producing an annual revenue of at least three hundred francs, has attained the age of twenty-five, and possesses the qualifications required by the canons received in France.

The bishops shall not ordain until the number of candidates for ordination has been submitted to the government and approved.

Section IV. Parish Priests

27. Priests shall enter upon their duties only after having taken at the hands of the prefect the oath prescribed by the convention concluded between the government and the Holy See. . . .

* * *

29. They shall be required to reside in their parishes.

* * *

32. No foreigner may serve in the functions of ecclesiastical ministry without government permission.

* * *

Title III. Worship

39. There shall be only one liturgy and catechism for all Catholic churches of France.

40. No priest may order extraordinary public prayers in his parish without the special permission of the bishop.

41. No holiday except Sunday may be established without government permission.

* * *

43. All clerics shall be dressed in the French manner, and in black.

Bishops may add the pastoral cross and violet stockings to this costume.

44. Domestic chapels and private oratories may not be established without express government permission, granted at the request of the bishop.

* * *

48. The bishop shall cooperate with the prefect to regulate the manner of calling the faithful to divine service by the ringing of bells. They cannot be rung for any other purpose without permission of the local police.

49. When the government orders public prayers the bishop shall cooperate with the prefect and the local military commandant as to the day, hour, and manner of execution of these orders.

* * *

51. The priests at the sermons of the parish masses shall pray . . . for the prosperity of the French Republic and the Consuls.

52. In their teachings they shall not indulge in any accusation, direct or indirect, either against individuals or against other religious bodies authorized in the state.

53. In the sermon they shall not declare anything distinct from the exercise of worship, except what may be ordered by the government.

54. They may give the nuptial benediction only to those who prove in good and due form that they have contracted marriage before the civil officer.

55. Registers kept by ministers of religion shall and may pertain only to the administration of sacraments and may in no case take the place of the registers ordered by law to authenticate the civil status of Frenchmen.

* * *

**Title IV. Delimitation of Archbishoprics, Bishoprics, and Parishes;
Buildings Intended for Worship and Ministers' Stipend**

Section I. Delimitation of Archbishoprics and Bishoprics

58. There shall be ten archbishoprics or metropolitan sees and fifty bishoprics in
France.

* * *

Section II. Delimitation of Parishes

* * *

62. No part of French territory may be erected into a living or subsidiary church
without express government authorization.

* * *

Section III. Stipend of Ministers

64. The stipend of archbishops shall be fifteen thousand francs.
65. The stipend of bishops shall be ten thousand francs.
66. Priests shall be divided into two classes.
The stipend of priests of the first class shall be set at fifteen hundred francs; that
of priests of the second class at one thousand francs.

* * *

69. Bishops shall draft regulations about the offerings which ministers of religion are authorized to receive for administering the sacraments. Regulations drafted
by bishops may not be published or otherwise put into execution until after approval
by the government.

Source: Jean B. Duvergier (ed.), *Collection complète des lois, décrets, ordonnances, règlements, avis du conseil d'état* (Paris, 1834–1906), XIII, 91–100.

SUGGESTIONS FOR BACKGROUND AND REFERENCE

References for Documents 28 and 38.

40   Organic Articles for Protestant Bodies

April 6, 1802 [18 Germinal, Year X]

French Protestantism, overwhelmed in the extreme period of the Revolution, partially revived under Napoleon. J. E. M. Portalis, the minister of
religion, at first proposed to leave Protestant pastors without state support, but a request for endowment from the Paris Protestants resulted in

financial arrangements that included reciprocal advantages for the government. An older Calvinist concern for the church's freedom was eclipsed in this vigorous assertion of state authority. The basis for government management, the consistorial church, was an artificial administrative convenience with no foundation in Reformed history or discipline. The provisions for Lutheranism were important in view of the large numbers of Rhineland Lutherans then included in France.

Title I. General Provisions for All Protestant Communions

1. No one may conduct worship unless he is French.

2. Neither Protestant churches nor their ministers may have relations with any foreign power or authority.

3. In their conduct of worship pastors and ministers of the different Protestant communions shall pray and have prayers said for the prosperity of the French Republic and for the Consuls.

4. No doctrinal or dogmatic decision or formulary, under the designation of *confession* or under any other designation, may be published or become the subject of instruction until the government has authorized its publication or promulgation.

5. No change in discipline may take place without the same authorization.

6. The Council of State shall be informed of every enterprise of ministers of religion and of all dissension which may arise among these ministers.

7. A stipend shall be provided for pastors of the consistorial churches. It is understood that the properties which these churches possess and the revenue from offerings established by usage or regulations shall be assigned to this stipend.

* * *

9. There shall be two academies or seminaries in the east of France for the education of ministers of the Augsburg Confession.

10. There shall be a seminary at Geneva for the education of ministers of the Reformed churches.

11. Teachers in all academies or seminaries shall be appointed by the First Consul.

12. No one may be chosen minister or pastor of a church of the Augsburg Confession unless he has studied for a fixed time in one of the French seminaries set aside for the education of ministers of that confession and presents a certificate in good form stating his time of study, ability, and good character.

13. No one may be chosen minister or pastor of a Reformed church unless he has studied in the seminary of Geneva and presents a certificate in the form stated in the preceding article.

14. Regulations concerning the administration and internal order of the seminaries, the number and quality of teachers, the manner of teaching and subjects of instruction, as well as the form of certificates or attestations of study, good conduct, and ability, shall be approved by the government.

Title II. The Reformed Churches

Section I. General Organization of These Churches

15. The Reformed churches of France shall have pastors, local consistories, and synods.

16. There shall be a consistorial church for six thousand persons of the same communion.

17. Five consistorial churches shall form the district of a synod.

Section II. Pastors and Local Consistories

18. The consistory of each church shall be composed of the officiating pastor or pastors of the church and of lay elders or notables chosen from the most heavily taxed citizens. The number of these notables may not fall below six nor exceed twelve.

19. The number of ministers or pastors in a single consistorial church may not be increased without government authorization.

20. Consistories shall supervise the maintenance of discipline, the administration of the church's property, and the administration of funds coming from alms.

* * *

24. Churches which have no present consistory shall form one. All members shall be elected by a meeting of the twenty-five Protestant heads of families who are most heavily taxed. This meeting shall take place only with the authorization and in the presence of the prefect or subprefect.

25. Pastors may be dismissed only when reasons for dismissal are presented to the government, which shall approve or reject them.

26. In case of death, voluntary resignation, or confirmed dismissal of a pastor, the consistory . . . shall choose a replacement by plurality of votes.

The certificate of election shall be presented to the First Consul for his approval . . . .

After approval has been given, he may serve only after having taken before the prefect the oath required of ministers of the Catholic religion.

27. All pastors presently serving are provisionally confirmed.

28. No church may extend from one department into another.

Section III. Synods

29. Each synod shall be composed of the pastor or one of the pastors, and one of the elders or notables from every church.

30. Synods shall supervise everything that pertains to the celebration of worship, the teaching of doctrine, and the conduct of ecclesiastical affairs. All decisions which issue from them, of whatever nature . . . , shall be submitted for government approval.

31. Synods may meet only when the government's permission has been granted.

Advance information shall be given to the councillor of state responsible for all matters concerning religion about the subjects to be considered. The assembly shall be held in the presence of the prefect or the subprefect and a copy of the report of deliberations shall be sent by the prefect to the councillor of state . . . who, in the shortest time possible, shall make his report to the government.

32. A synodal assembly may last only six days.

Title III. The Organization of Churches of the Augsburg Confession

Section I. General Provisions

33. Churches of the Augsburg Confession shall have pastors, local consistories, superintendencies [*inspections*], and general consistories.

Section II. Ministers or Pastors, and Local Consistories of Each Church

34. Provisions of Section II [of Title II] . . . shall be followed . . . .

Section III. Superintendencies

35. Churches of the Augsburg Confession shall be subordinate to superintendencies.

36. Five consistorial churches shall form the district of a superintendency.

37. Each superintendency shall be composed of a minister and an elder or notable from each church of the district. It may assemble only when government permission has been secured . . . . Each superintendency shall choose from its members two laymen and a cleric who shall take the title of superintendent and who shall be responsible for supervising the ministers and the maintenance of good order in the individual churches.

Choice of the superintendent and the two laymen shall be confirmed by the First Consul.

38. The superintendency shall assemble only with government authorization, in the presence of the prefect or subprefect and after having given advance information to the councillor of state . . . concerning subjects to be considered.

39. The superintendent shall visit the churches of his district . . . . He shall be responsible for convening the general assembly of the superintendency. No decision issuing from the general assembly . . . may be put into effect without having been submitted for government approval.

Section IV. General Consistories

40. There shall be three general consistories: one at Strassburg for the . . . departments of High and Low Rhine; another at Mainz for the departments of the Saar and Donnersberg; and the third at Cologne for the departments of Rhine-and-Moselle and of the Ruhr.

41. Each consistory shall be composed of a Protestant lay president, two ecclesiastical superintendents, and one deputy from each superintendency.

The president and the two ecclesiastical superintendents shall be appointed by the First Consul.

* * *

42. The general consistory may assemble only when government permission has been secured and in the presence of the prefect or subprefect. Advance information about subjects to be considered must be given to the councillor of state . . . . The assembly may not last longer than six days.

43. In the interim between one assembly and another, there shall be a directory composed of the president, the elder of the two ecclesiastical superintendents, and three laymen, of whom one shall be appointed by the First Consul. The two others shall be chosen by the general consistory.

Source: Jean B. Duvergier (ed.), *Collection complète des lois, décrets, ordonnances, règlements, avis du conseil d'état* (Paris, 1834–1907), XIII, 101–103.

SUGGESTIONS FOR BACKGROUND AND REFERENCE

B. C. Poland, *French Protestantism and the French Revolution, 1685–1815* (Princeton, 1957), pp. 253–279.
D. Robert, *Les églises reformées en France (1800–1830)* (Paris, 1961), pp. 69–132.
References for Documents 28 and 38.

✦ ✦ ✦

41   German Imperial Recess of 1803 (Extracts)

February 25, 1803[1]

France's annexation of the left bank of the Rhine, confirmed by the Treaty of Lunéville in 1801, was accomplished with the understanding that affected German territorial princes might receive compensation at the expense chiefly of ecclesiastical principalities east of the Rhine. This was basic to a fundamental reorganization of the Holy Roman Empire, formally approved by the Diet in 1803 but actually decided at Paris. One hundred and twelve states were liquidated, the principal beneficiaries being France's German allies, Bavaria, Baden, and Württemberg, and the principal victims the episcopal states (though free imperial cities and imperial knights also suffered). The three historic spiritual electorates of Mainz, Trier, and Cologne disappeared, together with the political sovereignty of some twenty-nine other bishops, and many Catholics became subject to Protestant governments. Exception was made for Napoleon's favorite, Karl Theodor von Dalberg, bishop of Regensburg, who was also given the see of Mainz and the primacy of the German church. The reorganization was accompanied by large-scale suppression of monasteries and seizure of church wealth, and ministered to the decline of Febronianism. The change marked the end of the ancient church of the Holy Roman Empire, which was itself to survive only three years more.

1. Enacted by Diet March 24; approved by emperor April 27.

[Earlier provisions of the document define in detail the territorial transfers.]

XXV. The see of Mainz is transferred to the cathedral church of Regensburg. The dignities of prince-elector-archchancellor of the Empire, as well as those of metropolitan archbishop and primate of Germany, shall be fixed there in perpetuity. The metropolitan jurisdiction extends over the former ecclesiastical provinces of Mainz, Cologne, and Trier (in so far as they are on the right bank of the Rhine and excepting the states of the king of Prussia) [and over part of the province of Salzburg].

* * *

XXXIV. All the property of the cathedral chapters and their officers is incorporated in the bishops' domains and passes with the bishoprics to the princes to whom these are assigned. In bishoprics divided among several princes, the said properties are incorporated in the respective portions.

XXXV. All properties of chapters, abbeys, and convents . . . of which express disposition has not been made in the preceding arrangements, are put at the free and full disposal of the respective territorial princes, both for the expenses of worship, instruction, and other foundations of public utility, and for the relief of their finances, under the express reservation:

Of the fixed endowment of cathedrals . . . .

Of pensions of suppressed clergy . . . .

* * *

XLII. The secularization of convents of cloistered nuns may be effected only with the agreement of the diocesan bishop, but convents of men shall be at the disposal of the territorial princes or their new owners, who may suppress or preserve them at their pleasure. Both may receive novices only with the consent of the territorial prince or the new possessor.

* * *

L. For their lifetimes and according to their different grades, all dispossessed ecclesiastical sovereigns are appointed a free lodging, suitable to their rank and status, with furnishings and table service. The prince-bishops and prince-abbots of the first rank shall have a summer residence also. It is understood that all furnishings that are personal property ought to be left to them entirely; but that part which belongs to the state ought to return to the latter after their decease.

LI. The maintenance of ecclesiastical sovereigns whose states pass wholly or in greatest part with their seats [*Residenzstädte*] to secular sovereigns may be determined, considering the diversity of their incomes, only in relation to the said incomes . . . .

* * *

LVII. The conventuals of the princely and of the imperial immediate abbeys shall continue to be supported in some community in a suitable manner and according to their former way of life. Those who withdraw with the permission of the sovereign shall receive a pension . . . .

* * *

LXI. The profits of sovereignty [*Regalien*], episcopal domains, possessions and revenues of the cathedral chapters fall to the new sovereign.

LXII. Archiepiscopal and episcopal dioceses remain in their present state until another diocesan organization is established, conformable to the laws of the Empire, on which shall depend also the future organization of cathedral chapters.

LXIII. The present public worship of each country is maintained against all attack and insult. In particular, the possession and peaceable enjoyment of the property of the church and endowments of schools . . . is left to each religion, in conformity with the stipulations of the Treaty of Westphalia. Nevertheless, the sovereign remains free to tolerate other religions and to grant them full enjoyment of civil rights.

Source: G. F. de Martens (ed.), *Recueil des principaux traités d'alliance, de paix, de trêve, de neutralité, de commerce, de limites, d'échange etc.*, 2d ed., VII (Göttingen, 1831), 483–519.

SUGGESTIONS FOR BACKGROUND AND REFERENCE

S. S. Biro, *German Policy of Revolutionary France: A Study in French Diplomacy during the War of the First Coalition, 1792–1797* (Cambridge, Mass., 1957).

H. A. L. Fisher, *Studies in Napoleonic Statesmanship: Germany* (Oxford, 1903), pp. 38–47, 163–172.

G. Goyau, *L'Allegmagne religieuse. Le catholicisme 1800–1870* (Paris, 1909–1910), I, 83–116.

K. D. Homig, *Der Reichsdeputationshauptschluss vom 25. Februar 1803 und seine Bedeutung für Staat und Kirche* (Tübingen, 1969).

J. Rovan, *Le catholicisme politique en Allemagne* (Paris, 1956), pp. 15–30.

References for Document 38.

42   Catechism of the French Empire (Extract)

1806

Napoleon's educational policy combined a genuine interest in educational reform with a determination to make instruction serve the aims of Bonapartist autocracy. Catholic catechetical instruction, already provided for in article 39 of the Organic Articles, was affected by this outlook. In March 1806, Portalis, the minister of religion, recommended the use of Bossuet's catechism of 1687 with appropriate alterations and additions, especially concerning the duties of subjects. The passage below represents the chief revision. A decree of April 4, 1806, required the exclusive use of this catechism in all Catholic churches of the Napoleonic empire.

Lesson VII. Continuation of the Fourth Commandment.

Q. What are the duties of Christians with respect to the princes who govern them, and what in particular are our duties towards Napoleon I, our Emperor?

A. Christians owe to the princes who govern them, and we owe in particular to Napoleon I, our Emperor, *love, respect, obedience, fidelity, military service* and the tributes laid for the preservation and defense of the Empire and of his throne; we also owe to him fervent prayers for his safety and the spiritual and temporal prosperity of the state.

Q. Why are we bound to all these duties towards our Emperor?

A. First of all, because God, who creates empires and distributes them according to His will, in loading our Emperor with gifts, both in peace and in war, has established him as our sovereign and has made him the minister of His power and His image upon the earth. *To honor and to serve our Emperor is then to honor and to serve God himself.* Secondly, because our Lord Jesus Christ by his doctrine as well as by His example, has Himself taught us what we owe to our sovereign: He was born the subject of Caesar Augustus; He paid the prescribed impost; and just as He ordered to render to God that which belongs to God, so he ordered to render to Caesar that which belongs to Caesar.

Q. Are there not particular reasons which ought to attach us more strongly to Napoleon I, our Emperor?

A. Yes; for it is he whom God has raised up under difficult circumstances to reestablish the public worship of the holy religion of our fathers and to be the protector of it. He has restored and preserved public order by his profound and active wisdom; he defends the state by his powerful arm; he has become the anointed of the Lord through the consecration which he received from the sovereign pontiff, head of the Universal Church.

Q. What ought to be thought of those who may be lacking in their duty towards our Emperor?

A. According to the Apostle Saint Paul, they would be resisting the order established by God himself and would render themselves *worthy of eternal damnation.*

Q. Will the duties which are required of us towards our Emperor be equally binding with respect to his lawful successors in the order established by the constitutions of the Empire?

A. Yes, without doubt; for we read in the Holy Scriptures, that God, Lord of heaven and earth, by an order of His supreme will and through His providence, gives empires not only to one person in particular, but also to his family.

Source: Frank M. Anderson (ed.), *The Constitutions and Other Select Documents Illustrative of the History of France 1789–1901* (Minneapolis, 1904), pp. 312–314. French text in André Latreille, *Le catéchisme impérial de 1806* (Paris, 1935), pp. 80–81.

SUGGESTIONS FOR BACKGROUND AND REFERENCE

A. Latreille, *Le catéchisme impérial de 1806* (Paris, 1935).
References for Document 38.

43   Württemberg Edict on Religion

October 15, 1806

Württemberg, Bavaria, and Baden were the chief beneficiaries of Napoleon's reorganization of the Holy Roman Empire. At the expense of Austria and lesser German states, they grew in territory and population and were ideologically influenced by France, especially after the formation of the Confederation of the Rhine in 1806. Large new religious minorities in these states necessitated revision in the legal status of religion, hitherto fixed by the sixteenth-century formula of *cuius regio eius religio*. Protestant Württemberg doubled in size of population during the Napoleonic era, and many of the new subjects were Roman Catholic. Frederick II (1797–1816), a student of the Prussian Frederick the Great, issued this law placing the three confessions on an equal footing. (In Catholic Bavaria the *Aufklärung* was more authentically represented by the Francophile Maximilian IV Joseph and his minister, Montgelas, friend of the Illuminati, who produced the similar Organic Law of March 24, 1809. Text in Chester Penn Higby, *The Religious Policy of the Bavarian Government during the Napoleonic Period* [New York, 1919], pp. 131–135.)

To secure to our royal subjects, belonging to any of the denominations of the Christian religion hitherto acknowledged, a free and unobstructed exercise of their religion in the whole extent of our kingdom, we . . . provide as follows:

1. Every Christian church, whether belonging to the two Protestant, or to the Catholic, confessions, has equal claims on our royal protection. Accordingly, we assure to every ecclesiastical community the continuance of the exercise of their religion, as heretofore practiced, and the enjoyment of their lands and revenues . . . as well as of the funds destined for the maintenance of their schools.

2. If at any place of our kingdom, where hitherto only one religion was practiced, the members of another confession should increase in number to such a degree, as to be able to form an ecclesiastical community, we will . . . allow them the free exercise of their religion . . . within the precincts of a church. Let it be understood, however, that the expenses required for the establishment of such worship must be defrayed without any charges and burdens on those members of the community that adhere to any other confession, or of their ecclesiastical endowments; inasmuch as we shall never permit one religious society to encroach on, or participate in, the use and enjoyment of the ecclesiastical lands, revenues, and establishments of any other religious society.

3. If the inhabitants of any place, dissenting from the confession established in the same, be incapable of forming a separate ecclesiastical community, they shall be at liberty, not only to resort to any neighboring church of their worship, but to invite among them a minister of their confession, with a view to religious instruction in their houses and to the education of their children, as well as in order to administer the sacraments. This invitation may also take place on occasions of christenings and

marriages, which acts are allowed . . . in private houses, when the . . . ministers shall be obliged . . . to give official notice of them to the parochial priest, who is charged to enter the same into the church register . . . . With respect to interments . . . the respective minister of the confession of any deceased person shall be allowed . . . to attend the funeral procession and to pronounce an oration at the grave. For the rest, those inhabitants who are not attached to the religion established in any place, so long as they form no separate church, shall be classed with the other parishioners, in whatever does not invade the freedom of their . . . worship or . . . consciences, and shall therefore . . . pay to the parochial clergy the *jura stolae* allowed by law.[1]

4. In appointing to places . . . no regard whatever shall in future be paid to the difference of the Christian confessions; . . . preference shall be given only to the most deserving, whether he be a member of the Catholic or of either of the Protestant churches.

5. Hereafter . . . every subject following any of the three Christian confessions, provided he [possess] all other points required by law, [is] to be entitled to the freedom of any place and to the full enjoyment of such rights as are connected with it.

6. To contract marriage with a person of a different Christian sect . . . there needs no dispensation . . . . The offspring of such marriages [are] . . . to be brought up in the religion of the father . . . . Parents, however, [are] . . . to be permitted to agree upon, and stipulate for, a separate education, according to the sex of their children, or for any other arrangement; provided that, if the father be a Lutheran, the sons are without any exception bred in that religion; and the agreements alluded to must be understood to have validity only if concluded before the magistracy of the husband. After attaining to years of discretion, children born in such marriages are at liberty to embrace . . . either Christian faith; individuals, however, holding any place under the king's civil government, [are] not to change their religion unless after previously informing us of it through the . . . head of the department to which they belong.

7. In marriages between persons of different religion, the consecration . . . [is] to be performed by the minister of the bridegroom. . . .

Source: [Great Britain, Foreign Office], *Supplementary Papers Relating to the Regulation of Roman Catholic Subjects in Foreign States* (1817), pp. 50–51. German text in M. Erzberger, *Die Säkularisation in Württemberg von 1802–1810* (Stuttgart, 1902), pp. 131–133.

SUGGESTIONS FOR BACKGROUND AND REFERENCE

F. H. Geffcken, *Church and State* (London, 1877), II, 1–22.

H. Hermelink, *Geschichte der evangelischen Kirche in Württemberg von der Reformation bis zur Gegenwart* (Stuttgart and Tübingen, 1949), pp. 283–329.

E. Holzle, *Württemberg in Zeitalter Napoleons und der deutschen Erhebung* (Stuttgart and Berlin, 1937), pp. 156–218.

1. Offerings to the clergy on special occasions, e.g., baptism or marriage.

44   Decree on Jewish Organization

March 17, 1808

The Revolution with its secular conception of citizenship fostered the emergence of Jews from their traditional environment of isolation and persecution. Granted citizenship in 1791, Jews were eventually made a part of Napoleon's religious settlement, perhaps partly to win European Jewish support. In 1806 a government-sponsored Jewish Assembly of Notables, assisted in 1807 by a "Grand Sanhedrin" made up chiefly of rabbis, prepared the consistorial plan sanctioned by decree of March 1808. The regulation also extended to Jews in the Rhenish, Westphalian, and Italian annexations to the French Empire. (However, not all of Napoleon's policies were directed toward assimilation, nor were they all benevolent; some decrees restricted Jewish legal and economic rights.)

The regulations approved in the general assembly of Jews held in Paris, December 10, 1806, shall be carried out and annexed to the present decree.

The deputies composing the assembly of Israelites, convoked by decree of May 30, 1806, having heard the report of the Commission of Nine, appointed to prepare the proceedings of the assembly, determining on the organization which it would be proper to give their coreligionists of the French Empire and the Kingdom of Italy regarding the practice of their religion and internal regulation, have unanimously adopted the following plan.

Art. 1. A synagogue and an Israelite consistory shall be established in each department containing two thousand individuals professing the religion of Moses.

2. In case there shall not be two thousand Israelites in a single department, the district of the consistorial synagogue shall include as many neighboring departments as shall be necessary to reach the requisite number. The seat of the synagogue shall always be in the city where the Israelite population is greatest.

3. In no case may there be more than one consistorial synagogue in a department.

4. No particular synagogue shall be established until application has been made by the consistorial synagogue to the competent authority. Each particular synagogue shall be administered by two notables and a rabbi, who shall be named by the competent authority.[1]

5. There shall be a grand rabbi for the consistorial synagogue.

6. The consistories shall be composed of a grand rabbi, of another rabbi when possible, and three other Israelites, of whom two shall be chosen from the residents of the town where the consistory is located.

7. The consistory shall be presided over by its oldest member, who shall take the title of *elder* of the consistory.

8. Some notables, to the number of twenty-five, chosen from the most heavily

---

1. Accompanying regulation specified nomination by departmental consistory and approval by central consistory.

taxed and respectable of Israelites, shall be named by competent authority in each consistorial district.[2]

9. These notables shall proceed to the election of members of the consistory, who must be approved by competent authority.[3]

10. No one may be a member of a consistory: (1) if he is not [at least] thirty years old; (2) if he has become bankrupt, unless he has been honorably rehabilitated; (3) if he is known to have practiced usury.

11. Every Israelite who wishes to settle in France or the Kingdom of Italy shall give notice to the consistory nearest the place where he locates within three months.

12. The duties of the consistory shall be:

(1) To see that the rabbis do not give, either in public or private, any instruction or explanation of the Law which does not conform to the answers of the assembly, confirmed as doctrinal decisions by the Grand Sanhedrin.

(2) To maintain order inside the synagogues, to watch over the administration of particular synagogues, to regulate the collection and use of sums intended for the expenses of the Mosaic worship, and to see that no assembly for prayers be formed, for cause or under pretext of religion, without explicit authorization.

(3) By all possible means to encourage the Israelites of the consistorial district to practice useful professions and to make known to authority those who have not acknowledged means of existence.

(4) Annually to give to authority knowledge of the number of Israelite conscripts of the district.

13. There shall be a central consistory composed of three rabbis and two other Israelites at Paris.[4]

14. The rabbis of the central consistory shall be chosen from the grand rabbis; and the other members shall be subject to the conditions of eligibility defined in article 10.

15. One member of the central consistory shall be retired annually, but he may always be reelected.

16. The remaining members shall provide for his replacement. The new member shall not be installed until he has been approved by competent authority.[5]

17. The duties of the central consistory shall be: (1) To correspond with consistories; (2) To supervise scrupulously the execution of the present regulations; (3) To denounce to competent authority all violations of the said regulations, whether by infraction or negligence; (4) To confirm the appointment of rabbis and to propose the removal of rabbis and members of the consistories to competent authority. . . .

2. Accompanying regulation specified appointment by the minister of the interior after nomination by the central consistory and recommendation by the prefects.

3. Accompanying regulation specified approval by the emperor after presentation by the minister of religion with the advice of the prefects.

4. Accompanying regulation required that the central consistory in its original form be composed of members of the Jewish Assembly or the Grand Sanhedrin appointed by the emperor on presentation by the minister of religion.

5. Accompanying regulation required approval by emperor on presentation by the minister of religion.

18. The election of the grand rabbi shall be by the twenty-five notables designated in article 8.

19. The new grand rabbi shall not enter on his duties until confirmed by the central consistory.

20. No rabbi may be elected: (1) if he is not a native or naturalized Frenchman, or Italian of the kingdom of Italy; (2) if he does not present an attestation of ability, subscribed by three Italian grand rabbis if he is Italian, or French grand rabbis if he is French; and from 1820 if he does not know the French language, if he is in France, or Italian, if he is in the kingdom of Italy; he who joins to the knowledge of Hebrew some knowledge of Greek and Latin shall be preferred, all other things being equal.

21. The duties of the rabbis are: (1) To teach religion; (2) To teach the doctrine contained in the decisions of the Grand Sanhedrin; (3) To urge obedience to the laws in all circumstances, notably and particularly to those relating to the defense of the nation, but to exhort more especially each year at the time of conscription, from the first call by the government until the complete execution of the law; (4) To present military service to Israelites as a sacred duty, and to declare to them that during the time of this service the Law exempts them from observances which might not be compatible with it; (5) To preach in the synagogues and recite there the common prayers for the emperor and the imperial family; (6) To celebrate marriages and pronounce divorces, without proceeding in any case until the interested parties have given satisfactory proof of civil marriage or divorce.

22. The stipend of the rabbis who are members of the central consistory shall be six thousand francs; that of the grand rabbis of the consistorial synagogues shall be three thousand francs; that of the rabbis of particular synagogues shall be fixed by the meeting of Israelites who requested the establishment of the synagogue; it may not be less than one thousand francs. Israelites of the respective districts may vote an increase of this stipend.

23. Each consistory shall propose to competent authority an assessment plan for Israelites of the district for the payment of the salary of the rabbis; other expenses of worship shall be determined and assessed on the request of the consistory by competent authority. Payment of rabbis who are members of the central consistory shall be levied proportionally on the sums collected in the different districts.

24. Each consistory shall name an Israelite, not a rabbi and not a member, to receive the sums collected in the district.

25. This collector shall pay rabbis quarterly, as well as paying the other expenses of worship, on an order signed by at least three members of the consistory. Annually on a fixed day, he shall render account to the consistorial assembly.

26. All rabbis who, after the implementation of the present regulations, are not employed but who wish to maintain their domiciles in France or the kingdom of Italy, shall be required to adhere, by an express declaration which they shall sign, to the decisions of the Grand Sanhedrin. The consistory which receives this declaration shall send a copy to the central consistory.

27. Rabbis who are members of the Grand Sanhedrin shall be preferred, as much as possible, to all others for the post of grand rabbi.

Source: Jean B. Duvergier (ed.), *Collection complète des lois, décrets, ordonnances, règlements, avis du conseil d'état* (Paris, 1834–1906), XVI, 250–252.

SUGGESTIONS FOR BACKGROUND AND REFERENCE

R. Anchel, *Napoléon et les juifs* (Paris, 1928).
F. Kobler, *Napoleon and the Jews* (New York, 1976).
S. Schwarzfuchs, *Napoleon, the Jews, and the Sanhedrin* (London, 1979).

45   Decrees Suppressing the Inquisition and Monastic Orders in Spain

December 4, 1808

Although the revolutionary upheaval in church-state relations, exported by Bonaparte, was felt in the Low Countries, Germany, Switzerland, and Italy, in no country was the impact greater than in conservative Spain. Laws of Charles IV in 1798 and 1805 had sanctioned seizure (with compensation) of some church property, but these measures had been conservatively applied and had produced slight effect. These Napoleonic decrees, issued during the 1808 military campaign, became part of the larger religious reorganization attempted by King Joseph Bonaparte, often with bloodshed. Though anti-French, Spanish liberalism sympathized with this ecclesiastical program and sought to continue it.

Decree Suppressing the Inquisition:

1. The Tribunal of the Inquisition is abolished as prejudicial to civil sovereignty and authority.

2. The property belonging to the Inquisition shall be sequestered and joined to the Spanish domain to serve as security for the *vales* [government bonds] and all other bills of the public debt.

3. The present decree shall be published and registered in all councils, courts, and tribunals in order that it may be executed as law of the state.

Decree Suppressing Monastic Orders:

Considering that the members of the various monastic orders in Spain are too numerous:

That, if a certain number of them is useful in aiding the ministers of the altar in the administration of the sacraments, the existence of too great a number is harmful to the prosperity of the state;

We have decreed and do decree as follows:

The number of convents presently in existence in Spain shall be reduced to a third. This reduction shall be accomplished by joining members of several convents of the same order into one house.

2. From the publication of the present decree, no admission to a novitiate or religious profession shall be permitted until the number of the religious of both sexes has been reduced to one-third of the number of said religious now in existence. Accordingly, within fifteen days all novices shall leave the convents to which they have been admitted.

3. All regular clergy who wish to renounce the common life and live as secular clergy shall be free to leave their houses.

4. The religious who renounce the common life in conformity with the preceding article shall enjoy a pension of which the amount shall be determined according to age, and which may not be less than 3,000 reals nor more than 4,000 reals.

5. First claim on the total property of [suppressed] convents . . . shall be the sum necessary to raise the bare portion of the parish priests, so that their minimum stipend shall be raised to 2,400 reals.

6. The [remaining] property of the suppressed convents . . . shall be joined to the Spanish domain and used as follows: (1), half of the said property to secure the *vales* and other bills of the public debt; (2), the other half to pay the provinces and cities for the expenses occasioned by the provisioning of the French and insurgent armies, and to indemnify the towns and country for the damages, the loss of houses, and all other losses occasioned by war.

Source: Correspondance de Napoléon I (Paris, 1865), XVIII, 104–105.

SUGGESTIONS FOR BACKGROUND AND REFERENCE

A. Fugier, *Napoléon et l'Espagne* (Paris, 1930).
H. C. Lea, *A History of the Inquisition in Spain* (New York, 1906–1907), IV, 399–418.

46   Decree Reuniting the Papal States to the French Empire

May 17, 1809

The immediate occasion of this annexation was the desire to tighten the Continental System against Britain, but relations between Bonaparte and the papacy had long been strained. French troops seized Rome in February 1808, and Pius, after excommunicating Napoleon, was removed to Grenoble, subsequently to Savona and Fontainebleau, where he refused to institute Napoleon's nominees to episcopal sees. Formal annexation of the Papal States to France in the form of two new departments was provided for in the *Senatus Consulte* of February 17, 1810. These events foreshadowed the assault on the temporal power of the papacy that was to dominate Italian politics in the nineteenth century.

Napoleon, Emperor of the French, King of Italy, Protector of the Confederation of the Rhine, etc., in consideration of the fact that when Charlemagne, Emperor of the French and our august predecessor, granted several counties to the Bishops of Rome he ceded these only as fiefs and for the good of his realm and Rome did not by reason of this cession cease to form a part of his empire; farther that since this association of spiritual and temporal authority has been and still is a source of dissensions and has but too often led the pontiffs to employ the influence of the former to maintain the pretentions of the latter and thus the spiritual concerns and heavenly interests which are unchanging have been confused with terrestrial affairs which by their nature alter according to circumstances and the policy of the time; and since all our proposals for reconciling the security of our armies, the tranquillity and the welfare of our people and the dignity and integrity of our Empire, with the temporal pretentions of the popes have failed, we have decreed and do decree what follows:

1. The Papal States are reunited to the French Empire.

2. The city of Rome, so famous by reason of the great memories which cluster about it and as the first seat of Christianity, is proclaimed a free imperial city. The organization of the government and administration of the said city shall be provided by a special statute.

3. The remains of the structures erected by the Romans shall be maintained and preserved at the expense of our treasury.

4. The public debt shall become an imperial debt.

5. The lands and domains of the pope shall be increased to a point where they shall produce an annual net revenue of two millions.

6. The lands and domains of the pope as well as his palaces shall be exempt from all taxes, jurisdiction or visitation and shall enjoy special immunities.

7. On the first of June of the present year a special consultus shall take possession of the Papal States in our name and shall make the necessary provisions in order that a constitutional system shall be organized and may be put in force on January first 1810.

Source: J. H. Robinson, *Napoleon and Europe*, vol. II of *Translations and Reprints from the Original Sources of European History* (Philadelphia, 1897), II, No. 2, 30–31. French text in *Correspondance de Napoléon I* (Paris, 1865), XIX, 18–19.

SUGGESTIONS FOR BACKGROUND AND REFERENCE

Cambridge Modern History (New York, 1903–1912), IX, 180–207.

A. Fugier, *Napoléon et l'Italie* (Paris, 1947), pp. 195–206.

E. E. Y. Hales, *The Emperor and the Pope* (London, 1962).

F. Nielsen, *The History of the Papacy in the Nineteenth Century* (London, 1906), I, 283–300.

M. O'Dwyer, *The Papacy in the Age of Napoleon and the Restoration: Pius VII, 1800–1823* (Lanham, Md., 1985), pp. 83–124.

J. M. Robinson, *Cardinal Consalvi, 1757–1824* (New York, 1987).

III

CATHOLIC RESURGENCE IN
THE NINETEENTH CENTURY

♦ ♦ ♦

47 Decree Restoring the Spanish Inquisition

July 21, 1814

The Spanish Inquisition, originally established by Ferdinand and Isabella in 1479 as a weapon against Marranos and Moriscos (relapsed Jews and Moslems), had been used to serve royal absolutism and to suppress Protestantism and freedom of thought before it was dissolved by Joseph Bonaparte in 1808. The revival by Ferdinand VII (1814–1833) in 1814 typified the reactionary politics of the Restoration Era. It lasted until the 1820 revolution.

The glorious title of Catholic, by which the kings of Spain are distinguished amongst other Christian princes, from their not tolerating any one in the kingdom who professes any other than the Roman Catholic Apostolic religion, has powerfully inclined my heart to employ all the means which God has placed in my hands in order to make myself worthy of that title. The past disturbances and the war which has afflicted for the space of six years all the provinces of the kingdom— foreign troops having remained in it during all this time, of various sects, and almost all of them infected with abhorrence and hatred of the Catholic religion— and the disorder which invariably follows these evils, in conjunction with the careless manner in which everything relating to the affairs of religion has been conducted, have given complete licence to the wicked to live according to their free will, and given rise to the introduction and establishment in the kingdom of many pernicious opinions, by the same means by which they are propagated in other countries.

Being desirous, therefore, of providing a remedy for so serious an evil, . . . I have thought that it would be proper . . . that the Tribunal of the Holy Office should return to the exercise of its jurisdiction.

Wise and virtuous prelates, many corporations, and persons of weight, both ecclesiastical as well as secular, have represented to me that Spain owes to this Tribunal the not having been contaminated, in the sixteenth century, with the errors which have caused such great affliction to other kingdoms; the nation flourishing at the same time in every kind of literature, in great men, and in sanctity and virtue.

One of the principal measures adopted by the Oppressor of Europe to sow corruption and discord, from which he derived such great advantages, was to destroy this Tribunal under the pretext that the state of knowledge would not admit of its existence any longer; and afterwards, the Cortes, called the General and

Extraordinary, under the same pretext, and the Constitution which they tumultuously made, abolished this Tribunal to the regret of the nation.

Wherefore the re-establishment of this Tribunal has been earnestly entreated of me; and acceding to the prayers and desires of the people, . . . I have resolved that the Council of the Inquisition and the other Tribunals of the Holy Office should return to and continue in the exercise of their jurisdiction, both the ecclesiastic, . . . and that royal jurisdiction which has been granted by kings, observing, in the exercise both of the one and of the other, the laws which were in force in 1808 and the laws and acts which, in order to avoid certain abuses and to moderate some privileges, it was thought necessary to make at different times.

But, moreover, in addition to these provisions, it may be necessary perhaps to establish others; and . . . I am desirous that, as soon as the Council of Inquisition is assembled, two of its individuals with two members of my royal council, all of them to be named by myself, should examine the form and mode of proceeding of the Holy Office in the causes which are brought before it, and the established mode of censuring and prohibiting books; and if in those forms I should find anything . . . which ought to be changed, they may propose it, and consult with me, that I may order that which is proper.

Source: British and Foreign State Papers (1812–1814) (London, 1841), I, 1102–1104.

SUGGESTIONS FOR BACKGROUND AND REFERENCE

W. J. Callahan, *Church, Politics and Society in Spain 1750–1874* (Cambridge, Mass., 1984), pp. 110 ff.

P. B. Gams, *Die Kirchengeschichte von Spanien* (Regensburg, 1862–1879), III, No. 2, 427 ff.

H. C. Lea, *A History of the Inquisition in Spain* (New York, 1906–1907), IV, 420–433.

48   *Sollicitudo Omnium Ecclesiarum* (Extract)

August 7, 1814

After dissolution of the order in 1773, Pius VII (1800–1823) approved the Jesuits in the Russian Empire in 1801 and Naples in 1804. One of his first acts after returning to Rome in May 1814 was to restore the order entirely, despite formal protests from some of the powers.

The catholic world demands, with unanimous voice, the re-establishment of the company of Jesus. We daily receive to this effect the most pressing petitions from our venerable brethren, the archbishops and bishops, and the most distinguished persons, especially since the abundant fruits which this company has produced . . . have been generally known. . . .

We should deem ourselves guilty of a great crime towards God, if, amidst these dangers of the christian republic, we neglected the aids which the special Providence of God has put at our disposal; and if, placed in the bark of Peter, tossed and assailed by continual storms, we refused to employ the vigorous and experienced rowers who volunteer their services, in order to break the waves of a sea which threatens every moment shipwreck and death. Decided by motives so numerous and powerful, we have resolved to do what we could have wished to have done at the commencement of our pontificate. After having by fervent prayers implored the Divine assistance, after having taken the advice and counsel of a great number of . . . the cardinals . . . , we have decreed . . . that all the concessions and powers granted by us solely to the Russian Empire and the kingdom of the Two Sicilies, shall henceforth extend to all our ecclesiastical states, and also to all other states. We therefore concede and grant to our well-beloved son, Thaddeo Barzozowski, at this time general of the company of Jesus, and to the other members of that company lawfully delegated by him, all suitable and necessary powers, in order that the said states may freely and lawfully receive all those who shall wish to be admitted into the regular order of the company of Jesus who, under the authority of the general, *ad interim,* shall be admitted and distributed, according to opportunity, in one or more houses, one or more colleges, and one or more provinces, where they shall conform their mode of life to the rules prescribed by St. Ignatius of Loyola . . . . We declare, besides, and grant power that they may . . . apply themselves to the education of youth in the principles of the catholic faith, to form them to good morals, and to direct colleges and seminaries; we authorize them to hear confessions, to preach the Word of God, and to administer the sacraments . . . . We take . . . under our immediate obedience, and that of the Holy See, all the colleges, houses, provinces, and members of this order; . . . always reserving to ourselves and the Roman Pontiffs, our successors, to prescribe and direct all that we may deem it our duty to prescribe and direct, to consolidate the said company more and more, to render it stronger, and to purge it of abuses, should they ever creep in . . . .

In fine, we recommend strongly in the Lord, the company and all its members to . . . the illustrious and noble princes and lords temporal, as well as to . . . the archbishops and bishops, and to all those who are placed in authority. . . .

We ordain that the present letters be inviolably observed, according to their form and tenour, in all time coming; . . . and this notwithstanding any apostolical constitutions and ordinances, especially the brief of Clement XIV of happy memory, beginning with the words *Dominus ac Redemptor noster,* . . . which we expressly abrogate, as far as contrary to the present order . . . .

Source: [House of Commons], *Report from the Select Committee Appointed to report the nature and substance of the Laws and Ordinances existing in Foreign States, respecting the Regulation of their Roman Catholic Subjects* . . . . (1816), pp. 424–426. Latin text, ibid.

SUGGESTIONS FOR BACKGROUND AND REFERENCE

R. Aubert et al., *The Church between Revolution and Restoration* (New York, 1981), pp. 206–209.

T. J. Campbell, *The Jesuits 1534–1921)* (London, 1921), pp. 605–715.

F. Nielsen, *The History of the Papacy in the Nineteenth Century* (London, 1906), I, 340–350.

J. Schmidlin, *Papstgeschichte der neuesten Zeit* (Munich, 1933–1936), I, 357–362.

✦ ✦ ✦ The Trusteeship Problem in the United States

49 New York Incorporation Act (Extract)

April 5, 1813

A complicated chapter in the history of the relations between Catholicism and American governments centers around church incorporation. American legal and religious tradition tended to shape ecclesiastical incorporation in a way that conflicted with the Catholic practice of hierarchical control of church property. This led to tension between the Roman Church and state governments and sometimes to bitter conflict within the churches themselves when lay trustees, relying on the statute, defied their bishops. New York in 1784 led the way with a measure that, without discrimination in favor of any particular denomination, permitted incorporation of church property under a general statute. This act was superseded by the more important incorporation act of 1813. Under both acts New York Catholicism was troubled with controversy and litigation.

. . . That it shall be lawful for the male persons of full age, belonging to any other church, congregation, or religious society [than the Episcopal and Dutch Reformed Churches, incorporated by special acts], now or hereafter to be established in this state, and not already incorporated, to assemble at the church meeting-house, or other place where they stately attend for divine worship, and, by plurality of voices to elect any number of discreet persons of their church, congregation or society, not less than three, nor exceeding nine in number, as trustees, to take the charge of the estate and property belonging thereto, and to transact all affairs relative to the temporalities thereof; and that at such election every male person of full age, who has stately worshipped with such church, congregation or society, and has formerly been considered as belonging thereto, shall be entitled to vote, and the said election shall be conducted as follows: the minister of such church, congregation or society, or in case of his death or absence, one of the elders or deacons, church wardens or vestrymen thereof, and for want of such officers, any other person being a member or a stated hearer in such church, congregation or society, shall publicly notify the congregation of the time when, and place where, the said election shall be held at least fifteen days before the day of election; . . . that on the said day of election, two of the elders or church wardens, and if there be no such officers, then two of the members of the said church, congregation or society, to be nominated by a majority of the members present, shall preside at such election . . . .

* * *

. . . That the trustees of every church, congregation or society, herein above mentioned, and their successors . . . are hereby authorised and empowered to take into their possession and custody all the temporalities belonging to such church, congregation or society, whether the same consist of real or personal estate, and whether the same shall have been given, granted or devised directly to such church congregation or society, or to any other person for their use; . . . and such trustees shall also have power to make rules and orders for managing the temporal affairs of such church, congregation or society, and to dispose of all monies belonging thereto, and to regulate and order the renting the pews in their churches and meeting-houses, and the perquisites for the breaking of the ground in the cemetery or churchyards . . . and all other matters relating to the temporal concerns and revenues of such church. . . .

Source: Laws of the State of New York [1812–1813] (Albany, 1813), II, 214–215.

SUGGESTIONS FOR BACKGROUND AND REFERENCE

P. J. Dignan, *History of the Legal Incorporation of Catholic Church Property in the United States (1784–1932)* (New York, 1935).

A. P. Stokes, *Church and State in the United States* (New York, 1950), III, 405–413.

50 *Non Sine Magno*

August 24, 1822

In Philadelphia the trusteeship issue in Roman Catholicism erupted with bitter violence in the 1820s. Controversy centered around the Rev. William Hogan, pastor of St. Mary's Cathedral, who was elected by lay trustees but removed by the bishop. In June 1821 the Philadelphia trustees addressed an appeal to American Catholics on "the Reform of Sundry Abuses in the Administration of our Church Discipline" in which they demanded "the exclusive right which always belonged to the Church, of electing our own Pastors and Bishops, and when a Bishop shall be so elected by the Trustees and congregations of each State, he shall be ordained in this country and receive the Bull, or approbation from Rome as a matter of course" (*Records of the American Catholic Historical Society of Philadelphia* [1914], XXV, 169–170). In the following year Pius VII addressed this brief to Archbishop Ambrose Maréchal of Baltimore and his suffragan bishops.

It was not without great grief we understood that the Church of Philadelphia has been for a long time so distracted by incessant discord and dissensions that schisms have arisen, perverse doctrines have been diffused, and that the affairs of the whole church itself are thrown into the greatest confusion. These disorders have originated principally from two causes, namely, from the senseless arrogance and nefarious proceedings of the priest William Hogan, and also from an abuse of power in those who administer the temporal properties of the church. For . . . this most abandoned priest, Hogan, despising and subverting the laws of the Church, has constituted himself judge of his own prelate . . . . But what strikes both us and the universal Church, not only with the greatest astonishment, but also with indignation, is . . . that this priest . . . could find many followers . . . who, neglecting and despising the authority of the bishop, would rather adhere to him than to their lawful pastor, from whom they have not hesitated to withdraw even the means necessary for the sustenance of life. This, indeed, is a most serious injury offered, not to the bishop only, but to us also and to this Apostolical See . . . . Are they ignorant that the Holy Ghost has placed the bishops to rule the Church of God? Whence it follows that bishops are the shepherds of the flock of Christ . . . . Are they ignorant that the order of the hierarchy has been so established . . . that priests must be subject to bishops and bishops to the supreme Vicar of Christ . . . ? Are they ignorant that it belongs not to Laymen to meddle with ecclesiastical judgments . . . ?

* * *

There is another circumstance which affords continual cause of discord and discontent, not only in Philadelphia, but also in many other places of the United States of America: the immoderate and unlimited right which trustees or administrators of the temporal properties of the churches assume, independently of the bishops. Indeed unless this be circumscribed by certain regulations, it may prove an eternal source of abuse and dissensions. Trustees ought therefore to bear in mind, that the properties that have been consecrated to divine worship for the support of the church and the maintenance of its ministers, fall under the power of the church, and since the bishops, by divine appointment, preside over their respective churches, they can not, by any means, be excluded from the care, superintendence and disposal of these properties. . . .

But that trustees and laymen should arrogate to themselves the right . . . of establishing for pastors priests destitute of legal faculties, and even not unfrequently bound by censures (as it appears was lately the case with regard to Hogan) and also of removing them at their pleasure, and of bestowing the revenues upon whom they please, is a practice new and unheard of in the Church. . . . For in that case the Church would be governed not by bishops, but by laymen, the shepherd would be subject to his flock, and laymen would usurp the power which was given by Almighty God to bishops. But those who are desirous of remaining in the bosom of their mother, the Holy Catholic Church, and of providing for their eternal salvation, are bound religiously to observe the laws of the Universal Church, and as the civil authorities must be obeyed in those things which are temporal, so also in those which are spiritual must the faithful comply with the laws of the Church . . . . In order then to avoid the dissensions and disturbances which frequently arise from the unbounded power of trustees, we have provided . . . that certain regulations and instructions concerning the choice and direction of trustees should be transmitted to you, to which, we are confident, the trustees will thoroughly conform themselves. . . .

Source: Records of the American Catholic Historical Society of Philadelphia (1914), XXV, 325–329. Latin text in D. C. Shearer (ed.), Pontificia Americana. A Documentary History of the Catholic Church in the United States (1784–1844) (Washington, D.C., 1933), pp. 128–131.

SUGGESTIONS FOR BACKGROUND AND REFERENCE

P. W. Carey, *People, Priests, and Prelates: Ecclesiastical Democracy and the Tensions of Trusteeism* (Notre Dame, 1987).

P. K. Guilday, *The Life and Times of John Carroll, Archbishop of Baltimore, 1735–1815* (New York, 1922), pp. 649 ff.

R. F. McNamara, "Trusteeism in the Atlantic States, 1785–1863," *Catholic Historical Review*, Vol. XXX, No. 2 (July 1944), pp. 135–154.

References for Document 49.

51   New York Incorporation Act

March 25, 1863

Problems of lay trusteeship subsided under episcopal censure, but legal adjustment to Roman Catholic ecclesiastical practice came more slowly. Bishop John Hughes of New York labored for a more favorable law in the 1850s, but the political climate, influenced by Know-Nothingism, was unsympathetic. In 1855 the state legislature even made clerical holding of church property illegal (though this was never enforced and was repealed in 1863). Finally, in 1863 a measure much more satisfactory to Catholics became law as an "act supplementary" to the 1813 statute.

1. It shall be lawful for any Roman Catholic church or congregation now or hereafter existing in this state, to be incorporated according to the provisions of this act; the Roman Catholic archbishop or bishop of the diocese in which such church may be erected or intended so to be, the vicar general of such diocese, and the pastor of such church for the time being, respectively, or a majority of them, may select and appoint two laymen, members of said church, and may, together with such laymen, sign a certificate in duplicate, showing the name or title by which they and their successors shall be known and distinguished as a body corporate by virtue of this act, which certificates shall be duly acknowledged or proved, in the same manner as conveyances of real estate; and one of such certificates shall be filed in the office of the secretary of state, and the other in the office of the clerk of the county in which such church may be erected or intended so to be; and thereupon such church or congregation shall be a body corporate, by the name or title expressed in such certificate, and the said persons so signing the same shall be the trustees thereof. The successors of any such archbishop, bishop, vicar general, or pastor, respectively, for the time being, shall, by virtue of his office, be the trustee of such

church, in place of his predecessor; and such laymen shall hold their office respectively for one year, and whenever the office of any such laymen shall become vacant by death, removal, resignation or otherwise, his successor shall be appointed in the same manner as herein provided for his original selection.

2. The trustees of every such church or congregation, and their successors, shall have all the powers and authority granted to the trustees of any church, congregation or society, by the fourth section of the act entitled "An act to provide for the incorporation of religious societies," passed April fifth, eighteen hundred and thirteen, and shall also have power to fix or ascertain the salary to be paid to any pastor or assistant pastor of such church, but the whole real and personal estate of any such church, exclusive of the church edifice, parsonage and school houses, together with the land on which the same may be erected, and burying places, shall not exceed the annual value or income of three thousand dollars; . . .

Source: Laws of the State of New York Passed at the Eighty-Sixth Session of the Legislature (Albany, 1863), pp. 65–66.

SUGGESTIONS FOR BACKGROUND AND REFERENCE

References for Document 49.

✦ ✦ ✦

52   Catholic Emancipation Act (Extracts)
April 13, 1829

The Union of Great Britain with Ireland in 1800 raised the Catholic problem in acute form. The number of Catholics in the United Kingdom was vastly increased, the issue was transferred from Dublin to Westminster, and the political circumstances attending the Union—Pitt's unfulfilled promise to effect Catholic emancipation—heightened agitation. Moreover, the extension of the vote to Catholics by the Dublin parliament in 1793 insured that Catholic views would be heard. The traditional opposition of crown, Tories, and Protestant opinion was overcome in the 1829 crisis when Daniel O'Connell, a Dublin barrister, won a Clare election with the aid of the Catholic Association, founded in 1823. O'Connell, a Catholic, was unable legally to qualify for Parliament, but the government, unwilling to face disorders and possibly revolt in Ireland, capitulated. Tory leaders drove the bill through Parliament. The immediate value of the concession was diminished by another act raising the property qualification, which greatly reduced the number of Irish Catholic voters. Few Catholic disabilities remained after the passage of the act.

WHEREAS by various Acts of Parliament certain Restraints and Disabilities are imposed on the Roman Catholic Subjects of His Majesty, to which other Subjects . . . are not liable: And Whereas it is expedient that such Restraints and Disabilities shall be from henceforth discontinued: And Whereas by various Acts certain Oaths and certain Declarations, commonly called the Declaration against Transubstantiation, and the Declaration against Transubstantiation and the Invocation of Saints and the Sacrifice of the Mass, as practised in the Church of Rome, are or may be required to be taken, . . . as Qualifications for sitting and voting in Parliament, and for the Enjoyment of certain Offices, Franchises, and Civil Rights: Be it enacted . . . , That from and after the Commencement of this Act all such parts of the said Acts as require the said Declarations . . . to be made . . . as a Qualification for sitting and voting in Parliament, or for the Exercise or Enjoyment of any Office, Franchise, or Civil Right, be . . . (save as hereinafter provided and excepted) hereby repealed.

II. . . . it shall be lawful for any Person professing the Roman Catholic Religion, being a Peer, or who shall . . . be returned as a member of the House of Commons, to sit and vote in either House of Parliament respectively, . . . upon taking and subscribing the following Oath, instead of the Oaths of Allegiance, Supremacy, and Abjuration:

"I, *A.B.*, do sincerely promise and swear that I will be faithful and bear true Allegiance to His Majesty King George the Fourth and will defend him to the utmost of my Power against all Conspiracies and Attempts whatever, which shall be made against his Person, Crown, or Dignity; and I will do my utmost Endeavour to disclose . . . all Treasons and traitorous Conspiracies . . . : And I do faithfully promise to maintain, support, and defend, to the utmost of my Power, the Succession of the Crown, which . . . stands limited to the Princess Sophia, Electress of Hanover, and the heirs of her Body, being Protestants; hereby utterly renouncing and abjuring any Obedience or Allegiance unto any other Person claiming or pretending a Right to the Crown of this Realm: And I do further declare, That it is not an Article of my Faith, and that I do renounce, reject, and abjure the Opinion, that Princes excommunicated or deprived by the Pope or any other Authority of the See of Rome may be deposed or murdered by their Subjects or by any Person whatsoever: And I do declare, That I do not believe that the Pope of Rome, or any other Foreign Prince, Prelate, Person, State, or Potentate, hath or ought to have any Temporal or Civil Jurisdiction, Power, Superiority, or Pre-eminence, directly or indirectly, within this Realm. I do swear that I will defend to the utmost of my Power the Settlement of Property within this Realm, as established by the Laws: And I do hereby disclaim, disavow, and solemnly abjure any Intention to subvert the present Church Establishment as settled by Law within this Realm: And I do solemnly swear, That I never will exercise any Privilege to which I am or may become entitled to disturb or weaken the Protestant Religion or Protestant Government in the United Kingdom . . . . So help me GOD."

* * *

V. . . . it shall be lawful for Persons professing the Roman Catholic Religion to vote at Elections of Members to serve in Parliament for England and for Ireland,

and also to vote at the Elections of Representative Peers of Scotland and of Ireland, and to be elected such Representative Peers, . . . upon taking . . . the Oath hereinbefore appointed . . . .

* * *

IX. . . . no Person in Holy Orders in the Church of Rome shall be capable of being elected to serve in Parliament as a Member of the House of Commons. . . .

X. . . . it shall be lawful for any of His Majesty's Subjects professing the Roman Catholic Religion to hold, exercise, and enjoy all Civil and Military Offices and Places of Trust or Profit under His Majesty, . . . and to exercise any other Franchise or Civil Right, except as hereinafter excepted, upon taking . . . the Oath hereinbefore appointed . . . .

* * *

XII. Provided also . . . That nothing herein contained shall extend . . . to enable any Person . . . professing the Roman Catholic Religion to hold or exercise the Office of . . . Justices . . . or of Regent of the United Kingdom . . . ; nor to enable any Person, otherwise than as he is now by Law enabled, to hold or enjoy the Office of Lord High Chancellor, Lord Keeper or Lord Commissioner of the Great Seal . . . or . . . Lord Lieutenant . . . of Ireland or . . . High Commissioner to the General Assembly of the Church of Scotland.

* * *

XIV. . . . it shall be lawful for any of His Majesty's Subjects professing the Roman Catholic Religion to be a Member of any Lay Body Corporate, and to hold any Civil Office or Place of Trust or Profit therein, and to do any Corporate Act or vote in any Corporate Election or other Proceeding, upon taking . . . the Oath hereby appointed . . . .

XV. Provided nevertheless . . . That nothing herein contained shall extend to authorize or empower any of His Majesty's Subjects professing the Roman Catholic Religion and being a Member of any Lay Body Corporate to give any Vote at, or . . . join in the Election, Presentation, or Appointment of any Person to any Ecclesiastical Benefice whatsoever or any Office . . . connected with the United Church of England and Ireland, or the Church of Scotland, being in the Gift, Patonage, or Disposal of such Lay Corporate Body.

XVI. Provided also . . . That nothing in this Act contained shall be construed to enable any Persons, otherwise than as they are now by Law enabled, to hold . . . any Office . . . belonging to the United Church of England and Ireland, or the Church of Scotland, or any Place . . . belonging to any of the Ecclesiastical Courts of Judicature . . . ; or any Office . . . belonging to any of the Universities . . . or Colleges or Halls of the said Universities, or the Colleges of Eton, Westminster, or Winchester, or any College or School . . . ; or to repeal, abrogate, or in any Manner to interfere with any local Statute . . . within any University, College, Hall, or School, by which Roman Catholics shall be prevented from being admitted thereto or from residing or taking Degrees therein: Provided also that nothing herein contained shall extend . . . to enable any Person, otherwise than as he is now by

Law enabled, to exercise any Right of Presentation to any Ecclesiastical Benefice whatsoever . . . .

* * *

XXIV. . . . And Whereas the Right and Title of Archbishops to their respective Provinces, of Bishops to their Sees, and of Deans to their Deaneries . . . have been settled . . . by Law; Be it therefore enacted, That if any Person . . . other than the Person thereunto authorized by Law shall assume or use the Name, Style, or Title of Archbishop of any Province, Bishop of any Bishopric, or Dean of any Deanery in England or Ireland, he shall for every such Offence forfeit . . . One hundred Pounds.

XXV. . . . if any Person holding any Judicial or Civil Office, or any Mayor, Provost, Jurat, Bailiff, or other Corporate Officer, shall . . . be present at any Place . . . for Religious Worship in England and Ireland, other than that of the United Church of England and Ireland, or in Scotland, other than that of the Church of Scotland, . . . in the Robe, Gown, or other peculiar Habit of his Office, or attend with the Ensign or Insignia . . . of . . . such his Office, such Persons shall . . . forfeit such Office and pay for every such Offence . . . One hundred Pounds.

XXVI. . . . if any Roman Catholic Ecclesiastic, or any Member of any of the Orders . . . shall . . . exercise any of the Rites or Ceremonies of the Roman Catholic Religion, or wear the Habits of his Order, save within the usual Places of Worship of the Roman Catholic Religion, or in private Houses, such Ecclesiastic or other Person shall . . . forfeit for every such Offence . . . Fifty Pounds.

* * *

XXVIII. And whereas Jesuits, and members of other Religious Orders . . . of the Church of Rome . . . are resident within the United Kingdom; and it is expedient to make Provision for the gradual Suppression and final Prohibition of the same therein; Be it therefore enacted, That every Jesuit, and every Member of any other Religious Order . . . of the Church of Rome . . . who at the time of the Commencement of this Act shall be within the United Kingdom, shall within Six Calendar Months . . . deliver to the Clerk of the Peace of the County or Place where such person shall reside . . . a Notice . . . which . . . such Clerk . . . shall . . . register amongst the Records of such County or Place . . . and shall forthwith transmit a Copy . . . to the Chief Secretary of the Lord Lieutenant . . . of Ireland . . . or . . . to One of His Majesty's Principal Secretaries of State . . . .

Source: 10 Geo. IV, c. 7; *The Statutes of the United Kingdom of Great Britain and Ireland [1829]* (London, 1829), pp. 49–57.

SUGGESTIONS FOR BACKGROUND AND REFERENCE

D. Gwynn, *The Struggle for Catholic Emancipation 1750–1829* (London, 1928).

E. Halevy, *A History of the English People in the Nineteenth Century* (London, 1924–1934), II, 237–306.

U. Henriques, *Religious Toleration in England, 1787–1833* (Toronto, 1961), pp. 136–174.

G. I. T. Machin, *The Catholic Question in English Politics, 1820–1830* (Oxford, 1964).

53　Belgian Constitution (Extract)

February 7, 1831

The brief religious provisions of the Belgian Constitution were significant as evidence of the first practical success of Catholic liberalism. During the late 1820s the political teachings of Félicité de Lamennais, the prophet of French Catholic liberalism, gained a hearing in Belgium. The political situation after 1815—the forced union with the Netherlands and the reactionary and Protestant policy of William I—suggested a national resistance, liberal and Catholic. Alliance between Catholics and Liberals made possible the 1830 Revolution, independence, and a constitution based on mutual compromise. Despite the breakdown of the alliance in the 1840s due to conflicts over education and the questionable validity of the Constitution from the standpoint of later papal pronouncements, the Belgian example encouraged Catholic liberalism elsewhere.

14. Religious liberty and freedom of public worship, as well as liberty to express opinions in all matters, are guaranteed, except for the suppression of offenses committed in the usage of these liberties.

15. No one shall be constrained to conform in any manner whatsoever to the forms or ceremonies of any religion, nor to observe its days of rest.

16. The state shall not interfere either in the appointment or the installation of ministers of any religion whatsoever, nor shall it forbid them to correspond with their superiors or to publish their proceedings, subject, in the latter case, to the ordinary responsibilities governing the press and publication.

Civil marriage ought always to precede the religious rite, subject to exceptions to be established by law if found necessary.

17. Instruction is free [of restraint]; every restrictive measure is forbidden; the suppression of offenses shall be regulated only by law. Public education at the cost of the state is likewise regulated by law.

Source: F.-R. and P. Dareste, *Les constitutions modernes* (Paris, 1928), I, 349–369.

SUGGESTIONS FOR BACKGROUND AND REFERENCE

R. Aubert et al., *The Church between Revolution and Restoration* (New York, 1981), pp. 271–282.

Cambridge Modern History (New York, 1903–1912), I, 517–544.

H. Haag, *Les origines du catholicisme libéral en Belgique (1788–1839)* (Louvain, 1950).

K. S. Latourette, *Christianity in a Revolutionary Age* (New York, 1958–1962), I, 426–429.

A. Simon, *L'Église catholique et les débuts de la Belgique indépendante* (Wetteren, 1949).

✦ ✦ ✦ Lamennais and the Beginnings of Catholic Liberalism

54 Act of Union (Extracts)

November 15, 1831

Hugues Félicité-Robert de Lamennais (1782–1854), the founder and prophet of nineteenth-century Catholic liberalism, began his political and clerical career as an ardent defender of legitimate monarchy and ultramontane Catholicism. His *Essai sur l'indifférence en matière de religion* (1817) secured for him a European reputation and the expressed approval of Leo XII. His passionate insistence on the church's freedom and his intense opposition to the surviving Gallicanism of Restoration government and bishops led to controversy, which became much more pronounced in the late 1820s when Lamennais renounced royalism and argued that the security and future of the church were best served by an alliance with democracy. After the 1830 revolution, Lamennais, with the help of enthusiastic friends, notably Count Charles de Montalembert and Jean Baptiste Henri Lacordaire, published *L'Avenir* (first issue, October 16, 1830) with the motto "God and Liberty" and a policy of vindicating mass suffrage, freedom of association and of press, and religious and educational liberty. Lamennais envisioned not only a popular Catholic renewal in France, but a new age of social and political transformation throughout Europe under Catholic and papal auspices. Accordingly, his party followed with keen interest the attempts of Catholics to win liberty in Ireland, Belgium, and Poland. In its last issue, November 15, 1831, *L'Avenir* published the projected *Acte d'Union* for Catholics and other crusaders for freedom. After suspending publication (primarily because of financial problems), Lamennais, Lacordaire, and Montalembert visited Rome in the vain attempt to secure Gregory XVI's approval for their doctrines.

Act of Union

PROPOSED TO ALL THOSE WHO, DESPITE THE MURDER OF POLAND, THE DISMEMBERMENT OF BELGIUM AND THE CONDUCT OF GOVERNMENTS WHICH CALL THEMSELVES LIBERAL, STILL HOPE FOR THE LIBERTY OF THE WORLD AND WISH TO WORK FOR IT

Preamble

Although Catholicism constitutes a perfect religious unity, Catholic nations may be in different positions with respect to defending their religious rights and the political liberties which are inseparable from them. This happens especially at a time of great crises, when one part of the world remains under the sway of old institutions, while the other part has entered into a new social situation. Such is the case with Catholics in Ireland, France, Belgium, and certain states of Germany—in a word, in all countries where constitutional government has taken root. This new situation forms ties between these Catholics which in themselves provide the bases for an unprecedented alliance.

[The development of liberty under constitutional government depends on the cooperation of all citizens. Moreover, the religious and political liberties desired by all peoples are independent of local issues and different forms of representative government.] Consequently, the same reason which inspires the organization in each country of a system of defense of all the rights authorized by its particular constitution should also lead to the establishment . . . of a vast united effort to defend, together with religious liberty, all the high and noble freedoms which are the common country of free peoples.

Catholics are called upon to give the world the model of this new type of association . . . . They are so called upon because of the great principle of unity which their religion comprehends, because of the peculiar character of Catholicism which . . . already constitutes a great moral federation of peoples. It falls to them to guide the development of liberty. Because, on the one hand, they have greater need of it than all others. Indeed, everything that happens in Europe demonstrates that where the Church is oppressed, religious liberty is regained only with the help of political liberties. But, on the other hand, it is also clear that liberty has need, and great need, of Catholics. Everywhere that liberty is separated from . . . those eternal principles of order and life which Catholicism always upholds and which without Catholicism succumb to the attack of irreligious scepticism, terrible disorders have marked its coming . . . . Hence this distrust, this fear which the name of liberty inspires in many people, and which, more than any other cause perhaps, obstructs its progress. Liberty will triumph . . . only if it develops in conjunction with order. The magnificent design which God reveals to Catholics is this conjunction in a future which it depends on Catholics to bring nearer. Not only are they fundamentally committed to order by all the strength of their convictions, but in them also the love of liberty revives with greatest sincerity, purity, and vigor . . . . In this work of regeneration . . . , they are destined to appear as the core of mankind striving to reestablish itself on the two foundations of liberty and order. And the *act of union* by which Irish, English, Belgian, German, and French—if we could only say Polish!—Catholics will declare to all the world their firm resolution to pledge themselves to the victory of this cause will be the herald of something great on earth.

This union should indeed rest on a political declaration which comprises the bases of the common liberty. All that may vary between nations, according to their particular conditions, necessarily remains outside this alliance. In joining peoples for the defense of interests of a higher order, this alliance should leave citizens of each country perfectly free in the area of their purely national interests . . . . The goal of the *Union* is to withdraw the spiritual in society from the interference of authority, and gradually and gently to encourage society's general tendency to manage its own material interests. Let Catholics, citizens of constitutional states, place themselves at the head of the progressive movement of society by adopting a declaration which sanctifies all these freedoms. Let them set up corresponding societies . . . to have it circulated in cities and the humblest villages . . . . Let it be covered with thousands of subscriptions . . . . Let these vigorous affirmations of the human conscience, echoing from the banks of the Seine to the heart of Germany and from the Belgian plains to the Irish seas, resound as one voice, as the purest, greatest cry for the salvation of the world.

* * *

For let no one mistake the character and object of this declaration. Catholics begin by signing it among themselves . . . because the faith which already unites them by such close and intimate bonds naturally prepares the way to their ready association in the cause of liberty. But in initiating this political union, they do not intend to limit it to their own religious beliefs. In their view every exclusive alliance would be an obstruction and a crime. In each constitutional state the rights which they defend are the public rights of all their fellow-citizens. In fighting for this cause they merge with the truly national party. . . . Thus the particular cause of Catholics is nothing but the general cause. Their chief desire is that its adherents grow in number and increase in strength through uniting. . . . They open the ranks of their alliance to every honest man, whatever his religious opinions, who gives his word and receives theirs in return. . . . If the preamble of the *act of union* is addressed particularly to Catholics, the *act of union* itself is framed so that every true adherent of equal liberty for all may sign it . . . . The reorganization of society depends on agreement . . . among good men who have the same idea of practical liberty with regard to contemporary society, and who are united by the same love of justice. They are naturally allied in the political realm, although in another realm they may be divided in views . . . . All distinctions of parties, founded on a different basis, are artificial and fraudulent and cannot last. [Soon a great judgment will take place, false and genuine liberals will be revealed, and a new age will dawn in which the rights of all will be respected by all.]

Catholics, our duty is to hasten this epoch . . . . We are ready for liberty. We are worthy of it, for we have already suffered much for it, and done much for the peace of the world. We can present heaven and earth with the long sacrifice of Ireland and the piety of Belgian liberty, pure as a prayer, and the tomb of that heroic Poland . . . whose glory will be as ineradicable in the memory of God and men as her bloodstains are on the purple of kings. Ancient peoples signed their treaties only by an altar where the blood of sacrifice flowed. We have had our great victims. Our *act of union* is consecrated.

Act of Union

We recognize the following principles as forming the basis of all genuine constitutional government.

I

The spiritual part of society ought to be completely freed from the interference of the political power. Accordingly:

1. Liberty of conscience and worship must be complete, of such a kind that the government does not interfere in any way, under any pretext, with the teaching, discipline, and ceremonies of religion.

2. Liberty of the press must not be shackled by any preventive measure, under whatever form this measure occurs.

3. Liberty of education must be as complete as liberty of religion, of which it is essentially part. It must be as complete as liberty of the press since, like the latter, it is part of the same liberty of ideas and the expression of opinions.

4. Liberty of intellectual, moral, and industrial associations rests on the same principles and should be sacred to the same rights.

Respecting each of these liberties, the right and duty of constitutional power consist only in repressing crimes and offenses which would materially attack either the complete and equal enjoyment of these same liberties for all or some other civil or political right of citizens.

II

Hence just as the spiritual part of society should be completely freed, constitutional power should be exerted only in the realm of material interests. And in this realm we acknowledge that it is necessary to seek a state of things in which all local affairs will be freely administered in common by those concerned, under the protection of authority—whatever be its form—directed thenceforth solely toward maintaining political unity and harmony between the various particular administrations, and toward providing for the general interest and defense of the state against external dangers.

III

And as society, which has justice for its basis, can make real advances only by a greater development and more extensive application of the law of justice and charity, we acknowledge that efforts should also be made immediately to elevate the minds and ameliorate the material conditions of the lower classes, in order to permit them to share more and more in social advantages.

We pledge ourselves to cooperate with all our power in the defense of these constitutional principles and the maintenance of the liberties declared above. We pledge ourselves to devote our civil and political rights to this cause, mutually promising help and assistance by all legal means and adhering with firm resolution to the present *act of union*. . . .

Source: L'Avenir, November 15, 1831, pp. 2–3.

SUGGESTIONS FOR BACKGROUND AND REFERENCE

J. M. S. Allison, *Church and State in the Reign of Louis Philippe* (Princeton, 1916).

G. Hourdin, *Lamennais: prophète et combattant de la liberté* (Paris, 1982).

H. Laski, *Authority in the Modern State* (New Haven, 1919), pp. 189–280.

J. Leflon, *La crise révolutionnaire, 1789–1846* (Paris, 1949), pp. 440–452.

C. S. Phillips, *The Church in France, 1789–1848: A Study in Revival* (London, 1929), pp. 206–258.

A. Vidler, *Prophecy and Papacy: A Study of Lamennais, the Church and the Revolution* (New York, 1954).

G. Weill, *Histoire du catholicisme libéral en France 1828–1908* (Paris, 1909), pp. 3–50.

55   *Mirari Vos* (Extracts)

August 15, 1832

Although Gregory XVI (1831–1846) granted an audience to Lamennais and his companions in March 1832, he declined to discuss the matters that had brought them to Rome and by implication made clear his dissatisfaction with the policies with which they were identified. Lamennais left Rome in July and had reached Munich when the encyclical *Mirari Vos,* sent with a covering letter from Cardinal Pacca (1756–1844), reached him. Condemnation, which had been requested by Austrian and French governments and some of the French hierarchy, may have been precipitated by Lamennais's announced intention to revive *L'Avenir.* The encyclical also reflected Rome's deep reaction to the revolts of 1831–1832 in the Papal States. Lamennais at once wrote a submission, declared the dissolution of *L'Avenir* and its supporting *Agence générale pour la défense de la liberté religieuse,* and retired to his country retreat at La Chesnaie. Reproduced below are passages from (A) the text of the encyclical, and (B) Cardinal Pacca's letter.

A. From *Mirari Vos:*

We speak . . . of things which you see with your own eyes, and which, in consequence, we all deplore with united tears. Active wickedness is triumphant . . . . The sanctity of holy things is despised . . . . Hence sound doctrine is perverted, and errors of every kind are audaciously disseminated. Neither laws of holy things, nor rights, nor institutions, nor any of the most sacred courses of discipline, are secure from the perverse audacity of babblers. *This our Roman chair of the blessed Peter, in which Christ has placed the main strength of the Church, is most furiously assailed . . . . The Divine authority of the Church is impugned . . . .* The obedience due to Bishops is infringed, and their rights are trampled under foot. Academies and schools resound horribly with novel and monstrous opinions, by which the Catholic faith is attacked—*no longer now, by secret undermining; but a horrible and nefarious warfare is openly and avowedly waged against her. . . .*

Hence, likewise, the restraint of our most holy religion being cast aside, (by which alone kingdoms stand, and the power and strength of authority is confirmed,) we behold the destruction of public order—the sapping of sovereignty, and the overthrow of all lawful power, spread far and wide. Which great mass of calamities must be traced primarily to the combination of those societies, into which whatever is sacrilegious, flagitious, and blasphemous in heresies, and in any of the most wicked sects, has *flowed, as into a common sewer, amidst a collection of all kinds of filth.*

* * *

. . . Let all remember, that the judgment upon the soundness of that doctrine with which the people are to be imbued, and the government and administration of the universal Church belongs to the Roman Pontiff . . . . It is the duty of every bishop to adhere most faithfully to the chair of Peter . . . . The priests must be subject to the bishops . . . ; and let them never forget that they are forbidden even by the ancient Canons to take any step in the ministry . . . , or to assume to themselves the office of teaching and preaching, without the sanction of the bishop . . . . Let it stand, therefore, . . . that all those who attempt anything in opposition to this prescribed order, are disturbing, so far as in them lies, the state of the Church.

It would, indeed, be a wicked thing . . . that the discipline which she has sanctioned, . . . should be assailed by a senseless freedom of opinion; or should be branded as opposed to the fixed principles of the law of nature, or be regarded as maimed and imperfect, and as subject to the civil authorities.

But, since it is plain . . . *that the Church has been instructed by Christ Jesus and his Apostles, and is taught by the Holy Ghost, daily suggesting to it all truth,—* it is manifestly absurd, and most highly injurious to it, that a certain *Restoration* and *Regeneration* should be pressed forward as being necessary for promoting its safety and increase; as if it could be supposed liable either to any defect, or obscurement, or other inconveniences of this kind: by which attempt, the innovators have this object in their view, *that the foundations of a new human institution may be laid;* and thus that may take place, which Cyprian abominates, *"that the Church, which is a Divine thing, may become a human one."*

* * *

We now proceed to speak of another most fertile source of evils, with which we lament to see the Church now afflicted, namely that "Indifferentism," or erroneous opinion, which by the artifice of wicked men has prevailed on every side; namely, that by any profession of faith whatsoever, the eternal salvation of a soul may be obtained, provided that the morals be honourable and upright.

* * *

And from this most filthy source of *"Indifferentism,"* flows that absurd and erroneous opinion, or rather mad conceit, that *liberty of conscience* is to be claimed and maintained for all! The way for which most pestilent error is prepared by that extensive and inordinate liberty of opinion, which is spreading far and wide, to the ruin of both Church and State: while some persons cease not to assert most impudently, that religion may derive from it a great advantage. But Augustine said, *"what is more fatal ruin to the soul, than liberty of error?"* For, if we remove every restraint by which men are kept in the path of truth, while their own natural inclination to evil throws them headlong into ruin, we may truly say, that the *pit of the abyss* is open . . . .

For, from thence come changes of men's minds, deadly corruption of youth; amongst the people, a contempt for divine rites, and for subjects and laws the most sacred. From thence, in a word, comes the chief and principal scourge of a state; since experience has proved . . . that states which were flourishing . . . have fallen to pieces through this one evil alone, namely, an ungoverned freedom of opinion, licentiousness of public harangues, and desire of innovation.

Towards this point tends that most vile, detestable, and never-to-be-sufficiently-execrated liberty of booksellers, namely, of publishing writings of whatsoever kind they please; a liberty which some persons dare with such violence of language to demand and promote.

We are horrified . . . when we behold the monstrous doctrines . . . which are disseminated far and wide on every side, by the vast multitude of books, and pamphlets, and tracts, small indeed in bulk, but exceeding large in mischievous intent . . . .

Yet there are some, alas! who are carried away to such a pitch of impudence, as to assert pertinaciously, that the foul deluge of errors springing from that source, is sufficiently compensated by some book or other, which amidst this great mass of depravity may be published in defence of religion and truth.

Beyond doubt, it is a crime, forbidden by every law of justice, that a certain and a great evil should deliberately be perpetrated, because there may be *hope* of some good to arise from it. . . .

Far different was the discipline of the Church in extirpating the infection of bad books, even in the days of the apostles; who, we read, publicly burned a vast quantity of books. . . .

This matter also occupied extremely the attention of the Fathers of Trent, who applied a remedy to so great an evil, by publishing a most salutary decree for compiling an Index of books in which improper doctrine was contained . . . .

So that, by this continual solicitude through all ages, with which this Holy Apostolic See has ever striven, to condemn suspected and noxious books, and to wrest them forcibly out of men's hands; it is most clear how false, rash, and injurious to the said Apostolic See . . . is the doctrine of those, who not only reject the Censorship of books . . . but even proceed . . . to assert, that it is contrary to the principles of equal justice, and dare deny to the Church, the right of enacting and employing it.

Since we have heard that in writings circulated amongst the public, certain doctrines are promulgated, by which the loyalty and submission due to princes is undermined, and the torch of rebellion is everywhere lighted up; the greatest care must be taken, that the people may not be thereby deceived and seduced from the path of rectitude.

Let them all bear in mind, that, according to the Apostle's admonition,—"There is no power but from God; and those which are, are ordained by God. He therefore who resisteth the power, resisteth the ordinance of God . . . ."

* * *

To this end uniformly tended the most wicked ravings and schemes of the Waldenses, Beguards, Wicliffites, and other sons of Belial of this stamp; who were the off-scourings and disgrace of the human race. . . . Nor is it from any other cause, that those old knaves exert all their powers, but that they may triumphantly congratulate themselves, with Luther, "that they are free from all," which object to obtain with more ease and readiness, they boldly undertake the most flagitious designs of every sort.

Nor can we augur more happy results, either to religion or monarchy, from the wishes of those who are anxious that the church should be separated from the state, and that the mutual concord of the empire and priesthood should be torn asunder. For it is certain, that these favourers of the most audacious liberty, do exceedingly fear that concord, which has ever been advantageous and salutary to both religious and civil interests.

Still, to other most sad causes of our solicitude, . . . there have been added certain associations, and set meetings; in which, as if by an union with the disciples of every false religion and worship, (under pretence indeed of a regard for religion, but, in truth, from a desire of prompting everywhere novelty and sedition,)—liberty of every kind is proclaimed; tumults are excited against the sacred and civil estate; even the most holy authority is disputed.

* * *

These, our common wishes for the preservation of the things both of church and state, may our dearest children in Christ, the sovereigns of kingdoms, second, both by their power and authority, which they may recollect were given to them, not only for the ruling of the world, but still more for the protection of the church.

Let them diligently bear in mind, that every exertion made for the welfare of the Church tends to their authority and tranquillity: nay, let them be persuaded, that the cause of religion ought to be even more regarded than that of their empire . . . .

B. From Cardinal Bartolommeo Pacca's Letter to Lamennais, August 16, 1832:

In the encyclical letter which the Holy Father has just addressed to patriarchs, archbishops, and bishops of the Catholic world . . . and of which you will find an attached copy which I am sending you by his express order, you will see . . . the doctrines which His Holiness condemns as contrary to the teaching of the Church, and those which it is necessary to follow, according to the holy and divine tradition and the constant maxims of the Apostolic See. Among the former are some which have been discussed and developed in *L'Avenir,* concerning which the successor of Peter could not remain silent.

However, the Holy Father . . . did not wish to forget the regard which he has for your person, as much on account of your great gifts as of your former services to religion. The encyclical will show you, *M. l'abbé,* that your name and even the titles of your writings whence are extracted the condemned principles have been altogether suppressed.

But as you love the truth and desire to know it in order to follow it, I am going to disclose frankly and in few words the principal points which, after the examination of *L'Avenir*, have most displeased His Holiness. They are:

First, he has been much pained to see that the editors have taken it upon them to discuss publicly and to decide the most delicate questions which pertain to the government of the Church and its supreme head, from which inevitably follows the disturbance of men's minds, and especially division among the clergy, which is always injurious to the faithful.

The Holy Father disapproves as well and even condemns the doctrines concerning *civil* and political liberty which, doubtless against your intentions, tend in their nature to excite and propagate everywhere the spirit of sedition and revolt on the part of subjects against their sovereigns. Now this spirit is in open opposition to the principles of the gospel and our holy Church which, as you well know, equally preaches obedience to peoples and justice to sovereigns.

The doctrines of *L'Avenir* on *liberty of worship* and *liberty of the press*, which have been discussed with such exaggeration and pushed so far by the editors are at once very reprehensible and opposed to the teaching, maxims, and practice of the Church. They have much astonished and pained the Holy Father; for if, in certain circumstances, prudence requires that they should be tolerated as a lesser evil, such doctrines can never be put forward by a Catholic as a good or desirable thing.

Finally, that which has increased the bitterness of the Holy Father beyond all measure is the *act of union proposed to all those who, despite the murder of Poland, the dismemberment of Belgium, and the conduct of governments which call themselves liberal, hope still for the liberty of the world and wish to work for it.* This . . . was published by *L'Avenir* when you had already solemnly indicated in the same journal your resolve to come to Rome with some of your collaborators to know the judgment of the Holy See on your doctrines, that is, in circumstances where many reasons should have recommended a halt. This observation could not escape the deep penetration of His Holiness; he condemns such an act in *substance* and *form*, and you, reflecting a little on its natural end . . . , will easily perceive that the results which it must produce can confuse it with other associations condemned several times by the Holy See.

This, *M. l'abbé*, is the message which His Holiness charges me to forward to you in confidence. He recalls with keen satisfaction the handsome and solemn engagement made by you at the head of your collaborators and published by the press of desiring to *imitate, according to the precept of the Savior, the humble docility of little children, by a submission without reservation to the Vicar of Jesus Christ.* This recollection comforts his heart. I am sure that your promise will be kept. . . .

Source: A. *The Encyclical Letter of Pope Gregory XVI, Bearing Date August 16th, 1832* (Dublin, 1833), pp. 1–5, 7–9, 11–12, 13–19; B. F. de La Mennais, *Affaires de Rome* (Paris, 1837), pp. 128–133. Latin text of *Mirari Vos* in *Acta Gregorii Papae XVI* (Rome, 1901), I, 169–174. For another English text of *Mirari Vos*, see Claudia Carlen (ed.), *The Papal Encyclicals 1740–1878* (Ann Arbor, Mich., 1990), pp. 235–241.

SUGGESTIONS FOR BACKGROUND AND REFERENCE

E. E. Y. Hales, *Revolution and Papacy 1769–1848* (New York, 1960), pp. 290–295.
New Catholic Encyclopedia (New York, 1967), Vol. X, "Bartolommeo Pacca."
J. Schmidlin, *Papstgeschichte der neuesten Zeit* (Munich, 1933–1936), I, 556–567.
References for Document 54.

56   *Singulari Nos* (Extract)

July 15, 1834

Though they formally submitted, Lamennais and his friends privately testified to their continued attachment to the principles of *L'Avenir* and assisted in the publication of a book sympathetic to the Polish revolution. When Rome required a simple and unqualified act of submission to the doctrines of *Mirari Vos,* Lamennais agreed in December 1833, but became increasingly embittered and despairing about the church. Distinguishing between Rome's legitimate ecclesiastical authority and the individual's freedom in temporal affairs and now seeking a Christian social transformation without ecclesiastical direction, Lamennais published his *Words of a Believer* in 1834. This poetic and apocalyptic work, "a *bonnet rouge* atop a cross," created a sensation and elicited the papal condemnation three months later. Subsequently, Lamennais parted from his associates of *L'Avenir* and drifted from the church. As a champion of republicanism and socialism, he won a seat in the National Assembly after the 1848 revolution, but quickly disillusioned, he abandoned politics after the Bonapartist coup of 1851.

It hardly seemed believable that he whom We welcomed with such good will and affection would so quickly forget Our kindness and desert Our resolution. . . . However, We have learned of the pamphlet written in French under the title *Paroles d'un croyant,* for it has been printed by this man and disseminated everywhere. . . .

We were very much amazed . . . when at first We understood the blindness of this wretched author . . . .

The mind shrinks from reading through those things in which the author tries to break the bond of loyalty and submission toward leaders. Once the torch of treason is ignited everywhere, it ruins public order, fosters contempt of government, and stimulates lawlessness. It overthrows every element of sacred and civil power. From this, the writer transposes the power of princes, through a new and wicked idea, to the power of Satan . . . , as if it were dangerous to divine law, even a work of sin. He brands the same marks of wickedness on the priests and rulers because of the conspiracy of crimes and labors in which he dreams they are joined against the rights of the people. Not content with such temerity, he thrusts forth every kind of opinion, speech, and freedom of conscience. He prays that everything will be favorable and happy for the soldiers who will fight to free liberty from tyranny, and he encourages groups and associations in the furious combat which engulfs everything . . . .

. . . Especially dangerous is the fact that holy Scriptures that have been tainted with the errors of this author are disseminated to the unwary. Acting as if he were sent and inspired by God, he speaks in the name of the Trinity and then uses Scriptures as a pretext for releasing people from the law of obedience. He twists the words of holy Scripture in a bold and cunning manner in order to firmly establish his depraved ravings. . . .

. . . By Our apostolic power, We condemn the book: . . . We decree that it be perpetually condemned. It corrupts the people by a wicked abuse of the word of God, to dissolve the bonds of all public order and to weaken all authority. It arouses, fosters, and strengthens seditions, riots, and rebellions . . .

Source: Claudia Carlen (ed.), *The Papal Encyclicals 1740–1878* (Ann Arbor, Mich., 1990), pp. 249–250. Latin text in *Acta Gregorii Papae XVI* (Rome, 1901), I, 433–434.

SUGGESTIONS FOR BACKGROUND AND REFERENCE

References for Documents 54 and 55.

✦✦✦ The Roman Revolution of 1848

57 Fundamental Statute for the Temporal Government of the States of the Church (Extracts)

March 14, 1848

At the time of his election Pius IX (1846–1878) was popular, comparatively young, and more inclined to experiment and reform than his predecessor. Popular enthusiasm mounted for a pontiff who granted a political amnesty, relaxed censorship, permitted a civil guard, consulted lay counsellors, and was believed sympathetic to national unification if the independence and sovereignty of the papacy could be safeguarded. Risings in other Italian states and the Paris revolt of 1848 led to expectations and demands in Rome that the Curia hesitantly and cautiously attempted to satisfy in this constitution.

General Provisions

I. The Sacred College of Cardinals, the electors of the Supreme Pontiff, forms a senate inseparable from him.

II. Two deliberative councils are instituted for the formation of laws—the High Council and the Council of Deputies.

III. Although all justice emanates from the sovereign and is administered in his name, the judicial order is independent in the application of the laws to individual cases, the right of pardon being always reserved to the sovereign himself. The judges of the collegiate tribunals are irremovable after having exercised their functions for three years . . . .

IV. No extraordinary tribunals or commissions can be instituted. Every one . . . shall be judged by the tribunal expressly determined by law . . . .

V. The Civic Guard is to be considered as a state institution . . . .

VI. No restriction can be placed upon personal liberty except in the cases and according to the forms prescribed by law. . . .

* * *

VIII. All property, whether of private individuals, of corporate bodies, or any pious or public institutions, contributes equally . . . to the state burdens, whoever may be its possessor. Whenever the Supreme Pontiff gives his sanction to laws on the taxes, he accompanies that sanction with a special "Apostolica," superseding the ecclesiastical immunity.

* * *

XI. The existing . . . political preventive censure [censorship] for the press is abolished, and repressive measures, to be determined by a special law, will be substituted for it. No innovation is made in the ecclesiastical censure, until the Supreme Pontiff may provide other regulations . . . .

XII. Public spectacles are regulated by preventive measures; theatrical compositions must be submitted to a censorship . . . .

XIII. The communal and provincial administration will be exercised by citizens and regulated by appropriate laws.

Of the High Council and of the Council of Deputies

XIV. The Supreme Pontiff convokes, prorogues, and closes the sessions of both the Councils. He dissolves that of the Deputies, summoning a new one within three months.

* * *

XIX. The members of the High Council are nominated for life by the Supreme Pontiff. Their number is not limited. They are required to have completed the age of thirty years and to be in the full exercise of their civil and political rights.

XX. [They are chosen from the ranks of distinguished clergy, ministers, and legislators; civil, military, administrative, and judicial officials; "proprietors with an annual income of 4,000 scudi from taxable capital possessed for six years"; and "persons who have deserved well of the state for distinguished services."]

* * *

XXII. The other council is composed of deputies chosen by the electors on the approximate basis of a deputy for every 30,000 souls.

[Articles XXIII and XXIV specify the economic and professional categories from which voters and deputies are to be drawn.]

XXV. The electors must have completed the age of twenty-five, the eligible that of thirty years: in both the full exercise of civil and political rights is indispensable, and therefore the profession of the Catholic religion, which is the necessary condition for the enjoyment of political rights in the state.

* * *

XXX. The members of both councils are [not accountable] for the opinions and votes given in the exercise of their functions. They cannot be arrested for debt during the session and the month immediately preceding and following it. Neither can they be arrested on criminal judgment . . . except by the consent of the council to which they belong.

* * *

Powers of the Two Councils

XXXIII. All laws in civil, administrative, and governmental matters are proposed, discussed, and voted in the two councils . . . .

* * *

XXXV. The proposal of the laws is made by the ministers, but may also emanate from either of the two councils, at the request of ten members. The propositions of the ministers shall always, however, have precedence.

XXXVI. The councils can never propose any law: (1) which regards ecclesiastical or mixed affairs; (2) which is contrary to the canons or to the discipline of the Church; (3) which tends to vary or modify the present statute.

* * *

XXXVIII. All discussions on the foreign diplomatico-religious relations of the Holy See are prohibited in the two councils.

* * *

XLI. All projects of laws . . . regarding: (1) the estimates and the expenditure of each year, (2) the creation, liquidation, or remission of state debts, (3) the imposts, leases, or any other cessions or alienations of the state revenues and property, shall always be first presented for the deliberation and vote of the Council of Deputies.

XLII. The direct taxation is voted for a year; the indirect may be established for several years.

* * *

XLVI. The Council of Deputies has alone the right of impeaching the ministers. Their trial, if laymen, belongs to the High Council . . . . [If they are clergy,] . . . trial is referred to the Sacred College . . . .

* * *

Of the Sacred Consistory

LII. When both councils have passed the proposal of a law, it shall be presented to the Supreme Pontiff, and proposed in the secret consistory. The pontiff, after hearing the vote of the cardinals, gives or withholds his sanction.

* * *

Of the Time When the Chair is Vacant

LVI. The death of the Supreme Pontiff suspends immediately and legally the sessions of both councils. They can never assemble during the vacancy of the Holy Chair . . . .

* * *

LVIII. The Sacred College . . . confirms the ministers, or substitutes others. Until this act has taken place the ministers remain in office. The ministry of foreign affairs passes immediately to the secretary of the Sacred College, which, however, has the power to entrust it to another person.

* * *

LXI. The rights of temporal sovereignty . . . reside during the vacancy . . . in the Sacred College . . . .

Of the Council of State

LXII. The Council of State will be composed of ten councillors, and of a body of auditors whose number will not exceed twenty-four—all to be nominated by the sovereign.

LXIII. The Council of State has the charge of drawing up . . . the projects of laws, the regulations for the public administration . . . .

Source: British and Foreign State Papers (1847–1848) (London, 1861), XXXVI, 879–887.

SUGGESTIONS FOR BACKGROUND AND REFERENCE

R. Aubert, *Le pontificat de Pie IX (1846–1848)* (Paris, 1952), pp. 27–39.
R. Aubert et al., *The Church in the Age of Liberalism* (New York, 1981), pp. 57–65.
Cambridge Modern History (New York, 1903–1912), XI, 65–95.
D. Demarco, *Pio IX e la rivoluzione romana del 1848* (Modena, 1947).
L. C. Farini, *The Roman State from 1815 to 1850* (London, 1851).

E. E. Y. Hales, *Pio Nono. A Study in European Politics and Religion in the Nineteenth Century* (London, 1954).

F. Nielsen, *History of the Papacy in the Nineteenth Century* (London, 1906), II, 102–182.

58 Papal Allocution of April 29, 1848 (Extracts)

This allocution to the cardinals was a turning point in the Roman movement of 1848 and in Pius IX's pontificate. Warnings from conservative advisers, the commotions in Rome, and the indignation of Austria and Germany over reported papal cooperation with the Italian nationalist movement all influenced the pope. To the dismay of liberals and nationalists, the allocution repudiated the unsettlement in Rome and Italy, restricted the use of papal troops to the defense of the Papal States, and disowned the interest awakened by Vincenzo Gioberti's *The Civil and Moral Primacy of the Italians* (1843) in an Italian union under papal presidency. In effect, the unification problem was left to Piedmont and Mazzini.

. . . But those are not now wanting who so speak of us, as if we were the chief author of the public commotions which have lately happened, not only in other parts of Europe, but likewise in Italy. From the Austrian parts, especially of Germany, we have learned that it is there spread about amongst the people that the Roman Pontiff . . . had excited the people of Italy to bring about unusual changes in public affairs. We have likewise learned that certain enemies of the Catholic religion hence seized the opportunity of inflaming the minds of the Germans with a fury of revenge, and of alienating them from the unity of this Holy See. Now . . . we know that it is our duty to . . . rebut the calumny . . . .

It is not unknown to you . . . that already from the late times of Pius VII . . . the chief princes of Europe had taken care to recommend to the Apostolic See that, in the administration of civil affairs, it should apply a more favorable rule, and one answering to the wishes of laymen. Afterwards, in the year 1831, these their counsels . . . were more solemnly made known by that celebrated Memorandum which the Emperors of Austria and Russia, and the Kings of France, of Britain, and of Prussia, judged proper to send by their ambassadors to Rome. In that writing also, among other things, was treated the question of calling . . . a Consulting Council, as well as that of restoring, or of enlarging, the constitution of municipalities, and of establishing provincial councils; moreover, of introducing the same and other institutions into all the provinces . . . , and of opening to laymen . . . all offices . . . .[1]

1. The memorandum was drawn up by the religious scholar and diplomat, Christian Karl Bunsen, on behalf of Prussia but subscribed by the Powers. French text in *British and Foreign State Papers* (1843–1844) (London, 1859), XXXII, 1385–1387; English translation in R. M. Johnston, *The Roman Theocracy and the Republic 1846–1849* (London, 1901), pp. 341–343.

It is concealed from no one that some of these were accomplished by Gregory XVI . . . . But these good acts of our predecessor appeared . . . not to be sufficient to secure the public utility and tranquillity . . . .

Therefore, we, when we were first . . . appointed in his place, . . . conceded a more copious pardon to those who had strayed from the fidelity due to the papal government, and thereupon hastened to institute some things which we had considered as conducive to the prosperity of its people. . . .

But truly after . . . our designs were brought about, not only our own, but the neighbouring people were seen to exult for joy, and so to extol us by public signs of congratulation and respect, that we were forced to endeavor to restrain, in this fair city especially, popular cries, applause . . . .

* * *

And would that the wished-for event had answered to our paternal voice and exhortations. But well known to every one are the public commotions of the people of Italy . . . . But if any one will contend that any way was opened to the issue of the self-same things, from those which at the beginning of our sacred sovereignty were by us benevolently and kindly done, he certainly in no manner whatever could ascribe it to our work . . . . Furthermore, nor could the above-mentioned people of Germany be angry with us, if it were not possible for us to restrain the ardor of those who, in our temporal State, resolved on applauding what was carried on against them in Upper Italy, and . . . on giving their assistance to the same cause with the other people of Italy. Since many other sovereigns, likewise, of Europe, far more powerful in military strength than we, equally could not withstand . . . the commotion of their people. In which condition of things we, however, willed no other command to our troops, sent to the confines of the papal territories, than that they should protect the integrity of the Papal States.

But when now some desire that we, . . . with the other people and sovereigns of Italy, should undertake a war against the Germans, we have . . . thought it our duty that . . . we clearly . . . declare that this is wholly abhorrent from our counsels, seeing that we . . . discharge on earth the office of Him who is the author of peace . . . and . . . embrace with equal paternal earnestness of love, all tribes, peoples, and nations. . . .

But in this place we cannot but repudiate . . . the crafty counsels . . . of those who would that the Roman Pontiff should preside over some new Republic, to be formed of all the people of Italy. Yea, the people themselves . . . we particularly warn . . . that they beware . . . of crafty counsels of this kind, . . . and that they firmly adhere to their sovereigns . . . . With regard, however, to us, we again and again declare that the Roman Pontiff directs all . . . his thoughts, cares, and desires, that the Kingdom of Christ, which is the Church, should daily increase: not, however, that the bounds should be widened, of the civil sovereignty with which Divine Providence willed this Holy See to be bestowed to protect its dignity and the free exercise of the Supreme Apostleship. Greatly, therefore, are they in error who think that our soul is seduced by the ambition of a more ample temporal dominion, that we should throw ourselves into the midst of the tumult of arms. . . .

Source: British and Foreign State Papers (1848–1849) (London, 1862), XXXVI, 1062–1066.

SUGGESTIONS FOR BACKGROUND AND REFERENCE

R. M. Johnston, *The Roman Theocracy and the Republic 1846–1849* (London, 1901).
References for Document 57.

59   Proclamation of the Roman Republic

February 9, 1849

The revolutionary sweep in Italy temporarily destroyed the pope's temporal sovereignty. The constitutional system had given rise to conflict between the pope and his ministers, and the national war against Austria threatened to compromise his position as international spiritual head. In November 1848 the moderate prime minister, Pellegrino Rossi, was assassinated, and after a week of further disorders, Pius fled to Neapolitan territory. Republicans, inspired by Mazzini, seized control, and the Constituent Assembly issued this special decree.

I. The papacy has forfeited in fact and of right the temporal government of the Roman state.

II. The Roman Pontiff shall have all the guarantees necessary to secure his independence in the exercise of his spiritual power.

III. The form of the government of the Roman state shall be a pure democracy, and it shall take the glorious name of the Roman Republic.

IV. The Roman Republic shall have with the rest of Italy such relations as the common nationality may require.

Source: British and Foreign State Papers (1854–1855) (London, 1865), XLV, 353. Italian text in Domenico Demarco, *Una rivoluzione sociale, la republica romana del 1849* (Naples, 1944), p. 95.

SUGGESTIONS FOR BACKGROUND AND REFERENCE

G. O. Griffith, *Mazzini, Prophet of Modern Europe* (London, 1932).
References for Documents 57 and 58.

✦ ✦ ✦ Reconstitution of the English Hierarchy

60   Cardinal Wiseman's Pastoral, "Out of the Flaminian Gate"

October 7, 1850

Catholic ecclesiastical administration, lost in England during the Reformation, was partially restored in the seventeenth century through the use of vicars-apostolic, bishops without regular diocesan authority. Catholic growth, partly due to Irish immigration, led to increasing the vicariates from four to eight in 1840, and in 1850 Cardinal Nicholas Wiseman (1802–1865) was able to announce the restoration of the hierarchy in this jubilant pastoral. The archbishopric of Westminster, held by Wiseman, was supported by twelve suffragan sees. Public feeling at this "papal aggression," coming soon after the conversion of John Henry Newman and others, was intense.

For on the twenty-ninth day of last month, . . . Pope Pius IX was graciously pleased to issue his letters apostolic, . . . wherein he substituted for the eight apostolic vicariates heretofore existing, one archiepiscopal or metropolitan and twelve episcopal sees, repealing at the same time and annulling all dispositions and enactments made for England by the Holy See with reference to its late form of ecclesiastical government.

And, by a brief dated the same day, his Holiness was further pleased to appoint us, though most unworthy, to the archiepiscopal see of Westminster, established by the above-mentioned letters apostolic, giving us at the same time the administration of the episcopal see of Southwark. So that at present, and till such time as the Holy See shall think fit otherwise to provide, we govern . . . the counties of Middlesex, Hertford, and Essex, as ordinary thereof, and those of Surrey, Sussex, Kent, Berks, and Hants, with the islands annexed, as administrator with ordinary jurisdiction.

Further, we have to announce to you . . . that, as if still further to add solemnity and honour before the church to this noble act of apostolic authority, and to give an additional mark of paternal benevolence towards the Catholics of England, his Holiness was pleased to raise me, in the private consistory of Monday, the 30th of September, to the rank of Cardinal . . . .

Then truly is this day to us a day of joy and exaltation of spirit, the crowning day of long hopes, and the opening day of bright prospects. How must the saints of our country, whether Roman or British, Saxon or Norman, look down from their seats of bliss with beaming glance upon this new evidence of the faith and church which led them to glory, sympathizing with those who have faithfully adhered to them through centuries of ill repute, for the truth's sake, and now reap the fruit of their patience and long suffering! And all those blessed martyrs of these later ages, who have fought the battles of the faith under such discouragement, who mourned, more than over their own fetters or their own pain, over the desolate ways of their own Sion and the departure of England's religious glory: oh! how must they bless God, who hath again visited His people, how take part in our joy, as they see the lamp of the temple again enkindled and rebrightening, as they behold the silver links of that chain which has connected their country with the See of Peter in its vicarial government changed into burnished gold; not stronger nor more closely knit, but more beautifully wrought and more brightly arrayed!

Source: The Times, October 29, 1850, p. 5.

SUGGESTIONS FOR BACKGROUND AND REFERENCE

B. Fothergill, *Nicholas Wiseman* (London, 1963), pp. 152–183.

S. W. Jackman, *Nicholas Cardinal Wiseman: A Victorian Prelate and His Writings* (Charlottesville, Va., 1977).

G. I. T. Machin, *Politics and the Churches in Great Britain, 1832–1868* (Oxford, 1977), pp. 210–228.

E. R. Norman, *Roman Catholicism in England: from the Elizabethan Settlement to the Second Vatican Council* (New York, 1986).

61   Ecclesiastical Titles Act (Extract)

August 1, 1851

Parliament in 1829 had provided that Catholic bishops were not to take territorial titles held by Anglican bishops, but this measure, the result of the uproar over Rome's decision to set up a Catholic hierarchy, went farther. Catholics largely ignored the act, which was never enforced. It was repealed in 1871.

WHEREAS divers of Her Majesty's Roman Catholic Subjects have assumed to themselves the Titles of Archbishop and Bishops of a pretended Province, and of pretended Sees or Dioceses, within the United Kingdom, under colour of an alleged Authority given to them . . . by certain Briefs, Rescripts, or Letters Apostolical from the See of Rome . . . : And whereas by the Act of the Tenth Year of King George the Fourth, Chapter Seven, . . . it was enacted, that if any Person . . . , other than the Person thereunto authorized by Law, should assume or use the Name, Style, or Title of Archbishop of any Province, Bishop of any Bishopric, or Dean of any Deanery, in England or Ireland, he should for every such Offence forfeit . . . One hundred pounds: And whereas it may be doubted whether the recited Enactment extends to the Assumption of the Title of Archbishop or Bishop of a pretended Province or Diocese . . . or Dean of any pretended Deanery . . . , not being the See, Province, or Diocese of any Archbishop or Bishop or Deanery of any Dean recognized by Law; but the Attempt to establish, under colour of Authority from the See of Rome or otherwise, such pretended Sees, Provinces, Dioceses, or Deaneries, is illegal and void: And whereas it is expedient to prohibit the Assumption of such Titles in respect of any Places within the United Kingdom: Be it therefore . . . enacted . . . That—

I. All such Briefs, Rescripts, or Letters Apostolical, and all and every the Jurisdiction, Authority, Pre-eminence, or Title conferred or pretended to be conferred thereby, are . . . unlawful and void.

II. . . . . That if, after the passing of this Act, any Persons shall obtain or cause to be procured from the Bishop or See of Rome, or shall publish or put in use within any Part of the United Kingdom, any such Bull, Brief, Rescript, or Letters Apostolical, . . . for the Purpose of constituting such Archbishops or Bishops . . . , or if any Person, other than a Person thereunto authorized by Law . . . , assume or use the Name, Style, or Title of Archbishop, Bishop, or Dean of any City, Town, or Place, or of any Territory or District . . . in the United Kingdom, . . . the Person so offending shall for every such Offence forfeit . . . One hundred pounds . . . .

Source: 14 & 15 Vict., c. 60; *A Collection of the Public General Statutes Passed in the Fourteenth and Fifteenth Year of the Reign of Her Majesty Queen Victoria [1851]* (London, 1851), pp. 419–421.

SUGGESTIONS FOR BACKGROUND AND REFERENCE

E. R. Norman, *Anti-Catholicism in Victorian England* (New York, 1968).
J. Prest, *Lord John Russell* (Columbia, S.C., 1972), pp. 319–330.
References for Document 60.

✦ ✦ ✦

62   Austrian Concordat (Extracts)

August 18, 1855

Catholic Austria long remained influenced by Febronianism and by the Josephinist tradition of state regulation and control of the church. Unlike many German states, beginning with Bavaria in 1817, which made concordats with Rome after the Vienna Congress, Austria was unwilling to relax controls until after 1848. Negotiations begun in 1853 resulted in the 1855 concordat, establishing Catholicism on a basis far more satisfactory to the church. This advantage was much qualified by the legislation and constitutional reorganization of 1867 and 1868, and in 1870 Austria revoked the agreement altogether, citing the Vatican Council and its definition of infallibility as the reason.

I. The Holy Apostolic Roman Catholic religion shall, with all the rights and privileges which it, according to the command of God and the stipulations of the ecclesiastical laws, must enjoy, be ever maintained unimpaired in the entire Empire of Austria . . . .

II. Since the pope of Rome by divine law possesses the primacy of honor as well as of judicial authority in the whole Church . . . , communication between the bishops, the clergy, the people, and the Holy See in spiritual matters and ecclesiastical affairs, will not be dependent on the necessity of demanding the consent of the sovereign, but will be perfectly free.

III. Archbishops, bishops, and all ordinaries will have free intercourse with the clergy and the people of their dioceses, in the discharge of their pastoral functions; they will also freely publish instructions and regulations on ecclesiastical affairs.

IV. Likewise archbishops and bishops will have freedom to exercise every right which pertains to them for the government of their dioceses, . . . and especially;

a. To constitute as their vicars, counsellors, and assistants in their administration all such ecclesiastics as they consider fitted . . . .

b. To admit into the clerical state . . . .

c. To erect smaller benefices, and after coming to an understanding with His Imperial Majesty, especially on the proper assignment of the revenues, to found, divide, or unite parishes.

d. To prescribe public prayers and other pious works . . . .

e. To convoke and to hold provincial councils and diocesan synods . . . and to publish their acts.

V. The entire education of the Catholic youth will in all public as well as private schools be in conformity with the doctrine of the Catholic religion; but the bishops . . . will order the religious instruction . . . and will keep careful watch that nothing opposed to Catholic truth and to moral purity be introduced . . . .

VI. No one will expound sacred theology, catechetic divinity, or religious doctrine in any public or private institution unless he have a mission and authority for that purpose from the bishop of the diocese, who is empowered to recall the same if he think fit. . . .

VII. In the colleges and middle schools for Catholic youth, Catholics alone will be appointed as professors or teachers . . . . The bishops, having consulted together on the subject, will appoint what books of instruction are to be employed in the said schools for religious teaching. . . .

VIII. All teachers of elementary Catholic schools will be subjected to the supervision of the Church. His Majesty will name the superintendents of the diocesan schools from men proposed by the bishop. In case sufficient provision has not been made for religious instruction in such schools, the bishop may freely appoint a clergyman to teach . . . the catechism. . . .

IX. Archbishops, bishops, and all ordinaries will . . . censure books which are injurious to religion and morality . . . . But the government will also prevent the dissemination of such books . . . .

X. As all ecclesiastical causes . . . belong solely and entirely to the tribunal of the Church, the ecclesiastical judge will take cognizance of them, and he will decide on marriage cases according to the holy canons, . . . only the civil effect of marriage being left to the secular judge. . . .

XI. Bishops are at liberty to inflict upon clergymen . . . the punishments prescribed by the holy canon laws, or even other penalties, . . . and to keep them under control in cloisters, seminaries, or houses set apart for this purpose. They shall in no wise be hindered from punishing with censures all believers who transgress the laws and regulations of the Church.

XII. The ecclesiastical court will decide on the right of patronage but the Holy See agrees that, when the question is about a lay right of patronage, the secular courts may judge . . . .

XIII. . . . the Holy See consents that the purely secular legal causes of the clergy, such as contracts, debts, inheritances, shall be considered and decided by the civil courts.

XIV. . . . the Holy See does not object to clergymen being summoned before the secular court on account of crimes and other misdemeanors . . . ; but it is incumbent on that court to inform the bishop of it without delay. . . . Clergymen will always suffer . . . imprisonment in places where they are separated from laymen. In case of condemnation for misdemeanor or transgression, they will be incarcerated in a monastery or some other religious house.

* * *

XVII. The episcopal seminaries will be kept up; and in cases where their income . . . is not fully sufficient, provision will be made for its increase . . . . The bishops will regulate and administer them . . . [and] will nominate the rectors and professors . . . .

XVIII. The Holy See will . . . erect new dioceses . . . when the spiritual benefit of believers demands it. But when such a case shall arise, it will come to an understanding with the imperial government.

XIX. His Majesty, in the choice of the bishops, whom . . . he may propose . . . to the Holy See for canonical installation, will hereafter take the advice of the bishops, more particularly of those belonging to the ecclesiastical province of the vacant see.

XX. The metropolitans and bishops . . . will take the following oath of allegiance before the emperor: "Upon God's holy gospel, and as it beseems a bishop, I swear and promise fidelity and obedience to Your Imperial Royal Apostolic Majesty and to your successors. I likewise swear . . . never to . . . take part in any design that can endanger public tranquillity and never, either within or without the realm, to enter into any connection open to suspicion, and should I learn that there is any danger threatening the state, I will leave nothing undone which may avail to ward off the same."

* * *

XXVI. The endowment of livings, the revenues of which are not adequate, . . . will be augmented as soon as possible . . . .

* * *

XXXIII. Inasmuch as during . . . the last troubles in many parts of the Austrian territory the ecclesiastical tithe has been abolished by the civil law, and as . . . it is impossible to re-establish it . . . , His Holiness . . . declares . . . that whilst reserving the right intact to levy the tithe where it still *de facto* exists, there shall be granted by the imperial government in other places, instead of the said tithe and as compensation for the same, to . . . every one who had the right of demanding tithe, a corresponding charge upon real property, or one upon the public debt of the state. . . .

Source: British and Foreign State Papers (1855–1856) (London, 1865), XLVI, 1069–1076. Latin text in A. Mercati (ed.), *Raccolta di Concordati su materie ecclesiastiche tra la Santa Sede e le autorità civili* (Rome, 1954), I, 821–830.

SUGGESTIONS FOR BACKGROUND AND REFERENCE

R. Aubert et al., *The Church in the Age of Liberalism* (New York, 1981), pp. 108–110.
F. Engel-Janosi, *Österreich und der Vatikan 1846–1918* (Vienna, 1958–1960), I, 61–142.
H. Geffcken, *Church and State* (London, 1877), II, 246–259.
M. Hussarek, "Die Verhandlung des Konkordats vom 18 August 1855. Ein Beitrag zur Geschichte des österreichischen Staatskirchenrechts," *Archiv für österreichische Geschichte* (1922), CIX, 447–811.
F. Nielsen, *The History of the Papacy in the Nineteenth Century* (London, 1906), II, 198–200.
J. Schmidlin, *Papstgeschichte der neuesten Zeit* (Munich, 1933–1936), II, 135–143.

✦✦✦ The Papacy and Italian Unification

63   Cavour's Speech of March 27, 1861 (Extract)

Cavour (1810–1861) hoped to crown his career as Sardinian statesman and chief architect of Italian unity by persuading the pope that surrendering temporal sovereignty would bring advantage rather than insecurity in a liberal state where irksome political controls over the church would be abandoned. Despite the failure of approaches to the Curia and the fear of some Italian nationalists that a free church might freely attack the new state, Cavour persisted in advocating this solution. The formula of the liberal program, *"libera chiesa in libero stato,"* perhaps borrowed from the French liberal, Montalembert, was most firmly enunciated in this parliamentary speech shortly before his death.

One thing remains to be done: convince the pontiff that the Church can be independent even by losing her temporal power. It seems impossible to me that the following argument, when presented to the pope in all sincerity and loyalty, will not be accepted: Holy Father, the temporal power is no longer a guarantee of independence for you. Renounce it, and we will give you that freedom for which you have been asking all great Catholic powers in vain for three centuries. Holy Father, you tried to wrest some portions of this freedom through concordats, but in compensation you had to grant some privileges—even worse than privileges, the use of spiritual weapons by those temporal powers willing to concede a bit of freedom to you. We are now offering you in full what you never were able to obtain from those powers which prided themselves on being your allies and faithful children. We are ready to proclaim in Italy this great principle: A free church in a free state. ([Members:] Very good!)

Your faithful friends agree with us that the temporal power, as it is, clearly cannot exist. They propose to you reforms which you, as pontiff, cannot make . . . . I can see your point when you assert it is not your task to proclaim religious freedom. You must teach certain doctrines, and therefore you cannot say it is well done that any kind of doctrine be taught by anybody. You cannot honor the advice of your sincere friends because they beg impossible things of you, and thus you have to remain in this abnormal status as the father of the faithful, obliged to keep your peoples under the yoke with foreign bayonets, or else to accept the principle of freedom, loyally and widely favored in the first-born Latin nation, the country where Catholicism is in its natural setting. . . .

No one can question the sincerity of these proposals of ours. I do not wish to become personal. But may I remind those colleagues of mine who were members of the other legislatures that I have always frankly proclaimed this principle since 1850 when, just a few days after I had been appointed a member of the Council of the Crown, I rejected the suggestion that all church property should be confiscated and clergymen be hired as salaried civil servants of the state.

May I point out, as evidence of the sincerity of our proposals, that they conform to our system, to our belief that freedom should permeate the entire religious and civil society. We want economic freedom, administrative freedom, full and absolute freedom of conscience. We want all political liberties consistent with public tranquillity. The structure we wish to frame will be all the more complete if we add to it that the principle of freedom be applied to the relations between church and state.

Source: Discorsi parlamentari del Conte Camillo di Cavour (Rome, 1872), XI, 346–348.

SUGGESTIONS FOR BACKGROUND AND REFERENCE

R. de Cesare, *The Last Days of Papal Rome, 1850–1870* (London, 1909).
A. Jemolo, *Church and State in Italy, 1850–1950* (Oxford, 1960), pp. 16–26.
D. Mack Smith, *Cavour* (New York, 1985), pp. 243–247.
G. Mollat, *La question romaine de Pie VI à Pie XI* (Paris, 1932), pp. 282–367.

64   Papal Protest on the Proclamation of the Italian Kingdom

April 15, 1861

Italian unification, achieved in the patriotic war against Austria from 1859 to 1860, was the product of resurgent nationalism, Piedmontese leadership, and French military assistance. Joining the Kingdom of the Two Sicilies with northern Italy required first military invasion, then annexation, of most of the Papal States, leaving only Rome and the area immediately surrounding it to the pope. Cavour's overtures to the Curia (October 1860 to February 1861) arguing for a settlement that would give Rome to Italy while leaving papal religious authority undisturbed were fruitless, and when the Italian kingdom was proclaimed March 17, 1861, Cardinal Antonelli (papal secretary of state) protested in this diplomatic circular. The encyclical *Jamdudum Cernimus,* dated March 18, defining the church's relationship to progress, liberalism, and modern civilization, also denounced spoliation of the Holy See.

A Catholic king, forgetful of every religious principle, despising every right, trampling upon every law, after having, little by little, despoiled the august head of the Catholic Church of the greatest and most flourishing portion of his legitimate possessions, has now taken to himself the title of King of Italy; with which title he has sought to seal the sacrilegious usurpations already consummated, and which his government has already manifested its intention of completing to the detriment of the patrimony of the Apostolic See. Although the Holy Father has solemnly protested . . . as he saw successive attacks made upon his sovereignty, he, nevertheless, is under the obligation of putting forth a fresh protest against the assumption of a title tending to legitimize the iniquity of so many facts.

It would here be superfluous to recall the holiness of the possession of the patrimony of the Church and the right the Supreme Pontiff has to it—an incontestable right, recognized at all times and by all governments. Therefore . . . the Holy Father will never be able to recognize the title of "King of Italy," arrogated to himself by the king of Sardinia, because it is injurious to justice and to the sacred property of the Church. On the contrary, he makes the most ample and formal protest against such an usurpation.

Source: The Annual Register, or a View of the History and Politics of the Year 1861 (London, 1862), pp. [187]–[188]. Italian text in *Civiltà cattolica,* 4th ser., Vol. X (1861), p. 497.

SUGGESTIONS FOR BACKGROUND AND REFERENCE

E. E. Y. Hales, *Pio Nono. A Study in European Politics and Religion in the Nineteenth Century* (New York, 1954), pp. 171–227.

F. Nielsen, *The History of the Papacy in the Nineteenth Century* (London, 1906), II, 200–238.

J. Schmidlin, *Papstgeschichte der neuesten Zeit* (Munich, 1933–1936), II, 66–80.

References for Document 63.

✦ ✦ ✦

65   Montalembert's Speeches at the Malines Congress (Extracts)

August 20–21, 1863

In 1863 Charles de Montalembert (1810–1870), then fifty-three years old and the most eminent of the French Catholic liberals, was invited to address a Catholic congress at Malines, presided over by Cardinal Sterckx and supported by prominent Belgian Catholics and by Cardinal Wiseman. He determined to deliver his *"testament politique."* He spoke twice, August 20 on Catholicism and democracy and August 21 on liberty of conscience. Although well received at Malines, the speeches raised much controversy in France and contest at Rome. After some delay, the papacy reproved Montalembert, but muted the censure by transmitting it in a private letter written by Cardinal Antonelli, papal secretary of state. Significant passages from both speeches are reproduced below as reported in the *Journal de Bruxelles.*

From the First Speech, August 20, 1863:

Perhaps I am wrong, but to my mind, Catholics, except in Belgium, are everywhere inferior to their opponents in public life because they have not yet resigned themselves to the great revolution which has given birth to modern society . . . . Many among them are still in heart and mind . . . of the old regime, that is, of the regime which accepted neither civil equality, political liberty, nor freedom of conscience.

This old regime had its great and good side. I do not presume to judge it here, and even less to condemn it. It is sufficient to remember only one defect, though a capital one: It is dead, and nowhere will it ever revive. (*Commotion.*)

Does this mean that the new order is irreproachable? Far from it. Will it everywhere keep its promises? Will it everywhere give the liberty that we expect from it? I doubt it. Until now it has not succeeded, and if necessary, I might undertake to show, for example, that there was in France one hundred years ago in 1763 a certain kind of independence, an order of guarantees, and of individual, local, and municipal liberties which no longer exists today. But that is not the question. The new society, democracy . . . exists . . . . In half of Europe it is already sovereign. Tomorrow it will be so in the other half, and it will alter neither in principle nor in nature as long as we live. . . .

* * *

As for me, I am not a democrat; but I am even less an absolutist. Above all, I try not to be blind. Full of deference and love for the past, in which there was much great and good, I do not slight the present and I try to study the future. Thus I look ahead, and everywhere I see only democracy. I see this flood rise, always rise, reach and overflow everything. As a man, I would be apt to fear it. As a Christian, I do not fear it, for at the same time that I see the flood I see also the ark. (*Long applause.*) On this immense sea of democracy with its depths, its whirlpools, its reefs, its dead calms and its storms, the Church alone may venture without distrust and fear. It alone will not be engulfed. It alone has the compass which never varies and the pilot who never fails.

* * *

The future of modern society depends on two problems: correcting democracy through liberty and reconciling Catholicism with democracy. (*Prolonged sensation.*)

The first is much the more difficult of the two. The natural affinities of democracy with despotism on the one hand, and with the revolutionary spirit on the other, are the great lesson of history and the great danger of the future. Forever tossed about between these two chasms, modern democracy painfully seeks its place and its moral equilibrium. It will find them only with the help of religion.

But if Catholics, condemned to live in the midst of democracy whether they like it or not, are to exert a creative and wholesome influence on it, they must know how to accept the vital conditions of modern society.

Above all, they must renounce the vain hope of witnessing the rebirth of a regime of privilege or an absolute monarchy favorable to Catholicism.

* * *

All things considered, I believe that the instincts, tendencies, and unyielding demands of democracy may be traced to two principles: first, the right of every man to aspire to anything—that is, political equality; second, the suppression of all privilege and all constraint in religion—that is, freedom of worship. . . . Once assured of these two victories, modern democracy sleeps soundly in false security about everything else. To instill in it the sense, taste, and need for public liberty, a sustained and noble effort is needed—an effort to which the Catholic conscience is more appropriate . . . than any other, for it is to the Catholic religion especially that it is important to see democracy become liberal and liberty again become Christian.

"God loves nothing in the world so much as the liberty of his Church," said St. Anselm . . . . Thus, for the Church liberty is the prime good, the prime necessity. But the Church can no longer be free except in the context of a general liberty. No particular liberty, and that of the Church least of all, may exist today except under the security of general liberty. It was otherwise in the great ages of Christian history . . . . But times have changed. The services performed by the Church as a privileged corporation are forgotten. Every privilege, however ancient, inoffensive, or legitimate it may be, offends our generation . . . .

* * *

Catholicism has every interest in combatting . . . whatever threatens and compromises modern society and liberty . . . . Absolutism, centralization, and demagogy are the great enemies of liberal democracy. They are also the forces which the Church encounters everywhere, armed and implacable against it.

The repulse of state encroachments, the consecration of the rights of property, respect for individual liberty, the establishment and maintenance of the right of association—these the progress and consolidation of democracy require. These the Church also should desire, for no [institution] will profit from them as much as it will.

* * *

Take one by one the most popular ideas and most accepted institutions at the heart of modern democracy. I challenge anyone to find among them a single one which is not acceptable or even advantageous to Catholics in the present state of the world.

The nineteenth century rightly boasts of having restored the idea of nationality. . . . Now where does this idea come from? Who baptized, blessed, instructed, shaped, and consecrated all the Christian nationalities? Who watched over their growth with the most maternal tenderness, if not the Church? . . . It is necessary to suppose the height of ingratitude on the one hand, and an abyss of stupidity on the other, to establish a conflict between the legitimate regeneration of oppressed nationalities and the unfailing motherhood of the Church.

Perhaps others will raise objection to universal suffrage. Universal suffrage! I am not its apologist; I am, on the contrary, its victim. (*Laughter.*) But it exists, and it threatens to win ground every day. . . . We old liberals . . . may well nourish grave apprehensions . . . concerning the possibility of reconciling the practice of universal suffrage with the intelligence and independence which representative government requires in the electorate. But all of us, victims or champions of universal suffrage, have the same interest in desiring . . . it to be enlightened, emancipated, and delivered from every abusive influence . . . . In what can this program wound the interests or rights of the Church? Why, moreover, should the Church . . . fear to be in contact with the masses on the field of electoral suffrage? . . . Has it not a thousand legitimate means of reaching the hearts, minds, and ears of the masses? And should it fail once, twice, even ten times, can it not hope with better right than any other for vigorous recoveries . . . ?

What shall we say of the great democratic principle of equality before the law, of the equal distribution of responsibilities and civil and social obligations? In what can it injure the Church, obstruct its action, or harm its principles? . . . Certainly, there is here a serious peril for political organization and social tranquillity . . . . But the Church! It has lived by it, and for eighteen centuries. (*Prolonged commotion.*) Indeed, has the Church ever acted otherwise— . . . never admitting in its powerful hierarchy any condition of birth or fortune, always calling to the highest offices . . . the most obscure of its children, having for the first pope a fisherman of Lake Tiberias, and . . . in the height of feudal aristocracy knowing no pontiff more illustrious or powerful than Saint Gregory VII, the son of a Tuscan carpenter? (*More bravos.*)

* * *

Liberty of instruction! . . . It is we who have especially and everywhere demanded it. It is we who especially and everywhere benefit from it. It is against us, exclusively against us, that it is continually disregarded or violated by force or ruse . . . .

Liberty of association! Again we above all benefit from it. To us especially it is . . . absolutely necessary for all our works of charity, instruction, devotion, and spiritual and penitential life. . . .

Liberty of the press! . . . Where would be our priests, our bishops, or even the pope himself in the present state of the world if the press was everywhere, as it is in certain countries, under the control of the government, censured, mutilated, smothered, and at the mercy of certain laymen? How would they begin to make truth, duty, and the true and supreme authority known to their flocks? God grant that I do not slight the abuses of the press or . . . demand . . . its absolute impunity and unlimited liberty! I am not even of those who believe that good books or journals may atone for all the evil done by bad journals and books. But I assert that in the countries that we represent here—France, England, Germany, and Italy—every arbitrary restriction imposed on the press will turn only to the advantage of the enemies of religion, serve only to enlarge the oppressive monopoly of the old journals, obstruct and suppress only the Catholic publications, freely pass only the poison and prevent only the antidote. . . .

From the Second Speech, August 21, 1863:

I fully admit the distinction . . . between *dogmatic intolerance* and *civil toleration,* the one inseparable from eternal truth and the other indispensable to modern society.

In agreement with the most authoritative interpreters of religion and philosophy, I hold that moral freedom gives me the faculty of choosing between good and evil, and not the right to choose evil. But to enlighten and determine my choice I wish to consult and hear only the Church and not the state.

It is not against the Church but against the state and against it alone that I claim this liberty of conscience, which is at once the right, the due, and the supreme danger of man. Far from suggesting the shadow of an attack on the spiritual power, I believe I multiply its strength a hundredfold . . . in proclaiming . . . the incompetence of the secular power and the unlawfulness of force and physical constraint in matters of faith . . . .

Having received moral liberty . . . from God . . . , I know that I should choose the true. But I do not want to be required by the state to believe what it believes true, because the state is not the judge of truth. However, the state . . . is required to protect me in the practice of the truth which I have chosen, . . . because I have found it alone true and superior to all others. This is what constitutes religious liberty which the modern state, the free state, is obliged to respect and guarantee, not only to each individual citizen, but to citizens meeting to profess and propagate their religion . . . .

* * *

. . . of all liberties . . . , liberty of conscience is in my eyes the most precious, sacred, legitimate, and necessary. I have loved and served all freedoms, but I am especially proud of having fought for that one. Even today, after so many years, so many battles and defeats, I can speak of it only with extraordinary emotion. Yes, all freedoms must be loved and served, but . . . religious freedom deserves the tenderest respect and requires the most absolute devotion . . . .

And yet—strange and melancholy circumstance!—this liberty, the most delicate and vulnerable of all . . . is almost everywhere . . . the least understood and respected, the least preserved from a thousand scurrilous or perfidious attacks which too often go unheeded or unpunished.

Moreover, . . . this enthusiastic devotion which I feel for religious liberty is not general among Catholics. They want it for themselves, but in this they win no great credit. . . . But religious liberty in itself, liberty of conscience for others, liberty for the religion which one denies and rejects—this disturbs and frightens many of us. If one seeks the sources of this fright, they can perhaps be discovered in three principles: Liberty of conscience is rejected by many Catholics, because they believe it to be of anti-Christian origin, because they see it appealed to especially by the enemies of the Church, and because it seems to them that we have more to lose than to gain from it.

Of these three objections, I truly do not know which is the least well founded and the most fanciful. I challenge all three of them with all my soul.

No, liberty of conscience has not an anti-Christian origin. On the contrary, it has the same origin as Christianity and the Church. It was created and placed in the world on the day when the first of popes, St. Peter, replied to the first of persecutors: *Non possumus.* "We cannot but speak the things which we have seen and heard. We cannot but obey God rather than you."

There is the cradle of liberty of conscience! . . .

No, liberty of conscience is by no means always appealed to by the enemies of the Church . . . . It is not against us that they invoke it. It is against us that they violate it . . . . In vain the rabble of superficial writers vie with one another in repeating that the Reformation was carried out in the name of liberty of conscience. Could they leave their tombs, the authors of the Reformation would vigorously disavow their modern panegyrists on this point. . . . Never has liberty of conscience been more odiously outraged than by Anglican Protestantism and the French Revolution, the two most formidable opponents of the Church. The penal code against English and Irish Catholics and the laws which followed the Civil Constitution of the Clergy in France suffice to show to what outrages the faith of Catholics is exposed under the ascendency of legislation which disowns religious liberty. Ah! Doubtless the history of Catholicism is not pure of this stain; . . . but in the eyes of every impartial judge the execrable cruelties of the Spanish Inquisition and the Revocation of the Edict of Nantes pale before the atrocities of the British Reformation and the French Terror.

No, finally, it is not the enemies of the Church who most need religious liberty; on the contrary, it is the Church which must demand it and take advantage from it everywhere. I will even say that in modern society we alone need it, for we alone alarm oppressors of religious conscience. (*Strong approval.*) The reason is very simple: we alone are a religion and a Church capable of resisting the masters of society, Caesars as well as demagogues, both of them infatuated with this horrible confusion of the two powers which is the ideal of all tyrannies.

* * *

Thus I am for liberty of conscience in the interest of Catholicism, without reservation or hesitation. . . . This leads me to a delicate but essential question. I shall approach it without evasion, because in all discussions of this nature I have always recognized the necessity of anticipating this too natural and often very sincere anxiety among opponents of Catholic liberty. Can one today ask liberty for the truth, that is for one's self . . . , and refuse it to error, that is to those who do not think as we do?

I reply plainly: No. Here, I well know, *incedo per ignes*. Also, I hasten to add once again that I intend only to express an individual opinion . . . . But I cannot today repress the conviction which reigns in my conscience and heart. . . . I feel a supreme horror for all the torment and violence done to humanity under pretext of serving or defending religion. The faggots lit by a Catholic hand fill me with as much horror as the scaffolds where the Protestants murdered so many martyrs. . . . The Spanish Inquisitor saying to the heretic, *"Truth or death,"* is as odious to me as the French terrorist saying to my grandfather, *"Liberty, fraternity or death."* (*Cheers.*) The human conscience has the right to require that these hideous alternatives never again be placed before it. (*More applause.*)

* * *

If good faith were banished from the world, said our King John, *it would have to be found again on the lips of a king of France.* Gentlemen, for the defense of our faith, let us all be kings of France. (*Prolonged bravos.*) . . . . Let us not give anyone the right to raise any doubt or suspicion concerning the justice, scrupulousness, and strict honesty of our intentions as of our conduct. Let us not appear to seek entry into modern society flying its colors, appealing to its principles, and claiming its guarantees so long as we are the weakest in order some day to turn against the rights of our enemies, under the pretext that *error has no rights*. After having said in other times, *"The Church asks for nothing but liberty, the liberty of all,"* let us never be swept on to say under the influence of an illusory protection: *"The Church alone ought to be free."*[1] Let us never imitate those in France under Louis Philippe and the Republic who demanded *liberty as in Belgium,* and as soon as they believed themselves the strongest, or what comes to the same thing, friends of the strongest, have not hesitated to say: "Liberty is good only for us, for *liberty ought to be fixed in proportionate measure to knowledge of the truth.* Now, we alone have the truth, and accordingly we alone ought to have liberty."[2] Why do they not see that acting and speaking thus furnishes enemies and false liberals with precisely the pretext they

1. The quotations are from Louis Veuillot's conservative Catholic and ultramontane organ, *Univers.* The first quotation is dated March 1848 and January 13, 1855; the second, March 30, 1853, and March 31, 1858.

2. *Univers,* November 14, 1854.

need against us? . . . Ah! I appeal to all honest and faithful hearts that hear me, and I appeal especially to the young people who will soon replace us in the struggle. I ask them to join me in rejecting in Catholic polemic all that would be inexcusable faithlessness in public or private life. Leave the monopoly of this faithlessness to enemies and persecutors of religion, to Caesarian or revolutionary democrats. Leave to them the work of betraying the principles they have elaborated, or destroying the agreements they have signed, of altering standards and principles at the direction of force and fortune, of suppressing everything which inconveniences them or does not fall into the narrow mould of their orthodox tyranny. . . .

* * *

We must demand of the state that it neither obstruct nor permit the obstruction of the observance of the laws of God and the Church and that it protect religious rights as all other rights. Society . . . owes me aid and protection in the exercise of my rights. It ought to prevent me from infringing on the rights of others, but it has no mission to force me to fulfill my duties. The state should protect me against whomever would hinder me from going to church, but the state which would lead me to church against my will would deservedly be as ridiculous as unbearable.

The mutual independence of Church and state, which is the great law of modern societies, does not entail their absolute separation, still less their mutual hostility. (*Agreement.*) This absolute separation is not at all an essential condition of religious or public liberty. Quite the contrary, it can very well be combined with terrible oppression. The French Revolution clearly demonstrated this. The free Church in the free state does not signify the Church at war with the state, the Church hostile or alien to the state. (*Approval.*) Church and state can and even should agree to reconcile their respective interests in order to give society, as well as the individual, such advantages and rights as this understanding alone can guarantee. Between the two there is a possible, lawful, and often necessary alliance which can and should be solid and lasting, but which also has mutual independence and autonomy as its fundamental condition. . . . In Belgium this alliance exists in fact as in law. Its conditions may be modified and improved with time. But the main lines have already been traced.

* * *

. . . In recapitulating all that I have taken too long to say, could we not deduce two conclusions? And first this one: . . . that religion has never been holier, stronger, and more fruitful than in the conditions of struggle to which Providence has led the nineteenth century. Who will guard the guards, said the prophet: *Quis custodiet custodes?* I reply: the enemy. It is the enemy who makes the sentinel stand guard.

Second, is it not permissible to believe that we are entering into a new era, one which may be called *the era of the liberty of the Church?*

I know that it is necessary to guard as much against utopia as against discouragement. . . . To speak plainly, I am not convinced that, except for some rare and too fleeting moments, the world has ever been much better than it is today. The evil was different, but it has always been very severe and very powerful. I no longer believe in the approaching advent of an era of restoration and universal prosperity. I believe simply in the coming of democracy . . . . Like all revolutions, this one will produce good and evil. The evil will be easy and popular, the good difficult and disputed. The eternal enemies of good will reappear in the corrupted propensities of human nature, with new obstacles emerging from the nature of modern circumstances. The virtues with which God has endowed his creature and those with which the Redeemer Jesus has endowed his Church will also reappear. The battle will be at least as violent as with former enemies of the spirit and the Church in eras of barbarism, feudalism, and absolute monarchy. But it will be at least as meritorious, fruitful, and glorious. To wage it, God furnishes us with new arms and new means of action, and in the great modern innovations—in publicity, equality, political liberty, the emancipation of the democratic masses, and the ease and wonderful rapidity of communications—they can already be seen. From this may emerge an era of complete liberty, unprecedented in her annals, for her that we have the good fortune to call our mother.

Source: [Charles Forbes] de Montalembert, *L'Église libre dans l'état libre* (Paris, 1863), pp. 10–12, 14–15, 18–19, 21–25, 68–69, 71–78, 80–82, 84, 86, 89–92, 94–102, 132–139, 142–144, 152–156.

SUGGESTIONS FOR BACKGROUND AND REFERENCE

A. Dansette, *Religious History of Modern France* (Freiburg, Germany, 1961), I, 295–308.
E. Lecanuet, *Montalembert* (Paris, 1909).
C. S. Phillips, *The Church in France, 1848–1907* (London, 1936), pp. 110–120.
G. Weill, *Histoire du catholicisme libéral en France* (Paris, 1909), pp. 159–168.

66 Syllabus of Errors (Extracts)

December 8, 1864

A commission of theologians had been given the task of preparing a condemnation of modern errors in 1854, but the famous syllabus did not appear until 1864 when it was attached to the encyclical *Quanta Cura*. Montalembert's Malines appearance and the Franco-Italian September Convention threatening the papacy's temporal power may have hastened publication. The errors had previously been identified in earlier papal pronouncements, but the syllabus attracted attention because it was interpreted as generalizing some condemnations that had previously been associated with particular events. From the time of its announcement, Catholic writers gave various interpretations to the syllabus, often cautioning that its correct meaning could not be found apart from the other papal pronouncements cited in the text (omitted below). By liberals everywhere it was regarded as a declaration of war, and in France its publication was officially prohibited.

V. Errors Concerning the Church and Her Rights.

19. The Church is not a true and perfect society fully free, nor does she enjoy her own proper and permanent rights given to her by her divine Founder, but it is the civil power's business to define what are the Church's rights, and the limits within which she may be enabled to exercise them.

20. The ecclesiastical power should not exercise its authority without permission and assent of the civil government.

21. The Church has not the power of dogmatically defining that the religion of the Catholic Church is the only true religion.

22. The obligation by which Catholic teachers and writers are absolutely bound is confined to those things alone which are propounded by the Church's infallible judgment, as dogmas of faith to be believed by all.

23. Roman Pontiffs and ecumenical councils have exceeded the limits of their power, usurped the rights of princes, and erred even in defining matters of faith and morals.

24. The Church has no power of employing force, nor has she any temporal power direct or indirect.

25. Besides the inherent power of the episcopate, another temporal power has been granted expressly or tacitly by the civil government, which may therefore be abrogated by the civil government at its pleasure.

26. The Church has no native and legitimate right of acquiring and possessing.

27. The Church's sacred ministers and the Roman Pontiff should be entirely excluded from all charge and dominion of temporal things.

28. Bishops ought not, without the permission of the government, to publish even letters apostolic.

29. Graces granted by the Roman Pontiff should be accounted as void, unless they have been sought through the government.

30. The immunity of the Church and of ecclesiastical persons had its origin from the civil law.

31. The ecclesiastical forum for the temporal causes of clerics, whether civil causes or criminal, should be altogether abolished, even without consulting, and against the protest of, the Apostolic See.

32. Without any violation of natural right and equity, that personal immunity may be abrogated, whereby clerics are exempted from the burden of undertaking and performing military services; and such abrogation is required by civil progress, especially in a society constituted on the model of a free rule.

33. It does not appertain exclusively to ecclesiastical jurisdiction by its own proper and native right to direct the teaching of theology.

34. The doctrine of those who compare the Roman Pontiff to a prince, free and acting in the universal Church, is the doctrine which prevailed in the Middle Age.

35. Nothing forbids that by the judgment of some general council or by the act of all peoples the supreme pontificate should be transferred from the Roman bishop and city to another bishop and another state.

36. The definition of a national council admits no further dispute, and the civil administration may fix the matter on this footing.

37. National churches separated and totally disjoined from the Roman Pontiff's authority may be instituted.

38. The too arbitrary conduct of Roman pontiffs contributed to the Church's division into East and West.

VI. Errors Concerning Civil Society, Considered Both In Itself and in Its Relations to the Church.

39. The state, as being the origin and fountain of all rights, possesses a certain right of its own, circumscribed by no limits.

40. The doctrine of the Catholic Church is opposed to the good and benefit of human society.

41. The civil power, even when exercised by a non-Catholic ruler, has an indirect negative power over things sacred; it has consequently not only the right which they call *exequatur*, but that right also which they call *appel comme d'abus*.

42. In the case of a conflict between the law of the two powers, civil law prevails.

43. The law power has the authority of rescinding, of declaring null, and of voiding solemn conventions (commonly called concordats) concerning the exercise of rights appertaining to ecclesiastical immunity which have been entered into with the Apostolic See, without this See's consent and even against its protest.

44. The civil authority may mix itself up in matters which appertain to religion, morals, and spiritual rule. Hence it can exercise judgment concerning those instructions which the Church's pastors issue according to their office for the guidance of consciences; nay, it may even decree concerning the administration of the holy sacraments and concerning the dispositions necessary for their reception.

45. The whole governance of public schools wherein the youth of any Christian state is educated, episcopal seminaries only being in some degree excepted, may and should be given to the civil power; and in such sense be given, that no right be recognized in any other authority of mixing itself up in the management of the schools, the direction of studies, the conferring of degrees, the choice or approbation of teachers.

46. Nay, in the very ecclesiastical seminaries, the method of study to be adopted is subject to the civil authority.

47. The best constitution of civil society requires that popular schools which are open to children of every class and that public institutions generally which are devoted to teaching literature and science and providing for the education of youth be exempted from all authority of the Church, from all her moderating influence and interference, and subjected to the absolute will of the civil and political authority [so as to be conducted] in accordance with the tenets of civil rulers and the standard of the common opinions of the age.

48. That method of instructing youth can be approved by Catholic men which is disjoined from the Catholic faith and the Church's power, and which regards exclusively, or at least principally, knowledge of the natural order alone and the ends of social life on earth.

49. The civil authority may prevent the bishops and faithful from free and mutual communication with the Roman Pontiff.

50. The lay authority has of itself the right of presenting bishops, and may require of them that they enter on the management of their dioceses before they receive from the Holy See canonical institution and apostolical letters.

51. Nay, the lay government has the right of deposing bishops from exercise of their pastoral ministry; nor is it bound to obey the Roman pontiff in those things which regard the establishment of bishoprics and the appointment of bishops.

52. The government may, in its own right, change the age prescribed by the Church for the religious profession of men and women, and may require religious orders to admit no one to solemn vows without its permission.

53. Those laws should be abrogated which relate to protecting the condition of religious orders and their rights and duties; nay, the civil government may give assistance to all those who may wish to quit the religious life which they have undertaken and to break their solemn vows; and in like manner it may altogether abolish the said religious orders, and also collegiate churches and simple benefices, even those under the right of a patron, and subject and assign their goods and revenues to the administration and free disposal of the civil power.

54. Kings and princes are not only exempted from the Church's jurisdiction, but also are superior to the Church in deciding questions of jurisdiction.

55. The Church should be separated from the state, and the state from the Church.

VII. Errors Concerning Natural and Christian Ethics.

56. The laws of morality need no divine sanction, and there is no necessity that human laws be conformed to the law of nature, or receive from God their obligatory force.

57. The sciences of philosophy and morals, and also the laws of a state, may and should withdraw themselves from the jurisdiction of divine and ecclesiastical authority.

* * *

63. It is lawful to refuse obedience to legitimate princes, and even rebel against them.

64. A violation of any most sacred oath or any wicked and flagitious action whatever repugnant to the eternal law is not only not to be reprobated, but is even altogether lawful and to be extolled with the highest praise when it is done for love of country.

* * *

IX. Errors Concerning the Roman Pontiff's Civil Princedom.

75. Children of the Christian and Catholic Church dispute with each other on the compatibility of the temporal rule with the spiritual.

76. The abrogation of that civil power which the Apostolic See possesses would conduce in the highest degree to the Church's liberty and felicity.

X. Errors Which Have Reference to the Liberalism of the Day.

✷ 77. In this our age it is no longer expedient that the Catholic religion should be treated as the only religion of the state, all other worships whatsoever being excluded.

78. Hence it has been laudably provided by law in some Catholic countries that men thither immigrating should be permitted the public exercise of their own several worships.

79. For truly it is false that the civil liberty of all worships, and the full power granted to all of openly and publicly declaring any opinions or thoughts whatever, conduces to more easily corrupting the morals and minds of peoples and propagating the plague of indifferentism.

✦ 80. The Roman Pontiff can and ought to reconcile and harmonize himself with progress, with liberalism and with modern civilization.

Source: The Dublin Review, New Series, Vol. IV (1865), pp. 516–529. Latin text, ibid.

SUGGESTIONS FOR BACKGROUND AND REFERENCE

R. Aubert, *Le pontificat de Pie IX* (Paris, 1952), pp. 245–261.
J. B. Bury, *History of the Papacy in the Nineteenth Century, 1864–1878* (London, 1930), pp. 1–46.
Cambridge Modern History (New York, 1903–1912), XI, 703–723.
E. E. Y. Hales, *Pio Nono. A Study in European Politics and Religion in the Nineteenth Century* (New York, 1954).
New Catholic Encyclopedia (New York, 1967), Vol. XIII, "Syllabus of Errors."
F. Nielsen, *The History of the Papacy in the Nineteenth Century* (London, 1908), II, 258–269.

67   Bishop Dupanloup's Interpretation of the Syllabus (Extracts)

1865[1]

The Syllabus of Errors gave rise to much discussion in the press. The most important interpretation of the document from the standpoint of Catholic liberalism was this pamphlet by Bishop Felix A. P. Dupanloup (1802–1878) of Orleans. Catholics troubled by the syllabus welcomed

---

1. Appeared January 23. J. Maurain, *La politique ecclésiastique du Second Empire de 1852 à 1869* (Paris, 1930), p. 716.

Dupanloup's argument, and over six hundred bishops were alleged to have expressed gratitude to the author. Rome did not pronounce further on the question, but Pius IX wrote a laudatory letter to the bishop, concluding with the wish that he "would devote himself the more energetically to explaining the true meaning of the Encyclical as he had more vehemently refuted erroneous interpretations of it" (C. S. Phillips, *The Church in France 1848–1907* [London, 1936], p. 125). The parts reproduced below are from the third and sixth sections of the first part of the pamphlet.

From "False Interpretations and True Principles":

Is it well understood in society what strictly follows from a condemned proposition? Or rather, considering the manner in which papal condemnations have been exaggerated, is it not something of which most who have written on the Encyclical are absolutely ignorant? No doubt I shall astonish them by reminding them of principles which are elementary not only in theology but in logic. For example:

It is an elementary rule of interpretation that the condemnation of a proposition as false, erroneous, and even as heretical does not necessarily imply the assertion of its *opposite*, which might often be another error, but only of its *contradiction*.

The *contradictory* proposition simply excludes the condemned proposition. The *opposite* goes beyond this simple exclusion. . . .

The pope condemns this proposition: "It is lawful to refuse obedience to legitimate princes." (Prop. 63)

They claim to conclude from this that, according to the pope, refusal of obedience is never lawful, and that it is necessary always to bow down before the will of princes. This is to go in one leap to the farthest extreme of the *opposite* and to make the Vicar of Jesus Christ bless the most brutal despotism and servile obedience to all the caprices of kings. It extinguishes the noblest of liberties, the holy liberty of conscience. And this is what is attributed to the pope!

There is another rule, no less elementary in interpretation, which must be observed if the condemned proposition is *universal* and *absolute;* for then it may often happen that the proposition is attacked only because of its universality and its too absolute sense.

Example: "The principle of nonintervention (as it is called) should be proclaimed and observed." (Prop. 62). . . .

Intervention no more than nonintervention can be an absolute rule.

The pope simply desires that nonintervention is not made into a universal principle, to be necessarily proclaimed, and always observed, as an axiom of international law. It is simply good sense. . . .

Nonintervention and intervention are courses, good or bad, just or unjust, wise or foolish, according to case and circumstance. . . . No government will accept the role of Don Quixote; but would it not also often be inhumanity . . . to require all the peoples of the earth, as a principle, to fold arms and do nothing while blood runs in streams in horrible fratricidal wars? And would it then be such a great sin if, for example, France and England intervened in America tomorrow to stop those frightful butcheries in which several million men have already perished?[2]

* * *

It is another rule of interpretation and good sense that each of the terms of a condemned proposition must be studied and weighed carefully to see on what the condemnation rests. . . .

Thus the pope condemns this proposition: "The Roman Pontiff can and ought to *reconcile and harmonize himself with modern civilization.*"

Therefore, they conclude, the papacy declares itself the irreconcilable enemy of *modern civilization.*

According to the newspapers, everything which constitutes modern civilization is an enemy of the Church, condemned by the pope.

This interpretation is quite simply an absurdity.

The words which should have been marked here are *reconcile* and *harmonize.*

In what our enemies designate under this vague complex name of *modern civilization* there is some good, some indifferent, and also some evil.

The pope does not have to reconcile himself with what is good or indifferent in modern civilization. To say so would be an impertinence and an insult, as if one would say to an honest man: "Reconcile yourself with justice."

The pope neither ought nor can reconcile or harmonize himself with what is evil. To suppose so would be a horror.

* * *

Still other rules: In the interpretation of condemned propositions, it is necessary to note all the terms and lightest nuances; for the flaw of a proposition often consists only in a nuance or word which alone is responsible for the error. Absolute propositions must be distinguished from relative propositions; for what might be admissible in hypothesis will often be false in thesis. Moreover, there are equivocal, dangerous propositions which may be condemned only because of this very ambiguity and the evil interpretation to which they may give rise, although they may have a good sense also. Finally, there are propositions—and the Syllabus includes several— which are condemned only in the sense of their authors, and not in the absolute sense of the separate words of the context. . . .

From "Religious Liberty":

. . . What the Church and the pope condemn is religious indifference, in other words, indifference in matters of religion, . . . that is, that religion, God, the soul, truth, virtue, the gospel or the Koran, Buddha or Jesus Christ, truth and falsehood, good and evil, all are the same. And to justify such errors, men have gone so far as

2. Confederate forces under Robert E. Lee surrendered at Appomattox Courthouse on April 9, 1865, less than three months after the publication of Dupanloup's work.

to say that *man himself makes the truth that he believes and the holiness that he worships.*

Behold what they would have had the pope approve . . . .

No! Forever no! God, the soul, virtue, truth, the future life, the distinction between good and evil, Jesus Christ and the gospel shall never be matters of indifference for us.

But to reject this insane and criminal indifference and the consequences of absolute license which spring from it—is this the same as rejecting toleration for men and the civil liberty of religions? It has never been so claimed, and all the theologians say the contrary.

Indeed, the popes have never meant to condemn governments which have believed that, according to the necessity of the times, they ought to write this toleration and liberty into their constitutions. Rather, the pope himself practices this at Rome . . . .

* * *

The distinction between the true and the false and the moral obligation to seek out and attach oneself to truth and spurn error is precisely what constitutes the philosophical mind and duty as well as the religious mind and duty. In this sense true religion is and must be exclusive and absolute, or else it is not true.

But in assuring to truth its rights and supreme place . . . , theologians, convinced that the civil liberty . . . of a dissenting religion . . . does not imply adherence to tolerated beliefs nor contradict Christian dogma, repeat when necessary the celebrated words of Fénelon to James II: "Grant civil toleration, not approving everything as indifferent, but suffering patiently all that God suffers and striving to win men back by gentle persuasion."

But there are men who, going far beyond these principles, would like to make the unlimited liberty of religions the universal ideal, absolute and mandatory for every age and nation. They would impose intellectual anarchy and the proliferation of sects on everyone—even on the pope and the Church—as the best state of society and the true religious and social optimum.

No! The pope does not believe such an ideal to be the best. For him and the Church there is another ideal. They must never be asked to change relative necessities into absolute truths nor elevate regrettable facts and unfortunate but tolerated divisions into dogmatic principles.

No! The ideal of the pope and the Church is not intellectual anarchy but harmony of minds, not the division of souls, but their unity. . . . Minds bound together in truth, and hearts bound together in love—this is the ideal of the pope and the Church.

* * *

[Catholic tradition, the Fathers and the saints, testify against the imposition of religion by force.]

If in the course of centuries there have been or if today there still are some areas of the world where the law of the Church has become the civil law, by the unity of faith and consensus of citizens . . . , does this mean that Church and state have acted there unlawfully? . . . .

Was not this the state of great European nations for centuries . . . ? Are the fruits of division so sweet? Is not unity of religion in a country such a value that one may legitimately try to preserve it?

The state of society where religious law had pervaded civil law was long the normal and general state of Europe. It continues to a certain degree in the largest and freest countries of the world. Has not England her Sunday law . . . ? Has she not her special days for fasts and public prayers? Does not the United States present the same spectacle? Has not President Lincoln continually called for prayers throughout the course of the war . . . ?

* * *

But does this mean that, circumstances having altered and law coming to change also, Catholics would slight Church and God by sincerely accepting . . . their country's constitution and the civil liberty of religions which it authorizes? Or that we talk of liberty when weak, but intend to deny it to others when we are strong?

Of all the accusations . . . against us, this one has always seemed to me . . . the most offensive, because it attacks our very honesty and honor.

* * *

The [true] inquisitors are these tutors of the modern world, divided among themselves, but agreed on this one point—Catholics must always be accused, slandered, and condemned. I smile when I hear it said that error is persecuted on earth. Rather, I see it triumphant while truth suffers violence everywhere. The pope confines himself to warnings, and he addresses only the faithful. But these men fulminate anathemas and presume to declare law to all humankind.

In the name of their *Credo* . . . they order revolution in Italy and exclusion and oppression in France, Belgium, Austria, and elsewhere. Christian or citizen—they demand that we choose between these two prime goods of man, instead of embracing them both. They mean to tear us from our oaths or our faith . . . .

The Church is always the true mother who does not desire her children to be cut in twain. Inflexible on principles, indulgent toward men, she permits, nay, bids every man to remain loyally submissive to his obligations as citizen and to the lawful constitution of his country.

Source: [Felix A. P. Dupanloup], *La convention du 15 septembre et l'encyclique du 8 décembre* (Paris, 1865), pp. 101–105, 122–123, 124–126, 130–135.

SUGGESTIONS FOR BACKGROUND AND REFERENCE

R. Aubert, "Monseigneur Dupanloup et le Syllabus," *Revue d'histoire ecclésiastique*, Vol. LI (1956), pp. 79–142, 471–512, 837–915.

———, *Le pontificat de Pie IX* (Paris, 1952), pp. 245–261.

E. E. Y. Hales, *Pio Nono. A Study in European Politics and Religion in the Nineteenth Century* (London, 1954), pp. 255–273.

F. Lagrange, *Life of Monseigneur Dupanloup, Bishop of Orleans* (London, 1885), II, 251–265.

J. Maurain, *La politique ecclésiastique du Second Empire de 1852 à 1869* (Paris, 1930), pp. 703–722.

C. S. Phillips, *The Church in France, 1848–1907* (London, 1936), pp. 120–125.

✦ ✦ ✦ The Vatican Council and Its Aftermath

68   Definition of Papal Infallibility (Extract)

July 18, 1870

The Vatican Council, much contemplated during the 1860s, finally opened in December 1869 and closed a month after the Italian seizure of Rome in October 1870. The celebrated definition of papal infallibility appeared in the fourth chapter of a constitution on the church presented to the Council, which accepted it on the last vote with 433 affirmatives, 2 negatives, and 55 abstaining. The issue raised lively discussion in Catholic circles and in the world press. Catholic opponents of the decision generally made their submission, but a few distinguished Catholics, of whom the most prominent was the Munich historian, Ignaz von Döllinger, declined to do so and broke with the church. Governments, Catholic and Protestant, generally disapproved. Bavaria and France considered intervention during the session, and Austria took the opportunity to denounce the 1855 concordat, charging that one of the signatories to the agreement had unilaterally changed its position.

Therefore, faithfully adhering to the tradition derived from the commencement of the Christian faith, to the glory of God our Saviour, to the exaltation of the Catholic religion, and to the salvation of Christian nations, *Sacro approbante Concilio,* we teach and define that it is a divinely revealed dogma: that the Roman Pontiff, when he speaks *ex Cathedrâ,* that is, when in discharge of his office of Pastor and Doctor of all Christians, he defines, in virtue of his supreme Apostolic authority, a doctrine of faith or morals to be held by the Universal Church, is endowed by the divine assistance promised to him in Blessed Peter, with that infallibility with which our divine Redeemer willed that the Church should be furnished in defining doctrine of faith or morals; and, therefore, that such definitions of the Roman Pontiff are irreformable of themselves and not in virtue of the consent of the Church.

But if any (which may God avert) shall presume to contradict this our definition, let him be anathema.

Source: The Dublin Review, New Series, Vol. XV (1870), p. 307. Latin text, ibid., pp. 504, 506.

SUGGESTIONS FOR BACKGROUND AND REFERENCE

R. Aubert, Le pontificat de Pie IX (Paris, 1952), pp. 311–367.
R. Aubert et al., The Church in the Age of Liberalism (New York, 1981), pp. 304–330.
J. B. Bury, History of the Papacy in the Nineteenth Century, 1864–1870 (London, 1930), pp. 75–142.
C. Butler, The Vatican Council (New York, 1930).
Cambridge Modern History (New York, 1903–1912), XI, 703–723.
E. E. Y. Hales, Pio Nono. A Study in European Politics and Religion in the Nineteenth Century (London, 1954), pp. 274–313.
A. B. Hasler, How the Pope Became Infallible (Garden City, N.Y., 1981).
G. MacGregor, The Vatican Revolution (London, 1958).

69   Abrogation of the Austrian Concordat (Extracts)

August 6, 1870

The end of the concordat of 1855 was forecast by a widening rift between Vienna and Rome. Never fully implemented, the agreement was much qualified by legislation establishing civil marriage and divorce, suppressing episcopal supervision of schools, and canceling theological students' exemption from military service. In 1860 the government unsuccessfully explored renegotiation of the concordat with Rome. Foreign policy, administered since 1868 by the Saxon Protestant and liberal Count Friedrich Ferdinand Beust (1809–1886), nullified attempts to draw Austria into disputes with Italy over the Roman Question and, while adhering to nonintervention respecting the Vatican Council, deprecated the "infallibility" issue. Parliamentary liberals demanded an end to the concordat as a "foreign" infringement on Austrian liberty. Following closely on the publication of the definition, Karl von Stremayr, minister of worship, on July 25, 1870, proposed repeal of the imperial patent of November 5, 1855, giving legal force to the concordat. Five days later Beust sent the dispatch, which the Austro-Hungarian chargé d'affaires, Palomba-Caracciolo, presented to Cardinal Antonelli on August 6. In the 1870s Austria set new policies on Catholic legal status and financial support, but there was no Kulturkampf as in Germany.

I authorize you to inform the papal government that the ministerial council has resolved upon the abrogation of the concordat. I believe that this decision is sufficiently justified by the actual circumstances. One cannot, without anxiety, maintain relations with a power that represents itself as unlimited and uncontrollable. To be sure, infallibility is to extend only to matters of faith and morals. Nonetheless, it is clear that he who cannot err also claims for himself the right to determine what is important for faith and morals, and thus he alone determines the limits of his competence.

The papal Encyclical of September 8, 1864 and its appended Syllabus amply demonstrated, before the proclamation of infallibility, to what matters infallibility is to be applied, in the view of the Holy See. Over against a power so constituted, the state, if it is unwilling to seize upon new measures, must at least reassert its entire freedom of action so that it may confront the encroachments which are almost inevitable.

[Hungary does not accept the legality of the concordat and therefore is under no obligation to cancel it. But Austria will be compelled to withdraw the imperial patent of November 5, 1855. The government prefers this course to that of prohibiting publication of the Vatican Decrees, which would be at variance with the liberal spirit of basic Austrian law.]

The imperial and royal government, however, is content to return to its entire freedom of action in order to be armed against eventual interference by the power of the church, which was established by the late council's decisions. This alteration, which has been accomplished in the person of one of the contracting parties, as well as the conditions which the other party insisted upon at the conclusion of the concordat, give the government the right, which it now invokes, to regard this act as annulled. In most cases the provisions of the concordat have become impossible to implement. For example, the rights and prerogatives of the Catholic church, which Article I seeks to assure, take on a completely new meaning and a completely different importance from the moment that papal infallibility is proclaimed. The teachings and discipline of the church, which is the subject of Article XXXIV, now come into new domains. The oath of the Austrian bishops, which according to the form prescribed in Article XX pledges loyalty to the emperor, loses its real value if it is to have no other significance than that acknowledged by the pope.

I could easily multiply these examples in support of my view that the Concordat of August 18, 1855 is actually and legally annulled through the decrees of the late council. May those in Rome take full account of the situation as it now stands. For our part, we merely state the facts of a situation which has been brought about without regard to our wishes. The imperial and royal government has not arbitrarily taken the initiative to dissolve the concordat. Rather, it has merely obeyed the necessity which the decisions of the church have forced upon it.

* * *

At the same time assure [the papal government] that nothing is farther from our wishes than to give the signal for a new conflict between the ecclesiastical and secular powers. . . . The state, in upholding its rights, will continue to maintain the rights and freedom of the church. . . .

Source: Alois Hudal, *Die Österreichische Vatikanbotschaft 1806–1918* (Munich, 1952), pp. 207–208.

SUGGESTIONS FOR BACKGROUND AND REFERENCE

F. F. von Beust, *Memoirs of Friedrich Ferdinand, Count von Beust* (London, 1887), II, 211–217.

F. Engel-Janosi, *Österreich und der Vatikan 1846–1918* (Vienna, 1958–1960), I, 143–180.

70   Resolutions of the Munich Old Catholic Congress

September 22–24, 1871

In Germany, following the example of the celebrated historian and theologian, Ignaz von Döllinger, some Catholics repudiated the Vatican decrees and then formed the Old Catholic communion. Since the bishops adhered to the Roman decisions, leadership was provided by academic men, especially at Munich, where the excommunicate Döllinger was elected rector of the university.[1] Basis for the Old Catholic communion was laid at the Munich congress, attended by three hundred sympathizers from Germany, Austria, Switzerland, France, and elsewhere, where these resolutions were adopted. Later, Old Catholics completed parish organization, established an episcopate, and secured canonical status from the Church of Utrecht. Prussia and some other German governments gave assistance, but the Kulturkampf soon adversely affected the movement by encouraging Catholic solidarity. In 1878 there were about 52,000 German Old Catholics. Thereafter the number declined. The movement was also significant in Switzerland.

1.[2] . . . We hold fast to the Old Catholic faith, as witnessed in Scripture and in tradition, and to the old Catholic worship. As rightful members of the Catholic Church, we refuse to be expelled either from Church communion or from the enjoyment of ecclesiastical and social rights proceeding from the same. We declare that the ecclesiastical censures with which we have been visited are arbitrary and objectless, and that we shall not suffer our consciences to be hindered thereby from active participation in Church communion. From the standpoint of the Confession of Faith contained in the Tridentine Creed, we reject the dogmas set up under Pope Pius IX in contradiction to the teaching of the Church and to the principles of the Apostolic Council, especially that of the infallible teaching office, and of the supreme jurisdiction of the pope.

2. We hold fast to the ancient constitution of the Church, and repudiate every attempt to thrust out the bishops from the immediate and independent direction of the separate churches. . . . According to the Tridentine Canon there exists a divinely instituted hierarchy of bishops, priests, and deacons. We acknowledge the primacy of the Roman bishop, as it was received by the Fathers . . . on the ground of Scripture. . . . [We declare that dogmas of faith can only be defined in accordance with Holy Scripture, and that the dogmatic decisions of a Council consistent with the conscious belief of the Catholic faithful and of theological thought must prove to be harmonious with the original delivered faith of the church.] We claim for the Catholic laity, for the clergy, and for scientific theology, the right of a voice and testimony in the enunciation of rules of faith.

---

1. Döllinger sympathized with the Old Catholic movement, but did not promote its institutionalization as a separate church nor sustain a formal relationship with the Old Catholic Church.

2. In several places this translation omits or condenses the German text. These places, as well as one condensed addition by the editor, have been indicated by ellipses or brackets. Paragraphing is also slightly different. See German text.

3. We aim, with the assistance of theological and canonical science, at a reform in the Church, which . . . may serve to abolish the faults and abuses at present existing, and especially meet the justifiable desire of the Catholic laity for constitutionally regulated participation in Church affairs, whereby, without danger to Church doctrinal union, the national views and requirements of the Catholic peoples may be recognised. We declare that the reproach of Jansenism against the Utrecht Church is causeless; there is no dogmatic difference between her and ourselves.[3] We hope for re-union with the Oriental-Greek and the Russian Churches, separation from these having been unnecessary and founded upon no irreconcilable dogmatic differences. In contemplation of the reform at which we aim, and in the progress of science and increased Christian culture, we hope for a gradual understanding with the Protestant and the Episcopal Churches.

4. We regard the culture of scientific knowledge as imperatively necessary in the training of the Catholic clergy. We look upon the exclusion (in boys' schools and in the higher seminaries, under the one-sided direction of the bishops) of the clergy from the intellectual training of the age, as dangerous, in consequence of their great influence, to civilisation, and as entirely inappropriate to the education of a morally virtuous, scientifically intelligent, and patriotic clergy. We demand for the so-called inferior clergy a position of dignity, and one protected against the arbitrary exercise of superior hierarchical power. We condemn the authority vested in the bishops of removing at discretion (*amovibilitas ad nutum*) priests with cure of souls, which was introduced by the French law, and has lately been more generally exercised.

5. We hold fast to the constitutions of our countries, which guarantee civil freedom and humanitarian culture [and reject the dogma of the papacy's fullness of power which threatens the state], and we assert our loyal and steadfast adhesion to our governments in the contest against the dogmatised Ultramontanism of the Syllabus.

6. As it is notorious that the present mischievous confusion . . . is the result of Jesuit activity, and as this Order has abused its power for the purpose of spreading and fostering in the hierarchy, the clergy, and the laity tendencies inimical to civilisation, dangerous to the State, and unpatriotic, and as again it inculcates and imposes a false and corrupting morality, we declare our conviction that peace, prosperity, and union in the Church, and just relations between it and civil society will be possible only when an end is made to the pernicious activity of this Order.

7. As members of that Catholic church not yet altered by the Vatican decrees, to which the States have guaranteed political acknowledgment and public protection, we maintain our right to all real goods and possessions of the Church.

Source: Theodorus [James Bass Mullinger], *The New Reformation* (London, 1875), pp. 126–127, 132–134. German text in *Stenographischer Bericht über die Verhandlungen des Katholiken-Congresses abgehalten vom 22, bis 24, September in München* (Munich, 1871), pp. 221–223.

3. The Utrecht church resulted from a Catholic schism when some French and Dutch churchmen rejected the bull *Unigenitus* (1713), condemning Jansenism.

SUGGESTIONS FOR BACKGROUND AND REFERENCE

K. S. Latourette, *Christianity in a Revolutionary Age* (New York, 1958–1962), I, 285–287.
C. B. Moss, *The Old Catholic Movement, Its Origins and History* (London, 1948).
W. J. S. Simpson, *Roman Catholic Opposition to Papal Infallibility* (London, 1909).
J. F. von Schulte, *Der Altkatholicismus: Geschichte seiner Entwicklung, inneren Gestaltung und rechtlichen Stellung in Deutschland* (Giessen, 1887).
Source for this document.

71 Gladstone's *Vatican Decrees in Their Bearing on Civil Allegiance* (Extracts)

1874

W. E. Gladstone (1809–1893) wrote this pamphlet as a private citizen, but his political position (he had resigned as prime minister in February 1874) lent his views a far from private importance. The Liberal leader was answered by Archbishop Manning and Lord Acton in *The Times,* but the most elaborate contribution was that of Newman in his *Letter to His Grace the Duke of Norfolk* (1874). Gladstone subsequently defended his viewpoint in the *Quarterly Review* (January 1875) and in a new essay, *Vaticanism* (London, 1875).

A century ago we began to relax that system of penal laws against Roman Catholics, at once pettifogging, base, and cruel . . . .

When this process had reached the point, at which the question was whether they should be admitted into Parliament, there arose a great and prolonged national controversy . . . . The arguments in its favour were obvious and strong, and they ultimately prevailed. But the strength of the opposing party had lain in the allegation that, from the nature and claims of the Papal power, it was not possible for the consistent Roman Catholic to pay to the crown . . . an entire allegiance, and that the admission of persons, thus self-disabled, to Parliament was inconsistent with the safety of the State and nation . . . .

An answer to this argument was indispensable; and it was supplied mainly from two sources. The Josephine laws, then still subsisting in the Austrian empire, and the arrangements which had been made after the peace of 1815 by Prussia and the German States . . . proved that the Papal Court could submit to circumstances, and could allow material restraints even upon the exercise of its ecclesiastical prerogatives. . . . But there were also measures taken to learn, from the highest Roman Catholic authorities of this country, what was the exact situation of the members of that communion with respect to some of the better known exorbitancies of Papal assumption. Did the Pope claim any temporal jurisdiction? Did he still pretend to the exercise of a power to depose kings, release subjects from their allegiance, and incite them to revolt? Was faith to be kept with heretics? Did the Church still teach the doctrines of persecution? . . . They were topics selected by way of sample; and the intention was to elicit declarations showing . . . that the Roman system, however strict in its dogma, was perfectly compatible with civil liberty, and with the institutions of a free State moulded on a different religious basis from its own.

Answers in abundance were obtained, tending to show that the doctrines of deposition and persecution, of keeping no faith with heretics, and of universal dominion, were obsolete beyond revival . . . .

But it was unquestionably felt that something more than the renunciation of these particular opinions was necessary in order to secure the full concession of civil rights to Roman Catholics. . . . What was really material therefore was, not whether the Papal chair laid claim to this or that particular power, but whether it laid claim to some power that included them all . . . . Did the Pope then claim infallibility? Or did he, either without infallibility or with it (and if with it, so much the worse), claim an universal obedience from his flock? And were these claims, either or both, affirmed in his Church by authority which even the least Papal of the members . . . must admit to be binding upon conscience?

* * *

All that remained was, to know what were the sentiments entertained on these vital points by the leaders and guides of Roman Catholic opinion nearest to our own doors. And here testimony was offered, which must not, and cannot, be forgotten. In part, this was the testimony of witnesses before the Committees of the two Houses in 1824 and 1825. I need quote two answers only, given by . . . Bishop Doyle.[1] He was asked,

"In what, and how far, does the Roman Catholic profess to obey the Pope?" He replied:

"The Catholic professes to obey the pope in matters which regard his religious faith: and in those matters of ecclesiastical discipline which have already been defined by the competent authorities."

And again:

"Does that justify the objection that is made to Catholics, that their allegiance is divided?"

"I do not think it does in any way. We are bound to obey the Pope in those things that I have already mentioned. But our obedience to the law, and the allegiance which we owe the sovereign, are complete, and full, and perfect, and undivided, inasmuch as they extend to all political, legal, and civil rights of the king or of his subjects. . . ."

Such is the opinion of the dead Prelate. . . . But the sentiments of the dead man powerfully operated on the open and trustful temper of this people to induce them to grant, at the cost of so much popular feeling and national tradition, the great and just concession of 1829. . . .

[Similar professions were made in 1826 by Vicars Apostolic in Britain and the Irish Catholic hierarchy.] Thus . . . Papal infallibility was most solemnly declared to be a matter on which each man might think as he pleased; the Pope's power to

---

1. James Warren Doyle (1786–1834), Roman Catholic Bishop of Kildare and Leighlin, was an Irish intellectual and political spokesman.

claim obedience was strictly and narrowly limited: it was expressly denied that he had any title, direct or indirect, to interfere in civil government. . . .

Since that time, all these propositions have been reversed. The Pope's infallibility, when he speaks *ex cathedra* on faith and morals, has been declared with the assent of the Bishops . . . , to be an article of faith, binding on the conscience of every Christian; his claim to the obedience of his spiritual subjects has been declared in like manner without any practical limit or reserve; and his supremacy, without any reserve of civil rights, has been similarly affirmed to include everything which relates to the discipline and government of the Church throughout the world. And these doctrines, we now know on the highest authority, it is of necessity for salvation to believe.

* * *

It seems not as yet to have been thought wise to pledge the Council in terms to the Syllabus and the Encyclical. That achievement is probably reserved for some one of its sittings yet to come. In the meantime it is well to remember, that this claim in respect of all things affecting the discipline and government of the Church, as well as faith and conduct, is lodged in open day by and in the reign of a Pontiff, who has condemned free speech, free writing, a free press, toleration of nonconformity, liberty of conscience, the study of civil and philosophical matters in independence of the ecclesiastical authority, marriage unless sacramentally contracted, and the definition by the State of the civil rights (*jura*) of the Church; who has demanded for the Church, therefore, the title to define its own civil rights, together with a divine right to civil immunities, and a right to use physical force . . . .

I submit, then, that . . . England is entitled to ask, and to know, in what way the obedience required by the Pope and the Council of the Vatican is to be reconciled with the integrity of civil allegiance?

* * *

Under circumstances such as these, it seems not too much to ask of them [Catholics] to confirm the opinion which we, as fellow-countrymen, entertain of them, by sweeping away, in such manner and terms as they may think best, the presumptive imputations which their ecclesiastical rulers at Rome, acting autocratically, appear to have brought upon their capacity to pay a solid and undivided allegiance; and to fulfill the engagement which their bishops, as political sponsors, promised and declared for them in 1825.

It would be impertinent, as well as needless, to suggest what should be said. . . . What is wanted, and that in the most specific form and the clearest terms, I take to be one of two things; that is to say, either—

I. A demonstration that neither in the name of faith, nor in the name of morals, nor in the name of the government or discipline of the Church, is the Pope of Rome able, by virtue of the powers asserted for him by the Vatican decree, to make any claim upon those who adhere to his communion, of such a nature as can impair the integrity of their civil allegiance; or else,

II. That, if and when such claim is made, it will, even although resting on the definitions of the Vatican, be repelled and rejected; just as Bishop Doyle, when he was asked what the Roman Catholic clergy would do if the pope intermeddled with their religion, replied frankly, "The consequence would be, that we should oppose him by every means in our power, even by the exercise of our spiritual authority."

In the absence of explicit assurances to this effect, we should appear to be led, nay, driven, by just reasoning upon that documentary evidence, to the conclusions:—

1. That the Pope, authorized by his Council, claims for himself the domain (a) of faith, (b) of morals, (c) of all that concerns the government and discipline of the Church.

2. That he in like manner claims the power of determining the limits of those domains.

3. That he does not sever them, by any acknowledged or intelligible line, from the domains of civil duty and allegiance.

4. That he therefore claims, and claims from the month of July, 1870, onwards with plenary authority, from every convert and member of his Church, that he shall "place his loyalty and civil duty at the mercy of another:" that other being himself.

* * *

What then is to be our course of policy hereafter? First let me say that, as regards the great Imperial settlement, achieved by slow degrees, which has admitted men of all creeds subsisting among us to Parliament, that I conceive to be so determined beyond all doubt or question, as to have become one of the deep foundation-stones of the existing Constitution. . . . I shall be guided hereafter, as heretofore, by the rule of maintaining equal civil rights irrespectively of religious differences; and shall resist all attempts to exclude the members of the Roman Church from the benefit of that rule. . . . Not only because the time has not yet come when we can assume the consequences of the revolutionary measures of 1870 to have been thoroughly weighed and digested by all capable men in the Roman Communion. Not only because so great a numerical proportion are . . . necessarily incapable of mastering, and forming their personal judgment upon, the case. Quite irrespectively even of these considerations, I hold that our onward even course should not be changed by follies, the consequences of which, if the worst come to the worst, this country will have alike the power and . . . the will to control. The State will, I trust, be ever careful to leave the domain of religious conscience free, and yet to keep it to its own domain; and to allow neither private caprice nor, above all, foreign arrogance to dictate to it in the discharge of its proper office. . . .

Source: W. E. Gladstone, *The Vatican Decrees in their Bearing on Civil Allegiance* (London, 1874), pp. 11–13, 14–15, 19–21, 29.

SUGGESTIONS FOR BACKGROUND AND REFERENCE

P. Magnus, *Gladstone, A Biography* (London, 1954).
H. C. G. Matthew, *Gladstone 1809–1874* (Oxford, 1986).

72   Archbishop Manning's Reply to Gladstone in
The Times

November 7, 1874

Henry Edward Manning (1808–1892), a Roman Catholic since 1851 and archbishop of Westminster since 1865, was a strong advocate of the infallibility definition. As head of the English Catholic community, he published this rejoinder to Gladstone in *The Times* on November 9.

This morning I received a copy of a pamphlet, entitled "The Vatican Decrees in their bearing on Civil Allegiance." I find in it a direct appeal to myself, both for the office I hold, and for the writings I have published. I gladly acknowledge the duty that lies upon me for both those reasons. I am bound by the office I bear not to suffer a day to pass without repelling from the Catholics of this country the lightest imputation upon their loyalty; and, for my teaching, I am ready to show that the principles I have ever taught are beyond impeachment upon that score.

It is true, indeed, that in page 57 of the pamphlet, Mr. Gladstone expresses his belief "that many of his Roman Catholic friends and fellow-countrymen" are, "to say the least of it, as good citizens as himself." But as the whole pamphlet is an elaborate argument to prove that the teaching of the Vatican Council renders it impossible for them to be so, I cannot accept this graceful acknowledgment, which implies that they are good citizens because they are at variance with the Catholic Church.

I should be wanting in duty to the Catholics of this country and to myself if I did not give a prompt contradiction to this statement, and if I did not with equal promptness affirm that the loyalty of our civil allegiance is not in spite of the teaching of the Catholic Church, but because of it.

The sum of the argument in the pamphlet just published to the world is this:—
That by the Vatican Decrees such a change has been made in the relations of Catholics to the civil power of States that it is no longer possible for them to render the same undivided civil allegiance as it was possible for Catholics to render before the promulgation of those Decrees.

In answer to this it is for the present sufficient to affirm:—

1. That the Vatican Decrees have in no jot or title changed either the obligations or the conditions of civil allegiance.

2. That the civil allegiance of Catholics is as undivided as that of all Christians, and of all men who recognize a divine or natural moral law.

3. That the civil allegiance of no man is unlimited, and therefore the civil allegiance of all men who believe in God, or are governed by conscience, is in that sense divided.

In this sense, and in no other, can it be said with truth that the civil allegiance of Catholics is divided. The civil allegiance of every Christian man in England is limited by conscience and the law of God and the civil allegiance of Catholics is limited neither less nor more.

The public peace of the British Empire has been consolidated in the last half-century by the elimination of religious conflicts and inequalities from our laws. The Empire of Germany might have been equally peaceful and stable if its statesmen had not been tempted in an evil hour to rake up the old fires of religious disunion. The hand of one man, more than any other, threw this torch of discord into the German Empire. The history of Germany will record the name of Dr. Ignatius Von Döllinger as the author of this national evil. I lament not only to read the name but to trace the arguments of Dr. Von Döllinger in the pamphlet before me. May God preserve these kingdoms from the public and private calamities which are visibly impending over Germany. The author of the pamphlet, in his first line, assures us that his "purpose is not polemical, but pacific." I am sorry that so good an intention should have so widely erred in the selection of the means.

But my purpose is neither to criticize nor to controvert. My desire and my duty, as an Englishman, as a Catholic, and as a pastor is to claim for my flock and for myself a civil allegiance as pure, as true, and as loyal as is rendered by the distinguished author of the pamphlet or by any subject of the British Empire.

Source: The Times, November 9, 1874, p. 9.

SUGGESTIONS FOR BACKGROUND AND REFERENCE

V. A. McClelland, *Cardinal Manning, His Public Life and Influence, 1865–1892* (London, 1962).

E. E. Reynolds, *Three Cardinals: Newman, Wiseman, Manning* (New York, 1958).

IV

PROTESTANT ISSUES THROUGH THE MID-NINETEENTH CENTURY

✦ ✦ ✦ Evangelical Union in Prussia

73 Frederick William III's Summons to Union

September 27, 1817

Ecclesiastical unity, long a Hohenzollern political aim, was promoted at the close of the Napoleonic era (which had added many new Rhenish Reformed subjects to Prussia). The time was considered propitious. The Enlightenment was thought to have minimized doctrinal differences between Lutheran and Reformed, Pietism had stressed their common Christian experience, and resurgent nationalism had provided a favorable emotional climate. After preliminary steps extending as far back as 1798, Frederick William III (1797–1840) seized the opportunity provided by the tercentenary of the Reformation to proclaim a religious but nondogmatic union. The announcement was greeted enthusiastically, but the king's attempt to impose a common liturgy after 1822 raised serious protest and eventually gave rise to the Old Lutheran movement. The union in Prussia was paralleled by similar mergers in other *Landeskirchen,* notably in the Palatinate, Hesse, and Baden.

As the history of their reigns and lives attests, my enlightened forefathers now resting in God, Elector John Sigismund, Elector George William, the Great Elector, King Frederick I, and King Frederick William I, dedicated themselves with devout sincerity to uniting the two separated Protestant churches, Reformed and Lutheran, into a single Evangelical Christian church in their dominions. Honoring their memories and wholesome intentions, I readily follow them, desiring . . . to establish in my realm a work pleasing to God. This work, which met with insuperable obstacles in the unfortunate sectarian spirit then prevailing, may now proceed under the influence of a better spirit which discards nonessentials yet holds fast to the principles of Christianity in which both confessions are agreed. I hope to see this work begun by the imminent tercentenary of the Reformation. Such a true religious union of both Protestant churches, which are separated now only by outward differences, conforms to the great purposes of Christianity. It agrees with the original aims of the Reformers. It finds support in the spirit of Protestantism. It strengthens a concern for the church. It promotes family piety. It will be the source of many useful improvements in church and school which until now have often been prevented only by confessional differences.

No difficulty arising from the proposal can stand against this healing union, so long sought after and now again so strongly desired, if only both sides earnestly and sincerely desire it in a true Christian spirit. For in this union the Reformed will not give way to the Lutherans nor vice versa, but both will become one new and quickened Evangelical Christian church . . . .

But however I may wish that the Reformed and Lutheran churches in my dominions share my well substantiated conviction, I respect their rights and freedoms. Accordingly, I am unwilling to force things or to decree or order anything on the subject. Besides, this union has true value only when people are neither prevailed upon nor indifferent, when the union is not merely one of outward form but one with roots and vitality in unity of hearts according to genuine Biblical principles.

Just as I shall myself celebrate the approaching tercentenary of the Reformation in this spirit by joining the existing Reformed and Lutheran Court and Garrison churches of Potsdam in one Evangelical Christian church and take holy communion with it, so also I hope that my own example may wholesomely influence all the Protestant congregations in my realm and inspire universal imitation in spirit and in truth. I leave the unifying structure of the union to the wise guidance of the consistories and to the godly zeal of the clergy and their synods. I am confident that the churches will gladly follow them in the true Christian spirit and that where attention is earnestly, sincerely, and unselfishly fixed on the essential issue and on the great and holy design itself, the form will easily be found. Thus, with simplicity and dignity the external form will issue from within. May the promised moment be not far off when all will gather into one flock under a common shepherd in one faith, one love, one hope!

Source: Carl Immanuel Nitzsch, *Urkundenbuch der Evangelischen Union mit Erläuterungen* (Bonn, 1853), pp. 125–127.

SUGGESTIONS FOR BACKGROUND AND REFERENCE

A. L. Drummond, *German Protestantism since Luther* (London, 1951), pp. 184–213.
H. Geffcken, *Church and State* (London, 1877), II, 168–187.
J. B. Kissling, *Der deutsche Protestantismus 1817–1917* (Münster, 1917–1918), I, 1–67.
K. S. Latourette, *Christianity in a Revolutionary Age* (New York, 1958–1962), II, 79–85.
K. D. Macmillan, *Protestantism in Germany* (Princeton, 1917), pp. 164–217.
New Schaff-Herzog Encyclopedia of Religious Knowledge (Grand Rapids, Mich., 1956), Vol. VII, "Lutherans," Part II.

74   Petition of Berlin Clergy and Cabinet-Order of 1834 (Extracts)

March 1, 1826; and February 28, 1834

The liturgy controversy became the burning issue in Prussia after 1822 and elicited the following two documents. The king's liturgy was based chiefly on older German liturgies and narrowly regulated the conditions and forms of worship. It was to be followed by all Protestant churches in Prussia. Distrusted as an administrative regulation lacking genuine religious basis, the liturgy was also criticized as theologically and aesthetically defective. F. D. E. Schleiermacher (1796–1839), the greatest theologian of the age and pastor of Trinity Church in Berlin, drew up the most celebrated protest, which was signed by eleven colleagues in 1826 but rejected by the king with explosive marginal comment. Eventually resistance, extreme in Silesia, resulted in Old Lutheran conventicles and religious persecution. In an 1834 edict the king tried to calm opposition by separating the union and liturgy issues and by promising security for the Reformation confessions. Separatism, however, was not to be tolerated. More moderate policies, including toleration of Old Lutherans, were inaugurated under Frederick William IV (1840–1861).

A. From the Petition of Berlin Clergy, March 1, 1826:

Many preachers have formally declared themselves in favor of accepting the new liturgy. Nonetheless, we believe we can maintain that, if one considers our Evangelical church as a whole, the diversity of liturgical forms has in no way been reduced by its introduction. Because nowhere has any current liturgy fallen into disuse. And where the new liturgy has been introduced in place of the [earlier] free selection [of liturgies], it has been made subject to that same freedom of choice . . . . And so in every province we now have one more form than before. . . . Besides, a falseness has entered into the handling of the matter which makes it impossible to trust that divine blessings accompany it. In part, the clergy have allowed themselves to be led to accept the new liturgy by the desire to please their superiors. This is indeed natural, but not justifiable in a matter where all personal concerns must be set aside.[1] And in part, superiors have multiplied all too greatly the measures by which subordinates were influenced . . . . In addition, the relations between congregations and their ministers have often been sadly rent, so that precisely on this issue the ministers' effectiveness has been altogether destroyed. This arises from the prejudice, reasonably harbored by the congregations, that when ministers work for the new liturgy they are chiefly[2] considering their own advantage and worldly position. Among the ministers themselves open discord has erupted which threatens to deteriorate all the more into passion and partisanship because those who were prevented by conscience from accepting the liturgy feel themselves neglected in every way.[3]

B. From the Cabinet-Order of February 28, 1834:

It can not but excite my just displeasure that the attempt has been made by some enemies of the peace of our Church, to mislead others by the misconceptions and

---

1. "An extremely impudent criticism, most wicked to make, and used as a cloak for disobedience!" [King's comment]

2. "Only through those who are spiteful, seeking to sow tares among the wheat, can such a prejudice have been disseminated, if it must be encountered now and then." [King's comment]

3. "A most insolent and criminal assertion." [King's comment]

incorrect views into which they themselves have fallen, with regard to the essence and object of the Union and the Liturgy. . . .

The Union does not signify or aim at any surrender of the existing Confessions of Faith, nor does it derogate from the authority they have hitherto possessed. In acceding to the Union, nothing is expressed but that spirit of charity and moderation which refuses to allow that the differences on certain dogmatic points are a sufficient ground for denying to the members of another Confession external Church-fellowship. The joining the Union is a matter of free choice, and the opinion is erroneous, that the introduction of the new Liturgy is necessarily connected therewith, or indirectly aims at that end. The latter rests on orders given by me; the former, as has been said, is a matter left to each person's voluntary decision. The Liturgy is only so far connected with the Union that the order of Divine Service prescribed in it, and the formularies set forth for the different rites of religion, inasmuch as they are according to Scripture, may be used to the common furthering of Christian piety and fear of God in those congregations which are composed of members of both Confessions without causing offense and objection. Further, the Liturgy is by no means intended as a substitute for the Confessions of Faith in the Evangelical Church, nor yet to be added to these as of like nature. Its sole object is to provide against all injurious license and confusion, and to establish an order for public worship and the official acts of the clergy which will be in accordance with the spirit of the Symbolical Books and based on the authority of the Evangelical Liturgies of the first period of the Reformation. Consequently, the prayer of those who, from dislike to the Union, also resist the introduction of the Liturgy, is to be rejected most earnestly and decidedly as one that cannot be entertained. Even in those Churches which have not joined the Union, the national Liturgy must be used, with the modifications allowed to each province in particular. Least of all, however, because it would be most unchristian, can it be permitted to the Union's enemies, in contradistinction to its friends, to constitute themselves a separate religious body.

Source: A. Wilhelm Dilthey (ed.), *Aus Schleiermacher's Leben. In Briefen* (Berlin, 1861–1863), IV, 450–452. King's comment from Erich Foerster, *Die Entstehung der preussischen Landeskirche unter der Regierung König Friedrich Wilhelms des Dritten* (Tübingen, 1905–1907), II, 423. B. Christian Charles Josias Bunsen, *Signs of the Times: Letters to Ernst Moritz Arndt on the Dangers to Religious Liberty in the Present State of the World* (New York, 1856), pp. 429–430. German text in K. A. von Kamptz (ed.), *Annalen der preussischen inneren Staats-Verwaltung* (Berlin, 1814–1840), XVIII, 74.

SUGGESTIONS FOR BACKGROUND AND REFERENCE

M. Redeker, *Schleiermacher: Life and Thought* (Philadelphia, 1973).
W. B. Selbie, *Schleiermacher, A Critical and Historical Study* (New York, 1913).
References for Document 73.

✦ ✦ ✦ Relaxation of Anglican Monopoly

75 Unitarian Relief Act (Trinity Act)

July 21, 1813

The Toleration Act (1689) did not benefit persons denying the Trinity, and the Blasphemy Act (1698) expressly provided for punishments, including imprisonment, for anti-Trinitarians. Though these penalties were not enforced and the Toleration Act was broadened in 1779 (permitting adherence to scripture "as commonly received among Protestant Churches" in place of subscription to the doctrinal articles of the Thirty-Nine Articles), Unitarians sought the removal of all statutory disqualifications. After success, they organized in 1819 the Unitarian Association for Protecting the Civil Rights of Unitarians for further security.

WHEREAS, in the Nineteenth Year of His present Majesty an Act was passed, intituled *An Act for the further Relief of Protestant Dissenting Ministers and Schoolmasters;* and it is expedient to enact as hereinafter provided; Be it therefore enacted . . . That so much of an Act passed in the First Year of . . . King William and Queen Mary, intituled *An Act for exempting His Majesty's Protestant Subjects dissenting from the Church of England from the Penalties of certain Laws,* as provides that that Act . . . should not extend . . . to give any Ease, Benefit or Advantage to Persons denying the Trinity as therein mentioned, be and the same is hereby repealed.

II. And be it further enacted, That the Provisions of another Act passed in the Ninth and Tenth Years of . . . William, intituled *An Act for the more effectual suppressing Blasphemy and Profaneness,* so far as the same relate to Persons denying . . . the Holy Trinity, be . . . repealed.

III. And whereas it is expedient to repeal an Act, passed in the Parliament of Scotland in the First Parliament of King Charles the Second, intituled *An Act against the Crime of Blasphemy;* and another Act, passed in . . . Scotland in the First Parliament of King William, intituled *An Act against Blasphemy;* which Acts respectively ordain the Punishment of Death; Be it therefore enacted, That the said Acts . . . are . . . repealed.

Source: 53 Geo. III, c. 160; *The Statutes of the United Kingdom of Great Britain and Ireland, 53 George III. 1813* (London, 1813), p. 797.

SUGGESTIONS FOR BACKGROUND AND REFERENCE

R. G. Cowherd, *The Politics of English Dissent* (New York, 1956), pp. 15–21.

U. Henriques, *Religious Toleration in England, 1787–1833* (Toronto, 1961), pp. 206–216.

K. S. Latourette, *Christianity in a Revolutionary Age* (New York, 1958–1962), II, 316–320.

E. M. Wilbur, *A History of Unitarianism in Transylvania, England, and America* (Cambridge, Mass., 1952), pp. 316–362.

76. Repeal of the Test and Corporation Acts (Extract)

May 9, 1828

The Restoration religious settlement, in the shape of the Test (1673) and Corporation (1661) Acts, had legally disqualified Dissenters from office by requiring communion in the Anglican church. Through the eighteenth century the acts had been rendered more or less ineffective by periodic indemnity acts, which excused violators from the statutory penalties, but Dissenters had long campaigned for complete repeal. Though the measure made little significant difference in political practice, it marked the official abandonment of the theory that church and state were one and that withdrawal from the church necessarily entailed forfeiture of some political privilege. The act left the Catholic position unchanged, but Catholic Emancipation was passed in the following year.

WHEREAS an Act was passed in the Thirteenth Year of . . . Charles the Second, intituled *An Act for the well governing and regulating of Corporations:* And Whereas another Act was passed in the Twenty-fifth Year of . . . Charles the Second, intituled *An Act for preventing Dangers which may happen from Popish Recusants:* And Whereas another Act was passed in the Sixteenth Year of . . . George the Second, intituled *An Act to indemnify Persons who have omitted to qualify themselves for Offices* . . . : And Whereas it is expedient that so much of the said several Acts . . . as imposes the Necessity of taking the Sacrament of the Lords' Supper according to the Rites or Usage of the Church of England, for the Purposes therein respectively mentioned, should be repealed; Be it therefore enacted . . . That so much and such Parts of the said several Acts . . . as require the . . . Persons . . . to take . . . the Sacrament of the Lord's Supper according to the Rites or Usage of the Church of England, for the several Purposes therein expressed, or to deliver a Certificate or make Proof of the Truth of such his or their receiving the said Sacrament . . . or as impose upon any such . . . Persons any Penalty, Forfeiture, Incapacity, or Disability whatsoever for or by reason of any Neglect or Omission to take . . . the said Sacrament . . . shall, from and immediately after the passing of this Act, be . . . repealed.

II. And Whereas the Protestant Episcopal Church of England and Ireland . . . and the Protestant Presbyterian Church of Scotland . . . are by the Laws of this Realm severally established, permanently and inviolably: And Whereas it is just and fitting that on the Repeal of such Parts of the said Acts . . . , a Declaration to the following Effect should be substituted in lieu thereof; Be it therefore enacted, That every Person who shall hereafter be placed, elected, or chosen in or to the Office of Mayor, Alderman, Recorder, Bailiff, Town Clerk or Common Councilman, or in or to any Office of Magistracy, or Place, Trust, or Employment relating to the Government of any City, Corporation, Borough, or Cinque Port within England and Wales or . . . Berwick-upon-Tweed, shall, within One Calendar Month next before or upon his Admission into any of the aforesaid Offices . . . subscribe the Declaration following:

"I, *A.B.*, do solemnly and sincerely, in the Presence of God, profess, testify, and declare, upon the true Faith of a Christian, That I will never exercise any Power, Authority, or Influence which I may possess by virtue of the Office of _____ to injure or weaken the Protestant Church as it is by Law established in England, or to disturb the said Church, or the Bishops and Clergy of the said Church, in the Possession of any Rights or Privileges to which such Church, or the said Bishops and Clergy, are or may be by Law entitled."

III. . . . the said Declaration shall be made . . . in the Presence of such Person . . . who, by the Charters or Usages of the said respective Cities, Corporations, Boroughs, and Cinque Ports, ought to administer the Oath for due Execution of the said Offices . . . and in default of such, in the Presence of Two Justices of the Peace . . . .

IV. . . . if any Person placed, elected, or chosen into any of the aforesaid Offices . . . shall omit . . . to make . . . the said Declaration . . . , such Placing, Election, or Choice shall be void . . . .

V. . . . every Person who shall hereafter be admitted into any Office . . . or . . . accept from His Majesty . . . any Patent, Grant, or Commission, and who . . . would by the Laws in force immediately before the passing of this Act, have been required to take the Sacrament . . . according to the Rites . . . of the Church of England, shall, within Six Calendar Months after his Admission to such Office . . . or his Acceptance of such Patent . . . subscribe the aforesaid Declaration . . . .

VI. . . . the aforesaid Declaration shall be made . . . in . . . the Court of Chancery, or in the Court of King's Bench, or at the Quarter Sessions . . . .

Source: 9 Geo. IV, c. 17; *The Statutes of the United Kingdom of Great Britain and Ireland, 9 George IV, 1828* (London, 1828), pp. 22–24.

SUGGESTIONS FOR BACKGROUND AND REFERENCE

R. Brown, *Church and State in Modern Britain 1700–1850* (London, 1991), pp. 206–211.

R. G. Cowherd, *The Politics of English Dissent* (New York, 1956), pp. 22–35.

R. W. Davis, "The Strategy of 'Dissent' in the Repeal Campaign, 1820–1828," *Journal of Modern History*, Vol. XXXVIII, No. 4 (December 1966), pp. 374–393.

E. Halevy, *A History of the English People in the Nineteenth Century* (London, 1924–1934), II, 237–306.

U. Henriques, *Religious Toleration in England, 1787–1833* (Toronto, 1961), pp. 54–98.

77 Jewish Relief Act

July 23, 1858

The first bill for Jewish emancipation was introduced into parliament in 1830, but success was not achieved until 1858. Before that time, Jews, while not disqualified from voting and permitted by a statute of 1845 to hold municipal office, could not sit in either house (because of the oath requiring Christian profession). Consequently, elections of Jews in 1847 and 1851 were set aside. This measure of 1858 permitted either house to modify the qualifying oath for Jewish members. Further security was provided by the Public Oaths Act of 1866.

I. Where it shall appear to either House of Parliament that a Person professing the Jewish Religion, otherwise entitled to sit and vote in such House, is prevented from so sitting and voting by his conscientious Objection to take the Oath . . . , such House, if it think fit, may resolve that thenceforth any Person professing the Jewish Religion, in taking the said Oath . . . may omit the Words "and I make this Declaration upon the true Faith of a Christian" . . . ; and the taking . . . of the Oath so modified shall, so far as respects the Title to sit and vote in such House, have the same Force and Effect as the taking . . . by other Persons of the said Oath in the Form required by the said Act.

II. In all other Cases, except for sitting in Parliament as aforesaid, or in qualifying to exercise the Right of Presentation to any Ecclesiastical Benefice in Scotland, whenever any . . . Subjects professing the Jewish Religion shall be required to take the said Oath, the Words "and I make this Declaration upon the true Faith of a Christian" shall be omitted.

III. Nothing herein contained shall extend . . . to enable any . . . Persons professing the Jewish Religion to hold or exercise the Office of Guardians and Justices of the United Kingdom, or of Regent . . . , or of Lord High Chancellor, Lord Keeper or Lord Commissioner of the Great Seal . . . , or . . . Lord Lieutenant or Deputy . . . of Ireland, or . . . High Commissioner to the General Assembly of the Church of Scotland.

IV. Where any Right of Presentation to any Ecclesiastical Benefice shall belong to any Office in the Gift or Appointment of Her Majesty . . . and such Office shall be held by a Person professing the Jewish Religion, the Right of Presentation shall devolve upon and be exercised by the Archbishop of Canterbury for the Time being . . . .

Source: 21 & 22 Vict., c. 49; *A Collection of the Public General Statutes, Passed in the Twenty-First and Twenty-Second Years of the Reign of Her Majesty Queen Victoria, 1858* (London, 1858), pp. 258–259.

SUGGESTIONS FOR BACKGROUND AND REFERENCE

A. Gilam, *The Emancipation of the Jews in England 1830–1860* (New York, 1982).
H. S. Q. Henriques, *The Jews and the English Law* (Oxford, 1908), pp. 265–305.
C. Roth, *A History of the Jews in England* (Oxford, 1941), pp. 239–267.

✦ ✦ ✦ Course of Separation
in the United States

78   *Baker* v. *Fales* (Dedham Case) (Extracts)

October Term, 1820

The quiet advance of Unitarianism within New England Congregationalism gave way to bitter controversy and division, especially after William
Ellery Channing's Baltimore sermon of 1819 candidly announced its
principles. The conflict produced a struggle in the courts for the control
of church property, the main legal question being the respective rights of
the parish or religious society and the church. The distinction was em-
bedded in New England history where the entire community had supported and attended religious worship, but church membership had been
restricted. Thus the parish comprised the voters whose taxes supported
local public worship, while the church was made up of communicants
who had evinced conversion and professed faith. The latter were more
likely to resist liberal innovations. The common use of "church" for
what was more accurately the parish raised a further complication
of which some use was made in the decision. In this Dedham case
the majority of the church refused to accept the minister elected by the
parish or to attend his ministry after his installation. Thereupon the
church minority, with the support of the parish, removed the former
deacons and appointed new ones, who brought suit for possession of the
church property. The defendant was a deacon supported by the church.
This Massachusetts Supreme Court judgment for the parish favored Unitarianism, compelling orthodox churchmen to build new meetinghouses
and reconsider the value of the Establishment. Their loss of confidence
in the state connection helped prepare the way for disestablishment in
1833. The court's opinion was delivered by Chief Justice Isaac Parker
(1768–1830).

. . . The defendant, as well as the plaintiffs, claims to be the deacon of the first
church in Dedham, and contends that the property, out of which the securities sued
for grew, belonged to the church as an ecclesiastical body, without any connection
with the parish, and that the conveyances were originally to the use of the church,
without any trust in favor of the parish. If this position can be maintained, it will
materially affect the question whether the plaintiffs, who were appointed deacons
by those members of the church who remained and acted with the parish, had
thereby acquired any right in the property . . . .

[The court here discussed historic conveyances to "the Church in Dedham" and judged that these were to be understood as grants to the church as trustee for the benefit of the parish.]

Hitherto we have gone upon the ground that, at the time when the earliest of these grants were made, there was a body of men in Dedham, known by the name of the *Dedham Church,* distinct from the *society* of Christians usually worshipping together in that town; and, even upon this hypothesis, we are satisfied that the church was intended to take nothing in the lands granted but estates in trust; and that, as the particular trusts intended must have been the providing for the public worship of God in Dedham, the inhabitants at large of that town, as parishioners or members of the religious society, were the proper *cestui que trusts,* because the effect of the grants was to relieve them from an expense they would otherwise have been obliged to bear, or forego all the benefits of a Christian ministry. But, in reverting to the history of those times, reason will be found to doubt the application of the term *church* as used in the grants, in the precise and limited sense in which it is now used.

Probably there was no very familiar distinction, at that time, between the church and the whole assembly of Christians in the town. We have had no evidence that the inhabitants were divided into two bodies, of church and society, or parish, keeping separate records, and having separate interests; but if the fact be otherwise than is supposed, there is no doubt that most of the inhabitants of the town were church members at that time. . . . a grant to *the church,* under such circumstances, could mean nothing else than a grant to the town . . . . That this was the state of things, will not be doubted by those who look into the ancient tracts and writings respecting the churches in New England. Before the migration of our ancestors to this country, . . . a Congregational church was . . . an assembly of Christians meeting together in the same place, for the public worship of God, under the same minister or ministers. Mr. Wise,[1] a writer on this subject, defines a particular church to be "a society of Christians meeting together in one place, under their proper pastors, for the performance of religious worship and the exercising of Christian discipline, united together by covenant," as most of those undoubtedly were who composed that society. *Parochia,* or *parish,* he says, signifies, in a church sense, a competent number of Christians dwelling near together, and having one bishop, pastor, &c. or more set over them. Therefore, parish, in this sense, is the same with a particular church or congregation . . . .

* * *

. . . From this account of the ancient state of things, it may well be conceived, that a person intending to give property to pious uses, and particularly for the support and maintenance of public worship . . . would denominate the donees—*the church,* meaning the whole society of worshipping Christians; and if his donation should be afterwards applied to the use of a few Christians, who had constituted themselves *the church,* instead of the whole society, his bounty would be perverted. The later grants from the proprietors were undoubtedly made for the same pur-

---

1. John Wise (1652–1725), Massachusetts Congregational divine, was author of *The Churches Quarrel Espoused* (1710) and *A Vindication of the Government of New England Churches* (1717).

poses . . . ; for, there being then but one church and one Christian society in Dedham, the proprietors, or the clerk who made the record, would be likely to adopt the phraseology which had been before used; and these grants should have the same construction as the earlier ones, although the distinction between church and town, or parish, might then have been known.

Considering, then, that the land granted was for the beneficial use of the assembly of Christians in Dedham, which were no other than the inhabitants of that town who constituted the religious society, within which the church was established, these inhabitants were the *cestui que trusts,* and the equitable title was vested in them, as long as they continued to constitute the assembly denominated the church in the grants.

* * *

And we are now brought to the question, whether the plaintiffs have proved themselves to be deacons of the *same church,* to which the grants were originally made, for the trusts before mentioned.

* * *

In whatever light ecclesiastical councils or persons may consider the question, it appears to us clear from the constitution and laws of the land, and from judicial decisions, that the body, which is to be considered the *first church in Dedham,* must be the *church* of the *first parish* in that town, as to all questions of property which depend upon that relation . . . .

If a church may subsist unconnected with any congregation or religious society, as has been urged in argument, it is certain that it has no legal qualities, and . . . cannot exercise any control over property which it may have had in trust for the society with which it had been formerly connected. That any number of the members of a church who disagree with their brethren, or with the minister, or with the parish, may withdraw from fellowship with them, and act as a church in a religious point of view . . . it is not necessary to deny . . . . But as to all civil purposes, the secession of a whole church from the parish would be an extinction of the church; and it is competent to the members of the parish to institute a new church, or to engraft one upon the old stock if any of it should remain; and this new church would succeed to all the rights of the old, in relation to the parish. This is not only reasonable, but it is conformable to the usages of the country; for, although many instances may have occurred of the removal of church members from one church or one place of worship to another, and no doubt a removal of a majority of the members has sometimes occurred, we do not hear of any church ceasing to exist, while there were members enough left to do church service. No particular number is necessary to constitute a church, nor is there any established quorum, which would have a right to manage the concerns of the body. . . . A church may exist, in an ecclesiastical sense, without any officers, as will be seen in the [Cambridge] Platform; and, without doubt, in the same sense a church may be composed only of *femes covert* and minors, who have no civil capacity. The only circumstance, therefore, which gives a church any legal character, is its connection with some regularly-constituted society; and those who withdraw from the society cease to be members of that particular church, and the remaining members continue to be the identical church. . . .

* * *

The consequences of the doctrine contended for by the defendant, will glaringly show the unsoundness of the principle upon which the argument is founded. The position is that, whenever property is given to a church, it has the sole control of it, and the members, for the time being, may remove to any other place, even without the commonwealth, and carry the property with them.

Now, property bestowed upon churches has always been given for some pious or benevolent purpose, and with a particular view to some associated body of Christians. The place in which the church is located, is generally had in view by the donor, either because he there had enjoyed the preaching of the gospel and the ordinances or because it was the place where his ancestors or his family and friends had assembled. . . . Thus, if a donation were made to the Old South church, Park-street church, Brattle-street church, or any other . . . , it must be supposed that the donor had in view the society of Christians worshipping in those places; and as his donation is intended to be perpetual, that he had regard to the welfare of successive generations, who might become worshipping Christians and church members in the same place. If the whole society should . . . remove to some other place in the same town, the identity might be preserved, and the bounty enjoyed as he intended it. But if the church alone should withdraw, and unite itself to some other church, or to a new and different congregation, it would be defeating his intentions to carry the property with them, and distribute the proceeds in a community for the members of which he may have never entertained any particular feelings of kindness.

* * *

It being . . . established that the members of the church, who withdrew from the parish, ceased to be the first church in Dedham, and that all the rights and duties of that body, relative to property intrusted to it, devolved upon those members who remained with and adhered to the parish; it remains to be considered whether the plaintiffs were duly chosen *deacons* of that church, and so became entitled to the possession of the property . . . .

The objection to the settlement of Mr. Lamson [the minister elected by the parish] rests altogether upon the supposition that there could be no legal settlement and ordination, unless the church, as a distinct body from the parish or congregation, had assented to his call . . . ; and it is upon this ground, also, that the ordaining council are supposed to have had no authority in the matter, they being invited by the parish and a minority of the members of the church, but not by the church itself, to which body, it is alleged, belongs solely the right of convening a council upon such occasions.

That the proceedings of the parish and the council were not conformable to the general usage of the country, cannot be denied. But the parish allege, in vindication . . . , their constitutional right to elect and contract with their minister, exclusively of any concurrence or control of the church; and the necessity they were under to proceed as they did, because the church had refused to concur . . . . That the parish have the constitutional right . . . cannot be questioned . . . . It is . . . provided [in the third article of the Declaration of Rights] "that the several towns, parishes, precincts, and other bodies politic or religious societies, shall at all times have the exclusive right of electing their public teachers, and of contracting with them for their support and maintenance." . . . All preexisting laws or usages must bow before this fundamental expression of the public will; and however convenient or useful it might be to continue the old form of electing or settling a minister, whenever a parish determines to assert its constitutional authority, there is no power in the state to oppose their claim.

* * *

We consider, then, the non-concurrence of the church in the choice of the minister, and in the invitation to the ordaining council, as in no degree impairing the constitutional right of the parish. That council might have refused to proceed, but the parish could not by that have been deprived of their minister. It was right and proper, as they could not proceed according to ancient usage . . . to approach as near to it as possible by calling a respectable council, and having their sanction in the ordination. . . . They ordained him over the parish only; but, by virtue of that act, founded upon the choice of the people, he became not only the minister of the parish, but of the church still remaining there, notwithstanding the secession of a majority of the members. . . . The church had a right to choose deacons, finding that the former deacons had abdicated their office, and thus no legal objection is found to exist against their right to maintain this action.

* * *

Indeed, we apprehend those are mistaken, who imagine that the cause of religion would be served . . . by restoring to the churches the power they once enjoyed, of electing the minister without concurrence of the people or congregation, or by the aid of a council which they might select to sanction their choice. Nothing would tend more directly to break up the whole system of religious instruction; for the people never would consent to be taxed for the support of men in whose election they had no voice. . . .

The authority of the church should be of that invisible, but powerful nature, which results from a superior gravity, piety, and devout example. It will then have its proper effect upon the congregation, who will cheerfully yield to the wishes of those who are best qualified to select the candidate. But as soon as it is challenged as a right, it will be lost. The condition of the members of a church is thought to be hard, where the minister elected by the parish is not approved by them. This can only be because they are a minority . . . . A difficulty of this nature surely would not be cured by returning to the old provincial system of letting the minority rule the majority; unless we suppose that the doctrines of a minister are of no consequence to any but church members. Besides, . . . there is no hardship, although there may be some inconvenience; for dissenting members of the church, as well as of the parish, may join any other church and society, or they may institute a new society . . . . It is true, if there are any parish funds, they will lose the benefit of them by removal; but an inconvenience of this sort will never be felt, when a case of conscience is in question.

Source: Eliphalet Baker and Another v. Samuel Fales, 16 Mass. 488.

SUGGESTIONS FOR BACKGROUND AND REFERENCE

G. E. Ellis, "The Church and the Parish in Massachusetts: Usage and Law," in *Unitarianism: Its Origin and History* (Boston, 1890), pp. 116–154.

L. W. Levy, *The Law of the Commonwealth and Chief Justice Shaw* (Cambridge, Mass., 1951), pp. 29–42.

J. C. Meyer, *Church and State in Massachusetts from 1740 to 1833* (Cleveland, 1930), pp. 160–183.

A. P. Stokes, *Church and State in the United States* (New York, 1950), III, 377–381.

E. M. Wilbur, *A History of Unitarianism in Transylvania, England, and America* (Cambridge, Mass., 1952), pp. 401–434.

79   Report of the Senate Committee on Sunday Mails (Extracts)

January 19, 1829

Controversy over Sunday mails reflected American differences concerning government homage to religious tradition. A law of 1810 requiring post offices to function every day awakened protest from Sabbatarians, especially in New York and New England. During the next twenty years they repeatedly placed the subject before Congress. In 1828, at a time when a Christian party in politics was being mooted, the General Union for Promoting the Observance of the Christian Sabbath was organized. Support came from some northern business interests and conservative politicians, while democrats and reformers were generally hostile. The Senate committee to which the petitions of mass protest were referred made its report through Senator Richard M. Johnson (1781–1850) of Kentucky. Preparation of the report may have been partly the work of O. B. Brown, a Baptist preacher and chief clerk of the Post Office Department, and Amos Kendall, Jacksonian journalist and political adviser. The statement, which achieved wide publicity and popularity (including official endorsement by several state legislatures), was regarded as a classic expression of Jacksonian insistence on entire religious neutrality and distrust of neotheocratic opinion and experiment. Subsequently, Johnson, as a member of the House of Representatives, wrote a second report on Sunday mails that was similarly influential.

That some respite is required from the ordinary vocations of life, is an established principle, sanctioned by the usages of all nations, whether Christian or pagan. One day in seven has also been determined upon as the proportion of time; and, in conformity with the wishes of the great majority of citizens of this country, the first day of the week, commonly called Sunday, has been set apart to that object. The principle has received the sanction of the National Legislature, so far as to admit a suspension of all public business on that day, except in cases of absolute necessity, or of great public utility. This principle the committee would not wish to disturb. . . . It should, however, be kept in mind that the proper object of government is to protect all persons in the enjoyment of their religious as well as civil rights, and not to determine for any whether they shall esteem one day above another, or esteem all days alike holy.

We are aware that a variety of sentiment exists among the good citizens of this nation on the subject of the Sabbath day; and our Government is designed for the protection of one, as much as for another. The Jews, who in this country are as free as Christians, and entitled to the same protection from the laws, derive their obligation to keep the Sabbath day from the fourth commandment of their decalogue, and, in conformity with that injunction, pay religious homage to the seventh day of the week, which we call Saturday. One denomination of Christians among us . . . agree with the Jews in the moral obligation of the Sabbath, and observe the same day. There are also many Christians among us who derive not their obligation to observe the Sabbath from the decalogue, but regard the Jewish Sabbath as abrogated. From the example of the Apostles of Christ, they have chosen the first day of the week, instead of that day set apart in the decalogue, for their religious devotions. . . . Many Christians again differ from these, professing to derive their obligation to observe the Sabbath from the fourth commandment of the Jewish decalogue, and bring the example of the Apostles, who appear to have held their public meetings for worship on the first day of the week, as authority for so far changing the decalogue as to substitute that day for the seventh. The Jewish Government was a theocracy, which enforced religious observances; and though the committee would hope that no portion of the citizens of our country could willingly introduce a system of religious coercion in our civil institutions, the example of other nations should admonish us to watch carefully against its earliest indication.

With these different religious views the committee are of opinion that Congress cannot interfere. It is not the legitimate province of the Legislature to determine what religion is true, or what is false. Our Government is a civil and not a religious institution. Our constitution recognises in every person the right to choose his own religion, and to enjoy it freely, without molestation. . . .

The transportation of the mail on the first day of the week, it is believed, does not interfere with the rights of conscience. The petitioners for its discontinuance appear to be actuated from a religious zeal, which may be commendable if confined to its proper sphere; but they assume a position better suited to an ecclesiastical than to a civil institution. They appear, in many instances, to lay it down as an axiom, that the practice is a violation of the law of God. Should Congress, in their legislative capacity, adopt the sentiment, it would establish the principle that the Legislature is a proper tribunal to determine what are the laws of God. It would involve a legislative decision in a religious controversy . . . . If this principle is once introduced, it will be impossible to define its bounds. Among all the religious persecutions with which almost every page of modern history is stained, no victim ever suffered but for the violation of what Government denominated the law of God. To prevent a similar train of evils in this country, the constitution has wisely withheld from our Government the power of defining the divine law. It is a right reserved to each citizen; and while he respects the equal rights of others, he cannot be held amenable to any human tribunal for his conclusions.

Extensive religious combinations to effect a political object are . . . always dangerous. This first effort of the kind calls for the establishment of a principle, which . . . would lay the foundation for dangerous innovations upon the spirit of the constitution, and upon the religious rights of the citizens. If admitted, it may be justly apprehended that the future measures of Government will be strongly marked, if not eventually controlled, by the same influence. All religious despotism commences by combination and influence; and when that influence begins to operate upon the political institutions of a country, the civil power soon bends under it; and the catastrophe of other nations furnishes an awful warning of the consequence.

Under the present regulations of the Post Office Department, the rights of conscience are not invaded. Every agent enters voluntarily, and, it is presumed, conscientiously, into the discharge of his duties, without intermeddling with the conscience of another. Post offices are so regulated as that but a small proportion of the first day of the week is required to be occupied in official business. In the transportation of the mail on that day, no one agent is employed many hours. Religious persons enter into the business without violating their own consciences, or imposing any restraints upon others. Passengers in the mail stages are free to rest . . . or to pursue their journeys, at their own pleasure. While the mail is transported on Saturday, the Jew and the Sabbatarian may abstain from any agency in carrying it, from conscientious scruples. While it is transported on the first day of the week, another class may abstain, from the same religious scruples. The obligation of Government is the same to both of these classes; and the committee can discover no principle on which the claims of one should be more respected than those of the other, unless it should be admitted that the consciences of the minority are less sacred than those of the majority.

It is the opinion of the committee that the subject should be regarded simply as a question of expediency, irrespective of its religious bearing. In this light it has hitherto been considered. Congress have never legislated upon the subject. It rests, as it ever has done, in the legal discretion of the Postmaster General, under the repeated refusals of Congress to discontinue the Sabbath mails. . . .

* * *

Nor can the committee discover where the system could consistently end. If the observance of a holiday becomes incorporated in our institutions, shall we not forbid the movement of an army, prohibit an assault in time of war, and lay an injunction upon our naval officers to lie in the wind while upon the ocean, on that day? . . . If the principle is once established that religion, or religious observances, shall be interwoven with our legislative acts, we must pursue it to its ultimatum. We shall, if consistent, provide for the erection of edifices for the worship of the Creator, and for the support of Christian ministers, if we believe such measures will promote the interests of Christianity. It is the settled conviction of the committee that the only method of avoiding these consequences, with their attendant train of evils, is to adhere strictly to the spirit of the constitution, which regards the General Government in no other light than that of a civil institution, wholly destitute of religious authority.

What other nations call religious toleration, we call religious rights. They are not exercised in virtue of governmental indulgence, but as rights, of which government cannot deprive any portion of citizens, however small. Despotic power may invade those rights, but justice still confirms them. Let the National Legislature once perform an act which involves the decision of a religious controversy, and it will have passed its legitimate bounds. The precedent will then be established, and the foundation laid for that usurpation of the divine prerogative in this country, which has been the desolating scourge to the fairest portions of the old world. Our constitution recognises no other power than that of persuasion for enforcing religious observances. Let the professors of Christianity recommend their religion by deeds of benevolence; by Christian meekness; by lives of temperance and holiness. . . . Government will find its legitimate object in protecting them. . . .

The petitioners do not complain of any infringement upon their own rights. They enjoy all that Christians ought to ask at the hand of any Government— protection from all molestation in the exercise of their religious sentiments.

Source: American State Papers (Washington, D.C., 1832–1861), Class VII (Post Office Department), pp. 211–212.

SUGGESTIONS FOR BACKGROUND AND REFERENCE

J. R. Bodo, *The Protestant Clergy and Public Issues 1812–1848* (Princeton, 1954), pp. 39–43.

A. M. Schlesinger, *The Age of Jackson* (Boston, 1945), pp. 136–140.

A. P. Stokes, *Church and State in the United States* (New York, 1950), II, 12–20.

80   Massachusetts Constitutional Amendment

November 11, 1833 (ratification date)

With disestablishment of Congregationalism in Connecticut in 1818, Massachusetts remained the last state to uphold a religious Establishment. Even in Massachusetts concessions to other denominations had so diluted the older Congregational state church system that its defenders claimed that its primary purpose was not to support a favored religious body, but to maintain the common Christianity. Opposition, led by Baptists and Jeffersonians, steadily grew, but attempts to separate religion from the state were unsuccessful after the Revolution and again in the constitutional revision of 1820. However, the Unitarian schism weakened conservative forces, and in 1833 voters overwhelmingly approved this eleventh amendment, which took the place of the third article of the Declaration of Rights in the 1780 constitution.

As the public worship of God, and instructions in piety, religion, and morality, promote the happiness and prosperity of a people, and the security of a republican government; therefore, the several religious societies of this commonwealth, whether corporate or unincorporate, at any meeting legally warned and holden for that purpose shall ever have the right to elect their pastors or religious teachers, to contract with them for their support, to raise money for erecting and repairing houses for public worship, for the maintenance of religious instruction, and for the payment of necessary expenses; and all persons belonging to any religious society shall be taken and held to be members, until they shall file with the clerk of such society a written notice declaring the dissolution of their membership, and thenceforth shall not be liable for any grant or contract which may be thereafter made or entered into by such society: and all religious sects and denominations demeaning themselves peaceably, and as good citizens of the commonwealth, shall be equally under the protection of the law; and no subordination of any one sect or denomination to another shall ever be established by law.

Source: Benjamin Perley Poore (ed.), *The Federal and State Constitutions Colonial Charters, and Other Organic Laws of the United States* (Washington, D.C., 1877), I, 975.

SUGGESTIONS FOR BACKGROUND AND REFERENCE

A. B. Darling, *Political Changes in Massachusetts, 1824–1848* (New Haven, 1925).
J. C. Meyer, *Church and State in Massachusetts from 1740 to 1833* (Cleveland, 1930), pp. 184–220.

81 *Vidal* v. *Girard's Executors* (Extract)

January Term, 1844

Stephen Girard, French-born Philadelphia financier and philanthropist, died in 1831 leaving the bulk of his estate for the founding of a school for poor white orphan boys. The will stated that "no ecclesiastic, missionary, or minister of any sect whatsoever, shall ever hold or exercise any station or duty whatever in the said college; nor shall any such person ever be admitted for any purpose, or as a visiter, within the premises appropriated to the purposes of the said college." The bequest was contested by some of Girard's heirs, and the case was eventually heard by the United States Supreme Court. There Daniel Webster, counsel for the heirs, argued that religion, as it sustained morals, had public utility and that undenominational Christianity was part of the common law of Pennsylvania. In a decision written by Justice Joseph Story (1779–1845), the Court unanimously upheld the will, despite partial agreement with Webster's argument, pointing out that religious and moral teachings might be inculcated by lay rather than clerical instruction.

The objection is, that the foundation of the College upon the principles and exclusions prescribed by the Testator, is derogatory and hostile to the Christian religion, and so is void, as being against the common law and public policy of Pennsylvania, and this for two reasons; first, because of the exclusion of all Ecclesiastics, Missionaries and Ministers of any sect, from holding or exercising any station or duty in the College, or even visiting the same; and secondly, because it limits the instruction to be given to the scholars to pure morality, and general benevolence, and a love of truth, sobriety and industry, thereby excluding by implication all instruction in the Christian Religion.

In considering this objection, the Court are not at liberty to travel out of the Record, in order to ascertain what were the private religious opinions of the Testator, of which, indeed, we can know nothing, nor to consider whether the scheme of education, by him prescribed, is such as we ourselves should approve, or as is best adapted to accomplish the great aims and ends of education.—Nor are we at liberty to look at general considerations of the supposed public interest and policy of Pennsylvania upon this subject, beyond what its Constitution and laws, and judicial decisions make known to us. The question, what is the public policy of a State, and what is contrary to it, if enquired into beyond these limits, will be found to be one of great vagueness and uncertainty. . . .

It is also said, and truly, that the Christian religion is a part of the common law of Pennsylvania; but this proposition is to be received with its appropriate qualifications, and in connection with the Bill of Rights of that State, as found in its Constitution of Government. The Constitution of 1790 . . . expressly declares, "That all men have a natural and indefeasible right to worship Almighty God according to the dictates of their own consciences; and no man can, of right, be compelled to attend, erect or support any place of worship, or to maintain any ministry against his consent; no human authority can, in any case whatever, control or interfere with the rights of conscience; and no preference shall ever be given, by law, to any religious establishments, or modes of worship." Language more comprehensive for the complete protection of every variety of religious opinion could scarcely be used; and it must have been intended to extend equally to all sects, whether they believed in Christianity or not, and whether they were Jews or infidels; so that we are compelled to admit, that although Christianity be a part of the common law of the State, yet it is so in this qualified sense, that its divine origin and truth are admitted, and therefore it is not to be maliciously and openly reviled and blasphemed against, to the annoyance of believers, or the injury of the public. Such was the doctrine of the Supreme Court of Pennsylvania, in Updegraph *vs.* the Commonwealth, 11 Serg. and Rawle, 394.

It is unnecessary for us, however, to consider what would be the legal effect of a devise in Pennsylvania for the establishment of a school or college for the propagation of Judaism or Deism, or any other form of Infidelity. Such a case is not to be presumed to exist in a Christian country; and therefore, it must be made out by clear and indisputable proofs. Remote inferences, or possible results, or speculative tendencies are not to be drawn or adopted for such purposes. There must be plain, positive and express provisions, demonstrating not only that Christianity is not to be taught, but that it is to be impugned or repudiated.

Now, in the present case, there is no pretence to say, that any such positive or express provisions exist, or are even shadowed forth in the Will. The Testator does not say that Christianity shall not be taught in the College, but only that no ecclesiastic of any sect shall hold or exercise any station or duty in the College. Suppose, instead of this, he had said that no person but a layman shall be an instructor, or officer, or visiter in the College, what legal objection could have been made to such a restriction? And yet the actual prohibition is in effect the same in substance. But it is asked; why are ecclesiastics excluded, if it is not because they are the stated and appropriate preachers of Christianity? The answer may be given in the very words of the Testator:—"In making this restriction, (says he,) I do not mean to cast any reflection upon any sect or person whatsoever: but as there is such a multitude of sects, and such a diversity of opinion amongst them, I desire to keep the tender minds of the orphans, who are to derive advantage from this bequest, free from the excitement which clashing doctrines and sectarian controversy are so apt to produce." Here, then, we have the reason given; and the question is not, whether it is satisfactory to us, nor whether the history of Religion does or does not justify such a sweeping statement; but the question is, whether the exclusion be not such as the Testator had a right, consistently with the Laws of Pennsylvania, to maintain, upon his own notions of religious instruction. Suppose the Testator had excluded all religious instructors but Catholics, or Quakers, or Swedenborgians; or to put a stronger case, he had excluded all religious instructors but Jews, would the bequest have been void on that account? Suppose he had excluded all lawyers, or all physicians, or all merchants from being instructors or visiters, would the prohibition have been fatal to the bequest? The truth is, that in cases of this sort, it is extremely difficult to draw any just and satisfactory line of distinction in a free country, as to the qualifications or disqualifications which may be insisted upon by the donor of a charity, as to those who shall administer or partake of his bounty.

But the objection, itself, assumes the proposition that Christianity is not to be taught, because ecclesiastics are not to be instructors or officers. But this is by no means a necessary or legitimate inference from the premises. Why may not laymen instruct in the general principles of Christianity, as well as ecclesiastics? There is no restriction as to the religious opinions of the instructors and officers. They may be, and, doubtless under the auspices of the city government, they will always be men, not only distinguished for learning and talent, but for piety, and elevated virtue, and holy lives and character. And we cannot overlook the blessings which such men, by their conduct as well as their instructions, may, nay must impart to their youthful pupils. Why may not the Bible, and especially the New Testament, without note or comment, be read and taught as a divine revelation, in the College—its general precepts expounded, its evidences explained, and its glorious principles of morality inculcated? What is there to prevent a work, not sectarian, upon the general evidences of Christianity, from being read and taught in the college by lay teachers? Certainly there is nothing in the Will that proscribes such studies. Above all, the

Testator positively enjoins, "That all the instructors and teachers in the College shall take pains to instil into the minds of the scholars the purest principles of morality, so that on their entrance into active life they may, from inclination and habit, evince benevolence towards their fellow-creatures, and a love of truth, sobriety and industry, adopting at the same time, such religious tenets as their matured reason may enable them to prefer." Now it may well be asked, what is there in all this, which is positively enjoined, inconsistent with the spirit or truths of Christianity? Are not these truths all taught by Christianity, although it teaches much more? Where can the purest principles of morality be learned so clearly or so perfectly, as from the New Testament? Where are benevolence, the love of truth, sobriety and industry, so powerfully and irresistibly inculcated as in the sacred volume? The Testator has not said how these great principles are to be taught, or by whom, except it be by laymen, nor what books are to be used to explain or enforce them. All that we can gather from his language is, that he desired to exclude sectarians and sectarianism from the College, leaving the instructors and officers free to teach the purest morality, the love of truth, sobriety and industry by all appropriate means; and of course, including the best, the surest and the most impressive. The objection then, in this view, goes to this, either that the Testator has totally omitted to provide for religious instruction in his scheme of education, (which, from what has been already said, is an inadmissible interpretation) or that it includes but partial and imperfect instruction in those truths. In either view, can it be truly said that it contravenes the known law of Pennsylvania upon the subject of charities, or is not allowable under the article of the Bill of Rights, already cited? Is an omission to provide for instruction in Christianity, in any scheme of school or college education a fatal defect, which avoids it according to the law of Pennsylvania? If the instruction provided for is incomplete and imperfect, is it equally fatal? These questions are propounded, because we are not aware that any thing exists in the Constitution or laws of Pennsylvania, or the judicial decisions of its tribunals, which would justify us in pronouncing that such defects would be so fatal . . . .

Looking to the objection, therefore, in a mere judicial view, which is the only one in which we are at liberty to consider it, we are satisfied that there is nothing in the devise establishing the College, or in the regulations and restrictions contained therein, which are inconsistent with the Christian religion, or are opposed to any known policy of the State of Pennsylvania.

Source: Arguments of the Defendants' Counsel, and Judgment of the Supreme Court, U.S. in the Case of Vidal and Another, Complainants and Appellants, versus the Mayor, &c. of Philadelphia, the Executors of S. Girard, and Others, Defendants & Appellees (Philadelphia, 1844), pp. 274–279 [2 Howard 127].

SUGGESTIONS FOR BACKGROUND AND REFERENCE

M. Baxter, *Daniel Webster and the Supreme Court* (Amherst, Mass., 1966), pp. 156–168.
L. Pfeffer, *Church, State, and Freedom* (Boston, 1933), pp. 212–214.
A. P. Stokes, *Church and State in the United States* (New York, 1952), III, 381–382.

82   Twelfth Annual Report of the Massachusetts Board of Education (Extracts)

November 24, 1848

New England, the leader in common school education, developed a public system that retained religious subjects in the curriculum, catechism, scripture reading, and texts of positive religious emphasis. The Massachusetts School Law of 1827, providing that the school committee "shall never direct any school books to be purchased or used, in any of the schools under their superintendence, which are calculated to favour any particular religious sect or tenet" (Anson Phelps Stokes, *Church and State in the United States* [New York, 1950], II, 53), reflected a shift to undenominational Christian teaching rather than to a secularized curriculum. Beginning in 1837, Horace Mann (1796–1859), secretary of the state Board of Education, reorganized and reconstructed the Massachusetts school system and through it had wide influence on all American education. In his last official report he defined the proper relations between religion and public education. Mann had been widely and inaccurately characterized as an opponent of religious education, a reputation he had already tried to combat in his Eighth Report (1844). Elsewhere Mann wrote to a critical clergyman, "I am in favor of religious instruction in our schools to the extremest verge to which it can be carried without invading those rights of conscience which are established by the laws of God and guaranteed to us by the Constitution of the State" (R. B. Culver, *Horace Mann and Religion in the Massachusetts Public Schools* [New Haven, 1929], p. 225).

It is a matter of notoriety, that the views of the Board of Education,—and my own, perhaps still more than those of the Board,—on the subject of religious instruction in our Public Schools, have been subjected to animadversion. Grave charges have been made against us, that our purpose was to exclude religion; and to exclude that, too, which is the common exponent of religion,—the Bible,—from the Common Schools of the State; or, at least, to derogate from its authority, and destroy its influence in them. . . .

It is known, too, that our noble system of Free Schools for the whole people, is strenuously opposed;—by a few persons in our own State, and by no inconsiderable numbers in some of the other states of this Union;—and that a rival system of "Parochial" or "Sectarian Schools," is now urged upon the public by a numerous, a powerful, and a well-organized body of men. It has pleased the advocates of this rival system . . . to denounce our system as irreligious and anti-Christian. . . .

In this age of the world, it seems to me that no student of history, or observer of mankind, can be hostile to the precepts and the doctrines of the Christian religion, or opposed to any institutions which expound and exemplify them . . . . In making this final Report, therefore, I desire to vindicate my conduct . . . .

* * *

The Colonial, Provincial, and State history of Massachusetts shows by what slow degrees the rigor of our own laws was relaxed, as the day-star of religious freedom slowly arose after the long, black midnight of the Past. It was not, indeed, until a very recent period, that all vestige of legal penalty or coercion was obliterated from our statute book, and all sects and denominations were placed upon a footing of absolute equality in the eye of the law. Until the ninth day of April, 1821, no person . . . was eligible to the office of Governor, Lieutenant Governor, or Counsellor, or to that of senator or representative in the General Court, unless he would make oath to a belief in the particular form of religion adopted and sanctioned by the State. And until the eleventh day of November, 1833, every citizen was taxable . . . for the support of the *Protestant* religion . . . . Nor was it until the tenth day of March, 1827 . . . that it was made unlawful to use the Common Schools of the State as the means of proselyting children to a belief in the doctrines of particular sects, whether their parents believed in those doctrines or not.

All know the energetic tendency of men's minds to continue in a course to which long habit has accustomed them. . . . A statute may be enacted, and may even be executed by the courts, long before it is ratified and enforced by public opinion. . . . And such was the case, in regard to the law of 1827, prohibiting sectarian instruction in our Public Schools. It was not easy for committees, at once, to withdraw or to exclude the books, nor for teachers to renounce the habits, by which this kind of instruction had been given. Hence, more than ten years subsequent to the passage of that law, at the time when I made my first educational and official circuits over the State, I found books in the schools, as strictly and exclusively *doctrinal* as any on the shelves of a theological library. I heard teachers giving oral instruction, as strictly and purely *doctrinal,* as any ever heard from the pulpit, or from the professor's chair. And more than this: I have now in my possession, printed directions, given by committee men to teachers, enjoining upon them the use of a catechism, in school, which is wholly devoted to an exposition of the doctrines of one of the denominations amongst us. . . .

In the first place, then, I believed these proceedings not only to be wholly unwarranted by law, but to be in plain contravention of law. And, in the next place, the Legislature had made it the express duty of the Secretary, "diligently to apply himself to the object of collecting information of the condition of the Public Schools, of the fulfilment of the duties of their office by all members of the school committees . . . ." I believed then, as now, that religious instruction in our schools, to the extent which the constitution and laws of the State allowed and prescribed, was indispensable to their highest welfare, and essential to the vitality of moral education. Then as now, also, I believed that sectarian books, and sectarian instruction, if their encroachments were not resisted, would prove the overthrow of the schools. While, on the one hand, therefore, I did deplore, in language as earnest and solemn as I was capable of commanding, the insufficiency of moral and religious instruction given in the schools; on the other hand, instead of detailing what I believed to be infractions of the law, in regard to sectarian instruction, I endeavoured to set forth what was supposed to be the true meaning and intent of the law. . . .

* * *

. . . That our Public Schools are not Theological Seminaries, is admitted. That they are debarred by law from inculcating the peculiar and distinctive doctrines of any one religious denomination amongst us, is claimed; and that they are also prohibited from ever teaching that what they do teach, is the whole of religion, or all that is essential to religion or to salvation, is equally certain. But our system earnestly inculcates all Christian morals; it founds its morals on the basis of religion; it welcomes the religion of the Bible; and, in receiving the Bible, it allows it to do what it is allowed to do in no other system,—*to speak for itself.* But here it stops, not because it claims to have compassed all truth; but because it disclaims to act as an umpire between hostile religious opinions.

The very terms, *Public School,* and *Common School,* bear upon their face, that they are schools which the children of the entire community may attend. Every man, not on the pauper list, is taxed for their support. But he is not taxed to support them as special religious institutions; if he were, it would satisfy, at once, the largest definition of a Religious Establishment. But he is taxed to support them, as a *preventive* means against dishonesty, against fraud, and against violence . . . . He is taxed to support schools, on the same principle that he is taxed to support paupers; because a child without education is poorer and more wretched than a man without bread. He is taxed to support schools, on the same principle that he would be taxed to defend the nation against foreign invasion . . . ; because the general prevalence of ignorance, superstition, and vice, will breed Goth and Vandal at home . . . . And, finally, he is taxed to support schools, because they are the most effective means of developing and training those powers and faculties in a child, by which, when he becomes a man, he may understand what his highest interests and his highest duties are; and may be, in fact, and not in name only, a free agent. . . . So the religious education which a child receives at school, is not imparted to him, for the purpose of making him join this or that denomination, when he arrives at years of discretion, but for the purpose of enabling him to judge for himself, according to the dictates of his own reason and conscience, what his religious obligations are, and whither they lead. But if a man is taxed to support a school, where religious doctrines are inculcated which he believes to be false, and which he believes that God condemns; then he is excluded from the school by the Divine law, at the same time that he is compelled to support it by the human law. This is a double wrong. It is politically wrong, because, if such a man educates his children at all, he must educate them elsewhere, and thus pay two taxes, while some of his neighbors pay less than their due proportion of one; and it is religiously wrong, because he is constrained, by human power, to promote what he believes the Divine Power forbids. The principle involved in such a course is pregnant with all tyrannical consequences. . . .

* * *

. . . the Massachusetts school system is not anti-Christian nor un-Christian. The Bible is the acknowledged expositor of Christianity. In strictness, Christianity has no other authoritative expounder. This Bible is in our Common Schools, by common consent. Twelve years ago, it was not in all the schools. Contrary to the genius of our government, if not contrary to the express letter of the law, it had been used for sectarian purposes,—to prove one sect to be right, and others to be wrong. Hence, it had been excluded from the schools of some towns, by an express vote. But since the law and the reasons on which it is founded, have been more fully explained and better understood; and since sectarian instruction has, to a great extent, ceased to be given, the Bible has been restored. I am not aware of the existence of a single town in the State, in whose schools it is not now introduced . . . .

If the Bible, then, is the exponent of Christianity; . . . if the Bible makes known those truths, which, according to the faith of Christians, are able to make men wise unto salvation; and if this Bible is in the schools, how can it be said that Christianity is excluded from the schools; or how can it be said that the school system, which adopts and uses the Bible, is an anti-Christian, or an un-Christian system? . . .

Is it not, indeed, too plain, to require the formality of a syllogism, that if any man's creed is to be found in the Bible, and the Bible is in the schools, then that man's creed is in the schools?

* * *

. . . In bidding an official Farewell to a system, with which I have been so long connected . . . I have felt bound to show, that, so far from its being an irreligious, and anti-Christian, or an un-Christian system, it is a system which recognizes religious obligations in their fullest extent; that it is a system which invokes a religious spirit, and can never be fitly administered without such a spirit; that it inculcates the great commands, upon which hang all the law and the prophets; that it welcomes the Bible, and therefore welcomes all the doctrines which the Bible really contains, and that it listens to these doctrines so reverently, that, for the time being, it will not suffer any rash mortal to thrust in his interpolations of their meaning, or overlay the text with any of the "many inventions" which the heart of man has sought out. It is a system, however, which leaves open all the other means of instruction,—the pulpits, the Sunday schools, the Bible classes, the catechism, of all denominations,—to be employed according to the preferences of individual parents. It is a system which restrains itself from teaching, that what it does teach is all that needs to be taught, or that should be taught; but leaves this to be decided by each man for himself, according to the light of his reason and conscience . . . .

Such, then, in a religious point of view, is the Massachusetts system of Common Schools. Reverently, it recognizes and affirms the sovereign rights of the Creator; sedulously and sacredly it guards the religious rights of the creature; while it seeks to remove all hinderances, and to supply all furtherances to a filial and paternal communion between man and his Maker. . . .

Source: [Horace Mann], *Twelfth Annual Report of the Board of Education* (Boston, 1849), pp. 103–104, 112–114, 116–118, 121–124, 139–140.

SUGGESTIONS FOR BACKGROUND AND REFERENCE

R. B. Culver, *Horace Mann and Religion in the Massachusetts Public Schools* (New Haven, 1929).

M. Curti, *The Social Ideas of American Educators* (New York, 1935), pp. 101–138.

N. G. McCluskey, *Public Schools and Moral Education: The Influence of Horace Mann,
William Torrey Harris and John Dewey* (New York, 1958), pp. 11–98.
J. Messerli, *Horace Mann* (New York, 1972).

✦ ✦ ✦ The Oxford Movement

83 Sermon on National Apostasy (Extracts)

July 14, 1833

The immediate occasion of the Oxford protest was the government's
plan for much needed reforms in ecclesiastical administration in Ireland
and England, but the movement sprang from a more fundamental reaction to the supposed threat of secular liberalism and the confessionally
neutral state. The conservative response stressed the divine institution of
the church and recalled men to its continuity and tradition. Of the Oxford
men, John Keble (1792–1866), with his Nonjuror antecedents, provided
the strongest link with the older Anglican Catholic tradition. Keble
preached this sermon before the Judges of Assize at St. Mary's, Oxford,
on the text, "As for me, God forbid that I should sin against the Lord in
ceasing to pray for you: but I will teach you the good and the right way"
(I Samuel xii. 23). In his *Apologia pro Vita Sua,* Newman wrote of the
event, "I have ever considered, and kept the day, as the start of the
religious movement of 1833." Reproduced below are passages from (A)
the Advertisement to the First Edition, and (B) the text of the Sermon on
National Apostasy.

A. From the Advertisement to the First Edition, July 22, 1833:

Since the following pages were prepared for the press, the calamity, in anticipation
of which they were written, has actually overtaken this portion of the Church of
God. The Legislature of England and Ireland, (*the members of which are not even
bound to profess belief in the Atonement,*) this body has virtually usurped the
commission of those whom our Saviour entrusted with *at least one voice* in making
ecclesiastical laws, on matters wholly or partly spiritual. The same Legislature has
also ratified, to its full extent, this principle;—that the Apostolical Church in this
realm is henceforth only to stand, in the eye of the State, as *one sect among many,*
depending, for any pre-eminence she may still appear to retain, merely upon the
accident of her having a strong party in the country.

It is a moment, surely, full of deep solicitude to all those members of the Church
who still believe her authority divine, and the oaths and obligations, by which they
are bound to her, undissolved and indissoluble by calculations of human expediency. Their anxiety turns not so much on the consequences, to the State, of what has

been done, (*they* are but too evident,) as on the line of conduct which they are bound themselves to pursue. How may they continue their communion with the Church *established,* (hitherto the pride and comfort of their lives,) without any taint of those Erastian Principles on which she is now avowedly to be governed? What answer can we make henceforth to the partisans of the Bishop of Rome, when they taunt us with being a mere Parliamentarian Church? And how, consistently with our present relations to the State, can even the doctrinal purity and integrity of the MOST SACRED ORDER be preserved?

B. From the text of the Sermon on National Apostasy:

What are the symptoms, by which one may judge most fairly, whether or no a nation, as such, is becoming alienated from God and Christ?

And what are the particular duties of sincere Christians, whose lot is cast by Divine Providence in a time of such dire calamity?

The conduct of the Jews, in asking for a king, may furnish an ample illustration of the first point: the behaviour of Samuel, then and afterwards, supplies as perfect a pattern of the second . . . .

I. The case is at least possible, of a nation, having for centuries acknowledged, as an essential part of its theory of government, that, as a Christian nation, she is also a part of Christ's Church, and bound, in all her legislation and policy, by the fundamental rules of that Church—the case is, I say, conceivable, of a government and people, so constituted, deliberately throwing off the restraint, which in many respects such a principle would impose on them, nay, disavowing the principle itself; and that, on the plea, that other states, as flourishing or more so in regard of wealth and dominion, do well enough without it. Is not this desiring, like the Jews, to have an earthly king over them, when the Lord their God is their King? . . .

To such a change, whenever it takes place, the immediate impulse will probably be given by some pretence of danger from without . . . . Pretences will never be hard to find; but, in reality, the movement will always be traceable to the same decay or want of faith, the same deficiency in Christian resignation and thankfulness, which leads so many, as individuals, to disdain and forfeit the blessings of the Gospel. . . .

* * *

One of the most alarming, as a symptom [of apostasy], is the growing indifference, in which men indulge themselves, to other men's religious sentiments. Under the guise of charity and toleration we are come almost to this pass; that no difference, in matters of faith, is to disqualify for our approbation and confidence, whether in public or domestic life. Can we conceal it from ourselves, that every year the practice is becoming more common, of trusting men unreservedly in the most delicate and important matters, without one serious inquiry, whether they do not hold principles which make it impossible for them to be loyal to their Creator, Redeemer, and Sanctifier? Are not offices conferred, partnerships formed, intimacies courted,—nay, (what is almost too painful to think of,) do not parents commit their children to be educated, do they not encourage them to intermarry, in houses, on which Apostolical Authority would rather teach them to set a mark, as unfit to be entered by a faithful servant of Christ?

* * *

. . . The point really to be considered is, whether, according to the coolest estimate, the fashionable liberality of this generation be not ascribable, in a great measure, to the same temper which led the Jews voluntarily to set about degrading themselves to a level with the idolatrous Gentiles? And, if it be true any where, that such enactments are forced on the Legislature by public opinion, is APOSTASY too hard a word to describe the temper of that nation?

The same tendency is still more apparent, because the fair gloss of candour and forbearance is wanting, in the surly or scornful impatience often exhibited, by persons who would regret passing for unbelievers, when Christian motives are suggested, and checks from Christian principles attempted to be enforced on their public conduct. . . .

For example:—whatever be the cause, in this country of late years, (though we are lavish in professions of piety,) there has been observable a growing disinclination, on the part of those bound by VOLUNTARY OATHS, to whatever reminds them of their obligation; a growing disposition to explain it all away. . . .

They will have the more reason to suspect themselves, in proportion as they see and feel more of that impatience under pastoral authority, which our Saviour Himself has taught us to consider as a never-failing symptom of an unchristian temper. "He that heareth you, heareth Me; and he that despiseth you, despiseth Me." Those words of divine truth put beyond all sophistical exception, what common sense would lead us to infer, and what daily experience teaches;—that disrespect to the Successors of the Apostles, as such, is an unquestionable symptom of enmity to Him, who gave them their commission at first, and has pledged Himself to be with them for ever. Suppose such disrespect general and national, suppose it also avowedly grounded not on any fancied tenet of religion, but on mere human reasons of popularity and expediency, either there is no meaning at all in these emphatic declarations of our Lord, or that nation, how highly soever she may think of her own religion and morality, stands convicted in His sight of a direct disavowal of His Sovereignty.

To this purpose it may be worth noticing, that the ill-fated chief, whom God gave to the Jews, as the prophet tells us, in His anger . . . —his first step in apostasy was, perhaps, an intrusion on the sacrificial office . . . . God forbid, that any Christian land should ever, by her prevailing temper and policy, revive the memory and likeness of Saul, or incur a sentence of reprobation like his. But if such a thing should be, the crimes of that nation will probably begin in infringement on Apostolical Rights; she will end in persecuting the true Church; and in the several stages of her melancholy career, she will continually be led on from bad to worse by vain endeavours at accommodation and compromise with evil. Sometimes toleration may be the word . . . ; sometimes state security . . . ; sometimes sympathy with popular feeling . . . .

[II. Following the scriptural text, the Church must fulfill the duties of intercession and remonstrance.]

Source: John Keble, Sermons Academical and Occasional (Oxford, 1847), pp. 127–128, 133–141.

SUGGESTIONS FOR BACKGROUND AND REFERENCE

G. Battiscombe, John Keble (London, 1963).

Y. Brillioth, The Anglican Revival (London, 1933).

O. J. Brose, Church and Parliament: The Reshaping of the Church of England, 1828–1860 (Stanford, 1939).

S. C. Carpenter, Church and People, 1789–1889 (London, 1933), pp. 146–174.

R. W. Church, The Oxford Movement: Twelve Years, 1833–1845 (London, 1891).

C. P. S. Clarke, The Oxford Movement and After (London, 1932).

G. C. Faber, The Oxford Apostles (London, 1933).

H. J. Laski, Studies in the Problem of Sovereignty (New Haven, 1917), pp. 69–120.

G. I. T. Machin, Politics and the Churches in Great Britain, 1832–1868 (Oxford, 1977), pp. 75–91.

84   Tract I

September 9, 1833

The extension of the movement beyond the university community was largely the work of the Tracts for the Times, "by members of the University of Oxford." This enterprise, planned in the summer of 1833, was designed to awaken Anglicanism to its historic Catholic faith and rally its defenders by means of brief, pointed messages contained in penny tracts. Between the first issue in September and the end of the year, twenty tracts, the first three by John Henry Newman (1801–1890), had been printed and widely distributed. They produced sensation and controversy at Oxford and throughout the country. Tract I was Newman's impassioned summons to the clergy to stand on "our apostolical descent."

Thoughts on the Ministerial Commission.
Respectfully Addressed to the Clergy.

I am but one of yourselves,—a Presbyter; and therefore I conceal my name, lest I should take too much on myself by speaking in my own person. Yet speak I must; for the times are very evil, yet no one speaks against them.

Is not this so? Do not we "look one upon another," yet perform nothing? Do we not all confess the peril into which the Church is come, yet sit still each in his own retirement, as if mountains and seas cut off brother from brother? Therefore suffer me, while I try to draw you forth from those pleasant retreats, which it has been our blessedness hitherto to enjoy, to contemplate the condition and prospects of our Holy Mother in a practical way; so that one and all may unlearn that idle habit, which has grown upon us, of owning the state of things to be bad, yet doing nothing to remedy it.

Consider a moment. Is it fair, is it dutiful, to suffer our Bishops to stand the brunt of the battle without doing our part to support them? Upon them comes "the care of all the Churches." This cannot be helped; indeed it is their glory. Not one of us would wish in the least to deprive them of the duties, the toils, the responsibilities of their high Office. And, black event as it would be for the country, yet, (as far as they are concerned,) we could not wish them a more blessed termination of their course, than the spoiling of their goods, and martyrdom.

To them then we willingly and affectionately relinquish their high privileges and honors; we encroach not upon the rights of the SUCCESSORS OF THE APOSTLES; we touch not their sword and crosier. Yet surely we may be their shield-bearers in the battle without offence; and by our voice and deeds be to them what Luke and Timothy were to St. Paul.

Now then let me come at once to the subject which leads me to address you. Should the Government and Country so far forget their GOD as to cast off the Church, to deprive it of its temporal honors and substance, *on what* will you rest the claim of respect and attention which you make upon your flocks? Hitherto you have been upheld by your birth, your education, your wealth, your connexions; should these secular advantages cease, on what must CHRIST's Ministers depend? Is not this a serious practical question? We know how miserable is the state of religious bodies not supported by the State. Look at the Dissenters on all sides of you, and you will see at once that their Ministers, depending simply upon the people, become the *creatures* of the people. Are you content that this should be your case? Alas! can a greater evil befal Christians, than for their teachers to be guided by them, instead of guiding? How can we "hold fast the form of sound words," and "keep that which is committed to our trust," if our influence is to depend simply on our popularity? Is it not our very office to *oppose* the world? can we then allow ourselves to *court* it? to preach smooth things and prophesy deceits? to make the way of life easy to the rich and indolent, and to bribe the humbler classes by excitements and strong intoxicating doctrine? Surely it must not be so;—and the question recurs, on *what* are we to rest our authority, when the State deserts us?

CHRIST has not left His Church without claim of its own upon the attention of men. Surely not. Hard Master He cannot be, to bid us oppose the world, yet give us no credentials for so doing. There are some who rest their divine mission on their own unsupported assertion; others, who rest it upon their popularity; others, on their success; and others, who rest it upon their temporal distinctions. This last case has, perhaps, been too much our own; I fear we have neglected the real ground on which our authority is built,—OUR APOSTOLICAL DESCENT.

We have been born, not of blood, nor of the will of the flesh, nor of the will of man, but of God. The Lord JESUS CHRIST gave His Spirit to His Apostles; they in turn laid their hands on those who should succeed them; and these again on others; and so the sacred gift has been handed down to our present Bishops, who have appointed us as their assistants, and in some sense representatives.

Now every one of us believes this. I know that some will at first deny they do; still they do believe it. Only, it is not sufficiently practically impressed on their minds. They *do* believe it; for it is the doctrine of the Ordination Service, which they have recognised as truth in the most solemn season of their lives. In order, then, not to prove, but to remind and impress, I entreat your attention to the words used when you were made Ministers of CHRIST's Church.

The office of Deacon was thus committed to you: "Take thou authority to execute the office of a Deacon in the Church of GOD committed unto thee: In the name," &c.

And the priesthood thus:

"Receive the HOLY GHOST, for the office and work of a Priest, in the Church of GOD, now committed unto thee by the imposition of our hands. Whose sins thou dost forgive, they are forgiven; and whose sins thou dost retain, they are retained. And be thou a faithful dispenser of the Word of GOD, and of His Holy Sacraments: In the name," &c.

These, I say, were words spoken to us, and received by us, when we were brought nearer to God than at any other time of our lives. I know the grace of ordination is contained in the laying on of hands, not in any form of words;—yet in our own case, (as has ever been usual in the Church,) words of blessing have accompanied the act. Thus we have confessed before GOD our belief, that through the Bishop who ordained us, we received the HOLY GHOST, the power to bind and to loose, to administer the Sacraments, and to preach. Now *how* is he able to give these great gifts? *Whence* is his right? Are these words idle, (which would be taking GOD's name in vain,) or do they express merely a wish, (which surely is very far below their meaning,) or do they not rather indicate that the Speaker is conveying a gift? Surely they can mean nothing short of this. But whence, I ask, his right to do so? Has he any right, except as having received the power from those who consecrated him to be a Bishop? He could not give what he had never received. It is plain then that he but *transmits;* and that the Christian Ministry is a *succession.* And if we trace back the power of ordination from hand to hand, of course we shall come to the Apostles at last. We know we do, as a plain historical fact; and therefore all we, who have been ordained Clergy, in the very form of our ordination acknowledged the doctrine of the APOSTOLICAL SUCCESSION.

And for the same reason, we must necessarily consider none to be *really* ordained who have not *thus* been ordained. For if ordination is a divine ordinance, it must be necessary; and if it is not a divine ordinance, how dare we use it? Therefore all who use it, all of *us,* must consider it necessary. As well might we pretend the Sacraments are not necessary to Salvation, while we make use of the offices of the Liturgy; for when GOD appoints means of grace, they are *the* means.

I do not see how any one can escape from this plain view of the subject, except, (as I have already hinted,) by declaring, that the words do not mean all that they say. But only reflect what a most unseemly time for random words is that, in which Ministers are set apart for their office. Do we not adopt a Liturgy, *in order to* hinder inconsiderate idle language, and shall we, in the most sacred of all services, write down, subscribe, and use again and again forms of speech, which have not been weighed, and cannot be taken strictly?

Therefore, my dear Brethren, act up to your professions. Let it not be said that you have neglected a gift; for if you have the Spirit of the Apostles on you, surely this *is* a great gift. "Stir up the gift of GOD which is in you." Make much of it. Show your value of it. Keep it before your minds as an honorable badge, far higher than that secular respectability, or cultivation, or polish, or learning, or rank, which gives you a hearing with the many. Tell *them* of your gift. The times will soon drive you to do this, if you mean to be still any thing. But wait not for the times. Do not be compelled, by the world's forsaking you, to recur as if unwillingly to the high source of your authority. Speak out now, before you are forced, both as glorying in your privilege, and to ensure your rightful honor from your people. A notion has gone abroad, that they can take away your power. They think they have given and can take it away. They think it lies in the Church property, and they know that they have politically the power to confiscate that property. They have been deluded into a notion that present palpable usefulness, produceable results, acceptableness to your flocks, that these and such like are the tests of your Divine commission. Enlighten them in this matter. Exalt our Holy Fathers, the Bishops, as the Representatives of the Apostles, and the Angels of the Churches; and magnify your office, as being ordained by them to take part in their Ministry.

But, if you will not adopt my view of the subject, which I offer to you, not doubtingly, yet (I hope) respectfully, at all events, CHOOSE YOUR SIDE. To remain neuter much longer will be itself to take a part. *Choose* your side; since side you shortly must, with one or other party, even though you do nothing. Fear to be of those, whose line is decided for them by chance circumstances, and who may perchance find themselves with the enemies of CHRIST, while they think but to remove themselves from worldly politics. Such abstinence is impossible in troublous times. HE THAT IS NOT WITH ME, IS AGAINST ME, AND HE THAT GATHERETH NOT WITH ME SCATTERETH ABROAD.

Source: Tracts for the Times (London, 1834–1840), I, No. 1, 1–4.

SUGGESTIONS FOR BACKGROUND AND REFERENCE

T. Kenny, *The Political Thought of John Henry Newman* (London, 1957).
I. T. Ker, *John Henry Newman. A Biography* (Oxford, 1990).
B. Martin, *John Henry Newman: His Life and Thought* (New York, 1982).
R. D. Middleton, *Newman at Oxford* (Oxford, 1950).
J. H. Newman, *Apologia pro Vita Sua* (London, 1887).
M. Trevor, *Newman* (London, 1962).
References for Document 83.

85 Tract XC (Extracts)

February 27, 1841 (publication)

Particularly after 1839, Newman began to doubt the validity of the *via media* and to consider the claims of Rome. This tract, the last published, argued for the legitimacy of a Catholic construction of the Anglican Thirty-Nine Articles. In the resulting outcry the charge of dishonesty was frequently raised. Heads of houses at Oxford made protest, and the Bishop of Oxford, Richard Bagot, required from Newman a promise that no more tracts would be published. Newman entered into a retirement broken only to announce his reception into the Roman Catholic Church in 1845. After temporary setback, the Oxford Movement revived later in the century under the leadership of E. B. Pusey.

Introduction.

It is often urged, and sometimes felt and granted, that there are in the Articles propositions or terms inconsistent with the Catholic faith . . . . The following Tract is drawn up with the view of showing how groundless the objection is . . . . That there are real difficulties to a Catholic Christian in the Ecclesiastical position of our Church at this day, no one can deny; but the statements of the Articles are not in the number; and it may be right at the present moment to insist upon this. If in any quarter it is supposed that persons who profess to be disciples of the early Church will silently concur with those of very opposite sentiments in furthering a relaxation of subscriptions, which, it is imagined, are galling to both parties, though for different reasons, and that they will do this against the wish of the great body of the Church, the writer of the following pages would raise one voice, at least, in protest against any such anticipation.

* * *

But these remarks are beyond our present scope, which is merely to show that, while our Prayer Book is acknowledged on all hands to be of Catholic origin, our Articles also, the offspring of an uncatholic age, are, through GOD's good providence, to say the least, not uncatholic, and may be subscribed by those who aim at being catholic in heart and doctrine. . . .

[In twelve sections Newman proceeds to interpret the Articles of Religion with respect to "Holy Scripture, and the Authority of the Church," "Justification by Faith only," "Works before and after Justification," "The Visible Church," "General Councils," "Purgatory, Pardons, Images, Relics, Invocation of Saints," "The Sacraments," "Transubstantiation," "Masses," "Marriage of Clergy," "The Homilies," "The Bishop of Rome."]

Conclusion.

One remark may be made in conclusion. It may be objected that the tenor of the above explanations is anti-Protestant, whereas it is notorious that the Articles were drawn up by Protestants, and intended for the establishment of Protestantism; accordingly, that it is an evasion of their meaning to give them any other than a Protestant drift, possible as it may be to do so grammatically, or in each separate part.

But the answer is simple:

1. In the first place, it is a *duty* which we owe both to the Catholic Church and to our own, to take our reformed confessions in the most Catholic sense they will admit; we have no duties toward their framers.

2. In giving the Articles a Catholic interpretation, we bring them into harmony with the Book of Common Prayer, an object of the most serious moment in those who have given their assent to both formularies.

3. Whatever be the authority of the Ratification prefixed to the Articles, so far as it has any weight at all, it sanctions the mode of interpreting them above given. For its injoining the "literal and grammatical sense," relieves us from the necessity of making the known opinions of their framers, a comment upon their text; and its forbidding any person to "affix any *new* sense to any Article," was promulgated at a time when the leading men of our Church were especially noted for those Catholic views which have been here advocated.

4. It may be remarked, moreover, that such an interpretation is in accordance with the well-known general leaning of Melanchthon, from whose writings our Articles are principally drawn, and whose Catholic tendencies gained for him that same reproach of popery, which has ever been so freely bestowed upon members of our own reformed Church.

* * *

5. Further: the Articles are evidently framed on the principle of leaving open large questions, on which the controversy hinges. They state broadly extreme truths, and are silent about their adjustment. For instance, they say that all necessary faith must be proved from Scripture, but do not say *who* is to prove it. They say that the Church has authority in controversies, they do not say *what* authority. They say that it may enforce nothing beyond Scripture, but do not say *where* the remedy lies when it does. They say that works *before* grace *and* justification are worthless and worse, and that works *after* grace *and* justification are acceptable, but they do not speak at all of works *with* GOD's aid, *before* justification. They say that men are lawfully called and sent to minister and preach, who are chosen and called by men who have public authority *given* them in the congregation to call and send; but they do not add *by whom* the authority is to be given. They say that councils called *by princes* may err; they do not determine whether councils called *in the name of* CHRIST will err.

6. Lastly, their framers constructed them in such a way as best to comprehend those who did not go so far in Protestantism as themselves. Anglo-Catholics then are but the successors and representatives of those moderate reformers; and their case has been directly anticipated in the wording of the Articles. It follows that they are not perverting, they are using them, for an express purpose for which among others their authors framed them. The interpretation they take was intended to be admissible; though not that which their authors took themselves. Had it not been provided for, possibly the Articles never would have been accepted by our Church at all. If, then, their framers have gained their side of the compact in effecting the reception of the Articles, let Catholics have theirs too in retaining the Catholic interpretation of them.

* * *

What has lately taken place in the political world will afford an illustration in point. A French minister, desirous of war, nevertheless, as a matter of policy, draws up his state papers in such moderate language, that his successor, who is for peace, can act up to them, without compromising his own principles.[1] The world, observing this, has considered it a circumstance for congratulation; as if the former minister, who acted a double part, had been caught in his own snare. It is neither decorous, nor necessary, nor altogether fair, to urge the parallel rigidly; but it will explain what it is here meant to convey. The Protestant Confession was drawn up with the purpose of including Catholics; and Catholics now will not be excluded. What was an economy in the reformers, is a protection to us. What would have been a perplexity to us then, is a perplexity to Protestants now. We could not then have found fault with their words; they cannot now repudiate our meaning.

1. Newman's reference is to the dismissal of Adolphe Thiers during the Mehemet Ali crisis and his replacement by François Guizot as the chief power in the French government.

Source: Tracts for the Times (London, 1834–1841), VI, No. 90, 2, 4, 80–83.

SUGGESTIONS FOR BACKGROUND AND REFERENCE

References for Documents 83 and 84.

✦ ✦ ✦

86   Act of Separation or Return [of the Congregation of Ulrum, Netherlands]

October 13, 1834

In the Netherlands, as in some other Reformed countries, the Evangelical Awakening produced a vigorous protest against the theological moderation and compromise inherited from the Enlightenment that dominated the state church. While many evangelicals sought to revitalize the national church, some came to feel that strict Calvinistic orthodoxy was best served by secession and a free church. Hendrik de Cock (1801–1842), a pastor at Ulrum in theologically conservative Groningen, criticized ministers and practices of the state church, and when deposed by synod, led the larger part of his congregation into separation. Similar secessions under other pastors, notably Hendrik Pieter Scholte, made possible the formation of the *Christelijke Gereformeerde Kerk* in 1836, which was harassed by fines and imprisonment at first, but won state toleration in 1840.

[1]We the undersigned, Deacons and Members of the Reformed congregation of Jesus Christ in Ulrum, having marked the decay in the Dutch Reformed Church for some

1. The Dutch text, a single paragraph and sentence, is broken into four parts in this translation for easier reading.

time, both in the mutilation or rejection of the teaching of our Fathers, based on God's Word, and in the corruption of the administration of the Holy Sacraments according to the ordinance of Christ in his Word, and in the almost total neglect of church discipline, all of which, according to our Reformed confession, art. 29, are the marks of the true Church; and having received . . . a Pastor and Teacher who presented to us the pure doctrine of our Fathers . . . putting it into practice both particularly and generally, thereby arousing the congregation to turn increasingly to regularity of faith and God's Holy Word in confession and conduct, . . . and also to refrain from serving God after man's commandments . . . by which means the congregation dwelt in peace and quiet.

However, this peace and quiet was disturbed by the unlawful and ungodly suspension of our unanimously beloved and esteemed Pastor and Teacher, because of his public testimony against false faith and polluted public worship . . . . Several entirely reasonable proposals were made both by our Pastor . . . and the remaining deacons . . . and repeatedly examination and judgment were requested according to God's Word, but everything was in vain. This most reasonable request was denied by the Classis, Provincial Council, and Synod, which contrariwise demanded . . . repentance, without indicating the offense from God's Holy Word, and demanded total submission to synodical regulations. . . .

By this means this Dutch Church Council is now made identical with the Papal church, which was rejected by our Fathers, not only because of the abovementioned decay, but also because God's Word is rejected and invalidated by church regulations and decisions . . . . Finally, by authority of the provincial Church Council the preaching of the Word of God by a publicly acknowledged Church preacher among us, the Reverend and very learned Mr. H. P. Scholte, Reformed teacher at Dovren and Gendren . . . in North Brabant has been forbidden, and the common meetings of believers, held with open doors, have been penalized by fine;—from all of which it has now become increasingly clear that the Dutch Reformed Church does not give credit to art. 29 of our confession;

Wherefore the undersigned declare here that, in accordance with the function of all believers, art. 28, they separate themselves from others who are not of the church and that they wish fellowship no longer with the Dutch Reformed Church until the latter returns to the true service of the Lord; and at the same time they declare their wish to practice fellowship with all true Reformed members and their desire to be united with each assembly based on God's infallible Word, . . . herewith testifying that we adhere to God's Holy Word and our old Formularies of unity in everything based on that Word, namely the Confession of Faith, the Heidelberg Catechism, and the Canons of the Synod of Dort . . . . Finally, we hereby declare that we keep our minister who was illegally suspended, acknowledging him as our lawfully called and ordained Pastor and Teacher.

Source: H. de Cock, *Acte van Afscheiding of Wederkeering* (Groningen, 1834), pp. 3–6.

SUGGESTIONS FOR BACKGROUND AND REFERENCE

M. G. Hansen, *The Reformed Church in the Netherlands* (New York, 1884), pp. 298–304.
M. E. Kluit, *Het Réveil in Nederland 1817–1854* (Amsterdam, 1936), pp. 159–199.

L. Knappert, *Geschiedenis der Nederlandsche Hervormde Kerk gedurende de 18e en 19e Eeuw* (Amsterdam, 1912), II, 272–313.

K. S. Latourette, *Christianity in a Revolutionary Age* (New York, 1958–1962), II, 239–249.

New Schaff-Herzog Encyclopedia of Religious Knowledge (Grand Rapids, Mich., 1952), Vol. V, "Holland," Part 2.

✦ ✦ ✦ The Scottish Disruption

87 Veto Act and Regulations

May 31 and June 2, 1834

The greatest source of division and controversy in the modern Scottish church was patronage. The legal rights of patrons, often crown or landlords, to impose their ministerial appointees on unwilling parishes contributed to several eighteenth-century schisms, but the General Assembly under the leadership of the rationalistic Moderates did not challenge the system. The situation was reversed when the Evangelical party, led by Thomas Chalmers (1780–1847), came to dominance in the nineteenth century and secured the Veto Act from the General Assembly.

I. OVERTURE and INTERIM ACT on CALLS.

Edinburgh, May 31. 1834.

The General Assembly declare, That it is a fundamental law of this Church, that no Pastor shall be intruded on any Congregation contrary to the will of the people; and, in order that this principle may be carried into full effect, the General Assembly, with the consent of a majority of the Presbyteries of this Church, do declare, enact, and ordain, That it shall be an instruction to Presbyteries, that if, at the moderating in a Call to a vacant pastoral charge, the major part of the male heads of families, members of the vacant congregation, and in full communion with the Church, shall disapprove of the person in whose favour the Call is proposed to be moderated in, such disapproval shall be deemed sufficient ground for the Presbytery rejecting such person, and that he shall be rejected accordingly, and due notice thereof forthwith given to all concerned; but that, if the major part of the said heads of families shall not disapprove of such person to be their pastor, the Presbytery shall proceed with the settlement according to the rules of the Church: And farther declare, that no person shall be held to be entitled to disapprove as aforesaid, who shall refuse, if required, solemnly to declare, in presence of the Presbytery, that he is actuated by no factious or malicious motive, but solely by a conscientious regard to the spiritual interests of himself or the congregation.

The General Assembly agree to transmit the above Overture to Presbyteries for their opinion, and, without a vote, convert the same into an Interim Act.

II. OVERTURE, WITH REGULATIONS, for carrying the above Act into effect.
Edinburgh, June 2, 1834.

* * *

1. That when any Presbytery shall have so far sustained a presentation to a parish as to be prepared to appoint a day for moderating in a Call to the person presented, they shall appoint one of their own number to preach in the Church of the parish on a day not later than the second Sunday thereafter; that he shall, on that day, intimate from the pulpit that the person presented will preach in that Church on the first convenient Sunday, so as it be not later than the third Sunday after such intimation; and that he shall at the same time intimate that on another day, to be fixed, not less than eight nor more than ten days after that appointed for the presentee to preach, the Presbytery will proceed, within the said Church, to moderate in a Call to such person to be Minister of the said parish in the usual way; but that the Presbytery, if they deem it expedient, may appoint the presentee to preach oftener than once . . . .

* * *

3. That if no special objections and no dissents by a major part of the male heads of families, being members of the Congregation and in full communion with the Church . . . shall be given in, the Presbytery shall proceed to the trials and settlement of the presentee . . . .

4. That it shall be competent to any one or more of the heads of families . . . to state any special objections to the settlement of the person presented . . . ; and that, if the objections appear to be deserving of deliberate consideration or investigation, the Presbytery shall delay the farther proceedings . . . till another meeting, to be then appointed, and give notice to all parties concerned . . . .

5. That if the special objections so stated affect the moral character or the doctrine of the Presentee, so that, if they were established, he would be deprived of his license or of his situation in the Church, the objectors shall proceed by libel, and the Presbytery shall take the steps usual in such cases.

6. That if the special objections relate to the insufficiency or unfitness of the Presentee . . . , the objectors shall not be required to become libellers, but shall simply deliver, in writing, their specific grounds for objecting to the settlement, and shall have full liberty to substantiate the same; upon all which the Presentee shall have an opportunity to be fully heard, and shall have all competent means of defence: That the Presbytery shall then consider these special objections, and if it shall appear that they are not sufficient or not well founded, they shall proceed to the settlement of the Presentee . . . : But if the Presbytery shall be satisfied that the . . . objectors have established that the Presentee is not fitted . . . , then they shall find that he is not qualified and shall intimate the same to the Patron, that he may forthwith present another person; it being always in the power of the different parties to appeal from the sentences pronounced by the Presbytery if they shall see cause.

* * *

8. That if the Dissents . . . do not amount . . . to the major part of the persons standing on the roll, and if there be no special objections remaining to be considered, the Presbytery shall proceed to the trials and settlement . . . .

9. That if it shall appear that Dissents have been lodged by an apparent majority of the persons on the said roll, the Presbytery shall adjourn the proceedings to another meeting, to be held not less than ten days nor more than fourteen days thereafter.

* * *

13. That in case the Presbytery shall at that meeting find that there is a majority of the persons on the roll still dissenting, it shall be competent to the Patron or the Presentee, or to any member of the Presbytery, to require all or any of the persons so dissenting to appear before the Presbytery, or a Committee of their number, at a meeting . . . to take place within ten days . . . and there and then to declare in terms of the resolution of the General Assembly; and if any such person shall fail to appear . . . or shall refuse to declare . . . , the name of such person shall be struck off the list of persons dissenting, and the Presbytery shall determine whether there is still a major part dissenting or not, and proceed accordingly.

14. That if the Presbytery shall find that there is at last a major part of the persons on the roll dissenting, they shall reject the person presented . . . ; and shall forthwith direct notice of this . . . to be given to the Patron, the Presentee, and the Elders of the parish.

15. That if the Patron shall give a presentation to another person within the time limited by law, the proceedings shall again take place in the same manner . . . .

16. That if no Presentation shall be given within the limited time to a person from whose settlement a majority on the roll do not dissent, the Presbytery shall then present *jure devoluto*.

17. That cases of presentation by the Presbytery *jure devoluto* shall not fall under the operation of the regulations in this and the relative act of Assembly, but shall be proceeded in according to the general laws of the Church applicable to such cases. But every person who shall have been previously rejected shall be considered as disqualified to be presented to that parish on the occasion of that vacancy.

18. That in order to ascertain definitely the persons entitled . . . to give in dissents, every Kirk-session . . . shall be required within two months after the rising of the present Assembly, to make out a list or roll of the male heads of families who are . . . Members of the Congregation and also regular Communicants, either in that parish or some other parish of the Church; of which, in the latter case, proper evidence shall be produced to the Kirk-session.

Source: The Principal Acts of the General Assembly of the Church of Scotland, Convened at Edinburgh, the 22d Day of May 1834 (Edinburgh, 1834), pp. 31–36.

SUGGESTIONS FOR BACKGROUND AND REFERENCE

S. J. Brown, *Thomas Chalmers and the Godly Commonwealth in Scotland* (Oxford, 1983).

R. Buchanan, *The Ten Years' Conflict: Being the History of the Disruption of the Church of Scotland* (Glasgow, 1849).

A. L. Drummond and J. Balloch, *The Scottish Church 1688–1843* (Edinburgh, 1973), pp. 180–265.

H. J. Laski, *Studies in the Problem of Sovereignty* (New Haven, 1917), pp. 27–68.

W. L. Mathieson, *Church and Reform in Scotland. A History from 1797 to 1843* (Glasgow, 1916).

H. Watt, *Thomas Chalmers and the Disruption* (Edinburgh, 1943).

88 Claim of Right (Extracts)

May 30, 1842

The Veto Act led to legal battles. In accordance with the act, patrons' nominees, rejected by the congregation, were denied installation by the presbytery, and they not unnaturally sought remedy in the courts. Decisions by the Scottish Court of Session and the House of Lords vindicated the rights of patrons and their appointees, judgments based on the position that the church's authority was derived from and dependent on the state. Further decisions invalidated the church's efforts to secure church extension and reunion with secession ministers, and awarded damages to those injured by acts of presbyteries pursuant to the Veto Act. Conversely, the 1842 General Assembly by a large majority asserted the church's right to free government and discipline from parliamentary and judicial intervention.

CLAIM, DECLARATION, and PROTEST anent the encroachments of the Court of Session.

Edinburgh May 30. 1842. Sess. 17

THE GENERAL ASSEMBLY of the CHURCH OF SCOTLAND, taking into consideration the solemn circumstances in which . . . this Church is now placed; and that, notwithstanding the securities for the government thereof by General Assemblies, Synods, Presbyteries, and Kirk-sessions, and for the liberties, government, jurisdiction, discipline, rights and privileges of the same, provided by the statutes of the realm, by the constitution of this country, as unalterably settled by the Treaty of Union, and by the oath, "inviolably to maintain and preserve" the same, required to be taken by each Sovereign at accession, as a condition precedent to the exercise of the royal authority; . . . these have been of late assailed by the very Court to which the Church was authorized to look for assistance and protection, to an extent that threatens their entire subversion, . . . hereby do solemnly . . . resolve and agree on the following Claim, Declaration, and Protest: That is to say:—

WHEREAS it is an essential doctrine of this Church, and a fundamental principle in its constitution, as set forth in the Confession of Faith . . . that "there is no other Head of the Church but the Lord Jesus Christ"; . . . and while the magistrate hath authority, and it is his duty . . . to take order for the preservation of purity, peace, and unity in the Church, yet "The Lord Jesus, as King and Head of his Church, hath therein appointed a government in the hand of Church officers distinct from the civil magistrate"; which government is ministerial, not lordly, and to be exercised in consonance with the laws of Christ, and with the liberties of his people:

[In support of the argument for independent jurisdiction, the claim at this point undertakes a detailed historical review, maintaining that the state has frequently, and particularly in acts of Parliament, the Revolutionary settlement, and the Treaty of Union with England, ratified the church's claim.]

AND WHEREAS . . . the Court of Session,—a tribunal instituted by special act of Parliament for the specific and limited purpose of "doing and administration of justice in all *civil actions,*" . . . have in numerous and repeated instances stepped beyond the province alloted to them by the Constitution . . . deciding not only "actions civil," but "causes spiritual and ecclesiastical,"—and that too even where these had no connection with the exercise of the right of patronage,—and have invaded the jurisdiction and encroached upon the spiritual privileges of the courts of this Church . . . : as for instance—

By interdicting Presbyteries . . . from admitting to a pastoral charge, when about to be done irrespective of the civil benefice attached thereto, or even where there was no benefice—no right of patronage—no stipend—no manse or glebe, and no place of worship, or any patrimonial right, connected therewith.

By issuing a decree requiring . . . a Church court to take on trial and admit to the office of the holy ministry . . . a probationer or unordained candidate for the ministry, and to intrude him also on the congregation, contrary to the will of the people;—both in this and in the cases first mentioned, invading the Church's exclusive jurisdiction in the admission of ministers, the preaching of the Word, and administration of sacraments—recognised by statute to have been "given by God" directly to the Church, and to be beyond the limits of the secular jurisdiction.

By prohibiting the communicants of the Church from intimating their dissent from a call proposed to be given to a candidate for the ministry to become their pastor.

By granting interdict against the establishment of additional ministers to meet the wants of an increasing population, as uninterruptedly practised from the Reformation to this day: against constituting a new kirk-session in a parish to exercise discipline; and against innovating on its existing state, "as regards pastoral superintendence, its kirk-session, and jurisdiction and discipline thereto belonging."

By interdicting the preaching of the Gospel and administration of ordinances throughout a whole district by any minister of the Church under authority of the Church Courts . . . .

By holding the members of inferior Church judicatories liable in damages for refusing to break their ordination vows and oaths . . . by disobeying . . . the sentences, in matters spiritual and ecclesiastical, of their superior Church judicatories . . . .

By interdicting the execution of the sentence of a church judicatory prohibiting a minister from preaching or administering ordinances within a particular parish, pending the discussion of a cause in the Church Courts as to the validity of his settlement therein.

By interdicting the General Assembly and inferior Church judicatories from inflicting Church censures . . . .

By suspending Church censures, inflicted by the Church judicatories in the exercise of discipline . . . .

By interdicting the execution of a sentence of deposition from the . . . ministry, pronounced by the General Assembly . . . .

By assuming to judge of the right of individuals elected members of the General Assembly to sit therein, and interdicting them from taking their seats . . . .

By, in the greater number of the instances above referred to, requiring the inferior judicatories of the Church to disobey the sentences . . . of the superior judicatories . . . .

* * *

AND WHEREAS farther encroachments are threatened . . . in actions now depending before the said Court, in which it is sought to have sentences of deposition from the . . . ministry reduced and set aside, and minorities of inferior judicatories authorized to take on trial and admit to the . . . ministry . . . .

AND WHEREAS the government and discipline of Christ's Church cannot be carried on . . . subject to the exercise by any secular tribunal of such powers as have been assumed by the said Court of Session:

AND WHEREAS this Church, highly valuing . . . her connection . . . with the State, and her possession of the temporal benefits thereby secured to her for the advantage of the people, must nevertheless, even at the risk and hazard of the loss of that connection and of these public benefits, . . . persevere in maintaining her liberties as a Church of Christ and in carrying on the government thereof on her own constitutional principles, and must refuse to intrude ministers on her congregations, to obey the unlawful coercion attempted . . . , or to consent that her people be deprived of their rightful liberties:

THEREFORE, the General Assembly, while . . . they fully recognise the absolute jurisdiction of the Civil Courts in relation to all matters whatsoever of a civil nature, and especially in relation to all the temporalities conferred by the State upon the Church, and the civil consequences attached by law to the decisions in matters spiritual of the Church courts—DO, in the name and on behalf of this Church, and of the Nation and People of Scotland, and under the sanction of the several statutes and the Treaty of Union herein before recited, CLAIM, as of RIGHT, That she shall freely possess and enjoy her liberties, government, discipline, rights, and privileges, according to law, . . . and that she shall be protected therein from the foresaid unconstitutional and illegal encroachments of the said Court of Session . . . .

AND they DECLARE that they cannot, in accordance with the Word of God, the authorized and ratified standards of this Church, and the dictates of their consciences, intrude ministers on reclaiming congregations, or carry on the government of Christ's Church, subject to the coercion attempted by the Court of Session . . . ; and that, at the risk and hazard of suffering the loss of the secular benefits conferred by the State, and the public advantages of an Establishment, they must, as by God's grace they will, refuse so to do; for, highly as they estimate these, they cannot put them in competition with the inalienable liberties of a Church of Christ . . . .

AND they PROTEST that all and whatsoever acts of the Parliament . . . passed without the consent of this Church and nation, in alteration of, or derogation to the aforesaid government, discipline, right, and privileges of this Church . . . , —as also, all and whatsoever sentences of courts in contravention of the same . . . are . . . void and null, and of no legal force or effect; and that, while they will accord full submission to all such acts and sentences in so far—though in so far only—as these may regard civil rights and privileges, . . . their said submission shall not be deemed an acquiescence therein, but that it shall be free to the members of this Church or their successors . . . when there shall be a prospect of obtaining justice, to claim the restitution of all such civil rights and privileges and temporal benefits and endowments . . . .

AND, FINALLY, the General Assembly call the Christian people of this kingdom, and all the Churches of the Reformation throughout the world, who hold the great doctrine of the sole headship of the Lord Jesus over his Church, to witness that it is for their adherence to that doctrine . . . and for the maintenance by them of the jurisdiction of the office-bearers, and the freedom and privileges of the members of the Church . . . that this Church is subjected to hardship, and that the rights so sacredly pledged and secured to her are put in peril; and they especially invite all the office-bearers and members of this Church . . . to stand by the Church, and by each other, in defence of the doctrine aforesaid and of the liberties . . . which rest upon it; and to unite in supplication to Almighty God that He would be pleased to turn the hearts of the rulers of this kingdom . . . ; or otherwise that he would give strength to this Church . . . to endure resignedly the loss of the temporal benefits of an establishment, and the personal sufferings and sacrifices to which they may be called . . . .

Source: The Principal Acts of the General Assembly of the Church of Scotland, Convened at Edinburgh, May 19, 1842 (Edinburgh, 1842), pp. 35–48.

SUGGESTIONS FOR BACKGROUND AND REFERENCE

References for Document 87.

89   Protest to the General Assembly

May 18, 1843

The men who formed the Free Church were not voluntarists; they prized a state church rightly constituted, but determined to abandon an unacceptable Establishment. As the Claim of Right did not convince Parliament, already sensitive to analogous issues raised by the Tractarians, the Disruption inevitably followed. At the opening meeting of the 1843 Assembly, Moderator David Welsh read the protest and led the withdrawal. The Scottish Free Church, immediately organized with Chalmers as moderator, won over a third of the ministers and influenced similar contests on the Continent, particularly among the Reformed.

WE, the undersigned Ministers and Elders, chosen as Commissioners to the General Assembly of the Church of Scotland, indicted to meet this day, but precluded from holding the said Assembly by reason of the circumstances hereinafter set forth, in consequence of which a free Assembly of the Church of Scotland, in accordance with the laws and constitution of the said Church, cannot at this time be holden— CONSIDERING that the Legislature, by their rejection of the CLAIM of RIGHT . . . and their refusal to give redress and protection against the jurisdiction assumed, and the coercion of late repeatedly attempted . . . by the Civil Courts, have recognised and fixed the conditions of the Church Establishment . . . to be such as these have been pronounced . . . by the said Civil Courts in their several recent decisions . . . .

[The protest here repeats in substance the objections to the court decisions enumerated in the Claim of Right.]

AND FARTHER, CONSIDERING that a General Assembly, composed in accordance with the laws and fundamental principles of the Church, in part of Commissioners themselves, admitted without the sanction of the Civil Court, or chosen by Presbyteries, composed in part of members not having that sanction, cannot be constituted as an Assembly of the Establishment without disregarding the law . . . .

AND FARTHER, CONSIDERING that such Commissioners as aforesaid would, as Members of an Assembly of the Establishment, be liable to be interdicted from exercising their functions, and to be subjected to civil coercion at the instance of any individual who might apply to the Civil Courts . . . .

AND CONSIDERING FURTHER, that civil coercion has already been . . . applied for and used, whereby certain Commissioners returned to the Assembly . . . have been interdicted from claiming their seats, . . . and certain Presbyteries have been by interdicts . . . prevented from freely choosing Commissioners to the said Assembly, whereby the freedom of such Assembly . . . has been forcibly obstructed and taken away.

AND FURTHER, CONSIDERING that in these circumstances a free Assembly of the Church of Scotland . . . cannot at this time be holden . . . .

AND CONSIDERING that, while heretofore as members of Church Judicatories . . . we held ourselves . . . bound to . . . maintain the jurisdiction vested in these Judicatories . . . , notwithstanding the decrees . . . of the Civil Courts, because we could not see that the State had required submission thereto as a condition of the Establishment, . . . we are now constrained to acknowledge it to be the mind and will of the State . . . that such submission . . . does form a condition of the Establishment . . . , and that as we cannot . . . comply with this condition, we cannot in conscience continue connected with, and retain the benefits of an Establishment, to which such condition is attached.

WE, THEREFORE . . . DO PROTEST that the conditions foresaid, while we deem them contrary to . . . the settlement . . . effected at the Revolution, and . . . guaranteed by the Act of Security and Treaty of Union, are also at variance with God's Word, in opposition to the doctrines and fundamental principles of the Church of Scotland, inconsistent with the freedom essential to the right constitution of a Church of Christ . . . .

AND WE FURTHER PROTEST, that any Assembly constituted in submission to the conditions now declared to be law, and under the civil coercion which has been brought to bear on the election of Commissioners to the Assembly . . . and on the Commissioners chosen thereto, is not . . . a lawful and free Assembly of the Church of Scotland . . . and that the Claim, Declaration, and Protest of the General Assembly . . . 1842, as the act of a free and lawful Assembly . . . shall be holden as setting forth the true constitution of the said Church . . . .

AND FINALLY, while firmly asserting the right and duty of the Civil Magistrate to maintain and support an establishment of religion in accordance with God's Word, and reserving to ourselves and our successors to strive by all lawful means . . . to secure the performance of this duty agreeably to the Scriptures . . . : WE PROTEST that in the circumstances in which we are placed, it is . . . lawful . . . to withdraw to a separate place of meeting for the purpose of taking steps . . . for separating in an orderly way from the Establishment . . . ; and we do now . . . withdraw accordingly, . . . but . . . with an assured conviction, that we are not responsible for any consequences that may follow from this our enforced separation from an Establishment which we loved and prized—through interference with conscience, the dishonour done to Christ's Crown, and the rejection of His sole and supreme authority as King in his Church.

Source: The Principal Acts of the General Assembly of the Church of Scotland, Convened at Edinburgh, May 18, 1843 (Edinburgh, 1843), pp. 19–22.

SUGGESTIONS FOR BACKGROUND AND REFERENCE

J. R. Fleming, *A History of the Church in Scotland, 1843–1874* (Edinburgh, 1927). References for Document 87.

✦ ✦ ✦

90   Resignation of the Clergy of Vaud

November 12, 1845

In French Switzerland, *le réveil*, the revival inspired partly from Scotland, produced tensions between evangelicals and the predominantly rationalistic ministry supported by the cantonal governments. The canton of Vaud, centering around Lausanne, was the scene of the chief disruption. In the 1820s conventicles appeared in defiance of the law, and some leaders of the *réveil* were banished. In 1839 the state discarded the historic Helvetic Confession as a binding formula and abolished the connectional structure of the church, leaving local congregations under government authority. Alexandre Vinet, the most celebrated Swiss intellectual and religious leader, resigned from the clergy at this time, but five further years of controversy occurred before the great Vaudois secession took place. In 1845 the Grand Council took steps to suppress the evangelical lectures and oratories and to withhold salaries of ministers associated with them. Pastors were ordered to read a pulpit proclamation justifying the government, and when the church courts acquitted those who refused, the government suspended them from the ministry. Two hundred and twenty-five of the 288 ministers of Vaud met November 11 and 12, and 153 signed this declaration. Most of the ministers but a minority of the laity left to form the Free Church, which suffered continuing harassments from the civil authorities until the 1850s. (In a similar disruption the Geneva Free Church was formed in 1849.)

The president and members of the Council of State:

By the double judgment which you pronounced on November 12, 1845 you have, on your sole authority, completely altered the Christian ministry in the national Church.

In this judgment you condemned and punished forty-two pastors and ministers for having refused to read from the pulpit the genuinely political proclamation of July 29.

You condemned them despite the precise text of the law of 1832 which required this refusal.

You condemned them in contempt of the acquittal verdict of the four classes.

By this judgment you have declared:

That in opposition to the constitution which says that "the law regulates the relations of Church and state," the Church, instead of being united to the state, is now subordinated to the state, instead of being regulated by the laws, is controlled by the arbitrary will of the Council of State;

That pastors are no longer to have benefit of the law;

That despite the precise text of the laws, the pastors are obliged to submit to every order of the executive authority;

That the civil magistrate has the right to have the pulpits of our churches taken over by agents to read proclamations at the time of divine service—proclamations which may announce other doctrines and interests than religious doctrines and spiritual interests.

We, the undersigned pastors and ministers, responsible for worship and religion, declare to you that we neither should nor will make ourselves instruments of such a claim.

In the same judgment of November 3 you condemned and punished three pastors for having praised God and declared the gospel in the Lausanne oratory, even for simply having been present at the worship of this oratory.

You condemned them, though they had violated no law.

You condemned them, despite God's Law which absolves them.

You condemned them in contempt of the unanimous acquittal verdict of the Lausanne classis.

By this judgment you have declared:

That the laws no longer protect the ministry, since you attribute force of law to your notices;

That God's law may no longer be the supreme rule of the Christian ministry in the national Church;

That pastors may no longer exercise their ministry of preaching except at hours fixed by authority, and if authority refuses it to them, they lose the right to meet with their parishioners to pray and expound the Word;

That, consequently, the civil authority assumes the right to alter the ministry of the pastors at its pleasure.

We, the undersigned pastors and ministers who have received this ministry of God and must render an account of it to Him, declare to you that we neither should nor will accept these fetters.

Accordingly, and in view of the arbitrary changes that you have wrought in the Christian ministry in the national Church, we declare to you that from this day we resign into your hands the official ecclesiastical functions that we exercise in the national Church. Until December 15 those of us who are not suspended will continue to exercise their functions. If we fix this delay, it is solely in order that the parishes may not be left uncared for and the state in difficulty.

By this resignation and the reasons that we have just given you, we protest before you and shall highly protest before the country that . . . it is your arbitrary measures which exclude us from the active service of our Church, so far as it is united with the state.

We declare that no political interest or personal view has motivated us.

At the same time we declare . . . that we stand ready to devote ourselves anew to the service of the national Church; but, for official functions, we may not do this until sufficient guarantees shall have protected us from measures similar to those by which you have assaulted the rights and liberties of our national Church and the Christian ministry of that Church.

Source: C. Archinard, *Histoire de l'église du canton de Vaud depuis son origine jusqu'aux temps actuels* (Lausanne, 1862), pp. 288–291.

SUGGESTIONS FOR BACKGROUND AND REFERENCE

R. Centlivres and J.-J. Fleury, *De l'église d'état à l'église nationale (1839–1863)* (Lausanne, 1963), pp. 1–26.

J. I. Good, *History of the Swiss Reformed Church since the Reformation* (Philadelphia, 1913), pp. 473–493.

K. S. Latourette, *Christianity in a Revolutionary Age* (New York, 1958–1962), II, 212–214.

B. W. Noel, *The History of the Formation of the Free Church of the Canton de Vaud, Switzerland* (London, n.d.).

E. Rambert, *Alexandre Vinet* (Lausanne, 1930).

Source for this document.

✦ ✦ ✦ The Revolutionary Movements of 1848

91 Swiss Constitution (Extracts)

September 12, 1848

Since the Reformation the Swiss cantons had separately determined which faith, Catholic or Reformed, would be supported by law. After 1830 ideas of political liberalism, security for individual rights, and a closer national union produced growing demands for revision of the weak pact of 1815. Resisting the trend six Catholic cantons united in the Sonderbund to protect religion and cantonal privilege, but the Diet in 1847 dissolved the league and exiled the Jesuits. The resulting civil war and defeat of the Sonderbund cleared the way for constitutional reorganization in 1848.

XLI. . . . 1. No Swiss belonging to a Christian profession can be denied the right to settle in any one of the Cantons, provided he is in possession of the following vouchers:

   a. A certificate of nativity or its equivalent.
   b. A certificate of good moral conduct.
   c. A certificate that he enjoys the rights and honors of citizenship; and if on
      demand he can prove that . . . he is enabled to support himself and family.

* * *

XLIV. The free exercise of religious worship is guaranteed to the acknowledged Christian professions throughout the whole extent of Switzerland.

To the Cantons, as well as to the Confederacy, is reserved the right to adopt measures necessary for maintaining public order and peace among the different denominations.

* * *

LVIII. The Order of Jesuits, and societies affiliated thereto, are not permitted to be domiciliated in any part of Switzerland.

Source: The Federal Constitution of the Swiss Confederation (Washington, D.C., 1858), pp. 15, 16, 18. German text in William E. Rappard, *Die Bundesverfassung der Schweizerischen Eidgenossenschaft 1848–1948* (Zurich, 1948), pp. 435–504.

SUGGESTIONS FOR BACKGROUND AND REFERENCE

Cambridge Modern History (New York, 1903–1912)), II, 234–261.
W. Oechsli, *History of Switzerland 1499–1914* (Cambridge, 1922), pp. 396–408.
U. Lampert, *Kirche und Staat in der Schweiz* (Freiburg, Germany, 1939).

92   Wichern's Speech at the Wittenberg Kirchentag (Extracts)

September 1848

Johann Hinrich Wichern (1808–1881), a Hamburg Lutheran of Pietist background, became familiar with working-class poverty through pastoral work and organized the *Rauhes Haus* for delinquent boys in 1833. The institution became famous, and Wichern's assistants won attention for their lay preaching, social rescue, and hospital and asylum work. Wichern's oratory at the Wittenberg Kirchentag was an attempt to arouse the Evangelical Church to a concern for an urban proletariat drifting from the church. The Inner Mission that resulted was responsible for much social and charitable endeavor, the different societies [*Vereine*] working under the direction of a coordinating board [*Central-Ausschuss*]. Wichern rejected systematic social reconstruction and relied on the gospel's power to bring about social regeneration. He and the Inner Mission remained politically conservative, condemned socialism, and enjoyed the confidence of the Prussian government. Yet many Lutheran conservatives viewed the movement with distrust. Passages reproduced below are from Wichern's first remarks (September 21), demanding a more prominent place on the agenda for discussion of the Inner Mission, and from his principal speech (September 22). The text is from the official Kirchentag transcript, but it is not perfectly or literally faithful to his words.

From the Session of September 21:

"A thorough historical study of the church . . . would disclose the kind of failing . . . which the year 1848 has made evident. The turning point of history, at which we now find ourselves, must also prove a turning point in the history of the Christian church, and especially in the history of the German Evangelical Church, if it is to enter into a new relationship with the people. These ideas, desires, and hopes have long been current in our church, and in the last decade they have won increasing attention in those circles which are urgently concerned about the people's welfare. Yet the difficulties and hindrances working against the realization of these hopes seemed numerous and insuperable. Then came last February with its terrors for our western neighbors, and it was followed by March with its disastrous events in our Fatherland.[1] But though the heart bled—and still bleeds—in agony at the revelation of the outrage and wretchedness and power of sin, yet for the eye of faith there lay hidden behind all this a new dawn, promising the revival of the church's faithful and saving work. We can only welcome the nearness of this day with quickening hope and joy. For with these events a day of God dawned as a day of

---

1. The Paris revolution in February brought about the collapse of the July Monarchy and the proclamation of the Second Republic. Riots in Vienna and Berlin in mid-March launched the German revolution.

salvation for the church in our dear Fatherland. It must and will become clear that our Evangelical Church must and can be a people's church, awakening the people through the gospel in a fresh way and with new power and touching them with a new breath of life from God. Actual beginnings have been made, though they may remain unknown to many. And I hail the present Kirchentag as a great and long sought step towards shaping our Evangelical Church into a true people's church, despite appearances that the church will suffer decline. . . ."

* * *

From the Session of September 22:

"The Inner Mission can be practiced within the individual and separate parishes. Here it is chiefly the concern of the practical minister, and it is often combined with the church's care for the poor. This in itself, however, cannot solve the problem. The Inner Mission reaches beyond the individual parishes. We Germans are not so'ely a settled people. We are also a nomadic people by the hundreds of thousands. Let us remember the itinerant journeymen whose countless numbers wander yearly throughout our Fatherland. As itinerants they have no home other than their lodgings, and until just recently no associates other than fellow-craftsmen.

". . . Things are happening [in these lodgings] which must be called unutterable in the sense of the Apostle, and only in a very select and confidential company could one speak of them. . . . Here the foundations of our modern revolutionary clubs were secretly laid. . . . How should we satisfy the religious needs of these hundreds of thousands? Whose office and duty is it to care for them? Who has labored here with God's Word? To what church and parish do these multitudes belong? Clearly, until recently no one has been concerned about them.

"In addition, there is a second and related field of the Inner Mission: the Germans outside Germany, chiefly in Europe. . . . This German diaspora in Europe again consists mainly of itinerant craftsmen and is to be found principally in the great European cities, especially Paris, Marseilles, Lyons, London, St. Petersburg, etc. What does the Evangelical Church of the Fatherland for all these? Two years ago those who talked earnestly about the dangers of communism among the Germans in Paris and London, for example, had to fear being laughed at or cut short. Circumstances have now taught otherwise. Those who knew how matters stood saw the threatening monster approach, and now the storm of a communist revolution has taken place. The artisans took more part in it than even the most realistic people were willing to recognize before this. Many of them had been personally and systematically trained in Paris for such barbarous activity. The police have long known many of these circumstances, but they did not believe that they might speak publicly of them and supposed that they could defeat the dangers with their own resources. The uninitiated can hardly imagine the astuteness and discretion of this indoctrination of artisans. One of the schools for direct preparation has been set up by the radical atheistic and communist party in French Switzerland. A veiled atheism, of course, has often been the chief means for the achievement of their ends. In a notorious book [*Das junge Deutschland in der Schweiz* (Leipzig, 1846)] which appeared two years ago . . . the author, W[ilhelm] Marr, as a traitor to his party, explains in detail the methods he and his fellows used. The main theme is, he says, that 'men must be made into personal enemies of God.' He boasts that he has prepared thousands of German craftsmen step by step for the organization. One condition for acceptance into the organization is a ringing 'No!' to the question: 'Do you believe in God?' . . . . The seat of all recent revolutionary upheaval with its blasphemous satanic underground activity is the clubs of the artisans. Their secret aims were known only to very few, even among the members of the executive committees. These clubs appeared unpretentiously and were often supported by many right-minded people in the nation, who, despite warnings, tolerantly let themselves be duped. These societies are usually directed by secret leaders and attempt to destroy all other artisans' associations which show some energy. The verses of a song which was sung recently in a meeting of small craftsmen in Hamburg may serve as an example of the spirit which is often dominant among the workers. After cursing kings and rich men, it goes on:

> A curse on God, who's blind and deaf,
> To whom we vainly prayed in faith,
> In whom we vainly hoped and trusted.
> He played with us and made us fools.

"Despite all this, I—as a Lutheran—recognize these men and Marr too with his comrades merely as baptized Christians and thus as objects of the Inner Mission, which must courageously attack this work of Satan with God's almighty Word."

* * *

For many years our lowest rabble has possessed and practiced what was brought to light by the newest development of philosophy in Feuerbach etc. with its ethical corollary [*Anhang*].[2] This explains the revolution. These communist ideas which are opposed to all sound political and moral, not to mention Christian, principles were added to this sham philosophy, adopted by so-called leaders of the people. And they were quickly grasped as motivation for revolution by the masses who rebelled. The quick intelligence and organizing ability of these circles explain the propaganda of the itinerant artisans, which can hardly be surpassed by any counter-propaganda and which spreads to all corners with government permission and protection. They also explain many other conditions, especially the long matured de-Christianization of people of all ranks—a situation in which revolution could spring up quickly as from a well-prepared soil. We can only marvel and praise God's grace that a people, undermined and poisoned in their deepest roots, could so long resist. For these fatal principles did not remain in the proletariat, but also rose to the heights of intellect and power.

What can be done? While this situation spread like a great net over all Europe and missionaries went out to the heathen in ever-increasing numbers, the solution lay near enough at hand: Employ missionary techniques in our own house, in the homeland. So the name of the Inner Mission came into existence in those circles

---

2. Ludwig Feuerbach (1804–1872), was a German philosopher, expositor of materialistic and antireligious doctrine.

which also promoted foreign missions. But the help which can be given this way is and remains incomplete if the perspective is not broadened to include government and political life. The state needs this work as much as the church. The deep moral foundations on which political life rests are shaken . . . .

* * *

From the outset charity for the destitute and the lost was a basic concern of the Evangelical Church. But to awaken the rich abundance of this love was reserved to a later, perhaps to the present, stage of development of the spirit of our church. Two of its most gifted men particularly labored for what was bound to come—Spener, by preaching the universal priesthood, and A. H. Franke through his celebrated work of charity at Halle.[3] But it was unfortunate that both then and until recently the work of rescuing love [*rettende Liebe*] was mainly concentrated on the youth and the poor. . . . A reformation, or rather a regeneration, of all our deepest relations is needed. The church is summoned to work for this new birth by new and renewed deeds and revelations of faith and love. . . . "Certainly the Inner Mission must now act politically. If it does not labor in this sense the church will perish with the state. To be sure, it is not its task to decide about forms of government or judge between political parties. Yet from this day on, one of its most serious concerns must be that every citizen be filled with the Christian spirit, regardless of the form of government."

. . . What Thiers said recently in the French National Assembly about the social problem of our time is excellent.[4] However, it is only negative. For the state in itself is not capable of directly supplying the solution to the entire problem, although it has now greatly promoted its solution indirectly by granting the great right of free association. If, in relation to this point, the church becomes aware of its high, national mission and makes use of this right as extensively as possible—if it recognizes, loves, and cultivates it in order to fill it with the Christian spirit, letting it develop in the direction of the Inner Mission . . . then it will be blessed as the deliverer of the whole society. Because by following this path the way would be open to the hearts of the whole German people as well as to all orders and degrees of public and private life . . . .

* * *

"My friends! One thing is needed. The Evangelical Church in its entirety must make this acknowledgment: The work of the Inner Mission is mine! . . . Rescuing love must become the great instrument with which the church proves the existence of faith. This love must burn in the church as God's bright torch, proclaiming that Christ has found expression in his people. As the whole Christ is revealed in the living word of God, so he also must be preached in the deeds of God, and the

---

3. Philipp Jakob Spener (1635–1705) and August Hermann Francke (1663–1727), were German theologians at Halle, identified with Pietist revival in German Lutheranism.

4. Adolphe Thiers (1797–1877), French journalist and statesman, was several times a minister under the July Monarchy, a moderate liberal in the Second Republic. His famous speech of September 13, 1848, endorsing a conservative republic, weighed the dangers of socialism.

highest, purest, most churchly of these deeds is rescuing love. If in this sense the word of the Inner Mission is accepted, then our church's promised day has dawned. Evangelical preachers must first gather together and do penance for all that has been neglected in this area. Through their repentance they must move the whole community to repentance. Indeed, is there anyone who could or would dare to refrain from repentance? Let us all humble ourselves before the Lord! Here is an accumulated guilt not of one but of all, a guilt not simply of this generation, but an inherited guilt from the centuries which now must be atoned for in this new dawning age of the world. This repentance would mark the division between the old and new ages in our church, and the new age and its harvest would be more glorious than the old with its conclusion. Because all who come out of repentance will rise up in faith to the great task of saving the people from sin and wretchedness through Christ's power and glory. . . ."

Source: Johann Hinrich Wichern, *Ausgewählte Schriften* (ed. Karl Janssen) (Gütersloh, Germany, 1958), I, 112, 114–116, 117, 121–122, 123–124.

SUGGESTIONS FOR BACKGROUND AND REFERENCE

G. Brakelmann, *Kirche und Sozialismus im 19. Jahrhundert* (Witten, Germany, 1966), pp. 15–109.
A. L. Drummond, *German Protestantism since Luther* (London, 1951), pp. 214–229.
M. Gerhardt, *Ein Jahrhundert Innere Mission. Die Geschichte des Central-Ausschusses für die Innere Mission der deutschen evangelischen Kirche* (Gütersloh, Germany, 1948)).
———, *Johann Hinrich Wichern. Ein Lebensbild* (Hamburg, 1927–1931).
K. S. Latourette, *Christianity in a Revolutionary Age* (New York, 1958–1962), II, 102–109.
F. J. Leenhardt, *La Mission interieure et sociale de l'église d'après Wichern* (Paris, 1931).
P. Schaff, *Germany: Its Universities, Theology, and Religion* (Philadelphia, 1857), pp. 405–418.
W. O. Shanahan, *German Protestants Face the Social Question* (Notre Dame, 1954).

93   Fundamental Rights of the German People (Extract)

March 28, 1849

The Frankfurt Assembly, the congress of German liberals made possible by the revolutionary upheaval, sought national unification and political freedom. Because the state churches were normally supports of autocracy, German liberalism had few vital links with official Protestantism, and the constitutional program of separation was regarded by the Evangelical churches as an attack. By contrast, Catholics, following the Belgian example, found some common ground with liberals in demands for freedom of press, association, and education. These Fundamental Rights were first proclaimed in December 1848 and finally placed in the Constitution of March 29, 1849, as Section VI. Religion was dealt with in Article V. But by May 1949 liberalism was in collapse, and the constitution was repealed by the restored Diet.

Every German has full freedom of belief and of conscience.

No one is obliged to disclose his religious convictions.

Every German is unrestricted in the common exercise of his religion at home or in public.

Committing a crime and violating a law in the practice of this freedom are to be punished according to law.

The enjoyment of civil and political privileges is neither dependent on nor restricted by religious profession. [However,] civil duties are not annulled thereby.

Every religious association regulates and administers its own concerns independently, but remains subject to the common laws of the land.

No religious association shall enjoy special prerogatives from the state above any other association. Henceforward there is no state church.

New religious associations may be formed; no recognition of their beliefs by the state is needed.

No one may be constrained [to participate] in a churchly observance or ceremony.

The future form of the oath shall read: "So help me God."

The civil validity of marriage depends only on the completion of the civil ceremony; the religious ceremony may occur only after the accomplishment of the civil ceremony.

Religious differences are not a civil hindrance to marriage.

Registry books are kept by the civil authorities.

Source: Ludwig Bergsträsser (ed.), *Die Verfassung des Deutschen Reiches vom Jahre 1849* (Bonn, 1913), pp. 79–81.

SUGGESTIONS FOR BACKGROUND AND REFERENCE

Cambridge Modern History (New York, 1903–1912), XI, 142–233.

F. Eyck, *The Frankfurt Parliament 1848–1849* (London, 1968), pp. 228–246.

H. Holborn, *A History of Modern Germany* (New York, 1959–1969), III, 45–98.

R. Lempp, *Die Frage der Trennung von Kirche und Staat im Frankfurter Parlament* (Tübingen, Germany, 1913).

J. Rovan, *Le catholicisme politique en Allemagne* (Paris, 1956), pp. 16–59.

94 Danish Constitution (Extracts)

June 5, 1849

One of the few enduring liberal gains from 1848 occurred in Denmark, hitherto a nation with strong absolutist traditions. The new constitution, drawn up by a popularly elected convention on the basis of a draft presented by the bishop-statesman, D. G. Monrad (1811–1887), viewed

Lutheranism as the national church rather than as a mere state Establishment. The promises of a new church constitution and an act for dissenters were not fulfilled, but in practice religious liberty was respected.

3. The Evangelical Lutheran Church is the National Church, and as such to be supported by the state.

* * *

6. The king must belong to the Evangelical Lutheran Church.

* * *

80. The state [constitution] of the National Church is to be regulated by law.

81. The citizens possess the right of forming communions to worship God in whatsoever way their convictions guide them, provided that nothing is taught or done contrary to morality or the public peace.

82. No person is bound to contribute personally to any other religious worship than his own. Everybody, however, who does not prove to be a member of one of the established creeds in the country, must pay to the school fund the tax established by law for the benefit of the National Church.

83. The relations of those religious denominations that differ from the National Church are to be regulated by law.

84. No one on account of his religious beliefs may be debarred access to the entire enjoyment of civil and political rights nor . . . escape the performance of any general obligation of a citizen.

Source: The Constitution or Fundamental Law for the Kingdom of Denmark as Passed by the United Diet on the 25th Day of May 1849 Approved and Sanctioned by His Majesty Frederic the Seventh June 5th 1849 (St. Croix, Christiansted, n.d.), pp. 2, 14–15.

SUGGESTIONS FOR BACKGROUND AND REFERENCE

Cambridge Modern History (New York, 1903–1912), XI, 691–696.

J. Danstrup, *A History of Denmark* (Copenhagen, 1948), pp. 94–124.

C. Goos and H. Hansen, *Das Staatsrecht des Königreichs Dänemark* (Tübingen, Germany, 1913), pp. 38–41.

H. Koch and B. Kornerup, *Den Danske Kirkes Historie* (Copenhagen, 1950–1958), VI, 351–361; VII, 1–33.

K. S. Latourette, *Christianity in a Revolutionary Age* (New York, 1958–1962), II, 149–150.

A. Nyholm, *Religion og Politik en Monrad Studie* (Copenhagen, 1947).

✦ ✦ ✦ Christian Socialism in Britain

95   "Workmen of England!"

April 12, 1848

Though not without some preparation earlier, British Christian Social-ism had its effective beginnings in the work of Charles Kingsley (1819–1875), Frederick Denison Maurice (1805–1872), and John M. F. Ludlow (1821–1911) in 1848 to 1852. All were disturbed by the rapid industrialization of English society, sympathized with the plight of the victimized workers, and deplored the sterility and insensitivity of the churches on the social question. The movements of 1848, particularly Chartism, gave each a sense of urgency and prompted decision. In April, Kingsley, a vigorous country parson destined for a literary career, sought out Maurice and Ludlow, and all determined to get out "placards for the walls, to speak a word for God with." The message, written by Kingsley, was posted in London on the morning of April 12.

Workmen of England!

You say that you are wronged. Many of you are wronged; and many besides yourselves know it. Almost all men who have heads and hearts know it—above all, the working clergy know it. They go into your houses, they see the shameful filth and darkness in which you are forced to live crowded together; they see your children growing up in ignorance and temptation, for want of fit education; they see intelligent and well-read men among you, shut out from a Freeman's just right of voting; and they see too the noble patience and self-control with which you have as yet borne these evils. They see it, and God sees it.

WORKMEN OF ENGLAND! You have more friends than you think for. Friends who expect nothing from you, but who love you, because you are their brothers, and who fear God, and therefore dare not neglect you, His children; men who are drudging and sacrificing themselves to get you your rights; men who know what your rights are, better than you know yourselves, who are trying to get for you something nobler than charters and dozens of Acts of Parliament—more useful than this "fifty thousandth share in a Talker in the National Palaver at Westminster"[1] can give you. You may disbelieve them, insult them—you cannot stop their working for you, beseeching you as you love yourselves, to turn back from the precipice of riot, which ends in the gulf of universal distrust, stagnation, starvation.

You think the Charter would make you free—would to God it would! The

---

1. Cf. Thomas Carlyle, *Past and Present* (London, 1843), p. 293: ". . . twenty-thousandth part of a Talker in our National Palaver . . . ." Carlyle earlier (1839) used similar expressions in *Chartism,* Chap. 9.

Charter is not bad; *if the men who use it are not bad!* But will the Charter make you free? Will it free you from slavery to ten-pound bribes? Slavery to beer and gin? Slavery to every spouter who flatters your self-conceit, and stirs up bitterness and headlong rage in you? That, I guess, is real slavery; to be a slave to one's own stomach, one's own pocket, one's own temper. Will the Charter cure *that?* Friends, you want more than Acts of Parliament can give.

Englishmen! Saxons! Workers of the great, cool-headed, strong-handed nation of England, the workshop of the world, the leader of freedom for 700 years, men say you have common-sense! then do not humbug yourselves into meaning "licence", when you cry for "liberty"; who would dare refuse you freedom? for the Almighty God, and Jesus Christ, the poor Man, who died for poor men, will bring it about for you, though all the Mammonites of the earth were against you. A nobler day is dawning for England, a day of freedom, science, industry!

But there will be no true freedom without virtue, no true science without religion, no true industry without the fear of God, and love to your fellow-citizens.

Workers of England, be wise, and then you *must* be free, for you will be *fit* to be free.

A WORKING PARSON

Source: [Fanny Kingsley] (ed.), *Charles Kingsley* (London, 1877), I, 156–157.

SUGGESTIONS FOR BACKGROUND AND REFERENCE

G. C. Binyon, *The Christian Socialist Movement in England* (London, 1931).
T. Christensen, *Origin and History of Christian Socialism 1848–54* (Aarhus, Denmark, 1962).
E. R. Norman, *The Victorian Christian Socialists* (Cambridge, 1987).
C. E. Raven, *Christian Socialism 1848–1854* (London, 1920).
M. F. Thorp, *Charles Kingsley 1819–1875* (Princeton, 1937).

96 "The New Idea"

November 2, 1850

Maurice, Kingsley, and Ludlow believed that the task of applying Christian principles to social and political questions required not only direct cooperation experiments, but a program of education through a new set of "Tracts for the Times" as well. Accordingly, they issued a series of short-lived journals: *Politics for the People* (April–July 1848), *Tracts on Christian Socialism* (1850), *The Christian Socialist* (1850–1851), and *Tracts of Priests and People* (1862). This manifesto by Ludlow in the opening issue of *The Christian Socialist* forcefully announced the group's aims. Anglican socialism's early experiments in producer cooperatives failed, but its ideas won increasing support and influenced modern Anglicanism and Labour politics.

The New Idea

A new idea has gone abroad into the world. That Socialism, the latest-born of the forces now at work in modern society, and Christianity, the eldest born of those forces, are in their nature not hostile, but akin to each other, or rather that the one is but the development, the outgrowth, the manifestation of the other, so that even the strangest and most monstrous forms of Socialism are at bottom but Christian heresies. That Christianity, however feeble and torpid it may seem to many just now, is truly but as an eagle at moult, shedding its worn-out plumage; that Socialism is but its livery of the nineteenth century (as Protestantism was its livery of the sixteenth) which it is even now putting on, to spread ere long its mighty wings for a broader and heavenlier flight. That Socialism without Christianity, on the one hand, is as lifeless as the feathers without the bird, however skilfully the stuffer may dress them up into an artificial semblance of life; and that therefore every socialist system which has endeavoured to stand alone has hitherto in practice either blown up or dissolved away; whilst almost every socialist system which has maintained itself for any time has endeavoured to stand, or unconsciously to itself has stood, upon those moral grounds of righteousness, self-sacrifice, mutual affection, common brotherhood, which Christianity vindicates to itself for an everlasting heritage. That Christianity on the other hand, in this nineteenth century of ours, becomes in its turn chilly and helpless when stripped of its social influences, or in other words, when divorced from Socialism; when cramped up within the four walls of its churches or chapels, and forbidden to go forth into the wide world, conquering and to conquer, to assert God's rightful dominion over every process of trade and industry, over every act of our common life, and to embody in due forms of organization every deepest truth of that faith committed to its charge. That, therefore, if Christ's gospel speaks true, and "ye cannot serve God and Mammon," that gospel is wholly incompatible with a political economy which proclaims self-interest to be the very pivot of social action. That if Christ's gospel speaks true, and "thou shalt love thy neighbour as thyself," that gospel cannot stand with a system of trade based wholly on the idea of Profit, *i.e.,* of taking more from our neighbour than we give to him, and which has adopted for its maxim to "buy cheap, and sell dear." But, finally, that if Christ's gospel be true, then it is compatible with those theories or systems which, however mistaken in their means, yet have for common object to bind up into fellowship, and not to divide by selfishness and rivalry, to substitute fair prices and living wages for a false cheapness and starvation its child, and which have adopted for their watchwords "Association" and "Exchange," instead of "Competition" and "Profit."

Such is the idea which this paper is intended to express; such is the idea which has given birth to the "Society for Promoting Working Men's Associations," of which it is intended to be the organ, and which has assigned for function to the Council of Promoters of that Society "to diffuse the principles of co-operation *as the practical application of Christianity to the purposes of trade and industry."* Do not let us be misunderstood. The members of those associations, nor even the writers of this paper, are required to make in words a profession of Christianity. The men who, claiming for themselves as their dearest privilege the title of "Christians," have yet, on the common ground of coöperative principles, of Socialism in a word, gladly accepted the fellowship of those for whom that title may have seemed hitherto but an insult or a mockery, these men have done so with their eyes open. They have done so, we repeat it, because they maintain Socialism to be essentially Christian, even when struggling against that blessed name; because they are taught by their Christianity, and many of them by their church, to recognise in every sceptic and infidel, a brother for whom Christ died. The fellowship which they have entered into, the common work in which they are engaged, involves for them no sacrifice of principle. It is their right to enter into that fellowship; it is their duty to carry on that work.

But more. The writers of this paper, we have said, need not all be professed Christians; still less need they be professed Churchmen. And yet, for many of those writers, to be members of the Church of England is but a lesser privilege than to be members of the Church of Christ. They too, as Churchmen, feel it their right and their duty to join this work. If others see in the marriage of Christianity with Socialism, the sole remedy for the present evils of society, they see in the Church of England the sole agent by which that remedy can be successfully applied. They are therefore Socialists by a double title,—as Christians and as Churchmen. They believe the formularies of the Church of England, whether of worship or of doctrine, to be alone adequate to the expression of those new feelings which are agitating the hearts of the masses, from one end of the British Isles,—ay, or of the Christian world,—to the other. They believe the constitution of the Church of England, even if overlaid here and there by the excrescences of State-tyranny, to be alone adaptable to the regular and organic embodiment of those new tendencies. They believe that no social reform can be thorough and practical without the help of the Church; they believe that no Church-reform can be living and permanent, which is not in harmony with social wants.

Some may say, indeed: Be Christian Socialists as much as you please; but why put the words in the very fore-front of your paper? Because there are times above all others in which it is needful for men to speak out what they mean. Because what we mean to speak out above all things is that new idea of the essential harmony between Christianity and Socialism. Because it is yet a disgrace, or at least a motive for distrust, to be a Christian among Socialists, or a Socialist among Christians. Because for men as conscious as we are of imperfection and sin, there would be spiritual affectation and pride to call ourselves simply Christians. Because there would be as much intellectual vanity and pretence to call ourselves simply Socialists, whilst several of us at least feel ourselves yet so ignorant of the science of co-operative organization.

If it be given to us to vindicate for Christianity its true authority over the realms of industry and trade; for Socialism its true character as the great Christian revolution of the nineteenth century, so that the title of "Socialist" shall be only a bugbear to the idle and to the wicked, and society, from the highest rank to the lowest, shall avowedly regulate itself upon the principle of co-operation, and not drift rudderless upon the sea of competition, as our let-alone political economists would have it do; then indeed we shall have achieved our task; and, in the meanwhile, we trust in God that no amount of obliquy, ridicule, calumny, neglect, shall make us desert it, so long as we have strength and means to carry on the fight. For a fight it is, and a long one, and a deadly one, a fight against all the armies of Mammon. Will the working men of England stand by us? We have no fear of the issue if they will.

Source: The Christian Socialist: A Journal of Association, November 2, 1850, pp. 1–2.

SUGGESTIONS FOR BACKGROUND AND REFERENCE

References for Document 95.

✦ ✦ ✦

97　French Protestant Constitution

March 26, 1852

Encouraged by the 1848 revolution, a national Reformed synod convened in Paris in September 1848 and drew up a new church constitution, which provided for presbyterial councils, regional synods, and a regularly convened general synod. This national synod was accorded no civil recognition, however, and the effective modification of the older Napoleonic settlement of 18 Germinal, Year X (April 8, 1802), came in the unilateral decree of the Bonapartist government in 1852. The constitution, together with a report to Louis Napoleon, was drawn up by the worship and instruction minister, Hippolyte Fortoul (1811–1856). It made some changes sympathetic to the Reformed tradition, reconstituting the parish councils, which had virtually disappeared in the artificial consistorial church, and doing away with the property qualification for electors. But the substitution of the Central Council for a general synod was alien to Reformed history and called forth spirited protest that strengthened the demand for separation from the state.

Report to the Prince-President of the French Republic.

Monseigneur, the position of the Reformed Church and the Church of the Augsburg Confession, particularly with respect to their relations with the government, has given occasion for frequent objections, either from the civil authority or from the Protestants themselves. Although effort has been made . . . to provide for some of the most urgent needs, the legislation still retains considerable gaps which should be closed . . . . [In the Lutheran churches, where "the principles of election and authority are combined," the latter principle is to be strengthened through the superior consistory and the directory.] The Reformed churches are ruled by presbyterial-synodical government. But this system, which has not functioned in its entirety for a long time, presents difficulties of application and perhaps does not permit the churches to enter usefully into relation with the government. In the interests of good organization . . . , requests have repeatedly been made for fifty years for the creation of a central consistory, analogous to that for the Israelite religion. This institution would be found an influential intermediary between the administration and the general consistories, an honest and effective representative of the respective interests. . . . From the beginning the unfortunate absence of this administrative machinery was obvious to councillor of state Portalis,[1] and the plan for a central commission was one of several measures by which the first organization of the Reformed Church was to have been completed. To remedy . . . the serious disadvantages arising from this lack of representation of the consistories I . . . propose, Monseigneur, that you set up a Central Council of the Reformed Churches at Paris. To impress an essential unity of viewpoint on the measure, this first assembly will be constituted by the head of state. The arrangements which I ask you to approve . . . are the application of the great principles proclaimed in 1789 and 1802 to assure both religious liberty and the tutelary influence of authority. . . .

* * *

Chapter I. Common Arrangements for the Two Protestant Religions

1. Each parish or section of the consistorial church shall have a presbyterial council composed at least of four lay members, at most of seven, and presided over by the pastor or by one of the pastors. A parish exists wherever the state remunerates one or several pastors. The presbyterial councils administer the parishes under the authority of consistories. They are elected by parochial suffrage, and half of the council must be elected every three years. Electors are members of the church whose names are carried on the parochial register.

2. Presbyterial councils of the principal towns of consistorial districts shall receive from the government the title of consistories and the powers which are attached thereto. In this case the number of members of the presbyterial council shall be doubled. All pastors of the consistorial district shall be members of the consistory, and each presbyterial council shall appoint a lay delegate thereto.

3. Like the presbyterial council, the consistory shall be reconstituted every three years. After each reorganization it elects its president from the pastors who are members, . . . subject to government approval. As much as possible, the president should reside in the chief town of the district. . . .

* * *

Chapter II. Special Arrangements for the Reformed Church

5. Pastors of the Reformed Church shall be appointed by the consistory. The presbyterial council . . . concerned may present a list of three candidates arranged in alphabetical order.

6. A Central Council of the Reformed churches . . . is hereby established in Paris. This council represents the churches to the government and head of state. It shall be summoned to consider such questions . . . as may be placed before it by the

---

1. Jean Portalis (1746–1807) was minister of religion under Napoleon I.

government or the churches . . . . For its initial organization it shall be composed of Protestant notables appointed by the government, and the two senior pastors of Paris.

7. When a professorial chair of the Reformed communion becomes vacant in the faculty of theology, the Central Council receives the votes of the consistories and transmits them, with its recommendation, to the minister.

Chapter III. Special Arrangements for the Church of the Augsburg Confession

8. Churches and consistories of the Augsburg Confession shall be placed under the authority of the superior . . . consistory, and of the directory.

9. The superior consistory shall be composed of: (1) two lay deputies for each superintendency [*inspection*], who may be chosen from outside the superintendency district; (2) the ecclesiastical superintendents; (3) a seminary professor, representative of his body; (4) the president of the directory, who is *ex officio* president of the superior consistory, and a lay member of the directory appointed by the government.

10. The superior consistory shall be convened by the government, either at the wish of the directory or of its own accord. It meets at least once a year. At the opening of the session, the directory makes a report of its administration. The superior consistory sees to the maintenance of the constitution and discipline of the church. It makes . . . regulations concerning internal administration . . . . It approves liturgical books and formularies which are used in worship or religious instruction. It has the right to supervise and investigate accounts of consistorial administration.

11. The directory shall be composed of a president, a lay member, and an ecclesiastical superintendent, appointed by the government; and of two deputies appointed by the superior consistory. The directory . . . nominates pastors and submits their appointment to the government . . . . It authorizes . . . with government approval, a pastor's transfer from one charge to another. It supervises the teaching and discipline of seminaries and of the Protestant colleges called *gymnasiums*. With government approval, it appoints teachers . . . . It gives its detailed recommendation concerning candidates to chairs of the theological faculty.

12. Ecclesiastical superintendents shall be appointed by the government on the request of the directory . . . .

13. The consistory of Paris will officially represent the superior consistory of Strassburg to the government . . . . The directory may specially designate a lay notable, residing at Paris, to represent it conjointly with the consistory.

Source: Jean B. Duvergier (ed.), *Collection complète des lois, décrets, ordonnances, règlements, avis du conseil d'état* (Paris, 1834–1906), III, 384–386.

SUGGESTIONS FOR BACKGROUND AND REFERENCE

G. de Felice, *History of the Protestants of France* (London, 1853), II, 316–339.
K. S. Latourette, *Christianity in a Revolutionary Age* (New York, 1958–1962), II, 228–229.

98   Canadian Clergy Reserves Act

December 18, 1854

Church-state issues in Canada during the first half of the nineteenth century were dominated by the tangled question of the "clergy reserves." Endowment of a Protestant clergy from income derived from reserved lands had been mandated by the Constitutional Act of 1791. By the 1820s increasing religious diversity had begun to challenge the Anglican contention that the Church of England was properly the exclusive beneficiary of the provision. Presbyterians especially asserted that since the Church of Scotland was also a state church in Britain, Presbyterian ministers should enjoy co-endowment. Other denominations, contending for religious equality, similarly laid claim to support as "Protestant clergy" or, like the Baptists, championed voluntaryism and secularization of the reserves. In 1840 the Westminster Parliament forbade future reservation of lands for support of religion and ordered that income from lands already sold be shared among several Protestant denominations, though Anglicans continued to receive the lion's share. This co-endowment arrangement was expected finally to settle the issue, but political reformers and increasing numbers of religious voluntaryists revived controversy at the end of the decade.

In 1853 the British Parliament authorized the Canadian legislature to formulate a solution. The basis of the subsequent act of 1854 was secularization of assets (the Municipalities Funds) with some protection for vested ecclesiastical interests. A special and controversial provision permitted clergy to commute their life interests to the benefit of denominations, from which commuted monies permanent invested endowments could then be funded. By voiding future government endowments and grants, the act practically severed historic ties between church and state, but the principle of separation was not explicitly declared. After passage of the act controversy gradually subsided, but remnants of state support (through the commutation provision) continued for Anglicans, Presbyterians, and Wesleyans, while some forty-four Anglican "Colbourne rectories," already endowed with glebe lands from the reserves in 1836, survived legal challenge.

1. The moneys arising from the Clergy Reserves in Upper Canada shall continue to form a separate Fund which shall be called The Upper Canada Municipalities Fund, and the moneys arising from the Clergy Reserves in Lower Canada shall continue to form a separate Fund, which shall be called The Lower Canada Municipalities Fund:

2. The Municipalities Fund for each section of the Province respectively, shall

From W. P. M. Kennedy (ed.), *Statutes, Treaties and Documents of the Canadian Constitution 1713–1929*, 2d ed. (London, 1930). Copyright, 1930, by Oxford University Press. Reprinted by permission of Oxford University Press.

consist of all moneys arising from the sale of Clergy Reserves in that section of the Province, whether now funded or invested either in the United Kingdom or in this Province, or remaining uninvested, or hereafter to arise from such sales, the Interest and Dividends of moneys forming part of such Fund, the interest upon Sales of Clergy Reserves in that Section of the Province, on credit, and rents, issues and profits arising from Clergy Reserves therein demised or to be demised for any term of years, and other casual and periodical incomings arising from Clergy Reserves therein, after deducting therefrom the actual and necessary expenses attending the sales of the said Clergy Reserves, and of managing the same and the Funds aforesaid: and the moneys forming the said Funds shall be paid into the hands of the Receiver General and shall be by him applied to the purposes hereinafter mentioned, under the authority of this Act, or any General or Special Order or Orders to be made by the Governor in Council.

II. The annual stipends or allowances which had been . . . assigned or given to the Clergy of the Churches of England and Scotland, or to any other Religious Bodies or denominations of Christians in either Section of the Province, and chargeable . . . on the Clergy Reserves . . . shall, during the natural lives or incumbencies of the parties receiving the same, . . . be the first charge on the Municipalities Fund for that Section of the Province, and shall be paid out of the same in preference to all other charges or expenses whatever: Provided always, that the annual allowance heretofore payable to the Roman Catholic Church in Upper Canada, and to the British Wesleyan Methodist Church for Indian Missions, shall continue to be payable during the twenty years next after the passing of this Act, and no longer.

III. And whereas it is desirable to remove all semblance of connection between Church and State, and to effect an entire and final disposition of all matters, claims and interests arising out of the Clergy Reserves by as speedy a distribution of their proceeds as may be: . . . the Governor in Council may, whenever he may deem it expedient, with the consent of the parties and Bodies severally interested, commute with the said parties such annual stipend or allowance for the value thereof, to be calculated at the rate of six per cent per annum, upon the probable life of each individual; and in the case of the Bodies above particularly specified in the second section of this Act, at the actual value of the said allowance at the time of commutation to be calculated at the rate aforesaid: and such commutation shall be paid accordingly out of that one of the Municipalities Funds upon which such stipend or allowance is made chargeable by this Act: Provided always, that no commutation shall take place but within one year next after the passing of this Act: Provided also, that in case of commutation with either of the said Bodies or Denominations, it shall not be lawful for them or either of them to invest the moneys paid for such commutation, or any part thereof, in Real Property of any kind whatsoever, under penalty of forfeiting the same to Her Majesty; and that the said bodies or denominations shall lay before the Legislature, whenever called on so to do, a statement of the manner in which said moneys shall have been invested or appropriated.

Source: 18 Vict., c. 2; W. P. M. Kennedy (ed.), *Statutes, Treaties and Documents of the Canadian Constitution 1713–1929* (London, 1930), pp. 516–519.

SUGGESTIONS FOR BACKGROUND AND REFERENCE

J. M. S. Careless, *The Union of the Canadas. The Growth of Canadian Institutions 1841– 1857* (Toronto, 1967), pp. 185–203.

J. S. Moir, *Church and State in Canada West: Three Studies in the Relation of Denominationalism and Nationalism, 1841–1867* (Toronto, 1959), pp. 27–81.

————, *The Church in the British Era. From the British Conquest to Confederation* (Toronto, 1972), pp. 180–183, 189–193.

A. Wilson, *The Clergy Reserves of Upper Canada: A Canadian Mortmain* (Toronto, 1968), pp. 197–222.

99   Swedish Religious Law of 1860 (Extracts)

October 26, 1860

Sweden, overwhelmingly Lutheran, maintained a vigorous state church, but the evangelical awakenings produced several pietistic and evangelical sects, of which the most important was the Mission Covenant. In the nineteenth century the numbers of Baptists and Methodists also increased. These bodies, supported by political liberalism, sought abandonment of the eighteenth-century Conventicle Act (1726) and of the legal requirement of banishment for those leaving the state church. Under Oscar I (1844–1859), with the liberal reformer, Louis de Geer, as minister of justice, the Conventicle Act was repealed in 1858. However, separate assemblies still could exist only under stern restrictions. The Repeal Decree stated:

> Unless special permission is granted, such a gathering may not occur at the time when the regular religious service of the parish takes place. Nor may the clergy of the parish, members of the [parochial] church council, or magistrates of the place be denied admission to a meeting for worship distinct from private family devotions. Should any illegality or disorder occur, the last-mentioned authority may disperse the meeting, if necessary. If someone who is not a minister or authorized for public preaching in conformity with church law appears at such a gathering as a religious teacher with preachings which could be considered as tending to church schism or contempt for the regular religious service or as otherwise undermining the sanctity of religion, it is the responsibility of the church council to forbid him to appear again in like capacity in the parish.

The Decree also stated that violations of these limits would be punished by fines of from fifty to three hundred rixdollars or imprisonment. (Per-Erik Lindorm, *Vårt Kristna Arv*, p. 304.)

This carefully measured religious freedom was clarified two years later by the Religious Law of 1860. This legislation described specific measures dissenters were to take in order to achieve legal recognition of separate religious standing. The bounds of liberty remained narrow;

nevertheless, the principle of a legal religious pluralism was acknowledged. Relaxation of rigor against sectaries was accompanied by greater
self-government and lay participation within the Church of Sweden,
notably in the organization of the *Kyrkomöte*, in the 1860s.

1. If Christian believers of another doctrine than the pure evangelical faith wish to
unite themselves in a congregation, they should make application to the king and at
the same time declare their belief and church order. If, after proper examination, the
king finds reason to approve the application, such an authorized separate (*främ-
mande*) religious body has the right freely to practice its religion within the limits set
by law and morality. However, public church practices and religious services must
be carried out only within the parish church, or chapel, or churchyard.

* * *

8. Adherents of separate confessions may not establish or open schools or other
institutions of learning except for believers in their own faith or their children. If the
contrary occurs, the school or institution of learning shall be closed and the director
of the same shall be fined from fifty to three hundred rixdollars.

* * *

14. If anyone departs from the pure evangelical doctrine and disregards his
pastor's instruction and warning he shall be admonished by the diocesan chapter or
its authorized representative. If he persists in his error and wishes to leave the
Swedish Church for a separate religious body, he should personally make application to the rector of the parish to which he belongs to have this recorded in the
church registry. However, he shall not be considered separated from the care of the
church before he has attained the age of eighteen and has been accepted by another
authorized religious body.

Source: Per-Erik Lindorm, *Vårt Kristna Arv,* p. 319.

SUGGESTIONS FOR BACKGROUND AND REFERENCE

Y. Brillioth and H. Holmquist, *Handbok i Svensk Kyrkohistoria* (Stockholm, 1940–1941),
    III, 62 ff.
K. S. Latourette, *Christianity in a Revolutionary Age* (New York, 1958–1962), II, 181–182.
J. Wordsworth, *The National Church of Sweden* (London, 1911), pp. 393 ff.
Source for this document.

V

CHURCH AND STATE, 1870–1917

✦ ✦ ✦ Religion and Education in Britain

100   Forster Education Act (Extracts)

August 9, 1870

Prior to 1833 the government accepted no responsibility for national elementary education. In that year annual grants-in-aid, £20,000 at first, were voted by Parliament, but schools remained financed largely by endowments and pupils' fees, and most were religiously controlled, usually by the Church of England. The establishment of a national system was provided for in the bill drawn up by W. E. Forster (1818–1886), Gladstone's education minister, authorizing local governments to set up schools wherever private schools were inadequate, such schools to be controlled by local school boards and maintained by national and local taxes and pupils' fees. Debate on the bill centered on the question of religious instruction. The bill included a conscience provision excusing children from religious observance or instruction in any school if their parent so desired. Yet Nonconformists feared Anglican advantage by the bill and finally forced an amendment, known as the Cowper-Temple clause, which excluded all denominational instruction from Board Schools. Government assistance to private schools, which determined their own religious policies, was continued and increased. Nonconformists were much dissatisfied with the measure, which began a long history of educational controversy in Britain. Only the religious provisions of the act are given here.

7. Every elementary school which is conducted in accordance with the following regulations shall be a public elementary school within the meaning of this Act; and every public elementary school shall be conducted in accordance with the following regulations (a copy of which regulations shall be conspicuously put up in every such school); namely,

(1.) It shall not be required, as a condition of any child being admitted into or continuing in the school, that he shall attend or abstain from attending any Sunday school, or any place of religious worship, or that he shall attend any religious observance or any instruction in religious subjects in the school or elsewhere, from which observance or instruction he may be withdrawn by his parent, or that he shall, if withdrawn by his parent, attend the school on any day exclusively set apart for religious observance by the religious body to which his parent belongs:

(2.) The time or times during which any religious observance is practised or instruction in religious subjects is given at any meeting of the school shall be either at the beginning or at the end or at the beginning and the end of such meeting, and shall be inserted in a time table to be approved by the Education Department, and to be kept permanently and conspicuously affixed in every schoolroom; and any scholar may be withdrawn by his parent from such observance or instruction without forfeiting any of the other benefits of the school:

(3.) The School shall be open at all times to the inspection of any of Her Majesty's inspectors, so, however, that it shall be no part of the duties of such inspector to inquire into any instruction in religious subjects given at such school, or to examine any scholar therein in religious knowledge or in any religious subject or book:

(4.) The school shall be conducted in accordance with the conditions required to be fulfilled by an elementary school in order to obtain an annual parliamentary grant.

* * *

14. Every school provided by a school board shall be conducted under the control and management of such board in accordance with the following regulations:

(1.) The school shall be a public elementary school within the meaning of this Act:

(2.) No religious catechism or religious formulary which is distinctive of any particular denomination shall be taught in the school.

Source: 33 & 34 Vict., c. 75; *The Public General Statutes Passed in the Thirty-Third & Thirty-Fourth Years of the Reign of Her Majesty Queen Victoria, 1870* (London, 1870), pp. 445–446, 448.

SUGGESTIONS FOR BACKGROUND AND REFERENCE

J. W. Adamson, *English Education 1789–1902* (Cambridge, 1930), pp. 345–386.
S. C. Carpenter, *Church and People, 1789–1889* (London, 1933), pp. 359–365.
M. Cruickshank, *Church and State in English Education* (London, 1963), pp. 1–68.
G. I. T. Machin, *Politics and the Churches in Great Britain 1869 to 1920* (Oxford, 1987), pp. 31–40.
M. Sturt, *Education of the People* (London, 1967).

101 Universities Tests Act

June 16, 1871

Since the Reformation, Oxford and Cambridge were unquestioned Anglican preserves. By legislation in the 1850s Parliament opened the two universities to Nonconformists, permitting them to come into residence and take degrees. The act of 1871 swept away the last remains of exclusiveness, throwing open all lay posts in colleges and universities without reference to religious profession. The act, though sponsored by the Churchman, Gladstone, was condemned by many Anglicans as marking the end of the older religious tradition of the universities, and opposition in the House of Lords, led by Salisbury, was vigorous though unavailing.

WHEREAS it is expedient that the benefits of the Universities of Oxford, Cambridge, and Durham, and of the colleges and halls now subsisting therein, as places of religion and learning, should be rendered freely accessible to the nation:

And whereas, by means of divers restrictions, tests, and disabilities, many of Her Majesty's subjects are debarred from the full enjoyment of the same:

And whereas it is expedient that such restrictions, tests, and disabilities should be removed, under proper safeguards for the maintenance of religious instruction and worship in the said universities . . . :

Be it enacted . . . as follows:

* * *

The word "office" includes every professorship other than professorships of divinity, every assistant or deputy professorship, public readership, prelectorship, lectureship, headship of a college or hall, fellowship, studentship, tutorship, scholarship, and exhibition, and also any office or emolument not in this section specified, the income of which is payable out of the revenues of any of the said universities, or of any college within the said universities, or which is held or enjoyed by any member as such of any of the said universities, or of any college . . . .

3. From and after the passing of this Act, no person shall be required, upon taking or to enable him to take any degree (other than a degree in divinity) within the Universities of Oxford, Cambridge, and Durham . . . or upon exercising . . . any of the rights and privileges . . . exercised by graduates . . . or upon taking or holding . . . any office . . . or upon teaching . . . or upon opening . . . a private hall or hostel in any of the said universities for the reception of students, to subscribe any article or formulary of faith, or to make any declaration or take any oath respecting his religious belief or profession, or to conform to any religious observance, or to attend or abstain from attending any form of public worship, or to belong to any specified church, sect, or denomination; nor shall any person be compelled . . . to attend the public worship of any church, sect, or denomination to which he does not belong: Provided that—

(1.) Nothing in this section shall render a layman or a person not a member of the Church of England eligible to any office or capable of exercising any right or privilege . . . which office, right, or privilege, under the authority of any Act of Parliament or any statute or ordinance of such university or college in force at the time of the passing of this Act, is restricted to persons in holy orders, or shall remove any obligation to enter into holy orders which is by such authority attached to any such office.

(2.) Nothing in this section shall open any office (not being an office mentioned in this section) to any person who is not a member of the Church of England, where such office is at the passing of this Act confined to members of the said Church by reason of any such degree as aforesaid being a qualification for holding that office.

4. Nothing in this Act shall . . . affect, . . . otherwise than is hereby expressly enacted, the system of religious instruction, worship, and discipline which now is . . . lawfully established in the said universities . . . .

5. The governing body of every college . . . shall provide sufficient religious instruction for all members thereof in statu pupillari belonging to the Established Church.

6. The Morning and Evening Prayer according to the Order of the Book of Common Prayer shall continue to be used daily as heretofore in the chapel of every college . . . .

7. No person shall be required to attend any college or university lecture to which he, if he be of full age, or, if he be not of full age, his parent or guardian, shall object upon religious grounds.

Source: 34 Vict., c. 26; *The Public General Statutes Passed in the Thirty-Fourth & Thirty-Fifth Years of the Reign of Her Majesty Queen Victoria, 1871* (London, 1871), pp. 191–193.

SUGGESTIONS FOR BACKGROUND AND REFERENCE

J. W. Adamson, *English Education 1789–1902* (Cambridge, 1930), pp. 415–418.
W. G. Addison, *Religious Equality in Modern England, 1714–1914* (London, 1944), pp. 141–144.
S. C. Carpenter, *Church and People, 1789–1889* (London, 1933), pp. 359–365.
L. E. Elliott-Binns, *Religion in the Victorian Era* (London, 1936), 319–325.
D. A. Winstanley, *Later Victorian Cambridge* (Cambridge, 1947), pp. 36–90.

✦ ✦ ✦ The Papacy and Italian Unification

102 Law of Papal Guarantees

May 13, 1871

Taking advantage of the Franco-Prussian War and the withdrawal of the French garrison at Rome, Italian troops forced their way into the city on September 22, 1870, and the subsequent annexation, approved by plebiscite in October, established the Roman Question as a major issue in Italian and European politics. Though Pius excommunicated the "usurpers," refused to surrender the Quirinal, and called international attention to his "imprisonment," the Italian government believed concil-iation possible. The Law of Guarantees, drawn up by the Destra heirs of Cavour, represented the Cavourist solution of "a free church in a free state." Much of the eighteenth-century regalist tradition of state control was discarded. Abroad the act was useful in reassuring Catholic govern-ments and populations, but at home it was attacked by the anticlerical Sinistra for yielding too much to the pontiff.

Title I. Prerogatives of the Supreme Pontiff and of the Holy See

1. The person of the Supreme Pontiff is sacred and inviolable.

2. Any attempt against the person of the Supreme Pontiff and the provocation to commit such an attempt shall be punished with the same penalty as similar offenses against the person of the King.

Public offenses and insults committed directly against the person of the Supreme Pontiff, by speech, by act, or by the means indicated in Art. 1 of the law of the press, shall be punished with the penalty fixed by Art. 19 of the said law.

The crimes above mentioned shall be proceeded against by the public prosecutor and tried by the Court of Assize.

The discussion of religious matters shall be entirely free.

3. The Italian government grants to the Supreme Pontiff, within the kingdom, sovereign honors, and guarantees to him the pre-eminence customarily accorded to him by Catholic sovereigns.

He may maintain the usual number of guards for his person and for the custody of the palaces . . . .

4. An annual income of 3,225,000 lire is reserved for the Holy See.

With this sum, equal to that of the Roman budget for "Holy Apostolic Palaces, Sacred College, Ecclesiastical Congregations, Secretary of State, and Diplomatic Corps abroad," it is intended to provide for the Supreme Pontiff and for the various ecclesiastical needs of the Holy See, for the ordinary and extraordinary maintenance and custody of the apostolic palaces and their annexes, for the compensation and pensions of the guards . . . and of the attachés of the pontifical court, and for casual expenses as well as for the regular maintenance and custody of the museums and library attached to the apostolic palaces, and for the compensation and pensions of their employees.

This dotation [endowment] shall be entered in the great book of the public debt as a perpetual and inalienable income in the name of the Holy See, and during the vacancy of the See, it shall continue to be paid . . . .

It shall remain free from every form of state, provincial, or communal taxation or other burden, and shall not be diminished even in case the Italian government should later decide to assume the expenses of the museums and of the library.

5. Besides the dotation . . . the Supreme Pontiff shall have the use of the apostolic Vatican and Lateran palaces with all buildings, gardens, and lands apper-taining thereto, and also the villa of Castel Gandolfo with all its appurtenances.

6. During the vacancy of the pontifical chair no judicial or political authority shall for any reason hinder or limit the personal liberty of cardinals.

The government shall see to it that assemblies of conclave and ecumenical councils are not disturbed by external violence.

7. No public official or agent of the public force in the performance of the duties of his office, shall enter the places or palaces which are the permanent or temporary residence of the Supreme Pontiff, or during the sessions of the ecumenical council or conclave, without the authorization of the pope, conclave, or council.

8. Papers, documents, books, or registers deposited in pontifical offices or congregations, invested with a purely spiritual character, shall be free from the legal processes of visit, search, or sequestration.

9. The Supreme Pontiff shall be entirely free to fulfil all the functions of his spiritual ministry, and to this end may affix to the doors of basilicas and churches of Rome notices relating to such ministry.

10. Ecclesiastics at Rome who officially take part in the promulgation of acts pertaining to the spiritual ministry of the Holy See shall not on this account be subjected to any examination, investigation, or control by the civil authorities.

Every foreigner invested with ecclesiastical office at Rome shall enjoy all the privileges and immunities of Italian citizens . . . .

11. Envoys of foreign governments to the Holy See shall be entitled within the kingdom to all the prerogatives and immunities accorded to other diplomatic agents, according to the usages of international law.

12. The Supreme Pontiff corresponds freely with the episcopacy and with the whole Catholic world, without any interference from the Italian government.

To this end he shall have the right to establish his own postal and telegraph offices at the Vatican or any of his other residences, served by employees chosen by himself.

The pontifical post-office may transmit sealed packages of correspondence directly to foreign offices, or may send them through the Italian offices. In either case transmission of dispatches or correspondence bearing the papal stamp shall be made free of charge within Italian territory.

Couriers sent out in the name of the Supreme Pontiff are, within the kingdom, placed on an equal footing with couriers of foreign governments.

Telegraphic connections between the pontifical telegraph system and that of the state shall be made at the expense of the state.

Telegrams sent to the state offices with pontifical authentication shall be received and transmitted within the kingdom in the same manner as telegrams of state, and without charge. . . .

13. Within the city of Rome and within the six subsidiary sees, the seminaries, academies, colleges, and other Catholic institutions founded for the education and training of ecclesiastics shall continue under the sole control of the Holy See, without any interference from the educational authorities of the state.

Title II. Relation of the State to the Church

14. Every special restriction upon the exercise of the right of members of the Catholic clergy to assemble is abolished.

15. The government renounces the right to an apostolic legation in Sicily, and to the appointment or nomination to the major benefices throughout the kingdom.

Bishops shall not be required to swear fidelity to the King.

Major and minor benefices may be conferred only upon Italian citizens, except in the city of Rome and in the subsidiary sees.

Nothing is changed with respect to the collation to benefices of royal patronage.

16. The *exequatur* and *placet regio* and all other forms of government authorization for the publication or execution of ecclesiastical acts are abolished.

But until otherwise provided by a special law mentioned in Art. 18, such *exequatur* and *placet regio* shall be required for acts disposing of ecclesiastical property and for appointments to major and minor benefices, except those in the city of Rome and in the subsidiary sees.

The provisions of the civil law relating to the creation and management of ecclesiastical institutions, and to the sale of their property, remain unchanged.

17. In matters of spiritual discipline there shall be no appeal from decisions of ecclesiastical authorities, nor shall such decisions be recognized or executed by the civil authorities.

The determination of the legal effects of such decisions and of other acts of the ecclesiastical authority shall belong to the civil authorities.

If, however, such acts are contrary to the laws of the state or opposed to public order, or encroach upon the rights of individuals, they shall be of no effect and shall be subject to the criminal laws, if they constitute offenses.

18. A future law shall provide for the reorganization, preservation and administration of the ecclesiastical property within the state. . . .

Source: Walter Fairleigh Dodd, *Modern Constitutions* (Chicago, 1909), II, 16–21. Italian text in *Gazzetta Ufficiale del Regno d'Italia*, No. 134, May 15, 1871.

SUGGESTIONS FOR BACKGROUND AND REFERENCE

Cambridge Modern History (New York, 1903–1912), XI, 529–544.

E. E. Y. Hales, *Pio Nono. A Study in European Politics and Religion in the Nineteenth Century* (New York, 1954), pp. 313–322.

S. W. Halperin, *Italy and the Vatican at War* (Chicago, 1939).

A. Jemolo, *Church and State in Italy 1850–1950* (Oxford, 1960), pp. 28–52.

K. S. Latourette, *Christianity in a Revolutionary Age* (New York, 1958–1962), I, 270–274.

G. Mollat, *La question romaine de Pie VI à Pie XI* (Paris, 1932), pp. 282–367.

L. P. Wallace, *The Papacy and European Diplomacy 1869–1878* (Chapel Hill, N.C., 1948).

103 *Ubi Nos* (Extracts)

May 15, 1871

As in Cavour's secret 1861 negotiations, the papacy rejected statutory guarantees as an adequate substitute for the freedom and security conferred by the lost temporal power. Thus the Roman Question was to trouble relations between Italy and the papacy for almost another six decades.

[The Piedmont government] has promoted certain empty immunities and privileges, commonly called "guarantees." . . . We have already delivered Our judgment on these immunities and provisions, and stigmatized their absurdity . . . .

But it is characteristic of the Piedmont Government to unite continuous, base pretense with shameless contempt for our papal rank and authority. . . . Accordingly, it has not ceased in the least to press on with the serious discussion and examination of these "guarantees" before the highest bodies in the kingdom, despite Our expressed judgment on these provisions. . . . It is unbelievable that they could have been produced here in Italy, whose chief glory has always been in the practice of the Catholic religion and in the Apostolic See.

* * *

Therefore We can submit to no agreement which would in any way destroy or diminish Our rights, which are the rights of God and of the Apostolic See. . . . Similarly, We never can and never shall allow or accept those "guarantees" devised by the Piedmont Government, whatever their motive. . . . These are offered under the guise of defending Our holy power and liberty in compensation for the civil rule they stripped Us of. But divine providence has willed this civil rule to be protection and strength for the Apostolic See; furthermore, legitimate and indisputable titles, as well as Our having possessed it for more than eleven centuries, confirm Our right to it. For if the Roman Pontiff were subject to the sway of another ruler, but no longer possessed civil power, neither his position nor the acts of the Apostolic ministry would be exempt from the authority of the other ruler. This ruler could be either a heretic or a persecutor of the Church or constantly at war with other rulers.

Indeed, is not this concession of "guarantees" itself the clearest proof that laws are being imposed on Us? God has given Us the authority of making laws in regard to the religious and moral order. . . . Will their observance and execution be right only because they are commanded and established by the will of lay powers? We, as the representative of blessed Peter, have received directly from God Himself all the prerogatives and all rights of authority which are necessary for ruling the universal Church . . . .

* * *

The rulers of the earth do not want the usurpation which We are suffering to be established and to thrive to the ruin of all authority and order. May God unite all rulers in agreement of mind and will. By removing all discord . . . and rejecting the ruinous counsels of the sects, may these rulers join in a common effort to have the rights of the Holy See restored. Then tranquillity will once again be restored to civil society.

From *The Papal Encyclicals,* ed. Claudia Carlen, I.H.M., 5 vols. (1981); reprint, Ann Arbor, Mich.: Pierian Press, 1990), © Claudia Carlen, used with permission.

Source: Claudia Carlen (ed.), *The Papal Encyclicals 1740–1878* (Ann Arbor, Mich., 1990), pp. 400–402. Latin text in *Acta Sanctae Sedis,* VI, 257–263.

SUGGESTIONS FOR BACKGROUND AND REFERENCE

References for Document 102.

✦ ✦ ✦

104   *Board of Education* v. *Minor* (Extracts)

December Term, 1872

Reflecting growing attack on the widespread practice of scripture reading in public schools, the Cincinnati Board of Education passed resolutions prohibiting religious instruction and reading of religious books, including the Bible, in the schools of the city. Opponents, decrying the impending "atheism" of the schools, asserted that Bible reading had been the practice in Cincinnati since the 1820s and that it was done without comment and from the version preferred by parents. They brought the case before the Superior Court of Cincinnati, which granted a perpetual injunction against the enforcement of the resolutions. Petition in error to the Supreme Court of Ohio resulted in a unanimous decision, written by Justice John Welch (1805–1891), reversing the Superior Court and upholding the Board of Education.

. . . We are not called upon as a court, nor are we authorized to say whether the Christian religion is the best and only true religion. There is no question before us of the wisdom or unwisdom of having "the Bible in the schools," or of withdrawing it therefrom. Nor can we . . . undertake to decide what religious doctrines, if any, ought to be taught, or where, when, by whom, or to whom it would be best they should be taught. These are questions which belong to the people and to other departments of the government.

The case . . . presents merely or mainly a question of the courts' rightful authority to interfere in the management and control of the public schools of the state. In other words, . . . has the court jurisdiction to interfere in the management and control of such schools, to the extent of enforcing religious instructions, or the reading of religious books therein . . . ?

* * *

Counsel for the defendants in error . . . claim to derive this authority of the court from the last clause in section 7, article 1, in connection with section 2, article 6, of the state constitution, which are as follows:

Sec. 7. ". . . Religion, morality, and knowledge . . . being essential to good government, it shall be the duty of the general assembly to pass suitable laws to protect every religious denomination in the peaceable enjoyment of its own mode of public worship, and to encourage schools and the means of instruction."

"Sec. 2. The general assembly shall make such provisions, by taxation or otherwise, as, with the income arising from the school trust fund, will secure a thorough and efficient system of common schools throughout the state; but no religious or other sect or sects shall ever have any exclusive right to, or control of, any part of the school funds of this state."

If we rightly comprehend the arguments, it is claimed on behalf of the defendants in error, (1) that these provisions in the constitution require and enjoin religious instructions, or the teaching of religious doctrines in the public schools, irrespective of the wishes of the people concerned therein; and (2) that this requirement and injunction rests, not upon the legislature alone, but, in the absence of legislative action for that purpose, is a law of the state, *proprio vigore,* binding upon the courts and people.

. . . the legislature have never passed any law enjoining or requiring religious instructions in the public schools, or giving the courts power in any manner . . . to direct or determine the particular branches of learning to be taught therein, or to enforce instructions in any particular branch or branches. The extent of legislative action . . . has been to establish and maintain a general system of common schools for the state, and to place their management and control exclusively in the hands of directors, trustees, or boards of education, other than the courts of the state . . . . While these laws do refer to other branches of learning in the schools, they nowhere enjoin or speak of religious instruction therein. They speak of the "morals" and "good conduct" of the pupils, and of the "moral character" of the teachers, but they nowhere require the pupil to be taught religion, or the teacher to be religious . . . .

* * *

There is a total absence, therefore, of any legislation looking to the enforcement of religious instruction, or the reading of religious books in the public schools; and we are brought back to the question, what is the true meaning and effect of these constitutional provisions . . . ? Do they enjoin religious instructions . . . ? and does this injunction bind the courts, in the absence of legislation? We are unanimous in the opinion that both these questions must be answered in the negative.

The clause relied upon as enjoining religious instructions . . . declares three things to be essential to good government, and for that reason requires the legislature to encourage "means of instruction" generally, and among other means, that of "schools." The three things . . . are "religion, morality, and knowledge." These three words stand in the same category, and in the same relation to the context; and if one of them is used in its generic or unlimited sense, so are all three. . . . The meaning is, that *true* religion, *true* morality, and *true* knowledge shall be promoted, by encouraging schools and means of instruction. The last named of these three words, "knowledge," comprehends in itself all that is comprehended in the other two words . . . . Nothing is enjoined, therefore, but the encouragement of means of instruction in general "knowledge"—the knowledge of *truth.* The fair interpretation seems to be, that true "religion" and "morality" are aided and promoted by the increase and diffusion of "knowledge" on the theory that "knowledge is the hand-maid of virtue," and that all three—religion, morality, and knowledge—are essential to good government. But there is no direction given as to what system of general knowledge, or of religion or morals, shall be taught. . . . To enjoin "instructions" in "knowledge," the knowledge of *truth* in all its branches—religious, moral, or otherwise—is one thing; and to declare *what* is truth—truth in any one or in all departments of human knowledge—and to enjoin the teaching of *that,* as truth, is quite another thing. To enjoin the latter, would be to declare that human knowledge had reached its ultimatum. This the constitution does not undertake to do, neither as to "religion," "morality," nor any other branch or department of human "knowledge." . . .

* * *

Equally plain is it to us, that if the supposed injunction to provide for religious instructions is to be found in the clauses of the constitution in question, it is one that rests exclusively upon the legislature. In both sections the duty is expressly imposed upon the "general assembly." The injunction is, to "pass suitable laws." Until these "laws" are passed, it is quite clear to us that the courts have no power to interpose. . . .

This opinion might well end here. Were the subject of controversy any other branch of instructions in the schools than religion, I have no doubt it might safely end here . . . . The case is of peculiar importance, however, in the fact that it touches our religious convictions . . . and threatens to disturb the harmonious working of the state government, and particularly of the public schools . . . . I deem it not improper, therefore, to consider briefly some of the points . . . argued by counsel, although really lying outside of the case proper, or only bearing on it remotely.

The real claim here is, that by "religion," in this clause . . . is meant "Christian religion," and that by "religious denomination" . . . is meant "Christian denomination." If this claim is well founded, I do not see how we can consistently avoid giving a like meaning to . . . "worship," "religious society," "sect," "conscience," "religious belief," throughout the entire section. To do so . . . would be to withdraw from every person not of Christian belief the guaranties therein vouchsafed, and to withdraw many of them from Christians themselves. In that sense the clause . . . would read . . . :

"Christianity, morality, and knowledge, however, being essential to good government, it shall be the duty of the general assembly to pass suitable laws to protect every *Christian* denomination in the peaceable enjoyment of its own mode of public worship, and to encourage schools and the means of instruction."

* * *

We are told that this word "religion" must mean "Christian religion" because "Christianity is a part of the common law of this country," lying behind and above its constitutions. Those who make this assertion can hardly be serious . . . . If Christianity is a *law* of the state, like every other law, it must have a *sanction.*

Adequate penalties must be provided to enforce obedience to all its requirements and precepts. No one seriously contends for any such doctrine . . . . The only foundation—rather, the only excuse—for the proposition, that Christianity is part of the law of this country, is the fact that it is a Christian country, and that its constitutions and laws are made by a Christian people. And is not the very fact that those laws do *not* attempt to *enforce* Christianity . . . itself a strong evidence that they *are* the laws of a Christian people, and that their religion is the best and purest of religions? . . . True Christianity asks no aid from the sword of civil authority. . . .

Legal Christianity is a solecism, a contradiction of terms. When Christianity asks the aid of government beyond mere *impartial protection,* it denies itself. Its laws are divine, and not human. Its essential interests lie beyond the reach and range of human governments. United with government, religion never rises above the merest superstition; united with religion, government never rises above the merest despotism; and all history shows us that the more widely and completely they are separated, the better it is for both . . . .

Source: Board of Education of the City of Cincinnati v. *John D. Minor et al.,* 23 Oh. St. 211.

SUGGESTIONS FOR BACKGROUND AND REFERENCE

H. M. Helfman, "The Cincinnati 'Bible War,' 1869–1870," *Ohio State Archaeological and Historical Quarterly,* Vol. IX, No. 4 (October 1951), pp. 369–386.

R. Michaelsen, "Common School, Common Religion? A Case Study in Church-State Relations, Cincinnati, 1869–1870," *Church History,* Vol. XXXVIII, No. 2 (June 1969), pp. 201–217.

L. Pfeffer, *Church, State, and Freedom* (Boston, 1953), pp. 374–382.

A. P. Stokes, *Church and State in the United States* (New York, 1950), II, 549–566.

✦ ✦ ✦ The German Kulturkampf

105 Pulpit Law

December 10, 1871

Although Bismarck (1815–1898) was not fully committed to the Kulturkampf until 1873, the conflict was foreshadowed by measures favoring Old Catholics and abolishing the Catholic section of the Worship Ministry in 1871. At the end of the year the famous Pulpit Law (*Kanzelparagraf*) was incorporated into the criminal code of the German Empire.

A minister of religion or any other spiritual person who shall in the exercise of his office publicly, and before a numerous assemblage of persons, or in a church or other place of religious worship, in presence of many people, treat of matters of state in a manner calculated to bring about a breach of the peace, shall be punished by imprisonment up to two years.

Source: Macmillan's Magazine, Vol. XXXI (1874–1875), p. 267. German text in Johannes B. Kissling, *Geschichte des Kulturkampfes im Deutschen Reiche* (Freiburg, Germany, 1913), II, 460.

SUGGESTIONS FOR BACKGROUND AND REFERENCE

M. Anderson, *Windthorst: a Political Biography* (Oxford, 1981), pp. 130–200.
R. Aubert et al., *The Church in the Industrial Age* (New York, 1981), pp. 26–45.
Cambridge Modern History (New York, 1903–1912), XII, 134–151.
G. Craig, *Germany 1866–1945* (New York, 1978), pp. 69–78.
E. Foerster, *Adalbert Falk, Sein Leben und Wirken als Preussischer Kultusminister* (Gotha, Germany, 1927).
J. Rovan, *Le catholicisme politique en Allemagne* (Paris, 1956), pp. 79–136.
E. Schmidt-Volkmar, *Der Kulturkampf in Deutschland 1871–1890* (Göttingen, Germany, 1962).
L. P. Wallace, *The Papacy and European Diplomacy 1869–1878* (Chapel Hill, N.C., 1948), pp. 187–301.

106   Anti-Jesuit Law

July 4, 1872

A more serious stage of the Kulturkampf was introduced in 1872 with a law governing state inspection of religious schools, the rupture of diplomatic relations with the Vatican, and this measure against the Jesuits. Bismarck was led to this contest by concern for the newly won unity of the Reich and by deep distrust of Catholic domestic and international politics. He doubted Catholic loyalty to the predominantly Protestant empire and remained disturbed by Catholic Bavaria's leadership of particularist forces. The Catholic Center party, second largest in the Reichstag, with its confessional basis and resistance to strong imperial government, aroused his hostility. He suspected that papal diplomacy and Catholic agitation over the Roman Question in the early 1870s were directed toward the reversal of Italian *and* German unification. Exploiting liberal reaction against the Vatican Council, Bismarck won passage for this measure against the Jesuits, reputedly pro-Polish and most ultramontane of orders. The law, passed by the Reichstag, applied to the entire Empire, but Bismarck's subsequent legislation was restricted to Prussia (though similar conflict occurred in other German states).

1. The Order of the Society of Jesus and orders and congregations related to it are excluded from the territory of the German Empire.

They are forbidden to erect establishments on the said territory. Existing establishments must be disbanded within a period to be determined upon by the Bundesrat, which period shall not exceed six months.

2. Members of the Order of the Society of Jesus or of orders and congregations related to it may, if foreigners, be expelled from German territory. If they are Germans, they may be assigned to a specified locality, or forbidden to inhabit a specified locality.

3. Directions and regulations necessary to carry out this law are left to the Bundesrat.

Source: Johannes B. Kissling, *Geschichte des Kulturkampfes im Deutschen Reiche* (Freiburg, Germany, 1913), II, 461.

SUGGESTIONS FOR BACKGROUND AND REFERENCE

References for Document 105.

107   Amendments to the Prussian Constitution

April 5, 1873

A barrier to Bismarck's proposed ecclesiastical legislation was the Prussian Constitution of 1850, Articles 15 and 18. Accordingly, the chancellor secured amendments that left the constitution in a form that would support the intended May Laws. (In this text the additions have been placed in italics.)

15. The Evangelical and the Roman Catholic Church, as well as every other religious society, orders and administers its affairs independently, *but remains subject to the laws of the state, and to the supervision of the state as defined by law.*

Under the same conditions, every religious society remains in the possession and enjoyment of the establishments required for its public worship, for education, and for charity, and of its endowments and funds.

* * *

18. The right of nomination, presentation, election, or confirmation in connection with the filling up of ecclesiastical offices, in so far as it appertains to the state as such, and does not rest upon patronage or special legal titles, is abolished.

The above, however, does not apply to the appointments of military chaplains or of spiritual persons in public institutions.

For the rest, the competence of the state in regard to the preparatory education, to the appointment and to the dismissal of clerical persons, and servants of religion, will be determined by laws which will likewise fix the limits of ecclesiastical discipline.

Source: Macmillan's Magazine, Vol. XXXI (1874–1875), p. 270. German text in Johannes B. Kissling, *Geschichte des Kulturkampfes im Deutschen Reiche* (Freiburg, Germany, 1913), II, 462.

SUGGESTIONS FOR BACKGROUND AND REFERENCE

References for Document 105.

108   May Laws (Extracts)

May 1873

Fruitless efforts to obtain concessions from Rome moved Bismarck to increase statutory curbs on Catholicism. Adalbert Falk (1827–1900), appointed Prussian minister of worship in 1872, was entrusted with drawing up the legislative program, which passed the Landtag in May 1873. There were four principal measures. One governed clerical education and appointment. Others provided for appeal from ecclesiastical discipline to a state court, limited discipline to strictly religious penalties, and established means for legal withdrawal from church. Greatest Catholic objection was made to government intrusion into the area of clerical appointments and discipline. The program was further strengthened by harsher measures in 1874 and 1875, of which the most important provided for civil marriage, severe punishment for refractory clergy, punitive suspension of state grants, and dissolution of religious orders. Resistance and disobedience were widespread, resulting in imprisonment and exile of bishops and priests, while the Center party increased its representation. Reproduced below are portions of (A) the law on education and appointment of clergy, and (B) the law on ecclesiastical discipline.

A. From the Law on Education and Appointment of Clergy, May 11, 1873:

I. General Provisions

1. Ecclesiastical office in any of the Christian churches may be conferred only on a German who has completed his academic preparation in accordance with provisions of the present law, and to whose appointment the government has raised no objection.

　2. The provisions of [article] 1 are applicable, whether the office is conferred on a permanent or revocable basis, and even when the appointment is simply that of a deputy or assistant. If there is danger in delay, an appointment of deputy or assistant may be made provisionally, reserving the right of the government to object.

　3. The provisions of [article] 1 are applicable, without prejudice to [article] 26,

when a clergyman already in office ([article] 2) is invested with another ecclesiastical office or when a revocable appointment is made into a permanent appointment.

II. Preparation for Ecclesiastical Offices

4. To be invested with an ecclesiastical office it is necessary to have taken a dismissory examination in a German *gymnasium*, completed three years of theological studies in a German state university, and passed a state academic examination.

5. The minister of ecclesiastical affairs is authorized to waive partially the required three years of studies in a German state university in consideration of prior university studies other than theology or of studies in a foreign state university or of other special studies.

6. Theological studies may be pursued in church seminaries in Prussia in existence at the time of promulgation of the present law and maintained for academic preparation of theologians, when the minister of ecclesiastical affairs authorizes the substitution of these studies for university studies.

However, this provision is applicable only to seminaries of places where no theological faculty exists, and it may be invoked only by students of the diocese in which the seminary is located.

The minister may not withhold the authorization . . . when the organization of the institution agrees with the provisions of the present law, and he has approved its plan of studies.

7. During the prescribed university studies students may not belong to an ecclesiastical seminary.

8. The state examination shall take place at the end of theological studies. Only those who have entirely satisfied the provisions of the present law concerning *gymnasium* and theological studies may be admitted to it.

The examination shall be public, and shall center on determining whether the candidate has attained the general academic knowledge required by his profession, especially in the fields of philosophy, history, and German literature.

The minister . . . shall regulate the details of the administration of this examination.

9. All ecclesiastical institutions maintained for the preparation of clergy (boys' seminaries, clerical seminaries, seminaries for preachers and priests, *Konvikte*,[1] etc.) are under state supervision.

Internal organization and regulation of discipline in these institutions and the plan of studies in boys' seminaries and *Konvikte* for youth, as well as in seminaries which have secured the authorization required in [article] 6, must be submitted to the governor [*Oberpräsident*] of the province by the directors of these institutions.

The institutions are subject to inspection by commissioners appointed by the governor.

10. Such institutions . . . may have as teachers or proctors only Germans to whose appointment the government has raised no objection and who have proved their academic competence according to the provisions of [article] 11.

The provisions of [articles] 2 and 3 are equally applicable.

---

1. *Konvikte:* Roman Catholic theological students at university (and Catholic boys at *gymnasium*) were often collected into these residential seminaries and colleges.

11. To be appointed to a boys' seminary or a *Konvikt* for youth, it is necessary to meet the conditions prescribed for corresponding appointments in a Prussian *gymnasium*. To be appointed to an institution of academic theological studies, it is necessary to meet the conditions required for teaching in a Prussian state university . . . .

* * *

13. For failure to observe the provisions contained in [articles] 9 to 11 or the regulations of public authorities, the minister . . . may withhold, until compliance, the state grants to the institution or he may close the institution.

* * *

14. It is henceforth forbidden to open boys' seminaries and *Konvikte* for youth ([article] 9) and to receive new pupils in existing institutions.

For admitting new pupils institutions may be closed by the minister . . . .

III. Appointment of Clergy

15. Ecclesiastical superiors must provide the governor with the name of the candidate . . . and the title of the office.

The same procedure is required for the transfer of a clergyman to another office . . . .

Within thirty days following this designation objection may be made to the appointment.

The right to object is vested in the governor.

16. Objection is valid: 1) when the candidate does not meet the required legal conditions . . . ; 2) when the candidate has been condemned . . . for a crime or misdemeanor punished by the Penal Code with imprisonment or loss of civil rights or loss of the right to fulfill public functions; 3) when there is reason to believe that the candidate will not observe the laws of the state or the ordinances of authority . . . or that he will disturb public peace.

The facts supporting the objection must be declared.

Appeal against the objection may be lodged with the Royal Court for Ecclesiastical Affairs within thirty days . . . .

The [appeal] judgment shall be final.

* * *

IV. Final Provisions

22. An ecclesiastical superior who confers an ecclesiastical office or approves an appointment to this office contrary to [articles] 1 to 3 shall be punished by a fine of 200 to 1000 thalers.

* * *

23. Whoever undertakes ecclesiastical functions in an office which has been conferred on him contrary to the provisions of [articles] 1 to 3 shall be punished by a fine not to exceed 100 thalers.

* * *

24. Whoever undertakes ecclesiastical functions after a legal judgment has nullified his capacity to fulfill an ecclesiastical office ([article] 21) shall be punished by a fine not to exceed 1000 thalers.

V. Transitional and Final Provisions

* * *

26. Provisions of the present law concerning proof of academic preparation and fitness are not applicable to persons who, before promulgation of the law, were provided with ecclesiastical office or have already qualified for filling such office.

Moreover, the minister . . . may exempt wholly or partly from the proof of preparation required by the law persons who before its promulgation were well advanced in preparing themselves for ecclesiastical office.

The minister . . . may also excuse foreigners from the conditions required by [article] 4 of the present law.

B. From the Law on Ecclesiastical Discipline, May 12, 1873:

I. General Provisions

1. The power of ecclesiastical discipline over church functionaries may be exercised only by German ecclesiastical authorities.

2. Ecclesiastical disciplinary penalties which infringe upon liberty or property may be imposed only after hearing the accused.

Removal from office (recall, replacement, suspension, compulsory retirement, etc.) must be preceded by regular legal procedure.

In every case the decision must be justified in writing.

3. Corporal punishments are not permitted as ecclesiastical penalties or means of discipline.

4. Fines may not exceed 30 thalers, or if the monthly stipend of the office is higher, the amount of that stipend.

5. The penalty of loss of liberty ([article] 2) may consist only in relegation to a place of discipline [*Demeritenanstalt*].

The banishment may not exceed three months and the execution of the penalty may neither begin nor continue against the will of the condemned.

Banishment to a foreign disciplinary house is prohibited.

6. The disciplinary houses are subject to state supervision. Their internal organization must be submitted for the approval of the governor of the province.

The governor has the right to order visitation of the disciplinary house and to be informed of its organization.

Within 24 hours the director of the institution must inform the governor of the admission of those under discipline and of the authority which prescribed the punishment. The director must keep a register of all under discipline, containing their names, the punishments ordered for them, and the time of their admission and departure. At the end of each year the register shall be sent to the governor.

7. Every ecclesiastical disciplinary decision which prescribes a fine of more

than 20 thalers, relegation to a disciplinary house for more than 14 days, or removal from office ([article] 2) must be communicated to the governor at the same time as to the person concerned.

The communication must contain reasons for the decision.

8. The governor may secure observance of the provisions of [articles] 5 to 7 . . . by fines which may not exceed 1000 thalers.

He may repeat the warning and the imposition of the penalty until the law is observed.

Moreover, he may close the disciplinary house.

9. Execution of ecclesiastical disciplinary decisions by means of state action may take place only when the governor has ratified them after examination.

II. Appeal to the State

10. Appeal to state authority ([article] 32) against decisions of ecclesiastical authorities . . . is permitted: 1) when the decision comes from an authority unrecognized by state laws; 2) when the provisions of [article] 2 have not been observed; 3) when the penalty is illegal; 4) when the penalty is imposed: a) because of an act or omission in compliance with state laws or regulations of authorities . . . ; b) because of the exercise or nonexercise of a public right of election and vote; c) because of exercise of appeal to state authority ([article] 32) on the basis of the present law.

* * *

III. Intervention of the State Without Appeal [Being Made to It]

24. Clergy who violate state laws pertaining to their office or to the performance of their ecclesiastical duties or the measures taken by authority . . . so flagrantly that their retention in office is incompatible with public order may, on the proposal of state authority, be relieved of their office by judicial decision.

Suspension from office involves legal incapacity to exercise office, loss of salary, and vacancy of office.

* * *

IV. Royal Court for Ecclesiastical Affairs

32. To judge matters covered in [articles] 10 to 23 and 24 to 30 . . . an authority called "The Royal Court for Ecclesiastical Affairs" shall be established in Berlin.

33. The court shall be composed of eleven members. The president and at least five of the other members must be official state judges. Oral discussion and judgment in each case shall take place with a quorum of seven members. The president and at least three of the assessors must belong to the judicial order.

* * *

34. The members of the court shall be appointed by the king on nomination of the ministry of state. Those who are already state officials shall be appointed for the duration of their chief post, and the other members for life.

* * *

35. The court judges in final resort and without appeal.

Source: Johannes B. Kissling, *Geschichte des Kulturkampfes im Deutschen Reiche* (Freiburg, Germany, 1913), II, 462–465, 466–467, 467–469, 471, 472.

SUGGESTIONS FOR BACKGROUND AND REFERENCE

References for Document 105.

✦ ✦ ✦

109   Public Worship Regulation Act (Extracts)

August 7, 1874

The development of ritual, a consequence of the Oxford Movement, was especially distasteful to many Victorians. The spread of ritual practices in the 1860s was rapid, and suits brought against innovating clergymen to compel observance of the accustomed worship were not markedly successful. (Ritualists contended that they were restoring lawful practices that mistakenly had been allowed to fall into disuse.) Anticipating parliament's intervention, Archbishop A. C. Tait (1811–1882), after consulting with the bishops, drew up a bill, which passed in a form less acceptable to the Church of England and was embarrassingly described by Disraeli as "a bill to put down ritualism." Prosecutions under the act resulted in several celebrated cases involving imprisonment of clergy, bringing the act into disrepute. Many bishops vetoed prosecution (being authorized to do so by the act), and many clergy believed the measure to be irritatingly Erastian. In the 1880s cases before the court set up by the act virtually disappeared.

7. The Archbishop of Canterbury and the Archbishop of York may, but subject to the approval of Her Majesty to be signified under Her Sign Manual, appoint from time to time a barrister-at-law who has been in actual practice for ten years, or a person who has been a judge of one of the Superior Courts of Law or Equity . . . to be . . . a judge of the Provincial Courts of Canterbury and York, hereinafter called the judge.

If the said archbishops shall not, within six months after the passing of this Act, or within six months after the occurrence of any vacancy in the office, appoint the said judge, Her Majesty may by Letters Patent appoint some person, qualified as aforesaid, to be such judge.

* * *

Every person appointed to be a judge under this Act shall be a member of the Church of England, and shall, before entering on his office, sign the declaration in

Schedule (A.) to this Act; and if at any time any such judge shall cease to be a member of the Church, his office shall thereupon be vacant.[1]

This section shall come into operation immediately after the passing of this Act.

8. If the archdeacon of the archdeaconry, or a churchwarden of the parish, or any three parishioners of the parish, within which archdeaconry or parish any church or burial ground is situate, . . . or in case of cathedral or collegiate churches, any three inhabitants of the diocese, being male persons of full age, who have signed and transmitted to the bishop under their hands the declaration contained in Schedule (A.) under this Act, and who have, and for one year . . . have had, their usual place of abode in the diocese . . . shall be of opinion,—

(1.) That in such church any alteration in or addition to the fabric, ornaments, or furniture thereof has been made without lawful authority, or that any decoration forbidden by law has been introduced into such church; or,

(2.) That the incumbent has within the preceding twelve months used or permitted to be used in such church or burial ground any unlawful ornament of the minister of the church, or neglected to use any prescribed ornament or vesture; or,

(3.) That the incumbent has within the preceding twelve months failed to observe, or to cause to be observed, the directions contained in the Book of Common Prayer relating to the performance, in such church or burial ground, of the services, rites, and ceremonies ordered by the said book, or has made or permitted to be made any unlawful addition to, alteration of, or omission from such services, rites, and ceremonies,—

such archdeacon, churchwarden, parishioners, or such inhabitants of the diocese, may . . . represent the same to the bishop, by sending to the bishop a form, as contained in Schedule (B.) to this Act, duly filled up and signed, and accompanied by a declaration . . . affirming the truth of the statements . . . : Provided, that no proceedings shall be taken under this Act as regards any alteration in or addition to the fabric of a church if such alteration . . . has been completed five years before the commencement of such proceedings.

9. Unless the bishop shall be of opinion, after considering the whole circumstances of the case, that proceedings should not be taken on the representation, (in which case he shall state in writing the reason for his opinion, and such statement shall be deposited in the registry of the diocese, and a copy thereof shall forthwith be transmitted to the person . . . who shall have made the representation, and to the person complained of,) he shall within twenty-one days . . . transmit a copy thereof to the person complained of, and shall require such person, and also the person making the representation, to state in writing within twenty-one days whether they are willing to submit to the directions of the bishop touching the matter . . . , without appeal; and, if they shall state their willingness . . . the bishop shall forthwith proceed to hear the matter . . . and shall pronounce such judgment and issue such monition (if any) as he may think proper, and no appeal shall lie from such judgment or monition. . . .

1. Schedule (A.) contained a formal declaration of membership in the Church of England.

If the person making the representation and the person complained of shall not, within the time aforesaid, state their willingness to submit to the directions of the bishop, the bishop shall forthwith transmit the representation . . . to the archbishop . . . [who] shall forthwith require the judge to hear the matter . . . within the diocese or province, or in London or Westminster.

The judge shall give not less than twenty-eight days notice to the parties of the time and place at which he will proceed to hear the matter . . . .

The person complained of shall within twenty-one days after such notice transmit to the judge, and to the person making the representation, a succinct answer . . . , and in default of such answer he shall be deemed to have denied the truth or relevancy of the representation.

In all proceedings . . . evidence shall be given vivâ voce, in open court, and upon oath; and the judge may . . . require and enforce the attendance of witnesses, and the production of evidences, books, or writings . . . .

Upon every judgment of the judge, or monition . . . , an appeal shall lie . . . to Her Majesty in Council. . . .

* * *

13. Obedience by an incumbent to a monition or order of the bishop or judge . . . shall be enforced, if necessary, . . . by an order inhibiting the incumbent from performing any service of the church, or otherwise exercising the cure of souls within the diocese for a term not exceeding three months; provided that at the expiration of such term the inhibition shall not be relaxed until the incumbent shall, by writing . . . , undertake to pay due obedience to such monition . . . ; provided that if such inhibition shall remain in force for more than three years . . . , or if a second inhibition in regard to the same monition shall be issued within three years from the relaxation of an inhibition, any benefice . . . held by the incumbent in the parish . . . shall thereupon become void, unless the bishop shall, for some special reason stated by him in writing, postpone for a period not exceeding three months the date at which . . . such benefice . . . shall become void . . . ; and . . . it shall be lawful for the patron of such benefice . . . to appoint . . . to the same as if such incumbent were dead . . . .

* * *

17. The duties appointed . . . to be performed by the bishop . . . shall in the case of a cathedral or collegiate church be performed by the visitor thereof.

If any complaint shall be made concerning the fabric, ornaments, furniture, or decorations of a cathedral or collegiate church, the person complained of shall be the dean and chapter, . . . and . . . the visitor, or the judge . . . shall have power to carry into effect the directions contained in such monition, and, if necessary, to raise the sum required to defray the cost thereof by sequestration of the profits of the preferments held in such cathedral or collegiate church by the dean and chapter thereof.

If any complaint shall be made concerning the ornaments of the minister in a cathedral or collegiate church, or as to the observance therein of the directions contained in the Book of Common Prayer . . . , the person complained of shall be the clerk in holy orders alleged to have offended . . . ; and the visitor or the judge . . . shall have the same power as to inhibition, and the preferment held in such cathedral or collegiate church . . . shall be subject to the same conditions as to avoidance, notice, and lapse . . . as are contained in this Act concerning an incumbent to whom a monition has been issued . . . .

Source: 37 & 38 Vict., c. 85; *The Public General Statutes Passed in the Thirty-Seventh & Thirty-Eighth Years of the Reign of Her Majesty Queen Victoria, 1874* (London, 1874), pp. 419–426.

SUGGESTIONS FOR BACKGROUND AND REFERENCE

J. Bentley, *Ritualism and Politics in Victorian Britain* (Oxford, 1978).
S. C. Carpenter, *Church and People, 1789–1889* (London, 1933), pp. 212–250.
P. J. Marsh, *The Victorian Church in Decline: Archbishop Tait and the Church of England, 1868–1882* (London, 1969), pp. 111–241.

110 French School Laws (Extracts)

1880–1886

The political alignment of Catholics and royalists versus anticlericals and republicans led militant defenders of the Third Republic to advocate the destruction of clerical influence in education. Indicting Catholic religious instruction and teaching by Catholic orders, they pressed for a national educational system organized according to the Masonic formula, "*l'obligation, la gratuité, la laicité.*" In the 1880s under the leadership of such politicians as Charles de Freycinet, Jules Ferry, and Paul Bert, much of this program was accomplished. Catholic institutions of higher education were deprived of university status, state faculties of Catholic theology were suppressed, and episcopal influence in the administration of public education was removed. By executive order the Jesuits were expelled, and unauthorized religious orders, involving over five thousand religious, were suppressed. The establishment of a state *lycée* system for girls was intended to diminish the religious influence on women. Vigorous reforms were pressed in primary education, with provision for departmental normal schools, abrogation of the teaching nun's letter of obedience as an equivalent of the teaching certificate, and abolition of tuition in the state schools. Bert's controversial law of March 28, 1882, made primary education compulsory and substituted morals and civics for religion. In 1886 all remaining teachers in state schools belonging to Catholic religious orders were ordered replaced. Early in the program the policy was apparently approved by voters in the 1881 elections. Catholic response to the "school without God" was extensive construction of rival Catholic schools throughout France. Passages from four important pieces of the program are reproduced below.)

A. From the Law of March 18, 1880:

1. The examinations and practical tests which determine the granting of degrees may be submitted only to the State Faculties.

* * *

3. Matriculation in the State Faculties is free.

4. In no case may private institutions of higher education take the name of university.

Certificates of studies awarded by them to students may not have the names of baccalaureat, licentiate, or doctorate.

5. University titles or degrees may be attributed only to those who have obtained them by examination or regular competition before professors or juries of the State Faculty.

B. From the Decrees of March 29, 1880:

First Decree

A period of three months from the present decree is granted to the unauthorized company or association called "of Jesus" to dissolve . . . and to evacuate the establishments which it occupies in the territory of the Republic.

This period shall be extended until August 31, 1880 for establishments in which literary or scientific instruction is given . . . .

Second Decree

1. Within three months from the promulgation of the present decree every unauthorized congregation or community is required to take the measures specified below to obtain verification and approval of its laws and regulations and legal recognition for each of its establishments presently existing.

2. The request for authorization must be filed, within the period above indicated, with the general secretariat of the prefecture of each of the departments where the association maintains one or more establishments.

Acknowledgment will be given for it.

The request will be transmitted to the minister of interior and worship who will examine the matter.

* * *

6. The request for authorization should include identification of the superior or superiors, their place of residence, and proof that this residence is and will remain in France. It should indicate whether the association extends to foreign countries or is confined to the Republic.

7. The following must be attached to the request for authorization: (1) a list of all members of the association indicating the birthplace and nationality of each member; (2) an account of assets and debts as well as revenues and expenses of

the association and of each of its establishments; (3) a copy of its statutes and regulations.

8. The required copy of the regulations should display the approval of the bishops and of the dioceses where the association has establishments and include a clause that the congregation or community is subject in spiritual things to the ordinary's jurisdiction.

9. All congregations or communities which have not made request for authorization with supporting documents within the period specified above shall suffer the full force of the laws.

C. From the Law of March 28, 1882:

1. Primary education includes:

Morals and civics;
Reading and writing;
French and French literature . . . . [and so forth]

2. Public primary schools shall be dismissed one day per week in addition to Sunday in order to permit parents to provide for religious education for their children outside the school buildings, if they wish to do so.

Religious education is optional in private schools.

3. Provisions of Articles 18 and 44 of the Law of March 14, 1850 giving ministers of religion the privilege of inspection [*droit d'inspection, de surveillance et de direction*] in public and private primary schools and infant schools are abolished, together with Paragraph 2 of Article 31 of the same law which gives consistories the right of presentation for instructors belonging to non-Catholic faiths.

4. Primary instruction is compulsory for children of both sexes from six to thirteen years. It may be given in primary or secondary institutions of education, either in public or private schools or in families by the father himself or by any person whom he chooses.

D. From the Law of October 30, 1886:

17. In public schools of every kind instruction is to be given only by lay personnel.

18. No new teaching appointment of a member of a religious order, male or female, may be made in departments where a normal school has functioned for four years . . . . In boys' schools the substitution of lay for religious personnel must be accomplished within five years from the promulgation of the present law.

Source: A. Debidour, *L'Église catholique et l'état sous la Troisième République (1870–1906)* (Paris, 1906–1909), I, 435–440, 445–446, 452–453.

SUGGESTIONS FOR BACKGROUND AND REFERENCE

E. M. Acomb, *The French Laic Laws (1879–1889)* (New York, 1941).

J. Brugerette, *Le prêtre français et la société contemporaine* (Paris, 1933–1938), II, 159–203.

G. Chapman, *The Third Republic of France: The First Phase, 1871–1894* (New York, 1962), pp. 148–159, 203–211.

A. Dansette, *Religious History of Modern France* (Freiburg, Germany, 1961), II, 40–57.

E. Lecanuet, *Les premières années du pontificat de Léon XIII (1878–1894)* (Paris, 1930–1931), pp. 46–179.

J. McManners, *Church and State in France 1870–1914* (New York, 1972), pp. 45–63.

C. S. Phillips, *The Church in France, 1848–1907* (London, 1936), pp. 184–210.

Source for this document, I, 201–370.

✦ ✦ ✦ Leo XIII on Church and State

111 *Immortale Dei* (Extracts)

November 1, 1885

Inheriting church-state conflicts in Germany, France, and Italy and some ill will occasioned by the Syllabus of Errors and the Vatican Council, Leo XIII (1878–1903), while not retreating from the principles of Pius IX, attempted a *démarche*. His detachment from the older legitimist political outlook, familiarity with modern society, accomplished diplomacy, and genuine desire to conciliate where possible enabled him to liquidate the Kulturkampf, guide French Catholics toward a *modus vivendi* with the Republic, and enhance papal prestige through a positive program for contemporary issues. Of Leo's great encyclicals, probably the most politically significant were *Quod Apostolici Muneris* (December 28, 1878), excluding socialism; *Diuturnum Illud* (June 29, 1881), stressing the legitimacy of the several forms of government and of popular participation in government; *Immortale Dei* (November 1, 1885); *Libertas Praestantissimum* (June 20, 1888); and *Graves de Communi* (January 18, 1901), cautioning against some forms of Christian democracy and defining legitimate Catholic popular action. The social document, *Rerum Novarum* (May 15, 1891), strove to make Catholic teaching relevant to the new civilization created by industrial capitalism. France, presenting greatest problems to Leo's diplomacy, elicited *Noblissima Gallorum Gens* (February 8, 1884) and *Au Milieu des Sollicitudes* (February 16, 1892) and figured prominently in the writing of others. The entire Leonine corpus is important; portions of the above letters of 1885, 1888, 1891, and 1892 are reproduced in the following pages.

Immortale Dei, though partly a response to special French problems, was probably the classic statement of Leo's political teaching. While the pope reasserted the ideal of a true and perfect Catholic society and defended it against compromise, he also considered what accommodations Catholics might lawfully make in the modern "neutral" state. This treatment of relative as well as absolute, of what may be possible or just in existing society as well as what is ultimately desirable gave apparent approval to an older Catholic distinction between "thesis" and "hypothesis," evident in Dupanloup's pamphlet on the Syllabus and still earlier in the *Civiltà Cattolica,* October 17, 1863. In France the encyclical was regarded as support for the Catholicism of Dupanloup and Montalembert, although its language was guarded and the Curia warned against unwarranted interpretation.

. . . But as no society can hold together unless some one be over all, directing all to strive earnestly for the common good; every civilized community must have a ruling authority, and this authority, no less than society itself, has its source in nature, and has, consequently, God for its author. Hence it follows that all public power must proceed from God. . . .

The right to rule is not necessarily, however, bound up with any special mode of government. It may take this or that form, provided only that it be of a nature to insure the general welfare. But whatever be the nature of the government, rulers must ever bear in mind that God is the paramount ruler of the world, and must set Him before themselves as their exemplar and law in the administration of the State. . . .

* * *

As a consequence, the State . . . is clearly bound to act up to the manifold and weighty duties linking it to God, by the public profession of religion. . . . Since, then, no one is allowed to be remiss in the service due to God, and since the chief duty of all men is to cling to religion in both its teaching and practice—not such religion as they may have a preference for, but the religion which God enjoins, and which certain and most clear marks show to be the only one true religion—it is a public crime to act as though there were no God. So, too, is it a sin in the State not to have care for religion, . . . or out of many forms of religion to adopt that one which chimes in with the fancy; for we are bound absolutely to worship God in that way which He has shown to be His will. All who rule, therefore, should hold in honor the holy name of God, and one of their chief duties must be to favor religion, to protect it, to shield it under the credit and sanction of the laws, and neither to organize nor enact any measure that may compromise its safety. This is the bounden duty of rulers to the people over whom they rule. . . .

* * *

Sad it is to call to mind how the harmful and lamentable rage for innovation which rose to a climax in the sixteenth century threw first of all into confusion the Christian religion, and next, by natural sequence, invaded the precincts of philosophy, whence it spread amongst all classes of society. From this source . . . burst forth all those later tenets of unbridled license which, in the midst of the terrible upheavals of the last century, were . . . boldly proclaimed as the principles . . . of that *new jurisprudence* which was . . . at variance on many points with not only the Christian, but even with the natural law.

Amongst these principles the main one lays down that as all men are alike by race and nature, so in like manner all are equal in the control of their life; that each one is so far his own master as to be in no sense under the rule of any other individual; that each is free to think on every subject just as he may choose, and to do whatever he may like to do; that no man has any right to rule over other men. In a society grounded upon such maxims, all government is nothing more nor less than the will of the people, and the people . . . is alone its own ruler. It does choose nevertheless some to whose charge it may commit itself, but in such wise that it makes over to them not the right so much as the business of governing, to be exercised, however, in its name.

The authority of God is passed over in silence, just as if there were no God . . . . Thus . . . a State becomes nothing but a multitude, which is its own master and ruler. . . . Moreover, it believes that it is not obliged to make public profession of any religion; or to inquire which of the very many religions is the only one true; or to prefer one religion to all the rest; or to show to any form of religion special favor; but, on the contrary, is bound to grant equal rights to every creed, so that public order may not be disturbed . . . .

* * *

Accordingly, it has become the practice . . . under this condition of public polity (now so much admired by many) either to forbid the action of the Church altogether, or to keep her in check and bondage to the State. . . . The drawing up of laws, the administration of State affairs, the godless education of youth, the spoliation and suppression of religious orders, the overthrow of the temporal power of the Roman Pontiff, all alike aim at this one end—to paralyze the action of Christian institutions, to cramp to the utmost the freedom of the Catholic Church, and to curtail her every single prerogative.

* * *

To hold therefore that there is no difference in matters of religion between forms that are unlike each other, and even contrary to each other, . . . leads in the end to the rejection of all religion . . . . And this is the same thing as atheism, however it may differ from it in name. . . .

So, too, the liberty of thinking, and of publishing, whatsoever each one likes, without any hindrance, is not in itself an advantage over which society can wisely rejoice. On the contrary, it is the fountain-head and origin of many evils. Liberty is a power perfecting man, and hence should have truth and goodness for its object.

* * *

This then is the teaching of the Catholic Church . . . . By the words and decrees [of the popes] . . . no one of the several forms of government is in itself condemned, inasmuch as none of them contain anything contrary to Catholic doctrine, and all of them are capable, if wisely and justly managed, to insure the welfare of the State. Neither is it blameworthy in itself . . . for the people to have a share . . . in the government: for at certain times, and under certain laws, such participation may not only be of benefit to the citizens, but may even be of obligation. Nor is there any reason why any one should accuse the Church of being . . . opposed to real and lawful liberty. The Church, indeed, deems it unlawful to place the various forms of divine worship on the same footing as the true religion, but does not, on that account, condemn those rulers who, for the sake of securing some great good or of hindering some great evil, allow patiently custom or usage to be a kind of sanction for each kind of religion having its place in the State. And in fact the Church is wont to take earnest heed that no one shall be forced to embrace the Catholic faith against his will, for, as St. Augustine wisely reminds us, "Man cannot believe otherwise than of his own free will."

In the same way the Church cannot approve of that liberty which begets a contempt of the . . . laws of God, and casts off the obedience due to lawful authority . . . . On the other hand, that liberty is truly genuine and to be sought after which . . . does not allow men to be the slaves of error . . . ; which, too, in public administration guides the citizens in wisdom and provides for them increased means of well-being; and which, further, protects the State from foreign interference.

This honorable liberty . . . the Church approves most highly . . . . And . . . whatever in the State is of chief avail for the common welfare; whatever has been usefully established to curb the license of rulers who are opposed to the true interests of the people, or to keep in check the leading authorities from unwarrantably interfering in municipal or family affairs;—whatever tends to uphold the honor, manhood, and equal rights of individual citizens;—of all these things . . . the Catholic Church has always been the originator, the promoter, or the guardian. Ever therefore consistent with herself, while . . . she rejects that exorbitant liberty which . . . ends in license or in thraldom, . . . she willingly . . . welcomes whatever improvements the age brings forth, if these really secure the prosperity of life here below . . . .

Therefore, when it is said that the Church is jealous of modern political systems, and that she repudiates the discoveries of modern research, the charge is a ridiculous and groundless calumny. Wild opinions she does repudiate . . . . But as all truth must necessarily proceed from God, the Church recognizes in all truth that is reached by research, a trace of the divine intelligence. And as all truth in the natural order is powerless to destroy belief in the teachings of revelation, but can do much to confirm it, . . . whatsoever spreads the range of knowledge will always be willingly . . . welcomed by the Church. . . .

. . . Our eyes are not closed to the spirit of the times. We repudiate not the assured and useful improvements of our age, but devoutly wish affairs of State to take a safer course than they are now taking, and to rest on a more firm foundation without injury to the true freedom of the people; for the best parent and guardian of liberty amongst men is truth. . . .

* * *

[Catholics must] take a prudent part in the business of municipal administration, . . . so that . . . public provision may be made for the instruction of youth in religion and true morality. Upon these things the well-being of every State greatly depends.

Furthermore, it is in general fitting and salutary that Catholics should . . . give their attention to national politics. . . .

It follows . . . that Catholics have just reasons for taking part in . . . public affairs.

For in so doing they assume not the responsibility of approving what is blameworthy in the actual methods of government, but seek to turn these very methods, so far as is possible, to the genuine and true public good . . . .

. . . it is the duty of all Catholics . . . to make use of popular institutions, so far as can honestly be done, for the advancement of truth and righteousness; to strive that liberty of action shall not transgress the bounds marked out by nature and the law of God; to endeavor to bring back all civil society to the pattern and form of Christianity which We have described. It is barely possible to lay down any fixed method by which such purposes are to be attained, because the means adopted must suit places and times widely differing from one another. Nevertheless, above all things, unity of aim must be preserved, and similarity must be sought after in all plans of action. . . .

* * *

But in matters merely political, as for instance the best form of government, and this or that system of administration, a difference of opinion is lawful. Those, therefore, whose piety is in other respects known, and whose minds are ready to accept . . . the decrees of the Apostolic See, cannot in justice be accounted bad men because they disagree as to subjects We have mentioned; and still graver wrong will be done them, if—as We have more than once perceived with regret—they are accused of violating, or of wavering in, the Catholic faith.

Source: John J. Wynne (ed.), *The Great Encyclical Letters of Pope Leo XIII* (New York, 1903), pp. 108–111, 114–115, 120–121, 122–124, 126–133. Latin text in *Acta Sanctae Sedis* (Rome, 1885), XVIII, 161–180.

SUGGESTIONS FOR BACKGROUND AND REFERENCE

A. Dansette, *Religious History of Modern France* (Freiburg, Germany, 1961), II, 58–111.

A. Debidour, *L'Église catholique et l'état sous la Troisième République (1870–1906)* (Paris, 1906–1909), II, 1–78.

E. T. Gargan, *Leo XIII and the Modern World* (New York, 1961).

K. S. Latourette, *Christianity in a Revolutionary Age* (New York, 1958–1962), I, 298–301, 307–310.

E. Lecanuet, *Les premières années du pontificat de Léon XIII (1878–1894)* (Paris, 1930–1931), pp. 285–608.

C. S. Phillips, *The Church in France, 1848–1907* (London, 1936), pp. 211–236.

J. Schmidlin, *Papstgeschichte der neuesten Zeit* (Munich, 1933–1936), II, 352–383.

E. Soderini, *The Pontificate of Leo XIII* (London, 1934).

112 *Libertas Praestantissimum* (Extracts)

June 20, 1888

Three years after *Immortale Dei* Leo amplified that encyclical's teaching on liberty in a new letter. *Libertas* argued that the church was not hostile to liberty but that liberty must properly include submission to God and not rest on denial of divine law and exaltation of human reason. Reproduced below are extracts indicating application of the pope's teaching to specific modern liberties.

What *Naturalists* or *Rationalists* aim at in philosophy, that the supporters of *Liberalism,* carrying out the principles laid down by Naturalism, are attempting in the domain of morality and politics. The fundamental doctrine of *Rationalism* is the supremacy of the human reason, which, refusing due submission to the divine and eternal reason, proclaims its own independence, and constitutes itself the supreme principle and source and judge of truth. Hence these followers of Liberalism . . . proclaim that every man is the law to himself; from which arises that ethical system which they style *independent* morality, and which, under the guise of liberty, exonerates man from any obedience to the commands of God, and substitutes a boundless license. The end of all this it is not difficult to foresee . . . . For, when once man is firmly persuaded that he is subject to no one, it follows that the efficient cause of the unity of civil society is not to be sought in any principle external to man, or superior to him, but simply in the free will of individuals; that the authority in the State comes from the people only; and that, just as every man's individual reason is his only rule of life, so the collective reason of the community should be the supreme guide in the management of all public affairs. Hence the doctrine of the supremacy of the greater number, and that all right and all duty reside in the majority. . . .

Moreover, . . . a doctrine of such character is most hurtful both to individuals and to the State. For once ascribe to human reason the only authority to decide what is true and . . . good, and the real distinction between good and evil is destroyed; honor and dishonor differ not in their nature, but in the opinion and judgment of each one; pleasure is the measure of what is lawful; and, given a code of morality which can have little or no power to restrain . . . the unruly propensities of man, a way is naturally opened to universal corruption. With reference also to public affairs: authority is severed from the true and natural principle whence it derives all its efficacy for the common good; and the law determining what it is right to do . . . is at the mercy of a majority. Now this is simply a road leading straight to tyranny. The empire of God over man and civil society once repudiated, it follows that religion, as a public institution, can have no claim to exist, and that everything that belongs to religion will be treated with complete indifference. Furthermore, . . . tumult . . . will be common amongst the people; and when duty and conscience cease to appeal to them, there will be nothing to hold them back but force . . . .

* * *

We must now consider briefly *liberty of speech* and liberty of the press. It is hardly necessary to say that there can be no such right as this, if it be not used in moderation, and if it pass beyond the bounds and end of all true liberty. For right is a moral power which . . . it is absurd to suppose that nature has accorded indifferently to truth and falsehood . . . . Men have a right freely and prudently to propagate . . . what things soever are true and honorable, so that as many as possible may possess them; but lying opinions . . . and vices . . . should be diligently repressed by public authority, lest they insidiously work the ruin of the State. The excesses of an unbridled intellect, which unfailingly end in the oppression of the untutored multitude, are no less rightly controlled by the authority of the law than are the injuries inflicted by violence upon the weak. And this all the more surely, because by far the greater part of the community is either absolutely unable, or able only with great difficulty, to escape from illusions and deceitful subtleties . . . . Thus . . . pernicious and manifold error . . . will easily prevail. Thus, too, license will gain what liberty loses; for liberty will ever be more free and secure, in proportion as license is kept in fuller restraint. In regard, however, to all matters of opinion which God leaves to man's free discussion, full liberty of thought and of speech is naturally within the right of every one; for such liberty never leads men to suppress the truth, but often to discover it . . . .

A like judgment must be passed upon what is called *liberty of teaching*. There can be no doubt that truth alone should imbue the minds of men . . . . For this reason it is plainly the duty of all who teach to banish error from the mind, and by sure safeguards to close the entry to all false convictions. From this it follows . . . that the liberty of which We have been speaking is greatly opposed to reason and tends absolutely to pervert men's minds, in as much as it claims for itself the right of teaching whatever it pleases—a liberty which the State cannot grant without failing it its duty. . . .

Wherefore, this liberty also . . . must be kept within certain limits . . . . Now truth . . . is of two kinds, natural and supernatural. Of natural truths, such as the principles of nature and whatever is derived from them immediately by our reason, there is a kind of common patrimony in the human race. On this . . . morality, justice, religion, and the very bonds of human society rest: and to allow people to go unharmed who violate or destroy it would be most impious . . . . But with no less religious care must we preserve that great and sacred treasure of the truths which God Himself has taught us. . . .

* * *

Another liberty is widely advocated, namely, *liberty of conscience*. If by this is meant that every one may, as he chooses, worship God or not, it is sufficiently refuted by the arguments already adduced. But it may also be taken to mean that every man . . . may follow the will of God and, from a consciousness of duty and free from every obstacle, obey His commands. This, indeed, is true liberty . . . —a liberty which the Church has always desired and held most dear. . . . And deservedly so; for this Christian liberty bears witness to the absolute and most just dominion of God over man, and to the chief and supreme duty of man towards God. . . .

By the patrons of *Liberalism,* however, who make the State absolute and omnip-
otent . . . , the liberty of which We speak . . . is not admitted; and whatever is
done for its preservation is accounted . . . an offence against the State. Indeed, if
what they say were really true, there would be no tyranny, no matter how monstrous, which we should not be bound to endure . . . .

The Church most earnestly desires that the Christian teaching . . . should pene-
trate every rank of society . . . . Yet, with the discernment of a true mother, the
Church weighs the great burden of human weakness and well knows the course
down which the minds and actions of men are in this our age being borne. For this
reason, while not conceding any right to anything save what is true and honest, she
does not forbid public authority to tolerate what is at variance with truth and justice,
for the sake of avoiding some greater evil, or of obtaining or preserving some
greater good. . . . But . . . the more a State is driven to tolerate evil the further is it
from perfection; and . . . the tolerance of evil which is dictated by political prudence should be strictly confined to the limits which its justifying cause, the public
welfare requires. Wherefore, if such tolerance would be injurious to the public
welfare and entail greater evils on the State, it would not be lawful . . . . And
although in the extraordinary condition of these times the Church usually acquiesces
in certain modern liberties, not because she prefers them in themselves, but because
she judges it expedient to permit them, she would in happier times exercise her own
liberty; and by persuasion, exhortation, and entreaty, would endeavor . . . to fulfil the duty assigned to her by God of providing for the eternal salvation of
mankind. . . .

Source: John J. Wynne (ed.), *The Great Encyclical Letters of Pope Leo XIII* (New York,
1903), pp. 145–146, 151–153, 155–158. Latin text in *Acta Sanctae Sedis* (Rome, 1887),
XX, 593–613.

SUGGESTIONS FOR BACKGROUND AND REFERENCE

References for Document 111.

113 *Rerum Novarum* (Extracts)

May 15, 1891

This encyclical, the most famous of Leo XIII's pronouncements, defined
Catholic social doctrine with reference to the problems of an industrial
society. Social philosophy and programs of social action had earlier been
explored by French and German Catholics, notably by Comte Albert de
Mun, founder of the *Cercles Catholiques d'Ouvriers,* and Wilhelm Emmanuel von Kettler, Bishop of Mainz. Leo himself had a familiarity with
modern industrialism extending back to his Brussels nunciature in the
1840s. In 1881 he placed Cardinal Mermillod of Lausanne over a commission to study the social question, and after 1885 gave his patronage to

the Catholic social congresses of the *Union de Fribourg*. This encyclical sought to clarify the rights and duties of employers and employees, expose the evils of socialism and individualistic capitalism, stress human solidarity and Christian charity, and warn against specific abuses in contemporary society to which the state might bring some appropriate remedies. The approval of Catholic associations assisted the development of Catholic trade unions, and the entire encyclical gave prominence and prestige to a developing Catholic social movement. The tradition was again invoked by Pius XI in *Quadragesimo Anno* in 1931.

That the spirit of revolutionary change, which has long been disturbing the nations of the world, should have passed beyond the sphere of politics and made its influence felt in the cognate sphere of practical economics is not surprising. The elements of the conflict now raging are unmistakable in the vast expansion of industrial pursuits and the marvellous discoveries of science; in the changed relations between masters and workmen; in the enormous fortunes of some few individuals, and the utter poverty of the masses; in the increased self-reliance and closer mutual combinations of the working classes; as also, finally, in the prevailing moral degeneracy. The momentous gravity of the state of things now obtaining fills every mind with painful apprehension; . . .

* * *

. . . the ancient workingmen's guilds were abolished in the last century, and no other organization took their place. . . . Hence by degrees it has come to pass that workingmen have been surrendered, all isolated and helpless, to the hardheartedness of employers and the greed of unchecked competition. The mischief has been increased by rapacious usury . . . . To this must be added the custom of working by contract, and the concentration of so many branches of trade in the hands of a few individuals; so that a small number of very rich men have been able to lay upon the . . . laboring poor a yoke little better than that of slavery itself.

To remedy these wrongs the Socialists, working on the poor man's envy of the rich, are striving to do away with private property . . . . They hold that by thus transferring property . . . to the community, the present mischievous state of things will be set to rights, inasmuch as each citizen will then get his fair share of whatever there is to enjoy. But their contentions are so clearly powerless to end the controversy that were they carried into effect the workingman himself would be among the first to suffer. They are, moreover, emphatically unjust, because they would rob the lawful possessor, bring State action into a sphere not within its competence, and create utter confusion in the community.

. . . when a man engages in remunerative labor, the . . . motive of his work is to obtain property, and thereafter to hold it as his very own. If one man hires out to another his strength or skill, he does so for the purpose of receiving in return what is necessary for sustenance and education; he . . . intends to acquire a right full and real, not only to the remuneration, but also to the disposal of such remuneration . . . . Thus, if he lives sparingly, saves money, and, for greater security, invests his savings in land, the land, in such case, is only his wages under another form; and, consequently, a workingman's little estate thus purchased should be as completely at his full disposal as are the wages he receives for his labor. But it is precisely in such power of disposal that ownership obtains, whether the property consist of land or chattels. Socialists, therefore, by endeavoring to transfer the possessions of individuals to the community at large, strike at the interests of every wage-earner . . . .

* * *

The great mistake . . . is to take up with the notion that class is naturally hostile to class, and that the wealthy and the workingmen are intended by nature to live in mutual conflict. So irrational and so false is this view, that the direct contrary is the truth. . . . Each needs the other . . . . Now in preventing such strife . . . , the efficacy of Christian institutions is marvellous . . . . First of all, there is no intermediary more powerful than Religion (whereof the Church is the interpreter and guardian) in drawing the rich and the poor bread-winners together, by reminding each class of its duties to the other, and especially of the obligations of justice. Thus Religion teaches the laboring man . . . to carry out honestly . . . all equitable agreements freely entered into; never to injure the property, nor to outrage the person, of an employer; never to resort to violence . . . nor to engage in riot or disorder . . . . Religion teaches the wealthy owner and the employer that their work-people are not to be accounted their bondsmen; that in every man they must respect his dignity and worth as a man and as a Christian; that labor is not a thing to be ashamed of . . . . Again, . . . the Church teaches that . . . the employer is bound to see that the worker has time for his religious duties; that he be not exposed to corrupting influences and dangerous occasions; and that he be not led away to neglect his home and family, or to squander his earnings. Furthermore, the employer must never tax his work-people beyond their strength, or employ them in work unsuited to their sex or age. His great and principal duty is to give every one a fair wage. Doubtless, before deciding whether wages are adequate, many things have to be considered; but wealthy owners and all masters of labor should be mindful of this—that to exercise pressure upon the indigent and the destitute for the sake of gain, and to gather one's profit out of the need of another, is condemned by all laws, human and divine.

* * *

. . . The foremost duty . . . of the rulers of the State should be to make sure that the laws and institutions, the general character and administration of the commonwealth, shall be such as of themselves to realize public well-being and private prosperity. . . . Now, a State chiefly prospers and thrives through moral rule, well-regulated family life, respect for religion and justice, the moderation and equal allocation of public taxes, the progress of the arts and of trade, the abundant yield of the land—through everything, in fact, which makes the citizens better and happier. Hereby, then, it lies in the power of a ruler to benefit every class in the State, and amongst the rest to promote to the utmost the interests of the poor . . . . And the more that is done for the benefit of the working classes by the general laws of the country, the less need will there be to seek for special means to relieve them.

There is another and deeper consideration . . . . As regards the State, the interests of all, whether high or low, are equal. The poor are members of the national community equally with the rich; . . . and . . . they are in every State very largely in the majority. It would be irrational to neglect one portion of the citizens and favor another; and therefore the public administration must duly and solicitously provide for the welfare and the comfort of the working classes . . . .

* * *

Whenever the general interest of any particular class suffers, or is threatened with mischief which can in no other way be met or prevented, the public authority must step in to deal with it. Now it interests the public, as well as the individual, that peace and good order should be maintained; that family life should be carried on in accordance with God's laws and those of nature; that religion should be reverenced and obeyed; that a high standard of morality should prevail . . . . If by a strike, or other combination of workmen, there should be imminent danger of disturbance to the public peace; or if . . . among the laboring population the ties of family life were relaxed; if religion were found to suffer through the operatives not having time and opportunity afforded them to practice its duties; if in workshops and factories there were danger to morals through the mixing of the sexes or from other harmful occasions of evil; or if employers laid burdens upon their workmen which were unjust, or degraded them with conditions repugnant to their dignity as human beings; finally, if health were endangered by excessive labor, or by work unsuited to sex or age—in such cases, . . . within certain limits, it would be right to invoke the aid and authority of the law. The limits must be determined by the nature of the occasion which calls for the law's interference—the principle being that the law must not undertake more, nor proceed further, than is required for the remedy of the evil or the removal of the mischief.

Rights must be religiously respected wherever they exist . . . . Still, when there is a question of defending the rights of individuals, the poor and helpless have a claim to especial consideration. The richer class have many ways of shielding themselves . . . ; whereas those who are badly off have no resources of their own to fall back upon, and must chiefly depend upon the assistance of the State.

. . . the chief thing to be realized is the safeguarding of private property by legal enactment and public policy. Most of all it is essential . . . to keep the multitude within the line of duty; for . . . neither justice nor the common good allows any individual to seize upon that which belongs to another . . . . [Most] workers prefer to better themselves by honest labor . . . . But there are not a few who are . . . eager for revolutionary change . . . . The authority of the State should intervene to put restraint upon such firebrands, to save the working classes from their seditious arts, and protect lawful owners from spoliation.

When working men have recourse to a strike, it is frequently because the hours of labor are too long, or the work too hard, or because they consider their wages insufficient. The grave inconvenience of this not uncommon occurrence should be obviated by public remedial measures; for such paralyzing of labor not only affects the masters and their work-people alike, but is extremely injurious to trade and to the general interests of the public; moreover, on such occasions, violence and disorder are generally not far distant . . . . The laws should forestall and prevent such troubles from arising; they should lend their influence and authority to the removal in good time of the causes which lead to conflicts between employers and employed.

* * *

. . . the first concern of all is to save the poor workers from the cruelty of greedy speculators, who use human beings as mere instruments of money-making. It is neither just nor human so to grind men down with excessive labor as to stupefy their minds and wear out their bodies. . . . Daily labor, therefore, should be so regulated as not to be protracted over longer hours than strength admits. . . . Those who work in mines and quarries . . . should have shorter hours . . . . And, in regard to children, great care should be taken not to place them in workshops and factories until their bodies and minds are sufficiently developed. . . . Women, again, are not suited for certain occupations . . . .

* * *

Wages, as we are told, are regulated by free consent, and therefore the employer, when he pays what was agreed upon, has done his part and seemingly is not called upon to do anything beyond. . . .

This mode of reasoning is . . . by no means convincing . . . . To labor is to exert one's self for the sake of procuring what is necessary for the purposes of life . . . . Hence a man's labor bears two notes or characters. First of all, it is *personal,* inasmuch as the exertion of individual strength belongs to the individual who puts it forth . . . . Secondly, man's labor is *necessary* . . . . Now, were we to consider labor so far as it is *personal,* merely, doubtless it would be within the workman's right to accept any rate of wages whatsoever; for in the same way as he is free to work or not, so is he free to accept a small remuneration or even none at all. But this is a mere abstract supposition; the labor of the workingman is not only his personal attribute, but it is *necessary;* and this makes all the difference. The preservation of life is the bounden duty of one and all . . . . It follows that each one has a right to procure what is required in order to live; and the poor can procure it in no other way than through work and wages.

Let it be then taken for granted that workman and employer should, as a rule, . . . agree freely as to the wages; nevertheless, there underlies a dictate of natural justice more imperious and ancient than any bargain between man and man, namely, that remuneration ought to be sufficient to support a frugal and well-behaved wage-earner.

* * *

In the last place—employers and workmen may of themselves effect much . . . by means of such associations and organizations as afford opportune aid to those who are in distress, and which draw the two classes more closely together. Among these may be enumerated societies for mutual help; various benevolent foundations established by private persons to provide for the workman, and for his widow or his orphans . . . ; and what are called "patronages," or institutions for the care of boys and girls, for young people, as well as homes for the aged.

The most important of all are workingmen's unions; for these virtually include all the rest. History attests what excellent results were brought about by the artificers' guilds of olden times. They were the means of affording not only many advantages to the workmen, but in no small degree of promoting the advancement of art . . . . Such unions should be suited to the requirements of this our age—an age of wider education, of different habits, and of far more numerous requirements in daily life. It is gratifying to know that there are actually in existence not a few associations of this nature, consisting either of workmen alone, or of workmen and employers together; but it were greatly to be desired that they should become more numerous and more efficient.

Source: John J. Wynne (ed.), *The Great Encyclical Letters of Pope Leo XIII* (New York, 1903), pp. 208–210, 218–220, 227–228, 230–232, 234–236, 238–239. Latin text in *Acta Sanctae Sedis* (Rome, 1890–1891), XXIII, 641–670.

SUGGESTIONS FOR BACKGROUND AND REFERENCE

J. McManners, *Church and State in France, 1870–1914* (New York, 1972), pp. 45–63.
L. P. Wallace, *Leo XIII and the Rise of Socialism* (Durham, N.C., 1966).
References for Document 111.

114   *Au Milieu des Sollicitudes* (Extracts)

February 16, 1892

The *ralliement,* the acceptance by Catholics of the Third Republic, was the aim of Leo XIII's French policy. Papal diplomacy was accordingly directed toward allaying the hostility of anticlerical politicians and statesmen and cautioning the Catholic leadership, overwhelmingly monarchist, against involvement in rightist conspiracy and agitation. The encyclicals *Immortale Dei, Libertas Praestantissimum,* and *Rerum Novarum* helped prepare Catholic opinion, as did also the minority of *abbés démocrates* who recognized republican preponderance and feared the permanent alienation of the population from religion. (On the republican side, chance of a rapprochement was increased by a desire to conciliate Catholic army and navy officers, recognition of Catholic usefulness in foreign and colonial affairs, appreciation of the Concordat as an instrument of religious control, and fear of socialism.) Explicit announcement of papal policy was made in the celebrated toast offered at a naval reception by Cardinal Lavigerie of Algiers, November 12, 1890: "But when the will of a people has plainly asserted itself and when the form of a government contains nothing contrary . . . to principles which alone can animate Christian and civilized nations; when, in order to rescue one's country from the abyss which endangers it, there is required adherence without reservation to that form of government, the moment has come to declare the matter at last settled, and, in order to put an end to our divisions, to sacrifice all that conscience . . . permits . . . ." Lavigerie added that "in speaking thus I am certain of not being disavowed by any authorized voice." (Antonin Debidour, *L'Église catholique et l'état sous la Troisième République 1870–1906* [Paris, 1906–1909], II, 499–500). Despite the great outcry that followed, Leo congratulated Lavigerie three months later and discouraged attempts to found a French Catholic political party in 1891. This encyclical, written in French, was the classic statement of the *ralliement*. Stressing acceptance of the Republic as obligatory and not merely permissive, the pope distinguished between government and legislation and warned against attacks on the Concordat or advocacy of separation. The message occasioned bitter controversy and division. Probably the policy won slow support in France, but it did not save Catholicism from embroilment in the Dreyfus Affair.

Various . . . governments have succeeded one another in France during the last century, each having its own distinctive form: the Empire, the Monarchy, and the Republic. By giving one's self up to abstractions, one could at length conclude which is the best . . . ; and in all truth . . . each of them is good, provided it lead straight to its end—that is to say, to the common good for which social authority is constituted; and . . . from a relative point of view, such and such a form . . . may be preferable because of being better adapted to the character and customs of such or such a nation. In this order of speculative ideas, Catholics, like all other citizens, are free to prefer one form of government to another precisely because no one of these social forms is, in itself, opposed to the principles of sound reason nor to the maxims of Christian doctrine. . . .

* * *

It were useless to recall that all individuals are bound to accept these governments and not to attempt their overthrow or a change in their form. Hence it is that the Church . . . has always condemned men who rebelled against legitimate authority and disapproved their doctrines. . . .

However, . . . whatever be the form of civil power in a nation, it cannot be considered so definitive as to have the right to remain immutable, even though such were the intention of those who, in the beginning, determined it. . . . But in regard to purely human societies, . . . time . . . operates great changes in their political institutions. On some occasions it limits itself to modifying something in the form of the established government; or, again, it will go so far as to substitute other forms for the primitive ones—forms totally different, even as regards the mode of transmitting sovereign power.

And how are these political changes . . . produced? They sometimes follow in the wake of violent crises, too often of a bloody character, in the midst of which pre-existing governments totally disappear; then anarchy holds sway, and soon public order is shaken to its very foundations and finally overthrown. From that time onward a *social need* obtrudes itself upon the nation . . . . Now, this social need justifies the creation and the existence of new governments, whatever form they take; since . . . these new governments are a requisite to public order . . . . Thence it follows that . . . all the novelty is limited to the political form of civil power, or to its mode of transmission; it in no wise affects the power considered in itself. This continues to be immutable and worthy of respect, as, considered in its nature, it is constituted to provide for the common good . . . . To put it otherwise, . . . civil power . . . is from God, always from God . . . .

Consequently, when new governments representing this immutable power are constituted, their acceptance is not only permissible but even obligatory . . . . This is all the more imperative because an insurrection stirs up hatred among citizens, provokes civil war, and may throw a nation into chaos and anarchy . . . .

Thus the wisdom of the Church explains itself in the maintenance of her relations with the numerous governments which have succeeded one another in France in less than a century, each change causing violent shocks. Such a line of conduct would be the surest and most salutary for all Frenchmen in their civil relations with the republic, which is the actual government of their nation. . . .

But a difficulty presents itself. "This Republic," it is said, "is animated by such anti-Christian sentiments that honest men, Catholics particularly, could not conscientiously accept it." This, more than anything else, has given rise to dissensions . . . . These regrettable differences would have been avoided if the very considerable distinction between *constituted power* and *legislation* had been carefully kept in view. In so much does legislation differ from political power and its form, that under a system of government most excellent in form legislation could be detestable; while quite the opposite under a regime most imperfect in form might be found excellent legislation. . . .

. . . Legislation is the work of men, invested with power . . . ; therefore it follows that, practically, the quality of the laws depends more upon the quality of these men than upon the form of power. The laws will be good or bad accordingly as the minds of the legislators are imbued with good or bad principles . . . .

That several years ago different important acts of legislation in France proceeded from a tendency hostile to religion, and therefore to the interests of the nation, is admitted by all . . . . Poor France! God alone can measure the abyss of evil into which she will sink if this legislation . . . will . . . continue in a course which must end in plucking from the minds and hearts of Frenchmen the religion which has made them so great.

And here is precisely the ground on which . . . upright men should unite as one to combat, by all lawful and honest means, these progressive abuses of legislation. The respect due to constituted power cannot prohibit this: unlimited respect and obedience cannot be yielded to all legislative measures, of no matter what kind, enacted by this same power. . . . Accordingly, such points in legislation as are hostile to religion and to God should never be approved; to the contrary, it is a duty to disapprove them. . . .

* * *

. . . We wish to touch upon two points . . . which, because so closely connected with religious interests have stirred up some division among Catholics. . . . One of them is the *Concordat* . . . . On the observance of this solemn, bi-lateral compact, always faithfully kept by the Holy See, the enemies of the Catholic religion do not themselves agree. . . . The more violent among them desire its abolition . . . . On the contrary, others, being more astute, wish, or rather claim to wish, the preservation of the Concordat: not because they agree that the State should fulfil toward the Church the subscribed engagements, but solely that the State may be benefited by the concessions made by the Church . . . . Of these two opinions which will prevail? We know not. We desired to recall them only to recommend Catholics not to provoke a secession by interfering in a matter with which it is the business of the Holy See to deal.

We shall not hold to the same language on another point, concerning the principle of the separation of the State and Church, which is equivalent to the separation of human legislation from Christian and divine legislation. . . . As soon as the State refuses to give to God what belongs to God, by a necessary consequence it refuses to give to citizens that to which, as men, they have a right; as . . . it cannot be denied that man's rights spring from his duty toward God. . . . In fact, to wish that the State would separate itself from the Church would be to wish . . . that the Church be reduced to the liberty of living according to the law common to all citizens. . . . It is true that in certain countries this state of affairs exists. It is a condition which, if it have numerous and serious inconveniences, also offers some advantages—above all when, by a fortunate inconsistency, the legislator is inspired by Christian principles—and, though these advantages cannot justify the false principle of separation nor authorize its defense, they nevertheless render worthy of toleration a situation which, practically, might be worse.

But in France, a nation Catholic in her traditions and by the present faith of the great majority of her sons, the Church should not be placed in the precarious position to which she must submit among other peoples; and the better that Catholics understand the aim of the enemies who desire this separation, the less will they favor it. To these enemies, . . . this separation means that political legislation be entirely independent of religious legislation . . . . But they make a reservation formulated thus: As soon as the Church, utilizing the resources which common law accords to the least among Frenchmen, will, by redoubling her native activity, cause her work to prosper, then the State intervening, can and will put French Catholics outside the common law itself. . . . In a word: the ideal of these men would be a return to paganism: the State would recognize the Church only when it would be pleased to persecute her.

Source: John J. Wynne (ed.), *The Great Encyclical Letters of Pope Leo XIII* (New York, 1903), pp. 255–260, 261–263. French and Latin texts in *Acta Sanctae Sedis* (Rome, 1891–1892), XXIV, 519–540.

SUGGESTIONS FOR BACKGROUND AND REFERENCE

J. Brugerette, *Le prêtre français et la société contemporaine* (Paris, 1933–1938), II, 323–370.

G. Chapman, *The Third Republic of France. The First Phase 1871–1894* (London, 1962), pp. 292–298.

A. C. Sedgwick, *Ralliement in French Politics, 1890 to 1898* (Cambridge, Mass., 1965), pp. 51–64.

References for Document 111.

✦ ✦ ✦

115   Law of Associations (Extracts)

July 1, 1901

The participation of some Catholics in rightist agitation during the Dreyfus Affair in the 1890s widened the gulf between the church and the Republic, despite Leo XIII's policy of *ralliement*. The government of republican defense under René Waldeck-Rousseau determined to curb the church and, alleging political and economic danger in the growth and wealth of religious orders, put through the Law of Associations requiring specific legislative acts of authorization for Catholic orders. These were denied for the most part, and after the 1902 elections and the establishment of a new cabinet under the extreme anticlerical, Émile Combes, the law was drastically enforced. Thousands of Catholic schools were closed.

Title III

13. No religious congregation may be formed without an authorization given by a law which shall determine the conditions of its operation.

No congregation may establish any new foundation except by virtue of a decree of the Council of State.

The dissolution of a congregation or the closing of any establishment may be declared by a cabinet decree.

14. No one shall be permitted to manage, either directly or through an intermediary, an educational institution of any kind whatsoever, nor to provide instruction therein if he belongs to an unauthorized religious congregation.

Violators shall be punished with the penalties provided by article 8, paragraph 2 [a fine of 16 to 5,000 francs and imprisonment from six days to one year]. In addition, the closing of the institution may be declared by judgment of condemnation.

15. Every religious congregation shall keep a statement of its receipts and expenses. It shall prepare annually the financial account of the past year and an inventoried statement of its real and personal property.

The complete list of its members, containing their patronymic names as well as the names under which they are designated in the congregation, their nationality, age and place of birth, and the date of their admission must be kept at the residence of the congregation.

On every request of the prefect, the congregation shall be required to produce . . . without alteration the accounts, statements, and lists above mentioned.

Representatives or directors of a congregation who have supplied false information or have refused to comply with the requests of the prefect in the cases provided for in the present article shall be punished with the penalties indicated by paragraph 2 of article 8.

16. Every congregation formed without authorization shall be declared unlawful.

Those who have taken part in it shall be punished with the penalties decreed by article 8, paragraph 2.

The penalty applicable to the founders or administrators shall be doubled.

* * *

18. Congregations existing at the time of the promulgation of the present law which have not been previously authorized or recognized must prove within the space of three months that they have taken the necessary steps to conform to its requirements.

In default of this proof, they shall be considered dissolved *ipso jure* [*de plein droit*]. It shall be the same with congregations to which authorization has been refused.

Liquidation of property retained by them shall take place in the courts. The court, at the request of the ministry, shall appoint . . . a liquidator who shall have all the powers of a sequestration administrator during the entire period of the liquidation.

The judgment ordering the liquidation shall be made public in the form prescribed for legal announcements.

Property and assets belonging to members of the congregation prior to their admission to the congregation, or which may have fallen to them since, either by inheritance *ab intestat* in direct or collateral line, or by legacy or bequest in the direct line, shall be restored to them.

* * *

Property and assets acquired in free title which have not been specifically assigned by gift to a charitable work may be reclaimed by the donor, his heirs or interested parties . . . .

* * *

After the passage of six months, the liquidator shall proceed to the sale by judicial process of all real property which may not have been reclaimed or assigned to a charitable work.

The product of the sale, as well as all movable assets, shall be deposited with the deposit and consignment fund.

* * *

The regulation of public administration . . . shall determine the grant in capital or life annuity which shall be assigned from assets remaining [after the deductions earlier provided for] to members of the dissolved congregation who may not have assured means of support or who may prove that they have contributed by their personal labor to the acquisition of the assets being distributed.

Source: Antonin Debidour, *L'Eglise catholique et l'état sous la Troisième République* (Paris, 1906–1909), II, 541–544.

SUGGESTIONS FOR BACKGROUND AND REFERENCE

J. Brugerette, *Le prêtre français et la société contemporaine* (Paris, 1933–1938), II, 415–516.

A. Dansette, *Religious History of Modern France* (Freiburg, Germany, 1961), II, 166–206.

E. Lecanuet, *Les signes avant-coureurs de la séparation: les dernières années de Léon XIII et l'avènement de Pie X 1894–1910* (Paris, 1930), pp. 225–472.

J. McManners, *Church and State in France, 1870–1914* (New York, 1972), pp. 118–139.

P. Nourrisson, *Histoire légale des congrégations religieuses en France depuis 1789* (Paris, 1928), II, 1–125.

M. O. Partin, *Waldeck-Rousseau, Combes, and the Church: The Politics of Anti-Clericalism, 1899–1905* (Durham, N.C., 1969).

C. S. Phillips, *The Church in France, 1848–1907* (London, 1936), pp. 259–289. Source for this document.

116   Balfour Education Act (Extracts)

December 18, 1902

In addition to substituting county and borough governments for the earlier school boards and providing for secondary and technical education, this new act achieved the integration of church schools in the national educational system. Though the Cowper-Temple arrangement for undenominational religious teaching was retained in the "provided" schools (formerly Board Schools), the section placing church schools on the local rates raised much controversy. (The school managers were to provide and maintain the buildings, while the government paid the costs of education.) The change saved many Anglican and Roman Catholic schools and raised educational standards, but Nonconformists objected on principle to public support of church schools. Resistance, including conscientious refusal to pay taxes, was prolonged.

Part II
Higher Education

2.—(1) The local education authority shall consider the educational needs of their area and take such steps as seem to them desirable, after consultation with the Board of Education, to supply or aid the supply of education other than elementary, and to promote the general co-ordination of all forms of education . . . .

* * *

4.—(1) A council, in the application of money under this Part of this Act, shall not require that any particular form of religious instruction or worship or any religious catechism or formulary which is distinctive of any particular denomination shall or shall not be taught, used or practised in any school, college or hostel aided but not provided by the council, and no pupil shall, on the ground of religious belief, be excluded from or placed in an inferior position in any school, college or hostel provided by the council, and no catechism or formulary distinctive of any particular religious denomination shall be taught in any school, college or hostel so provided, except in cases where the council, at the request of parents of scholars, at such times and under such conditions as the council think desirable, allow any religious instruction to be given in the school, college or hostel otherwise than at the cost of the council: Provided that, in the exercise of this power, no unfair preference shall be shown to any religious denomination.

(2) In a school or college receiving a grant from, or maintained by, a council under this Part of this Act,

(a) A scholar attending as a day or evening scholar shall not be required, as a condition of being admitted into or remaining in the school or college, to attend or abstain from attending any Sunday school, place of religious worship, religious observance or instruction in religious subjects in the school or college or elsewhere; and

The times for religious worship or for any lesson on a religious subject shall be conveniently arranged for the purpose of allowing the withdrawal of any such scholar therefrom.

Part III
Elementary Education

5. The local education authority shall, throughout their area, have the powers and duties of a school board and school attendance committee . . . , and shall also be responsible for and have the control of all secular instruction in public elementary schools not provided by them; and school boards and school attendance committees shall be abolished.

* * *

7.—(1) The local education authority shall maintain and keep efficient all public elementary schools within their area which are necessary, . . . ; but, in the case of a school not provided by them, only so long as the following conditions and provisions are complied with:—

(a) The managers of the school shall carry out any directions of the local education authority as to the secular instruction to be given in the school, including any directions with respect to the number and educational qualifications of the teachers . . . , and for the dismissal of any teacher on educational grounds; . . . but no direction given under this provision shall be such as to interfere with reasonable facilities for religious instruction during school hours;

(b) The local education authority shall have power to inspect the school;

(c) The consent of the local education authority shall be required to the appointment of teachers, but that consent shall not be withheld except on educational grounds; and the consent of the authority shall also be required to the dismissal of a teacher, unless the dismissal be on grounds connected with the giving of religious instruction in the school;

* * *

(6) Religious instruction given in a public elementary school not provided by the local education authority shall, as regards its character, be in accordance with the provisions (if any) of the trust deed relating thereto, and shall be under the control of the managers: Provided that nothing in this subsection shall affect any provision in a trust deed for reference to the bishop or superior ecclesiastical or other denominational authority, so far as such provision gives to the bishop or authority the power of deciding whether the character of the religious instruction is or is not in accordance with the provisions of the trust deed.

(7) The managers of a school maintained but not provided by the local education authority shall have all powers of management required for the purpose of carrying out this Act, and shall (subject to the powers of the local education authority under this section) have the exclusive power of appointing and dismissing teachers.

Source: 2 Edw. VII, c. 42; *The Public General Acts Passed in the Second Year of the Reign of His Majesty King Edward the Seventh* (London, 1902), pp. 126–130.

SUGGESTIONS FOR BACKGROUND AND REFERENCE

J. W. Adamson, *English Education 1789–1902* (Cambridge, 1930), pp. 450–471.

M. Cruickshank, *Church and State in English Education* (London, 1963), pp. 69–112.

G. I. T. Machin, *Politics and the Churches in Great Britain, 1869 to 1921* (Oxford, 1987), pp. 260–273.

B. Sacks, *The Religious Issue in the State Schools of England and Wales, 1902–1914* (Albuquerque, 1963).

117   Chinese-American Treaty of 1903 (Extract)

October 8, 1903

Led by Great Britain, the Western powers greatly accelerated their penetration of China in the second half of the nineteenth century. As a result, Chinese religious policy was deeply affected by European interests and ideas and by the needs of missionaries, predominantly British and American. The Treaty of Nanking (1842) and subsequent imperial edicts (1844, 1846) granted freedom of worship in five treaty ports, and more sweeping concessions—missionary travel in the interior and protection of converts—were covered in treaties of 1858 to 1860. Henceforth religious policy was not a domestic concern to be determined unilaterally by the Chinese government, but a treaty issue with Western states acting as guarantors of religious toleration. A high point in this development was reached in the treaties following the Boxer Rebellion. Article XIV of the American treaty enlarged on previous rights and expressly secured the missionary right to acquire property. Ratifications were exchanged January 13, 1904.

XIV. The principles of the Christian religion, as professed by the Protestant and Roman Catholic Churches, are recognized as teaching men to do good and to do to others as they would have others do to them. Those who quietly profess and teach these doctrines shall not be harassed or persecuted on account of their faith. Any person, whether citizen of the United States or Chinese convert, who, according to these tenets, peaceably teaches and practises the principles of Christianity shall in no case be interfered with or molested therefor. No restrictions shall be placed on Chinese joining Christian churches. Converts and non-converts, being Chinese subjects, shall alike conform to the laws of China, and shall pay due respect to those in authority, living together in peace and amity; and the fact of being converts shall not protect them from the consequences of any offence they may have committed before or may commit after their admission into the church, or exempt them from paying legal taxes levied on Chinese subjects generally, except taxes levied and contributions for the support of religious customs and practices contrary to their faith. Missionaries shall not interfere with the exercise by the native authorities of their jurisdiction over Chinese subjects; nor shall the native authorities make any distinction between converts and non-converts, but shall administer the laws without partiality, so that both classes can live together in peace.

Missionary Societies of the United States shall be permitted to rent and to lease in perpetuity, as the property of such societies, buildings, or land in all parts of the Empire for missionary purposes and, after the title-deeds have been found in order and duly stamped by the local authorities, to erect such suitable buildings as may be required for carrying on their good work.

Source: British and Foreign State Papers (1903–1904) (London, 1908), XCVII, 729–730.

SUGGESTIONS FOR BACKGROUND AND REFERENCE

F. R. Dulles, *China and America: The Story of Their Relations since 1784* (Princeton, 1946), pp. 1–122.

K. S. Latourette, *A History of Christian Missions in China* (New York, 1929).

V. Purcell, *Boxer Uprising* (Cambridge, 1963).

P. A. Varg, *Missionaries, Chinese, and Diplomats: The American Protestant Missionary Movement in China, 1890–1952* (Princeton, 1958), pp. 3–146.

✦ ✦ ✦

118   *Motu Proprio* on Catholic Action (*Fin Dalla Prima*) (Extract)

December 18, 1903

Encouraged by *Rerum Novarum,* Catholic social organization in the late nineteenth century found expression in political parties, labor unions, cooperatives, credit unions, information bureaus, and other significant agencies. However, controversy over the interpretation of social policy erupted in parts of the popular Catholic movement in the 1890s, and Leo XIII's last great social encyclical, *Graves de Communi* (1901), repudiated advanced interpretations of Catholic democracy and emphasized Christian charity and ecclesiastical direction. Under Pius X (1903–1914) and his secretary of state, Merry del Val, the warning was strongly amplified.

[Catholic action is necessary and praiseworthy. But among Catholic forces differences have arisen, which have "produced discussions unfortunately too vivacious" and which threaten to create divisions. The rules to be followed have been traced in Leo XIII's encyclicals and the Instruction of the Sacred Congregation for Extraordinary Ecclesiastical Affairs of January 27, 1902. We have summarized them in the following articles, "which will constitute the fundamental plan of Catholic popular action."]

Fundamental Regulations.

I. Human society, as established by God, is composed of unequal elements, just as the different parts of the human body are unequal; to make them all equal is impossible, and would mean the destruction of human society. (Encyclical, "Quod Apostolici Muneris.")

II. The equality existing among the various social members consists only in this: that all men have their origin in God the Creator, have been redeemed by Jesus Christ, and are to be judged and rewarded or punished by God exactly according to their merits or demerits. (Encyclical, "Quod Apostolici Muneris.")

III. Hence it follows that there are, according to the ordinance of God, in human society princes and subjects, masters and proletariat, rich and poor, learned and ignorant, nobles and plebeians, all of whom, united in the bonds of love, are to help one another to attain their last end in heaven, and their material and moral welfare here on earth. (Encyclical, "Quod Apostolici Muneris.")

IV. Of the goods of the earth man has not merely the use, like the brute creation, but he has also the right of permanent proprietorship—and not merely of those things which are consumed by use, but also of those which are not consumed by use. (Encyclical, "Rerum Novarum.")

V. The right of private property, the fruit of labor or industry, or of concession or donation by others, is an incontrovertible natural right; and everybody can dispose reasonably of such property as he thinks fit. (Encyclical, "Rerum Novarum.")

VI. To heal the breach between rich and poor, it is necessary to distinguish between justice and charity. There can be no claim for redress except when justice is violated. (Encyclical, "Rerum Novarum.")

* * *

Obligations of Justice.

[Here follows a digest of the "obligations of justice" for both the workingman and the capitalist, as explained in Leo XIII's *Rerum Novarum*.]

Christian Democracy.

XII. This end is especially aimed at by the movement of Christian Popular Action of Christian Democracy in its many and varied branches. But Christian Democracy must be taken in the sense already authoritatively defined. Totally different from the movement known as "Social Democracy," it has for its basis the principles of Catholic faith and morals—especially the principle of not injuring in any way the inviolable right of private property. (Encyclical, "Graves de Communi.")

XIII. Moreover, Christian Democracy must have nothing to do with politics, and never be able to serve political ends or parties; this is not its field; but it must be a beneficent movement for the people, and founded on the law of nature and the precepts of the gospel. (Encyclical, "Graves de Communi," Instructions of the S. Cong. of E.E. Affairs.)

Christian Democrats in Italy must abstain from participating in any political action—this is under present circumstances forbidden to every Catholic *for reasons of the highest order*. (Instructions as cited.)

XIV. In performing its functions, Christian Democracy is bound most strictly to depend upon ecclesiastical authority, and to offer full submission and obedience to the bishops and those who represent them. There is no meritorious zeal or sincere piety in enterprises, however beautiful and good in themselves, when they are not approved by the pastor. (Encyclical, "Graves de Communi.")

XV. In order that the Christian Democratic movement in Italy may be united in its efforts, it must be under the direction of the Association of Catholic Congresses and Committees, which, during many years of fruitful labor, has deserved so well of Holy Church, and to which Pius IX and . . . Leo XIII . . . entrusted the charge of directing the whole Catholic movement, always, of course, under the auspices and guidance of the bishops. (Encyclical, "Graves de Communi.")

Catholic Writers.

XVI. Catholic writers must, in all that touches religious interests and the action of the Church in society, subject themselves entirely in intellect and will, like the rest of the faithful, to their bishops and to the Roman Pontiff. They must above all take care not to anticipate the judgments of the Holy See in this important matter. (Instruction as cited.)

XVII. Christian Democratic writers must, like all other Catholic writers, submit to the previous examination of the ordinary all writings which concern religion, Christian morals and natural ethics, by virtue of the Constitution "Officiorum et munerum" (Art. 41). By the same Constitution ecclesiastics must obtain the previous consent of the ordinary for publication of writings of a merely technical character. (Instruction.)

XVIII. They must, moreover, make every effort and every sacrifice to ensure that charity and harmony may reign among them. When causes of disagreement arise, they should, instead of printing anything on the matter in the papers, refer it to the ecclesiastical authority, which will then act with justice. And when taken to task by the ecclesiastical authority, let them obey promptly without evasion or public complaints—the right to appeal to a higher authority being understood when the case requires it; and it should be made in the right way. (Instruction.)

XIX. Finally, let Catholic writers take care, when defending the cause of the proletariat and the poor, not to use language calculated to inspire aversion among the people of the upper classes of society. Let them refrain from speaking of redress and justice when the matter comes within the domain of charity only, as has been explained above. Let them remember that Jesus Christ endeavored to unite all men in the bond of mutual love, which is the perfection of justice, and which carries with it the obligation of working for the welfare of one another. (Instruction.)

The foregoing fundamental rules we . . . renew . . . in all their parts, and we ordain that they be transmitted to all Catholic committees, societies and unions of every kind. All these societies are to keep them exposed in their rooms and to have them read frequently at their meetings. We ordain, moreover, that Catholic papers publish them in their entirety and make declaration of their observance of them— and, in fact, observe them religiously; failing to do this they are to be gravely admonished, and if they do not then amend, let them be interdicted by ecclesiastical authority.

Source: The American Catholic Quarterly Review, Vol. XXIX (1904), pp. 234–239. Latin text in *Acta Sanctae Sedis* (Rome, 1903–1904), XXXVI, 339–345.

SUGGESTIONS FOR BACKGROUND AND REFERENCE

M. P. Fogarty, *Christian Democracy in Western Europe, 1820–1953* (Notre Dame, 1957).
F. A. Forbes, *Life of Pius X* (London, 1918).
C. Ledré, *Pie X* (Paris, 1952).

✦✦✦ Separation of Church and State in France

119   Vatican Diplomatic Circular on President Loubet's Roman Visit

April 28, 1904

Though separation of church and state had long been desired by some extreme French anticlericals, the final successful campaign owed much to the furor created by this note—"the act of Pius X which surely contributed most to separation," according to one close (though anti-clerical) student of the subject (Antonin Debidour, *L'Église catholique et l'état sous la Troisième République,* II, 394). The plan for a state visit of President Loubet to Rome in 1904 had advantages for both France and Italy. The absorption of France's ally, Russia, in the Japanese conflict made France anxious for Italian friendship, while Italy welcomed French confirmation of her Roman position. Shortly before his death Leo XIII had informed France that if the visit were made, the president could not be received at the Vatican. Pius X strongly emphasized this policy through this protest, issued by Secretary of State Merry del Val (1865–1917) while Loubet was in Rome and sent to governments with diplomatic representation at the Holy See. The socialist leader, Jean Jaurès, obtained and published the text in *L'Humanité.* The outcry affected public and parliamentary opinion, the French ambassador was ordered home, and (after additional friction) diplomatic relations with the Vatican were terminated at the end of July.

The coming to Rome of M. Loubet, President of the French Republic, on a state visit to Victor Emmanuel III has been an event of such exceptional gravity that the Holy See cannot allow it to pass without calling it to the most serious attention of the government which Your Excellency represents.

It is scarcely necessary to recall that heads of Catholic states, joined as such by special ties to the Supreme Pastor of the Church, have the duty of showing him greater consideration, in comparison with sovereigns of non-Catholic states, in all that concerns his dignity, independence, and absolute rights. This duty, until now recognized and observed by all notwithstanding the weightiest considerations of politics, alliance, or relationship, was incumbent all the more on the first magistrate of the French Republic, who, without having any of these special motives, presides instead over a nation which is united by the closest traditional relations to the Roman papacy, which enjoys signal privileges by virtue of a bilateral pact with the Holy See, which has a large representation in the Sacred College of Cardinals and consequently in the government of the Universal Church, and which by singular favor possesses the protectorate of Catholic interests in the East. Accordingly, if some head of a Catholic nation would commit a grave offense against the Sovereign Pontiff by coming to pay respects at Rome—that is, at the very seat of the Papal See and even in the apostolic palace—to him who against all justice withholds the pope's civil sovereignty and thereby restrains his necessary liberty and independence, this offense has been all the greater when committed by M. Loubet; and if, despite this, the papal nuncio has remained at Paris, it is due only to very grave reasons of a nature in every way special. The declaration of M. Delcassé[1] to the French Parliament that this visit implied no hostile intent toward the Holy See can alter neither its character nor significance; for the offence is intrinsically in the act, so much the more in that the Holy See had not failed to warn this same [French] government.

And public opinion, in France as much as Italy, has not failed to see the offensive character of this visit, deliberately sought by the Italian government with the object of procuring by this means the weakening of the rights of the Holy See . . . .

Source: Felix Stoerk (ed.), *Nouveau recueil général de traités et autres actes relatifs aux rapports de droit international,* 2d Ser. (Leipzig, 1905), XXXII, 243–244.

SUGGESTIONS FOR BACKGROUND AND REFERENCE

J. Brugerette, *Le prêtre français et la société contemporaine* (Paris, 1933–1938), II, 523–554.

A. Dansette, *Religious History of Modern France* (Freiburg, 1961), II, 207–264.

A. Debidour, *L'Église catholique et l'état sous la Troisième République (1870–1906)* (Paris, 1906–1909), II, 339–484.

K. S. Latourette, *Christianity in a Revolutionary Age* (New York, 1958–1962), I, 408–415.

E. Lecanuet, *Les signes avant-coureurs de la séparation: les dernières années de Léon XIII et l'avènement de Pie X, 1894–1910* (Paris, 1930), pp. 473–588.

J. McManners, *Church and State in France, 1870–1914* (New York, 1972), pp. 140–165.

C. S. Phillips, *The Church in France, 1848–1907* (London, 1938), pp. 275–288.

120   Separation Law (Extracts)

December 9, 1905

In June 1903 a parliamentary committee was appointed to consider several private members' bills for separation of church and state. This committee, led chiefly by the socialist Aristide Briand (1862–1932), decided narrowly for separation, and after the fall in January 1905 of Premier Combes, who distrusted the policy, the bill was introduced for

---

1. Theophile Delcassé (1852–1923) was a Radical statesman and French foreign minister from 1898 to 1905.

debate. Recent events—the controversy over religious congregations, the Dreyfus Affair, diplomatic tensions with the Vatican—created a political climate favorable to action. The bill passed the Chamber by 341 to 233 votes on July 3, 1905. The Senate concurred December 6, and the measure was promulgated three days later. The statute destroyed the Napoleonic religious settlement. Not only was the Concordat of 1801 terminated, but state association with the other recognized religions—Protestantism and Judaism—was brought to an end. It marked the triumph of the anticlerical tradition and the end of an era in the history of French Catholicism.

Chapter I. Principles

1. The Republic assures liberty of conscience. It guarantees the free practice of religion, subject only to the restrictions enacted below in the interest of public order.

2. The Republic neither recognizes, subsidizes, nor provides salaries for any religion. Consequently, from the first day of January next after the promulgation of the present law, all expenses related to the practice of religion shall be suppressed in the budgets of the state, the departments, and the communes. Nevertheless, there may still be included in the said budgets expenses related to the provision of chaplains and intended to assure the free practice of religion in public institutions, such as *lycées,* colleges, schools, hospitals, asylums, and prisons.

Public religious establishments are hereby suppressed, subject to the provisions of Article 3.

Chapter II. Assignment of Property. Pensions

3. The establishments ordered suppressed by Article 2 shall continue to function provisionally, according to their present regulations, until the assignment of their property to the associations provided for by Chapter IV, and at latest until the expiration of the period stated below.

After the promulgation of the present law, agents of the Public Lands Administration shall proceed to a descriptive inventory and assessment: (1) of the real and personal property of the said establishments; (2) of the property of the state, the departments, and the communes, of which the establishments have the use.

This double inventory shall be drawn up in concert with the legal representatives of the ecclesiastical establishments . . . .

The agents responsible for the inventory shall have the right to inspect all title-deeds and documents useful to their work.

4. Within one year from the promulgation of the present law, the real and personal property of the *menses* [ancient endowments], vestries, presbyterial councils, consistories, and other public religious establishments . . . shall be transferred by the legal representatives of those establishments to the associations . . . which shall be legally formed according to the provisions of Article 19 for the practice of that religion in the former districts of the said establishments.

5. That part of the property designated in the preceding article which issues from the state and is not [legally] burdened [with responsibility] to a pious foundation created subsequent to the Law of 18 Germinal, Year X, shall revert to the state.

* * *

6. The associations to which are assigned the property of suppressed ecclesiastical establishments shall be held responsible for the debts of those establishments . . . .

* * *

7. Personal or real property devoted to a charitable purpose or to any purpose other than the practice of religion shall be assigned by the legal representatives of the ecclesiastical establishments to public services or institutions, or to services or institutions of public utility, the purpose of which is in accord with that of the said property. Such assignment must be approved by the prefect of the department . . . . When approval is denied, the issue shall be settled by decree of the Council of State.

* * *

9. In default of any association to take over the property of a public religious establishment, such property shall be assigned by decree to the communal institutions for poor relief or charity . . . .

In case of dissolution of an association, the property which has been conveyed to it . . . shall be assigned by decree of Council of State either to similar associations in the same district or, in default of such, in neighboring districts, or to the institutions mentioned in the first paragraph of the present article.

* * *

11. Ministers of religion who, at the promulgation of the present law, have completed their sixtieth year and for at least thirty years have filled ecclesiastical positions remunerated by the state shall receive an annual pension for life equal to three-fourths of their salary.

Those who are more than forty-five years old and for at least twenty years have filled ecclesiastical positions remunerated by the state shall receive an annual pension for life equal to half their salary.

Pensions granted by the two preceding paragraphs shall not exceed 1,500 francs.

In case of death of such pensioners, the pensions shall be transferable, to the extent of half of their amount, in favor of the widow and minor orphans . . . , and to the extent of a quarter in favor of a widow without minor children. When the orphans reach their majority their pension shall cease *ipso facto*.

Ministers of religion presently salaried by the state who are not in the situations stated above shall, during the four years following the suppression of the Budget of Religions, receive an allowance equal to their entire salary for the first year, to two-thirds for the second year, to half for the third year, and to one-third for the fourth year.

However, in communes with less than 1000 inhabitants, and for ministers of religion who continue to fulfill their functions in the same, the duration of each of the four periods stated above shall be doubled.

Departments and communes may, under the same conditions as the state, grant to ministers of religion presently salaried by them pensions or allowances established on the same basis and for the same period.

* * *

Chapter III. Ecclesiastical Buildings

12. Buildings which have been placed at the disposal of the nation and which . . . are used for public worship . . . or for the lodging of their ministers (cathedrals, churches, chapels, temples, synagogues, archbishops' and bishops' houses, presbyteries, seminaries), together with their outbuildings, and the furnishings contained therein . . . are and shall remain the property of the state, the departments, and the communes. . . .

For these buildings, . . . including the faculties of Protestant theology, the procedure shall be in accordance with the provisions of the following articles.

13. Buildings used for public worship, together with their furnishings, shall be left gratuitously at the disposal of the public religious establishments, and afterwards of the associations called upon to replace them to which the property of such establishments shall have been assigned by application of the provisions of Chapter II.

This possession shall be terminated, and if need be transferred, by decree, with a right of appeal to the Council of State in its judicial capacity: (1) if the beneficiary association is dissolved; (2) if, apart from cases of absolute necessity [*force majeure*], the practice of worship has ceased for more than six consecutive months; (3) if the preservation of the building or its furnishings . . . is endangered by neglect of repairs . . . ; (4) if the association ceases to fulfill its object, or if the buildings are diverted from their appointed use; (5) if the association fails to satisfy the requirements of Article 6 or the last paragraph of the present article or the provisions relating to historical monuments.

The secularization of these buildings may, in the above cases, be decided by decree of the Council of State. Apart from these cases, secularization may be accomplished only by a law.

Buildings hitherto set aside for religions, in which worship has not been celebrated for one year previous to the present law, as well as those buildings which are not claimed by a religious association within two years after the promulgation of the law, may be secularized by decree.

The same shall apply for buildings, the secularization of which has been claimed before June 1, 1905.

Public religious establishments, and afterwards the beneficiary associations, shall be held responsible for repairs of every kind, as well as for the cost of insurance and other charges connected with the buildings and the furnishings therein.

14. Archbishops' and bishops' houses, presbyteries, and their appurtenances, *grands séminaires,* and Protestant theological colleges shall be left gratuitously at

the disposal of the public religious establishments and afterwards of the associations provided for in Article 13, as follows: archbishops' and bishops' houses for two years; presbyteries in communes where the minister of religion is resident, *grands séminaires,* and Protestant theological colleges for five years from the promulgation date of the present law.

With respect to these buildings, the establishments and associations are subject to the obligations provided for by the last paragraph of Article 13. However, they shall not be held responsible for major repairs.

* * *

When the period of gratuitous possession expires, free disposal of the buildings shall revert to the state, the departments, or the communes.

The cost of housing now borne by the communes which have no presbytery . . . shall remain at their charge for a period of five years. In case of dissolution of the association, it shall terminate *ipso facto.*

* * *

Chapter IV. Associations for the Practice of Religion

18. The associations formed to provide for the cost, maintenance, and public worship of a religion must be constituted in conformity with . . . the law of July 1, 1901. . . .

19. These associations must have the practice of a religion for their exclusive object. They must have a minimum membership:

In communes of fewer than 1,000 inhabitants, of seven persons;

In communes of 1,000 to 20,000 inhabitants, of fifteen persons;

In communes of more than 20,000 inhabitants, of twenty-five adult persons, domiciled or resident in the ecclesiastical district.

Any of their members may withdraw at any time after payment of the assessments that are due, and those of the current year . . . .

At least once a year . . . acts of financial management and legal administration of the property performed by the directors and managers shall be submitted to the authority of the general meeting of the members of the association for their ratification.

The associations may receive, in addition to the assessments provided for in Article 6 of the law of July 1, 1901, the proceeds of alms and collections for the expenses of worship. They may receive recompense: for religious ceremonies . . . ; for the renting of pews and seats; for supplying objects for funeral services in religious buildings, and for the decoration of those buildings.

* * *

They may not, under any form whatsoever, receive subsidies from the state, the departments, or the communes. But sums allowed for repairs to registered monuments will not be considered as subsidies.

20. These associations may . . . [combine to] form unions having a central administration or directorate . . . .

* * *

22. The associations and unions may use their available resources for the formation of a reserve fund sufficient to assure the expenses and support of the religion, which [resources] may not in any case be diverted to other purposes . . . .

* * *

Chapter V. Regulation of Worship

25. Meetings for worship held in places belonging to a religious association or placed at its disposal must be public. . . . They may be held only after a declaration has been made . . . indicating the place where they will be held.

A single declaration is sufficient for all the regular, periodical, or occasional meetings held during the year.

26. It is forbidden to hold political meetings in places regularly used for worship.

27. Ceremonies, processions, and other public demonstrations of religion shall continue to be regulated in accordance with Articles 95 and 97 of the municipal law of April 5, 1884.

Bell ringing shall be regulated by municipal decree and, in case of disagreement between the mayor and the president or director of the religious association, by order of the prefect.

* * *

28. It is forbidden in the future to erect or fix any religious sign or emblem on public monuments or in any public place whatsoever, with the exception of buildings used for worship, places of burial in cemeteries, monuments for the dead, and museums or exhibitions.

* * *

34. Any minister of religion who, in places where the services of such religion are held, shall, by discourse, by reading, by distribution or posting of written or printed notices, publicly insult or defame a citizen in public office, shall be punished with a fine of 500 to 3,000 francs and imprisonment from one month to one year, or one of these two penalties singly.

* * *

35. If a discourse delivered or a document posted or publicly distributed in places where worship is held contains a direct provocation to resist the execution of the laws or the legal acts of public authority, or tends to arouse or arm one group of citizens against others, the offending minister of religion shall be punished with imprisonment of three months to two years, without prejudice to the penalties for

complicity in cases where provocation has been followed by sedition, revolt, or civil war.

* * *

Chapter VI. General Regulations

* * *

39. Young men who as ecclesiastical students have obtained the dispensation [from military service] . . . shall continue to benefit by it . . . on condition that at the age of twenty-six years they are provided with a position as minister of religion salaried by a religious association . . . .

40. For eight years from the promulgation of the present law, ministers of religion shall be ineligible for the municipal council in communes where they exercise their ecclesiastical functions.

Source: Jean B. Duvergier (ed.), *Collection complète des lois, décrets, ordonnances, règlements, avis du conseil d'état* (Paris, 1834–1905), CV, 586–623.

SUGGESTIONS FOR BACKGROUND AND REFERENCE

J. Brugerette, *Le prêtre français et la société contemporaine* (Paris, 1933–1938), II, 555–608.

L. V. Méjan, *La séparation des églises et de l'état* (Paris, 1959).

P. Sabatier, *Disestablishment in France* (New York, 1906).

W. Schurer, *Aristide Briand und die Trennung von Kirche und Staat in Frankreich* (Basel, 1939).

G. Suarez, *Briand: sa vie, son oeuvre, avec son journal et de nombreux documents inédits* (Paris, 1938–1952), I, 387–464.

References for Document 119.

121   *Vehementer* (Extracts)

February 11, 1906

The heart of the new system that the Separation Law was expected to establish lay in the highly controversial provisions for *associations cultuelles,* the predominantly lay bodies to be formed locally for the practical management and upkeep of religious worship in the parishes. Though some Catholics believed that a *modus vivendi* could be worked out, Catholic argument generally saw in these provisions a challenge to clerical authority and canon law. Pius X, possibly fearful of international consequences of yielding, rejected concession. *Vehementer* condemned the Separation Law as a violation of the Christian idea of society, denounced the unilateral rejection of the Concordat of 1801 as a departure from the law of nations, and dismissed the law's provisions for *associations cultuelles.*

[The Separation Law is disastrous to both society and religion, but it is not surprising, considering the recent trend of religious policy in France. Marriage legislation, secularization of schools and hospitals, dispersal of religious congregations, and other outrages were steps intended to eventuate in complete and official separation.]

That the state must be separated from the Church is a thesis absolutely false . . . . Based . . . on the principle that the state must not recognize any religious cult, it is . . . guilty of a great injustice to God; for the Creator of man is also the Founder of human societies, and preserves their existence as He preserves our own. We owe Him, therefore, not only a private cult, but a public and social worship to honor Him. Besides, it is an obvious negation of the supernatural order. It limits the action of the state to the pursuit of public prosperity during this life only, which is but the proximate object of political societies; and it occupies itself in no fashion (on the plea that this is foreign to it) with their ultimate object, which is man's eternal happiness . . . . It also upsets the order providentially established by God in the world, which demands a harmonious agreement between the two societies, the civil and the religious . . . . It follows necessarily that there are many things belonging to them in common in which both societies must have relations with one another. . . . Finally, it inflicts great injury on society itself, for it cannot either prosper or last long when due place is not left for religion . . . .

* * *

And the ties that consecrated this union [in France] should have been doubly inviolable from the fact that they were sanctioned by oath-bound treaties. The Concordat entered upon by the Sovereign Pontiff and the French government was . . . a bilateral contract binding on both parties . . . . Hence the same rule applied to the Concordat as to all international treaties, viz., the law of nations, which prescribes that it could not be in any way annulled by one alone of the contracting parties. . . .

The extent of the injury inflicted on the Apostolic See by the unilateral abrogation of the Concordat is notably aggravated by the manner in which the state has effected this abrogation. It is a principle admitted without controversy . . . that the breaking of a treaty should be previously and regularly notified . . . to the other contracting party . . . . Yet not only has no notification of this kind been made to the Holy See, but no indication whatever on the subject has been conveyed to it. . . .

If we now proceed to examine . . . the law . . . , we find therein fresh reason for protesting still more energetically. When the state broke the bonds of the Concordat and separated itself from the Church it ought, as a natural consequence, to have left her her independence . . . . Nothing of the kind has been done. We recognize in the law many exceptional and odiously restrictive provisions, the effect of which is to place the Church under the domination of the civil power. . . .

For the provisions of the new law are contrary to the constitution on which the Church was founded by Jesus Christ. The Scripture teaches us, and the tradition of the Fathers confirms the teaching, that the Church is the mystical body of Christ, ruled by the *Pastors* and *Doctors* . . . . It follows that the Church is essentially an *unequal* society, that is, a society comprising two categories of persons, the pastors and the flock, those who occupy a rank in the different degrees of the hierarchy and the multitude of the faithful. So distinct are these categories that with the pastoral body only rests the necessary right and authority for promoting the end of that society and directing all its members towards its end; the one duty of the multitude is to allow themselves to be led, and, like a docile flock, to follow the pastors. . . . The Law of Separation, in opposition to these principles, assigns the administration and the supervision of public worship . . . to an association formed of laymen. To this association it assigns a special form and a juridical personality, and considers it alone as having rights and responsibilities . . . in all matters appertaining to religious worship. It is this association which is to have the use of the churches and sacred edifices, which is to possess ecclesiastical property, real and personal, which is to have at its disposition (though only for a time) the residences of the bishops and priests and the seminaries; which is to administer the property, regulate collections and receive the alms and the legacies destined for religious worship. As for the hierarchical body of pastors, the law is completely silent. And if it does prescribe that the associations of worship are to be constituted in harmony with the general rules of organization of the cult whose existence they are designed to assure, . . . care has been taken to declare that in all disputes which may arise relative to their property, the Council of State is the only competent tribunal. These associations of worship are therefore placed in such a state of dependence on the civil authority that the ecclesiastical authority will, clearly, have no power over them. . . .

Besides, nothing more hostile to the liberty of the Church . . . could well be conceived. For, with the existence of the association of worship, the Law of Separation hinders the pastors from exercising the plenitude of their authority . . . over the faithful, when it attributes to the Council of State supreme jurisdiction over these associations and submits them to a whole series of prescriptions not contained in common law, rendering their formation difficult and their continued existence more difficult still; when, after proclaiming the liberty of public worship, it proceeds to restrict its exercise by numerous exceptions; when it despoils the Church of the internal regulation of the churches in order to invest the state with this function; when it thwarts the preaching of Catholic faith and morals and sets up a severe and exceptional penal code for clerics—when it sanctions all these provisions . . . , does it not place the Church in a position of humiliating subjection and, under the pretext of protecting public order, deprive peaceable citizens, who still constitute the vast majority in France, of the sacred right of practising their religion? Hence it is not merely by restricting the exercise of worship . . . that the state injures the Church, but by putting obstacles to her influence . . . . Thus, for instance, the state has not been satisfied with depriving the Church of the religious orders . . . , but it must also deprive her of the resources which constitute the human means necessary for her existence and the accomplishment of her mission.

In addition . . . , the Law of Separation also violates . . . the rights of property of the Church. . . . The resources furnished by Catholic liberality for the maintenance of Catholic schools, and the working of various charitable associations connected with religion, have been transferred to lay associations in which it would be idle to seek for a vestige of religion. In this it violates not only the rights of the Church, but the . . . purpose of the donors and testators. It is also a subject of keen grief to us that the law . . . proclaims as property of the state, departments, or communes the ecclesiastical edifices dating from before the Concordat. True, the law concedes the gratuitous use of them, for an indefinite period, to the associations of worship, but it surrounds the concession with so many and so serious reserves that in reality it leaves to the public powers the full disposition of them. Moreover, we entertain the gravest fears for the sanctity of those temples. . . . For they are certainly in danger of profanation if they fall into the hands of laymen.

When the law, by the suppression of the Budget of Public Worship, exonerates the state from the obligation of providing for the expenses of worship, it violates an engagement contracted in a diplomatic convention . . . . When the French government assumed in the Concordat the obligation of supplying the clergy with a revenue sufficient for their decent subsistence and for the requirements of public worship, the concession was not a merely gratuitous one—it was an obligation assumed by the state to make restitution, at least in part, to the Church whose property had been confiscated during the first Revolution. On the other hand, when the Roman Pontiff in this same Concordat bound himself and his successors . . . not to disturb the possessors of property thus taken from the Church, he did so only on one condition: that the French government should bind itself in perpetuity to endow the clergy suitably and to provide for the expenses of divine worship.

* * *

Hence, . . . we . . . condemn the law . . . for the separation of Church and state as deeply unjust to God, whom it denies, and as laying down the principle that the Republic recognizes no cult. We . . . condemn it as violating the natural law, the law of nations, and fidelity to treaties; as contrary to the divine constitution of the Church, to her essential rights and to her liberty; as destroying justice and trampling under foot the rights of property which the Church has acquired by many titles and, in addition, by virtue of the Concordat. We . . . condemn it as gravely offensive to the dignity of this Apostolic See, to our own person, to the episcopacy and to the clergy and all the Catholics of France. Therefore, we protest solemnly and with all our strength against the introduction, the voting, and the promulgation of this law . . . .

Source: The American Catholic Quarterly Review, Vol. XXXI (1906), pp. 209–217. Latin text in *Acta Sanctae Sedis* (Rome, 1906), XXXIX, 3–16.

SUGGESTIONS FOR BACKGROUND AND REFERENCE

M. J. M. Larkin, "The Vatican, French Catholics, and the *Associations Cultuelles," Journal of Modern History,* Vol. XXXVI, No. 3 (September 1964), pp. 298–317.
J. McManners, *Church and State in France, 1870–1914* (New York, 1972), pp. 166–175.
References for Documents 119 and 120.

122   Religious Worship Law (Extracts)

January 2, 1907

The failure to find common ground for compromise left France with an apparently insuperable religious problem. The plan of the Separation Law could not be implemented; no *associations cultuelles* were formed. Strict enforcement of the statute required the seizure of ecclesiastical property and the closing of the churches, but the government, which in any case had no use for the church buildings, shrank from this extreme. For their part, the bishops decided to surrender the churches only to force. Consequently, the government sought a way out of this impasse by this law of 1907, permitting Catholics to use the forfeited church property through an association formed in accordance with the Law of Associations (1901) or through individuals making declaration of public meeting under a law of 1881—one declaration to cover the entire year.

1. From the promulgation of the present law, the state, the departments, and the communes shall recover by absolute title the free disposal of the archbishops' and bishops' residences, presbyteries, and seminaries . . . if their use has not been claimed by an association formed within the year following the promulgation of the Law of December 9, 1905, in conformity with the provisions of the said law.

* * *

2. Property of ecclesiastical establishments which has not been claimed by associations formed within the year following the promulgation of the Law of December 9, 1905 . . . shall be assigned by absolute title, from the promulgation of the present law, to communal establishments for charity or benevolence under the conditions fixed by article 9, paragraph 1 of the said law, without prejudice to the grants to be effected through application of articles 7 and 8, in cases concerning property encumbered by an appropriation distinct from the exercise of religious worship.

3. After the expiration of one month from promulgation of the present law, the allowances conferred by application of article 11 of the Law of December 9, 1905 to ministers of religion who continue to exercise their functions shall be suppressed *ipso jure* in the ecclesiastical districts where the conditions prescribed by the Law of December 9, 1905 or by the present law have not been fulfilled . . . .

* * *

4. Independently of the associations subject to the provisions of Title IV of the Law of December 9, 1905 the public exercise of religious worship may be assured either by means of associations regulated by the Law of July 1, 1901 . . . or by means of meetings held under individual initiative by virtue of the Law of June 30, 1881, and according to the provisions of article 25 of the Law of December 9, 1905.

5. In default of associations for worship, buildings assigned to the exercise of religious worship, as well as their furnishings, shall, subject to voidance in cases

provided for by the Law of December 9, 1905, continue at the disposal of the faithful and ministers of religion for practice of their religion.

Gratuitous use thereof may be granted either to the associations for worship formed in conformity with articles 18 and 19 of the Law of December 9, 1905, or to associations formed by virtue of the already cited provisions of the Law of July 1, 1901, to assure the continuation of the public exercise of worship, or to ministers of religion whose names must be included in the declarations prescribed by article 25 of the Law of December 9, 1905.

Source: Antonin Debidour, *L'Église catholique et l'état sous la Troisième République* (Paris, 1906–1909), II, 601–602.

SUGGESTIONS FOR BACKGROUND AND REFERENCE

References for Documents 119 and 120.

123 *Une Fois Encore* (Extracts)

January 6, 1907

Only a few days after the promulgation of the new law on worship, the Vatican replied, rejecting the proposal for annual declarations for permission to occupy religious edifices. After this encyclical, and as other attempts to arrive at a legal settlement were unavailing, the government adopted a policy of connivance at Catholic worship and occupancy of the confiscated property. A law of March 28, 1907, abolished the requirement of a declaration for public meetings. With this "settlement" the French Catholic Church was left insecure, illegal, and financially crippled, but also independent of government direction.

Once again the serious events which have been precipitated in your noble country compel Us to write to the Church of France to sustain her in her trials, and to comfort her in her sorrow. . . .

* * *

This persecution which she is reproached as having provoked, and which they declare they have refused, is now being actually inflicted upon her. Have they not within these last days evicted from their houses even the bishops who are most venerable . . . , driven the seminarists from the *grands* and *petits séminaires,* and entered upon the expulsion of the curés from their presbyteries? The whole Catholic world has watched this spectacle with sadness . . . .

As for the ecclesiastical property which we are accused of having abandoned, . . . this property was partly the patrimony of the poor and . . . , more sacred still, of the dead. It was not permissible to the Church to abandon or surrender it; she could only let it be taken from her by violence. . . . Consequently, to declare ecclesiastical property unclaimed on a given date unless the Church had by then created within herself a new organism; to subject this creation to conditions in rank opposition to the divine constitution of the Church . . . ; to transfer this property to third parties . . . , and finally to assert that in thus acting there was no spoliation of the Church but only a disposal of the property abandoned by her—this is not merely argument of transparent sophistry but adding insult to the most cruel spoliation. . . . In any case it would have been easy for the state not to have subjected the formation of *associations cultuelles* to conditions in direct opposition to the divine constitution of the Church which they were supposed to serve.

* * *

As regards the annual declaration demanded for the exercise of worship, it did not offer the full legal security which one had a right to desire. Nevertheless . . . the Church could, in order to avoid greater evils, have brought herself to tolerate this declaration. But by providing that the "curé or officiating priest would no longer," in his church "be anything more than an occupier without any judicial title or power to perform any acts of administration," there has been imposed on ministers of religion in the very exercise of their ministry a situation so humiliating and vague that, under such conditions, it was impossible to accept the declaration.

There remains for consideration the law recently voted by the two Chambers.

From the point of view of ecclesiastical property, this law is a law of spoliation and confiscation, and it has completed the stripping of the Church. . . . Her ownership, indisputable from every point of view, had been, moreover, officially sanctioned by the state, which could not consequently violate it. From the point of view of the exercise of worship, this law has organized anarchy; it is the consecration of uncertainty and caprice. Uncertainty [exists] whether places of worship, always liable to be diverted from their purpose, are meanwhile to be placed, or not placed, at the disposition of the clergy and faithful. . . . Public worship will be in as many diverse situations as there are parishes in France; in each parish the priest will be at the discretion of the municipal authority. And thus an opening for conflict has been organized from one end of the country to the other. On the other hand, there is an obligation to meet all sorts of heavy charges, whilst at the same time there are draconian restrictions upon the resources by which they are to be met. . . .

It is easy to see . . . that this law is an aggravation of the Law of Separation, and we can not therefore do otherwise than condemn it.

Source: The American Catholic Quarterly Review, Vol. XXXII (1907), pp. 138–142. Latin text in *Acta Sanctae Sedis* (Rome, 1907), XL, 3–11.

SUGGESTIONS FOR BACKGROUND AND REFERENCE

References for Documents 119, 120, and 121.

✦ ✦ ✦

124   Condemnation of *Le Sillon* (Extracts)

August 25, 1910

Le Sillon in France and Romolo Murri's *Lega democratica nazionale* in Italy were articulate and experimental Catholic social movements of the turn of the nineteenth century. Founded by an ex-soldier, Marc Sangnier (1873–1950), *Le Sillon* recruited successfully from Catholic students, intellectuals, the army, and workingmen. Through study-circles Sangnier promoted adherence to the Republic, social reform, and Christianized democracy. Though approved by Leo XIII and—at first—by Pius X, the movement incurred the hostility of French conservatives and employers, challenged traditional positions on liberty and authority, and by inattention to clerical direction disturbed the hierarchy and raised the issue of agreement with Pius X's *motu proprio* of 1903. After 1906 Sangnier, fearing condemnation, modified the bases of the movement, gave less stress to Catholic inspiration, received non-Catholics into membership, and emphasized simple political democracy. In Italy the modernist Murri was excommunicated in 1909. But in France Sangnier submitted to the censure of 1910 and dissolved *Le Sillon*. (The reorganization on diocesan lines, ordered at the end of the document, was unsuccessful.) The statement delimited the scope and nature of social and political action lawful to Catholic democracy.

[The pope has hesitated to inform the bishops concerning the Sillon because of the nobility of the movement's leaders and adherents. Following *Rerum Novarum*, the Sillon has performed praiseworthy work among the working classes. Yet the Sillon went astray because its youthful founders were inadequately grounded in history, philosophy, and theology, and could not rightly meet social problems and prevent liberal and Protestant infiltration. The Sillon cannot escape the direction of ecclesiastical authority, for its leaders proclaim "a social doctrine and religious and philosophic principles for the reconstruction of society upon a new plan," and "they appeal to the Gospel interpreted in their own manner, and . . . to a disfigured and diminished Christ." Therefore, their purposes appertain to "the moral domain, which is the proper domain of the Church."]

In effect, the Sillon puts forward as a programme the elevation and regeneration of the working classes. But in this matter the principles of Catholic doctrine are fixed . . . . Our predecessor . . . reminded them of this . . . . He denounced "a certain democracy which goes so far in perversity as to attribute . . . sovereignty to the people and to aim at the suppression and the leveling down of the classes." At the same time, Leo XIII laid down for Catholics a programme of action . . . . But what have the leaders of the Sillon done? . . . . they have openly rejected the programme . . . and adopted one diametrically opposed to it . . . .

* * *

In order not to be accused of judging too hastily . . . the social theories of the Sillon, we wish to review their essential points.

The Sillon is nobly solicitous for human dignity, but it understands that dignity in the manner of certain philosophers of whom the Church does not at all feel proud. The first element of that dignity is liberty, understood in the sense that, except in the matter of religion, each man is autonomous. From this fundamental principle it draws the following conclusions: today the people are in tutelage under an authority distinct from themselves; they ought to free themselves from it: *political emancipation*. They are dependent upon employers who hold their instruments of labor, exploit them, oppress them and degrade them; they ought to shake off the yoke: *economic emancipation*. Finally, they are ruled by a caste, called the directing caste, to whom their intellectual development gives an undue preponderance in the direction of affairs; they must break away from their domination: *intellectual emancipation*. The leveling down of conditions from this triple point of view will establish equality amongst men, and this equality is true human justice. . . .

* * *

First of all, in politics the Sillon does not abolish authority; . . . but it wishes to divide it, or rather to multiply it in such a way that each citizen will become a kind of king. Authority, it is true, emanates from God, but it resides first of all in the people and is obtained from them by means of election, or, better still, selection, without at the same time leaving the people and becoming independent of them; it will be external but in appearance only; in reality it will be internal, because it will be an accepted authority.

Proportions being preserved, it will be the same in the economic order. Taken away from a particular class, the mastership will be so well multiplied that each workingman will himself become a sort of master. The system by which it is intended to realize this economic ideal is not that of socialism; it is the system of co-operation sufficiently multiplied to provoke a fruitful competition and to safeguard the independence of the workingmen who will not be bound down to any single one of the co-operative forces.

We come now to the principal element, the moral element. Since . . . authority is much reduced, another force is necessary to take its place . . . . This new principle . . . is the love of professional interest and of public interest . . . . Imagine a society in which in each one's soul, with the innate love of individual and family welfare, reigns the love of professional and public welfare, in which in each one's conscience these loves are so subordinate that the welfare of a superior character always takes its place before the welfare of an inferior—could not such a society almost do without authority and does it not offer the ideal of human dignity . . . ? Snatched away from the narrowness of private interests, . . . the human heart . . . would embrace all comrades of the same profession, all compatriots, all men. Here is human greatness and nobility, the idea realized by the celebrated trilogy, liberty, equality, fraternity.

These three elements . . . are subordinated one to the other and . . . the moral element is the principle [*sic*]. In effect, no political democracy can exist if it has not profound points of connection in economic democracy. In their turn, neither . . . is possible if they have not mutually their roots in a state of mind in which the conscience is invested with proportionate moral responsibilities and energies. But supposing . . . this state of mind, . . . economic democracy will naturally arise out of it [the moral element] . . . ; and, similarly . . . , out of the co-operative regime will arise political democracy: and political and economic democracy, the latter bearing the other, will find themselves fixed in the very conscience of the people on unshakable bases.

* * *

This rapid explanation . . . shows you clearly how much reason we have to say that the Sillon opposes doctrine to doctrine, that it builds its state on a theory contrary to Catholic truths . . . .

The Sillon places public authority first of all in the people, from whom it then flows to rulers in such a manner, however, that it continues to reside in the people. . . . No doubt the Sillon holds that that authority, which it places first of all in the people, descends from God . . . . But . . . Leo XIII refuted in advance this attempt to reconcile Catholic doctrine with the error of philosophism. "For," he continues, ". . . those who preside over the government . . . may . . . be chosen by the will and the judgment of the multitude without repugnance or opposition to Catholic doctrine. But if this choice marks out the governor, it does not confer upon him the authority to govern; it does not delegate the power, it designates the person who will be invested with it."

For the rest, if the people are the holders of power, what becomes of authority? It is a shadow, a myth . . . .

* * *

The Sillon . . . therefore sows amongst your Catholic youth erroneous and fatal notions upon authority, liberty and obedience. The same is to be said with regard to justice and equality. It strives, it says, to attain an era of equality, which, owing to that fact alone, would be an era of greater justice. Thus to it every inequality of condition is an injustice, or at least a diminution of justice! A principle supremely contrary to the nature of things, productive of jealousy and injustice and subversive of all social order. Thus democracy alone will inaugurate the reign of perfect justice! Is it not an insult to other forms of government . . . ?

* * *

Finally, at the base of all the falsifications of fundamental social views . . . the Sillon places a false idea of human dignity. According to it, man will not be truly man . . . except . . . when he shall have acquired a conscience enlightened, . . . able to do without a master, obeying only itself and capable of assuming and discharging the greatest responsibilities . . . . These are the big words by which the sentiment of human pride is exalted . . . .

* * *

We close here our consideration of the errors of the Sillon. . . . But we must now go on to observe the influence of these errors on the practical conduct and social action of the Sillon.

The doctrines of the Sillon do not keep within the domain of abstract philosophy. They are taught to Catholic young people and efforts are made to make them live. The Sillon regards itself as the nucleus of the state of the future and accordingly reflects it as closely as possible. Thus, there is no hierarchy of government in the Sillon. The elite by whom it is directed emerge from the rank and file by selection, that is to say, they make their position by their moral authority and their qualities. . . . Studies are carried on without a master . . . . The study clubs are veritable intellectual co-operative societies . . . . Even the priest, on entering, lowers the eminent dignity of his priesthood, and by a strange reversal of roles becomes a scholar, placing himself on a level with his young friends . . . .

In these democratic customs and the theories on the ideal state inspired by them, you will see . . . the secret cause of the lack of discipline with which you have so often had to reproach the Sillon. . . . You represent the hierarchy, social inequalities, authority, obedience—worn out institutions to which their minds . . . can no longer bow . . . . It has come to this: Our Catholic young people are inspired with distrust of the Church their Mother; they are told that for nineteen centuries she has failed to build up society on its true foundations; that she has not understood the social notions of authority, liberty, equality, fraternity, and human dignity; that the great bishops and kings who have created and governed France so gloriously have not been able to provide their people with real justice or happiness because they had not the same ideal as the Sillon.

The breath of the Revolution has passed this way, and we may conclude that if the social doctrines of the Sillon are erroneous, its spirit is dangerous and its education disastrous.

* * *

There was a time when the Sillon as such was formally Catholic. In the matter of moral force it recognized but . . . the Catholic force, and it was wont to proclaim that democracy would be Catholic or would not exist at all. A moment came when it changed its mind. It left to each one his religion or his philosophy. It ceased to call itself Catholic, and for the formula "the democracy will be Catholic" it substituted this other, "the democracy will not be anti-Catholic," any more than it will be anti-Jewish or anti-Buddhist. It was the period at which the Sillon attained its highest influence. For the construction of the future state they appealed to all the workers of all the religions and all the sects. They asked them only to embrace the same social ideal, to respect all beliefs, and to bring with them a certain supply of moral force. . . .

* * *

The result of this promiscuousness and labor, the beneficiary of this cosmopolitan social action, can only be a democracy which will be neither Catholic nor Protestant, nor Jewish; a religion (for Sillonism, its chiefs state, is a religion) more universal than the Catholic Church, uniting all men . . . .

And now . . . we ask . . . where is the Catholicism of the Sillon? Alas! this organization which formerly afforded such excellent hopes . . . has been mastered in its course by the modern enemies of the Church and forms only a miserable affluent of the great movement of apostasy organized in all countries for the establishment of a universal Church which shall have neither dogmas nor hierarchy, neither rule for the mind nor curb for the passions, and which, under the pretext of liberty and human dignity, would bring back to the world . . . the legal reign of cunning and of force, of the oppression of the weak—of those who suffer and toil.

[Moreover, since society should be organized to "enable every one of good will to gain a legitimate share of temporal happiness," the bishops are urged to take an active role.] And to this end, . . . you will choose some [priests] . . . who possess doctors' degrees in philosophy and theology and who are thoroughly acquainted with the history of ancient and modern civilization, and you will set them to the study . . . of social science, so that you can place them at the proper time in charge of your Catholic social movement. But let not those priests allow themselves to be led astray . . . . Let them be convinced that . . . the Church . . . has not to free herself from the past, and that it is enough for her to take up again . . . the organisms broken by the Revolution and to adapt them . . . to the new situation created by the material evolution of contemporary society: for the true friends of the people are neither revolutionaries nor innovators, but traditionalists.

We desire that the Sillonist youth, freed from their errors, far from offering any obstacle to this work, . . . should bring to it a loyal and efficacious assistance . . . and with befitting submission.

. . . As to the members of the Sillon, we desire that they should be divided according to the dioceses, in order to work, under the direction of their respective bishops, for the Christian and Catholic regeneration of the people . . . . These diocesan groups will for the moment be independent of one another; and in order to show clearly that they have broken with the errors of the past, they will take the name of *Catholic Sillons* . . . . It is needless to say that every Catholic Sillonist will remain free to entertain his political preferences, provided they are purified of everything that is not . . . entirely conformable to the doctrine of the Church. . . .

Source: The American Catholic Quarterly Review, Vol. XXXV (1910), pp. 693–711. Latin text in *Acta Apostolicae Sedis* (Rome, 1910), II, 607–633.

SUGGESTIONS FOR BACKGROUND AND REFERENCE

E. Barbier, *Histoire du catholicisme libéral et du catholicisme social en France du concile du Vatican à l'avènement de S. S. Benoit XV (1870–1914)* (Bordeaux, 1924), IV, 371–592.

C. Breunig, "Condemnation of the Sillon: An Episode in the History of Christian-Democracy in France," *Church History*, Vol. XXVI, No. 3 (September 1957), pp. 227–244.

J. Brugerette, *Le prêtre français et la société contemporaine* (Paris, 1933–1938), III, 217–235.

A. Dansette, *Religious History of Modern France* (Freiburg, Germany, 1961), II, 112–137, 265–290.

A. Hoog, *Histoire du catholicisme social en France 1871–1931* (Paris, 1946), pp. 1–190.

E. Lecanuet, *La vie de l'église sous Léon XIII* (Paris, 1930), pp. 603–702.

J. McManners, *Church and State in France, 1870–1914* (New York, 1972), pp. 94–103, 170–173.

A. Vidler, *A Century of Social Catholicism, 1820–1920* (London, 1964), pp. 112–140.

125   Federal Council "Social Creed"

December 9, 1912

Though the "social gospel" movement in American Protestantism matured in the nineteenth century, official church action did not come until after 1900. Then most of the leading denominations established commissions for social study and action that attempted to educate church people, establish sympathetic relations with the labor movement, and mitigate social antagonisms. An early official statement of importance was the social program endorsed by the Methodist Baltimore Conference in 1908 and adopted in large measure by the newly formed Federal Council of Churches of Christ in America. In 1912 the Federal Council altered its social creed to this form, which was to stand until 1932. Though the social movement probably represented a minority of church people and was sometimes viewed with distrust, this comprehensive statement marked the beginning of a deeper Protestant involvement in contemporary social and political issues that grew stronger with the years. (A comparable Catholic milestone in social policy appeared in "The Bishops' Program of Social Reconstruction," adopted in 1919 by the National Catholic War Council. See *Our Bishops Speak . . . 1919–1951* [Milwaukee, 1952], pp. 243–260.)

The Churches must stand:

1. For equal rights and complete justice for all men in all stations of life.

2. For the protection of the family, by the single standard of purity, uniform divorce laws, proper regulation of marriage, and proper housing.

3. For the fullest possible development for every child, especially by the provision of proper education and recreation.

4. For the abolition of child labor.

5. For such regulation of the conditions of toil for women as shall safeguard the physical and moral health of the community.

6. For the abatement and prevention of poverty.

7. For the protection of the individual and society from the social, economic, and moral waste of the liquor traffic.

8. For the conservation of health.

9. For the protection of the worker from dangerous machinery, occupational diseases, and mortality.

10. For the right of all men to the opportunity for self-maintenance, for safeguarding this right against encroachments of every kind, and for the protection of workers from the hardships of enforced unemployment.

11. For suitable provision for the old age of the workers, and for those incapacitated by injury.

12. For the right of employees and employers alike to organize, and for adequate means of conciliation and arbitration in industrial disputes.

13. For a release from employment one day in seven.

14. For the gradual and reasonable reduction of the hours of labor to the lowest practicable point, and for that degree of leisure for all which is a condition of the highest human life.

15. For a living wage as a minimum in every industry, and for the highest wage that each industry can afford.

16. For a new emphasis upon the application of Christian principles to the acquisition and use of property, and for the most equitable division of the product of industry that can ultimately be devised.

Source: The Outlook, December 21, 1912, p. 851.

SUGGESTIONS FOR BACKGROUND AND REFERENCE

A. I. Abell, *The Urban Impact on American Protestantism 1865–1900* (New York, 1962).

J. Dombrowski, *The Early Days of Christian Socialism in America* (New York, 1936).

C. H. Hopkins, *The Rise of the Social Gospel in American Protestantism, 1865–1915* (New Haven, 1940).

H. F. May, *Protestant Churches and Industrial America* (New York, 1949).

D. B. Meyer, *The Protestant Search for Political Realism, 1919–1941* (Berkeley, 1960).

R. M. Miller, *American Protestantism and Social Issues, 1919–1939* (Chapel Hill, N.C., 1958).

E. B. Sanford, *Origin and History of the Federal Council of the Churches of Christ in America* (Hartford, Conn., 1916).

126   Mexican Constitution of 1917 (Extracts)

January 31, 1917

In the second half of the nineteenth century, church and state conflicts became common in Latin America, where the clergy were identified with the conservative landed classes in resisting agrarian and political reconstruction in the interests of the impoverished peasantry and Indians. In Mexico the anticlerical tradition, born in ecclesiastical opposition to the national struggle against Spain, matured in the Juarez program of the 1850s, which indicted the landed wealth and political and educational influence of the church. Yet the clerical position was not seriously undermined until the 1910 revolution. The new Constitution of 1917 inaugurated a bitter and violent conflict, which occasionally erupted into civil war and dominated Mexican politics for decades. Strife was greatest after 1926 when President Calles sought to give effect to the religious provisions of the Constitution and again between 1934 and 1937 under President Cárdenas. In the contest much ecclesiastical property was secularized and some areas were deprived of priests and sacraments. The

From *British and Foreign State Papers,* CXI (1917–1918) (London, 1921). Copyright, 1921, by H. M. Stationery Office. Reprinted by permission of the publisher.

struggle subsided at the end of the decade, but left a heritage of political bitterness comparable to that of France or Spain.

3. Instruction is free; that given in public institutions of learning shall be secular. Primary instruction, whether higher or lower, given in private institutions shall likewise be secular.

No religious corporation nor minister of any religious creed shall establish or direct schools of primary instruction.

* * *

24. Everyone is free to embrace the religion of his choice and to practise all ceremonies, devotions or observances of his respective creed, either in places of public worship or at home, provided they do not constitute an offence punishable by law.

Every religious act of public worship shall be performed strictly within the places of public worship, which shall be at all times under governmental supervision.

* * *

From Article 27:

(2) The religious institutions known as churches, irrespective of creed, shall in no case have legal capacity to acquire, hold or administer real property or loans made on such real property; all such real property or loans as may be at present held by the said religious institutions, either on their own behalf or through third parties, shall vest in the nation, and anyone shall have the right to denounce property so held. Presumptive proof shall be sufficient to declare the denunciation well-founded. Places of public worship are the property of the nation, as represented by the Federal Government, which shall determine which of them may continue to be devoted to their present purposes. Episcopal residences, rectories, seminaries, orphan asylums or collegiate establishments of religious institutions, convents or any other buildings built or designed for the administration, propaganda, or teaching of the tenets of any religious creed shall forthwith vest, as of full right, directly in the nation, to be used exclusively for the public services of the Federation or of the States, within their respective jurisdictions. All places of public worship which shall later be erected shall be the property of the nation.

(3) Public and private charitable institutions for the sick and needy, for scientific research, or for the diffusion of knowledge, mutual aid societies or organizations formed for any other lawful purpose shall in no case acquire, hold or administer loans made on real property, unless the mortgage terms do not exceed ten years. In no case shall institutions of this character be under the patronage, direction, administration, charge or supervision of religious corporations or institutions, nor of ministers of any religious creed or of their dependents, even though either the former or the latter shall not be in active service.

* * *

130. The Federal authorities shall have power to exercise in matters of religious worship and outward ecclesiastical forms such intervention as by law authorized. All other officials shall act as auxiliaries to the Federal authorities.

The Congress shall not enact any law establishing or forbidding any religion whatsoever.

Marriage is a civil contract. Marriage and all other acts relating to the civil status of individuals shall appertain to the exclusive jurisdiction of the civil authorities in the manner and form by law provided, and they shall have the force and validity given them by said laws.

A simple promise to tell the truth and to comply with obligations contracted shall subject the promiser, in the event of a breach, to the penalties established therefor by law.

The law recognizes no juridical personality in the religious institutions known as churches.

Ministers of religious creeds shall be considered as persons exercising a profession, and shall be directly subject to the laws enacted on the matter.

The State Legislatures shall have the exclusive power of determining the maximum number of ministers of religious creeds, according to the needs of each locality. Only a Mexican by birth may be a minister of any religious creed in Mexico.

No ministers of religious creeds shall, either in public or private meetings, or in acts of worship or religious propaganda, criticize the fundamental laws of the country, the authorities in particular or the government in general; they shall have no vote, nor be eligible to office, nor shall they be entitled to assemble for political purposes.

Before dedicating new temples of worship for public use, permission shall be obtained from the Department of the Interior [*Gobernación*]; the opinion of the governor of the respective State shall be previously heard on the subject. Every place of worship shall have a person charged with its care and maintenance, who shall be legally responsible for the faithful performance of the laws on religious observances within the said place of worship, and for all objects used for purposes of worship.

The caretaker of each place of public worship, together with ten citizens of the place, shall promptly advise the municipal authorities as to the person charged with the care of the said place of worship. The outgoing minister shall . . . give notice of any change, for which purpose he shall be accompanied by the incoming minister and ten other citizens of the place. The municipal authorities, under penalty of dismissal and fine, not exceeding 1,000 pesos for each breach, shall be responsible for the exact performance of this provision; they shall keep a register of the places of worship and another of the caretakers thereof. . . . The municipal authorities shall likewise give notice to the Department of the Interior through the State governor of any permission to open to the public use a new place of worship, as well as of any change in the caretakers. . . .

Under no conditions shall studies carried on in institutions devoted to the professional training of ministers . . . be given credit or granted any other dispensation . . . which shall have for its purpose the accrediting of the said studies in official institutions. Any authority violating this provision shall be punished criminally, and all such dispensation of privilege be null and void, and shall invalidate . . . the professional degree towards the obtaining of which the infraction of this provision may in any way have contributed.

No periodical publication which . . . is of a religious character, shall comment upon any political affairs of the nation, nor publish any information regarding the acts of the authorities . . . or of private individuals, in so far as the latter have to do with public affairs.

Every kind of political association whose name shall bear . . . any indication relating to any religious belief is hereby strictly forbidden. No assemblies of any political character shall be held within places of public worship.

No minister of any religious creed may inherit, either on his own behalf or by means of a trustee or otherwise, any real property occupied by any association of religious propaganda or religious or charitable purposes. Ministers of religious creeds are incapable legally of inheriting by will from ministers of the same religious creed or from any private individual to whom they are not related by blood within the fourth degree. . . .

No trial by jury shall ever be granted for the infraction of any of the preceding provisions.

Source: British and Foreign State Papers (1917–1918) (London, 1921), XCI, 779, 785, 787–788, 828–830.

SUGGESTIONS FOR BACKGROUND AND REFERENCE

W. H. Callcott, *Liberalism in Mexico, 1857–1929* (Stanford, 1931).

C. C. Cumberland, *Mexican Revolution: Genesis under Madero* (Austin, 1952).

R. E. Quirk, *The Mexican Revolution and the Catholic Church, 1910–1929* (Bloomington, Ind., 1973), pp. 79–112.

VI

THE LATEST ERA: SINCE THE RUSSIAN REVOLUTION

✦✦✦ The Orthodox Church
and the Bolsheviks

127 Patriarch Tikhon's Pastoral

February 1, 1918 [January 19, Old Style]

The 1917 revolution and the establishment of the provisional government gave Russian Orthodoxy a brief period of freedom. With the approval of the government, an Orthodox sobor of more than five hundred delegates met in August 1917 and reorganized the Russian Church, naming Tikhon (1866–1925), Metopolitan of Moscow, as the first patriarch since the reign of Peter the Great. Tikhon, chosen by lot from three nominees, was the least popular but most moderate of the candidates and had long experience in the hierarchy, including nine years as head of the church in North America. His enthronement (November 21) followed closely on the Communist seizure of power, and the next five years of his career were filled with political struggle. Early Bolshevik decrees confiscated church lands and buildings, ended state salaries for clergy, nationalized schools (including church secondary schools and theological academies and seminaries), provided for civil marriage and divorce, and transferred the keeping of civil registers from clergy to government bureaus. Tikhon's anathema, published in the absence of the sobor but later approved by it, represented the opening of the long conflict between Orthodoxy and the Bolshevik regime.

The Lord will deliver us from this present evil world. (Gal. i. 4.)

The Holy Orthodox church of Christ is at present passing through difficult times in the Russian Land; the open and secret foes of the truth of Christ began persecuting that truth, and are striving to destroy the work of Christ by sowing everywhere in place of Christian love the seeds of malice, hatred, and fratricidal warfare.

The commands of Christ regarding the love of neighbor are forgotten or trampled upon; reports reach us daily concerning the astounding and beastly murders of wholly innocent people, and even of the sick upon their sick-beds, who are guilty perhaps only of having fulfilled their duty to the Fatherland, and of having spent all their strength in the service of the national welfare. This happens not only under cover of the nocturnal darkness, but openly in daylight, with hitherto unheard of

From Matthew Spinka, *The Church and the Russian Revolution* (New York, 1927). Copyright, 1927, by The Macmillan Company. Reprinted by permission of the author.

audacity and merciless cruelty, without any sort of trial and despite all right and lawfulness, and it happens in our days almost in all the cities and villages of our country, as well as in our capital, and outlying regions (Petrograd, Moscow, Irkutsk, Sevastopol, and others).

All this fills our heart with a deep and bitter sorrow and obliges us to turn to such outcasts of the human race with stern words of accusation and warning, in accordance with the command of the holy apostle: "them that sin reprove in the sight of all, that the rest also may be in fear." (I Tim. v. 20.)

Recall yourselves, ye senseless, and cease your bloody deeds. For what you are doing is not only a cruel deed; it is in truth a satanic act, for which you shall suffer the fire of Gehenna in the life to come, beyond the grave, and the terrible curses of posterity in this present, earthly life.

By the authority given us by God, we forbid you to present yourselves for the sacraments of Christ, and anathematize you, if you still bear the name of Christians, even if merely on account of your baptism you still belong to the Orthodox church.

I adjure all of you who are faithful children of the Orthodox church of Christ, not to commune with such outcasts of the human race in any matter whatsoever: "cast out the wicked from among you." (I Cor. v. 13.)

The most cruel persecution has likewise arisen against the holy church of Christ: the blessed sacraments, sanctifying the birth of man into the world, or blessing the marital union of the Christian family, have been pronounced unnecessary and superfluous; the holy churches are subjected either to destruction by reason of the gunfire directed against them (*e.g.* the holy cathedrals of the Moscow Kremlin), or to plunder and sacrilegious injury (*e.g.* the Chapel of the Savior in Petrograd). The saintly monasteries revered by the people (as the Alexandro-Nevsky and Pochaevsky monasteries) are seized by the atheistic masters of the darkness of this world and are declared to be in some manner national property; schools, supported from the resources of the Orthodox church to train the ministers of churches and teachers of the faith, are declared superfluous, and are turned either into training institutes of infidelity or even directly into nurseries of immorality.

Property of monasteries and Orthodox churches is alienated from them under the guise of being national property, but without any right and even without any desire to act in accordance with the lawful will of the nation. . . . Finally, the government which is pledged to uphold right and truth in Russia, and to guarantee liberty and order everywhere, manifests only the most unbridled caprice and crassest violence over all and especially in dealing with the holy Orthodox church.

Where are the limits to such mockery of the church of Christ? How and wherein may the attacks upon it by its raging enemies be stopped?

We appeal to all of you, believing and faithful children of the church: rise up in defense of our injured and oppressed holy Mother!

The enemies of the church seize rule over her and her property by force of death-dealing weapons; but you rise to oppose them with the strength of your faith, with your own nation-wide outcry which would stop those senseless people and would show them that they have no right to call themselves protagonists of the people's welfare, initiators of a new life in accordance with the national ideal, for they are directly against the conscience of the people.

And if it should become necessary to suffer in behalf of the cause of Christ, we invite you, beloved children of the church, to suffer along with us in accordance with the words of the holy apostle: "Who shall separate us from the love of God? Shall tribulation, or anguish, or persecution or famine, or nakedness, or peril, or sword?" (Romans viii. 35.)

And you, brethren hierarchs and clergy, do not lose even an hour in your spiritual task, and with fiery zeal call upon your members to defend the impugned rights of the Orthodox church; convene religious gatherings; appeal not because of necessity, but take your place in the ranks of spiritual warriors of your own free choice, and oppose to the external violence the force of your genuine spirituality; we then positively affirm that the enemies of the church of Christ shall be shamed and shall be dispersed by the might of the cross of Christ, for the promise of the divine Cross-bearer is immutable: "I will build my church, and the gates of hell shall not prevail aginst it." (Matt. xvi. 18.)

Source: Matthew Spinka, *The Church and the Russian Revolution* (New York, 1927), pp. 118–121. Russian text in Alexander Vvedensky, *Tserkov i Gosudarstvo, 1918–1922* (Moscow, 1923), pp. 114–116.

SUGGESTIONS FOR BACKGROUND AND REFERENCE

P. B. Anderson, *People, Church and State in Modern Russia* (New York, 1944).
G. Buss, *The Bear's Hug: Religious Belief and the Soviet State* (London, 1987), pp. 17–34.
J. S. Curtiss, *Church and State in Russia: The Last Years of the Empire, 1900–1917* (New York, 1940).
———, *The Russian Church and the Soviet State, 1917–1950* (Boston, 1953).
W. C. Fletcher, *The Russian Orthodox Church Underground 1917–1970* (Oxford, 1974).
D. Pospielovsky, *The Russian Church under the Soviet Regime, 1917–1982* (New York, 1984).
R. Rössler, *Kirche und Revolution in Russland: Patriarch Tichon und der Sowjetstaat* (Cologne, 1969).
N. S. Timasheff, *Religion in Soviet Russia, 1917–1942* (New York, 1942).
A. Wuyts, *Le patriarcat russe au concile de Moscou de 1917–1918* (Rome, 1941).
Source for this document.

128 Separation Decree

February 5, 1918 [January 23, Old Style]

Early Bolshevik ecclesiastical legislation was crowned by this comprehensive Separation Law, signed by Lenin and eight commissars, which secularized the state and deprived churches of all property and legal status. It marked the official end of the thousand-year-old confessional state of "holy Russia." The sobor condemned the decree as "an inimical attempt upon the life of the Orthodox church," and "an act of open persecution." It further warned that participating in the publication of the law or in attempts to implement it was "not reconcilable with membership in the Orthodox church" and would subject transgressors "to the heaviest penalties, to the extent of excommunicating them from the church . . ." (Matthew Spinka, *The Church and the Russian Revolution* [New York, 1927], p. 127). The decree was only partially enforced. While it lost state subsidies, land and other financial resources, and schools, the church temporarily retained many church buildings and seminaries and continued to perform the registration function.

1. The church is separated from the state.

2. Within the territory of the Republic the passing of any local laws or regulations limiting or interfering with freedom of conscience or granting special rights or privileges to citizens because they belong to a certain faith is forbidden.

3. Every citizen has a right to adopt any religion or not to adopt any at all. Every legal restriction connected with the profession of certain faiths or with the non-profession of any faith is now abolished.

Note: Official acts shall make no mention of a citizen's faith.

4. State or semi-official public functions are not to be accompanied by religious ceremonies or rituals.

5. Religious performances may be carried on freely in so far as they do not disturb the public order or encroach upon the rights of citizens of the Russian Republic. Local authorities have the right to take the necessary measures to preserve order and safeguard the rights of citizens.

6. No one can decline to carry out his civic duties on the ground of his religious views. Exception to this ruling may be made by special decisions of the people's court provided one civic duty is substituted for another.

7. Religious oaths are abolished. In case of necessity a solemn promise will suffice.

8. All civil acts are performed exclusively by the civic authorities [in charge of] the department for the registration of marriages and births.

9. The school is separated from the church. The teaching of religion in state and public schools, as well as in private schools where general subjects are taught, is forbidden. Citizens may study or teach religious subjects privately.

10. Church and religious societies are subject to the same laws and regulations as private societies and unions. They do not enjoy any special privileges or subsidies from the state or from local institutions.

11. The levying of obligatory collections or imposition for the benefit of church or religious societies is forbidden. These organizations are forbidden also to coerce or punish their members.

12. Church and religious societies have no right to own property. They do not have the rights of a legal person.

13. All property in Russia now owned by churches and religious organizations is henceforth the property of the people. Buildings and objects that are needed for

religious services revert to the free use of religious organizations by special arrangement with the central or local [Soviet] authorities.

Source: James Bunyan and H. H. Fisher (eds.), *The Bolshevik Revolution 1917–1918* (Stanford, 1934), pp. 590–591. Russian text in *Sobranie Uzakonenii i Rasporiazhenii Rabochego i Krestianskogo Pravitelstva*, 1918, No. 18, pp. 272–273.

SUGGESTIONS FOR BACKGROUND AND REFERENCE

A. Kischkowsky, *Die sowjetische Religionspolitik und die Russische Orthodoxe Kirche* (Munich, 1957).
References for Document 127.

129   Instructions of the Patriarch and the Sobor to the Church (Extracts)

February 28, 1918 [February 15, Old Style]

Bolshevik decrees ending state aid and providing for uncompensated confiscation of church property aimed at the destruction of the economic basis of the church. Moreover, in many districts peasants had already appropriated church lands on their own initiative. The sobor condemned such measures and summoned Orthodox faithful to resist. Leagues of laymen were organized in many places, attracting conservative or tsarist leaders. The church also encouraged the formation of parents' and teachers' associations in defense of the schools. These instructions, issued jointly by the patriarch and the sobor, sought to organize clergy, parochial brotherhoods, education societies, and other Orthodox resistance. This organized opposition produced processions, demonstrations, riots, and loss of life on a large scale, but did not force the Bolsheviks to alter policy.

The new conditions of Church life demand of Church workers, especially local ones, extraordinary care and unusual efforts, in order that requisite spiritual work may be carried on with good success, regardless of the obstacles to be met and even persecution. The Holy Assembly and Holy Patriarch direct the general method to be followed at the present time by the spiritual pastors; inviting them to independent action under the present difficult conditions and cautioning against possible erroneous action on their part, propose the following instructions:

CALL TO THE PRIESTS:

1. Priests are invited to be strictly on guard in protecting the Holy Church in the heavy years of persecution, to encourage, strengthen and unite the believers, for defense against attacks on the freedom of the Orthodox Faith and to strengthen the prayers for the enlightenment of the doubting.

2. The Priests should encourage the good intentions of the believers directed towards the defense of the Church.

Organizations of the Church

3. Parishioners and worshipers of all parish and other churches should be organized into united societies whose duty it shall be to defend all the sacred things and other church property against violation.

4. These organizations must have an educational and charitable character as also a name, and can be presided over by a layman or priest; but should not be called either Church or religious societies, as all church and religious societies are by virtue of a new decree deprived of all legal rights.

5. In extreme cases these societies can declare themselves the owners of church property, in order to save them from seizure at the hands of the non-Orthodox or even those of another faith. Let the Church and church property remain in the hands of the Orthodox believing in God and devoted to the Church.

6. The Superiors, sister superiors and brothers of monasteries, hermitages and resting houses to be appointed by similar united societies from among local residents and regular worshipers of the parish and all loyal parishioners.

7. The principals and teachers in church educational institutions shall establish relations with the parents of the pupils and the employees of the united societies for the protection of educational societies from seizure, and guarantee of their future activity for the benefit of the Church as also the well-being of the Orthodox people.

8. These societies must firmly demand and endeavor by all means to ensure that the situation in the educational institutions shall remain strictly intact pending further orders of the church authorities.

9. Teachers of religion in the non-ecclesiastical educational institutions should by all means in their power extend their influence over the councils of educators and parents so that they may firmly defend the instruction of religion in educational institutions and cooperate with every new effort of the same for the benefit of religious training and education.

10. The removal by force of the clergy and members of the parish or monks from the monasteries should under no circumstances be permitted. In case of forceful removal, by the congregation or other persons, of the clergy from the posts occupied by them, the diocesan authority does not fill their places but demands the reappointment of those removed to their former posts, as also the re-establishing of their rights. Every interference with a priest or member of the parish should be reported to the Church authorities, which alone have the authority, after investigating the matter, to remove priests and church employees from the parish.

11. If it should be established that the forceful removal was due to the request of any member of the clergy, the guilty person is subject to an episcopal tribunal and strict punishment, denied the right of clerical duties and is expelled from the clergy.

12. Church vessels and other appurtenances of the church service should be protected by all possible means against desecration and destruction, and for this reason they should not be removed from safe depositories; the latter should be constructed in such a manner that they might not be easily opened by robbers.

13. In case of attempted seizure of church vessels, appurtenances of the Church service, church registers and other church property, the same should not be surrendered voluntarily, inasmuch as (a) Church vessels and other appurtenances of

church service are blessed for church use and the congregation should not even touch them, (b) Church registers are indispensable for church uses, and the secular authorities, if in need of same, should see to the preparation of them themselves, (c) Church property belongs to the Holy Church, and the clergy and all Orthodox people are merely their guardians.

14. In cases of attack by despoilers or robbers of church property, the church people should be called to the defense of the Church, sound the alarm and send out runners, etc.

15. Should the seizure nevertheless take place, it is absolutely necessary to make a report thereof, signed by witnesses with an accurate description of the articles seized, indicating by name those guilty of the seizure, and forthwith to report thereon to the diocese.

[Articles 16–27 deal with excommunication of guilty persons, and Articles 28–31 with marriages.]

32. Until further notice of the Church authorities, it is obligatory to enter promptly in the books of record the births, certificates of baptism, marriages and deaths in the usual manner.

33. The collecting by the clergy of statistical data and the forwarding of same to the civil authorities is not compulsory on the clergy. However, the representatives of the civil authorities must have access to the Church Records for the copying of information required by them under the supervision of members of the diocese.

Source: Paul B. Anderson, *People, Church and State in Modern Russia* (New York, 1944), pp. 68–71. Russian text in Alexander Vvedensky, *Tserkov i Gosudarstvo, 1918–1922* (Moscow, 1923), pp. 203–205.

SUGGESTIONS FOR BACKGROUND AND REFERENCE

References for Document 127.

130 Instructions of the Justice Commissariat on the Separation Decree

August 24, 1918

The meaning of the Decree of Separation of Church and State became clearer when the Justice Commissariat issued these detailed instructions a half year later. To carry out these directions, "liquidation sections" were attached to executive committees of provincial soviets, but in some areas there was no real enforcement until 1919 or 1920 (despite the two-month time limit stated in Article 24). The work secured to the state the wealth and invested capital of the church, but in most cases parish churches, complying with the law, were permitted to function. Efforts of the church to escape penalty by using laymen's societies were disallowed by the instructions. The educational provisions of these directives were further clarified by a law of March 1919 prohibiting instruction in religious doctrine to children under eighteen. Appended to the instructions was a pattern contract to be entered into by groups using church buildings for worship.

1. The decree . . . applies to: a) The following churches: The Orthodox, The Old Believers' Church, the Roman Catholic Church of all Rites, the Armenian-Gregorian, and the Protestant Church, and the following Creeds: the Jewish, the Mohammedan, the Buddhist-Lamaite; b) all other private religious associations formed for . . . worship according to any religious cult, . . . and also c) all associations membership in which is limited solely to persons of one and the same creed, and which, be it even under the guise of charity, education, or other aims, serve the purpose of rendering direct support and assistance to any religious cult whatsoever (in the shape of maintaining the ministers of such cult, or institutions of the cult, etc.).

2. All associations mentioned in Article I under the Decree . . . are deprived of the rights of a juridical person. Individual members of such associations shall have the right to arrange only collections for the purpose of acquiring property for religious purposes, and for satisfying other religious needs.

3. Charitable, educational, and other similar associations mentioned in clause "c" of Article I, as well as those of them which, although veiling their religious aims under the guise of charity or education, etc., spend money for religious purposes, shall be closed, all their property being turned over by the Soviet . . . to the corresponding Commissariats or Departments.

Property Intended for the Observance of Religious Rites

4. All property which, at the time the Decree . . . was promulgated, was under the management of the Orthodox Ecclesiastical Department and other religious . . . institutions . . . shall . . . be transferred to the direct management of the local Soviets . . . on conditions laid down in the following articles.

5. The local Soviet . . . shall make it incumbent upon the representatives of the former ecclesiastical departments or other persons belonging to the given religious creed, in whose actual possession and management is the church and all other property for . . . worship, to compile in triplicate, a specification of all property intended specially for . . . religious rites. According to such specification the Soviet . . . takes over the property from . . . the said religious cult, and hands it over, together with the specification, for use free of charge, to such local inhabitants of the same religious creed who want to use such property; the second copy of the specification, with the signatures of those who have taken the property over, shall be kept in the local Soviet . . . , while the third copy is to be sent to the Commissariat of Education.

6. The number of local inhabitants required for obtaining the use of such ritual property shall be fixed by the local Soviet . . . , but cannot be less than 20 persons.

7. If the representatives of the abolished Ecclesiastical Department, or those persons in whose actual possession the given property is, refuse to produce the required specification, . . . the local Soviet . . . shall check such property and compile a list of it in the presence of the group of persons to whom such property is to be handed over, . . . before witnesses summoned from the number of local inhabitants, and shall turn it over to the group . . . who have stated their wish to receive such ritual property for . . . worship.

8. Those who have taken over the property for use shall undertake: (I.) to keep it carefully . . . ; (II.) to keep the said property in good repair, and cover . . . expenses for heating, insurance, protection, payment of debts, local taxes and dues, etc.; (III.) to make use of such property solely for . . . religious requirements; (IV.) to make good all losses . . . ; (V.) to keep a detailed specification of all ritual property and to enter in this specification all subsequently added articles . . . (presented as gifts, transferred from other churches, etc.), provided they are not the private property of individual citizens; (VI.) to admit freely and unrestrictedly, at times when divine service is not going on, persons authorized by the Soviet . . . to make periodical revisions and inspections of the property; and (VII.) in case the Soviet . . . should disclose pilferings and malpractices, to immediately surrender such property to the said Soviet, whenever requested to do so. All the above conditions are to be introduced into the agreement which is to be concluded by the aforesaid group of citizens with the local Soviet . . . .

9. Churches and houses of prayer of historic, artistic, and archeological value shall be transferred in accordance with a special instruction elaborated by the Museum Section of the Commissariat of Education.

10. All local inhabitants of the corresponding religion shall have the right to sign the agreement mentioned in Articles 5 to 8 also after the transfer of the said property, and they shall thus acquire the right to participate in the administration of the ritual property . . . .

11. In case there is nobody desirous to take over . . . the ritual property, the local Soviet . . . shall make a public offer three times through . . . the local press, and exhibit a notice . . . on the doors of the houses of prayer.

12. If after the expiration of one week after the last publication there is no application for taking over the property . . . , the local Soviet . . . shall notify the Commissariat of Education of this. In its communication the Soviet . . . shall state the time at which the given house of prayer was built, pointing out its merits from an economic, historic, and artistic point of view, and mentioning for what purpose it is proposed to utilize the building . . . .

13. On receipt of a reply from the Commissariat of Education, the Soviet . . . will carry out the suggestion of the Commissariat . . . , or, if there are none, its own notions on this point.

14. So-called sacred objects . . . kept in buildings not utilized for religious purposes may be handed over either to a group . . . belonging to the corresponding religious creed in accordance with the rules laid down in Articles 5 to 8, or else be turned over to the corresponding institutions of the Soviet Republic.

15. The erection of new churches and houses of prayer shall be permitted unrestrictedly on the condition that general technical rules applying to building work are observed. Estimates and plans . . . are subject to approval of the Architectural Commission of the local Soviet . . . . Completion of such building work shall be guaranteed by the builders by depositing with the State Treasury a certain sum to be fixed by the Soviet . . . , which sum shall be paid back in installments to cover building expenses . . . . Possession of the thus constructed church is to be given in conformity with Articles 5 to 8 of the present Instruction.

Other Property

16. All other property of Church and religious associations which does not serve special religious or ritual purposes, also property of the abolished departments, such as: buildings, landed property, country estates, works, candle factories and other factories, fishing grounds, hospices, hotels, funds, and generally speaking, all property yielding profit . . . which has . . . not yet been taken over by the Soviet institutions, shall immediately be confiscated . . . .

* * *

20. All capital belonging to the abolished religious departments and Church or other religious associations, which may be in the hands of private persons or organizations, shall be claimed . . . within a fortnight. The holders of such monies, if they fail to comply . . . , shall be held criminally and civily liable for embezzlement of such sums.

* * *

24. All measures in connection with the confiscation of Church or religious property must be completed not later than within two months after the present Instruction has been published . . . .

* * *

Birth, Marriage and Death Registration Books

26. All registration books of all religious creeds and covering all previous years, which . . . have until now not been taken away from the ecclesiastical authorities . . . shall without delay be turned over to the Provincial (Oblast) Birth, Marriage and Death Registries.

27. Registration books covering all previous years from all urban and rural churches of any creed are subject to immediate seizure by the Soviet . . . . After the books have been seized, servants of the cult shall have the right to take copies from such registration books, if they need them . . . .

28. In conformity with the prohibition to make on passports, or other official documents . . . endorsements relating to the religious creed of citizens, it shall likewise be prohibited to make . . . endorsements concerning the performance of certain religious rites (such as baptism, confirmation, circumcision, marriage, burial, etc.) as well as divorces pronounced by servants of religious cults . . . .

Religious Ceremonies and Rites

29. In state and other public premises . . . it shall be absolutely prohibited:

a) To conduct religious rites . . . .
b) To exhibit religious images of any description . . . .

30. The local Soviet authorities shall adopt every suitable measure to eradicate such practices . . . .
Note: The removal of religious images of artistic or historic value, as well as decisions concerning their further fate, shall be attended to with the consent of the Commissariat of Education.

31. Religious processions, and the performance of religious rites in streets and public places, shall be permitted only by written permission of the local Soviet authorities . . . .

32. The local Soviet authorities shall remove, or cause the . . . concerned persons to remove, from churches and other houses of prayer . . . all articles offending the religious feelings of the labor masses, such as: . . . inscriptions . . . in memory of any persons who were members of the dynasty overthrown by the People, or its supporters.

Religious Instruction and Teaching

33. In view of the separation of School and Church, instruction in any creed must not in any case be permitted in state, public, and private educational establishments, with the exception of purely theological establishments.

34. All credits voted for religious instruction in schools shall be immediately stopped, and leaders of religious creeds shall be deprived of all rations and supplies hitherto issued to them. No state or other public institution shall have the right to issue the instructors of religion any monies . . . .

35. The buildings of spiritual, educational and training establishments of any creed, as well as of the parish church schools, shall, as national property, be turned over to the local Soviets . . . or to the Commissariat of Education.
Note: The Soviets . . . may lease or let such buildings for the purpose of establishing in them special training establishments of any religious creed, on general conditions applicable to all citizens, and with the knowledge of the Commissariat of Education.

Source: Boleslaw Szczesniak (ed.), *The Russian Revolution and Religion* (Notre Dame, 1959), pp. 40–46.

SUGGESTIONS FOR BACKGROUND AND REFERENCE

References for Document 127.

✦ ✦ ✦

131 Weimar Constitution (Extract)

August 11, 1919

The German religious situation was greatly affected by World War I and the 1918 Revolution, with widespread defection from the churches and decline of theological scholarship. Protestantism, traditionally monarchist and closely tied to the Hohenzollern empire, seemed unsuited to the liberal republic, which relied chiefly on the Social Democratic and Catholic Center parties for leadership. The Weimar Constitution provided for a complex partial disestablishment of religion. On the one hand, the historic princely involvement in ecclesiastical administration and legislation was not continued by the postwar state. (This in itself required fundamental reconstruction of church government and doctrine.) Yet the *Landeskirchen* remained territorial churches, clearly distinguished from the free churches, enjoying state subsidies for clergy and assistance in collecting revenue, and theoretically ministering to all who did not expressly repudiate their services. While Protestantism remained somewhat disorganized and distrustful of the new arrangements, German Catholicism, with stronger organization, a history of greater independence, and a more flexible political tradition, fared better.

Section III.—Religion and Religious Bodies

135. All inhabitants of the Federation enjoy full liberty of faith and of conscience. The undisturbed practice of religion is guaranteed by the Constitution, and is under state protection. The general laws of the state remain unaffected hereby.

136. Civil and political rights and duties are neither dependent upon nor restricted by the practice of religious freedom.

The enjoyment of civil and political rights, as well as admission to official posts, are independent of religious creed.

No one is bound to disclose his religious convictions. The authorities have the right to make enquiries as to membership of a religious body only when rights and duties depend upon it, or when the collection of statistics ordered by law requires it.

No one may be compelled to take part in any ecclesiastical act or ceremony, or to participate in religious practices, or to make use of any religious form of oath.

137. There is no state church.

Freedom of association is guaranteed to religious bodies. There are no restrictions as to the union of religious bodies within the territory of the Federation.

Each religious body regulates and administers its affairs independently, within the limits of the general laws. It appoints its officials without the co-operation of the state, or of the civil community.

Religious bodies acquire legal rights in accordance with the general regulations of the civil code.

Religious bodies remain corporations with public rights in so far as they have been so up to the present. Equal rights shall be granted to other religious bodies upon application, if their constitution and the number of their members offer a guarantee of permanence. Where several such religious bodies holding public rights combine to form one union this union becomes a corporation of a similar class.

Religious bodies forming corporations with public rights are entitled to levy taxes on the basis of the civil tax-rolls, in accordance with the provisions of state law.

Associations adopting as their work the common encouragement of a world-philosophy shall be placed upon an equal footing with religious bodies.

So far as the execution of these provisions may require further regulation, this is the duty of states legislatures.

138. State connections with religious bodies, depending upon law, agreement or special legal titles, are dissolved by state legislation. The principles for such action shall be laid down by the Federal Government.

Ownership and other rights of religious bodies and unions to their institutions, foundations and other property devoted to purposes of public worship, education or charity, are guaranteed.

139. Sundays and holidays recognized by the state shall remain under legal protection as days of rest from work and for the promotion of spiritual purposes.

140. The members of the armed forces shall be allowed the necessary free time for the performance of their religious duties.

141. Religious bodies shall have the right of entry for religious purposes into the army, hospitals, prisons, or other public institutions, so far as is necessary for the arrangement of public worship or the execution of pastoral offices, but every form of compulsion must be avoided.

Source: British and Foreign State Papers (1919) (London, 1922), CXII, 1085–1087. German text in G. Anschütz (ed.), *Die Verfassung des Deutschen Reichs vom 11. August 1919* (Berlin, 1933), pp. xii–xxxxviii.

SUGGESTIONS FOR BACKGROUND AND REFERENCE

D. R. Borg, *The Old Prussian Church and the Weimar Republic* (Hanover, N.H., 1984).

H. Cazelles, *Église et état en Allemagne de Weimar aux premières années du IIIe Reich* (Paris, 1936), pp. 36–109.

A. L. Drummond, *German Protestantism since Luther* (London, 1951), pp. 258–278.

E. Eyck, *A History of the Weimar Republic* (Cambridge, Mass., 1962), I, 1–79.

H. H. Kramm, "Organization and Constitution of the German Protestant Churches," *Church Quarterly Review,* Vol. CXXXCIII (April 1944), pp. 87–98.

K. S. Latourette, *Christianity in a Revolutionary Age* (New York, 1958–1962), IV, 247–257.

132 Church Assembly Act

December 23, 1919

The revival of Convocation in 1852 after more than a century of silence failed to provide the church with the effective instrument of decision and expression that many Anglicans desired. Convocation was archaic, excessively bound by tradition, exclusively clerical, and provincial rather than national in scope. While the Lambeth Conferences spoke for the world Anglican communion after 1867, need for a national church council continued and was only partly satisfied by the deliberative Representative Church Council (composed of the two convocations and lay delegates) after 1904. In 1914 the two archbishops appointed a committee that formulated a plan for a National Assembly of the Church of England, made up of three houses of bishops, clergy, and laity, the last elected every five years by lay members of the diocesan conferences. This assembly would be capable of passing measures to which parliament would be requested to give the authority of law. After parliamentary enactment of this Church of England Assembly (Powers) Act in 1919, the law became an issue in the Prayer Book controversy of the 1920s.

2.—(1) There shall be a Committee of members of both Houses of Parliament styled "The Ecclesiastical Committee."

(2) The Ecclesiastical Committee shall consist of fifteen members of the House of Lords nominated by the Lord Chancellor and fifteen members of the House of Commons nominated by the Speaker of the House of Commons, to be appointed on the passing of this Act to serve for the duration of the present Parliament and thereafter to be appointed at the commencement of each Parliament to serve for the duration of that Parliament.

* * *

(3) The powers and duties of the Ecclesiastical Committee may be exercised and discharged by any twelve members thereof, and the Committee shall be entitled to sit and to transact business whether Parliament be sitting or not, and notwithstanding a vacancy in the membership of the Committee. Subject to the provisions of this Act, the Ecclesiastical Committee may regulate its own procedure.

3.—(1) Every measure passed by the Church Assembly shall be submitted by the Legislative Committee [of the Church Assembly] to the Ecclesiastical Committee, together with such comments and explanations as the Legislative Committee may deem it expedient or be directed by the Church Assembly to add.

(2) The Ecclesiastical Committee shall thereupon consider the measure so submitted to it, and may, at any time during such consideration, either of its own motion or at the request of the Legislative Committee, invite the Legislative Committee to a conference to discuss the provisions thereof . . . .

(3) After considering the measure, the Ecclesiastical Committee shall draft a

report thereon to Parliament stating the nature and legal effect of the measure and its views as to the expediency thereof, especially with relation to the constitutional rights of all His Majesty's subjects.

(4) The Ecclesiastical Committee shall communicate its report in draft to the Legislative Committee, but shall not present it to Parliament until the Legislative Committee signify its desire that it should be so presented.

(5) At any time before the presentation of the report to Parliament the Legislative Committee may, either on its own motion or by direction of the Church Assembly, withdraw a measure from further consideration by the Ecclesiastical Committee; but the Legislative Committee shall have no power to vary a measure of the Church Assembly either before or after conference with the Ecclesiastical Committee.

(6) A measure may relate to any matter concerning the Church of England, and may extend to the amendment or repeal in whole or in part of any Act of Parliament, including this Act:

Provided that a measure shall not make any alteration in the composition or powers or duties of the Ecclesiastical Committee, or in the procedure in Parliament prescribed by section four of this Act.

(7) No proceedings of the Church Assembly in relation to a measure shall be invalidated by any vacancy in the membership of the Church Assembly or by any defect in the qualification or election of any member thereof.

4. When the Ecclesiastical Committee shall have reported to Parliament on any measure . . . , the report, together with the text of such measure, shall be laid before both Houses of Parliament forthwith . . . and thereupon, on a resolution being passed by each House of Parliament directing that such measure in the form laid before Parliament should be presented to His Majesty, such measure shall be presented to His Majesty, and shall have the force and effect of an Act of Parliament on the Royal Assent being signified thereto in the same manner as to Acts of Parliament . . . .

Source: 9 & 10 Geo. V, c. 76; *The Public General Acts Passed in the Ninth and Tenth Years of the Reign of His Majesty King George the Fifth* (London, 1919), pp. 348–350.

SUGGESTIONS FOR BACKGROUND AND REFERENCE

G. K. A. Bell, *Randall Davidson, Archbishop of Canterbury* (London, 1935), II, 956–980.

C. F. Garbett, *Church and State in England* (London, 1950), pp. 100–140.

R. Lloyd, *The Church of England in the Twentieth Century* (London, 1947–1950), I, 246–253.

J. Marchant (ed.), *The Future of the Church of England* (New York, 1926), pp. 107–115.

S. Neill, *Anglicanism* (Harmondsworth, 1958), pp. 391–394.

133   Church of Scotland Act

July 28, 1921

In the late nineteenth and early twentieth centuries most of the ecclesiastical schisms of Scottish history were healed. For the most part those divisions had arisen not from doctrinal causes, but from a determination to vindicate the church's freedom. By the Patronage Act of 1874, acknowledging the congregation's rights in the naming of pastors, Parliament removed the chief grievance. However, successful negotiations required the further assurance given in this act of 1921, fully declaring the church's liberty. Reunion of the United Free Church with the Church of Scotland was officially proclaimed in 1929. (The United Free Church was itself a union, accomplished in 1900, between the Free Church of the Disruption of 1843 and the United Presbyterian Church, the heir of the Secession and Relief Schisms of the eighteenth century.)

WHEREAS certain articles declaratory of the constitution of the Church of Scotland in matters spiritual have been prepared with the authority of the General Assembly of the Church, with a view to facilitate the union of other Churches with the Church of Scotland, which articles are set out in the Schedule to this Act . . . :

And whereas it is expedient that any doubts as to the lawfulness of the Declaratory Articles should be removed:

Be it therefore enacted . . . as follows:—

1. The Declaratory Articles are lawful articles, and the constitution of the Church of Scotland in matters spiritual is as therein set forth, and no limitation of the liberty, rights and powers in matters spiritual therein set forth shall be derived from any statute or law affecting the Church of Scotland in matters spiritual at present in force, it being hereby declared that in all questions of construction the Declaratory Articles shall prevail, and that all such statutes and laws shall be construed in conformity therewith and in subordination thereto, and all such statutes and laws in so far as they are inconsistent with the Declaratory Articles are hereby repealed and declared to be of no effect.

* * *

Schedule
Articles Declaratory of the Constitution of the Church
of Scotland in Matters Spiritual

I. The Church of Scotland is part of the Holy Catholic or Universal Church; . . . . The Church of Scotland adheres to the Scottish Reformation; receives the Word of God which is contained in the Scriptures . . . as its supreme rule of faith and life; and avows the fundamental doctrines of the Catholic faith founded thereupon.

II. The principal subordinate standard of the Church . . . is the Westminster Confession . . . . Its government is Presbyterian . . . . Its system and principles of worship, orders, and discipline are in accordance with "The Directory for the Public Worship of God," "The Form of Presbyterial Church Government," and "The Form of Process," . . . .

III. This Church is in historical continuity with the Church of Scotland which was reformed in 1560, whose liberties were ratified in 1592, and for whose security provision was made in the Treaty of Union of 1707. . . . As a national Church representative of the Christian Faith of the Scottish people it acknowledges its distinctive call and duty to bring the ordinances of religion to the people in every parish of Scotland through a territorial ministry.

IV. This Church, as part of the Universal Church wherein the Lord Jesus Christ has appointed a government in the hands of Church office-bearers, receives from Him, its Divine King and Head, and from Him alone, the right and power subject to no civil authority to legislate, and to adjudicate finally, in all matters of doctrine, worship, government, and discipline in the Church, including the right to determine all questions concerning membership and office in the Church, the constitution and membership of its Courts, and the mode of election of its office-bearers, and to define the boundaries of the spheres of labour of its ministers and other office-bearers. Recognition by civil authority of the separate and independent government and jurisdiction of this Church in matters spiritual, in whatever manner such recognition be expressed, does not in any way affect the character of this government and jurisdiction as derived from the Divine Head of the Church alone, or give to the civil authority any right of interference with the proceedings or judgments of the Church within the sphere of its spiritual government and jurisdiction.

V. This Church has the inherent right, free from interference by civil authority, but under the safeguards for deliberate action and legislation provided by the Church itself, to frame or adopt its subordinate standards, to declare the sense in which it understands its Confession of Faith, to modify the forms of expression therein, or to formulate other doctrinal statements, and to define the relation thereto of its office-bearers and members . . . .

VI. This Church acknowledges the divine appointment and authority of the civil magistrate within his own sphere, and maintains its historic testimony to the duty of the nation acting in its corporate capacity to render homage to God, to acknowledge the Lord Jesus Christ to be king over the nations, to obey His laws, to reverence His ordinances, to honour His Church, and to promote in all appropriate ways the Kingdom of God. The Church and the State owe mutual duties to each other, and acting within their respective spheres may signally promote each other's welfare. The Church and the State have the right to determine each for itself all questions concerning the extent and the continuance of their mutual relations in the discharge of these duties and the obligations arising therefrom.

VII. The Church of Scotland . . . recognises the obligation to seek and promote union with other Churches . . . ; and it has the right to unite with any such Church without loss of its identity on terms which this Church finds to be consistent with these Articles.

VIII. The Church has the right to interpret these Articles, and, subject to the safeguards for deliberate action and legislation provided by the Church itself, to modify or add to them . . . .

Source: 11 & 12 Geo. V, c. 29; *The Public General Acts Passed in the Eleventh and Twelfth Years of the Reign of His Majesty King George the Fifth* (London, 1921), pp. 86–89.

SUGGESTIONS FOR BACKGROUND AND REFERENCE

J. R. Fleming, *A History of the Church in Scotland, 1875–1929* (Edinburgh, 1933).
————, *The Story of Church Union in Scotland* (London, 1929).
R. Sjolinder, *Presbyterian Reunion in Scotland, 1907–1921* (Edinburgh, 1962).

✦ ✦ ✦ Orthodoxy: The Schism and the Soviet Government

134 Proclamation of the Progressive Clergy of Petrograd

May 13, 1922

As in the French Revolution, political pressures produced a schism in the church. Orthodox leadership—patriarch, sobor, and hierarchy—was generally hostile to bolshevism and sought the overthrow of the regime, which it believed would soon collapse in any case. During the Civil War many churchmen openly supported the Whites, and the émigré Karlovtsi Sobor, meeting in Yugoslavia in 1921, appealed for Western assistance to effect a tsarist restoration. Patriarch Tikhon, already accused of collusion with tsarist clergy abroad, rejected government demands for the contribution of the church's consecrated vessels to relieve suffering in the famine of 1921 and 1922. His policy of resistance was followed by bloody clashes in the parishes, sensational state trials of clergy, and finally his own house arrest. Within Orthodoxy a minority opposition to this leadership and policy became vocal in 1922. Led by leftist priests, notably Alexander Vvedensky and V. D. Krasnitsky, some clergy demanded the adjustment of the church to the new order. The movement also drew strength from long-standing hostility of "white" (married, parochial) clergy toward "black" (monastic, episcopal) clergy, and called for greater lay participation and theological and liturgical reform in the church. These clerical critics, soon to be organized as the Living Church, first announced their opposition to patriarchal policy in a published letter of twelve priests on the famine crisis. After Tikhon's arrest,

From Matthew Spinka, *The Church and the Russian Revolution* (New York, 1927). Copyright, 1927, by The Macmillan Company. Reprinted by permission of the author.

"representatives of the progressive clergy of Petrograd" pressed the attack with this fuller proclamation, printed in *Izvestia*.

Brethren and sisters in Christ!

In the course of the last few years, in accordance with the will of God, without which nothing in the world comes to pass, the Workers-Peasants' government came into power in Russia.

It took upon itself the task of liquidating the heavy consequences of the World War, a struggle with the famine, epidemics, and the remaining disorders of the governmental life.

The church, in the meantime, remained aloof from this great struggle for truth and the well-being of humanity.

The heads of the church were on the side of the enemies of the people.

This became manifest, in so far as every current incident was accompanied by a counter-revolutionary uprising within the church. Such things happened more than once. At the present time, similar sad occurrences have taken place before our own eyes, in the matter of converting the church treasures into bread for the starving. Such an act should have been an occasion for a joyous manifestation of love for the perishing brother, but it was converted into a conspiracy against the government.

It resulted in bloodshed. Blood was shed that the hungering Christ might not be aided.

By the refusal to help the starving, churchmen were attempting to bring about the overthrow of the government. The proclamation of Patriarch Tikhon became the standard around which rallied the counter-revolutionists, outwardly disguised in ecclesiastical garb.

But the wider masses of the people and the majority of the rank and file of the clergy did not heed their call. The popular conscience condemned those guilty of shedding blood, and the death of those who succumbed to the famine falls with a heavy reproach upon those who wished to exploit the national calamity for their own political ends.

We, the undersigned clergy of the Orthodox church, representing the opinions of wide ecclesiastical circles, condemn the actions of those hierarchs and those pastors who are guilty of organizing opposition to the governmental authorities in the matter of aiding the starving and in other undertakings for the good of the workers.

The church by its very essence should represent a society of love and truth, and not a political organization, or a counter-revolutionary party.

We consider it necessary that a local Sobor be called without delay for a trial of those who are guilty of the ruin of the church, as well as to order the ecclesiastical government, and to establish normal relations with the Soviet authorities. The civil war which is carried on by the supreme administration against the government must be stopped.

Every faithful and loving son of the church will doubtless approve our petition with which we appealed to the government authorities, asking to grant us the permission to call a local Sobor speedily for the purpose of ordering the church and pacifying the national life.

Source: Matthew Spinka, *The Church and the Russian Revolution* (New York, 1927), pp. 196–197. Russian text in *Izvestiya,* No. 106, May 14, 1922.

SUGGESTIONS FOR BACKGROUND AND REFERENCE

References for Document 127.

135   Clerical Memorandum to Tikhon

May 18, 1922

The schism actually developed in the exchanges of the pro-Soviet clergy with Tikhon in May 1922. Three days after his indictment and arrest (May 9), a delegation of clergy visited the patriarch, charged him with counterrevolutionary policies and responsibility for the ruin of religion and demanded his withdrawal from ecclesiastical administration. Accordingly, Tikhon renounced his authority and named the conservative Metropolitan Agathangel as his deputy. On May 18 a further demand was made on Tikhon that he turn over the patriarchal chancery to the "progressive" party until the arrival of Agathangel. This petition was accepted by the patriarch who wrote across the top of the memorandum: "The persons named below are ordered to take over and transmit to the Most Reverend Metropolitan Agathangel, upon his arrival in Moscow, and with the assistance of Secretary Numerov, the synodical business; [administration of] the Moscow eparchy [to be entrusted] to the Most Reverend Innocent, bishop of Klinsk, and before his arrival to the Most Reverend Leonid, bishop of Vernensk, with the assistance of the departmental chief Nevsky." The metropolitan never took up his charge, and the socialist clergy, now organized as the Provisional Superior Church Administration, proclaimed themselves high canonical authority in the church. For a time the Living Church movement, encouraged by the government, won wide support in Russia and some recognition from foreign patriarchs. It was troubled with internal dissension and declined after 1925.

In view of the abdication of your holiness from the administration of the church until the time of the calling of the Sobor, and of your transfer of authority to one of the elder hierarchs, the church remains at present, as a matter of fact, without any kind of administration.

That circumstance shows itself extraordinarily detrimental to the course of general church life, and especially in Moscow, exciting thereby a great disturbance of minds.

We, the undersigned, have petitioned the governmental authorities for permission to open the chancery of your holiness and start its functioning.

By the present letter we filially ask for your holiness' blessing upon it, in order that the harmful cessation in the administration of church affairs be terminated.

Your substitute, then, upon his arrival, will immediately enter upon the discharge of his duties.

For these labors in the chancery, until such time as the final formation of the administration under the headship of your substitute be accomplished, we temporarily engage bishops now at liberty in Moscow.

Source: Matthew Spinka, *The Church and the Russian Revolution* (New York, 1927), pp. 202, 201. Russian text in *Vestnik Svyashchennogo Sinoda Pravoslavnoy Rossiiskoy Tserkvi,* No. 2, 1925, p. 18.

SUGGESTIONS FOR BACKGROUND AND REFERENCE

References for Document 127.

136   Sobor Condemnation of Tikhon

May 3, 1923

Part of the program of the Living Church was the convening of a second sobor to establish desired reforms. This sobor, with membership carefully screened, met April 29, 1923, endorsed the October Revolution, condemned the Karlovtsi Sobor, and approved important revisions of church law, including provision for "white" married bishops and remarried priests. Its most important act was this resolution repudiating the 1917 Sobor and setting forth the offenses of Tikhon, reducing him to lay status, and abolishing the patriarchate. The patriarch, still imprisoned, was not present, and no real trial was held. The reformers now regarded their position as established, but actually the deposition was uncanonical, the decision of a party rather than the church. Tikhon, formally notified of the decision, denied its legality and sought to maintain his position against the insurgents.

Having heard the report of Archpriest A. Vvedensky, the All-Russian Local Sobor of the Orthodox Church witnesses before the church and before all mankind that at present the world has become divided into two classes: capitalists-exploiters, and the proletariat, by whose toil and blood the capitalistic world builds its prosperity. No one in the world but the Soviet government of Russia has undertaken a struggle against this social evil. Christians cannot remain indifferent spectators of that struggle. The Sobor declares capitalism to be a mortal sin, and the fight against it to be sacred for Christians. The Sobor sees in the Soviet government the world leader toward fraternity, equality, and international peace. The Sobor denounces the international and domestic counter-revolution, and condemns it with all its religious and moral authority.

The Sobor calls upon every honest Christian citizen of Russia to go forth to battle, in united front, under the guidance of the Soviet government, against the world-evil of social wrong.

The Holy Sobor of 1923 of the Orthodox Church, having deliberated on the condition of the church during the time of the revolution, has resolved:

1. Beginning with the summer of 1917, responsible leaders of the church assumed a definitely counter-revolutionary point of view. The church must reëstablish the unity of the tsarist Russia—such was the slogan which the church chose to follow (having been so closely bound with tsarism prior to the revolution). The Sobor of 1917, composed largely of representatives of the reactionary clergy as well as of the high nobility, property owners, and members of reactionary political parties, became at the very outset a definitely political counter-revolutionary gathering which merely covered all these actions with the name of Christ the Savior. The Sobor fought against the revolution. It did not recognize even the Provisional Government, and after October this struggle assumed perfectly incredible proportions.

After the meeting of the Sobor, Patriarch Tikhon continued this counter-revolutionary activity. He became the leader and standard-bearer of all opponents of the Soviet government. He drove the church into the counter-revolutionary struggle.

The Holy Sobor of 1923 of the Orthodox Church condemns the counter-revolutionary struggle and its methods, which are the methods of man-hatred. Especially does the Sobor of 1923 deplore the anathematization of the Soviet government and of all who recognize it. The SOBOR DECLARES this anathematization TO HAVE NO FORCE.

2. The Sobor of 1923 condemns all those who have followed this path and persuaded others to follow them. And this applies, first of all, to the responsible leader of our church life, Patriarch Tikhon. Whereas Patriarch Tikhon served the counter-revolution instead of sincerely serving Christ, and, since he is the person who was supposed to direct properly all ecclesiastical life, but as on the contrary he led astray the broad masses of the church, the Sobor regards Tikhon as an apostate from the original commands of Christ and a traitor to the church. On the basis of the canons of the church, it hereby declares him to be DEPRIVED OF HIS CLERICAL ORDERS AND MONKHOOD, AND RELEGATED TO HIS ORIGINAL LAY CONDITION.

HEREAFTER PATRIARCH TIKHON IS LAYMAN BASIL BELAVIN.

3. The representatives of the reformist church movement have severed all connection with the counter-revolution, and have thereby earned for themselves the disapprobation of all reactionary churchmen. The Holy Sobor of 1923 declares that all such interdictory measures have no force whatever. On the contrary, the Sobor approves the courage of these men and their devotion to the church, which they have rescued from the hands of the counter-revolution and are restoring to Christ the Savior.

4. The Holy Sobor urges all churchmen to abandon all attempts to use the

church for temporal political schemes, for the church belongs to God and must serve Him only. There must be no place in the church for counter-revolution. The Soviet government is not a persecutor of the church. In accordance with the constitution of the Soviet government, all citizens are granted genuine religious freedom of conscience. The decree regarding the separation of the church from the state guarantees such freedom. The freedom of religious equally with anti-religious propaganda affords the believers an opportunity to defend by argument the merits of their purely religious convictions. Hence churchmen must not see in the Soviet authority the antichrist; on the contrary, the Sobor calls attention to the fact that the Soviet authority is the only one throughout the world which will realize, by governmental methods, the ideals of the Kingdom of God. Therefore every faithful churchman must not only be an honorable citizen, but also fight with all his might, together with the Soviet authority, for the realization of the Kingdom of God upon earth.

5. Condemning the former patriarch Tikhon as a leader of counter-revolution and not of the church, the Sobor holds that the very restoration of the patriarchate was a definitely political counter-revolutionary act. The ancient church knew no patriarch and was governed conciliarly; hence the Holy Sobor hereby abolishes the restored patriarchate: hereafter the church shall be governed by the Sobor.

6. Condemning counter-revolution within the church, punishing its leaders, abolishing the institution of the patriarchate itself, and recognizing the existing governmental authority, the Sobor creates normal conditions of peaceful progress of ecclesiastical life. Henceforth all church life should be based upon two principles: (1) with respect to God, upon a genuine devotion of church people to the original commands of Christ the Savior; (2) with respect to the government, upon the principle of separation of the church from the state.

Building upon these foundations, the church will become what it ought to be; a loving, laboring company of those who believe in God, his Christ, and his truth.

Source: Matthew Spinka, *The Church and the Russian Revolution* (New York, 1927), pp. 240–244. Russian text in *Deyaniya Drugago Vserossiiskago Pomestnago Sobora 1923 goda* (Moscow, 1923), pp. 6–8.

SUGGESTIONS FOR BACKGROUND AND REFERENCE

References for Document 127.

137 Tikhon's Confession

June 16, 1923

Tikhon's spectacular recantation of past policy and appeal for reconciliation with the Bolshevik government resulted in his sudden release from detention and cancellation of his trial. The patriarch won not only his freedom but a greatly strengthened position against the Living Church. The government's motives are conjectural. Freeing the patriarch may have been useful to Soviet propaganda abroad, while at the same time it quickened the internal struggle within Orthodoxy. Moreover, Tikhon's break with the past and accommodation to the Soviet order, which seems to have been genuine, made him an acceptable instrument to advance government interests. The remainder of his life, devoted to battle against the schismatics, demonstrated loyalty to the regime. This appeal was addressed to the Supreme Court. Despite the confession of counter-revolutionary activity, the patriarch later denied the charge in a statement for the *Manchester Guardian*.

Appealing with the present declaration to the Supreme Court of the Russian Soviet Federation of Socialistic Republics, I regard it as my duty, dictated by my pastoral conscience, to declare the following:

Having been nurtured in a monarchist society, and until my arrest having been under the influence of anti-Soviet individuals, I was filled with hostility against the Soviet authorities, and at times my hostility passed from passivity to active measures, as in the instance of the proclamation on the occasion of the Brest-Litovsky peace in 1918, the anathematizing of the authorities in that same year, and finally, the appeal against the decree regarding the removal of church treasures in 1922. All my anti-Soviet acts, with the exception of a few inexactitudes, were stated in the act of accusation drawn up by the Supreme Court. Acknowledging the correctness of the accusations of the Supreme Court and its sentence as conforming to the clauses of the criminal code, I repent of all my actions directed against the government and petition the Supreme Court to change its sentence and to set me free.

I declare hereby to the Soviet authorities that henceforth I am no more an enemy to the Soviet government, and that I have completely and resolutely severed all connections with the foreign and domestic monarchists and the counter-revolutionary activity of the White Guards.

Source: Matthew Spinka, *The Church and the Russian Revolution* (New York, 1927), pp. 250–251. Russian text in *Izvestiya*, No. 141, June 27, 1923.

SUGGESTIONS FOR BACKGROUND AND REFERENCE

References for Document 127.

✦ ✦ ✦

138   *Pierce* v. *Society of Sisters* (Extracts)

June 1, 1925

Post–World War I nationalism contributed to the enactment in 1922 of an Oregon Compulsory Education Act. The measure, secured by popular petition and referendum, required all children to attend only public schools. The law was challenged by the Roman Catholic Society of Sisters, an order of teaching nuns, and by the Hill Military Academy. In 1925 it had not yet been judicially determined that the Fourteenth Amendment incorporated the guarantees of the First Amendment. Consequently, the case was not argued or decided on the basis of the First Amendment's security for religious liberty, but on the issue of protecting property jeopardized by state action. Yet this case is commonly considered the most important constitutional foundation of the parochial school system in the United States. The decision was delivered by Justice James McReynolds (1862–1946).

The challenged Act . . . requires every parent, guardian or other person having control or charge or custody of a child between eight and sixteen years to send him "to a public school for the period of time a public school shall be held during the current year" in the district where the child resides; and failure so to do is declared a misdemeanor. . . . The manifest purpose is to compel general attendance at public schools by normal children . . . who have not completed the eighth grade. And without doubt enforcement of the statute would seriously impair, perhaps destroy, the profitable features of appellees' business and greatly diminish the value of their property.

Appellee, the Society of Sisters, is an Oregon corporation, organized in 1880, with power to care for orphans, educate and instruct the youth, establish and maintain academies or schools, and acquire necessary real and personal property. It has long devoted its property and effort to the secular and religious education and care of children, and has acquired the valuable good will of many parents and guardians. . . . In its primary schools many children . . . are taught the subjects usually pursued in Oregon public schools during the first eight years. Systematic religious instruction and moral training according to the tenets of the Roman Catholic Church are also regularly provided. All courses of study, both temporal and religious, contemplate continuity of training under appellee's charge; the primary schools are essential to the system and the most profitable. It owns valuable buildings, especially constructed and equipped for school purposes. The business is remunerative . . . . The Compulsory Education Act of 1922 has already caused the withdrawal from its schools of children who would otherwise continue, and their income has steadily declined. The appellants, public officers, have proclaimed their purpose strictly to enforce the statute.

After setting out the above facts the Society's bill alleges that the enactment conflicts with the right of parents to choose schools where their children will receive appropriate mental and religious training, the right of the child to influence the parents' choice of a school, the right of schools and teachers therein to engage in a useful business or profession, and is accordingly repugnant to the Constitution and void. And, further, that unless enforcement of the measure is enjoined the corporation's business and property will suffer irreparable injury.

* * *

. . . The court ruled that the Fourteenth Amendment guaranteed appellees against the deprivation of their property without due process of law consequent upon the unlawful interference by appellants with the free choice of patrons, present and prospective. It declared the right to conduct schools was property and that parents and guardians, as a part of their liberty, might direct the education of children by selecting reputable teachers and places. Also, that these schools were not unfit or harmful to the public, and that enforcement of the challenged statute would unlawfully deprive them of patronage and thereby destroy their owners' business and property. . . .

No question is raised concerning the power of the State reasonably to regulate all schools, to inspect, supervise and examine them, their teachers and pupils; to require that all children of proper age attend some school, that teachers shall be of good moral character and patriotic disposition, that certain studies plainly essential to good citizenship must be taught, and that nothing be taught which is manifestly inimical to the public welfare.

The inevitable practical result of enforcing the Act . . . would be destruction of appellees' primary schools, and perhaps all other private primary schools . . . within . . . Oregon. These parties are engaged in a kind of undertaking not inherently harmful, but long regarded as useful and meritorious. Certainly there is nothing in the present records to indicate that they have failed to discharge their obligations to patrons, students or the State. And there are no peculiar circumstances or present emergencies which demand extraordinary measures relative to primary education.

Under the doctrine of *Meyer* v. *Nebraska,* 262 U.S. 390, we think it entirely plain that the Act of 1922 unreasonably interferes with the liberty of parents and guardians to direct the upbringing and education of children under their control. As often heretofore pointed out, rights guaranteed by the Constitution may not be abridged by legislation which has no reasonable relation to some purpose within the competency of the State. The fundamental theory of liberty upon which all governments in this Union repose excludes any general power of the State to standardize its children by forcing them to accept instruction from public teachers only. The child is not the mere creature of the State; those who nurture him and direct his destiny have the right, coupled with the high duty, to recognize and prepare him for additional obligations.

* * *

Generally it is entirely true . . . that no person in any business has such an interest in possible customers as to enable him to restrain exercise of proper power of the State upon the ground that he will be deprived of patronage. But the injunctions here sought are not against the exercise of any *proper* power. Plaintiffs asked protection against arbitrary, unreasonable and unlawful interference with their patrons and the consequent destruction of their business and property. Their interest is clear and immediate . . . .

Source: Pierce, Governor of Oregon, et al. v. *Society of Sisters,* 268 U.S. 510.

SUGGESTIONS FOR BACKGROUND AND REFERENCE

P. B. Kurland, *Religion and the Law* (Chicago, 1961), pp. 26–28.
L. Pfeffer, *God, Caesar and the Constitution* (Boston, 1975), pp. 253–257.
A. P. Stokes, *Church and State in the United States* (New York, 1950), II, 733–741.

139 Resolution of the Upper House of Convocation of Canterbury on Prayer Book Revision

July 11, 1929

Prayer Book revision, considered formally by convocations since 1906, was embodied in a measure overwhelmingly accepted by the Church Assembly and forwarded to Parliament. Many liturgical changes were noncontroversial, but provision for an alternative communion service and reservation of the sacrament raised fears that revision was designed to advance the "Romanizing" views of the Anglo-Catholic minority.[1] (The Malines conversations between Anglicans and Catholics [1921–1926] had already alarmed the evangelical wing of the church.) The measure passed the House of Lords by 241 to 88 but was lost in the House of Commons by 238 to 205 in December 1927. A second revision, written with a view to meeting objections but still retaining reservation of the sacrament, was rejected in the Commons in June 1928 by a vote of 266 to 220. These decisions created much dissatisfaction with the Church Assembly Act and the prevailing system of church-state relations among many churchmen. They argued that the non-Anglican vote in Parliament had thwarted the worship most desired by the national Anglican community, and Archbishop Randall Davidson (1848–1930) and other leaders expressed concern for the independent spiritual authority of the church. Despite much talk of voluntary separation from the state, the bishops decided instead on a policy of conscientious disregard of the parliamentary votes in permitting services consistent with the 1928 revision (even though the 1662 Book remained the lawful liturgy). This "solution," officially enacted by the bishops on the archbishop's motion,

---

1. For the history and theological significance of the practice of retaining the bread consecrated at the Eucharist, see F. L. Cross and E. A. Livingstone (eds.), *The Oxford Dictionary of the Christian Church,* 2d ed. (New York, 1974), "Reservation."

produced some liturgical diversity, but was practically successful in restoring peace to the church and quieting extreme demands.

The worship of God is in every generation a primary concern of the Church. For many years the Church of England has been engaged in an endeavour to amend the existing laws of public worship so as to make fuller provision for the spiritual needs of the Church and to bring order into the variety of usage which has become prevalent. This endeavour has for the present failed. It is impossible and undesirable to bring back the conduct of public worship strictly within the limits of the Prayer-book of 1662. Accordingly the Bishops, having failed to secure the statutory sanction which was desired and sought, are compelled in the present situation to fulfil by administrative action their responsibility for the regulation of public worship.

On September 20, 1928, the Bishops announced that they intended to consult the clergy and laity of their dioceses. These consultations have now been held in almost every diocese, and, in view of the information gained and desires expressed, the Bishops hereby resolve that, in the exercise of their administrative discretion, they will in their respective dioceses consider the circumstances and needs of parishes severally, and give counsel and directions. In these directions the Bishops will conform to the principles which they have already laid down, namely:—

(1) That during the present emergency and until further order be taken the Bishops, having in view the fact that the Convocations of Canterbury and York gave their consent to the proposals for deviations from and additions to the Book of 1662, as set forth in the Book of 1928, being laid before the National Assembly of the Church of England for final approval, and that the National Assembly voted final approval to these proposals, cannot regard as inconsistent with loyalty to the principles of the Church of England the use of such additions or deviations as fall within the limits of these proposals. For the same reason they must regard as inconsistent with Church order the use of any other deviations from or additions to the Forms and Orders contained in the Book of 1662.

(2) That accordingly the Bishops, in the exercise of that legal or administrative discretion, which belongs to each Bishop in his own Diocese, will be guided by the proposals set forth in the Book of 1928, and will endeavour to secure that the practices which are consistent neither with the Book of 1662 nor with the Book of 1928 shall cease.

Further: (3) That the Bishops, in the exercise of their authority, will only permit the ordinary use of any of the Forms and Orders contained in the Book of 1928 if they are satisfied that such use would have the good will of the people as represented in the Parochial Church Council, and that in the case of the Occasional Offices the consent of the parties concerned will always be obtained.

Source: The Times, July 9, 1929, p. 16; ibid., July 12, 1929, p. 19.

SUGGESTIONS FOR BACKGROUND AND REFERENCE

G. K. A. Bell, *Randall Davidson, Archbishop of Canterbury* (London, 1935), II, 1325–1359.

R. Currie, "Power and Principle: The Anglican Prayer Book Controversy, 1927–1930," *Church History,* Vol. XXXIIII, No. 2 (June 1964), pp. 192–205.

C. Garbett, *Church and State in England* (London, 1950), pp. 204–226.

A. Hastings, *A History of English Christianity 1920–1985* (London, 1986), pp. 203–208.

D. Martin and P. Mullen (eds.), *No Alternative: The Prayer Book Controversy* (Oxford, 1981).

H. L. Stewart, *A Century of Anglo-Catholicism* (London, 1929), pp. 319–397.

✦ ✦ ✦ Soviet Religious Settlement

140 Declaration of Metropolitan Sergei

July 29, 1927 [July 16, Old Style]

The death of Tikhon threw the church into further confusion. The imprisonment or exile of many bishops rendered impractical the calling of a sobor to choose a new patriarch, if indeed the government would have permitted it. Acting heads of the church were arrested, and rival churchmen contested for the leadership. Meanwhile, the Living Church continued to claim authority. In 1926 the situation clarified with the emergence of Sergei (1867–1944), Metropolitan of Nizhni Novgorod, as leader of the patriarchal group. Sergei, an able hierarch of long standing and a member of the Holy Synod both before and after the Revolution, had sided briefly with the Living Church but returned to allegiance to Tikhon in 1924. Believing legalization was essential for the church's survival, Sergei took the lead in finding a *modus vivendi.* By existing law only local congregations could register with the authorities and obtain legal sanction, while the structure and hierarchical administration of the church possessed no validity. Sergei, pledging the church to civil loyalty and abstention from politics, made request for legalization in June 1926, but the petition was not accepted by the government until after the passage of another year, further negotiation, and concession. Success was announced by Sergei in this declaration to "all faithful members of the Holy All-Russian Church." The metropolitan's work won greater toleration for Orthodoxy from the government, though at the cost of entire political subservience. While the policy was bitterly assailed by some churchmen, it speeded the decline of the schismatics and the restoration of greater ecclesiastical unity under Sergei.

Among the cares of our late most holy father, Patriarch Tikhon, before his death, was the placing of our Russian Church in a legalized relation to the Soviet govern-

From Matthew Spinka, *The Church in Soviet Russia* (New York, Oxford University Press, 1956). Copyright, 1956, Oxford University Press. Reprinted by permission of the publisher.

ment and thus securing for the Church the possibility of a fully legal and peaceful existence. Dying, the Patriarch exclaimed: "I would need to live another three short years!" And indeed, if the unexpected demise had not cut short his holy labors, he would have carried this undertaking to its completion. Unfortunately, various circumstances, and principally the activities of the enemies of the Soviet government abroad, among whom were found not only the rank and file of the faithful of our Church, but their leaders as well, and which aroused on the part of the government a just distrust against all Church functionaries, hampered his efforts. Thus it was not granted him to see his efforts completed during his life.

Now that the lot of being the temporary vicar of the Primate of our Church has fallen on me, the unworthy Metropolitan Sergei, it has also become my duty to continue the efforts of the deceased in striving by all means to bring about a peaceful ordering of our Church affairs. My efforts in this direction, shared with me by the Orthodox archpastors, have not remained fruitless; with the establishment of the temporary Holy Synod, the hope for bringing into proper state and order all of our ecclesiastical administration has been strengthened, and confidence in the possibility of peaceful life and activity within the limits of law has been increased. Now, when we are almost at the very goal of our efforts, the provocative acts of our enemies abroad still continue: murders, arsons, airplane flights, explosions, and other similar occurrences of underground war are plainly seen by us all. These acts disturb the peaceful tenor of life, create an atmosphere of mutual distrust, and all manner of suspicion. Hence, it is so much more needful for our Church, and therefore the duty of all of us to whom her interests are dear, who desire to bring her on the road of legalized and peaceful existence, to show that we, as Church functionaries, are not enemies of our Soviet government and do not participate in these senseless intrigues, but are at one with our nation and our government.

To manifest these sentiments is the first goal of our present task (mine and the Synod's). Therefore, we wish to inform you that in May of the current year, upon my request and with the permission of the government, we organized the temporary Holy Synod to assist the deputy Guardian (of the Patriarchate). It is composed of the undersigned members.[1] There are still absent the Most Reverend Metropolitan Arseny of Novgorod, who has not yet arrived, and the Archbishop Sebastian of Kostroma, who is ill. Our endeavor to secure the permission for the Synod to begin its task of administering the Orthodox All-Russian Church has been crowned with success.

At present our Orthodox Church in the Union possesses not only canonical, but also fully legal, centralized administration consonant with civil laws. We furthermore hope that this legalization will be gradually extended to the lower ecclesiastical administrations: archdiocesan, regional, etc. Is it necessary to enlarge upon the significance of the consequences of the change that has occurred in the status of our Orthodox Church, of her clergy, and all her functionaries and institutions?

Let us raise our grateful prayers to the Lord who has been so gracious to our

---

1. Seraphim, metropolitan of Tver; Sylvester, archbishop of Vologda; Alexei, archbishop of Khytin; Anatoly, archbishop of Samara; Pavel, archbishop of Vyatka; Filipp, archbishop of Zvenigorod; Konstantin, bishop of Sumy; Sergei, bishop of Serpukhov.

holy Church. Let us also express, in behalf of the entire nation, our gratitude to the Soviet government for this attention to the spiritual needs of the Orthodox population, and at the same time let us assure the government that we will not abuse its confidence reposed in us.

Addressing ourselves, with God's blessing, to our synodal labors, we clearly realize the magnitude of our task . . . . We need to show not in words, but in deeds, that not only people indifferent to Orthodoxy, or those who reject it, may be faithful citizens of the Soviet Union, loyal to the Soviet government, but likewise the most fervent adherents of Orthodoxy, to whom it is as precious with all its canonical and liturgical treasures as truth and life. We wish to remain Orthodox and at the same time to recognize the Soviet Union as our civil fatherland whose joys and successes are our joys and successes, and whose misfortunes are our misfortunes. Every blow directed against the Union, be it war, boycott, or any other common disaster, or even a hole-and-corner murder as the one that occurred in Warsaw, we acknowledge as a blow directed against us. . . .[2]

We may be hindered only . . . by an insufficient recognition of the seriousness of that which has occurred in our country. Many people have misunderstood the establishment of the Soviet regime, regarding it as a fortuitous event; hence, as something not binding upon them.

People have forgotten that for a Christian there are no fortuitous events, and that what has occurred in our land, as everywhere and at all times, has been the work of God's providence, undeviatingly leading every nation toward its predestined goal. To such people, refusing to recognize "the signs of the times," to break with the former regime or even with the monarchy without breaking with Orthodoxy, may appear impossible. Such an attitude, expressed in words and deeds by certain ecclesiastical groups, has aroused the Soviet government's suspicion and has hindered the efforts of the holy Patriarch to establish peaceful relations between the Church and the Soviet government. Not in vain does the Apostle tell us that we may live in godliness, "quietly and peaceably," only if we submit to the lawful government (I Tim. 2:2); otherwise, we ought to leave the community. Only arm-chair visionaries can suppose that such an immense community as our Orthodox Church, with all its organizations, may peacefully exist in this country, hiding itself from the government. Now when our patriarchate, fulfilling the will of the late Patriarch, has decisively and undeviatingly embarked on the path of loyalty, people of the above-mentioned tendencies must, turning about and leaving their own political sympathies behind, bring to the Church only their faith and work with us only in the name of that faith; or, if they cannot immediately make the change, they must at least cease to interfere with us, temporarily refraining from all activity. We are confident that they will again and very soon return to co-operation with us, having become convinced that the change has taken place only in our relation to the regime, while the faith and the Orthodox life remain unaltered.

The problem of the émigré clergy under these circumstances is especially poignant. The openly anti-Soviet actions of some archpastors and pastors, greatly detri-

---

2. The murder of the Soviet minister to Poland, Peter Voikoff, by a young tsarist émigré had taken place in June 1927.

mental to the relations between the government and the Church, have forced the late Patriarch, as is known, to depose the Synod abroad (April 23/May 5, 1922). Nevertheless, the Synod has continued to exist hitherto, and has not changed its politics. Moreover, by its pretentions to rule, it has lately divided the ecclesiastical community abroad into two camps. In order to put an end to this state of affairs, we demanded from the clergy abroad a written promise of their complete loyalty to the Soviet government in all their public activities. Those who fail to make such a promise, or to observe it, shall be expelled from the ranks of the clergy subject to the Moscow patriarchate. We think that having set up such limits, we shall be secure against all unexpected happenings abroad. On the other hand, our demand may perhaps cause many to pause and consider whether the time has not come to revise their attitude toward the Soviet regime, so as not to be cut off from their native Church and land.

We deem it no less weighty a task to prepare and issue a call for the Second All-Russian Sobor which would choose no longer a temporary, but the permanent central Church administration and which would also deal with those "usurpers of power" in the Church who are tearing the robe of Christ asunder. The order and the time of the call, the subjects of discussion of the Sobor, and all other details will be worked out later. We shall at present only express our firm conviction that the future Sobor, having solved many of the most painful problems of the Church's inner life, will at the same time give its final approval, with one mind and voice, to the task undertaken by us in establishing regular relations between our Church and the Soviet regime.

Source: Matthew Spinka, *The Church in Soviet Russia* (New York, 1956), pp. 161–165. Russian text in *Patriarkh Sergii, i ego dukhovnoe nasledstvo* (Moscow, 1947), pp. 58–63.

SUGGESTIONS FOR BACKGROUND AND REFERENCE

References for Document 127.
Source for this document, pp. 51–100.

141　Law of April 8, 1929 (Extracts)

While the policy of Metropolitan Sergei saved the organization of the Patriarchal Church, it did not affect the campaign against religion. The League of the Militant Godless, founded in 1925, carried on energetic propaganda. With the launching of the first Five Year Plan in 1928 the Soviet government intensified efforts to drive out religious faith as a vestige of nonsocialist society. Persecution and severe restriction of religious activity were the rule until partial relaxation in the mid-1930s. The most important legislation in this campaign was this statute on the legal position of religious organizations. While making some concessions, such as permission for religious congresses, local and central organizations, parochial fund raising, and new prayer houses, the law imposed broad prohibitions, particularly in Article 17. Furthermore, by interpretation the law permitted religious instruction of children only by parents and not by priests. The legislation was particularly injurious to the growing sects outside Orthodoxy.

2. A religious association of believers of any cult shall be registered as a religious society or group of believers.

A citizen may only belong to one religious (cult) association (society or group).

3. A religious society is a local association of believers, having attained the age of eighteen years, of one and the same cult, belief, conviction and doctrine, and numbering not less than twenty persons, who have combined for the purpose of making provision for their requirements in the matter of religion. Those believers who, owing to lack of numbers, are unable to form a religious society, may form a group of believers. Religious societies and groups of believers have no juridical rights.

4. A religious society or group of believers may only carry on its activities after registration . . . .

* * *

10. Believers belonging to a religious society with the object of making provision for their requirements in the matter of religion may lease under contract, free of charge, from the Sub-District (Volost) or Regional (Rayon) Executive Committee or from the Town Soviet, special buildings for the purpose of worship and objects intended exclusively for the purposes of their cult.

Furthermore, believers . . . may use for religious meetings other buildings which have been placed at their disposal by private persons or by local Soviets and Executive Committees. . . .

* * *

17. Religious associations may not (a) create mutual credit societies, co-operatives or commercial undertakings, or in general use the property at their disposal for other than religious purposes; (b) give material assistance to their members; (c) organize for children, young people and women special prayer or other meetings, or, generally, meetings, groups, circles or departments for biblical or literary study, sewing, working or the teaching of religion, &c., or organize excursions, children's playgrounds, public libraries or reading rooms, or organize sanatoria and medical assistance.

Only books necessary for the purposes of the cult may be kept in the buildings and premises used for worship.

18. The teaching of any form of religious belief in state, public and private teaching and educational establishments is prohibited. Such teaching is permitted exclusively at special theological courses organized by citizens of the U.S.S.R. by special permission of the Commissariat for Internal Affairs . . . .

19. The work of ministers of religion, religious preachers and instructors, &c.,

shall be restricted to the area in which the members of their religious association reside, and to the place where the premises used for worship are situated.

* * *

20. Religious societies and groups of believers may organize local, All-Russian and All-Union religious congresses and conferences, but they must obtain permission on each occasion . . . .

* * *

22. Religious congresses and the executive bodies elected by them do not possess the rights of a juridical person and, in addition, may not—

(a) form any kind of central fund for the collection of voluntary gifts from believers;
(b) make any form of enforced collection;
(c) own religious property, receive the same on contract, obtain the same by purchase or hire premises for religious meetings;
(d) conclude any form of contract or deal.

* * *

25. Property necessary for the observance of the cult, whether handed over under contract to the believers forming the religious society or newly acquired by them or given to them for the purposes of the cult, is nationalized . . . .

* * *

40. Upon the liquidation of a place of worship religious property shall be disposed of as follows:—

(a) All articles of platinum, gold or silver, or cloth of gold or silver, and precious stones shall be placed to the credit of the funds of the state and shall be handed over to the local financial body or administrative body of the People's Commissariat for Education, if these articles are on their list, for disposal at their discretion.
(b) All articles of historical, artistic or museum value shall be handed over to the administrative body of the Commissariat for Education.
(c) Other articles (icons, robes, banners, covers, &c.) having special significance in the observance of the cult, shall be handed over to the believers for transfer to another place of worship of the same cult . . . .
(d) Articles in general use (bells, furniture, carpets, chandeliers, &c.) shall be placed to the credit of the funds of the state and handed over to the local financial body or administrative body of the educational authorities, if these articles are on their list, for disposal at their discretion.
(e) Cash and consumable property such as incense, candles, oil, wine, wax, wood, and coal, which are necessary for the execution of the contract or for the performance of religious services, shall not, if the society contin-

ues to exist after the liquidation of the place of worship, be subject to appropriation.

* * *

45. The construction of new places of worship may take place at the desire of religious societies provided that the usual technical building regulations and the special regulations laid down by the People's Commissariat for Internal Affairs are observed.

* * *

54. Members of groups of believers and religious societies may raise subscriptions among themselves and collect voluntary offerings, both in the place of worship itself and outside it, but only amongst the members of the religious association concerned and only for purposes connected with the upkeep of the place of worship and the religious property, for the engagement of ministers of religion and for the expenses of their executive body.

Any form of forced contribution in aid of religious associations is punishable under the Criminal Code of the R.S.F.S.R.

Source: Decree of the All-Russian Central Executive Committee and the Council of People's Commissars respecting Religious Associations April 8, 1929 (London, 1930), pp. 2, 3, 4, 5–6, 8–9, 11, 12.

SUGGESTIONS FOR BACKGROUND AND REFERENCE

A. Y. Vyshinsky, *The Law of the Soviet State* (New York, 1948), pp. 605–610. References for Document 127.

142   Constitution of the U.S.S.R. (Extract)

December 5, 1936

In another shift in government policy, the violence of the antireligious campaign was tempered in the mid-1930s. The change was represented in the Stalin Constitution of 1936. The R.S.F.S.R. Constitution of 1918 had repeated church-state separation in Article 13: "To secure for the toilers real freedom of conscience, the church is separated from the state, and the schools from the church, and freedom of religious and antireligious propaganda is recognized as the right of every citizen." And Article 65 had disfranchised "monks and clergymen of all religious denominations." (For the 1918 Constitution see James Bryan [ed.], *Intervention, Civil War, and Communism in Russia April–December 1918* [Baltimore, 1936], pp. 507–524.) An amendment in 1929 had terminated the right to religious propaganda, and this formula was retained in the 1936 document. However, Stalin's view that clergy were no longer dangerous was evident in Article 135 restoring voting rights. In the remaining years before World War II additional concessions of minor importance were made, but the government remained hostile, and some clergy suffered in the 1937 and 1938 purges.

Article 124.

In order to ensure to citizens freedom of conscience, the church in the USSR is separated from the state, and the school from the church. Freedom of religious worship and freedom of anti-religious propaganda is recognized for all citizens.

Source: Constitution (Fundamental Law) of the Union of Soviet Socialist Republics (Washington, D.C., 1945) (published by U.S.S.R. embassy), p. 26.

SUGGESTIONS FOR BACKGROUND AND REFERENCE

References for Documents 127 and 141.

✦ ✦ ✦

143　Lateran Accord (Extracts)

February 11, 1929

In the twentieth century the Roman Question, while still a troubling presence in Italian politics, lost the capacity to create diplomatic crises or to invoke the bitterness of the nineteenth century. World War I, the postwar Communist danger, and the Vatican's relaxation of the *non expedit* all worked toward a better relationship to which Mussolini and the Fascists fell heir in 1922. Though personally anticlerical, Mussolini cultivated the church for political advantage, preserving Catholic instruction in schools and suppressing the Freemasons in 1925. The papacy viewed government policy favorably in comparison with previous liberal and socialist anticlericalism, and gave no support to the Catholic Popular party, the Fascists' chief rivals. In 1926 Pius XI (1922–1939) authorized Cardinal Pietro Gasparri, secretary of state, to respond to Mussolini's invitation for negotiations. The agreement, announced in 1929, comprised a treaty (establishing the miniature Vatican State), a financial convention, and a concordat. (Only parts of the treaty and concordat are reproduced here.) Though the closing of the Roman Question produced great satisfaction in Italy and enhanced Fascist prestige, controversy soon broke out between the church and the regime over youth and education.

From the Treaty Between the Holy See and Italy:

Art. 1. Italy recognises and reaffirms the principle embodied in article 1 of the statute of the Kingdom dated the 4th March, 1848, according to which the Roman Catholic Apostolic religion is the sole religion of the State.

2. Italy recognises the sovereignty of the Holy See in the international domain as an attribute inherent in its nature and in conformity with its traditions and the requirements of its mission in the world.

3. Italy recognises the full ownership and the exclusive and absolute dominion and sovereign jurisdiction of the Holy See over the Vatican, as at present constituted, together with all its appurtenances and endowments; by this means is created the Vatican City . . . .

* * *

4. The sovereignty and exclusive jurisdiction over the Vatican City, which Italy recognises as appertaining to the Holy See, precludes any intervention therein on the part of the Italian Government and any authority other than that of the Holy See.

* * *

6. Italy shall ensure . . . an adequate supply of water to the Vatican City in ownership.

Italy shall further provide for communication with the State railways by means of the construction of a railway station within the Vatican City . . . and by the running on the Italian railways of carriages belonging to the Vatican.

It shall also provide for the direct connexion with other States of the telegraph, telephone, radiotelegraph, radiotelephone and postal services in the Vatican City.

Finally, Italy shall also provide for the co-ordination of the other public services.

* * *

8. Considering the person of the Supreme Pontiff as sacred and inviolable, Italy declares any attempt against the same, and any incitement to commit such an attempt, to be punishable with the same penalties as are prescribed in the case of an attempt . . . against the person of the King.

Offences and public insults committed within Italian territory against the . . . Supreme Pontiff by means of speeches, acts and writings, shall be punished in the same manner as offences . . . against the King.

* * *

10. The Church dignitaries and persons belonging to the Papal Court, . . . even when not citizens of the Vatican, shall be always . . . exempt from military service, jury obligations and every service of a personal character.

12. Italy recognises the right of the Holy See to active and passive legation in accordance with the general rules of international law.

Envoys of foreign Governments to the Holy See shall continue to enjoy . . . all the privileges and immunities appertaining to diplomatic agents . . . .

. . . Italy undertakes . . . to leave free the correspondence from all States, including belligerents, to the Holy See and *vice versa,* and to allow the free access of bishops from all parts of the world to the Apostolic See.

* * *

14. Italy recognises the full ownership by the Holy See of the pontifical palace of Castel Gandolfo, together with all . . . appendages . . . .

* * *

19. Diplomatic officers and envoys of the Holy See, diplomatic officers and envoys of foreign Governments accredited to the Holy See, and dignitaries of the Church . . . shall be admitted without further formality to the City across Italian territory. . . .

20. Goods arriving from foreign countries and destined for the Vatican City, or for institutions or offices of the Holy See outside the City, shall always be admitted in transit over Italian territory . . . with entire exemption from customs or octroi duty.

21. All cardinals shall enjoy in Italy the honours due to Princes of the blood. Those resident in Rome, even outside the Vatican City, shall for all purposes be regarded as citizens of the latter.

When the Pontifical See is vacant Italy shall . . . ensure that there be no impediment to the free transit and access of Cardinals across Italian territory to the Vatican . . . .

Italy shall further ensure that within Italian territory surrounding the Vatican City no acts are committed which may in any manner disturb the meetings of the Conclave.

* * *

24. As regards the sovereignty appertaining to it in the international sphere, the Holy See declares that it desires to remain . . . aloof from rivalries of a temporal nature between other States and from international congresses convened to deal with them, unless the contending parties make a joint appeal to its mission of peace. In any event the Holy See reserves the right to exercise its moral spiritual influence.

Consequently, the Vatican City shall always . . . be regarded as neutral and inviolable territory.

* * *

26. The Holy See considers that by the agreements signed this day there is adequately assured to it everything that is necessary for making provision, with the requisite liberty and independence, for the pastoral administration of the diocese of Rome and the Catholic Church in Italy and throughout the world; it declares the Roman question to be finally and irrevocably settled and therefore eliminated, and it recognises the Kingdom of Italy under the dynasty of the House of Savoy, with Rome as the capital of the Italian State.

Italy on her part recognises the State of the Vatican City under the sovereignty of the Supreme Pontiff.

From the Concordat Between the Holy See and Italy:

Art. 1. In accordance with article 1 of the treaty, Italy shall assure to the Catholic Church the free exercise of spiritual power and the free and public exercise of worship, as well as of its jurisdiction in ecclesiastical matters, in accordance with . . . the present concordat. Where it is necessary Italy shall afford to ecclesiastics the protection of her authorities for the acts of their spiritual ministry.

Having regard to the sacred character of the Eternal City, . . . the centre of the Catholic world and the goal of pilgrimages, the Italian Government shall adopt measures to prevent in Rome all that may conflict with that character.

2. The Holy See shall communicate and correspond freely with the bishops, the clergy and the whole Catholic world . . . .

Similarly, so far as concerns their pastoral ministry, the bishops shall communicate and correspond freely with their clergy and with all the faithful.

Both the Holy See and the bishops may freely publish and also affix in the interior and at the outside doors of the buildings set aside for worship or at the offices of their ministry the instructions, ordinances, pastoral letters, diocesan notices and other documents . . . .

* * *

3. Theological students, those of the last two years of their theological preparation for ordination and novices of religious institutions may . . . postpone the fulfilment of their military service obligations from year to year until their 26th year.

Clergy ordained *in sacris* and members of religious orders who have taken vows are exempt from military service, except in the event of general mobilisation. In that case, priests will be drafted to the armed forces . . . but will continue to wear clerical dress in order that they may exercise their sacred office among the troops under . . . the military ordinary . . . .

Nevertheless, priests with a cure of souls shall be exempt from answering the call in the event of general mobilisation. . . .

4. Ecclesiastics and members of religious orders shall be exempt from service on juries.

5. No ecclesiastic may be engaged or remain in an employment or office of the Italian State or of public bodies subordinate thereto without the consent of the diocesan ordinary.

* * *

7. Ecclesiastics may not be required by magistrates . . . to give information regarding persons or matters known to them by reason of their sacred office.

8. In the event of an ecclesiastic or a member of a religious order being brought before a criminal magistrate for a crime, the King's Procurator must immediately inform the ordinary of the diocese . . . and . . . transmit to him officially the result of the enquiry and any judicial sentence passed, whether of first instance or of appeal.

In the event of arrest the ecclesiastic . . . shall be treated with the consideration due to his status and rank in the hierarchy.

In the event of an ecclesiastic . . . being sentenced, the punishment shall, if possible, be served in establishments separate from those destined for laymen, unless the competent ordinary has reduced the convicted person to lay status.

* * *

19. The selection of archbishops and bishops shall appertain to the Holy See.

Before proceeding to the appointment of an archbishop or diocesan bishop or coadjutor *cum jure successionis,* the Holy See shall communicate to the Italian Government the name of the person selected in order to ensure that the latter have no objection of a political nature to such appointment. . . .

20. Before taking over their dioceses bishops shall take an oath of allegiance to the Head of the State in the following terms:—

"Before God and His Holy Apostles I swear . . . allegiance to the Italian state . . . . I swear . . . to respect, and to cause to be respected by my clergy, the King and the Government established in accordance with the constitutional laws of the State. I further swear . . . that I will enter into no agreement nor attend any council which may be prejudicial to the interests of the Italian State and to public order, and that I will not permit my clergy to participate in such. As it is my concern to promote the welfare and interests of the Italian State I will endeavour to prevent any evil which may threaten it."

21. The bestowal of ecclesiastical benefices shall devolve upon the ecclesiastical authorities.

Appointments of persons to benefices shall be confidentially notified by the competent ecclesiastical authorities to the Italian Government, and such appointment shall not take effect until 30 days after such notification.

Within this period the Italian Government shall, in the event of serious objections to the appointment, confidentially inform the ecclesiastical authority thereof. Should the divergence of views be maintained the ecclesiastical authorities shall submit the case to the Holy See.

* * *

30. The . . . administration of property belonging to any ecclesiastical institution or religious association shall be carried out under the . . . control of the . . . Church, any intervention . . . of the Italian State being excluded . . . .

The Italian State recognises the right of ecclesiastical institutions and religious associations to acquire property, subject to the provisions of the civil laws governing acquisitions by juridical persons.

Pending further agreement to the contrary the Italian Government shall continue to make good any deficiencies in the revenue of ecclesiastical benefices by the grant of subventions . . . .

* * *

34. Desiring to restore to . . . marriage . . . a dignity in conformity with the Catholic traditions of its people, the Italian State recognises the civil effects of the sacrament of marriage as governed by canon law.

Notices of marriage . . . shall be published at the communal offices as well as at the parish church.

Immediately after the ceremony the parish priest shall explain to the parties the civil effects of the marriage and read the articles of the Civil Code concerning the rights and duties of married persons. He shall draw up the marriage certificate, an exact copy of which he shall forward within 5 days to the commune . . . .

Actions for the nullity of marriage and the annulment of marriages solemnised but not consummated shall be reserved to the competence of ecclesiastical courts . . . .

* * *

35. As regards secondary schools kept by ecclesiastical or religious bodies, the institution of State examinations with effective parity of conditions for candidates from Government institutions and from the aforesaid schools, shall be maintained.

36. Instruction in Christian doctrine according to . . . Catholic tradition is regarded by Italy as the foundation and crown of public instruction. She therefore agrees that the religious teaching now given in the public elementary schools shall be further developed in the secondary schools . . . .

This instruction shall be given by means of teachers and professors, priests or members of religious orders, approved by the ecclesiastical authorities, with assistance from lay teachers . . . who shall . . . be furnished with a certificate of qualification issued by the ordinary . . . .

The revocation of this certificate . . . shall forthwith deprive the teacher of the capacity to teach.

Only text-books approved by the ecclesiastical authorities shall be used for such religious teaching . . . .

37. In order to facilitate the religious instruction and attendance at religious services of youths . . . the Avanguardisti and Balilla[1] . . . shall arrange their timetables . . . as to form no impediment to . . . religious duties on Sundays and feasts of obligation.

* * *

43. The Italian State recognises the organisations subordinate to the "Azione Cattolica Italiana" [Catholic Action] in so far as these, as laid down by the Holy See, pursue their activities outside any political party and in the direct subordination to the hierarchy of the Church . . . .

The Holy See takes the opportunity . . . to renew the prohibition against Italian ecclesiastics and members of religious orders becoming members contending in favour of any political party whatever.

Source: British and Foreign State Papers (1929, Part I) (London, 1934), CXXX, 792–813. Italian text in *Acta Apostolicae Sedis* (Rome, 1929), XXI, 209–295.

1. Fascist military youth organizations, the *Balilla* for boys under fourteen and the *Avanguardia* recruited from the *Balilla*

SUGGESTIONS FOR BACKGROUND AND REFERENCE

D. A. Binchy, *Church and State in Fascist Italy* (Oxford, 1941).
P. Hughes, *Pope Pius the Eleventh* (New York, 1937), pp. 195–228.
A. Jemolo, *Church and State in Italy, 1850–1950* (Oxford, 1960), pp. 182–277.
P. Kent, *The Pope and the Duce: the International Impact of the Lateran Agreements* (London, 1981).
J. F. Pollard, *The Vatican and Italian Fascism 1929–1932* (Cambridge, 1985).

144   *Non Abbiamo Bisogno* (Extracts)

June 29, 1931

The signing of the Lateran Accord briefly preceded the inauguration of a second and more absolute stage in Fascist dictatorship in which the totalitarian regime inevitably collided with the church. Conflict came over the youth program of Catholic Action. In May 1931, after harassing Catholic leaders and accusing Catholic Action of anti-Fascist activity, the government ordered the closing of Catholic youth offices. Pius XI (1922–1939) replied with this encyclical, rejecting Fascist charges against the church and asserting Catholic rights in education. (In September 1931, tension relaxed. The government again permitted Catholic Action, while the church placed Catholic youth directly under episcopal authority, dropped sports programs, carefully related educational and social activities to religious ends, and avoided political entanglements.)

Already on several occasions . . . we have protested against the campaign of false and unjust accusations which preceded the disbanding of the associations of the young people and of the university students affiliated with Catholic Action. It was a disbanding which was carried out in a way and with the use of tactics which would give the impression that action was being taken against a vast and dangerous organization of criminals. And the proceedings were directed against young men and young women who are certainly some of the best among the good . . . . It is noteworthy that even among the officers of the law charged to carry out these orders of suppression, there were many who were ill at ease . . . .

However, in sad contrast to the manner of acting of these officials, there were how many acts of mistreatment and of violence, extending even to the striking of blows and the drawing of blood! How many insults in the press, how many injurious words and acts against things and persons, not excluding Ourself . . . . And all of this sad accompaniment of irreverences and of violence took place in the presence of and with the participation of members of a political party some of whom were in uniform, and . . . with such a passive acquiescence on the part of the civil authorities and the police as to make one necessarily think of some uniform directions received from some high authority. . . .

* * *

As is well known, We have repeatedly and solemnly affirmed and protested that Catholic Action, both from its very nature and essence (the participation and the collaboration of the laity with the Apostolic Hierarchy) and by Our precise and categorical directions and dispositions, is outside and above every political party. We have also affirmed and protested that We are sure that in Italy Our directions and dispositions have been faithfully obeyed and followed. . . .

* * *

And We do not wish to omit mentioning another guarantee that Catholic Action will abstain from politics, . . . and that is that Catholic Action has been, is, and will always be, under the dependence of the Episcopate . . . . When the Popular Party was dissolved and passed out of existence, those who formerly belonged to Catholic Action continued to belong to Catholic Action, and they submitted themselves with perfect discipline to the fundamental law of Catholic Action, that is, abstention from every political activity, and so did all those who on that occasion asked to be received as members. And with what justice and charity could these people have been expelled or not admitted to Catholic Action when they possessed the necessary qualifications required by the constitution? The regime and the party which seemed to attribute such a fearful and feared strength to those who belonged to the Popular Party for particular reasons should show themselves grateful to Catholic Action, which removed them precisely from that sphere and required them to make a formal pledge not to carry out any political activities, to limit themselves to religious ones. . . . We cannot be grateful to one who, after putting out of existence socialism and anti-religious organizations (Our enemies and not alone Ours), has permitted them to be so generally readmitted, as all see and deplore, and has made them even more strong and dangerous inasmuch as they are now hidden and also protected by their new uniform. . . .

* * *

. . . it is clear that these accusations—of political activity by Catholic Action, manifest or disguised hostility of some of its partisans against the regime and the party, as well as its being also the eventual . . . haven of the refugees who up to the present hostility have been spared through the banner of Catholic Action . . . —are nothing but a pretext or a cumulation of pretexts.

We dare to say that even Catholic Action itself is only a pretext. That which was desired and . . . attempted was to tear away . . . from the Church, the young, and all the young. So very true is this that, after having talked so much about Catholic Action, aim was taken only at the associations of the young, nor were these attacks limited to associations of the young affiliated with Catholic Action. Then afterward, they were extended and broadened so that the tumultuous measure embraced associations of a simply devotional character . . . .

This essential point is very largely . . . confirmed . . . by many antecedent statements made by personalities more or less responsible, and also by persons representative of the regime and of the party . . . .

* * *

And here We find Ourselves in the presence of a contrast between authentic affirmations on the one hand and not less authentic facts on the other hand, which reveal . . . the proposal, already in great part actually put into effect, to monopolize . . . the young, from the tenderest years up to manhood and womanhood, and all for the exclusive advantage of a party, of a regime based on ideology which clearly resolves itself into a . . . real pagan worship of the state, which is no less in contrast with the natural rights of the family than it is in contradiction to the supernatural rights of the Church. To propose and promote such a monopoly, to persecute for this reason Catholic Action . . . is truly . . . to prevent children from going to Jesus Christ, since it impedes them from going to His Church and even arrives at the point of snatching them with violence from the bosom of both . . . .

The Church . . . has never contested the rights and the duties of the state concerning the education of its citizens . . . ; rights and duties which are unchallengeable as long as they remain within the limits of the state's proper competency . . . .

* * *

The Church . . . is certainly acting within the limits of its mandate, not only when it puts into souls the first indispensable beginnings and elements of supernatural life, but also when it . . . encourages the growth of this supernatural life . . . and in the ways . . . which . . . seem suitable also with the purpose of preparing capable and efficient collaborators with the apostolic Hierarchy and clergy. . . .

It was Jesus Christ Himself who laid the first foundations of Catholic Action. It was Christ Himself Who, choosing and educating the Apostles and Disciples as collaborators in His Divine Apostolate, gave an example which at once was followed by the first holy Apostles . . . .

It is, consequently, an unjustified pretense . . . to come to teach the Church and its Head what is sufficient . . . for the education and Christian formation of souls . . . .

. . . it is a grave and destructive error to believe . . . that the work of the Church done by Catholic Action . . . is . . . made superfluous by the religious instruction in the schools and on ecclesiastical assistance of the associations of youth of the party and . . . regime. Both are certainly necessary. Without them the schools and the associations would inevitably and quickly become . . . pagan things. Necessary, therefore, they are, but they are not sufficient. As a matter of fact, with such religious instructions and such ecclesiastical assistance the Church . . . can develop only a minimum of her spiritual . . . effectiveness . . . in an environment which does not depend on the Church . . . subject to immediate superiors often little or not at all favorably disposed and occasionally exercising by the example of their lives an influence contrary to their words.

* * *

A conception of the state which makes the young generations belong entirely to it without any exception from the tenderest years up to adult life cannot be reconciled by a Catholic with the Catholic doctrine nor can it be reconciled with the natural right of the family. It is not possible . . . to reconcile with Catholic doctrine the pretense that the Church and the Pope must limit themselves to the external practices of religion, such as Mass and the Sacraments, and then to say that the rest of education belongs to the state.

* * *

. . . what is to be thought about the formula of an oath which even little boys and girls are obliged to take about executing orders without discussion, from an authority which . . . can give orders against all truth and justice and in disregard of the rights of the Church and its souls . . . and to have them swear to serve with all their strength, even to the shedding of blood, the cause of a revolution that snatches the youth from the Church and from Jesus Christ and which educates its own young forces to hatred, to deeds of violence, and to irreverence, not excluding the person of the Pope himself . . . . When you place the question in such terms the answer from the Catholic point of view and also from a human point of view is, inevitably, only one . . . : such an oath as it stands is illicit.

Source: Encyclical Letter of His Holiness, Pope Pius XI Issued June 29, 1931 (Washington, D.C., 1931), pp. 7–8, 12–13, 14–15, 19–26. Italian text in *Acta Apostolicae Sedis* (Rome, 1931), XXIII, 285–312.

SUGGESTIONS FOR BACKGROUND AND REFERENCE

References for Document 143.

✦ ✦ ✦ Protestantism and Nazi Germany

145 German Christian Platform

May 26, 1932

The nationalist extremism of postwar Germany found expression in the neopagan racist German Faith Movement and, in a party that had much more significance for German Protestantism, the German Christians. Led by Pastor Joachim Hossenfelder (b. 1899), the German Christians demanded an Aryan church corresponding to the "German spirit," politically Nazi, and embracing all German Protestants. Practically this program meant uniting all *Landeskirchen* into a single *Reichskirche* with Nazi leadership and ideology and authoritarian government. The principles of the movement were formally set forth in a Berlin convention that met June 6, 1932. (However, interpretation of German Christian views varied widely among adherents.) With the coming to power of the Nazis in the next year, German Christian leaders sought to impress these principles on a reorganized German church.

1. These directives are to demonstrate to all believing Germans the means and objectives by which they can achieve a new order in the church. These directives are not intended to be a creed or to replace one; neither are they intended to undermine the confessional foundations of the Evangelical Church. They are a dedicated way of life [*Lebensbekenntnis*].

2. We are fighting for the merger of the 29 churches embraced by the German Evangelical Church Federation into one evangelical *Reichskirche* . . . .

3. The [voting] list "German Christians" will be no church-political party in the usual sense. It applies to all Christians of German type. The age of parliamentarianism has had its day, and in the church as well. Church-political parties have no religious mandate to represent church people and they obstruct the lofty aim of becoming one [united] people of the church. We want a living *Volkskirche* which is the expression of all the spiritual force of our people.

4. We take our stand on the basis of positive Christianity. We avow an affirmative type of Christian faith, as conformable to the German spirit of Luther and heroic piety.

5. We wish to bring to recognition in our church the reawakened German feeling for life and to make our church vigorous. In the fateful battle for German freedom and future, the church has proved to be too feeble in its leadership. The church has not yet mobilized for decisive struggle against God-hating Marxism and the foreign-spirited Center Party, but instead has reached an accord with the political parties which represent these forces. We wish our church to fight at the head of the decisive struggle for the existence or annihilation of our nation. It dare not stand apart or even disavow the freedom-fighters.

6. We demand a change in the church constitution (political clause) and battle against religion-hating, nation-hating Marxism and its Christian socialist fellow-supporters of all shades. We miss in this church constitution the trusting reliance on God and the mission of the church. The way into the Kingdom of God leads through battle, cross and sacrifice, not through false peace.

7. We see in race, nationality, and nation orders of life granted and entrusted to us by God; to preserve them is for us a commandment of God. Therefore racial mixing is to be opposed. . . .

8. We see in home missions [*Inner Mission*], rightly understood, a living Christianity of action [*Tat-Christentum*] which, according to our understanding, is rooted not in mere pity but in submission to God's will and in thankfulness for Christ's death on the cross. Mere pity is "charity" and becomes arrogance, coupled with bad conscience, and effeminates a nation. We know something of Christian duty and love toward the helpless, but we demand also the safeguarding of the nation from the unfit and inferior. The *Inner Mission* must on no account contribute to the degeneration of our folk. It has moreover to keep distant from economic adventures . . . .

9. In the mission to the Jews we see a serious danger for our nationality. It is the

entryway for foreign blood into our national body. It has no right to exist compared with foreign missions. We reject the mission to the Jews in Germany, as long as the Jews have rights of citizenship and by this means present the danger of racial decay and bastardization. . . . Marriage between Germans and Jews is particularly to be forbidden.

10. We want an Evangelical Church which is rooted in nationhood, and we reject the spirit of a Christian cosmopolitanism. We want to overcome the pernicious manifestations which have sprung up from this spirit—such as pacifism, internationalism, Freemasonry, etc.—through faith in the national mission granted to us by God. The membership of an Evangelical minister in a lodge of Freemasons is not permissible.

These ten points of the "German Christians" are a call to rally, and they form in large measure the direction of the future Evangelical *Reichskirche,* which by preserving confessional peace will develop the powers of our Reformation faith into the best of the German nation.

Source: Joachim Beckmann (ed.), *Evangelische Kirche im Dritten Reich (Kirchliches Jahrbuch für die Evangelische Kirche in Deutschland)* (Gütersloh, Germany, 1948), pp. 4–6.

SUGGESTIONS FOR BACKGROUND AND REFERENCE

A. C. Cochrane, *The Church's Confession under Hitler* (Philadelphia, 1962).
J. S. Conway, *The Nazi Persecution of the Churches 1933–1945* (London, 1968).
R. P. Ericksen, *Theologians under Hitler: Gerhard Kittel, Paul Althaus, and Emanuel Hirsch* (New Haven, 1985).
E. Helmreich, *The German Churches under Hitler: Background, Struggle, and Epilogue* (Detroit, 1978).
K. S. Latourette, *Christianity in a Revolutionary Age* (New York, 1958–1962), IV, 257–269.
P. Matheson, *The Third Reich and the Christian Churches* (Grand Rapids, Mich., 1981).
K. S. Scholder, *The Churches and the Third Reich* (Philadelphia, 1988).

146 Evangelical Church Constitution (Extracts)

July 11, 1933

Nazi and German Christian pressure moved the Evangelical Church Federation to appoint a committee to produce a constitution for a new *Reichskirche.* Completed in great haste, the constitution provided for government by a synod and Reichsbishop and protection for the three confessions. The basic question was who would administer the new church. With Nazi support the German Christians tried to force acceptance of a Nazi former army chaplain, Ludwig Müller, as Reichsbishop, but the Federation instead named Friedrich von Bodelschwingh of the Inner Mission. Government insistence forced Bodelschwingh to resign, and summer elections, accompanied by propaganda and terrorism, made

Müller Reichsbishop in September 1933. German Christians also obtained control of several *Landeskirchen,* notably that of Prussia.

At this time when Almighty God is letting our German people pass through a new historical era the German Evangelical Churches unite in carrying on and perfecting the unity brought about by The German Evangelical Church Federation and forming with one accord one

GERMAN EVANGELICAL CHURCH

It unites the confessions arising out of the Reformation and co-existing with equal rights in a solemn league and bears thereby testimony: One Body, and one Spirit, one Lord, one Faith, one Baptism, one God and Father of us all, who is over all, and through all and in all.

The German Evangelical Church has enacted the following Constitution:

1. The inviolable foundation of the German Evangelical Church is the Gospel of Jesus Christ, as testified to us in the Holy Scriptures and brought to light again in the creeds of the Reformation. The full powers which the Church needs for her mission are thereby determined and limited.

2. (1) The German Evangelical Church is divided into member churches (*Landeskirchen*) . . . .

(3) The Landeskirchen remain independent in confession and worship.

(4) The German Evangelical Church may give to the Landeskirchen direction for their constitutions, in so far as these are not bound by confession. It has to promote and guarantee legal unity among the Landeskirchen in the domain of administration and jurisprudence.

(5) Leading office-holders of the Landeskirchen are appointed after consultation with The German Evangelical Church.

(6) All ecclesiastical office-holders shall, on entering office, be called upon to pledge themselves to the Constitution of The German Evangelical Church.

3. (1) The German Evangelical Church regulates the whole of German ecclesiastical legal existence.

(2) It arranges its relationship to the State.

(3) It determines its attitude towards outside religious bodies.

* * *

5. (1) The head of the Church is the Lutheran Reichs-Bishop.

(2) The Reichs-Bishop is assisted by a Spiritual Council.

(3) A German Evangelical National Synod co-operates in the appointment of the Church Government and in legislation.

(4) Advisory Chambers guarantee to the living forces inherent in the German Evangelical soul free creative co-operation in the service of the Church.

6. (1) The Reichs-Bishop represents The German Evangelical Church. He is called upon to give visible expression to the coherent church life in the Landeskirchen and to guarantee a homogeneous leadership for the work of The German Evangelical Church. He takes all necessary measures for the safe-guarding of the Constitution.

(2) The Reichs-Bishop installs the members of the Spiritual Council in their

offices. He meets the leading office-holders of the Landeskirchen regularly for discussion and consultation. He nominates and dismisses the officials of The German Evangelical Church.

[(3) The Reichs-Bishop is competent to perform all spiritual] functions, especially to preach, to issue proclamations in the name of The German Evangelical Church and to order extraordinary penitential and festive services.[1]

* * *

(5) The Reichs-Bishop is proposed to the National Synod by the official leaders of the Landeskirchen together with the Spiritual Council and appointed to the bishopric by the National Synod.

* * *

7. (1) The Spiritual Council is called upon under the leadership of the Reichs-Bishop to govern The German Evangelical Church and to legislate.

(2) It consists of three theologians and one jurist member. In appointing the theologians attention shall be paid to the confessional character inherent in The German Evangelical Church. . . .

(3) It is the especial task of the theological members to strengthen the spiritual bond of the Landeskirchen with The German Evangelical Church . . . .

(4) The members of the Spiritual Council are appointed by the Reichs-Bishop. The theological members are proposed to the Reichs-Bishop by the official leaders of the Landeskirchen. . . .

* * *

8. (1) The German Evangelical National Synod consists of sixty members. Two thirds are sent by the German Evangelical Landeskirchen out of their Synods and governments. One third is chosen by The German Evangelical Church from persons who have done prominent service in the Church.

* * *

(3) The National Synod is convened by the Reichs-Bishop at least once a year. . . . Place and time of the session is fixed by the Reichs-Bishop.

* * *

10. The Laws of The German Evangelical Church are decreed by the National Synod in cooperation with the Spiritual Council or by the latter alone. They are drawn up by the Reichs-Bishop and published in the Official Gazette . . . .

* * *

12. (1) The Constitution may be altered by law in so far as provisions relating to confession or worship are not involved. This law requires the consent of two thirds

---

1. Typographical error in translation of this paragraph has been corrected by reference to German text.

of the present members of the National Synod or the unanimous approval of the Spiritual Council.

(2) Any alteration of the Constitution that affects the structure of the executive bodies of The German Evangelical Church must be made law by the co-operation of the National Synod.

Source: Charles S. Macfarland, *The New Church and the New Germany* (New York, 1934), pp. 181–186. German text in Joachim Beckmann (ed.), *Evangelische Kirche im Dritten Reich* (Gütersloh, Germany, 1948), pp. 17–20.

SUGGESTIONS FOR BACKGROUND AND REFERENCE

References for Document 145.
Source for this document.

147   Church Aryan Law (Extracts)

September 6, 1933

Nazi racism led to laws excluding Jews from schools and universities, professions, and public service. While the new Evangelical Constitution did not contain an Aryan Paragraph, Bishop Müller signified his intention of introducing the racial distinction into the church. Accordingly, the new church law of the Old Prussian Union excluded from the ministry or other church office persons of non-Aryan descent or married to non-Aryans. While the policy did not want for some plausible and scholarly defenses, such as that of Emanuel Hirsch of Göttingen, some pastors and professors protested vigorously. (For the statement of the theological faculty of the University of Marburg, see Charles S. Macfarland, *The New Church and the New Germany* [New York, 1934], pp. 188–191.)

I

1. Only he may be called as clergyman or official of the general church administration who possesses the prescribed training for his career and who appears unreservedly for the national State and the German Evangelical Church.

2. He who is not of Aryan extraction or is married to a person of non-Aryan extraction may not be called as clergyman or official of the general church administration. Clergymen and officials of Aryan extraction who enter into marriage with a person of non-Aryan extraction are to be dismissed.

Decision concerning who is to be regarded as a person of non-Aryan extraction shall be according to provisions of the law of the Reich.

* * *

III

1. Clergymen and officials whose previous practice offers no security that at all times they appear unreservedly for the national State and the German Evangelical Church may be retired.

2. Clergymen or officials of non-Aryan extraction or married to persons of non-Aryan extraction are to be retired.

3. Application of Section 2 may be waived in cases of persons who have rendered exceptional services toward the advancement [*Aufbau*] of the church in the German spirit.

4. Provisions of Section 2 are not valid for clergymen or officials who have already since August 1, 1914 been clergymen or officials of the church, of the Reich, of a [German] state [*Land*], or of any other corporation of public law, or who were at the front for the German Reich or its allies in the World War or whose fathers or sons fell in the World War.

Source: Joachim Beckmann (ed.), *Evangelische Kirche im Dritten Reich* (Gütersloh, Germany, 1948), pp. 24–25.

SUGGESTIONS FOR BACKGROUND AND REFERENCE

C. S. Macfarland, *The New Church and the New Germany* (New York, 1934), pp. 62–84. References for Document 145.

148 Barmen Confession

May 29–31, 1934

Resistance to the Nazis and the German Christians was soon organized and expanded as the government's program became clearer. Led chiefly by Karl Barth (1886–1968), then professor at Bonn, the opposition group denounced the nationalist heresy and protested the decision of the Old Prussian Union synod to Aryanize the church. In 1933 the Pastors' Emergency League was formed with the vow drafted by Martin Niemöller (1892–1984):

"1. I engage to execute my office as Minister of the Word, holding myself bound to the Holy Scriptures and to the Confessions of the Reformation as the true exegesis of the Holy Scriptures.

"2. I engage to protest, irrespective of the sacrifice involved, against every violation of this Confessional position.

"3. I hold myself responsible to the utmost of my ability for those who are persecuted on account of this Confessional position.

"4. Under this vow I testify that a violation of the Confessional position is perpetrated by the application of the Aryan paragraph within the Church of Christ." (Arthur Frey, *Cross and Swastika* [London, 1938], pp. 143–144.)

The league won support from about twenty-five hundred pastors. (About the same number supported the German Christians.) More opposition exploded when Nazis attacked the Old Testament and suppressed the Evangelical youth movement. The Confessing Church now emerged. Its leaders, convinced that organs of church government were held by men bent on destroying historic German Protestantism, summoned the May organizational synod at Barmen with representatives from United, Lutheran, and Reformed churches. Support for the Confessing Church was conspicuous from men of Reformed or United traditions. Some Lutherans, while distrustful of Nazis, were less pronounced in opposition and suspicious of the interfaith cooperation typified by Barmen.

1. Summons to the Evangelical Churches and Christians in Germany.

The Confessional Synod of the German Evangelical Church met in Barmen from 29th to 31st May, 1934. Here representatives from all the German Confessional Churches found themselves at one in confession of the one Lord of the One, Holy, Apostolic Church. In loyalty to this their confession members of Lutheran, Reformed and United Churches sought for a common message for the trouble and tribulation of the Church in our days. With gratitude to God they verily believe that the common message has been given to them. They aimed neither at founding a new Church, nor forming a Union. For nothing was further from their thoughts than the abolition of the Confessional position of our Churches. Their desire was rather, in fidelity, to resist unanimously the destruction of the Confession of Faith, and so, of the Evangelical Church in Germany. In opposition to the attempts to unify the German Evangelical Church by means of false doctrine, by the use of force, and of insincere practices, the Confessional Synod declares: *The unity of the Evangelical Churches in Germany can only come into being from the Word of God in faith through the Holy Spirit. Only so does the Church become renewed.*

Therefore the Confessional Synod calls the Churches to place themselves in prayer behind it and to range themselves solidly around their pastors and teachers who are loyal to the Confession.

Do not let yourselves be misled by frivolous speeches, pretending that we oppose the unity of the German People! Do not listen to the deceivers who twist our intention to make it seem that we want to rend the unity of the German Evangelical Church or to forsake the Confessions of our fathers!

Try the spirits whether they are of God! Try also the words of the Confessional Synod of the German Evangelical Church to see whether they agree with the Holy Scriptures and with the Confessions of our fathers. If you find that we contradict Scripture, do not listen to us! But if you find that we are standing upon Scripture, then let no fear nor temptation keep you from travelling with us the way of faith and obedience to the Word of God . . . .

* * *

3. Theological Declaration of the Present Position of the German Evangelical Church.

The German Evangelical Church is . . . a federation of Confessional Churches of equal status, having their roots in the Reformation. The theological basis for the union of these Churches is stated in Art. 1 and Art. 2, 1 of the Constitution . . . .

We . . . declare that we jointly stand on the ground of the . . . Church as a federation of German Confessional Churches. We are united by the Confession of the One Lord of the One, Holy, Catholic and Apostolic Church.

We declare publicly before all the Evangelical Churches of Germany that our common cause in this Confession and so also the unity of the German Evangelical Church are most seriously imperilled. They are threatened by the methods of teaching and acting employed by the ruling Church party, that of the German Christians, and by the government of the Church run by them, methods which became more and more visible in the first year of the existence of the German Evangelical Church. This threat consists in the fact that the basic principles which unite the German Evangelical Church are continually and systematically being thwarted and made ineffective by alien principles, held both by the leaders and spokesmen of the German Christians and also by the Government of the Church. When these principles are acknowledged, then, according to all the Confessions that hold sway amongst us, the Church ceases to be Church. When therefore these principles are acknowledged, the German Evangelical Church as a federation of Confessional Churches becomes impossible.

As members of the Lutheran, Reformed and United Churches we may and must to-day raise our voices in common in this cause. For the very reason that we want to be and to continue faithful to our various Confessions, we must not keep silence, since we believe that in a time of common trouble and tribulation a common message has been given us to deliver. We leave it to God to determine what this signifies for the inter-relations of the Confessional Churches.

In face of the errors of the "German Christians" and the present Reich Church Government, errors which ruin the Church and so shatter the unity of the German Evangelical Church, we make profession of the following Gospel truths.

1. "I am the way, the truth and the life. No man cometh unto the Father but by me." (John xiv.)

"Verily, verily, I say unto you, He that entereth not by the door into the sheepfold, but climbeth up some other way, the same is a thief and a robber. I am the door: by me if any man enter in, he shall be saved." (John x. 1, 9.)

Jesus Christ, as He is testified to us in Holy Scripture, is the one Word of God which we have to hear and which we have to trust and obey in life and death.

We reject the false doctrine that the Church might and must acknowledge as sources of its proclamation, except and beside this one Word of God, still other events, powers, forms and truths as God's revelation.

2. "Jesus Christ is of God made unto us wisdom, and righteousness, and sanctification, and redemption." (1 Cor. i. 30.)

As Jesus Christ is God's Word of forgiveness of all our sins, in the same way and with the same seriousness, He is God's mighty claim upon our whole life.

Through Him we get happy liberation from the godless bondage of this world into free, thankful service of His creatures.

We reject the false doctrine that there are realms of our life in which we belong not to Jesus Christ, but to other masters, realms where we do not need to be justified and sanctified by Him.

3. "But speaking the truth in love, we may grow up into Him in all things, which is the head, even Christ, from whom the whole body is fitly joined together." (Eph. iv. 15, 16.)

The Christian Church is the community of brethren in which Jesus Christ, present as its Lord, acts in Word and Sacrament through the Holy Spirit. In the midst of the world of sin, it has, as the Church of pardoned sinners, to witness, by its faith and by its obedience, by its message and order of life, that it is only His property, that it lives and can live only by His consolation and by His orders, in expectation of His coming.

We reject the false doctrine that the Church is permitted to form its message or its order according to its own desire or according to prevailing philosophical or political convictions.

4. "Ye know that the princes of the Gentiles exercise dominion over them, and they that are great exercise authority over them. But it shall not be so among you: but whosoever will be great among you, let him be your minister." (Matt. xx. 25, 26.)

The various offices in the Church do not set up any lordship of some over others, but they make possible the carrying out of that ministry which is entrusted to and enjoined upon the whole congregation.

We reject the false doctrine that the Church is able or at liberty apart from this ministry to give itself or to accept special "leaders" equipped with power to rule.

5. "Fear God. Honour the King." (1 Pet. ii. 17.)

Scripture tells us that, in the as yet unredeemed world in which the Church exists the State has by divine appointment the task of seeing to and maintaining—by the fullest exercise of human insight and human capacity, by means of the threat of force and by means of the use of force—law and peace. With gratitude and reverence towards God the Church acknowledges the benefit of this order which He has appointed. It is a reminder of God's Kingdom, of God's commandment and righteousness, and so, of the responsibility of both rulers and ruled. It trusts and obeys the power of that Word through which God sustains all things.

We reject the false doctrine that the State should or could go beyond its special task and become the sole and total order of human life, thus fulfilling also the Church's vocation.

We reject the false doctrine that the Church should or could go beyond its special task and assume functions and dignities of the State, thus itself becoming an organ of the State.

6. "Lo, I am with you alway, even unto the end of the world." (Matt. xxviii. 20.)
"The Word of God is not bound." (2 Tim. ii. 9.)

The Church is commissioned—and in this lies its freedom—to this task: in Christ's stead and so in the service of His Word and Work, to deliver, by means of Preaching and Sacrament, to all men the message of the free grace of God.

We reject the false doctrine that the Church could assume a human sovereignty over the Word and Work of the Lord, and place these at the service of any arbitrarily chosen wishes, aims or plans.

The Confessional Synod of the German Evangelical Church declares that it sees in the recognition of these truths and in the rejection of these errors the indispensable theological basis of the German Evangelical Church as a federation of Confessional Churches. It invites all those who are able to accept their declaration to keep these theological principles in mind in their decisions in Church politics. It asks all whom it concerns to return to the unity of faith, love and hope.

Verbum Dei manet in aeternum.

Source: Arthur Frey, *Cross and Swastika* (London, 1938), pp. 149–157. German text in Joachim Beckmann (ed.), *Evangelische Kirche im Dritten Reich* (Gütersloh, Germany, 1948), pp. 62–65.

SUGGESTIONS FOR BACKGROUND AND REFERENCE

V. Barnett, *For the Soul of the People: Protestant Protest against Hitler* (New York, 1992), pp. 47–73.
J. Bentley, *Martin Niemöller* (New York, 1984), pp. 42–130.
References for Document 145.

149 Dahlem Declaration

October 20, 1934

Church conflict was violent after the Barmen Synod as the government attempted to exact a loyalty oath to Hitler from all pastors and to incorporate, against aroused opposition, those *Landeskirchen* that had not yet been absorbed into the *Reichskirche*. In Bavaria and Württemberg where the attack went strongest, defense of the Lutheran leadership assumed the character of a widespread resistance movement. The Confessing Church now set up organs of church government. At the Dahlem (Berlin) Synod it proclaimed itself the legitimate German Evangelical Church and issued this Dahlem Declaration asserting the church's right to determine its own constitution. Accompanying these resolutions was an appeal to the congregations: "Let those come openly to our side who are resolved to drive from the Church unrighteousness and violence, lying and heresy, who are minded to let the Word of God have its place as sole saving power, who are convinced that in matters of Church doctrine and organization the Church alone is called to decide—Come to us! Unite with us in the struggle." Though harassed and persecuted, the Confessing Church, by organizing, effectively ended the threat of a

From Arthur Frey, *Cross and Swastika* (London, 1938). Translated by J. Strathearn McNab. Copyright, 1938, by SCM Press, Limited. Reprinted by permission of the publisher.

united Nazi-controlled Protestantism. In remaining years before World War II it continued heroic resistance, though at great disadvantage from restrictions on publication, suppression of schools, tax penalties, and imprisonment of pastors. Protestant opposition to Hitler was further weakened by some disagreement on policy. Some, often associated with the "intact" (uncoordinated with *Reichskirche*) Lutheran *Landeskirchen*, regarded the Barmen-Dahlem position as too advanced and counseled further efforts at cooperation with the government.

By means of the Police Force the Reich Church Government has followed up its removal of the Government of the Church in Hesse with the removal of those of Württemberg and Bavaria. Thereby the disorganization which had already prevailed for long in the Evangelical Church and which had been evident since the summer of 1933 has reached such a height that we feel ourselves compelled to make the following declaration.

I

1. The first and fundamental article of the Constitution of the German Evangelical Church of 11th July, 1933, says:

"The inviolable basis of the German Evangelical Church is the Gospel of Jesus Christ as it is testified to in the Holy Scriptures and as it has come anew to light in the Confessions of the Reformation. By this means the authority that the Church needs for its mission is determined and delimited."

This article has actually been set aside by the instructions, laws and measures of the Reich Church Government, thereby the Christian basis of the German Evangelical Church has been destroyed.

2. The National Church which the Reich Bishop is aiming at with the watchword "One State, One People, One Church" means that the Gospel is invalidated so far as the German Evangelical Church is concerned and the message of the Church surrendered to the powers of this world.

3. The usurped autocracy of the Reich Bishop and his legal administrator has set up an impossible Papacy in the Evangelical Church.

4. Inspired by the spirit of a false unscriptural revelation, the Church Government has punished obedience to Scripture and Confession as recalcitrance.

5. The anti-Scriptural introduction of the temporal leadership-principle into the Church and the consequent demand of an unconditioned obedience has bound the office-bearers of the Church to the Church Government instead of to Christ.

6. The elimination of the Synods has, in contravention of the Biblical and Reformation doctrine of the priesthood of all believers reduced the congregations to silence and deprived them of their rights.

II

1. All the protests, warnings and admonitions which we have raised, taking our stand on Scripture and Confession, have been in vain. On the contrary, the Reich

Church Government, appealing to the Führer and using and getting the co-operation of political forces, has continued ruthlessly its work of destroying the Church.

2. The violent measures adopted against the South German Churches have destroyed all possibility of retaining what has come from the past in the renewal of Church organization.

3. This has necessitated the Church emergency legislation, which we are compelled to proclaim to-day.

III

1. We assert: The Constitution of the G[erman] E[vangelical] C[hurch] is shattered. Its legitimate organs no longer exist. The men who have usurped Church Government in the Reich and in the Regions have, by their actions, divorced themselves from the Christian Church.

2. The Confessional Synod of the GEC creates new organs of government by virtue of the Church Emergency legislation of those Churches, congregations and clerical office-bearers who are bound by Scripture and Confession. For the work of governing and representing the GEC as a federation of Confessionally ordered Churches it appoints the Council of Brethren of the GEC and from that body the Council of the GEC to act as executive. Both organs are formed and organized in accord with the Confessions.

3. We urge congregations, their Ministers and Elders not to take any directions from the hitherto existing Reich Church Government or its officials, and to withdraw from co-operation with those who are willing to remain obedient to this Church Government. We urge them to hold to the instructions of the Confessional Synod of the GEC and of the organs recognized by it.

IV

We transmit this our Declaration to the Reich Government begging it to note the decision taken in it, and asking it to recognize that in matters concerning the Church, its doctrine and organization, the Church, without prejudice to the State's right of oversight [i.e., in financial matters], is alone called to judge and decide.

Source: Arthur Frey, *Cross and Swastika* (London, 1938), pp. 179–183. German text in Joachim Beckmann (ed.), *Evangelische Kirche im Dritten Reich* (Gütersloh, Germany, 1948), pp. 76–77.

SUGGESTIONS FOR BACKGROUND AND REFERENCE

References for Document 145.

✦ ✦ ✦ Catholicism and Nazi Germany

150 German Concordat (Extracts)

July 20, 1933

Under the Weimar Republic, Catholicism enjoyed a religious revival, while increasing its political influence through the Center party, which usually held the balance of power. Freedom from state restrictions, partial financial support, and favorable concordats with Bavaria (1924), Prussia (1929), and Baden (1932) all benefited the German church. But some Catholics distrusted the Republic and its policies and withheld support from the Center, while Bavarian Catholics formed a separate party. Hitler's rise to power divided Catholics. Some bishops condemned his doctrines, but other influential Catholics viewed the Nazis as security against any threat from the left. Franz von Papen (1879–1969), Hitler's Catholic vice-chancellor, negotiated this concordat with Cardinal Eugenio Pacelli (later Pope Pius XII). Many provisions paralleled those of Mussolini's agreement of 1929. Like other German political parties, the Center was dissolved.

Art. 1. The German Reich guarantees liberty of profession and of public exercise of the Catholic religion.

It recognises the right of the Catholic Church, within the limits of the general laws in force, freely to regulate and administer its own affairs and, within the sphere of its own competence, to issue laws and ordinances which are binding on its members.

2. The concordats concluded with Bavaria, (1924), Prussia (1929), and Baden (1932) remain in force . . . . As regards the other States the provisions agreed upon in the present concordat apply in their entirety. These provisions are also obligatory for the three above-mentioned States in regard to matters which are not regulated in the State concordats . . . .

In [the] future the conclusion of concordats with individual States will only be effected in agreement with the Government of the Reich.

3. In order to cultivate good relations between the Holy See and the German Reich an Apostolic Nuncio will reside, as hitherto, in the capital of the German Reich and an Ambassador of the German Reich will be accredited to the Holy See.

4. The Holy See enjoys full liberty to communicate . . . with the bishops, the clergy, and all who are members of the Catholic Church . . . . The same applies to the bishops and other diocesan authorities in their communications with the faithful, in everything which appertains to their pastoral office.

The instructions, ordinances, pastoral letters, official diocesan bulletins and all other acts . . . issued by the ecclesiastical authorities within the limits of their competence (article 1, paragraph 2) may be published freely . . . .

5. In the exercise of their priestly activities ecclesiastics shall enjoy the protection of the State to the same degree as the officials of the State. The latter will prevent . . . insults to their persons or to their capacity as ecclesiastics, as well as any disturbances in the acts of their ministry . . . .

6. Clerics and members of religious orders are exempt from the obligation of assuming public office and charges which, according to . . . Canon Law, are not compatible with . . . religious status. This applies in particular to the office of assessor, juryman and member of tax commissions or of financial tribunals.

7. In order to hold an appointment or office under the State or under any public corporation . . . , ecclesiastics [must] obtain the "nihil obstat" of their diocesan ordinary . . . .

8. The revenues enjoyed by ecclesiastics by reason of their office are exempt from distraint to the same extent as the salaries and emoluments of officials of the Reich and of the States.

9. Ecclesiastics may not be required by magistrates . . . to give information on . . . matters confided to them in the exercise of their cure of souls . . . .

* * *

13. Parishes and other similar Catholic ecclesiastical communities, parochial and diocesan associations, episcopal sees, dioceses and chapters, orders and religious associations as also the patrimonial institutes, foundations and revenues of the Catholic Church, administered by ecclesiastical bodies, preserve or acquire a juridical personality for purposes of the civil courts according to the ordinary rules of State law. . . .

14. The Catholic Church has in principle the right freely to confer all ecclesiastical offices and benefices without the co-operation of the State or of the communes, with the exception of the cases contemplated in the concordats mentioned in article 2. . . .

(1) Catholic priests who occupy an ecclesiastical charge in Germany, or who carry on activities in the cure of souls or in education, must—

(a) be German citizens;

(b) have obtained a leaving certificate entitling them to study at a German high school;

(c) have, for at least 3 years, studied philosophy and theology in a German State high school, a German ecclesiastical academical institute or a Pontifical high school in Rome.

(2) Before issuing Bulls for the appointment of archbishops, bishops, a coadjutor *cum jure successionis* or a *praelatus nullius,* the name of the person chosen shall be communicated to the *Reichsstatthalter* [representative of the Reich] in the state in question in order to ascertain that there are no objections of a general political character against him.

15. Orders and religious associations are not subjected by the State to any special restrictions in regard to their foundation, residence, number and—except in the case of article 15, paragraph 2—the capacity of their members, their activity in the cure of souls, their teaching, nursing and works of charity, or in the regulation of their affairs and in the administration of their property.

Superiors of religious orders who have their residence in the German Reich must possess German nationality. Provincial and general superiors resident outside . . . the German Reich, even if of another nationality, have the right to visit their houses situated in Germany.

The Holy See will take care that in the case of religious houses existing within the German Reich the provincial organisation shall be regulated in such a manner that they are not, so far as possible, subjected to foreign provincial superiors. Exceptions may be made, in agreement with the Government of the Reich . . . .

16. Bishops, before taking possession of their dioceses, shall take an oath of allegiance before the *Reichsstatthalter* in the competent State or before the President of the Reich . . . :—

"Before God and the holy Gospels I swear and undertake, as becomes a bishop, loyalty to the German Reich and to the State of _____. I swear and promise to respect and to make my clergy respect the Government established according to the constitutional laws of the State. Zealous, as it is my duty to be, of the welfare and interest of the German State, I will strive, in the exercise of the sacred ministry entrusted to me, to avert any injury which may threaten it."

17. The ownership and other rights of public corporations, institutes, foundations and associations of the Catholic Church over their property shall be guaranteed . . . .

* * *

20. Without prejudice to other agreements in force the church has the right to found, for the training of the clergy, schools of philosophy and theology exclusively dependent on the ecclesiastical authorities, so long as no subsidy is required from the State.

The foundation, direction and management of seminaries and ecclesiastical colleges appertain entirely to the ecclesiastical authorities . . . .

21. The teaching of the Catholic religion in elementary, technical, secondary and high schools is part of the ordinary curriculum, and will be imparted in conformity with the principles of the Catholic Church.

In religious instruction special attention will be devoted to educating the pupil to a consciousness of his patriotic, civil and social duties, according to the maxims of the faith and of the moral Christian law, the same also applying to all other teaching.

The programme of religious teaching and the choice of text-books will be settled in agreement with the superior ecclesiastical authorities, who will be given the opportunity to examine, in agreement with the scholastic authorities, whether the scholars receive religious instruction in conformity with the doctrines and requirements of the Church.

22. The appointment of teachers of the Catholic religion will be settled in agreement between the bishop and the Government of the particular State.

Teachers whom the bishop . . . has declared to be unfit to impart religious instruction may not be employed . . . .

23. The maintenance of Catholic confessional schools and the erection of new

buildings are guaranteed. In all communes in which parents, or others on their behalf, so request, elementary Catholic schools will be erected, provided that the number of the pupils renders it possible to carry on the school . . . .

24. In all elementary Catholic schools such teachers only will be employed as belong to the Catholic Church and guarantee to comply with the special requirements of the Catholic confessional school.

In the programme for the general professional training of teachers there must be institutes which ensure that Catholic teachers shall be trained in a manner corresponding to the particular requirements of the Catholic confessional school.

25. Orders and religious associations are authorised to found and direct private schools . . . .

For admission to the post of teacher and for appointment as teacher in the elementary, secondary and high schools, the ordinary requirements apply for members of orders and religious associations.

* * *

27. . . . The direction of the spiritual care of the army is vested in the military bishop. His ecclesiastical appointment will be made by the Holy See . . . in agreement with the Reich . . . .

The . . . appointment of military chaplains . . . is made by the military bishop, after consultation with the competent authority of the Reich. . . .

* * *

31. Catholic organisations and associations with exclusively religious, cultural and philanthropic aims which, as such, are dependent on the ecclesiastical authorities, will receive protection . . . .

Catholic organisations which, in addition . . . have other aims, including social and professional, will enjoy . . . the protection mentioned in article 31, paragraph 1, in so far as they afford guarantees to pursue their activities outside any political party.

The list of organisations . . . which come under the terms of this article will be drawn up by the Government of the Reich and the German episcopate in agreement.

In so far as there are juvenile organisations—sporting or otherwise—supported by the Reich or by particular States, care will be taken that a regular fulfilment of their religious duties on Sundays and other festivals is rendered possible . . . , and that they are not obliged to act in any way incompatible with their convictions and their religious and moral duties.

32. In view of the present special circumstances in Germany and in consideration of the guarantees . . . of the present concordat, . . . the Holy See will issue orders excluding ecclesiastics and members of religious orders from membership of political parties and from activities on behalf of such parties.

Source: British and Foreign State Papers (1933) (London, 1938), CXXXVI, 697–704. German and Italian texts in *Acta Apostolicae Sedis* (Rome, 1933), XXV, 389–414.

SUGGESTIONS FOR BACKGROUND AND REFERENCE

G. Adriányi et al., *The Church in the Modern Age* (New York, 1981), pp. 63–77.
P. Hughes, *Pope Pius the Eleventh* (New York, 1937).
K. S. Latourette, *Christianity in a Revolutionary Age* (New York, 1958–1962), IV, 176–189.
G. Lewy, *The Catholic Church and Nazi Germany* (New York, 1964).
N. Micklem, *National Socialism and the Roman Catholic Church* (New York, 1939).
J. Rovan, *Le catholicisme politique en Allemagne* (Paris, 1956), pp. 212–252.

151   *Mit Brennender Sorge* (Extracts)

March 14, 1937

Despite the 1933 Concordat, friction inevitably developed between Roman Catholicism and Hitlerism. Nazi condemnation of the Old Testament, conflicts over education, attacks on monastic clergy, and violations of the concordat were all issues leading to this protest of Pius XI. The government responded by closing or suspending the German firms that printed and published the encyclical. The letter was in German, addressed to the archbishops and bishops of Germany.

1. With deep anxiety and increasing dismay, We have for some time past beheld the sufferings of the Church, and the steadily growing oppression of those men and women who, loyally professing their faith in thought and deed, have remained true to her . . . .

* * *

[The failure of the 1933 Concordat to bring peace cannot be blamed on the church or the pope. Rather, the "lessons of the past years" disclose "machinations that from the beginning had no other aim than a war of exterminations." Where the pope planted peace, others sowed "discord, hatred, calumny," "secret and open enmity against Christ and His Church."]

6. . . . When once the time shall have come to place before . . . the world these Our endeavors, all right-minded persons will know where they have to look for those who kept the peace, and where for those who broke it . . . . We have stood faithful to the terms of the agreement. But . . . to change the meaning of the agreement, to evade the agreement, to empty the agreement of all its significance, and finally more or less openly to violate the agreement, has been made the unwritten law of conduct by the other party.

* * *

9. Take care . . . that first of all belief in God, the primary and irreplaceable foundation of all religion, be preserved true and unadulterated in German lands. He is not a believer in God who uses the word of God rhetorically but he who associates with the sacred word the true and worthy idea of God.

* * *

11. He who replaces a personal God with a weird impersonal Fate supposedly according to ancient pre-Christian German concepts denies the wisdom and providence of God, that "reacheth from end to end mightily and ordereth all things sweetly" and directs everything for the best. Such a one cannot claim to be numbered among those who believe in God.

12. He who takes the race, or the people, or the State, or the form of Government, the bearers of the power of the State or other fundamental elements of human society—which in the temporal order of things have an essential and honorable place—out of the system of their earthly valuation, and makes them the ultimate norm of all, even of religious, values, and deifies them with an idolatrous worship, perverts and falsifies the order of things created and commanded by God. . . .

13. Beware . . . of the growing abuse in speech and writing, of using the thrice Holy name of God as a meaningless label for a more or less capricious form of human search and longing. . . . Our God is the personal, superhuman, almighty, infinitely perfect God, one in the Trinity of persons, threefold in the unity of the Divine essence, the Creator of the universe, the Lord and King in whom the history of the world finds fulfillment, Who suffers and can suffer no other god beside Him.

14. This God has given His commandments in His capacity as Sovereign. They apply regardless of time and space, country or race. As God's sun shines on all that bear human countenance, so does His law know no privileges or exceptions. The rulers and the ruled, crowned and uncrowned, high and low, rich and poor, all alike are subject to His law. . . . This claim to obedience comprehends every walk of life, in which moral questions demand a settlement in harmony with God's law and consequently the adjustment of transitory human legislation to the structure of the immutable law of God. Only superficial minds can lapse into the heresy of speaking of a national God, of a national religion; only such can make the mad attempt of trying to confine within the boundaries of a single people, within the narrow blood stream of a single race, God the Creator of the world, the King and Lawgiver of all peoples . . . .

* * *

18. The fulness of divine revelation has appeared in Jesus Christ, the incarnate Son of God. . . . The sacred books of the Old Testament are all God's Word, an organic part of His revelation. Corresponding to the gradual unfolding of the revelation, the dimness of the time preceding the full noon day of the redemption hovers over them. As is inevitable in the case of books of history and law, they are the reflections in many particulars of human imperfection, weakness and sin. Side by side with infinitely much that is high and noble, they relate the dissipation and worldliness that occurred time and again among the covenanted people who bore the revelation and promise of God.

19. . . . He who wants to see the Biblical history and the wisdom of the Old Testament banished from the Church and school, blasphemes the Word of God [and] the Almighty's plan of salvation, makes the . . . limited mind of man judge over the divine plan of history. He denies belief in the real Christ, . . . Who took His human nature from that people which was to nail Him to the cross. He stands uncomprehendingly before the world-drama of the Son of God Who opposed to the felony of His crucifiers the Divine high-priestly action of the Redeemer's death and thus brought the Old Testament to its fulfilment and completion in the New, by which it is superseded.

20. The climax of revelation reached in the Gospel of Jesus Christ is definite, is obligatory for ever. This revelation knows no addition from the hand of man, above all, knows no substitution and no replacement by arbitrary "revelations" that certain speakers of the present day wish to derive from the myth of blood and race. . . .

* * *

24. In your districts . . . voices are raised in ever louder chorus urging men on to leave the Church. Among the spokesmen there are many who, by reason of their official position, seek to create the impression that leaving the Church . . . is a particularly convincing . . . form of profession of loyalty to the present State. With cloaked and with manifest methods of coercion, by intimidation, by holding out the prospect of economic, professional, civic and other advantages, the loyalty of Catholics and especially of . . . Catholic officials to their faith is put under a pressure that is as unlawful as it is unworthy . . . . But . . . for the believer the way of heroic fortitude is the only way of salvation. When the tempter or oppresser comes to him with the Judas-like suggestion to leave the Church, then, even at the cost of heavy, earthly sacrifices he can only reply in the words of the Saviour: "Begone, Satan: for it is written: The Lord thy God thou shalt adore and Him only shalt thou serve." But to the Church he will say: Thou my Mother . . . may my tongue cleave to my palate, if I . . . should turn traitor to the promises of my baptism. . . .

* * *

27. Revelation, in the Christian sense, is the word of God to man. To use the same word for the "whispered inspirations" of blood and race, for the manifestations of the history of a people, is confusing in any case. Such false coinage does not deserve to be received into the vocabulary of a believing Christian.

* * *

29. Immortality in the Christian sense is the continuance of the life of a man after temporal death, as a personal individual, to be rewarded or punished eternally. To designate with the word immortality the collective continued enjoyment of life in association with the continued existence of one's people on earth for an undetermined length of time in the future, is to pervert and falsify one of the principal truths of the Christian faith . . . .

* * *

32. Humility in the spirit of the Gospel and prayer for the help of God's grace are compatible with self-respect, self-confidence and heroic purpose. The Church of Christ, that in all ages up to the present time counts more confessors and voluntary martyrs than any other body, does not need to receive instruction from such quarters about heroic purposefulness and heroic achievement. In its shallow twaddle about Christian humility being self-abasement and unheroic conduct, the disgusting pride of these reformers mocks itself.

33. Grace, in the loose sense of the term, can be said to be everything that the creature receives from the Creator. Grace in the proper and Christian sense of the word embraces, however, the supernatural manifestations of divine love, the loving kindness and working of God, whereby He raises man to that inward participation of life with Himself, that is called in the New Testament sonship of God. . . . The repudiation of this supernatural elevation of grace on account of the supposedly peculiar German type of being, is an error and an open challenge to a fundamental truth of Christianity. . . .

* * *

36. The believer has an inalienable right to profess his faith and put it into practice in the manner suited to him. Laws that suppress or make this profession and practice difficult contradict the natural law.

37. Conscientious parents, aware of their duty in the matter of education, have a primary and original right to determine the education of the children . . . in the spirit of the true faith . . . . Laws or other regulations concerning schools that disregard the rights of parents . . . , or by threat and violence nullify those rights, contradict the natural law and are utterly and essentially immoral.

* * *

41. . . . If the State founds a State-Youth to which all are obliged to belong, then it is—without prejudice to the rights of Church associations—an obvious, an inalienable right of the young men . . . and of their parents responsible for them before God, to demand that this obligatory organization should be cleansed of all manifestations of a spirit hostile to Christianity . . . .

42. No one has any intention of obstructing the youth of Germany on the road that is meant to bring them to the realization of true popular union, to the fostering of the love of freedom, to steadfast loyalty to the fatherland. What We object to . . . is the intentional and systematically fomented opposition which is set up between these educational purposes and those of religion. Therefore we call out to youth: . . . He who sings the song of loyalty to his earthly country must not, in disloyalty to God, to his church, to his eternal country, become a deserter and a traitor. You are told a great deal about heroic greatness, in designed and false contrast to the humility and patience of the Gospel. Why is silence kept about the heroism of moral struggle? Why is it not told you that the preservation of baptismal innocence represents an heroic action . . . ? A great deal is told you of human weaknesses in the history of the Church. Why is nothing said of the great deeds that accompany her on her way through the centuries . . . ? You are told a great deal of

the exercises of sport. Undertaken with discretion, the cult of physical fitness is a benefit for youth. But now so much time is devoted to it . . . that no account is taken of the harmonious development of mind and body, of what is due to family life, of the commandment to keep holy the Lord's day. . . . With confidence We expect from practicing Catholic youth that, in the difficult circumstances of obligatory State organization, they will insist unflinchingly on their right to keep Sunday in a Christian manner, that in the cult of physical fitness they will not forget the interests of their immortal souls . . . .

* * *

47. We address a particularly hearfelt greeting to Catholic parents. . . . When the attempt is made to desecrate the tabernacle of a child's soul sanctified in baptism by an education that is hostile to Christ; . . . then it is the duty of every professing Christian . . . to keep his conscience clear of any culpable cooperation in such dreadful work . . . . The formal maintaining of religious instruction, especially when controlled . . . by those who are not competent, in the framework of a school that in other departments systematically and invidiously works against the same religion, can never be a justification for a believing Christian to give his free approval to such a school that aims at destroying religion . . . . Meanwhile do not forget this: from the bond of responsibility established by God that binds you to your children, no earthly power can loose you. No one of those who today are oppressing you in the exercise of your rights in education and pretend to free you from your duty in this matter, will be able to answer for you to the Eternal Judge when He asks you the question: "Where are those I have given you?" May everyone of you be able to answer: "Of them thou hast given me, I have not lost anyone."

Source: Encyclical Letter of His Holiness, Pope Pius XI Issued March 14, 1937 (Washington, D.C., 1937), pp. 1–4, 6–11, 16–19, 20–21, 24–28, 31–32. German text in *Acta Apostolicae Sedis* (Rome, 1937), XXIX, 145–167.

SUGGESTIONS FOR BACKGROUND AND REFERENCE

The Persecution of the Catholic Church in the Third Reich, Facts and Documents (New York, 1942).
References for Document 150.

✦✦✦ United States Supreme Court Interpretations of Separation

152 *Cantwell v. Connecticut* (Extracts)

May 20, 1940

The religious guarantees of the First Amendment originally bound only the federal government (though in fact state constitutions often had similar provisions and no state churches had existed since 1833). In 1868 the Fourteenth Amendment passed with its celebrated due process clause (Section 1): "All persons born or naturalized in the United States, and subject to the jurisdiction thereof, are citizens of the United States and of the State wherein they reside. No State shall make or enforce any law which shall abridge the privileges or immunities of citizens of the United States; nor shall any State deprive any person of life, liberty, or property, without due process of law; nor deny to any person within its jurisdiction the equal protection of the laws." The application of the amendment to civil liberties has been primarily a twentieth-century development. Though occasionally invoked in support of religious freedoms, the Fourteenth Amendment was expressly declared to extend the safeguards of the First Amendment over state actions respecting religion in the Cantwell case. The case involved three Jehovah's Witnesses engaged in religious propaganda on the streets of New Haven. They were arrested and charged with violating a Connecticut law requiring a license for soliciting contributions and with the common law offense of inciting breach of the peace. Convictions on these counts were reversed by the Supreme Court in this decision written by Justice Owen J. Roberts (1875–1955).

First. We hold that the statute, as construed and applied to the appellants, deprives them of their liberty without due process of law in contravention of the Fourteenth Amendment. The fundamental concept of liberty embodied in that Amendment embraces the liberties guaranteed by the First Amendment. The First Amendment declares that Congress shall make no law respecting an establishment of religion or prohibiting the free exercise thereof. The Fourteenth Amendment has rendered the legislatures of the states as incompetent as Congress to enact such laws. The constitutional inhibition of legislation on the subject of religion has a double aspect. On the one hand, it forestalls compulsion by law of the acceptance of any creed or the practice of any form of worship. Freedom of conscience and freedom to adhere to such religious organization or form of worship as the individual may choose cannot be restricted by law. On the other hand, it safeguards the free exercise of the chosen form of religion. Thus the Amendment embraces two concepts,—freedom to believe and freedom to act. The first is absolute, but in the nature of things, the second cannot be. Conduct remains subject to regulation for the protection of society. The freedom to act must have appropriate definition to preserve the enforcement of that protection. In every case the power to regulate must be so exercised as not, in attaining a permissible end, unduly to infringe the protected freedom. No one would contest the proposition that a state may not, by statute, wholly deny the right to preach or to disseminate religious views. . . . It is equally clear that a state may by general and non-discriminatory legislation regulate the times, the places, and the manner of soliciting upon its streets, and of holding meetings thereon; and may in other respects safeguard the peace, good order and comfort of the community, without unconstitutionally invading the liberties protected by the Fourteenth Amendment. The appellants are right in their insistence that the Act in question is not such a regulation. If a certificate is procured, solicitation is permitted without restraint but, in the absence of a certificate, solicitation is altogether prohibited.

The appellants urge that to require them to obtain a certificate as a condition of soliciting support for their views amounts to a prior restraint on the exercise of their religion within the meaning of the Constitution. The State insists that the Act, as construed by the Supreme Court of Connecticut, imposes no previous restraint upon the dissemination of religious views or teaching but merely safeguards against the perpetration of frauds under the cloak of religion. Conceding that this is so, the question remains whether the method adopted by Connecticut to that end transgresses the liberty safeguarded by the Constitution.

The general regulation, in the public interest, of solicitation, which does not involve any religious test and does not unreasonably obstruct or delay the collection of funds, is not open to any constitutional objection, even though the collection be for a religious purpose. . . .

It will be noted, however, that the Act requires an application to the secretary of the public welfare council of the State; that he is empowered to determine whether the cause is a religious one, and that the issue of a certificate depends upon his affirmative action. . . . His decision to issue or refuse it involves appraisal of facts, the exercise of judgment, and the formation of an opinion. . . . Such a censorship of religion as the means of determining its right to survive is a denial of liberty protected by the First Amendment and included in the liberty which is within the protection of the Fourteenth.

The State asserts that if the licensing officer acts arbitrarily, capriciously, or corruptly, his action is subject to judicial correction. . . . It is suggested that the statute is to be read as requiring the officer to issue a certificate unless the cause in question is clearly not a religious one; and that if he violates his duty his action will be corrected by a court.

To this suggestion there are several sufficient answers. The line between a discretionary and a ministerial act is not always easy to mark and the statute has not been construed by the State court to impose a mere ministerial duty on the secretary of the welfare council. . . . Moreover, the availability of a judicial remedy for abuses in the system of licensing still leaves that system one of previous restraint . . . . A statute authorizing previous restraint upon the exercise of the guaranteed freedom by judicial decision after trial is as obnoxious to the Constitution as one providing for like restraint by administrative action.

Nothing we have said is intended even remotely to imply that, under the cloak of religion, persons may, with impunity, commit frauds upon the public. . . . Without doubt a state may protect its citizens from fraudulent solicitation by requiring a stranger in the community . . . to establish his identity and his authority to act for the cause which he purports to represent. The state is likewise free to regulate the time and manner of solicitation generally, in the interest of public safety, peace, comfort or convenience. But to condition the solicitation of aid for the perpetuation of religious views or systems upon a license, the grant of which rests in the exercise of a determination by state authority as to what is a religious cause, is to lay a forbidden burden upon the exercise of liberty protected by the Constitution.

Second. We hold that, in the circumstances disclosed, the conviction of Jesse Cantwell on the fifth count must be set aside. Decision as to the lawfulness of the conviction demands the weighing of two conflicting interests. The fundamental law declares the interest of the United States that the free exercise of religion be not prohibited and that freedom to communicate information and opinion be not abridged. The state of Connecticut has an obvious interest in the preservation and protection of peace and good order within her borders. . . .

* * *

The offense known as breach of the peace embraces a great variety of conduct destroying or menacing public order . . . . It includes not only violent acts but acts and words likely to produce violence in others. No one would have the hardihood to suggest that the principle of freedom of speech sanctions incitement to riot or that religious liberty connotes the privilege to exhort others to physical attack upon those belonging to another sect. When clear and present danger of riot, disorder, interference with traffic upon the public streets, or other immediate threat to public safety, peace, or order, appears, the power of the state to prevent or punish is obvious. Equally obvious is it that a state may not unduly suppress free communication of views, religious or other, under the guise of conserving desirable conditions. Here we have a situation analogous to a conviction under a statute sweeping in a great variety of conduct under a general and indefinite characterization, and leaving to the executive and judicial branches too wide a discretion in its application.

* * *

We find in the instant case no assault or threatening of bodily harm, no truculent bearing, no intentional discourtesy, no personal abuse. On the contrary, we find only an effort to persuade a willing listener to buy a book or to contribute money . . . .

In the realm of religious faith, and in that of political belief, sharp differences arise. . . . To persuade others to his own point of view, the pleader, as we know, at times resorts to exaggeration, to vilification of men who have been, or are, prominent in church or state, and even to false statement. But the people of this nation have ordained in the light of history, that, in spite of the probability of excesses and abuses, these liberties are, in the long view, essential to enlightened opinion and right conduct on the part of the citizens of a democracy.

The essential characteristic of these liberties is, that under their shield many types of life, character, opinion and belief can develop unmolested and unobstructed. Nowhere is this shield more necessary than in our own country for a people composed of many races and of many creeds. There are limits to the exercise of these liberties. . . .

Although the contents of the [phonograph] record not unnaturally aroused animosity, we think that, in the absence of a statute narrowly drawn to define and punish specific conduct as constituting a clear and present danger to a substantial interest of the State, the petitioner's communication, considered in the light of the constitutional guarantees, raised no such clear and present menace to public peace and order as to render him liable to conviction of the common law offense in question.

Source: Cantwell et al. v. *State of Connecticut,* 310 U.S. 296.

SUGGESTIONS FOR BACKGROUND AND REFERENCE

P. B. Kurland, *Religion and the Law* (Chicago, 1961), pp. 51–65.

L. Pfeffer, *Church, State, and Freedom* (Boston, 1953), pp. 529–543.

V. W. Rotnem and F. G. Folsom, Jr., "Recent Restrictions upon Religious Liberty," *American Political Science Review,* Vol. XXXVI, No. 6 (December 1942), pp. 1053–1068.

J. M. Snee, "Religious Disestablishment and the Fourteenth Amendment," *Washington University Law Quarterly* (December 1954), pp. 371–407.

A. P. Stokes, *Church and State in the United States* (New York, 1950), I, 575–593.

H. H. Stroup, *The Jehovah's Witnesses* (New York, 1945).

153 *West Virginia State Board of Education* v. *Barnette* (Extracts)

June 14, 1943

Collision between the interests of religious freedom and national unity elicited significant constitutional decisions from the Court in the Gobitis and Barnette cases. As in the Cantwell case, the Jehovah's Witnesses provided the challenge to the law, in this instance refusing to observe "idolatrous" patriotic ritual—the flag salute and the pledge of allegiance —in public schools. In *Minersville School District* v. *Gobitis,* 310 U.S. 586, the Court, through Justice Frankfurter, denied their appeal, arguing for the political responsibilities of all citizens and the superior claims of national security and unity. Justice Stone provided the lone dissent. Public and professional criticism of the decision was widespread, and in 1942 the Federal District Court of West Virginia reopened the question by staying the West Virginia State Board of Education from enforcing flag salute in the case of Witness Walter Barnette. Appeal to the Supreme Court resulted in this six-to-three reversal of the Gobitis judgment. Three judges—Black, Douglas, and Murphy—had changed their views. The Court, through Justice Robert H. Jackson (1892–1954), stressed freedom of speech rather than religious freedom in the decision and carefully refuted arguments it had followed three years earlier. (Justice Frankfurter's dissent maintained the Gobitis judgment.)

The Gobitis decision . . . *assumed* . . . that power exists in the State to impose the flag salute discipline upon school children in general. The Court only examined and rejected a claim based on religious beliefs of immunity from an unquestioned general rule. The question which underlies the flag salute controversy is whether such a ceremony so touching matters of opinion and political attitude may be imposed upon the individual by official authority . . . . We examine rather than assume existence of this power and, against this broader definition of issues in this case, re-examine specific grounds assigned for the Gobitis decision.

* * *

2. It was also considered in the Gobitis case that functions of educational officers in states, counties and school districts were such that to interfere with their authority "would in effect make us the school board for the country." . . .

The Fourteenth Amendment, as now applied to the States, protects the citizen against the State itself and all of its creatures—Boards of Education not excepted. These have, of course, important, delicate, and highly discretionary functions, but none that they may not perform within the limits of the Bill of Rights. That they are educating the young for citizenship is reason for scrupulous protection of Constitutional freedoms of the individual, if we are not to strangle the free mind at its source and teach youth to discount important principles of our government as mere platitudes.

Such Boards are numerous and their territorial jurisdiction often small. But small and local authority may feel less sense of responsibility to the Constitution, and agencies of publicity may be less vigilant in calling it to account. . . . There are village tyrants as well as village Hampdens, but none who acts under color of law is beyond reach of the Constitution.

3. The Gobitis opinion reasoned that this is a field "where courts possess no marked and certainly no controlling competence," that it is committed to the legislatures as well as the courts to guard cherished liberties and that it is constitutionally appropriate to "fight out the wise use of legislative authority in the forum of public opinion and before legislative assemblies rather than to transfer such a contest to the judicial arena," since all the "effective means of inducing political changes are left free." . . .

The very purpose of a Bill of Rights was to withdraw certain subjects from the vicissitudes of political controversy, to place them beyond the reach of majorities and officials and to establish them as legal principles to be applied by the courts. One's right to life, liberty, and property, to free speech, a free press, freedom of worship and assembly, and other fundamental rights may not be submitted to vote; they depend on the outcome of no elections.

In weighing arguments of the parties it is important to distinguish between the due process clause of the Fourteenth Amendment as an instrument for transmitting the principles of the First Amendment and those cases in which it is applied for its own sake. The test of legislation which collides with the Fourteenth Amendment, because it also collides with the principles of the First, is much more definite than the test when only the Fourteenth is involved. Much of the vagueness of the due process clause disappears when the specific prohibitions of the First become its standard. The right of a State to regulate, for example, a public utility may well include, so far as the due process test is concerned, power to impose all of the restrictions which a legislature may have a "rational basis" for adopting. But freedoms of speech and of press, of assembly, and of worship may not be infringed on such slender grounds. They are susceptible of restriction only to prevent grave and immediate danger to interests which the state may lawfully protect. It is important to note that while it is the Fourteenth Amendment which bears directly upon the State it is the more specific limiting principles of the First Amendment that finally govern this case.

* * *

4. Lastly, and this is the very heart of the Gobitis opinion, it reasons that "National unity is the basis of national security," that the authorities have "the right to select appropriate means for its attainment," and hence reaches the conclusion that such compulsory measures toward "national unity" are constitutional. . . . Upon the verity of this assumption depends our answer in this case.

National unity as an end which officials may foster by persuasion and example is not in question. The problem is whether under our Constitution compulsion as here employed is a permissible means for its achievement.

Struggles to coerce uniformity of sentiment in support of some end thought essential to their time and country have been waged by many good as well as by evil men. . . . As first and moderate methods to attain unity have failed, those bent on its accomplishment must resort to an ever-increasing severity. As governmental pressure toward unity becomes greater, so strife becomes more bitter as to whose unity it shall be. Probably no deeper division of our people could proceed from any provocation than from finding it necessary to choose what doctrine and whose program public educational officials shall compel youth to unite in embracing. . . . Those who begin coercive elimination of dissent soon find themselves exterminating dissenters. Compulsory unification of opinion achieves only the unanimity of the graveyard.

It seems trite but necessary to say that the First Amendment to our Constitution was designed to avoid these ends by avoiding these beginnings. There is no mysticism in the American concept of the State or of the nature or origin of its authority. We set up government by consent of the governed, and the Bill of Rights denies those in power any legal opportunity to coerce that consent. Authority here is to be controlled by public opinion, not public opinion by authority.

The case is made difficult not because the principles of its decision are obscure but because the flag involved is our own. Nevertheless, we apply the limitations of the Constitution with no fear that freedom to be intellectually and spiritually diverse or even contrary will disintegrate the social organization. To believe that patriotism will not flourish if patriotic ceremonies are voluntary and spontaneous instead of a compulsory routine is to make an unflattering estimate of the appeal of our institutions to free minds. We can have intellectual individualism and the rich cultural diversities that we owe to exceptional minds only at the price of occasional eccentricity and abnormal attitudes. When they are so harmless to others or to the State as those we deal with here, the price is not too great. But freedom to differ is not limited to things that do not matter much. That would be a mere shadow of freedom. The test of its substance is the right to differ as to things that touch the heart of the existing order.

If there is any fixed star in our constitutional constellation, it is that no official, high or petty, can prescribe what shall be orthodox in politics, nationalism, religion, or other matters of opinion or force citizens to confess by word or act their faith therein. If there are any circumstances which permit an exception, they do not now occur to us.

We think the action of the local authorities in compelling the flag salute and pledge transcends constitutional limitations on their power and invades the sphere of intellect and spirit which it is the purpose of the First Amendment to our Constitution to reserve from all official control.

Source: West Virginia State Board of Education et al. v. *Barnette et al.,* 319 U.S. 624.

SUGGESTIONS FOR BACKGROUND AND REFERENCE

H. W. Barber, "Religious Liberty v. Police Power: Jehovah's Witnesses," *American Political Science Review,* Vol. XLI, No. 2 (April 1947), pp. 226–247.

W. G. Fennell, "The 'Reconstructed Court' and Religious Freedom: The Gobitis Case in Retrospect," *New York University Law Quarterly Review,* Vol. XIX, No. 1 (November 1941), pp. 31–48.

A. W. Johnson and F. H. Yost, *Separation of Church and State in the United States* (Minneapolis, 1948), pp. 175–186.

P. B. Kurland, *Religion and the Law* (Chicago, 1961), pp. 41–47.

L. Pfeffer, *Church, State, and Freedom* (Boston, 1953), pp. 510–528.

A. P. Stokes, *Church and State in the United States* (New York, 1950), I, 600–616.

References for Document 152.

154 *Everson* v. *Board of Education* (Extracts)

February 10, 1947

Education, always an area of friction in issues of church and state, occupied the foreground in the constitutional cases of the 1940s. Measures relating to parochial schools and desired chiefly by Catholics were passed in some states and attacked by opponents as indirect government aid to religion. An important early case (1930) was *Cochran* v. *Louisiana State Board of Education,* 281 U.S. 370, where the Supreme Court declined to overturn legislation supplying parochial pupils with textbooks purchased with public money. (The Louisiana law, however, was challenged on the issue of diverting a public tax to private purposes rather than on the First Amendment.) Legal argument supporting such legislation often stressed the principle of welfare benefit to the child rather than subsidy to the school. The Everson case arose from a New Jersey provision in 1941 permitting local boards of education to provide students with transportation to all nonprofit schools. The Ewing board thereupon took steps to refund the transportation expenses of children commuting to public and Catholic high schools in Trenton. Counsel for taxpayer, Everson, argued the case on the First Amendment applicable to the states through the Fourteenth Amendment. The Court, while unanimously stressing the importance of maintaining the wall of separation, split five to four on the immediate issue, upholding the New Jersey law. Justice Hugo Black (1886–1971) wrote the decision, which was criticized in vigorous dissents by Justices Jackson and Wiley Rutledge (1894–1949). Below are passages from all three opinions.

From the Opinion of the Court:

New Jersey cannot consistently with the "establishment of religion" clause of the First Amendment contribute tax-raised funds to the support of an institution which teaches the tenets and faith of any church. On the other hand, other language of the amendment commands that New Jersey cannot hamper its citizens in the free exercise of their own religion. Consequently, it cannot exclude individual Catholics, Lutherans, Mohammedans, Baptists, Jews, Methodists, Non-believers, Presbyterians, or the members of any other faith, *because of their faith, or lack of it,* from receiving the benefits of public welfare legislation. While we do not mean to intimate that a state could not provide transportation only to children attending public schools, we must be careful in protecting the citizens of New Jersey against state-established churches, to be sure that we do not inadvertently prohibit New Jersey from extending its general state law benefits to all its citizens without regard to their religious belief.

Measured by these standards, we cannot say that the First Amendment prohibits New Jersey from spending tax-raised funds to pay the bus fares of parochial school pupils as a part of a general program under which it pays the fares of pupils attending public and other schools. It is undoubtedly true that children are helped to get to church schools. There is even a possibility that some of the children might not be sent to the church schools if the parents were compelled to pay their children's bus fares out of their own pockets when transportation to a public school would have been paid for by the State. . . . Moreover, state-paid policemen, detailed to protect children going to and from church schools from the very real hazards of traffic, would serve much the same purpose . . . as state provisions intended to guarantee free transportation of a kind which the state deems to be best for the school children's welfare. And parents might refuse to risk their children to . . . traffic accidents going to and from parochial schools, the approaches to which were not protected by policemen. Similarly, parents might be reluctant to permit their children to attend schools which the state had cut off from . . . ordinary police and fire protection, connections for sewage disposal, public highways and sidewalks. Of course, cutting off church schools from these services, so separate and so indisputably marked off from the religious function, would make it far more difficult for the schools to operate. But such is obviously not the purpose of the First Amendment. That Amendment requires the state to be a neutral in its relations with groups of religious believers and non-believers; it does not require the state to be their adversary. State power is no more to be used so as to handicap religions, than it is to favor them.

This Court has said that parents may, . . . under state compulsory education laws, send their children to a religious rather than a public school if the school meets the secular educational requirements . . . . It appears that these parochial schools meet New Jersey's requirements. The State contributes no money to the schools. . . . Its legislation, as applied, does no more than provide a general program to help parents get their children, regardless of their religion, safely and expeditiously to and from accredited schools.

The First Amendment has erected a wall between church and state. That wall must be kept high and impregnable. We could not approve the slightest breach. New Jersey has not breached it here.

From Justice Jackson's Dissent:

Whether the taxpayer constitutionally can be made to contribute aid to parents of students because of their attendance at parochial schools depends upon the nature of those schools and their relation to the Church. The Constitution says nothing of education. It lays no obligation on the states to provide schools and does not undertake to regulate state systems of education . . . . But they cannot, through school policy any more than through other means, invade rights secured to citizens by the Constitution . . . . One of our basic rights is to be free of taxation to support a transgression of the constitutional command that the authorities "shall make no law respecting an establishment of religion, or prohibiting the free exercise thereof. . . ."

The function of the Church school is a subject on which this record is meager. It shows only that the schools are under superintendence of a priest and that "religion is taught as part of the curriculum." But we know that such schools are parochial only in name—they, in fact, represent a world-wide and age-old policy of the Roman Catholic Church.

* * *

It is no exaggeration to say that the whole historic conflict in temporal policy between the Catholic church and non-Catholics comes to a focus in their respective school policies. The Roman Catholic Church . . . takes what, from the viewpoint of its own progress and the success of its mission, is a wise estimate of the importance of education to religion. It does not leave the individual to pick up religion by chance. It relies on early and indelible indoctrination in the faith and order of the Church . . . .

Our public school, if not a product of Protestantism, at least is more consistent with it than with the Catholic culture and scheme of values. It is a relatively recent development dating from about 1840. It is organized on the premise that secular education can be isolated from all religious teaching so that the school can inculcate all needed temporal knowledge and also maintain a strict and lofty neutrality as to religion. The assumption is that after the individual has been instructed in worldly wisdom he will be better fitted to choose his religion. . . .

I should be surprised if any Catholic would deny that the parochial school is a vital, if not the most vital, part of the Roman Catholic Church. . . . Catholic education is the rock on which the whole structure rests, and to render tax aid to its Church school is indistinguishable to me from rendering the same aid to the Church itself. . . .

It is of no importance in this situation whether the beneficiary of this expenditure of tax-raised funds is primarily the parochial school and incidentally the pupil, or whether the aid is directly bestowed on the pupil with indirect benefits to the school. The state cannot maintain a Church and it can no more tax its citizens to furnish free carriage to those who attend a Church. The prohibition against establishment of religion cannot be circumvented by a subsidy, bonus or reimbursement of expense to individuals for receiving religious instruction and indoctrination.

The Court, however, compares this to other subsidies and loans to individuals and says, "Nor does it follow that a law has a private rather than a public purpose because it provides that tax-raised funds will be paid to reimburse individuals on account of money spent by them in a way which furthers a public program. . . ." Of course, the state may pay out tax-raised funds to relieve pauperism, but it may not under our Constitution do so to induce or reward piety. It may spend funds to secure old age against want, but it may not spend funds to secure religion against skepticism. . . .

It seems to me that the basic fallacy in the Court's reasoning, which accounts for its failure to apply the principles it avows, is in ignoring the essentially religious test by which beneficiaries of this expenditure are selected.[1] A policeman protects a Catholic, of course—but not because he is a Catholic; it is because he is a man and a member of our society. The fireman protects the Church school—but not because it is a Church school; it is because it is property, part of the assets of our society. Neither the fireman nor the policeman has to ask before he renders aid "Is this man

1. In a footnote the Court had set aside the issue of a violation of the equal protection clause of the Fourteenth Amendment with the observation: "Although the township resolution authorized reimbursement only for parents of public and Catholic school pupils, appellant does not allege, nor is there anything in the record which could offer the slightest support to an allegation, that there were any children in the township who attended and would have attended, but for want of transportation, any but public and Catholic schools. It will be appropriate to consider the exclusion of students of private schools operated for profit when and if it is proved to have occurred, is made the basis of a suit by one in a position to challenge it, and New Jersey's highest court has ruled adversely to the challenger . . . ."

or building identified with the Catholic Church?" But before these school authorities draw a check to reimburse for a student's fare they must ask just that question, and if the school is a Catholic one they may render aid . . . , while if it is of any other faith or is run for profit, the help must be withheld. To consider the converse of the Court's reasoning will best disclose its fallacy. . . . Could we sustain an Act that said police shall protect pupils on the way to or from public schools and Catholic schools but not while going to and coming from other schools, and firemen shall extinguish a blaze in public or Catholic school buildings but shall not put out a blaze in Protestant Church schools or private schools operated for profit? . . .

The Court's holding is that this taxpayer has no grievance because the state has decided to make the reimbursement a public purpose and therefore we are bound to regard it as such. . . . But it cannot make public business of religious worship or instruction, or of attendance at religious institutions of any character. There is no answer to the proposition . . . that the effect of the . . . Amendment . . . was to take every form of propagation of religion out of the realm of things which could directly or indirectly be made public business and thereby be supported in whole or in part at taxpayers' expense. That is a difference which the Constitution sets up between religion and almost every other subject matter of legislation, a difference which goes to the very root of religious freedom and which the Court is overlooking today.

From Justice Rutledge's Dissent:

The [First] Amendment's purpose was not to strike merely at the official establishment of a single sect, creed or religion, outlawing only a formal relation such as had prevailed in England and some of the colonies. Necessarily it was to uproot all such relationships. But the object was broader than separating church and state in this narrow sense. It was to create a complete and permanent separation of the spheres of religious activity and civil authority by comprehensively forbidding every form of public aid or support for religion. . . .

"Religion" appears only once in the Amendment. But the word governs two prohibitions and governs them alike. It does not have two meanings, one narrow to forbid "an establishment" and another, much broader, for securing "the free exercise thereof." "Thereof" brings down "religion" with its entire and exact content, no more and no less, from the first into the second guaranty, so that Congress and now the states are as broadly restricted concerning the one as they are regarding the other.

No one would claim today that the Amendment is constricted, in "prohibiting the free exercise" of religion, to securing the free exercise of some formal or creedal observance, of one sect or of many. It secures all forms of religious expression, creedal, sectarian or nonsectarian, wherever and however taking place, except conduct which trenches upon the like freedoms of others or clearly and presently endangers the community's good order and security. . . . And on this basis parents have been held entitled to send their children to private, religious schools. . . . Accordingly, daily religious education commingled with secular is "religion" within the guaranty's comprehensive scope. So are religious training and teaching in whatever form. The word connotes the broadest content, determined not by the form or formality of the teaching or where it occurs, but by its essential nature regardless of those details.

"Religion" has the same broad significance in the twin prohibition concerning "an establishment." The Amendment was not duplicitous. "Religion" and "establishment" were not used in any formal or technical sense. The prohibition broadly forbids state support, financial or other, of religion in any guise, form or degree. It outlaws all use of public funds for religious purposes.

II

No provision of the Constitution is more closely tied to or given content by its generating history than the religious clause of the First Amendment. The history includes . . . the . . . struggle for religious freedom in America, more especially in Virginia, of which the Amendment was the direct culmination. In the documents of the times, particularly of Madison, . . . is to be found irrefutable confirmation of the Amendment's sweeping content.

* * *

The climax [in the Virginia movement for religious freedom] came in the legislative struggle of 1784–1785 over the Assessment Bill. . . . This was nothing more nor less than a taxing measure for the support of religion . . . . So long as it singled out a particular sect for preference it incurred the active and general hostility of dissentient groups. It was broadened to include them, with the result that some subsided temporarily in their opposition. As altered, the bill gave to each taxpayer the privilege of designating which church should receive his share of the tax. In default of designation the legislature applied it to pious uses. But what is of the utmost significance here, "in its final form the bill left the taxpayer the option of giving his tax to education."

Madison was unyielding at all times, opposing . . . the general and non-discriminatory as he had the earlier particular and discriminatory assessments proposed. . . . Madison . . . maneuvered deferment of final consideration until November, 1785. And before the Assembly reconvened . . . he issued his historic Memorial and Remonstrance.

* * *

As the Remonstrance discloses throughout, Madison opposed every form and degree of official relation between religion and civil authority. For him religion was a wholly private matter beyond the scope of civil power either to restrain or to support. . . . State aid was no less obnoxious or destructive to freedom and to religion itself than other forms of state interference. . . . Hence he sought to tear out the institution not partially but root and branch, and to bar its return forever.

In no phase was he more unrelentingly absolute than in opposing state support or aid by taxation. Not even "three pence" contribution was thus to be exacted from any citizen for such purpose. . . . Not the amount but "the principle of assessment was wrong." And the principle was as much to prevent "the interference of law in religion" as to restrain religious intervention in political matters. In this field the authors of our freedom would not tolerate "the first experiment on our liberties" or "wait till usurped power had strengthened itself by exercise, and entangled the question in precedents." . . . Nor should we.

* * *

Compulsory attendance upon religious exercises went out early in the process of separating church and state . . . . Test oaths and religious qualifications for office followed later. . . . Hence today, apart from efforts to inject religious training or exercises and sectarian issues into the public schools, the only serious surviving threat . . . is through use of the taxing power to support religion, religious establishments, or establishments having a religious foundation whatever their form or special religious function.

Does New Jersey's action furnish support for religion by use of the taxing power? Certainly it does, if the test remains undiluted as Jefferson and Madison made it, that money taken by taxation from one is not to be used or given to support another's religious training or belief, or indeed one's own. Today as then the furnishing of "contributions of money for the propagation of opinions which he disbelieves" is the forbidden exaction and the prohibition is absolute for whatever measure brings that consequence and whatever amount may be sought or given to that end.

Source: Arch R. Everson, appellant, v. *Board of Education of the Township of Ewing et al.,* 330 U.S. 1.

SUGGESTIONS FOR BACKGROUND AND REFERENCE

R. F. Drinan, *Religion, the Courts, and Public Policy* (New York, 1963).

A. W. Johnson and F. H. Yost, *Separation of Church and State in the United States* (Minneapolis, 1948), pp. 152–164.

R. Kramer et al., "Religion and the State," *Law and Contemporary Problems,* Vol. XIV, No. 1 (1949), pp. 1–159.

P. B. Kurland, *Religion and the Law of Church and State and the Supreme Court* (Chicago, 1962).

D. H. Oaks (ed.), *The Wall between Church and State* (Chicago, 1963).

L. Pfeffer, *Church, State, and Freedom* (Boston, 1953), pp. 470–478.

A. P. Stokes, *Church and State in the United States* (New York, 1950), II, 642–758. See especially II, 694–715.

155 *McCollum* v. *Board of Education* (Extracts)

March 8, 1948

Concern for the religious education of their children in public schools led some church leaders to advocate "released time" from regular studies for religious instruction by appropriate representatives of the parents' faith.

Versions of the program differed in detail, but the movement enjoyed much Protestant, and eventually considerable Catholic favor. (Jewish support was more rare.) Several states passed enabling statutes, and the programs were upheld in state courts. The program in Champaign, Illinois, which made direct use of the public schools, was unsuccessfully challenged before the state supreme court by a "rationalist" parent. Appeal to the United States Supreme Court followed. Mindful of the recent Everson doctrines on separation, held by both the majority and minority, counsel for the Board of Education asked the Court to reverse its opposition to nonpreferential government aid to religion and its application of the First Amendment to the states through the Fourteenth Amendment. In a decision by Justice Black, the Court invalidated the Champaign "released time" program. There was a concurring opinion by Justice Frankfurter and a dissent by Justice Reed. Only the decision is reproduced here.

In 1940 interested members of the Jewish, Roman Catholic, and a few of the Protestant faiths formed . . . the Champaign Council on Religious Education. They obtained permission from the Board of Education to offer classes in religious instruction to public school pupils in grades four to nine inclusive. Classes were made up of pupils whose parents signed printed cards requesting that their children be permitted to attend; they were held weekly, thirty minutes for the lower grades, forty-five minutes for the higher. The council employed the religious teachers at no expense to the school authorities, but the instructors were subject to the approval and supervision of the superintendent of schools. The classes were taught in three separate religious groups by Protestant teachers, Catholic priests, and a Jewish rabbi, although for the past several years there have apparently been no classes instructed in the Jewish religion. Classes were conducted in the regular classrooms of the school building. Students who did not choose to take the religious instruction were not released from public school duties; they were required to leave their classrooms and go to some other place in the school building for pursuit of their secular studies. On the other hand, students who were released from secular study for the religious instructions were required to be present at the religious classes. Reports of their presence or absence were to be made to their secular teachers.

The foregoing facts . . . show the use of tax-supported property for religious instruction and the close cooperation between the school authorities and the religious council in promoting religious education. The operation of the State's compulsory education system thus assists and is integrated with the program of religious instruction carried on by separate religious sects. Pupils compelled by law to go to school for secular education are released in part from their legal duty upon the condition that they attend the religious classes. This is beyond all question a utilization of the tax-established and tax-supported public school system to aid religious groups to spread their faith. And it falls squarely under the ban of the First Amendment (made applicable to the States by the Fourteenth) as we interpreted it in *Everson* v. *Board of Education* . . . .

* * *

Recognizing that the Illinois program is barred by the First and Fourteenth Amendments if we adhere to the views expressed both by the majority and the minority in the *Everson* case, counsel for the respondents challenge those views as dicta and urge that we reconsider and repudiate them. They argue that historically the First Amendment was intended to forbid only government preference of one religion over another, not an impartial governmental assistance of all religions. In addition they ask that we distinguish or overrule our holding in the *Everson* case that the Fourteenth Amendment made the "establishment of religion" clause of the First Amendment applicable as a prohibition against the States. After giving full consideration . . . we are unable to accept either of these contentions.

To hold that a state cannot consistently with the First and Fourteenth Amendments utilize its public school system to aid any or all religious faiths or sects in the dissemination of their doctrines and ideals does not, as counsel urge, manifest a governmental hostility to religion or religious teachings. A manifestation of such hostility would be at war with our national tradition as embodied in the First Amendment's guaranty of the free exercise of religion. For the First Amendment rests upon the premise that both religion and government can best work to achieve their lofty aims if each is left free from the other within its respective sphere. Or, as we said in the Everson case, the First Amendment has erected a wall between Church and State which must be kept high and impregnable.

Here not only are the state's tax-supported public school buildings used for the dissemination of religious doctrines. The State also affords sectarian groups an invaluable aid in that it helps to provide pupils for their religious classes through use of the State's compulsory public school machinery. This is not separation of Church and State.

Source: People of State of Illinois ex rel. McCollum v. *Board of Education of School Dist. No. 71, Champaign County, Ill., et al.,* 333 U.S. 203.

SUGGESTIONS FOR BACKGROUND AND REFERENCE

R. F. Cushman, "Public Support of Religious Education in American Constitutional Law," *Illinois Law Review,* Vol. XLV, No. 3 (July–August 1950), pp. 333–356.

A. W. Johnson and F. H. Yost, *Separation of Church and State in the United States* (Minneapolis, 1948), pp. 74–99.

D. W. Kucera, *Church-State Relationships in Education in Illinois* (Washington, D.C., 1955).

J. M. Lassiter, "The McCollum Decision and the Public School," *Kentucky Law Review,* Vol. XXXVII, No. 4 (May 1949), pp. 402–411.

L. Pfeffer, *Church, State, and Freedom* (Boston, 1953), pp. 313–351.

A. P. Stokes, *Church and State in the United States* (New York, 1950), II, 488–641. See especially II, 495–522.

References for Document 154.

156   *Zorach* v. *Clauson* (Extracts)

April 28, 1952

In the four years after 1948 the extent of the prohibition contained in the McCollum judgment was much discussed. Many "released time" programs continued, relying partly on the qualification in Justice Frankfurter's opinion: "We do not consider, as indeed we could not, school programs not before us which, though colloquially characterized as 'released time,' present situations differing in aspects that may well be constitutionally crucial." In 1952 the Court met the issue again in this Zorach case. Zorach, an Episcopalian, brought an action against the New York Board of Education to force abandonment of its "released time" program, based on a state statute of 1940. Unlike Champaign, New York permitted no use of school space for religious instruction. Failure in state courts led plaintiffs to appeal to the Supreme Court, which in a six-to-three decision upheld the New York system. The decision, written by Justice William O. Douglas (1898–1980), made some use of the religious nation concept prominent in Justice Reed's dissent in the McCollum case. Spirited dissents from Justices Black, Frankfurter, and Jackson underlined the division of the Court. Passages from the decision and from the Black dissent are reproduced below.

From the Opinion of the Court:

New York City has a program which permits its public schools to release students during the school day so that they may leave the school buildings and school grounds and go to religious centers for religious instruction or devotional exercises. A student is released on written request of his parents. Those not released stay in the classrooms. The churches make weekly reports to the schools, sending a list of children who have been released from public school but who have not reported for religious instruction.

This "released time" program involves neither religious instruction in public school classrooms nor the expenditure of public funds. All costs, including the application blanks, are paid by the religious organizations. The case is therefore unlike *McCollum* v. *Board of Education* . . . .

Appellants, who are taxpayers and residents of New York City and whose children attend its public schools, challenge the present law, contending it is in essence not different from the one involved in the *McCollum* case. Their argument . . . reduces itself to this: the weight and influence of the school is put behind a program for religious instruction; public school teachers police it, keeping tab on students who are released; the classroom activities come to a halt while the students who are released for religious instruction are on leave; the school is a crutch on which the churches are leaning for support in their religious training; without the cooperation of the schools this "released time" program, like the one in the *McCollum* case, would be futile and ineffective. . . .

* * *

There cannot be the slightest doubt that the First Amendment reflects the philosophy that Church and State should be separated. And so far as interference with the "free exercise" of religion and an "establishment" of religion are concerned, the separation must be complete and unequivocal. . . . The First Amendment, however, does not say that in every and all respects there shall be a separation of Church and State. Rather, it studiously defines the manner, the specific ways, in which there shall be no concert or union or dependency one on the other. That is the common sense of the matter. Otherwise the state and religion would be aliens to each other—hostile, suspicious, and even unfriendly. Churches could not be required to pay even property taxes. Municipalities would not be permitted to render police or fire protection to religious groups. . . . Prayers in our legislative halls; the appeals to the Almighty in the messages of the Chief Executive; the proclamations making Thanksgiving Day a holiday; "so help me God" in our courtroom oaths—these and all other references to the Almighty that run through our laws, our public rituals, our ceremonies would be flouting the First Amendment. . . .

We would have to press the concept of separation of Church and State to these extremes to condemn the present law on constitutional grounds. . . .

* * *

We are a religious people whose institutions presuppose a Supreme Being. We guarantee the freedom to worship as one chooses. We make room for as wide a variety of beliefs and creeds as the spiritual needs of man deem necessary. We sponsor an attitude on the part of government that shows no partiality to any one group and that lets each flourish . . . . When the state encourages religious instruction or cooperates with religious authorities by adjusting the schedule of public events to sectarian needs, it follows the best of our traditions. For it then respects the religious nature of our people and accommodates the public service to their spiritual needs. To hold that it may not would be to find in the Constitution a requirement that the government show a callous indifference to religious groups. That would be preferring those who believe in no religion over those who do believe. Government may not finance religious groups nor undertake religious instruction nor blend secular and sectarian education nor use secular institutions to force one or some religion on any person. But we find no constitutional requirement which makes it necessary for government to be hostile to religion and to throw its weight against efforts to widen the effective scope of religious influence.

* * *

In the *McCollum* case the classrooms were used for religious instruction and the force of the public school was used to promote that instruction. Here . . . the public schools do no more than accommodate their schedules . . . . We follow the *McCollum* case. But we cannot expand it to cover the present released time program unless separation of Church and State means that public institutions can make no adjustments of their schedules to accommodate the religious needs of the people. We cannot read into the Bill of Rights such a philosophy of hostility to religion.

From Justice Black's Dissent:

I see no significant difference between the invalid Illinois system and that of New York here sustained. Except for the use of the school buildings in Illinois, there is no difference between the systems which I consider even worthy of mention. In the New York program, as in that of Illinois, the school authorities release some of the children on the condition that they attend the religious classes, get reports on whether they attend, and hold the other children in the school building until the religious hour is over. As we attempted to make categorically clear, the *McCollum* decision would have been the same if the religious classes had not been held in the school buildings. We said:

> Here *not only* are the state's tax-supported public school buildings used for the dissemination of religious doctrines. The State *also* affords sectarian groups an invaluable aid in that it helps to provide pupils for their religious classes through use of the State's compulsory public school machinery. *This* is not separation of Church and State." (Emphasis supplied.) . . .

McCollum thus held that Illinois could not constitutionally manipulate the compelled classroom hours of its compulsory school machinery so as to channel children into sectarian classes. Yet that is exactly what the Court holds New York can do.

* * *

Here the sole question is whether New York can use its compulsory education laws to help religious sects get attendants presumably too unenthusiastic to go unless moved to do so by the pressure of this state machinery. That this is the plan, purpose, design and consequence of the New York program cannot be denied. The state thus makes religious sects beneficiaries of its power to compel children to attend secular schools. Any use of such coercive power by the state to help or hinder some religious sects or to prefer all religious sects over nonbelievers or vice versa is just what I think the First Amendment forbids. In considering whether a state has entered this forbidden field the question is not whether it has entered too far but whether it has entered at all. New York is manipulating its compulsory education laws to help religious sects get pupils. This is not separation but combination of Church and State.

The Court's validation of the New York system rests in part on its statement that Americans are "a religious people whose institutions presuppose a Supreme Being." This was at least as true when the First Amendment was adopted; and it was just as true when eight Justices of this Court invalidated the released time system in *McCollum* on the premise that a state can no more "aid all religions" than it can aid one. It was precisely because Eighteenth Century Americans were a religious people divided into many fighting sects that we were given the constitutional mandate to keep Church and State completely separate. . . . Now as then, it is only by wholly isolating the state from the religious sphere and compelling it to be completely neutral, that the freedom of each and every denomination and of all non-believers can be maintained. It is this neutrality the Court abandons today when it treats New York's coercive system as a program which *merely* "encourages religious instruction or cooperates with religious authorities." The abandonment is all the more dangerous to liberty because of the Court's legal exaltation of the orthodox and its derogation of unbelievers.

Under our system of religious freedom, people have gone to their religious sanctuaries not because they feared the law but because they loved their God. . . . The spiritual mind of man has thus been free to believe, disbelieve, or doubt, without repression, great or small, by the heavy hand of government. . . . Before today, our judicial opinions have refrained from drawing invidious distinctions between those who believe in no religion and those who do believe. The First Amendment has lost much if the religious follower and the atheist are no longer to be judicially regarded as entitled to equal justice under law.

Source: Zorach et al. v. Clauson et al., 343 U.S. 306.

SUGGESTIONS FOR BACKGROUND AND REFERENCE

L. Pfeffer, *Church, State, and Freedom* (Boston, 1953), pp. 351–373.
F. J. Sorauf, "Zorach v. Clauson: The Impact of a Supreme Court Decision," *American Political Science Review*, Vol. LIII, No. 3 (September 1959), pp. 777–791.
References for Documents 154 and 155.

✦ ✦ ✦ Postwar Tensions Behind the Iron Curtain

157 Agreement of Hungary with the Hungarian Reformed Church

October 7, 1948

The shock of Communist decrees for sweeping reorientation of East European church life created religious upheaval in most countries between the end of World War II and 1950.[1] At first the reorganizations

---

1. Partial exception may be made for Russia itself, where Orthodox services in the war and the need for national unity reduced tensions. With Stalin's express approval, Sergei had been elected patriarch in 1943, the League of the Militant Godless suspended publication, priests were permitted to teach religion to children, and (in the following year) a theological institute opened in Moscow. The most important

may have appeared to be only consistent with the region's traditional Erastian arrangements, aiming at comprehensive state control rather than destruction of religion, but Marxist monopoly of education and extensive antireligious propaganda quickly revealed the likelihood of open enmity, oppression, and suffering in the near future. In all countries Communist governments pressed for nationalization of church property and institutions, severance of ecclesiastical ties with the West, the removal of "uncooperative" church leaders, the promotion of "progressive" factions among clergy and laity, and the creation of new legal machinery for harsh controls. Often this religious revolution was promoted, not only by legislation and bureaucratic rigidity, but also by "voluntary" agreements with deferential or intimidated church officials.

In Hungary, where the largest Protestant community beyond Germany was found, the Communists first sought to advance religious reorganization through compacts with the Reformed and Lutheran churches. In contrast to the violent resistance of Catholicism, the Protestant mood of repentance for social injustice, Naziism, and the war was attuned to a more limited opposition. Both churches suffered state seizure of property and schools and suppression of press and youth organizations, but many churchmen attempted genuine cooperation with the regime. In April 1948 the Reformed Church Synodical Council formally recognized the new order, approved agrarian reorganization and nationalization of industry, and offered assistance. In the same month, Reformed Bishop Laszlo Ravasz, chief opponent of Communist pressures, bowed to government demands for his resignation. In June this agreement was drawn up and given final approval in October 1948. A similar concordat with the Lutheran church was authorized in December 1948. Despite later efforts to work with the government, Protestants found Communist hostility unrelaxed. The revolt in 1956 and its aftermath intensified pressures.

1. In order to arrive at a new regulation of the status of the church in the Hungarian Republic the government . . . and the Hungarian Reformed Church appoint a permanent joint committee for drafting new laws concerning religious matters among which first of all a bill concerning the religion of children should be prepared. The legislative body of the church will amend its ecclesiastical laws in accordance with the new national legislation on religion.

---

legal concession was the constitutional statute on church organization that the sobor was permitted to adopt in 1945, providing for effective discipline under patriarch and hierarchy. (English translation in Robert Tobias, *Communist-Christian Encounter in East Europe* [Indianapolis, 1956], pp. 298–301. See also the analysis of A. A. Bogolepov, "The Statutes of the Russian Orthodox Church of 1945," *St. Vladimir's Seminary Quarterly,* Vol. II, New Series, No. 3 [Summer 1958], pp. 23–39.) This improved legal position of the church continued after the war, when the ecclesiastical imperialism of the Moscow patriarchate was politically useful to expanding Russian influence.

From Vladimir Gsovski (ed.), *Church and State Behind the Iron Curtain* (New York, 1955). Copyright, 1955, by the Free Europe Committee.

2. The government . . . declares . . . that it shall recognize and guarantee . . . the full enjoyment of religious freedom. . . .

3. The Government . . . deems that the following activities belong to the free sphere of church activities: the performance of worship in churches, suitable public buildings, private homes and open places; the teaching of the Bible in churches, schools, private homes and congregational houses; missionary work through denominational newspapers and other publications; disseminating the Bible . . . ; holding congregational and national ecclesiastical conferences . . . for evangelization, the compulsory teaching of religion in the schools, and the performance of charitable work. For this purpose the Hungarian Government permits the church to use, where needed, without charge . . . the classrooms or other suitable rooms of the public schools for worship, Sunday schools, Bible lectures, choir and other religious . . . meetings . . . at any time except during the regular periods of teaching until the congregations have secured other buildings for their purposes.[2]

* * *

4. The Government . . . respects . . . those duties of the Church which concern inspiring its members to perform good deeds and especially to take care of the poor, the abandoned, the aged and orphans. . . . For this purpose the State will protect the right of the Church to maintain and expand charitable institutions and to collect charitable donations. . . .

5. The Government . . . recognizes the manifest endeavor of the Reformed church to realize the principle: "A Free Church in a Free State."

The Government . . . declares its willingness to grant subventions temporarily to the Reformed Church as stated below until its financial condition improves.

(a) The Hungarian Republic secures the subvention to the personnel in the amount equal to the salaries of public servants from June 30, 1948 to December 31, 1948, and thereafter for the following five years. The . . . subsidy . . . shall be reduced . . . January 1, 1954, and the government shall continue to furnish the remaining 75 per cent until December 31, 1958. During the period from January 1, 1959 to December 31, 1963, 50 per cent of the present government subsidy shall be paid, while . . . from January 1, 1964 to December 31, 1968, 25 per cent shall be paid. All government subsidies shall cease on December 31, 1968.

* * *

(c) The Government . . . continues to pay a subsidy for the construction, reconstruction, and equipment of buildings of the . . . Church. . . . This subsidy shall be reduced every five years in a manner similar to the reduction of the subsidy for personnel and . . . shall cease on December 31, 1968.

* * *

(e) The Government shall pay the pensions of the Reformed ministers and the widows and children of members of the National Pension Fund in accordance with the rules governing the pensions of public servants. . . .

2. In small communities Reformed worship had often been held in the church school.

6. The . . . Church . . . shall incorporate prayers for the Hungarian Republic, for the head of the State, for the Government and for the well-being and peace of the Hungarian people in its "Order of Worship," and shall conduct worship . . . on national holidays. It declares that the new hymn book to be published in the near future contains hymns suitable for such occasions.

7. The . . . Church takes notice . . . that all schools other than the public schools together with the boarding houses connected with them will be socialized by legislative action. The enforcement of the nationalization of Calvinist schools shall be guided by the following arrangement.

(a) The government shall take over into the civil service as of July 1, 1948, the entire former teaching and other personnel of the nationalized schools. . . .

(b) The buildings of the nationalized schools, the boarding houses organically connected with them, and their lands . . . shall pass into government ownership. . . .

* * *

(d) Nationalization shall not apply to institutions which are exclusively ecclesiastical in nature and are not institutions of public education, i.e., theological academies, ministers' training institutes, deacons' and deaconess' training schools, and training schools for missionaries or other church workers.

* * *

(f) The Government . . . recognizes . . . that mandatory religious instruction must also henceforth be held at schools of a public character in complete freedom. The question of religious instruction is to be settled anew in one way or another by the new law concerning religious matters, with special consideration to the followers of the free churches and to those who are not affiliated with any religion.

Source: Vladimir Gsovski (ed.), *Church and State Behind the Iron Curtain* (New York, 1955), pp. 134–137.

SUGGESTIONS FOR BACKGROUND AND REFERENCE

A. Bereczky, *Hungarian Christianity in the New Hungarian State* (Birmingham, England, 1950).

K. S. Latourette, *Christianity in a Revolutionary Age* (New York, 1958–1962), IV, 351–353.

P. Sager (ed.), *Die Schul- und Wissenschaftspolitik der Ungarischen Volksrepublik, 1945–1956* (Bern, 1958), pp. 1–41.

H. Seton-Watson, *The East European Revolution* (New York, 1951), pp. 190–202, 282–295.

Source for this document, pp. 77–108.

158   Cardinal Mindszenty's Last Pastoral

November 18, 1948

Hungarian Catholicism, privileged and powerful before World War II, suffered a dramatic reversal of fortune under postwar communism. Drastic land reforms; suppression of Catholic organizations, press, and religious orders; and nationalization of schools effected the change. Vigorous resistance was marshaled by Cardinal Joseph Mindszenty (1892–1975), archbishop of Esztergom and Prince Primate of Hungary after 1945. In 1947 Mindszenty encouraged Catholic solidarity through urging special devotion to the Virgin and proclaiming her protection for Hungary. In the following year he excommunicated those responsible for the seizure of Roman Catholic schools. His last pastoral suggests consciousness of crisis and expectation of arrest (which came in December 1948). The Mindszenty case was the most dramatic confrontation of Catholicism and postwar communism, and the cardinal's trial and confession (repudiated in advance before arrest) were skilfully used by the state to weaken Catholic opposition. (Sentenced to life imprisonment, Mindszenty took refuge in the American legation during the 1956 revolt.)

For many weeks attempts have been made to stage "resolutions" directed against me in all the townships and village communities of Hungary. I am blamed for counter-revolutionary plots and activities hostile to the people, because of the Marian celebrations in 1947–1948. It is complained as a result, that adjustment of relations between the Church and the State was frustrated and demand is made that these "activities detrimental to the welfare of the people" should cease.

The goal of those celebrations in honor of Our Lady was the deepening of the traditional Hungarian devotion to the Blessed Virgin and the strengthening of faith. Never were purely political matters made the subject of speeches on those occasions. . . .

The purpose of the Marian Days was achieved. The Bishops of Hungary . . . testified to this. . . . They identified themselves with me against the attacks which were launched against the Marian Days. This same testimony has been given by the millions who represent the majority of public opinion. . . . Against their heroic patience measures had to be adopted which degrade those who employ them— measures that stand in opposition to the principle of religious freedom, guaranteed by democratic laws. . . .

As to the legal aspect of these "resolutions," it should be noted: In spite of many official promises, no elections of local autonomous administrations have been held since the Second World War, except in Budapest. Consequently all these decisions of "resolutions" staged in counties, townships and villages lack any legal basis. The signatures to them have been wrung from the people under threats of loss of bread

From *Cardinal Mindszenty Speaks* (New York, 1949). Copyright, 1949, by Longmans, Green & Co.

and liberty. The country is condemned to silence and public opinion is made a mere frivolous jest. Democratic "freedom of speech" in this country means that any opinion that differs from the official one is silenced. If a man dares to raise his voice in contradiction, he is dismissed from his position for criticism of democracy. . . . I feel the deepest sympathy for those who have been forced into such a position. I have been greatly impressed and deeply moved by many wonderful examples of unflinching courage and loyalty.

. . . We asked the Government to publish those letters of mine to which such strong exception has been taken, and to submit them to the judgment of world opinion. But this has not been done. . . .

As to the fact that between Church and State—or perhaps we should say "parties"—no agreement has yet been reached, everyone knows that the Church was invited to negotiate an agreement only after a delay of three months, although she had repeatedly and publicly declared her willingness to enter into negotiations. At first it was announced that the questions . . . must be settled by mutual agreement. When, however, the Church was at last invited to negotiate, the main point— the problem of the schools—had already been settled by the State. The church, of course, was forced to play the role of scapegoat.

* * *

I look on calmly at this artificial whipping up of the waves. In the place where I stand, not by the grace of any party, but by the grace and confidence of the Holy See, seething waters are not an extraordinary phenomenon. History lives in change.

Of my predecessors, two were killed in action, two were robbed of all their possessions, one was taken prisoner and deported, one was assassinated, our greatest one was exiled. . . .

Of all my predecessors, however, not one stood so bare of all means as I do. Such a systematic and purposeful net of propaganda lies—a hundred times disproved and yet a hundred times spread anew—has never been organized against the seventy-eight predecessors in my office. I stand for God, for the Church, and for Hungary. This responsibility has been imposed upon me by the fate of my nation which stands alone, an orphan in the whole world. Compared with the sufferings of my people, my own fate is of no importance.

I do not accuse my accusers. If I am compelled to speak out from time to time and to state the facts as they are, it is only the misery of my people and the urge of truth which force me to do so.

I pray for a world of truth and love. I pray for those who, in the words of our Lord, "know not what they do." I forgive them from the bottom of my heart.

Source: Cardinal Mindszenty Speaks (New York, 1949), pp. 209–212.

SUGGESTIONS FOR BACKGROUND AND REFERENCE

J. Broun, *Conscience and Captivity, Religion in Eastern Europe* (London, 1988), pp. 127–133.

O. Chadwick, *The Christian Church in the Cold War* (London, 1992), pp. 67–72.

J. Kozi-Horvath, *Cardinal Mindszenty—Confessor and Martyr of Our Time* (Chichester, 1979).

K. S. Latourette, *Christianity in a Revolutionary Age* (New York, 1958–1962), IV, 191–195.

159 Decree Abolishing the Romanian Uniate Church

December 1, 1948

In the Ukraine, Galicia, Ruthenia, and Romania, Communist policy early focused on the absorption of the Uniate (Eastern rite) Catholics by the more easily dominated Orthodox. Orthodoxy was the dominant religion in Romania, but the Catholic community was second in size and divided between the Latin rite and the Uniates. Although the 1948 constitution assured freedom of religion, the government adopted policies of severe repression toward Catholics, indicting their westward orientation and Vatican ties. The Orthodox Church, by contrast, was exploited as a useful instrument of government, particularly after the election of Patriarch Justinian in May 1948. Justinian called for the end of the Vatican concordat and the reintegration of the Uniates into the national church. The concordat was denounced in July, and in October an Orthodox synod "accepted" the "return" of the Uniates. Since by government estimate 75 percent of the Uniates had become Orthodox, Uniate property was transferred to the Orthodox in accordance with the Law of Cults of August 4, 1948. This decree of December 1948 was the epitaph of the Romanian Uniates.

Art. 1. As a result of the return of the local communities (parishes) of the Greek-Catholic (Uniate) cult to the Rumanian Orthodox cult, and in conformity with art. 13 of the decree No. 177/1948, the central statutory organizations of this cult, e.g., the metropolitanate, the bishoprics, the chapters, the orders, the congregations, the archparishes, the monasteries, the foundations, the associations, as well as all other institutions and organizations, under any other name, cease to exist.

Art. 2. The entire property of any description, belonging to the organizations and institutions shown as under art. 1 above, with the express exception of the former parishes, accrues to the Rumanian state. The latter will take possession immediately.

An interdepartmental commission, composed of the delegates of the Ministries of Finance, Agriculture, Education and the Home Office, will decide upon the fate of this property, and may allocate part of it to the Rumanian Orthodox Church, or to its various component parts.

From Ion Ratiu, "The Communist Attack on the Catholic and Orthodox Churches in Rumania," *The Eastern Churches Quarterly,* Vol. VIII. Reprinted by permission of *The Eastern Churches Quarterly.*

Source: Ion Ratiu, "The Communist Attack on the Catholic and Orthodox Churches in Rumania," *The Eastern Churches Quarterly,* Vol. VIII, No. 3 (July–September 1949), pp. 185–186.

SUGGESTIONS FOR BACKGROUND AND REFERENCE

J. Broun, *Conscience and Captivity, Religion in Eastern Europe* (London, 1982), pp. 199–207.

O. Chadwick, *The Christian Church in the Cold War* (London, 1992), pp. 51–69.

A. Cretzianu (ed.), *Captive Rumania: A Decade of Soviet Rule* (New York, 1956), pp. 165–203.

V. Gsovski (ed.), *Church and State Behind the Iron Curtain* (New York, 1955), pp. 253–293.

K. S. Latourette, *Christianity in a Revolutionary Age* (New York, 1958–1962), IV, 207–208, 533–537.

Source for this document, pp. 163–197.

160   Czech Law on Church Affairs

September 14, 1949

Czech Communists, in power after the coup of February 1948, attempted to exploit a national tradition of qualified loyalty to Roman Catholicism arising from the Hussite Reformation and from patriotic resistance to Catholic Austria in the nineteenth century. They suppressed Catholic schools, press, and lay organizations, seized landed property, and launched a schismatic progovernment "Catholic Action" movement. In October 1949 the state established a Government Bureau for Church Affairs to "see to it that Church life develops in accordance with the Constitution and the principles of the people's democratic order. . . ." It was competent to supervise all churches, but was concerned chiefly with Catholicism. In addition, the National Assembly passed this law, to take effect November 1, providing for state financial support of the churches, political approval of clergy, and general surveillance. Four days later a cabinet decree interpreted the act in detail for Catholics. The Catholic bishops' petition of October 21 was ignored, and later resistance led to ruptured diplomatic relations with the Vatican, the suppression of monasteries and free seminaries, and the arrest of bishops and priests.

Sec. 1— . . . the Government shall grant emoluments to the clergymen of Churches and religious associations who with the consent of the Government either perform strictly religious functions, or are employed in Church administration or in establishments for the training of clergymen. The Government Bureau for Church

From Vladimir Gsovski (ed.), *Church and State Behind the Iron Curtain* (New York, 1955). Copyright, 1955, by the Free Europe Committee.

Affairs may exceptionally in agreement with the Ministry of Finance also grant emoluments to clergymen who are engaged in other activities.

Sec. 2—Government consent may be granted only to ministers of religion who are Czechoslovak citizens, are politically reliable, are irreproachable, and who otherwise meet the general requirements for employment with the Government. The Government Bureau for Church Affairs may waive the requirement of citizenship in cases deserving special consideration.

Sec. 3— . . . The Cabinet shall establish . . . the basic salary, the rates of increases and the methods of granting them, the requirements for granting additional pay according to rank, and its amount, as well the requirements of granting an efficiency bonus. . . .

Sec. 4— . . . Clergymen entitled to emoluments shall also be entitled to compensation for travel, moving, and other expenses. . . .

Sec. 5— . . . Clergymen performing strictly religious functions are under the obligation to teach religion in schools, without remuneration, unless there is another arrangement for the teaching of religion. . . .

Sec. 6— . . . Social benefits, in particular allocations for dependent children and pension benefits for a clergyman and members of his family shall be granted in accordance with provisions for governmental employees. . . .

Sec. 7—Activities and Appointment of Clergymen. (1) Only those persons may carry on the activities of a minister of religion (preacher and the like) in a Church or religious association who have obtained the consent of the Government therefor and have taken an oath.

(2) Every employment (by election or appointment) of such persons shall require the consent of the Government, given in advance.

(3) Vacant posts must be filled within 30 days. If this is not done, the Government may take the necessary measures to secure the regular performance of the religious functions, Church administration, or the education of clergymen.

Sec. 8—Expenses of Upkeep. (1) The Government shall reimburse Churches and religious associations for regular expenses of upkeep relating to the divine service, to other religious functions, and to the Church administration in accordance with their budgets, as approved [by the Government Bureau for Church Affairs].

(2) The Government may grant a special subsidy for extraordinary expenses of upkeep if they are justified.

Sec. 9—Budgets. (1) Representatives of Churches and religious associations as well as managers of Church property must prepare budgets and final accounts and submit them for approval to the Government Bureau for Church Affairs.

(2) The budgets of current expenses of upkeep shall be set up in conformity with actual needs, in accordance with the rules for the drafting of the Government budget. . . .

Sec. 10—Property. (1) The Government shall supervise the property of the Churches and religious associations.

(2) The representatives of Churches and religious associations as well as managers of Church property shall take an inventory of all personal property, real property, and property rights of the Churches and religious associations, their branches, communities, institutions, foundations, Churches, prebends, and funds,

and shall submit them to the Government Bureau for Church Affairs within three months. . . .

(3) Any disposal or encumbering of the property of Churches and religious associations shall require the consent of the Government administration, given in advance.

* * *

Sec. 12—Schools for the Education of Clergymen. The Government shall maintain schools and institutions for education of clergymen.

Sec. 13—Penal Provisions. Acts or omissions contrary to this law . . . shall be punished, if they are not punishable by the courts, by the County People's Committees as administrative offenses with a fine not to exceed 100,000 Czechoslovak crowns. According to the gravity of the offense a substitute penalty of imprisonment not to exceed six months, shall simultaneously be determined in cases where the fine cannot be collected.

Source: Vladimir Gsovski (ed.), *Church and State Behind the Iron Curtain* (New York, 1955), pp. 42–45.

SUGGESTIONS FOR BACKGROUND AND REFERENCE

K. S. Latourette, *Christianity in a Revolutionary Age* (New York, 1958–1962), IV, 195–200.

L. Nemec, *Church and State in Czechoslovakia Historically, Juridically, and Theologically Documented* (New York, 1955).

G. N. Schuster, *Religion Behind the Iron Curtain* (New York, 1954), pp. 61–97.

R. Tobias, *Communist-Christian Encounter in East Europe* (Indianapolis, 1956), pp. 488–523.

161   Agreement Between Poland and the Catholic Bishops

April 14, 1950

In Poland Communist religious policy was cautious by reason of the nation's strong historical and patriotic bonds to Roman Catholicism (which also commanded at least nominal support from about 95 percent of the population). Although the government denounced the Concordat of 1925, interference with the church did not become severe until 1949. But in 1950 the government secularized *Caritas,* the Catholic welfare organization, seized church lands (spared in the earlier 1945 nationalization), and attempted to detach the lower clergy from dependence on the episcopate. This intense campaign was temporarily relaxed when the bishops endorsed this important accord with the state, which they later explained as arising from a desire to prove goodwill and secure peaceful coexistence. Loose wording in the agreement accommodated conflicting interpretations, and late in 1952 the anti-Catholic campaign recovered momentum with trials of clergy, the requirement of government approval for all ecclesiastical appointments (Decree of February 9, 1953), and the monastic confinement of Cardinal Wyszynski. Reproduced below are passages from the accord and the accompanying protocol. ("Recovered Territories" in Article III is a Polish term for annexations of former German territory.)

From the Agreement:

I. The Episcopate shall urge that . . . the clergy teach the faithful respect for the law and the authorities of the State.

II. The Episcopate shall urge that . . . the clergy call upon the faithful to intensify their work for the reconstruction of the country. . . .

III. The Polish Episcopate states that economic, historical, cultural and religious reasons and also historic justice demand that the Recovered Territories should belong to Poland forever. Basing itself on the premise that the Recovered Territories form an inseparable part of the Republic, the Episcopate shall address a request to the Holy See that those Church administrations now holding the rights of residential bishoprics shall be converted into permanent episcopal dioceses.

IV. To the extent of its ability the Episcopate shall oppose activities hostile to Poland and particularly the anti-Polish revisionist actions of a part of the German clergy.

V. The principle that the Pope is the competent and supreme authority of the Church refers to matters of faith, morals, and Church jurisdiction; in other matters, however, the Episcopate is guided by the interests of the Polish State.

VI. Basing itself on the premise that the mission of the Church can be fulfilled within various social and economic systems established by secular authority, the Episcopate shall explain to the clergy that it should not oppose the development of cooperatives in rural areas since the cooperative movement is based essentially on the ethical element in human nature directed toward voluntary social solidarity which has as its goal the welfare of all.

VII. In accordance with its principles and in condemnation of all acts against the Polish State, the Church shall oppose particularly the misuse of religious feelings for anti-State purpose.

VIII. The Church . . . shall combat the criminal activities of underground bands and shall denounce and punish under canon law those clergymen who are guilty of participation in any underground activities against the Polish State.

* * *

X. Religious instruction in schools:

A. The Government does not intend to reduce the present status of religious instruction in schools; the program of religious instruction will be worked out by school authorities together with representatives of the Episcopate; the schools will be supplied with appropriate textbooks; lay and clerical instructors of religion shall be treated on an equal footing with teachers of other subjects; supervisors of religious instruction shall be appointed by the school authorities in consultation with the Episcopate.

B. The authorities will not place obstacles in the way of students wishing to participate in religious practices outside the schools.

C. While existing schools which are Catholic in character shall be continued, the Government shall require that these schools carry out instructions loyally and fulfill the program as determined by State authorities.

D. Schools run by the Catholic Church will enjoy the privileges of State schools in accordance with the general principles defined by the appropriate laws and the regulations of the school authorities.

X. Where a school is established which provides no religious instruction . . . , those Catholic parents who so desire shall have the right . . . to send their children to schools where religion is taught.

XI. The Catholic University of Lublin shall be permitted to continue the present scope of its activities.

XII. Catholic associations shall enjoy the same rights as heretofore after satisfying all requirements provided in the decree concerning associations. . . .

XIII. The Church shall have the right and the opportunity to conduct its activities in the fields of charity, welfare, and religious education within the framework of existing regulations.

XIV. The Catholic press and Catholic publications shall enjoy privileges as defined by appropriate laws and the regulations of the authorities, and on an equal basis with other publications.

XV. No obstacles shall be placed in the way of public worship, traditional pilgrimages and processions. In accordance with the requirements for maintaining public order, arrangements for such ceremonies shall be made in consultation between Church and administrative authorities.

XVI. The status of military chaplains shall be defined by special regulations to be worked out by military authorities in agreement with representatives of the Episcopate. . . .

* * *

XIX. Religious orders shall have full freedom of activity within the limits of their calling and within the framework of existing laws.

From the Protocol:
1. . . . in order to normalize relations between the State and Church, . . . "Caritas" is being transformed into the Association of Catholics for Aid to the Poor and Needy. The Association shall carry on its activities through branches corresponding to the administrative divisions of the country, [and] the Episcopate shall make it possible for those members of the clergy who wish to do so to work in this Association. . . .

2. The Polish Government, in carrying out the law for "the transfer of Church

lands to State ownership" . . . shall consider the needs of the bishops and of church institutions in order to provide assistance. . . .

3. The Church Fund shall place adequate sums at the disposal of diocesan bishops.

4. Implementing the law on military service, the military authorities shall make necessary arrangements for students of religious seminaries to enable them to complete their studies; ordained priests and monks who have taken their vows shall not be called to active military service, but will be transferred to the reserve corps and qualified for military service.

Source: Robert Tobias, *Communist-Christian Encounter in East Europe* (Indianapolis, 1956), pp. 410–413.

SUGGESTIONS FOR BACKGROUND AND REFERENCE

E. Dolan, "Post-War Poland and the Church," *The American Slavic and East European Review*, Vol. XIV, No. 1 (February 1955), pp. 84–92.

V. Gsovski (ed.), *Church and State Behind the Iron Curtain* (New York, 1955), pp. 159–241.

K. S. Latourette, *Christianity in a Revolutionary Age* (New York, 1958–1962), IV, 200–206.

R. C. Monticone, *The Catholic Church in Communist Poland, 1945–1985: Forty Years of Church-State Relations* (Boulder, Colo., 1986), pp. 9–25.

G. N. Shuster, *Religion Behind the Iron Curtain* (New York, 1954), pp. 130–163.

R. Staar, *Poland 1944–1962: The Sovietization of a Captive People* (Baton Rouge, La., 1962), pp. 241–269.

E. Valkenier, "Catholic Church in Communist Poland, 1945–1955," *Review of Politics*, Vol. XVIII (July 1956), pp. 305–326.

162   Pastoral of the Berlin-Brandenburg Church

April 23, 1950

Communist-controlled East Germany was the homeland of the Lutheran Reformation and its population was overwhelmingly Protestant. As in Poland, government policy was at first cautious and less openly oppressive than in other Iron Curtain countries. Churches kept their lands (though impossible production quotas were set), religious education was permitted in the schools, and East Germans participated in the *Evangelische Kirche in Deutschland* (EKD), the all-German federation of *Landeskirchen* formed in 1945. But Communist pressure on youth, publication, education, and charity was unrelenting, and official encouragement was given to atheism. Protestant policy avoided both rebellion and compliance; it accepted the regime, sought relief through negotiation and protest, appealed to law and courts, and testified to its beliefs. The chief Protestant leader was Otto Dibelius (1880–1967), bishop of Berlin-Brandenburg, an opponent of Hitler who had joined in the formation of the EKD and served as one of the World Council presidents. His protest of April 20, 1950, to Prime Minister Grotewohl against government hostility and anti-Christian pressures was followed by this pastoral, signed by Dibelius and other church leaders. The government denounced these protests (and a similar statement by Cardinal Von Preysing) as illegal acts, and in the 1950s imposed new restrictions. Yet Protestant vitality in the East was sometimes reported to be greater than in the Federal Republic.

Our Lord Jesus Christ speaks unto us, saying, "The truth shall make you free." And this truth is none other than He Himself, the Crucified and Risen Saviour. He is our comfort and our strength, and Him do we proclaim unto all men, even amid the great troubles of our time.

Today more than ever before we find ourselves encompassed by oppressed and uneasy consciences. The people of our parishes cry without ceasing to their church leaders and pastors and elders, "Help us. We are constrained to say things that, out of regard for truthfulness, we cannot say. We are compelled to engage in doings in which we cannot join with a quiet mind. We have to acquiesce in decisions we cannot approve. We are in constant peril of losing our liberty, our employment, our daily bread, if we refuse to do as others do." And this situation has grown sensibly more acute with the intensifying of the campaign on behalf of the National Front. Especially heart-rending are the appeals of parents who say that their children are becoming more and more accustomed, under the pressure of their schools and colleges and youth organizations, to say and write what they do not think, that the Christian faith is being made contemptible to them and teachers are seeking to persuade them that there is no God and that Christ never lived at all.

Our people should know that the church leaders of the Eastern Zone have submitted these facts, frankly and seriously, to the highest authorities of the State. They were answered that many of these occurrences were not sanctioned by the Government, and that cases mentioned by name would be investigated. . . . But we are concerned not with individual cases, but with the whole set-up of public life. We feel obliged, therefore, to declare our views as follows:

1. The Evangelical Church confesses to the truth that is Christ Jesus. This truth is not compatible with the materialist outlook on life. We protest, therefore, against the propagation of this philosophy as the sole valid truth in schools, in colleges, in administrative bodies and in State-supported organizations. No governing power has the right to force upon anyone a philosophy that runs counter to his faith and his conscience. We call upon the members of our congregations to bear witness, gladly and resolutely, wherever their faith is assailed either overtly or covertly, that Christ is our Lord and that we are His, body and soul.

2. Jesus Christ, Who is the truth, frees us from the power of the lie. It is a sin to coerce men by violence into falsehood, and to seduce mere children into the same.

We most earnestly beseech all those now active in public affairs not to take on themselves the guilt of such a sin.

3. Truth, which is Jesus Christ, likewise makes us free to love our neighbour even when he is our enemy. Where hatred is preached against nations, against races or classes, against individuals, the Christian is called upon to love. Whatever happens, he must not be accessory to acts of violence or to any propaganda of hate. And should he himself become the victim of such dealings, he must not answer force with force, but must seek strength from God to withstand through endurance.

4. Truth, which we confess in our Lord Jesus Christ, binds us to one another in a fellowship of faith and charity. Where one falls victim to violence, it is the duty of the rest to come to his assistance, and to prove by their actions that he who suffers without cause is deserving of redoubled esteem and affection.

5. Truth, in which we take comfort, is the voice of the Lord, Who will not break the bruised reed nor quench the smoking flax. We know how many have not the strength to resist pressure from without. And being men such as know their own weakness, we commend ourselves and you to the forgiveness of God. . . . Only let none allow his conscience to lose its edge, and come to feel a life filled daily with falsehoods to be a thing inevitable and of no moment!

6. Finally, we proclaim even unto them that still close their ears to the call of Christ that His truth is to make them also free. Without Him, we are one and all, even if we will not admit it, most poor and pitiable and troubled creatures. He alone makes us free to be fellow-beings and brethren one of another.

Source: Robert Tobias, *Communist-Christian Encounter in East Europe* (Indianapolis, 1956), pp. 546–547.

SUGGESTIONS FOR BACKGROUND AND REFERENCE

[O. Dibelius], "Church and State in Berlin-Brandenburg," *Ecumenical Review,* Vol. III, No. 3 (April 1951), pp. 279–283.

O. Dibelius, *In the Service of the Lord* (London, 1965).

R. F. Goeckel, *The Lutheran Church and the East German State: Political Conflict and Change under Ulbricht and Honecker* (Ithaca, N.Y., 1990).

K. S. Latourette, *Christianity in a Revolutionary Age* (New York, 1958–1962), IV, 284–287.

G. M. Schuster, *Religion Behind the Iron Curtain* (New York, 1954), pp. 32–60.

R. W. Solberg, *God and Caesar in East Germany* (New York, 1961).

✦ ✦ ✦ Protestant Reorientation in the New China

163   The Christian Manifesto

May 13, 1950

After years of conflict with the Kuomintang, the victorious Chinese Communists formally inaugurated their rule in October 1949. The sweeping revolution in Chinese life required reorientation of all religions, Tao, Moslem, and Buddhist, as well as Christian. Because of its foreign ties, Chinese Christianity was especially vulnerable. The government denied Protestant and Catholic missionaries entry into the country, and those already present were confined to cities of residence. Aliens were driven from official positions in churches and church institutions. Foreign financial aid was terminated. Pressure increased after Chinese intervention in the Korean war, and by 1952 most missionaries had left the country. The government strongly promoted Catholic and Protestant factions willing to accommodate to the regime. Protestant leadership for this Christian Manifesto came from a group of Shanghai churchmen, led by YMCA secretary Y. T. Wu (Wu Yao-tsung) (b. 1893), a former student at Union Seminary (New York), social gospeler, and pacifist. Joined by northern Protestant representatives, the Shanghai leaders had three interviews with Premier Chou En-lai in May 1950, at the last of which (May 13) Wu's draft of the manifesto received government approval. Church criticism prompted minor changes in the text, but continuing dissatisfaction caused some churchmen to withdraw from the movement. The manifesto was published in July 1950, and a campaign for subscriptions ultimately claimed 400,000 signatures. (In Catholicism, anticommunism and loyalty to Rome made for especially bitter resistance, but churchmen of the Catholic Patriotic Association were in control by 1958.)

Protestant Christianity has been introduced to China for more than a hundred and forty years. During this period it has made a not unworthy contribution to Chinese society. Nevertheless, . . . not long after Christianity's coming to China, imperialism started its activities here; and since the principal groups of missionaries who brought Christianity to China all came themselves from these imperialistic countries, Christianity consciously or unconsciously, directly or indirectly, became related with imperialism. Now that the Chinese revolution has achieved victory, these imperialistic countries will not rest passively content. . . . They will certainly seek to contrive by every means the destruction of what has actually been achieved; they may also make use of Christianity to forward their plot of stirring up internal dissension, and creating reactionary forces in this country. It is our purpose in publishing the following statement to heighten our vigilance against imperialism, to make known the clear political stand of Christians in New China, to hasten the building of a Chinese church whose affairs are managed by the Chinese themselves, and to indicate the responsibilities that should be taken up by Christians throughout the whole country in national reconstruction in New China. We desire to call upon all Christians in the country to exert their best efforts in putting into effect the principles herein presented.

The Task in General

Christian churches and organizations give thoroughgoing support to the "Common Political Platform," and under the leadership of the government oppose imperialism, feudalism, and bureaucratic capitalism, and take part in the effort to build an independent, democratic, peaceable, unified, prosperous, and powerful New China.

Fundamental Aims

(1) Christian churches and organizations in China should exert their utmost efforts, and employ effective methods, to make people in the churches everywhere recognize clearly the evils that have been wrought in China by imperialism; recognize the fact that in the past imperialism has made use of Christianity; purge imperialistic influences from within Christianity itself; and be vigilant against imperialism, and especially American imperialism, in its plot to use religion in fostering the growth of reactionary forces. At the same time, the churches and organizations should call upon Christians to participate in the movement opposing war and upholding peace, and teach them thoroughly to understand and support the government's policy of agrarian reform.

(2) Christian churches and organizations in China should take effective measures to cultivate a patriotic and democratic spirit among their adherents in general, as well as a psychology of self-respect and self-reliance. The movement for autonomy, self-support, and self-propagation hitherto promoted in the Chinese church has already attained a measure of success. This movement from now onwards should complete its tasks within the shortest possible period. At the same time, self-criticism should be advocated, all forms of Christian activity re-examined and readjusted, and thoroughgoing austerity measures adopted, so as to achieve the goals of a reformation in the church.

Concrete Methods

(1) All Christian churches and organizations in China that are still relying upon foreign personnel and financial aid should work out concrete plans to realize within the shortest possible time their objective of self-reliance and rejuvenation.

(2) From now onwards, as regards their religious work, Christian churches and organizations should lay emphasis upon a deeper understanding of the nature of Christianity itself, closer fellowship and unity among the various denominations,

the cultivation of better leadership personnel, and reform in systems of church organization. As regards their more general work, they should emphasize anti-imperialistic, anti-feudalistic and anti-bureaucratic-capitalistic education, together with such forms of service to the people as productive labor, teaching them to understand the New Era, cultural and recreational activities, literacy education, medical and public health work, and care of children.

Source: Francis Price Jones (ed.), *Documents of the Three-Self Movement, Source Materials for the Study of the Protestant Church in Communist China* (New York, 1963), pp. 19–20.

SUGGESTIONS FOR BACKGROUND AND REFERENCE

G. T. Brown, *Christianity in the Peoples Republic of China* (Atlanta, 1983) pp. 75–86.
R. Bush, *Religion in Communist China* (Nashville, 1970), pp. 170–208.
C. Cary Elwes, *China and the Cross: A Survey of Missionary History* (New York, 1957), pp. 181–285.
F. P. Jones, *The Church in Communist China* (New York, 1962).
K. S. Latourette, *Christianity in a Revolutionary Age* (New York, 1958–1962), V, 371–411.
L. T. Lyall, *Come Wind, Come Weather, The Present Experience of the Church in China* (Chicago, 1960).
L. M. Outerbridge, *The Lost Churches of China* (Philadelphia, 1952).
F. A. Varg, *Missionaries, Chinese, and Diplomats: The American Protestant Missionary Movement in China, 1890–1952* (Princeton, 1958), pp. 274–318.

164   Declaration of the Peking Chinese Christian Conference

April 1951

The chief means whereby Chinese Protestantism was drawn into conformity with Communist policy was the Three Self Reform Movement. Advocating "self-support, self-government, self-propagation," the movement justified the government's uncompensated confiscation of mission properties and Christian institutions and skilfully exploited an older Chinese Christian restlessness under missionary authority and paternalism. The movement was formally launched at a Peking conference called for April 16 to 21 by the government Religious Affairs Bureau. Convened ostensibly to guide organizations that had been in receipt of American aid, the conference recognized the Three Self Reform Committee, of which Y. T. Wu was chairman, and inaugurated a denunciation campaign against individual missionaries and Chinese allegedly under Western influences. This statement, supposedly representing the opinion of the 151 delegates, was released at the conclusion of the conference.

At this time when the strength of peace is growing among the people of the world, imperialism has already reached its last days. The encroachment of American imperialism in Korea and Taiwan is a final show of strength before death. American imperialism is now arming Japan and Western Germany, preparing to attain its aggressive objectives, once again preparing to kill multitudes of people, but it will not attain its objective. In Korea it has already met the force of the people of China and Korea—it will yet experience in the end defeat and death.

We strongly oppose this American imperialistic aggressive plan, . . . the use of atomic weapons, . . . a separate peace treaty with Japan and . . . rearming Japan, . . . rearming Western Germany. We wish to unite with all Christians in the world who love peace and oppose all schemes of American imperialism to break up peace programs.

But most Christians in the world are good. It is the wicked imperialists who use the church as their tool of aggression. In July 1950 the Executive Committee of the World Council of Churches met in Toronto, Canada, and passed a resolution concerning the war in Korea, branding the North Korean government as an aggressor. . . .

This resolution distorts truth. . . . This resolution . . . echoes the voice of the United States Congress. . . . We express our wish to expose U.S. imperialism, which . . . over a hundred years has made use of the church's work in evangelism and cultural activities to carry out its sinister policy. In our Manifesto of September 1950 we emphasized the breaking-off of relations between the church in China and imperialism. . . .

On December 29, 1950 the Legislative Yuan of the Central People's Government published the "Plan to control cultural, educational and relief organizations and religious bodies receiving American financial aid." At this present meeting, we have discussed the draft proposed by the Government concerning the plan to be adopted by Protestant religious bodies receiving American financial grants. We have also heard the reports of Government leaders and had detailed discussions. We recognize that the plan of the . . . Government for the protection of the Protestant church is certainly careful, complete and very satisfactory. The Fifth Article of the Common Platform guarantees the people's freedom of religion and belief; moreover, we have received freedom of religion and belief, and this state of affairs has greatly encouraged and strengthened Protestant Christians in self-government, self-support and independent evangelism. . . . American imperialism wishes to use the method of freezing assets to cause these Protestant churches and enterprises dependent upon foreign funds to fall into despair. But the People's Government has helped us to progress toward a bright future. We believe that the Chinese Protestant church, relying upon God, and under the eminent guidance of Chairman Mao, with the encouragement and help of the Government, will be able to make full use of its own strength to raise up a purer, fitter and more perfect Christian enterprise to serve the people.

We call upon fellow-Christians in the whole country:

(1) To resolutely support and carry out the Central Government Legislative Yuan's "Plan of control for all cultural, educational and relief organizations and religious bodies receiving American financial aid," also the regulations concerning registration for [such organizations having] transactions in foreign exchange, ... And finally, *to thoroughly, permanently and completely sever all relations with*

American missions and all other missions, thus realizing self-government, self-support, and self-propagation in the Chinese church.

(2) To enthusiastically take part in the "Oppose-America, Support-Korea" Movement, [and] . . . carry out the patriotic program. *Every local church, every church body, every Christian publication must implement the "oppose-America help-Korea" propaganda and make* [it] *known to every Christian.*

(3) To support the Common Program, support the Government land reform policy and support the Government in the repression of anti-revolutionaries, obey all Government laws, positively respond to the Government commands, and exert every effort in the reconstruction of the nation. We want to be more alert, to resolutely reject the blandishments of imperialism, *to assist the Government to discover and punish anti-revolutionary and corrupt elements within the Protestant church;* to resolutely oppose the secret plans of imperialists and reactionaries who wish to destroy the Three-Self Movement; also encourage and spread the movement in each church and Christian organization and denounce imperialists and anti-revolutionary evil elements.

(4) To increase patriotic education, greatly enlarge the study movement in order to increase the political consciousness of Christians. Finally, we call upon all Christians to continue to promote and enlarge the campaign to secure signatures to revolutionary documents and firmly resolve to make effective the Three-Self mission of the church, and with the highest enthusiasm welcome the unlimited, glorious future of the People's Republic of China.

Source: Francis Price Jones (ed.), *Documents of the Three-Self Movement. Materials for the Study of the Protestant Church in Communist China* (New York, 1963), pp. 19–20.

SUGGESTIONS FOR BACKGROUND AND REFERENCE

References for Document 163.

✦ ✦ ✦ United States Supreme Court: Termination of Religious Practices in the Public Schools

165   *Engel* v. *Vitale* (Extract)

June 25, 1962

Prescribed prayer in public schools was invalidated in this decision, written by Justice Black. In 1951 the New York State Board of Regents recommended to school boards the following "nonsectarian" prayer, to be recited aloud in each classroom at the beginning of each school day: "Almighty God, we acknowledge our dependence upon Thee, and we beg Thy blessings upon us, our parents, our teachers and our Country." When introduced in New Hyde Park, the practice was challenged by parents of ten pupils as a violation of the First Amendment. The exercise was accompanied by no compulsion or comment, and a divided New York Court of Appeals upheld the Regents' prayer. When the United States Supreme Court struck down the custom, only Justice Stewart dissented.

We think that by using its public school system to encourage recitation of the Regents' prayer, the State of New York has adopted a practice wholly inconsistent with the Establishment Clause. There can, of course, be no doubt that New York's program of daily classroom invocation of God's blessings as prescribed in the Regents' prayer is a religious activity. . . .

The petitioners contend among other things that the state laws requiring or permitting use of the Regents' prayer must be struck down as a violation of the Establishment Clause because that prayer was composed by governmental officials as a part of a governmental program to further religious beliefs. For this reason, petitioners argue, the State's use of the Regents' prayer in its public school system breaches the constitutional wall of separation between Church and State. We agree with that contention since we think that the constitutional prohibition against laws respecting an establishment of religion must at least mean that in this country it is no part of the business of government to compose official prayers for any group of the American people to recite as a part of a religious program carried on by government.

* * *

By the time of the adoption of the Constitution, our history shows that there was a widespread awareness among many Americans of the dangers of a union of Church and State. These people knew, some of them from bitter personal experience, that one of the greatest dangers to the freedom of the individual to worship in his own way lay in the Government's placing its official stamp of approval upon one particular kind of prayer or one particular form of religious services. . . . The First Amendment was added to the Constitution to stand as a guarantee that neither the power nor the prestige of the Federal Government would be used to control, support or influence the kinds of prayer the American people can say. . . . Under that Amendment's prohibition against governmental establishment of religion, as reinforced by the provisions of the Fourteenth Amendment, government in this country, be it state or federal, is without power to prescribe by law any particular form of prayer which is to be used as an official prayer in carrying on any program of governmentally sponsored religious activity.

There can be no doubt that New York's state prayer program officially establishes the religious beliefs embodied in the Regents' prayer. The respondents' argument to the contrary, which is largely based upon the contention that the Regents' prayer is "non-denominational" and the fact that the program, as modified and approved by state courts, does not require all pupils to recite the prayer but permits those who wish to do so to remain silent or be excused from the room, ignores the essential nature of the program's constitutional defects. Neither the fact that the prayer may be denominationally neutral, nor the fact that its observance on the part of the students is voluntary can serve to free it from the limitations of the Establishment Clause, as it might from the Free Exercise Clause, of the First Amendment, both of which are operative against the States by virtue of the Fourteenth Amendment. . . . The Establishment Clause, unlike the Free Exercise Clause, does not depend upon any showing of direct governmental compulsion and is violated by the enactment of laws which establish an official religion whether those laws operate directly to coerce nonobserving individuals or not. This is not to say, of course, that laws officially prescribing a particular form of religious worship do not involve coercion of such individuals. When the power, prestige and financial support of government is placed behind a particular religious belief, the indirect coercive pressure upon religious minorities to conform to the prevailing officially approved religion is plain. But the purposes underlying the Establishment Clause go much further than that. Its first and most immediate purpose rested on the belief that a union of government and religion tends to destroy government and to degrade religion. The history of governmentally established religion, both in England and in this country, showed that whenever government had allied itself with one particular form of religion, the inevitable result had been that it had incurred the hatred, disrespect and even contempt of those who held contrary beliefs. That same history showed that many people had lost their respect for any religion that had relied upon the support of government to spread its faith. The Establishment Clause thus stands as an expression of principle . . . that religion is too personal, too sacred, too holy, to permit its "unhallowed perversion" by a civil magistrate. Another purpose of the Establishment Clause rested upon an awareness of the historical fact that governmentally established religions and religious persecutions go hand in hand. . . . The New York laws officially prescribing the Regents' prayer are inconsistent both with the purposes of the Establishment Clause and with the Establishment Clause itself.

It has been argued that to apply the Constitution in such a way as to prohibit state laws respecting an establishment of religious services in public schools is to indicate a hostility toward religion or toward prayer. Nothing, of course, could be more wrong. The history of man is inseparable from the history of religion. And . . . many people have devoutly believed that "more things are wrought by prayer than this world dreams of." . . . And there were men of this same faith in the power of prayer who led the fight for adoption of our Constitution and also for our Bill of Rights. . . . These men knew that the First Amendment, which tried to put an end to governmental control of religion and of prayer, was not written to destroy either. They knew rather that it was written to quiet well-justified fears . . . arising out of an awareness that governments of the past had shackled men's tongues to make them speak only the religious thoughts that government wanted them to speak and to pray only to the God that government wanted them to pray to. It is neither sacrilegious nor antireligious to say that each separate government in this country should stay out of the business of writing or sanctioning official prayers and leave that purely religious function to the people themselves and to those the people choose to look to for religious guidance.

Source: Engel et al. v. *Vitale et al., 370 U.S. 421.*

SUGGESTIONS FOR BACKGROUND AND REFERENCE

E. Cahn, "On Government and Prayer," *New York University Law Review,* Vol. XXXVII, No. 6 (December 1962), pp. 981–1000.
P. G. Kauper, "Prayer, Public Schools and the Supreme Court," *Michigan Law Review,* Vol. LXI, No. 6 (April 1963), pp. 1031–1068.
L. Pfeffer, *God, Caesar, and the Constitution* (Boston, 1975), pp. 168–227.
A. E. Sutherland, Jr., "Establishment According to Engel," *Harvard Law Review,* Vol. LXXVII, No. 1 (November 1962), pp. 25–52.

166 *Abington School District* v. *Schempp* (Extract)

June 17, 1963

Although regular readings from the Bible had been judicially invalidated in several states, the practice was required or permitted by law in other states, often with provision for the use of different versions of the Bible and for the excused absence of objecting students. In 1963 the Court struck down the practice in a single decision applicable to two similar cases from Pennsylvania and Maryland. The Pennsylvania law stated: "At least ten verses from the Holy Bible shall be read, without comment, at the opening of each public school on each school day. Any child shall be excused from such Bible reading, or attending such Bible reading, upon the written request of his parent or guardian." The Schempp family's suit alleged violation of rights under the First and Fourteenth Amendments. The decision was read by Justice Tom Clark (1899–1977). As in *Engel* v. *Vitale,* Justice Potter Stewart dissented. The passage reproduced below is an extract from the decision.

These companion cases present the issues in the context of state action requiring that schools begin each day with readings from the Bible. . . . In light of the history of the First Amendment and of our cases interpreting and applying its requirements, we hold that the practices at issue and the laws requiring them are unconstitutional under the Establishment Clause, as applied to the states through the Fourteenth Amendment.

* * *

The wholesome "neutrality" of which this Court's cases speak thus stems from a recognition of the teachings of history that powerful sects or groups might bring about a fusion of governmental and religious functions or a concert or dependency of one upon the other to the end that official support of the State or Federal Government would be placed behind the tenets of one or of all orthodoxies. This the Establishment Clause prohibits. And a further reason for neutrality is found in the Free Exercise Clause, which recognizes the value of religious training, teaching and observance and, more particularly, the right of every person to freely choose his own course with reference thereto, free of any compulsion from the state. This the Free Exercise Clause guarantees. Thus, . . . the two clauses may overlap. As we have indicated, the Establishment Clause has been directly considered by this Court eight times in the past score of years and, with only one Justice dissenting on the point, it has consistently held that the clause withdrew all legislative power respecting religious belief or the expression thereof. The test may be stated as follows: what are the purpose and the primary effect of the enactment? If either is the advancement or inhibition of religion then the enactment exceeds the scope of legislative power as circumscribed by the Constitution. That is to say that to withstand the strictures of the Establishment Clause there must be a secular legislative purpose and a primary effect that neither advances nor inhibits religion. . . . The Free Exercise Clause . . . withdraws from legislative power, state and federal, the exertion of any restraint on the free exercise of religion. . . . Hence it is necessary in a free exercise case for one to show the coercive effect of the enactment as it operates against him in the practice of his religion. The distinction between the two clauses is apparent—a violation of the Free Exercise Clause is predicated on coercion while the Establishment Clause violation need not be so attended.

Applying the Establishment Clause principles to the cases at bar we find that the States are requiring the selection and reading at the opening of the school day of verses from the Holy Bible and the recitation of the Lord's Prayer by the students in unison. These exercises are prescribed as part of the curricular activities of students who are required by law to attend school. They are held in the school buildings under the supervision and with the participation of teachers. . . . The trial court in No. 142 [the Pennsylvania case] has found that such an opening exercise is a religious ceremony and was intended by the State to be so. We agree with the trial court's finding. . . . Given that finding the exercises and the law requiring them are in violation of the Establishment Clause.

There is no such specific finding as to the religious character of the exercises in No. 119 [the Maryland case], and the State contends (as does the State in No. 142) that the program is an effort to extend its benefits to all public school children without regard to their religious belief. Included within its secular purposes, it says, are the promotion of moral values, the contradiction to the materialistic trends of our times, the perpetuation of our institutions and the teaching of literature. . . . But even if its purpose is not strictly religious, it is sought to be accomplished through readings, without comment, from the Bible. Surely the place of the Bible as an instrument of religion cannot be gainsaid, and the State's recognition of the pervading religious character of the ceremony is evident from the rule's specific permission of the alternative use of the Catholic Douay version as well as the recent amendment permitting nonattendance at the exercises. None of these factors is consistent with the contention that the Bible is here used either as an instrument for nonreligious moral inspiration or as a reference for the teaching of secular subjects.

The conclusion follows that in both cases the laws require religious exercises and such exercises are being conducted in direct violation of the rights of the appellees. . . . Nor are these required exercises mitigated by the fact that individual students may absent themselves upon parental request, for that fact furnishes no defense to a claim of unconstitutionality under the Establishment Clause. . . . Further, it is no defense to urge that the religious practices here may be relatively minor encroachments on the First Amendment. The breach of neutrality that is today a trickling stream may all too soon become a raging torrent. . . .

It is insisted that unless these religious exercises are permitted a "religion of secularism" is established in the schools. We agree, of course, that the State may not establish a "religion of secularism" in the sense of affirmatively opposing or showing hostility to religion. . . . We do not agree, however, that this decision in any sense has that effect. In addition, it might well be said that one's education is not complete without a study of comparative religion or the history of religion and its relationship to the advancement of civilization. It certainly may be said that the Bible is worthy of study for its literary and historic qualities. Nothing we have said here indicates that such study of the Bible or of religion, when presented objectively as part of a secular program of education, may not be effected consistent with the First Amendment. But the exercises here do not fall into these categories. They are religious exercises, required by the States in violation of the command of the First Amendment that the Government maintain strict neutrality, neither aiding nor opposing religion.

Finally, we cannot accept that the concept of neutrality, which does not permit a State to require a religious exercise even with the consent of the majority of those affected, collides with the majority's right to free exercise of religion. While the Free Exercise Clause clearly prohibits the use of state action to deny the rights of free exercise to *anyone*, it has never meant that a majority could use the machinery of the State to practice its beliefs. . . .

Source: School District of Abington Township, Pennsylvania, et al. v. *Schempp et al.*, 374 U.S. 203.

SUGGESTIONS FOR BACKGROUND AND REFERENCE

D. E. Boles, *The Bible, Religion, and the Public School* (Ames, Iowa, 1961).

J. W. Harrison, "The Bible, the Constitution and Public Education," *Tennessee Law Review*, Vol. XXIX, No. 3 (Spring 1962), pp. 363–418.

A. W. Johnson and F. H. Yost, *Separation of Church and State in the United States* (Minneapolis, 1948), pp. 33–73.

L. Pfeffer, *God, Caesar, and the Constitution* (Boston, 1975), pp. 168–227.

L. H. Pollak, "Public Prayers in Public Schools," *Harvard Law Review*, Vol. LXXVII, No. 1 (November 1963), pp. 62–78.

✦ ✦ ✦

167 Vatican Council Declaration on Religious Freedom (Extracts)

December 7, 1965

The accession of John XXIII (1958–1963) marked the beginning of a broad movement of *aggiornamento,* ecumenism, and reform in the Catholic Church. To forward this policy the pope called the second Vatican Council, which met in four sessions between 1962 and 1965 (the last three sessions under his successor, Paul VI). While the Council's declaration on religious liberty was widely supported, it was notably advocated by the American episcopate and reflected the thought of the American Jesuit, John Courtney Murray. It was opposed by a minority drawn largely from southern Europe and Latin America. Temporarily postponed at the close of the third session, the declaration "on the right of the person and of communities to social and civil freedom in matters religious" was at last given decisive approval by a vote of 1,997 to 224 on September 21, 1965. It was promulgated on December 7 in an amended form (stressing Catholicism as the one true church, to meet some conservative objections). The statement was expected to strengthen religious liberty in some Catholic countries and to encourage movements toward Christian unity.

The document is too long for extensive reproduction. Below are extracts discussing religious freedom in relation to the individual, the religious community, the family, civil society, and the church.

2. This Vatican Synod declares that the human person has a right to religious freedom. This freedom means that all men are to be immune from coercion on the part of individuals or of social groups and of any human power, in such wise that in matters religious no one is to be forced to act . . . contrary to his own beliefs. Nor is anyone to be restrained from acting in accordance with his own beliefs, whether privately or publicly, whether alone or in association with others, within due limits.

The Synod further declares that the right to religious freedom has its foundation in the very dignity of the human person, as this dignity is known through the revealed Word of God and by reason itself. This right . . . is to be recognized in the constitutional law whereby society is governed. Thus it is to become a civil right.

It is in accordance with their dignity as persons—that is, beings endowed with reason and free will and therefore privileged to bear personal responsibility—that all men should be at once impelled by nature and also bound by a moral obligation to seek the truth, especially religious truth. They are also bound to adhere to the

From Walter M. Abbott (ed.), *The Documents of Vatican II* (New York, 1966). Copyright, 1966, by The America Press. Reprinted by permission of the publisher.

truth, once it is known, and to order their whole lives in accord with the demands of truth.

However, men cannot discharge these obligations in a manner in keeping with their own nature unless they enjoy immunity from external coercion as well as psychological freedom. Therefore the right to religious freedom has its foundation, not in the subjective disposition of the person, but in his very nature. In consequence, the right to this immunity continues to exist even in those who do not live up to their obligation of seeking the truth and adhering to it. Nor is the exercise of this right to be impeded, provided that the just requirements of public order are preserved.

3. Further light is shed on the subject if one considers that the highest norm of human life is the divine law—eternal, objective, and universal—whereby God orders, directs, and governs the entire universe. . . . Man has been made by God to participate in this law, with the result that . . . he can come to perceive ever increasingly the unchanging truth. Hence every man has the duty, and therefore the right, to seek the truth in matters religious, in order that he may with prudence form for himself right and true judgments of conscience, with the use of all suitable means.

Truth, however, is to be sought after in a manner proper to the dignity of the human person and his social nature. The inquiry is to be free, carried on with the aid of teaching or instruction, communication and dialogue. In the course of these, men explain to one another the truth they have discovered, or think they have discovered, in order thus to assist one another in the quest for truth. Moreover, as the truth is discovered, it is by a personal assent that men are to adhere to it.

On his part, man perceives and acknowledges the imperatives of the divine law through the mediation of conscience. In all his activity a man is bound to follow his conscience faithfully, in order that he may come to God. . . . It follows that he is not to be forced to act in a manner contrary to his conscience. Nor, . . . is he to be restrained from acting in accordance with his conscience. . . .

For, of its very nature, the exercise of religion consists before all else in those internal, voluntary, and free acts whereby man sets the course of his life directly toward God. No merely human power can either command or prohibit acts of this kind.

However, the social nature of man itself requires that he should give external expression to his internal acts of religion; that he should participate with others in matters religious; that he should profess his religion in community. Injury, therefore, is done to the human person and to the very order established by God for human life, if the free exercise of religion is denied in society when the just requirements of public order do not so require.

There is a further consideration. The religious acts whereby men, in private and in public and out of a sense of personal conviction, direct their lives to God transcend by their very nature the order of terrestrial and temporal affairs. Government, therefore, ought indeed to take account of the religious life of the people and show it favor, since the function of government is to make provision for the common welfare. However, it would clearly transgress the limits set to its power were it to presume to command or inhibit acts that are religious.

4. The freedom or immunity from coercion in matters religious which is the endowment of persons as individuals is also to be recognized as their right when they act in community. Religious bodies are a requirement of the social nature both of man and of religion itself.

Provided the just requirements of public order are observed, religious bodies rightfully claim freedom in order that they may govern themselves according to their own norms, honor the Supreme Being in public worship, assist their members in the practice of the religious life, strengthen them by instruction, and promote institutions in which they may join together. . . .

Religious bodies also have the right not to be hindered, either by legal measures or by administrative action on the part of government, in the selection, training, appointment, and transferral of their own ministers, in coummunicating with religious authorities and communities abroad, in erecting buildings for religious purposes, and in the acquisition and use of suitable funds or properties.

Religious bodies also have the right not to be hindered in their public teaching and witness to their faith, whether by the spoken or by the written word. However, in spreading religious faith and in introducing religious practices, everyone ought . . . to refrain from any . . . action which might seem to carry a hint of coercion or of a kind of persuasion that would be dishonorable or unworthy, especially when dealing with poor or uneducated people. . . .

5. Since the family is a society in its own original right, it has the right freely to live its own domestic religious life under the guidance of parents. Parents, moreover, have the right to determine . . . the kind of religious education that their children are to receive.

Government . . . must acknowledge the right of parents to make a genuinely free choice of schools. . . . The use of this freedom . . . is not to be made a reason for imposing unjust burdens on parents, whether directly or indirectly. Besides, the rights of parents are violated if their children are forced to attend lessons or instructions which are not in agreement with their religious beliefs. The same is true if a single system of education, from which all religious formation is excluded, is imposed upon all.

6. The common welfare . . . consists in . . . conditions of social life under which men enjoy the possibility of achieving their own perfection. . . . Hence this welfare consists chiefly in the protection of the rights, and in the performance of the duties, of the human person. Therefore the care of the right to religious freedom devolves upon the people as a whole, upon social groups, upon government, and upon the Church and other religious Communities. . . .

The protection and promotion of the inviolable rights of man ranks among the essential duties of government. Therefore government is to assume the safeguard of the religious freedom of all its citizens, in an effective manner, by just laws and by other appropriate means. Government is also to help create conditions favorable to the fostering of religious life, in order that the people may be truly enabled to exercise their religious rights and to fulfill their religious duties, and also in order that society itself may profit by the moral qualities of justice and peace which have their origin in men's faithfulness to God and to His holy will.

If, in view of peculiar circumstances obtaining among certain peoples, special

legal recognition is given . . . to one religious body, it is at the same time imperative that the right of all citizens and religious bodies to religious freedom should be
recognized and made effective in practice.

Finally, government is to see to it that the equality of citizens before the law,
which is itself an element of the common welfare, is never violated, for religious
reasons, whether openly or covertly. Nor is there to be discrimination among
citizens.

It follows that a wrong is done when government imposes upon its people, by
force or fear or other means, the profession or repudiation of any religion, or when
it hinders men from joining or leaving a religious body. All the more is it a violation
of the will of God and of the sacred rights of the person and the family of nations,
when force is brought to bear in any way in order to destroy or repress religion,
either in the whole of mankind or in a particular country or in a specific community.

7. The right to religious freedom is exercised in human society: hence its
exercise is subject to certain regulatory norms. In the use of all freedoms the moral
principle of personal and social responsibility is to be observed. . . .

Furthermore, society has the right to defend itself against possible abuses committed on pretext of freedom of religion. It is the special duty of government to
provide this protection. However, government is not to act in arbitrary fashion or in
an unfair spirit of partisanship. Its action is to be controlled by juridical norms
which are in conformity with the objective moral order.

These norms arise out of the need for effective safeguard of the rights of all
citizens and for peaceful settlement of conflicts of rights. They flow from the need
for an adequate care of genuine public peace. . . . They come, finally out of the
need for a proper guardianship of public morality.

* * *

9. The declaration of this Vatican Synod on the right of man to religious
freedom has its foundation in the dignity of the person. The requirements of this
dignity have come to be more adequately known to human reason, through centuries
of experience. What is more, this doctrine of freedom has roots in divine revelation,
and for this reason Christians are bound to respect it all the more conscientiously.

Revelation does not indeed affirm in so many words the right of man to immunity from external coercion in matters religious. It does, however, disclose the
dignity of the human person in its full dimensions. It gives evidence of the respect
which Christ showed toward the freedom with which man is to fulfill his duty of
belief in the Word of God. It gives us lessons too in the spirit which disciples of
such a Master ought to make their own and to follow in every situation. In particular, religious freedom in society is entirely consonant with the freedom of the act of
Christian faith.

10. It is one of the major tenets of Catholic doctrine that man's response to God
in faith must be free. Therefore no one is to be forced to embrace the Christian faith
against his own will. This doctrine is contained in the Word of God and it was
constantly proclaimed by the Fathers of the Church. The act of faith is of its very
nature a free act. Man, redeemed by Christ the Savior and through Christ Jesus
called to be God's adopted son, cannot give his adherence to God revealing Himself

unless the Father draw him to offer to God the reasonable and free submission of faith.

It is therefore completely in accord with the nature of faith that in matters religious every manner of coercion on the part of men should be excluded. In consequence, the principle of religious freedom makes no small contribution to the creation of an environment in which men can without hindrance be invited to Christian faith and embrace it of their own free will, and profess it effectively in their whole manner of life.

* * *

12. The Church therefore is being faithful to the truth of the gospel, and is following the way of Christ and the apostles when she recognizes, and gives support to, the principle of religious freedom. . . . Throughout the ages, the Church has kept safe and handed on the doctrine received from the Master and from the apostles. In the life of the People of God, . . . there have at times appeared ways of acting which were less in accord with the spirit of the gospel or even opposed to it. Nevertheless, the doctrine of the Church that no one is to be coerced into faith has always stood firm. . . .

13. Among the things which concern the good of the Church and indeed the welfare of society here on earth—things therefore which are always and everywhere to be kept secure and defended against all injury—this certainly is preeminent, namely, that the Church should enjoy that full measure of freedom which her care for the salvation of men requires. This freedom is sacred, because the only-begotten Son endowed with it the Church which He purchased with His blood. It is so much the property of the Church that to act against it is to act against the will of God. The freedom of the Church is the fundamental principle in what concerns the relations between the Church and governments and the whole civil order.

In human society and in the face of government, the Church claims freedom for herself in her character as a spiritual authority, established by Christ the Lord. Upon this authority there rests, by divine mandate, the duty of going out into the whole world and preaching the gospel to every creature. The Church also claims freedom for herself in her character as a society of men who have the right to live in society in accordance with the precepts of Christian faith.

* * *

At the same time, the Christian faithful, in common with all other men, possess the civil right not to be hindered in leading their lives in accordance with their conscience. Therefore, a harmony exists between the freedom of the Church and the religious freedom which is to be recognized as the right of all men and communities and sanctioned by constitutional law.

* * *

15. The fact is that men of the present day want to be able freely to profess their religion in private and in public. Religious freedom has already been declared to be a civil right in most constitutions, and it is solemnly recognized in international documents. The further fact is that forms of government still exist under which,

even though freedom of religious worship receives constitutional recognition, the powers of government are engaged in the effort to deter citizens from the profession of religion and to make life difficult and dangerous for religious Communities.

This sacred Synod greets with joy the first of these two facts, as among the signs of the times. With sorrow, however, it denounces the other fact, as only to be deplored. The Synod exhorts Catholics, and it directs a plea to all men, most carefully to consider how greatly necessary religious freedom is, especially in the present condition of the human family.

All nations are coming into even closer unity. Men of different cultures and religions are being brought together in closer relationships. There is a growing consciousness of the personal responsibility that weighs upon every man. All this is evident.

Consequently, in order that relationships of peace and harmony may be established ·and maintained within the whole of mankind, it is necessary that religious freedom be everywhere provided with an effective constitutional guarantee, and that respect be shown for the high duty and right of man freely to lead his religious life in society.

Source: Walter M. Abbott (ed.), *The Documents of Vatican II* (New York, 1966), pp. 678–690, 692–696. Latin text, "Dignitatis Humanae Personae," *Acta Apostolicae Sedis* (1966) (Rome, 1967), LVIII, 929–946.

SUGGESTIONS FOR BACKGROUND AND REFERENCE

G. A. Bull, *Vatican Politics at the Second Vatican Council, 1962–5* (London, 1966).

A. Hastings (ed.), *Modern Catholicism: Vatican II and After* (London, 1990).

T. T. Love, "John Courtney Murray, S.J.: Liberal Roman Catholic Church-State Theory," *Journal of Religion,* Vol. 45, No. 3 (July, 1965), pp. 211–224.

J. C. Murray, *The Problem of Religious Freedom* (Westminster, Md., 1965).

K. Rahner, *Toleranz in der Kirche* (Freiburg im Breisgau, 1977).

R. E. Tracy, "Letter from the Council: Steps toward Declaration on Religious Liberty," *America,* Vol. 113, No. 15 (October 9, 1965), pp. 397–399.

R. M. Wiltgen, *The Rhine Flows into the Tiber: A History of Vatican II* (Devon, England, 1979).

V. A. Yzermans (ed.), *American Participation in the Second Vatican Council* (New York, 1967), pp. 617–676.

✦ ✦ ✦ Religion and Racial Policy in South Africa

168   Anglican Bishops' Protest Against Apartheid

March 6, 1957

South Africa's white settlement began in the mid-seventeenth century, but in the twentieth century the politically and economically dominant whites did not exceed one-fifth of the population. The vast majority were black (and divided by tribal allegiances); large colored and Indian minorities were also important. Compounding ethnic complexity was the division of whites (and colored and some blacks) into competing language cultures—Afrikaans and English. Of particular importance in modern South African history was the aspiration of many white Afrikaners to combat both nonwhite dissension and the established English urban culture and to reshape the nation as a European-dominated, Afrikaans-speaking society. The National Party, founded in 1913 and consistently in power after 1948, pursued this goal through "apartheid" or separateness, an amalgam of historic social segregation, racial doctrine, religious apologetic and paternalism, and the quest for political and economic security. Rapid implementation of apartheid theory into law after 1948 coincided with increasing political consciousness on the part of nonwhite peoples, much of it focused by the African National Congress, founded in 1912.

Segregation enacted for sexual relations, residential areas, employment, transport, and public amenities was extended to religion by the Native Laws Amendment Act (1957), which by enforcing restrictions on nonwhites entering white areas, mandated segregated worship. The policy elicited protest from English-language Protestant and Catholic churches (which had large nonwhite majorities), though white laity do not always appear to have supported clerical leadership in this regard; response of the several churches of the Dutch Reformed Afrikaans tradition was far more ambiguous. Of the English churches the Anglican communion was largest. Led by Geoffrey Clayton (1884–1957), archbishop of Cape Town, its bishops sent a letter of warning to the prime minister and thus embarked on what was to be the religious response to apartheid during the next three decades—conscientious disobedience to laws deemed unchristian.

It appears to us that, as far as the Anglican Church is concerned, churches and congregations in every urban area within the Union, even those mainly attended by Europeans, will be affected by this clause. . . .

We desire to state that we regard the . . . Clause as an infringement of religious freedom in that it makes conditional on the permission of the Minister of Native Affairs:

(a) The continuance in existence of any church or parish constituted after January 1, 1938 in an urban area, except in a location, which does not exclude Native Africans from public worship;

(b) The holding of any service in any church in an urban area, except in a location, in which a Native African would be admitted if he presented himself;

(c) The attendance of any Native African at any synod or church assembly held in an urban area outside a location.[1]

The Church cannot recognise the right of an official of a secular Government to determine whether or where a member of the Church of any race (who is not serving a sentence which restricts his freedom of movement) shall discharge his religious duty of participation in public worship or to give instructions to the minister of any congregation as to whom he shall admit to membership of that congregation.

Further, the Constitution of the Church of the Province of South Africa provides for the synodical government of the Church. In such synods, bishops, priests and laymen are represented without distinction of race or colour. Clause 29 (c) makes the holding of such synods dependent upon the permission of the Minister of Native Affairs.

We recognise the great gravity of disobedience to the law of the land. We believe that obedience to secular authorities, even in matters about which we differ in opinion, is a command laid upon us by God. But we are commanded to render unto Caesar the things which be Caesar's, and to God the things that are God's. There are therefore some matters which are God's and not Caesar's, and we believe that the matters dealt with in Clause 29 (c) are among them.

It is because we believe this that we feel bound to state that if the Bill were to become law in its present form we should ourselves be unable to obey it or to counsel our clergy and people to do so.

Source: Cape Times, March 9, 1957.

SUGGESTIONS FOR BACKGROUND AND REFERENCE

J. W. De Gruchy, *The Church Struggle in South Africa* (Grand Rapids, Mich., 1986).

A. Paton, *Apartheid and the Archbishop: The Life and Times of Geoffrey Clayton* (New York, 1973).

M. E. Worsnip, *Between the Two Fires: the Anglican Church and Apartheid, 1948–1957* (Pietermaritzburg, South Africa, 1991).

1. "Location" signifies an area officially set apart for nonwhite settlement and residence.

169 Cottesloe Consultation Statement (Extracts)

December 1960

Racial strife exploded with riots and a bloody confrontation at Sharpe-ville in 1960, calling world attention to South Africa's social turmoil and controversial race policies. In response the World Council of Churches sponsored a conference of the churches of Cape Province and Transvaal at Cottesloe near Johannesburg, December 7 to 14, 1960. Since the conference included both the English churches and the large and influential Afrikaner Nederduitse Gereformeerde Kerk (NGK), then a member of the WCC, "widely divergent convictions" were expressed on the policy of apartheid. As a result, the consensus "statement" was necessarily moderate and compromising, though article 6 challenged a basic presupposition of apartheid in the affirmation that "no one who believes in Jesus Christ may be excluded from any Church on the grounds of his colour or race." Participation in Cottesloe was a critical moment for the Reformed communion and might have led to a gradual moderation of apartheid through Afrikaans religious influence. Instead, government outrage, public criticism, and dissension within the NGK eventuated in its withdrawal from the WCC. Thirteen years later, in 1974, the church adopted a declaration, based on biblical and theological argument, defending South Africa's racial course.

The general theme of our seven days together has been the Christian attitude towards race relations. We are united in rejecting all unjust discrimination. Nevertheless, widely divergent convictions have been expressed on the basic issues of apartheid. They range on the one hand from the judgment that it is unacceptable in principle, contrary to the Christian calling and unworkable in practice, to the conviction on the other hand that a policy of differentiation can be defended from the Christian point of view, that it provides the only realistic solution to the problems of race relations and is therefore in the best interests of the various population groups.

Although proceeding from these divergent views, we are nevertheless able to make the following affirmations. . . .

The Church of Jesus Christ, by its nature and calling, is deeply concerned with the welfare of all people, both as individuals and as members of social groups. It is called to minister to human need in whatever circumstances and forms it appears, and to insist that all be done with justice. In its social witness the Church must take cognizance of all attitudes, forces, policies, and laws which affect the life of a people; but the Church must proclaim that the final criterion of all social and political action is the principles of Scripture regarding the realization of all men of a life worthy of their God-given vocation. . . .

1. We recognize that all racial groups who permanently inhabit our country are a part of our total population, and we regard them as indigenous. Members of all

From John De Gruchy and Charles Villa-Vicencio (eds.), *Apartheid is a Heresy* (Cape Town, 1983). Copyright, 1983, by David Philip Publishers Ltd. Reprinted by permission of the publisher.

these groups have an equal right to make their contribution towards the enrichment of the life of their country and to share in the ensuing responsibilities, rewards and privileges.

2. The present tension in South Africa is the result of a long historical development and all groups bear responsibility for it. This must also be seen in relation to events in other parts of the world. The South African scene is radically affected by the decline of the power of the West and by the desire for self-determination among the peoples of the African continent.

3. The Church has a duty to bear witness to the hope which is in Christianity both to white South Africans in their uncertainty and to non-white South Africans in their frustration.

4. In a period of rapid social change the Church has a special responsibility for fearless witness within society.

5. The Church as the body of Christ is a unity and within this unity the natural diversity among men is not annulled but sanctified.

6. No one who believes in Jesus Christ may be excluded from any Church on the grounds of his colour or race. The spiritual unity among all men who are in Christ must find visible expression in acts of common worship and witness, and in fellowship and consultation on matters of common concern.

* * *

10. There are no Scriptural grounds for the prohibition of mixed marriages. The well-being of the community and pastoral responsibility require, however, that due consideration should be given to certain factors which may make such marriages inadvisable.

11. We call attention once again to the disintegrating effects of migrant labour on African life. No stable society is possible unless the cardinal importance of family life is recognized, and, from the Christian standpoint, it is imperative that the integrity of the family be safeguarded.

12. It is now widely recognized that the wages received by the vast majority of the non-white people oblige them to exist well below the generally accepted minimum standard for healthy living. . . .

13. The present system of job reservation must give way to a more equitable system of labour. . . .

14. Opportunities must be provided for the inhabitants of the Bantu races to live in conformity with human dignity.

15. It is our conviction that the right to own land wherever he is domiciled, and to partake in the government of his country, is part of the dignity of the adult man, and for this reason a policy which permanently denies to non-white people the right of collaboration in the government of the country of which they are citizens cannot be justified.

16. (a) It is our conviction that there can be no objection in principle to the direct representation of coloured people in Parliament. (b) We express the hope that consideration will be given to the application of this principle in the foreseeable future.

17. In so far as nationalism grows out of a desire for self-realization, Christians

should understand and respect it. The danger of nationalism is, however, that it may seek to fulfil its aim at the expense of the interests of others and that it can make the nation an absolute value which takes the place of God. The role of the Church must therefore be to help to direct national movements towards just and worthy ends.

Source: John De Gruchy and Charles Villa-Vicencio (eds.), *Apartheid is a Heresy* (Cape Town, 1983), pp. 149–151.

SUGGESTIONS FOR BACKGROUND AND REFERENCE

D. Balia, *Christian Resistance to Apartheid: Ecumenism in South Afrika* (Hamburg, 1939).

A. Boesak, *Black and Reformed: Apartheid, Liberation and the Calvinist Tradition* (Maryknoll, N.Y., 1984).

J. W. De Gruchy, *The Church Struggle in South Africa* (Grand Rapids, Mich., 1986), pp. 62–69.

J. H. P. Serfontein, *Apartheid Change and the NG Kerk* (Emmarentia, South Africa, 1982).

C. Villa-Vicencio, *Trapped in Apartheid* (Maryknoll, N.Y., 1988).

170 "A Message to the People of South Africa" (Extracts)

May 1968

The Christian Council, transformed into the South African Council of Churches in 1968, represented most of the English churches and the nonwhite Reformed Mission church, Nederduitse Gereformeerde Sendingkerk, the only Afrikaans church that remained in ecumenical communion with other churches. In 1968 the SACC issued "A Message to the People of South Africa," which was endorsed by nearly all member churches. The "Message" went beyond the more temporizing Cottesloe statement, rejecting apartheid entirely as a false gospel irreconcilable with Christian faith. The "Message" also made clear the fundamental schism between Christian imperatives and the South African social and political system and warned that "we must obey God rather than men."

We, in this country, and at this time, are in a situation where a policy of racial separation is being deliberately effected with increasing rigidity. The effects of this are to be seen in a widening range of aspects of life—in political, economic, social, educational and religious life; indeed, there are few areas even of the private life of the individual which are untouched by the effects of the doctrine of racial separation. In consequence, this doctrine is being seen by many not merely as a temporary political policy but as a necessary and permanent expression of the will of God, and as the genuine form of Christian obedience for this country. But this doctrine, together with the hardships which are deriving from its implementation, forms a programme which is truly hostile to Christianity and can serve only to keep people away from the real knowledge of Christ.

There are alarming signs that this doctrine of separation has become, for many, a false faith, a novel Gospel which offers happiness and peace for the community and for the individual. It holds out to men a security built not on Christ but on the theory of separation and the preservation of their racial identity. It presents separate development of our race-groups as a way for the people of South Africa to save themselves. Such a claim inevitably conflicts with the Christian Gospel, which offers salvation, both social and individual, through faith in Christ alone.

This false offer of salvation is being made in this country in the name of Christianity. Therefore, we believe that the Church must enable all our people to distinguish between this false, novel Gospel and the true eternal Gospel of Jesus Christ. We believe that it is the Church's duty to enable our people to discriminate more carefully between what may be demanded of them as subjects or citizens of the State of South Africa and what is demanded of them as disciples of Jesus Christ. . . .

The first Christians, both Jews and Gentiles, discovered that God was creating a new community in which differences of race, nation, culture, language and tradition no longer had power to separate man from man. . . . The most significant features of a man are the characteristics which enable him to be a disciple of Christ—his ability to respond to love, to make choices, to work as a servant of his fellowmen; these are the gifts of the grace of God at work in the individual person; and to insist that racial characteristics are more important than these is to reject our own humanity as well as the humanity of the other man.

But in South Africa, everyone is expected to believe that a man's racial identity is the most important thing about him. Until a man's racial identity is established, virtually no decisions can be taken; but, once it is established it can be stated where he can live, whom he can marry, what work he can do, what education he can get, whose hospitality he can accept, where he can get medical treatment, where he can be buried—and the answer to multitudes of other questions can be supplied once this vital fact is established. . . . This amounts to a denial of the central statements of the Gospel. It is opposed to the Christian understanding of the nature of man and community. It, in practice, severely restricts the ability of Christian brothers to serve and know each other, and even to give each other simple hospitality. It arbitrarily limits the ability of a person to obey the Gospel's command to love his neighbour as himself. . . .

The Bible's teaching about creation has nothing to say about the distinctions between races and nations. God made man—the whole human race—in his image. . . . Where differences between people are used as badges or signs of opposing groups, this is due to human sin. . . . Any scheme which is claimed to be Christian must also take account of the reconciliation already made for us in Christ. The policy of separate development does not take proper account of these truths. It promises peace and harmony between the peoples of our country not by a faithful and obedient pursuit of the reconciliation wrought by Christ, but through separation, which, being precisely the opposite course, is a demonstration of unbelief and distrust in the power of the Gospel. Any demonstration of the reality of reconciliation would endanger this policy; therefore the advocates of this policy inevitably find themselves opposed to the Church if it seeks to live according to the Gospel and if it shows that God's grace has overcome our hostilities. A thorough policy of racial separation must ultimately require that the Church should cease to be the Church.

* * *

Many of our people believe that their primary loyalty must be to their group or tradition or political doctrine, and that this is how their faithfulness will be judged. But this is not how God judges us. In fact, this kind of belief is a direct threat to the true salvation of many people, for it comes as an attractive substitute for the claims of Jesus. . . . But God judges us, not by our faithfulness to a sectional group, but by our willingness to be made new in the community of Christ. We believe that we are under an obligation to state that our country and Church are under God's judgment, and that Christ is inevitably a threat to much that is called "the South African way of life." We must ask ourselves what features of our social order will have to pass away if the lordship of Christ is to be fully acknowledged and if the peace of God is to be revealed as the destroyer of our fear.

But we believe that Christ is Lord, and that South Africa is part of his world. . . . And so we wish to put to every Christian person in this country the question which we ourselves are bound to face each day, to whom, or to what, are you truly giving your first loyalty, your primary commitment? Is it to a subsection of mankind, an ethnic group, a human tradition, a political idea; or to Christ?

Source: John De Gruchy and Charles Villa-Vicencio (eds.), *Apartheid is a Heresy* (Cape Town, 1983), pp. 155–159.

SUGGESTIONS FOR BACKGROUND AND REFERENCE

J. W. De Gruchy, *The Church Struggle in South Africa* (Grand Rapids, Mich., 1986), pp. 115–127.
References for Document 169.

171   *Status Confessionis* Resolve of the Nederduitse Gereformeerde Sendingkerk

October 1982

Intensification of racial conflict characterized the 1970s as the government attempted mass population removals, and the ANC, banned since 1960, retaliated with violence and industrial sabotage. In the early 1980s the government announced reforms, dismantling some features of the apartheid system and improving conditions for Indians, colored, and urban Africans with residential rights though not for the mass of the black population. But by 1982 momentum for reform was halted by "hard-liner" defections from the National Party and rightist election successes. With the silencing of other protest leaders, black and colored churchmen gained prominence as opponents of the state's social agenda. Notable among them were Desmond Tutu, Anglican archbishop of Cape Town, and Allan Boesak, statesman of the Reformed Mission Church (NG Sendingkerk) and in 1982 president of the World Alliance of Reformed Churches. In that year the WARC, meeting in Ottawa, judged apartheid to be a Christian heresy and suspended the NGK and the smaller Nederduitsch Hervormde Kerk (NHK) from membership until they abandoned theological justification for South African racial policy. The NHK immediately withdrew; the NGK, resolving that the WARC action was "taken from a standpoint of liberation theology . . . in conflict with the Bible and Reformed theology," declined to withdraw but declared that "for practical purposes" it no longer regarded itself as a full member.

This action by the Mission Church completed the rupture. Entrenched among the Afrikaans-speaking colored population, the NG Sendingkerk was a product of Reformed missionary endeavor and the practice of segregated worship, instituted in the mid-nineteenth century. Following the Ottawa decision, its synod confirmed apartheid as heresy and broke its relation with the NGK, thereby repudiating the segregation that had brought it into being a century earlier. (In 1986 the NGK, reflecting shifts in South African opinion and politics, again condemned racism as sin and agreed that segregation lacked biblical imperative and harmony with Christian morality.)

The political and ecclesiastical order of South Africa is an order within which irreconcilability has been elevated to a fundamental social principle within which, in spite of supposed good intentions, the greed and prejudice of the powerful and the privileged are entrenched at the cost of those who are powerless and without privileges. . . .

Apartheid is a system within which people are separated from one another, *and kept apart from one another.*

The possibility that these groups *can* be brought together and that peaceful coexistence *can* replace tension and conflict is ruled out as a matter of principle. Therefore, ethnic groups, to the extent that this is possible, must be compelled, by law if necessary, to remain separate from one another, because the bringing of these groups of people together will necessarily result in conflict and the mutual threatening of one another.

* * *

The visible effect of reconciliation between God and man is the existence of the Church as a *reconciling community of people,* a unified community. The message of reconciliation is entrusted to this Church. The invitation is extended to the world and to all people who inhabit it to reconcile themselves to God and to one another. In Christ, the Church says, there is new hope, there are new possibilities for the world. Sinfulness and hatred, enmity and separation need not be the last word, but rather reconciliation and peace. Christ has made this possible.

The Church will always bear witness to the fact that no order of communal living which fundamentally affirms the irreconcilability of people and groups of people can be regarded as acceptable. Such a point of departure binds people to their past history of enmity and hate—it invalidates the Gospel.

We do not simply present one or more Bible texts. It is always easy to use biblical texts to one's own end. . . .

No! The touchstone for apartheid is the essential biblical message of reconciliation. If it fails here, a few disparate biblical texts cannot save it. . . .

* * *

Racism is an ideology of racial domination which includes a belief in the inherent, cultural and biological inferiority of certain races and racial groups. It is also a political and an economic system that determines the unequal treatment of these groups at the level of law, structures and institutions. Racism does not merely concern the attitude of people, it is also structural. It does not merely concern the *feeling* of inferiority in relation to another person or group, but the *system* of political, social and economic domination. . . . Where this racism is regimentally imposed in Church and communal structures it denies the community of believers the possibility of being human and it denies the reconciling and the humanizing work of Christ.

In South Africa apartheid in the Church and in society leans to a significant extent on the theological and moral justification of the system. Apartheid is therefore a pseudo-religious ideology as well as a political policy. It allows itself to be validated within the realms of both Church and state, and in so doing it influences and structurally controls the entire South African society. . . .

Because the secular Gospel of apartheid threatens in the deepest possible way the witness of reconciliation in Jesus Christ and the unity of the Church . . . , the NG Mission Church . . . declares that this constitutes a *status confessionis* for the Church of Jesus Christ. (A *status confessionis* means that we regard this matter as a concern about which it is impossible to differ without it affecting the integrity of our communal confession as Reformed Churches.)

We declare that apartheid (separate development) is a sin, that the moral and theological justification of it makes a mockery of the Gospel, and that its consistent disobedience to the Word of God is a theological heresy. . . .

According to the conviction of the Synod the NGK believes in the ideology of apartheid. . . . Therefore . . . we can do no other than with the deepest regret accuse the NGK of theological heresy and idolatry. This is done in the light of her theologically formulated standpoint and its implementation in practice.

* * *

The Synod resolves that its decision regarding the *status confessionis* be officially handed to the NGK at its General Synod sitting in Pretoria and that it also be sent to the different regional synods.

The NG Mission Church regrets that its relationship with the NGK is seriously threatened. The Synod is of the opinion that the road of reconciliation can only be walked if the NGK confesses its guilt . . . and concretely demonstrates her repentance by working out what the consequences of this confession of guilt mean in both Church and state. . . .

Source: John De Gruchy and Charles Villa-Vicencio (eds.), *Apartheid is a Heresy* (Cape Town, 1983), pp. 175–181.

SUGGESTIONS FOR BACKGROUND AND REFERENCE

G. D. Cloete and D. J. Smit (eds.), *A Moment of Truth: The Confession of the Dutch Reformed Mission Church* (Grand Rapids, Mich., 1984).
References for Document 169.
Source for this document.

✦✦✦ Latin American Catholicism and Liberation Theology

172 Medellín Conference of Latin American Bishops (Extracts)

September 1968

In the mid-twentieth century "liberation theology" became a significant component of Latin American Catholicism. During colonial centuries the church had been closely and often uncritically allied with Spanish state and culture, a pattern only slightly modified by nineteenth-century independence and republicanism. But by the end of the century political liberalism, religious indifference, and anticlericalism sapped Catholic vitality, and "secularization" made an appearance, especially among the urban bourgeoisie. Not until the 1930s were new stirrings evident. Then, as economic depression weakened liberal confidence and reactionary authoritarian regimes revived (sometimes with religious support), a Catholic intellectual quickening began to develop, stimulated by both European and Latin American theologians and social theorists. Organizationally also, revitalization was signaled by the founding of the General Conference of the Latin American Episcopate at Rio de Janeiro in

1955 and the presence of over six hundred Latin American bishops at Vatican II in the 1960s. Of immense importance at the common level was the spontaneous growth of the "grass-roots" institution (*comunidad de base*), where small clusters of neighbors organized to discuss problems and resist oppression—an institution that soon became vital to popular church life.

These influences came together at the second General Conference at Medellín in 1968 to give focus to an emerging Catholic social policy. At the opening Paul VI stressed social justice but cautioned against revolution or violence. The final Conference statement ventured beyond this restraint, and though easily approved, was controversial. Its language reflected Brazilian leadership and disturbed both curial and episcopal conservatives, notably the Columbian hierarchy. Eschewing ideas of liberalism or "progress," it declared solidarity with the poor and indicted exploitation by both regional conservatives and international capitalism. While deploring violence and warning that its use would create new evils, the Conference also called attention to the "institutionalized violence" of a repressive status quo and guardedly conceded that force might be inevitable in extreme circumstances. Nonetheless, principal stress fell on the church's role in awakening and instructing oppressed and apolitical masses through organization, education, and mobilization of public conscience. After 1968 the movement produced a large literature, conflicting interpretations, and controversy, while criticism attacked its alleged dependence on Marxian categories. Reproduced below is a passage from the document on "Peace."

As the Christian believes in the productiveness of peace in order to achieve justice, he also believes that justice is a prerequisite for peace. He recognizes that in many instances Latin America finds itself faced with a situation of injustice that can be called institutionalized violence, when, because of a structural deficiency of industry and agriculture, of national and international economy, of cultural and political life, "whole towns lack necessities . . . ," thus violating fundamental rights. This situation demands all-embracing courageous, urgent and profoundly renovating transformations. We should not be surprised, therefore, that the "temptation to violence" is surfacing in Latin America. One should not abuse the patience of a people that for years has borne a situation that would not be acceptable to any one with any degree of awareness of human rights. . . .

We would like to direct our call in the first place, to those who have a greater share of wealth, culture and power. We know that there are leaders in Latin America who are sensitive to the needs of the people and try to remedy them. They recognize that the privileged many times join together, and . . . pressure those who govern, thus obstructing necessary changes. . . . . Therefore, we urge them not to take advantage of the pacifist position of the Church in order to oppose, either actively or passively, the profound transformations that are so necessary. If they jealously retain their privileges, and defend them through violence, they are responsible to history for provoking "explosive revolutions of despair." The peaceful future of the countries of Latin America depends to a large extent on their attitude.

Also responsible for injustice are those who remain passive for fear of the sacrifice and personal risk implied by any courageous and effective action. Justice, and therefore peace, conquer by means of a dynamic action of awakening (concientizacion) and organization of the popular sectors, which are capable of pressing public officials who are often impotent in their social projects without popular support.

We address ourselves, finally, to those who, in the face of injustice and illegitimate resistance to change, put their hopes in violence. . . . .

If it is true that revolutionary insurrection can be legitimate in the case of evident and prolonged "tyranny that seriously works against the fundamental rights of man, and which damages the common good of the country," whether it proceeds from one person or from clearly unjust structures, it is also certain that violence or "armed revolution" generally "generates new injustices, introduces new imbalances and causes new disasters, one cannot combat a real evil at the price of a greater evil."[1]

If we consider, then, the totality of the circumstances of our countries, and if we take into account the Christian preference for peace, the enormous difficulty of a civil war, the logic of violence, the atrocities it engenders, the risk of provoking foreign intervention, . . . the difficulty of building a regime of justice and freedom while participating in a process of violence, we earnestly desire that the dynamism of the awakened and organized community be put to the service of justice and peace.

* * *

To us, the Pastors of the Church, belongs the duty to educate the Christian conscience. . . . It is also up to us to denounce everything which, opposing justice, destroys peace. . . .

To awaken in individuals and communities, principally through mass media, a living awareness of justice, infusing in them a dynamic sense of responsibility and solidarity.

To defend the rights of the poor and oppressed . . . urging our governments and upper classes to eliminate anything which might destroy social peace: injustice, inertia, venality, insensibility.

To favor integration, energetically denouncing the abuses and unjust consequences of the excessive inequalities between poor and rich, weak and powerful.

To be certain that our preaching, liturgy and catechesis take into account the social and community dimensions of Christianity. . . .

To achieve in our schools, seminaries and universities a healthy critical sense of the social situation and foster the vocation of service. . . .

To invite various Christian and non-Christian communities to collaborate in this fundamental task of our times.

1. Quotations are from Paul VI's encyclical, *Populorum progressio.*

To encourage and favor the efforts of the people to create and develop their own grass-roots organizations for the redress and consolidation of their rights and the search for true justice. . . .

To urge a halt and revision in many of our countries of the arms race. . . . The struggle against misery is the true war that our nations should face. . . .

To denounce the unjust action of world powers that works against self-determination of weaker nations who must suffer the bloody consequences of war and invasion, and to ask competent international organizations for effective and decisive procedures.

Source: Second General Conference of Latin American Bishops, *The Church in the Present-Day Transformation of Latin America in the Light of the Council* (Washington, D.C., 1973), pp. 61–65.

SUGGESTIONS FOR BACKGROUND AND REFERENCE

P. Berryman, *Liberation Theology: Essential Facts about the Revolutionary Movement in Latin America* (New York, 1986).

L. Boff, *Ecclesiogenesis: The Base Communities Reinvent the Church* (Maryknoll, N.Y., 1986).

E. L. Cleary, *Crisis and Change: The Church in Latin America Today* (Maryknoll, N.Y., 1985).

J. L. Mecham, *Church and State in Latin America: A History of Politico-Ecclesiastical Relations* (Chapel Hill, N.C., 1969).

D. E. Mutchler, *The Church as a Political Factor in Latin America* (New York, 1971). Source for this document.

173   Puebla Conference of Latin American Bishops (Extracts)

February 1979

Criticism of liberation theology and the Medellín documents became more spirited in the 1970s and coincided with other conservative currents in Latin America. Unsettlement over Vatican II decisions, economic recession and political unrest, fear of communism, and the rise of reactionary military regimes in prominent states muted the impact of the Medellín message. The cautious mood was also evident in the choice in 1972 of Alfonso Lopez Trujillo, a Columbian conservative, as secretary-general of CELAM, the organization of the Latin American episcopate.

Preparation for the Third General Conference of Bishops at Puebla, Mexico, reflected these trends. The preliminary document issued by the secretariat in 1977 emphasized the dangers of secularization, gave less prominence to the desperation of the poor, guarded hierarchical authority, and stressed the spiritual vocation of the church. Membership of the Conference was also more conservative than that of Medellín. Widespread criticism, both before and during the sessions, brought substantial changes in the document, and the motif of "preferential option for the poor" was preserved. However, cautions against priestly involvement in political strife, stress on ideologies as the source of violence, and warnings about the use of Marxian analysis marked some shift in emphasis from Medellín. (Unlike the former conference, Puebla submitted documents to Rome for curial revision before publication.) Reprinted below are extracts from the conclusions on "Evangelization, Ideologies, and Politics."

Speaking in general, . . . the Church feels it has a duty and a right to be present in this [political] area of reality. For Christianity is supposed to evangelize the whole of human life, including the political dimension. So the Church criticizes those who would restrict the scope of faith to personal or family life; who would exclude the professional, economic, social, and political orders as if sin, love, prayer, and pardon had no relevance in them.

* * *

The Church recognizes the proper autonomy of the temporal order. . . . This holds true for governments, parties, labor unions, and other groups in the social and political arena. The purpose that the Lord assigned to his Church is a religious one; so when it does intervene in the sociopolitical arena, it is not prompted by any aim of a political, economic, or social nature. . . .

Insofar as the political arena is concerned, the Church is particularly interested in distinguishing between the specific functions of the laity, religious, and those who minister to the unity of the Church—i.e., the bishop and his priests.

We must distinguish between two notions of politics and political involvement. First, in the broad sense politics seeks the common good. . . . Its task is to spell out the fundamental values of every community. . . . It also defines the ethics and means of social relationships. In this broad sense politics is of interest to the Church, and hence to its pastors, who are ministers of unity. . . .

So the Church helps to foster the values that should inspire politics. . . . And it does this with its testimony, its teaching, and its varied forms of pastoral activity.

Second, the concrete performance of this fundamental political task is normally carried out by groups of citizens. They resolve to pursue and exercise political power in order to solve economic, political, and social problems in accordance with their own criteria or ideology. Here, then, we can talk about "party politics." Now even though the ideologies elaborated by such groups may be inspired by Christian doctrine, they can come to differing conclusions. No matter how deeply inspired in church teaching, no political party can claim the right to represent all the faithful because its concrete program can never have absolute value for all. . . .

Party politics is properly the realm of lay people. . . . Their lay status entitles them to establish and organize political parties, using an ideology and strategy that is suited to achieving their legitimate aims.

In the social teaching of the Church lay people find the proper criteria deriving from the Christian view of the human being. For its part the hierarchy will demonstrate its solidarity by contributing to their adequate formation and their spiritual life, and also by nurturing their creativity. . . .

Pastors, on the other hand, must be concerned with unity. So they will divest themselves of every partisan political ideology that might condition their criteria and attitudes. They then will be able to evangelize the political sphere as Christ did, relying on the Gospel without any infusion of partisanship or ideologization. . . .

Priests, also ministers of unity, and deacons must submit to the same sort of personal renunciation. If they are active in party politics, they will run the risk of absolutizing and radicalizing such activity. . . .

* * *

Faced with the deplorable reality of violence in Latin America, we wish to express our view clearly. Condemnation is always the proper judgment of physical and psychological torture, kidnapping, the persecution of political dissidents or suspect persons, and the exclusion of people from public life because of their ideas. If these crimes are committed by the authorities entrusted with the task of safeguarding the common good, then they defile those who practice them, notwithstanding any reasons offered.

The Church is just as decisive in rejecting terrorist and guerrilla violence, which becomes cruel and uncontrollable when it is unleashed. Criminal acts can in no way be justified as the way to liberation. Violence inexorably engenders new forms of oppression and bondage, which usually prove to be more serious than the ones people are allegedly being liberated from. But most importantly violence is an attack on life, which depends on the Creator alone. And . . . when an ideology appeals to violence it thereby admits its own weakness and inadequacy.

Our responsibility as Christians is to use all possible means to promote the implementation of nonviolent tactics in the effort to re-establish justice in economic and sociopolitical relations. . . .

* * *

Of the many different definitions of ideology that might be offered, we apply the term here to any conception that offers a view of the various aspects of life from the standpoint of a specific group in society. The ideology manifests the aspirations of this group, summons its members to a certain kind of solidarity and combative struggle, and grounds the legitimacy of these aspirations on specific values. Every ideology is partial because no one group can claim to identify its aspirations with those of society as a whole. Thus an ideology will be legitimate if the interests it upholds are legitimate and if it respects the basic rights of other groups in the nation. Viewed in this positive sense, ideologies seem to be necessary for social activity, insofar as they are mediating factors leading to action.

But in themselves ideologies have a tendency to absolutize the interests they uphold, the vision they propose, and the strategy they promote. In such a case they really become "lay religions." People take refuge in ideology as an ultimate explanation of everything. . . .

But ideologies should not be analyzed solely in terms of their conceptual content. In addition, they are dynamic, living phenomena of a sweeping and contagious nature. They are currents of yearning tending toward absolutization, and they are powerful in winning people over and whipping up redemptive fervor. . . . Their slogans, typical expressions, and criteria can easily make their way into the minds of people who are far from adhering voluntarily to their doctrinal principles. . . . This aspect calls for constant vigilance and re-examination. And it applies both to ideologies that legitimate the existing situation and to those that seek to change it.

* * *

Neither the Gospel nor the Church's social teaching deriving from it are ideologies. On the contrary, they represent a powerful source for challenging the limitations and ambiguities of all ideologies. The ever fresh originality of the gospel message must be continually clarified and defended against all efforts to turn it into an ideology.

* * *

In Latin America we are obliged to analyze a variety of ideologies:

a. First, there is capitalist liberalism, the idolatrous worship of wealth in individualistic terms. . . . The illegitimate privileges stemming from the absolute right of ownership give rise to scandalous contrasts, and to a situation of dependence and oppression on both the national and international levels. . . .

b. Second, there is Marxist collectivism. With its materialist presuppositions, it too leads to the idolatrous worship of wealth—but in collectivist terms. . . .

The driving force behind its dialectics is class struggle. Its objective is a classless society, which is to be achieved through a dictatorship of the proletariat; but in the last analysis this really sets up a dictatorship of the party. . . . Some believe it is possible to separate various aspects of Marxism—its doctrine and its method of analysis in particular. But we would remind people of the teaching of the papal magisterium on this point. . . .

We must also note the risk of ideologization run by theological reflection when it is based on a praxis that has recourse to Marxist analysis. The consequences are the total politicization of Christian existence, the disintegration of the language of faith into that of the social sciences, and the draining away of the transcendental dimension of Christian salvation. . . .

c. In recent years the so-called Doctrine of National Security has taken a firm hold on our continent. . . . It is bound up with a specific politico-economic model with elitist and verticalist features, which suppresses participation of the people in political decisions. In some countries of Latin America this doctrine justifies itself as the defender of the Christian civilization of the West. . . .

* * *

In propounding an absolutized view of the human being to which everything, including human thought, is subordinated, ideologies and political parties try to use the church or deprive it of its legitimate independence. This manipulation of the church . . . may derive from Christians themselves, and even from priests and religious, when they proclaim a gospel devoid of economic, social, cultural, and political implications. In practice this mutilation comes down to a kind of complicity with the established order, however unwitting.

Other groups are tempted in the opposite direction. They are tempted to consider a given political policy to be of primary urgency, a precondition for the church's fulfillment of its mission. They are tempted to equate the Christian message with some ideology and subordinate the former to the latter, calling for a "rereading" of the gospel on the basis of a political option. But the fact is that we must try to read the political scene from the standpoint of the gospel, not vice versa.

Traditional integrism looks for the Kingdom to come principally through a stepping back in history and reconstructing a Christian culture of a medieval cast. This would be a new Christendom, in which there was an intimate alliance between civil authority and ecclesiastical authority.

The radical thrust of groups at the other extreme falls into the same trap. It looks for the Kingdom to come from a strategic alliance between the Church and Marxism, and it rules out all other alternatives. For these people it is not simply a matter of being Marxists, but of being Marxists in the name of the faith.

Source: John Eagleson and Philip Scharper (eds.), *Puebla and Beyond* (New York, 1979), pp. 194–202.

SUGGESTIONS FOR BACKGROUND AND REFERENCE

G. MacEoin and Nivita Riley, *Puebla: A Church Being Born* (New York, 1980). Source for this document.
References for Document 172.

✦ ✦ ✦ Russian Orthodoxy and Post-Stalinist Repression

174 Solzhenitsyn's Lenten Letter to Patriarch Pimen (Extracts)

"Fourth Week of Lent, 1972"

Russian Orthodoxy (which, unlike the East European churches, ostensibly functioned in church-state separation) passed through alternating states of severity and relaxation in the second half of the century. During World War II Soviet pressure on the church had become less evident. The Kremlin had seen need for national solidarity, and Orthodoxy had patriotically supported the war effort. Moreover, churches that had reopened in German-occupied territory were generally permitted to continue after the enemy had been driven out. For fifteen years after the war this more permissive government posture prevailed, allowing the revival of theological seminaries and congregations. Then in 1960 Khrushchev inaugurated a new persecution that closed thousands of churches and imposed a new church constitution (1961) by which the freedom of priests to carry out parish duties was drastically reduced. Against these pressures the hierarchy raised few objections; when two priests, Gleb Yakunin and Nikolai Eshliman, sent a letter of protest to Patriarch Alexei (December 1965), they were suspended from priestly functions.

It was against this background that Alexander Solzhenitsyn (1918–), the celebrated writer, Nobel Prize winner, and dissident, directed this Lenten Letter to Patriarch Pimen, poignantly portraying the decay of Russian Christianity and urging the hierarchy to defend the church, even to martyrdom. Pimen made no answer, but a priest from Pskov, Sergei Zheludkov (b. 1909), defended the hierarchy's policy of patient resignation in a reply (dated Easter, 1972), of which a small part is reproduced below.

A. From Solzhenitsyn's Lenten Letter:

The past half-century has already been lost beyond hope, it is pointless to attempt to rescue the present, but how are we to save the future of our country—the future which will consist of the children of today? The true, profound fate of our country ultimately depends on whether the rightness of force will finally become rooted

From Alexander Solzhenitsyn, *A Lenten Letter to Pimen Patriarch of All Russia* (Minneapolis, 1972). Translated by Keith Armes. Copyright, 1972, by Burgess Publishing. Reprinted by permission of the publisher.

in the understanding of the people or whether the force of rightness will emerge from its eclipse and again shine forth. Will we succeed in restoring in ourselves at least some Christian characteristics, or will we lose *all* of those that still remain to us and surrender ourselves up to the calculations of self-preservation and personal advantage?

The study of Russian history during the last few centuries convinces one that the whole of our history would have taken a far more humane and harmonious course if the Church had not renounced her independence. . . . Gradually we have come to lose that radiant Christian ethical atmosphere in which over a period of thousands of years were established our mores, way of life, view of the world and folklore. . . . We are losing the last tokens and characteristics of a Christian people—how is it possible that this should not be the principal concern of the Russian Patriarch? . . .

It is now six years since two most honorable priests, Yakunin and Eshliman, wrote a well-known letter to your predecessor, confirming by their self-critical example that the pure flame of the Christian faith had not yet been extinguished in our native land. In full detail and with abundance of proof they pictured to him the voluntary internal enslavement, amounting to self-destruction, to which the Russian Church had been reduced. . . . And what reply did they receive? The simplest and crudest: they were punished for saying the truth by being forbidden to perform services. . . .

Six years since everything was said out loud—and what has changed? For every working church there are twenty churches which have been demolished and destroyed irrecoverably and twenty abandoned and desecrated. Is there a sight more heartrending than these skeletons of churches, the property of birds and store-keepers? How many towns and villages are there in our country where the nearest church is 100 or even 200 Kilometers away? . . . Any attempt by church volunteers, religious donors or the faithful in their legacies to restore even the smallest church is blocked by the one-sided laws respecting the so-called separation of church and state. We scarcely even dare to ask about bellringing—but why should Russia be deprived of her ancient ornament, of her best voice? But what use is it to talk of churches? Even a copy of the Gospel is nowhere to be had. . . .

Six years have passed—and has anything been successfully defended by the Church? The entire administration of the Church, the appointment of parish priests and bishops (including those who commit outrages with the aim of making it easier to deride and destroy the Church), everything is controlled by the Committee on Religious Affairs just as secretly as before. Such a church, directed dictatorially by atheists, is a sight which has not been seen for two millennia. All the property of the Church has been surrendered to their control, as well as the use of the Church funds, the coppers dropped into the collection plates by devout fingers. . . . The priests are deprived of their rights in their parishes, remaining entrusted solely with the holding of services; however, they are not allowed even to leave their churches in order to cross the threshold to visit a sick man or go to the cemetery; to do so they are obliged to ask official permission from the City Council.

What arguments can one find to convince oneself that the systematic destruction of the spirit and body of the Church under the direction of atheists is the best means of preserving it? Preservation for whom? Evidently not for Christ. Preservation—but how? By lying? But after this lying who is to perform the Eucharist?

Most holy lord! . . . Do not give us reason to suppose, do not make us think that for the prelates of the Russian Church temporal power is above heavenly power and that temporal responsibility is more fearful than responsibility before God.

Let us not craftily pretend either before others or, above all, in our prayers that external fetters are stronger than our spirit. It was no easier at the time of the birth of Christianity, but nevertheless Christianity withstood everything and flourished. And it showed us the way, the way of sacrifice. He who is deprived of all material strength will finally always be triumphant through sacrifice. Within our memory our priests and fellow-believers have undergone just such a martyrdom worthy of the first centuries of Christianity. Then they were thrown to the lions, while today they can lose only their material welfare.

In these days, as you kneel before the cross, set up for Easter in the middle of the church, ask our Lord: what other aim can there be for your service amongst the people, who have almost lost both the spirit of Christianity and the very semblance of Christians?

B. From Zheludkov's Reply to Solzhenitsyn:

The *full truth* is that the legal Church organisation cannot be *an island of freedom* in our strictly unified society, directed from a single Centre. There may be various opinions as to the historical significance of such a strictly unified and controlled social system. The most extreme judgment is that in our country literature and art are perishing, economics and science are lagging behind, morality is decaying, the people are becoming dull and stupid. . . . At the price of its own culture our nation saved Europe from the Tatars and saved the whole world from fascism; today it is undergoing a grandiose experiment, on view to the whole world, that is not leading anywhere. This is the opinion of some. Others . . . cherish bright hopes. . . . But one thing I must state with great conviction. There exists this strictly centralised system and within it, surprisingly, is preserved an alien body—the Russian Ortho-dox Church. It exists in very strictly determined conditions. We are *not permitted* to work at the religious education of children, or of adults, just as we are not permitted to do many other things necessary for the existence of real church life. *We are permitted only one thing*—to conduct divine worship in our churches, whereby it is supposed that this is something from the past preserved only for a disappearing generation.

What can we do in such a situation? Should we say: all or nothing? Should we try to go underground, which in the present system is unthinkable? Or should we try somehow to accept the system and for the present make use of those opportunities that are permitted? The Russian hierarchy took the latter decision.

Hence today all the evil about which you very rightly wrote. . . . But there was

From Gerhard Simon, *Church, State and Opposition in the U.S.S.R.* (London, 1974). Copyright, 1974. Reprinted by permission of the publisher, C. Hurst and Co., London.

no other choice. . . . You justly wrote about the abuses that have not existed during two thousand years of Christian history. But never, never before have our completely unique conditions of human existence been known.

This is the whole truth. The late Patriarch Alexi, unable to answer the accusations of the two priests in words, answered in deeds—he forbade them to serve as priests and thereby he involuntarily confirmed the relative truth of their argument. . . . Our present Patriarch Pimen also has no opportunity of answering you in word. By what deed do you suppose he could answer you? Only by giving up his position. . . . One of the consequences of your accusatory letter will be a still greater discrediting of the Church hierarchy in the eyes of those who do not understand the whole truth. . . .

There must be no unwillingness for sacrifice and martyrdom in the Church of Christ. We have enough willing martyrs, both inside and outside the Church. . . . I would say that our duty today is to give due appreciation to their deeds, and ourselves each one to work as best we can in the opportunities open to us. In particular, there is now a problem of the Christian education of children in the scattered families of the emergent Christian intelligentsia. In general, we must make a healthy acknowledgment of reality: the Russian Church hierarchy in its present composition and in our present system cannot in any significant way affect the system. It is easy and safe . . . to accuse the bishops, but in fact the work of the Lord today is hard. The destiny of the Russian Church is inseparably linked to the fate of the people. If "there is a future," then there will also inevitably be a renaissance of Russian Christianity.

Source: A. Alexander Solzhenitsyn, *A Lenten Letter to Pimen Patriarch of All Russia* (Minneapolis, 1972), pp. 6–8; B. Gerhard Simon, *Church, State and Opposition in the U.S.S.R.* (London, 1974), pp. 206–208.

SUGGESTIONS FOR BACKGROUND AND REFERENCE

M. Bourdeaux (ed.), *Religious Liberty in the Soviet Union* (1976).

G. Buss, *The Bear's Hug: Religious Belief and the Soviet State* (London, 1987).

J. Ellis, *The Russian Orthodox Church* (Bloomington, Ind., 1986).

N. Eshliman and G. Yakunin, *A Cry of Despair from Moscow Churchmen* (New York, 1966).

W. C. Fletcher, *Soviet Believers: The Religious Sector of the Population* (Lawrence, Kans., 1981).

N. Nielsen, *Solzhenitsyn's Religion* (Nashville, 1975).

D. Pospielovsky, *The Russian Church under the Soviet Regime 1917–1982* (New York, 1984).

M. Scammell, *Solzhenitsyn: A Biography* (New York, 1984).

175   Declaration of the Christian Committee for the Defence of Believers' Rights

December 27, 1976

In the absence of effective resistance by the hierarchy, three Orthodox churchmen, of whom the dissident priest, Gleb Yakunin (1934–   ), was the most prominent, undertook to organize the Christian Committee for the Defence of Believers' Rights.[1] Six months later the committee sent a lengthy critique of the new draft Soviet Constitution (June 1977) to L. I. Brezhnev, then chairman of the Constitutional Commission, protesting official atheism, and warning that "IF THIS DRAFT IS ACCEPTED, THEN IN ALL SERIOUSNESS BELIEVERS WILL FACE AN AGONISING QUESTION: CAN THEY, WITHOUT PREJUDICE TO THEIR RELIGIOUS CONSCIENCE, REMAIN CITIZENS OF A STATE WHICH PROCLAIMS BY LAW THAT NATIONAL ATHEISM IS ITS GOAL?"[2] The initial declaration of the committee, justifying its existence and explaining its aims and intentions, is reproduced below.

It is the inalienable natural right of every man to believe in God and to live in accordance with his belief. In principle, this right is acknowledged in the Basic Legislation of the USSR Soviet State Constitution. However, in practice, the principle of freedom of conscience proclaimed in the Constitution comes up against considerable difficulties as regards the attitude to religion of a government which is constructing a non-religious society. This attitude is expressed not only in the character of existing legislation, but also in the violation by the state administrative authorities of even those rights which believers legally possess. Religious believers form a significant proportion of the population in our country, and a normalisation of their legal position is vitally necessary for the State, since it proclaims itself to be lawful and wholly representative.

Because of this, we considered it our Christian and civil duty to form the Christian Committee for the Defence of Believers' Rights in the USSR.

At present, the bishops of the Russian Orthodox Church and the leaders of other religious organizations do not concern themselves with the defence of believers' rights, for a variety of reasons. In such circumstances, the Christian community has to make the legal defence of believers its own concern.

The Committee's aim is to help believers to exercise their right of living in accordance with their convictions. The Committee intends:

1. To collect, study and distribute information on the situation of religious believers in the USSR.

1. In addition to Yakunin, the Declaration was signed by Varsonofi Khaibulin (hiero-deacon) and Viktor Kapitanchuk (secretary of the committee).

From *Religion in Communist Lands*, Vol. VI, No. 1 (1978). Copyright, 1978, by Keston College, publisher. Reprinted by permission of the publisher.

2. *Religion in Communist Lands*, Vol. VI, No. 1 (1978), p. 36.

2. To give legal advice to believers when their civil rights are infringed.
3. To appeal to state institutions concerning the defence of believers' rights.
4. To conduct research, as far as this is possible, to clarify the legal and factual position of religion in the USSR.
5. To assist in putting Soviet legislation on religion into practice.

The Committee has no political aims. It is loyal to Soviet laws. The Committee is ready to cooperate with social and state organizations, in so far as such cooperation can help in improving the position of believers in the USSR.

The Committee is made up of members of the Russian Orthodox Church. For centuries, Orthodoxy was the State religion in our country. Orthodox churchmen often allowed the State to use forcible methods to restrict the religious freedom of other denominations. As we acknowledge that any use of compulsion against people on the grounds that they are not Orthodox or belong to a different faith is contrary to the Christian spirit, we consider it our especial duty to take the initiative in defending the religious freedom of all believers in our country, regardless of denomination.

We ask our fellow Christians to pray that God may help us in our human frailty.

Source: Religion in Communist Lands, Vol. VI, No. 1 (1978), pp. 33–34.

SUGGESTIONS FOR BACKGROUND AND REFERENCE

References for Document 174.

176 Appeal to the Ecumenical Patriarch by the Christian Committee for the Defence of Believers' Rights (Extracts)

April 11, 1978

In April 1978 the Orthodox Church undertook a formal celebration of the sixtieth anniversary of the restoration of the patriarchate (after the long interruption begun by Peter the Great in 1700). In contrast to the official commemoration, the CCDBR seized the occasion to publish an open appeal to the Orthodox Ecumenical Patriarch, Demetrios, detailing the sufferings of the Russian church under Soviet oppression. The committee not only criticized the hierarchy for serving the atheist state and failing to defend the faithful, but raised a fundamental theological issue: Were not the hierarchs, in their segregation of cult and Christian life, guilty of separating the two natures of Christ, in a manner reminiscent of ancient Christological heresies?

From *Religion in Communist Lands,* Vol. VII, No. 2 (1979). Copyright, 1979, by Keston College, publisher. Reprinted by permission of the publisher.

We were . . . happy to learn that you, Your Holiness, in your Christmas Message, called upon leaders of the Churches and heads of government to declare 1977 a year of religious freedom. . . . Your appeal also had a special significance for us, because we could not and cannot count upon open approval for activity in defence of believers' rights from the topmost hierarchy of the Russian Orthodox Church. The hierarchy, according to its vocation, ought to be the first to speak out in defence of persecuted and oppressed Christians, and to call upon all its spiritual children to fight for the flouted rights of the Church, just as the All-Russian Council (*Sobor*) of 1917–18 and the great Primate of the Russian Church, Patriarch Tikhon, did. It is not our aim to condemn the hierarchy of our Mother Church for deviating from its pastoral duty. For 50 years now it has followed the course chosen by Metropolitan Sergi Stragorodsky at a time when a storm of infernal malice, unknown in the two thousand year history of the Ecumenical Church, rained down upon the ship of the Russian Church. The enemies of Christianity succeeded not only in physically destroying all the greatest strengths of the Russian Church, but also in delivering her an enormous spiritual blow. . . .

The episcopate's rejection of the charisma of confession, as expressed in its official renunciation of the martyrs and confessors of freedom for the Church, and its false statements about the prosperity and freedom of the Russian Church, led to a situation where the duty of a church leader to intercede for the people was forgotten. And this led gradually to complete blindness and deafness towards the needs of the Church's spiritual children, and to the extensive erosion of pastoral and ecclesiological consciousness.

To our eyes, it seems that the great St. Seraphim's prophecy, widely known in the Russian Church, is being fulfilled. God revealed to St. Seraphim that a time would come when the leaders of the Russian Church would deviate from the observance of Orthodoxy in all its purity, for they would teach *human* doctrines and commandments, and their hearts would be far from God. The leading hierarchs . . . are not only failing to defend their spiritual children. Under the conditions of a State which is dominated by an ideology hostile to Christianity, the struggle to preserve outward well-being has so transformed the minds of church leaders that they are beginning to do what is completely unacceptable . . . : merging Christianity, and its hopes and aspirations, with the ideology of the adversaries of the Church of Christ.

In 1977 a new Soviet Constitution was adopted . . . which patently discriminated against the rights of believers. As an alternative to the constitutionally proclaimed freedom of anti-religious propaganda believers are merely granted freedom for "the performance of a religious cult," and certainly not freedom for religious preaching or missionary activity. . . . But even the freedom to perform a religious cult becomes a fiction when, in the face of the insistently felt need of believers to participate in the liturgy and the Church's sacraments, the authorities refuse to open Orthodox churches. In the last 25 years, we do not know of a single case where a new Orthodox community has been registered. . . .

In recent years pressure on the Church has been intensified. More and more often local authorities have forced Orthodox parishes to accept as churchwardens people who have previously had no connection whatever with the parish. At the same time, truly believing parishioners who attempt to become members of the [parish council] with the aim of restoring health to parish life, are prevented from doing so. . . . Recently some Moscow churches were forbidden to accept people younger than 35–40 into the church choir. For more than ten years now it has been obligatory for churches to register the documents of people being baptized, or the documents of parents in cases where children are being baptized. Lists of those who have registered are systematically passed on to the local authorities, after which those whose names appear on the lists are subjected to administrative pressure. . . . In their attempts to make life difficult for the Orthodox monasteries, the authorities have also begun to subject to administrative treatment even believers who send parcels and remittances of money to the monasteries by post. . . .

In Christ the Saviour the fullness of the Godhead is united, unconfused but inseparable, with the fullness of human nature and human energies. In relation to the Church, the Body of Christ, this means that there is no kind of human activity which is not called to adoration, to following exclusively "the divine and all-powerful will." There is no sphere of human creativity which cannot be inspired by the all-hallowing grace of God. . . . But it is not only the atheists, the builders of a godless society, the originators of legislation which permits the Church only to "perform a religious cult," who oppose this. How are we to reconcile with the demands of Orthodox ecclesiology the recent statement by Patriarch Pimen . . . that in their liturgical life the members of the Russian Church are guided by the canons of Orthodoxy, but in their working and public lives by the principles proclaimed 60 years ago by the October Revolution, that is, principles aimed at completely depriving all humanity of God? . . . Within the confines of the church the clergy are required to observe church canons, but outside the limits of "performing a religious cult" they must be guided by these canons only insofar as they do not contradict the general policy of destroying religion and the discriminatory legislation in particular. Anyone who carries out missionary work not only risks being persecuted by the state organs, but also risks receiving canonical prohibitions from his superior in the Church. The latter, moreover, is inspired by "the interests of the well-being of the Church," and reacts with exaggerated sharpness to its instability and vulnerability. . . .

To preach about the complete invulnerability and "everlasting freedom" of the Church is an example of ecclesiological monophysitism in its extreme Docetic form. "The Church is always free, do not be concerned about the freedom of the Church" is what even highly authoritative elders preach from the pulpit, affirming as they do so the complete illusoriness of the Church's sufferings and its legal limitations, just as the Docetists affirmed the illusoriness of the suffering of Christ's human nature. Ecclesiological monothelitism is represented by extreme distrust of all human creativity and human activity, including activity in defence of people's rights. It essentially denies that God can act in history through the human will and the creative activity of man. In the minds of the episcopate and a significant portion of the clergy, both these diametrically opposed types of unorthodox ecclesiology co-exist peacefully and even united in hostility to and suspicion of, or indifferent aloofness to, human rights activity, to campaigns for the opening of churches and registration of new communities. It is not rare for the bishops to use their authority against such undertakings of zealots for the faith, with the intention of stifling their enthusiasm. . . .

If the forces of Ecumenical Orthodoxy, and its free voice, do not come to the aid of the captive Russian Church, then only divine intervention will be able to save us. . . .

This year is the 60th anniversary of the Patriarchate of the Russian Church. Sixty years ago, at the All-Russian Council (*Sobor*), the synodal form of church administration, dependent on the authority of the State was overthrown. The Council decided that henceforward the Russian Church was "independent of the State and, guided by its dogmatic and canonical principles, would in church legislative, administrative and judicial affairs enjoy the rights of self-determination and self-government." . . .

Your Holiness! It is essential that concerted efforts should be made by the fraternal Orthodox Churches to study the tenets of Orthodoxy in the context of the contemporary world, which is secularized or openly hostile to the Church. It is essential to clarify the fundamental ecclesiological principles by which the Church must be guided in its mutual relations with State and society. . . .

The sickness of the Russian Church is a serious one. But we believe that the Lord, he who raised Lazarus after four days, will not abandon us in his mercy. Prostrating ourselves before you . . . we beg for your especial prayers, and those of all Orthodox Christians, for the revival of the Russian Church to the glory of Our Lord Jesus Christ.

Source: Religion in Communist Lands, Vol. VII, No. 2 (1979), pp. 191–194.

SUGGESTIONS FOR BACKGROUND AND REFERENCE

References for Document 174.

✦ ✦ ✦ United States Supreme Court: Contemporary Tensions in American Religion

177 *Epperson v. Arkansas* (Extracts)

November 12, 1968

Despite the humiliation of the religious antievolution cause in the Tennessee Scopes trial in 1925, opposition to the teaching of evolution persisted in much of American fundamentalism, where defense of the verbal inerrancy of scripture was regarded as a dogmatic essential. Moreover, in the 1960s opponents of evolution in the schools began to develop a new tactic, formulating a theory of origins called "creationism," which offered no offense to biblical narrative and which they believed might serve as a "scientific" alternative to Darwin. Arkansas, which had a tradition of hostility to evolution in education, was the new arena of legal conflict in the 1960s and 1970s. In 1965 Susan Epperson, a Little Rock teacher, challenged the statutory ban on teaching evolution (despite the fact that no prosecutions had ever occurred under the state's 1928 law). The case, carried on appeal to the Supreme Court, resulted in the voiding of the statute as contrary to the First and Fourteenth Amendments.

After the Epperson judgment, Arkansas turned to an "equal time" strategy mandating that schools must provide for the exposition of "creation science" as well as evolution. This alternative was also disallowed by a federal district court (*McLean* v. *Arkansas Board of Education*) in 1976, but debate over the claim of "creationism" to a place in the school curriculum has not been silenced.

The opinion of the Court was delivered by Justice Abe Fortas (1910–1982).

. . . While study of religions and of the Bible from a literary and historic viewpoint, presented objectively as part of a secular program of education, need not collide with the First Amendment's prohibition, the State may not adopt programs or practices in its public schools or colleges which "aid or oppose" any religion. . . . This prohibition is absolute. It forbids alike the preference of a religious doctrine or the prohibition of theory which is deemed antagonistic to a particular dogma. . . .

. . . The State's undoubted right to prescribe the curriculum for its public schools does not carry with it the right to prohibit, on pain of criminal penalty, the teaching of a scientific theory or doctrine where that prohibition is based upon reasons that violate the First Amendment. . . .

In the present case, there can be no doubt that Arkansas has sought to prevent its teachers from discussing the theory of evolution because it is contrary to the belief of some that the Book of Genesis must be the exclusive source of doctrine as to the origin of man. No suggestion has been made that Arkansas' law may be justified by considerations of state policy other than the religious views of some of its citizens. It is clear that fundamentalist sectarian conviction was and is the law's reason for existence. Its antecedent, Tennessee's "monkey law," candidly stated its purpose to make it unlawful "to teach any theory that denies the story of the Divine Creation of man as taught in the Bible, and to teach instead that man has descended from a lower order of animals." Perhaps the sensational publicity attendant upon the *Scopes* trial induced Arkansas to adopt less explicit language. It eliminated Tennessee's reference to "the story of the Divine Creation of man" as taught in the Bible, but there is no doubt that the motivation for the law was the same: to suppress the teaching of a theory which, it was thought, "denied" the divine creation of man.

Arkansas' law cannot be defended as an act of religious neutrality. Arkansas did not seek to excise from the curricula of its schools and universities all discussion of the origin of man. The law's effort was confined to an attempt to blot out a particular theory because of its supposed conflict with the Biblical account, literally read. Plainly, the law is contrary to the mandate of the First, and in violation of the Fourteenth, Amendment to the Constitution.

Source: Epperson et al. v. Arkansas, 393 U.S. 97.

SUGGESTIONS FOR BACKGROUND AND REFERENCE

D. E. Boles, *The Bible, Religion and the Public Schools* (New York, 1961).
P. Kurland, *Church and State: The Supreme Court and the First Amendment* (Chicago, 1975).
R. Morgan, *The Supreme Court and Religion* (New York, 1972).
L. Pfeffer, *God, Caesar, and the Constitution* (Boston, 1975), pp. 220–224.

178 *Lemon v. Kurtzman* (Extracts)

June 28, 1971

In the 1960s private schools, often church-related and usually Catholic, had benefited from laws whereby financial assistance could be made available for certain educational functions. Thus Pennsylvania in 1968 granted public funds to defer costs of teachers' salaries, textbooks, and instructional aids in private schools; in 1969 Rhode Island supplemented wages of instructors of secular subjects in such schools. Both states' arrangements were disallowed by this 1971 decision, the Pennsylvania practice by unanimous judgment and the Rhode Island statute with only the single qualified dissent of Justice Byron R. White. The opinion, written by Chief Justice Warren E. Burger (1907–1986), stressed the entanglement test: the statutes failed to qualify constitutionally because in administering such practices, states would have to keep continuous surveillance to confirm that aid was used for secular purposes only. Moreover, politics would inevitably divide on religious lines if legislatures were called upon to vote funds for church-related institutions.

"Parochial aid" measures had been chiefly sought by Catholic schools, though some Protestant leaders, fearful of "secularism," and some politicians (including President Nixon) favored such legislation. While the decision added to financial crisis for some Catholic school systems, it did not invalidate indirect aid (such as health, bus, or lunch programs). Moreover, the issue did not die; it resurfaced in new ways in proposals for tax credits, parent reimbursement, various "voucher" arrangements, and other legislative stratagems.

Every analysis in this area must begin with consideration of the cumulative criteria developed by the Court over many years. Three such tests may be gleaned from our cases. First, the statute must have a secular legislative purpose; second, its principal or primary effect must be one that neither advances nor inhibits religion . . . ; finally, the statute must not foster "an excessive government entanglement with religion." . . .

Inquiry into the legislative purposes of the Pennsylvania and Rhode Island statutes affords no basis for a conclusion that the legislative intent was to advance religion. On the contrary, the statutes themselves clearly state that they are intended to enhance the quality of the secular education in all schools covered by the compulsory attendance laws. There is no reason to believe the legislatures meant anything else.

* * *

The two legislatures, however, have also recognized that church-related elementary and secondary schools have a significant religious mission and that a substantial portion of their activities is religiously oriented. They have therefore sought to create statutory restrictions designed to guarantee the separation between secular and religious educational functions and to ensure that State financial aid supports only the former. All these provisions are precautions taken in candid recognition that these programs approached, even if they did not intrude upon, the forbidden areas under the Religious Clauses. We need not decide whether these legislative precautions restrict the principal or primary effect of the programs to the point where they do not offend the Religious Clauses, for we conclude that the cumulative impact of the entire relationship arising under the statutes in each State involves excessive entanglement between government and religion.

* * *

Our prior holdings do not call for total separation between church and state; total separation is not possible in an absolute sense. Some relationship between government and religious organizations is inevitable. . . . Fire inspections, building and zoning regulations, and state requirements under compulsory school-attendance laws are examples of necessary and permissible contacts. . . . Judicial caveats against entanglement must recognize that the line of separation, far from being a "wall," is a blurred, indistinct, and variable barrier. . . .

In order to determine whether the government entanglement with religion is excessive, we must examine the character and purposes of the institutions that are benefited, the nature of the aid that the State provides, and the resulting relationship between the government and the religious authority. . . .

(a) Rhode Island Program

The District Court made extensive findings on the grave potential for excessive entanglement that inheres in the religious character and purpose of the Roman Catholic elementary schools of Rhode Island, to date the sole beneficiaries of the Rhode Island Salary Supplement Act.

The church schools involved in the program are located close to parish churches. This understandably permits convenient access for religious exercises since instruction in faith and morals is part of the total educational process. The school buildings contain identifying religious symbols such as crosses on the exterior and crucifixes, and religious paintings and statues either in the classrooms or hallways. Although only approximately 30 minutes a day are devoted to direct religious instruction, there are religiously oriented extracurricular activities. Approximately two-thirds of the teachers in these schools are nuns of various religious orders. Their dedicated efforts provide an atmosphere in which religious instruction and religious vocations are natural and proper parts of life in such schools. Indeed, as the District Court found, the role of teaching nuns in enhancing the religious atmosphere has led the parochial school authorities to attempt to maintain a one-to-one ratio between nuns and lay teachers in all schools rather than to permit some to be staffed almost entirely by lay teachers.

On the basis of these findings the District Court concluded that the parochial schools constituted "an integral part of the religious mission of the Catholic Church." The various characteristics of the schools make them "a powerful vehicle for transmitting the Catholic faith to the next generation." This process of inculcating religious doctrine is, of course, enhanced by the impressionable age of the pupils in primary schools particularly. In short, parochial schools involve substantial religious activity and purpose.

The substantial religious character of these church-related schools gives rise to entangling church-state relationships of the kind the Religious Clauses sought to avoid. Although the District Court found that concern for religious values did not inevitably or necessarily intrude into the content of secular subjects, the considerable religious activities of these schools led the legislature to provide for careful governmental controls and surveillance by state authorities in order to ensure that state aid supports only secular education.

The dangers and corresponding entanglements are enhanced by the particular form of aid that the Rhode Island Act provides. Our decisions from *Everson* to *Allen* have permitted the States to provide church-related schools with secular, neutral, or nonideological services, facilities, or materials. Bus transportation, school lunches, public health services, and secular textbooks supplied in common to all students were not thought to offend the Establishment Clause. We note that the dissenters in *Allen* seemed chiefly concerned with the pragmatic difficulties involved in ensuring the truly secular content of the textbooks provided at state expense.

In *Allen* the Court refused to make assumptions, on a meager record, about the religious content of the textbooks that the State would be asked to provide. We cannot, however, refuse here to recognize that teachers have a substantially different ideological character from books. In terms of potential for involving some aspect of faith or morals in secular subjects a textbook's content is ascertainable, but a teacher's handling of a subject is not. We cannot ignore the danger that a teacher under religious control and discipline poses to the separation of the religious from the purely secular aspects of pre-college education. The conflict of functions inheres in the situation.

In our view the record shows these dangers are present to a substantial degree. The Rhode Island Roman Catholic elementary schools are under the general supervision of the Bishop of Providence and his appointed representative, the Diocesan

Superintendent of Schools. In most cases, each individual parish, however, assumes the ultimate financial responsibility for the school, with the parish priest authorizing the allocation of parish funds. With only two exceptions, school principals are nuns appointed either by the Superintendent or the Mother Provincial of the order whose members staff the school. By 1969 lay teachers constituted more than a third of all teachers in the parochial elementary schools, and their number is growing. They are first interviewed by the superintendent's office and then by the school principal. The contracts are signed by the parish priest, and he retains some discretion in negotiating salary levels. Religious authority necessarily pervades the school system.

* * *

We need not and do not assume that teachers in parochial schools will be guilty of bad faith or any conscious design to evade the limitations imposed by the statute and the First Amendment. We simply recognize that a dedicated religious person, teaching in a school affiliated with his or her faith and operated to inculcate its tenets, will inevitably experience great difficulty in remaining religiously neutral. Doctrines and faith are not inculcated or advanced by neutrals. With the best of intentions such a teacher would find it hard to make a total separation between secular teaching and religious doctrine. . . .

We do not assume, however, that parochial school teachers will be unsuccessful in their attempts to segregate their religious beliefs from their secular educational responsibilities. But the potential for impermissible fostering of religion is present. The Rhode Island Legislature has not, and could not, provide state aid on the basis of a mere assumption that secular teachers under religious discipline can avoid conflicts. The State must be certain, given the Religion Clauses, that subsidized teachers do not inculcate religion—indeed the State here has undertaken to do so. To ensure that no trespass occurs, the State has therefore carefully conditioned its aid with pervasive restrictions. An eligible recipient must teach only those courses that are offered in the public schools and use only those texts and materials that are found in the public schools. In addition the teacher must not engage in teaching any course in religion.

A comprehensive, discriminating, and continuing state surveillance will inevitably be required to ensure that these restrictions are obeyed and the First Amendment otherwise respected. Unlike a book, a teacher cannot be inspected once so as to determine the extent and intent of his or her personal beliefs and subjective acceptance of the limitations imposed by the First Amendment. These prophylactic contacts will involve excessive and enduring entanglement between state and church.

There is another area of entanglement in the Rhode Island program that gives concern. The statute excludes teachers employed by nonpublic schools whose average per-pupil expenditures on secular education equal or exceed the comparable figures for public schools. In the event that the total expenditures of an otherwise eligible school exceed this norm, the program requires the government to examine the school's records in order to determine how much of the total expenditures is attributable to secular education and how much to religious activity. This kind of state inspection and evaluation of the religious content of a religious organization is fraught with the sort of entanglement that the Constitution forbids. It is a relationship pregnant with dangers of excessive government direction of church schools and hence of churches. . . .

[The decision continues with a review of the Pennsylvania program, which is omitted here.]

A broader base of entanglement of yet a different character is presented by the divisive political potential of these state programs. In a community where such a large number of pupils are served by church-related schools, it can be assumed that state assistance will entail considerable political activity. Partisans of parochial schools, understandably concerned with rising costs and sincerely dedicated to both the religious and secular educational missions of their schools, will inevitably champion this cause and promote political action to achieve their goals. Those who oppose state aid, whether for constitutional, religious, or fiscal reasons, will inevitably respond and employ all of the usual political campaign techniques to prevail. Candidates will be forced to declare and voters to choose. It would be unrealistic to ignore the fact that many people confronted with issues of this kind will find their votes aligned with their faith.

Ordinarily, political debate and division, however vigorous or even partisan, are normal and healthy manifestations of our democratic system of government, but political division along religious lines was one of the principal evils against which the First Amendment was intended to protect. . . . To have States or communities divide on the issues presented by state aid to parochial schools would tend to confuse and obscure other issues of great urgency. . . . It conflicts with our whole history and tradition to permit questions of the Religion Clauses to assume such importance in our legislatures and in our elections that they could divert attention from the myriad issues and problems that confront every level of government.

* * *

The potential for political divisiveness related to religious belief and practice is aggravated in these two statutory programs by the need for continuing annual appropriations and the likelihood of larger and larger demands as costs and populations grow. The Rhode Island District Court found that the parochial school system's "monumental and deepening financial crisis" would "inescapably" require larger annual appropriations subsidizing greater percentages of the salaries of lay teachers. Although no facts have been developed in this respect in the Pennsylvania case, it appears that such pressures for expanding aid have already required the state legislature to include a portion of the state revenues from cigarette taxes in the program.

* * *

Finally, nothing we have said can be construed to disparage the role of church-related elementary and secondary schools in our national life. Their contribution has been and is enormous. . . .

The merit and benefits of these schools, however, are not the issue before us in these cases. The sole question is whether state aid to these schools can be squared with the dictates of the Religion Clauses. Under our system the choice has been made that government is to be entirely excluded from the area of religious instruction and churches excluded from the affairs of government. The Constitution decrees that religion must be a private matter for the individual, the family, and the institutions of private choice, and that while some involvement and entanglement are inevitable, lines must be drawn.

Source: Lemon et al. v. *Kurtzman, Superintendent of Public Instruction of Pennsylvania, et al.,* 403 U.S. 602.

SUGGESTIONS FOR BACKGROUND AND REFERENCE

D. E. Boles, "Religion and the Public Schools in Judicial Review," *Journal of Church and State*, Vol. 26, No. 1 (Winter 1984), pp. 55–71.

L. Pfeffer, *God, Caesar, and the Constitution* (Boston, 1975), pp. 276–288.

"The Sacred Wall Revisited—The Constitutionality of State Aid to Nonpublic Education following Lemon v. Kurtzman and Tilton v. Richardson," *Northwestern University Law Review*, Vol. 67, No. 1 (March–April 1972), pp. 118–145.

J. E. Wood, "Religion and Education in American Church-State Relations," *Journal of Church and State*, Vol. 28, No. 1 (Winter 1984), pp. 31–54.

————, *Religion, the State, and Education* (Waco, Tex., 1984).

179 *Bob Jones University* v. *United States* (Extracts)
May 24, 1983

In this case and the companion case of Goldsboro Christian Schools, South and North Carolina institutions, the public policy of racial non-discrimination contested with the claim of religious liberty. Seeking to enforce a national policy against discrimination in education, the Internal Revenue Service in 1970 disallowed tax exempt status for private schools maintaining racial admissions criteria. Bob Jones University, religiously opposed to racial intermarriage on the basis of an alleged biblical injunction, excluded black students by policy and had its exempt status revoked. (After 1971 the university accepted blacks married within their race; after 1975 it accepted unmarried blacks but prohibited interracial dating or marriage.) In response the university claimed a violation of the free exercise of religion under the First Amendment and brought suit in the courts. The decision, written by Chief Justice Warren E. Burger, denied relief, justifying limitation on religious liberty in order to attain an "overriding governmental interest." Justice William H. Rehnquist alone dissented.

Section 501(c)(3) provides that "corporations . . . organized and operated exclusively for religious, charitable . . . or educational purposes" are entitled to tax exemption. Petitioners argue that the plain language of the statute guarantees them tax-exempt status. They emphasize the absence of any language in the statute expressly requiring all exempt organizations to be "charitable" in the common-law sense, and they contend that the disjunctive "or" separating the categories in 501(c)(3) precludes such a reading. Instead, they argue that if an institution falls within one or more of the specified categories it is automatically entitled to exemption, without regard to whether it also qualifies as "charitable." . . .

It is a well-established canon of statutory construction that a court should go beyond the literal language of a statute if reliance on that language would defeat the plain purpose of the statute. . . .

Section 501(c)(3) therefore must be analyzed and construed within the framework of the Internal Revenue Code and against the background of the congressional purposes. Such an examination reveals unmistakable evidence that, underlying all relevant parts of the Code, is the intent that entitlement to tax exemption depends on meeting certain common-law standards of charity—namely, that an institution seeking tax-exempt status must serve a public purpose and not be contrary to established public policy.

* * *

We are bound to approach these questions with full awareness that determinations of public benefit and public policy are sensitive matters with serious implications for the institutions affected; a declaration that a given institution is not "charitable" should be made only where there can be no doubt that the activity involved is contrary to a fundamental public policy. But there can no longer be any doubt that racial discrimination in education violates deeply and widely accepted views of elementary justice. . . . Over the past quarter of a century, every pronouncement of this Court and myriad Acts of Congress and Executive Orders attest a firm national policy to prohibit racial segregation and discrimination in public education.

An unbroken line of cases following Brown v. Board of Education establishes beyond doubt this Court's view that racial discrimination in education violates a most fundamental national public policy, as well as rights of individuals.

* * *

Few social or political issues in our history have been more vigorously debated and more extensively ventilated than the issue of racial discrimination, particularly in education. Given the stress and anguish of the history of efforts to escape from the shackles of the "separate but equal" doctrine of Plessy v. Ferguson . . . it cannot be said that educational institutions that, for whatever reasons, practice racial discrimination, are institutions exercising "beneficial and stabilizing influences in community life," . . . or should be encouraged by having all taxpayers share in their support by way of special tax status.

There can thus be no question that the interpretation . . . announced by the IRS in 1970 was correct. . . . It would be wholly incompatible with the concepts underlying tax exemption to grant the benefit of tax-exempt status to racially discriminatory educational entities, which "exert a pervasive influence on the entire educational process."

* * *

Petitioners contend that, even if the Commissioner's policy is valid as to non-religious private schools, that policy cannot constitutionally be applied to schools that engage in racial discrimination on the basis of sincerely held religious beliefs. As to such schools, it is argued that the IRS construction . . . violates their free exercise rights under the Religion Clauses of the First Amendment. This contention presents claims not heretofore considered by this Court in precisely this context.

This Court has long held the Free Exercise Clause of the First Amendment to be an absolute prohibition against governmental regulation of religious beliefs. . . . However, "not all burdens on religion are unconstitutional. . . . The state may justify a limitation on religious liberty by showing that it is essential to accomplish an overriding governmental interest." . . .

On occasion this Court has found certain governmental interest so compelling as to allow even regulations prohibiting religiously based conduct. In Prince v. Massachusetts . . . for example, the Court held that neutrally cast child labor laws prohibiting sale of printed materials on public streets could be applied to prohibit children from dispensing religious literature. The Court found no constitutional infirmity in "excluding [Jehovah's Witnesses children] from doing there what no other children may do." . . . Denial of tax benefits will inevitably have a substantial impact on the operation of private religious schools, but will not prevent those schools from observing their religious tenets.

The governmental interest at stake here is compelling. . . . [The] Government has a fundamental, overriding interest in eradicating racial discrimination in education—discrimination that prevailed, with official approval, for the first 165 years of this Nation's constitutional history. That governmental interest substantially outweighs whatever burden denial of tax benefits places on petitioners' exercise of their religious beliefs.

Source: Bob Jones University v. United States, 461 U.S. 574.

SUGGESTIONS FOR BACKGROUND AND REFERENCE

C. O. Galvin and N. Dennis, "A Tax Policy Analysis of *Bob Jones University v. United States*," *Vanderbilt Law Review*, Vol. 36, No. 6 (November 1985), pp. 1353–1382.
D. M. Kelley, "A New Meaning for Tax Exemption?" *Journal of Church and State*, Vol. 25, No. 3 (Autumn 1983), pp. 415–426.
References for Documents 177 and 178.

180   *Mueller* v. *Allen* (Extracts)

June 29, 1983

A new and more ambiguous form of public assistance to parochial schools was the issue in this Minnesota case. State statutes of 1955, 1976, and 1978 allowed state income tax deductions for expenses incurred by taxpayers (tuition, textbooks, and transportation) in educating their elementary and secondary school-age children. When the practice was challenged on First Amendment grounds, the Court acknowledged difficulty in declaring a judgment consistent with past decisions. On the one hand, indirect aid had been judged constitutional, while contributions to instructional expenses had been struck down. In this instance the Court split but narrowly upheld the Minnesota statutes, concluding that they met the tripartite test defined in *Lemon* v. *Kurtzman* that such laws must have a secular purpose, neither advance nor inhibit religion, and not result in excessive government entanglement with religion. The opinion was written by Justice William H. Rehnquist (1924–   ).

Strong dissent was recorded by Justices Thurgood Marshall, William J. Brennan, Harry A. Blackmun, and John Paul Stevens, arguing that the laws had the direct and immediate effect of advancing religion. (Judicial uncertainty was underscored two years later when the Court returned to a more separationist stance in two companion cases: *Grand Rapids School District* v. *Ball* nullified classes in "leased" classrooms in private schools taught by public school teachers and *Aguilar* v. *Felton* invalidated a New York program that supplied public school teachers to religious schools to support remedial education.)

The general nature of our inquiry . . . has been guided, since the decision in *Lemon* v. *Kurtzman* . . . by the "three-part" test . . . :

> "First, the statute must have a secular legislative purpose; second, its principal or primary effect must be one that neither advances nor inhibits religion . . . ; finally, the statute must not foster 'an excessive government entanglement with religion.'" . . .

While this principle is well settled, our cases have also emphasized that it provides "no more than a helpful signpost" in dealing with Establishment Clause challenges. . . .

Little time need be spent on the question of whether the Minnesota tax deduction has a secular purpose. Under our prior decisions, governmental assistance programs have consistently survived this inquiry even when they have run afoul of other aspects of the *Lemon* framework. . . . This reflects, at least in part, our reluctance to attribute unconstitutional motives to the States, particularly when a plausible secular purpose for the State's program may be discerned from the face of the statute.

A State's decision to defray the cost of educational expenses incurred by parents—regardless of the type of schools their children attend—evidences a purpose that is both secular and understandable. An educated populace is essential to the political and economic health of any community, and a State's efforts to assist parents in meeting the rising cost of educational expenses plainly serves this secular purpose. . . .

We turn therefore to the more difficult but related question whether the Minnesota statute has "the primary effect of advancing the sectarian aims of the nonpublic schools." . . . In concluding that it does not, we find several features of the Minnesota tax deduction particularly significant. First, an essential feature of Minnesota's arrangement is the fact that Minnesota statute 290.09, subd. 22, is only one among many deductions—such as those for medical expenses . . . and charitable contributions . . . —available under the Minnesota tax laws. Our decisions consistently have recognized that traditionally "legislatures have especially broad latitude in creating classifications and distinctions in tax statutes" . . . , in part because the "familiarity with local conditions" enjoyed by legislators especially enables them to "achieve an equitable distribution of the tax burden." . . . [T]he Minnesota Legislature's judgment that a deduction for educational expenses fairly equalizes the tax burden of its citizens and encourages desirable expenditures for educational purposes is entitled to substantial deference.

Other characteristics of 290.09, subd. 22, argue equally strongly for the provision's constitutionality. Most importantly, the deduction is available for educational expenses incurred by *all* parents, including those whose children attend public schools and those whose children attend nonsectarian private schools or sectarian private schools. . . .

* * *

We also agree with the Court of Appeals that, by channeling whatever assistance it may provide to parochial schools through individual parents, Minnesota has reduced the Establishment Clause objections to which its action is subject. It is true, of course, that financial assistance provided to parents ultimately has an economic effect comparable to that of aid given directly to the schools attended by their children. It is also true, however, that under Minnesota's arrangement public funds become available only as a result of numerous private choices of individual parents of school-age children. . . . It is noteworthy that all but one of our recent cases invalidating state aid to parochial schools have involved the direct transmission of assistance from the State to the schools themselves. . . . Where, as here, aid to parochial schools is available only as a result of decisions of individual parents, no "imprimatur of state approval" . . . can be deemed to have been conferred on any particular religion or on religion generally.

* * *

Petitioners argue that, notwithstanding the facial neutrality of 290.09, subd. 22, in application the statute primarily benefits religious institutions. Petitioners rely . . . on a statistical analysis of the type of persons claiming the tax deduction. They contend that most parents of public school children incur no tuition expenses . . . and that other expenses deductible under 290.09, subd. 22, are negligible in value; moreover, they claim that 96% of the children in private schools in 1978–1979 attended religiously affiliated institutions. . . .

We need not consider these contentions in detail. We would be loath to adopt a rule grounding the constitutionality of a facially neutral law on annual reports reciting the extent to which various classes of private citizens claimed benefits under the law. Such an approach would scarcely provide the certainty that this field stands in need of, nor can we perceive principled standards by which such statistical evidence might be evaluated. . . .

Finally, private educational institutions, and parents paying for their children to attend these schools, make special contributions to the areas in which they operate. . . . If parents of children in private schools choose to take especial advantage of the relief provided . . . , it is no doubt due to the fact that they bear a particularly great financial burden in educating their children. More fundamentally, whatever unequal effect may be attributed to the statutory classification can fairly be regarded as a rough return for the benefits . . . provided to the State and all taxpayers by parents sending their children to parochial schools. . . .

Thus, we hold that the Minnesota tax deduction for educational expenses satisfies the primary effect inquiry of our Establishment Clause cases.

Turning to the third part of the *Lemon* inquiry, we have no difficulty in concluding that the Minnesota statute does not "excessively entangle" the State in religion. The only plausible source of the "comprehensive, discriminating, and continuing state surveillance," . . . necessary to run afoul of this standard would lie in the fact that state officials must determine whether particular textbooks qualify for a deduction. In making this decision, state officials must disallow deductions taken for "instructional books and materials used in the teaching of religious tenets, doctrines or worship, the purpose of which is to inculcate such tenets, doctrines or worship." . . . Making decisions such as this does not differ substantially from making the types of decisions approved in earlier opinions of this Court.

Source: Mueller et al. v. *Allen et al.*, 463 U.S. 388.

SUGGESTIONS FOR BACKGROUND AND REFERENCE

Washington University Law Review, Vol. 61, No. 1 (Spring 1983), pp. 269–286. References for Document 178.

✦ ✦ ✦ East European Christianity in Crisis: Issues of Resistance, Accommodation, Survival

After the initial shock presented by the establishment of Communist regimes with draconian statutory and bureaucratic controls, East European Christianity passed into a somber era, four decades (c. 1950–1990) of protracted tension, exhaustion, and depression. Conflicts varied in detail from country to country, but most encounters produced common hardships and defeats—legal status but stifling political restraints, isolation from ecumenical or international contacts, bans on religious education and charity, closure of churches and seminaries, splits between collaborating and resisting clergy, government rejection of clerical and episcopal appointments, impoverishment of parishes and clergy of all ranks, discrimination against religious laity, atheistic education for the young, censorship, persecution, arrest, imprisonment, and liquidation of dissent. The several communions dealt differently with these challenges. Orthodoxy, enured to centuries of state authoritarianism and caesaropapism, ventured only limited protest. Protestants, dominant only in East Germany and a minority presence in Hungary, Romania, and Czechoslovakia, sometimes made genuine efforts to adjust and enter into productive dialogue with Marxists. Catholic official policy passed through stages: confrontation after Pius XII excommunicated Communists in 1949, Paul VI's more compliant *Ostpolitik* and search for *détente* after 1963, and the Polish John Paul II's stiffening support for suffering churches after 1978.

Each Communist regime developed its own level of hostility. East Germany eventually evolved a pattern of negotiated coordination and— relative to other eastern states—became less restrictive. By contrast, Czechoslovakia and Bulgaria were consistently antagonistic, seeking the decay and collapse of religious belief and organization. Between these poles, Hungary, Romania and Poland engaged in a more complex pattern of hostility, tactical compromise, and manipulation as they sought to devitalize religion with varying degrees of success. In the later 1980s all governments began to experience greater difficulty in intimidating the younger postwar generation, which increasingly rejected the failed strategies of accommodation and demanded greater freedom and comprehensive reforms. Nonetheless—apart from Poland—religion seldom played a major role in the eventual overthrow of the discredited Communist regimes at the turn of the decade.

Literature of religious protest was often denied legal expression and had to appear furtively as *samizdat* publication. Sometimes such protest carried official ecclesiastical support (as in Poland), but often (since official church structures were frequently co-opted by the state and organized opposition was impossible) it took the form of fugitive protest pieces authored by small dissident groups or even by individuals. Reproduced below are documents of five notable conflicts that express the struggle, anguish, and internal divisions created in East European Christianity under Marxist conduct of church-state relations.

181   Polish Bishops' Rejection of Decree on Clerical Appointments

May 1953

The Catholic Church enjoyed a far stronger position in Poland than in any other East European country. Historically identified with Polish nationalism and (unlike other Marxist states) free from any long-standing Erastian tradition, Catholicism also commanded the support of over 90 percent of the population. Consequently, the Communist government, with limited popular mandate, found enormous difficulty in establishing effective controls over religion. The accord with the bishops in 1950 (Document 161) brought no peace and soon broke over issues of religion in the schools and episcopal appointments. Therefore the history of church-state relations in the four decades after 1950 followed a repeated pattern: elaborate government restrictions, spirited hierarchical resistance, frequent confrontation and crisis, then concession and compromise when popular insurrection threatened or renewed efforts at manipulation and subordination when greater stability was recovered. The Communist party used various techniques: confiscation of assets, closing of seminaries, eradication of religious education, sponsorship of collaborating "patriotic priests," takeover of Catholic charities, imposition of heavy taxation, a ban on building new churches, arrest and imprisonment of opponents. The much smaller Orthodox and Protestant bodies fared better; official policy sought to break the Catholic religious "monopoly," and indeed Polish non-Catholic churches may have experienced some greater freedoms under Communism than they had known before the war.

Catholic response was robust. Illegal churches were built, religious literature was clandestinely published, catechetical centers replaced outlawed religious instruction, and popular devotion (such as the "Great Novena" of the early 1960s) was actively promoted. Leadership in counterattack belonged to the autocratic, conservative, and fiercely anti-Communist cardinal-primate, Stefan Wyszynski (1901–1981). The primate's political guidance was shrewd, and while his frequent and open defiance led to arrest and imprisonment for a term, government subjugation of religion was not advanced thereby. Of all East European churches, Polish Catholicism was the most outspoken, audacious, and assertive.

The pattern was fixed early in the Marxist regime's history. Three years after the 1950 accord, the state decreed its intent to appoint and dismiss all priests and bishops unilaterally. Wyszynski called the Polish episcopate to Cracow where the following defiance was drafted. The state, terming the opposition treasonable, had nine bishops (including the primate) and about nine hundred priests under confinement by the end of the year. Yet by 1956 disorders and riots compelled the government to new compromise.

Considering it their highest duty, the Polish Episcopate draw attention to the tragic fate of the Church in Poland; to the symptoms of oppression and its causes; and to

From Polish White Paper, as printed in Janice Broun, *Conscience and Captivity. Religion in Eastern Europe* (Washington, D.C., 1988). Copyright, 1988, by Ethics and Public Policy Center. Reprinted by permission of the publisher.

the sources from which flow the concern, anxiety, and exasperation of the broad masses of the Catholic community.

The main cause of this state of affairs is the hatred which is destroying the strength of our country. . . . We have not abandoned our desire for a peaceful solution and collaboration in the important task of a successful settlement of relations between Church and State in accordance with the agreement reached on April 14, 1950. However, in the present state of affairs, it depends solely on the sincere good will of the government whether internal peace and reciprocal harmony, which are so essential, will be genuinely achieved. It depends on the government's forsaking its radical, destructive hatred towards Catholicism, and abandoning its aim of subjugating the Church and turning it into an instrument of the State.

We wish the government to understand clearly what the decree on appointments to clerical offices really means for the structure of the Church. We therefore remind it that by this act, which is illegal according to the Constitution, the State has assumed the right of constant intrusion in the internal affairs of the Church. This intrusion sometimes interferes with priests' consciences, and involves a willful and systematic subjection of church jurisdiction to its own will.

The situation is inadmissible, from the point of view of the Church, firstly because the Church's jurisdiction pertains to strictly religious, internal, and supernatural matters, such as teaching God's revelation, expounding Christian morals, administering the Holy Sacraments, organizing religious services, and providing spiritual guidance for the souls and consciences of the people. In the name of what rights could such strictly religious matters be submitted to the authority of the State, which by its nature pertains to matters exclusively secular and temporal—more especially if that authority is based on a materialistic and anti-religious ideology, and filled with destructive hatred towards the Church? Everyone, even atheists, should see that such dependence is quite impossible. That was why Lenin justly condemned the subjugation of the Church to the State as a "cursed and disgraceful" thing.

Secondly, this is an impossibility for the Church because, in accordance with its unalterable constitution, with regard to which even the pope is helpless, there is not and cannot be in that Catholic community another juridical authority besides that which flows from above, from the Pope and the bishops.

Therefore, whenever the secular authority willfully tries to seize ecclesiastical jurisdiction, it usurps something which does not belong to it. . . .

Aware of our apostolic mission, we solemnly declare that we cannot consider this decree as legal and binding, because it is inconsistent with the Constitution of the Polish People's Republic, and violates the laws of God and of the Church. "One should obey God rather than men." We are not refusing to take into consideration the motives and the suggestions of the government. But in fulfilling church positions we must be directed by divine and by ecclesiastical law, and we must appoint only those priests whom we consider, in our conscience, as fit and worthy. We find it difficult to overlook how little worthy of their positions, especially the more important ones, are those who have yielded to external political pressure. . . . We are not allowed to place the things of God on the altar of Caesar. *Non possumus!*

We are conscious of the special tasks and duties of the Catholic priest towards his country, and that is why we have often reminded our priests of them. . . . But we also demand, emphatically, that our priests should not be torn away from religious duties; they should not be drawn into political affairs which are alien to their vocation; that political pressure aimed at using them as instruments in the struggle of the State against the Church should be stopped; and they should not be forced to break the oath by which they pledged loyalty to the Church and their bishops. In short, in accordance with the principle of separation of Church and State, as guaranteed in our Constitution, the State must abstain from intruding in the religious, spiritual, and internal affairs of the Church. . . .

Source: Janice Broun, *Conscience and Captivity. Religion in Eastern Europe* (Washington, D.C., 1988), pp. 333–334.

SUGGESTIONS FOR BACKGROUND AND REFERENCE

R. C. Monticone, *The Catholic Church in Communist Poland, 1945–1985: Forty Years of Church-State Relations* (Boulder, Colo., 1986).

B. Szajkowski, *Next to God—Poland: Politics and Religion in Contemporary Poland* (New York, 1983).

N. C. Nielsen, *Revolutions in Eastern Europe. The Religious Roots* (Maryknoll, N.Y., 1991), pp. 65–84.

Source for this document, pp. 163–198.

182   ALRC Appeal to the Romanian Council of State (Extracts)

July 5, 1978

Though Romania's Uniates and The Lord's Army—the evangelical wing of Romanian Orthodoxy—were suppressed in 1948 and other religious groups experienced persecution during the late 1950s and early 1960s, Romania relaxed tensions during the 1970s and acquired a reputation in the West for successful management of religion without marked ruthlessness or violence. Church deference to state control, especially in Orthodoxy, yielded benefits: growing numbers, permission for new churches, successful theological institutions, and an increasing clergy. In 1977 and 1978, however, protest developed among Baptists, Romania's fastest-growing denomination.

In February 1977 opposition to a Baptist leadership subservient to the state surfaced at the Bucharest Congress of Baptist Churches. Protests against excessive regulation of churches and antireligious discrimination in education and employment were made. The denomination obediently denounced and punished dissidents, but in April 1978, nine

From *Religion in Communist Lands,* Vol. VII, No. 3 (1979). Copyright, 1979, by Keston College, publisher. Reprinted by permission of the publisher.

Baptists organized the Christian Committee for the Defence of Religious Freedom and Freedom of Conscience (ALRC). The organizers sought to broaden its base by seeking human rights and religious freedom for all Romanians. In July the committee addressed the appeal to the government, reproduced below.

Through arrest, imprisonment, and forced emigration the ALRC was quickly destroyed and its supporters expelled from the Baptist Union. The episode emphasized that accommodation and coordination between church and regime must remain under rigorous state control.

We welcome the recent reforms proposed by our leaders in the economic field, in legislation and other areas, except in the field of religion where the same methods have been practised for 30 years. This has created tension between Church and State, and leads to permanent suffering among the faithful.

As this situation cannot remain static, affecting as it does not only the work of the Christian Church but also Romania's prestige in the world, we consider a change of attitude to be absolutely essential.

Therefore, we demand from the central organs of the Party and from the State the following:

1. The right of religious associations to exist undisturbed and to be recognized by law. In this connection we demand the right of the Roman Catholic Church to have a recognized juridical statute; the re-establishment of the Greek Catholic Church, which was disbanded by the Romanian State in 1948; the re-integration of the Church of the Reformed Seventh-day Adventists; official recognition of the evangelical movement, "The Lord's Army" within the framework of the Romanian Orthodox Church; the right of religious associations . . . to join international religious organizations without official approval.

2. The right to practise religion in church, private homes and in public without official approval, as well as the right to preach, to baptize and to officiate at open-air meetings. The right to carry out pastoral work without restriction, anywhere in our country, especially in hospitals, old people's homes and prisons. The right of priests and pastors to lecture and preach wherever they are invited and by whatever confession.

3. The right to make church appointments: to appoint leaders, hierarchs, priests, pastors and theological professors. We demand an end to interference by the Department of Cults . . . ; the end of identity cards and permits for priests and pastors, as well as the annulment of the obligation to be "recognized" or "approved" before taking up a post. The annulment of a "ceiling" for the appointment of clergy and the right to create new parishes according to the desire of the faithful. . . .

4. The right to build, to buy or hire places of worship without the approval of the Department of Cults. . . . The right to own church property, liturgical objects, donations. The right to receive money donations, material help, cult objects from Christians abroad. . . .

5. The right to express religious opinions in public as does atheist propaganda at present. Free dialogue between Christians and Marxists and on the radio, television and in the press. The right of Christians to reply in the press of the United Socialist

Front . . . to atheist propaganda and attacks, as all the 14 religious cults are members of this association.

6. The right to print and distribute religious literature. . . .

The right to have a free religious press, and an end to censorship by the Department of Cults. The publication of religious magazines, regularly, in quantities necessary to meet the demand. Publicity in the magazines on all aspects of the cult, as well as on cases of religious persecution. . . .

The right of any confession to have its own printing press and to own a duplicating machine.

The right to disseminate and sell religious literature and the Bible in Romanian, Hungarian, German, Serbian, English, French through colporteurs, bookshops and kiosks. . . .

7. The right to give religious instruction to children and young people. The right for priests and pastors to hold catechism classes freely; to hold meetings for prayer and Bible study; to organize excursions. The right to give religious instruction to young Christians in school, just as classes in Marxism are held for non-believers.

The right of parents to give religious instruction to their children and to have a say in the type of cultural activities their children should join. An end to the sabotage of Sundays and Christian feast-days in schools and institutions. Respect for Sunday as a day of rest.

An end to enforced indoctrination of children and young people with atheist and materialist ideas.

8. The right to carry out charitable work. . . .

9. The right to found centres for theological instruction at university level . . . and freedom for those who are chosen to be ordained. . . .

10. The right to hold . . . congresses without the approval of the Ministry. The right to invite foreigners to take part in these. The right to subscribe to foreign reviews.

11. The right for Christians to have access to higher posts in the economy, education, university life, the diplomatic service, etc. The right to be promoted. . . .

12. The right of Churches and religious associations to have access to television, radio, the press, and to be able to broadcast on Sundays and other religious feast-days.

13. The right of the faithful to warn the authorities about the persecution of those hierarchs who are also Members of Parliament.

14. The right to re-open all closed churches, and the right of all pastors and clergy, who were dismissed arbitrarily, to be reinstated. . . .

15. The right of young Christians in the Army to have a Bible, prayer-book, etc.

16. The right of Romanian Christians to refuse to sign an oath of loyalty to the Communist Party, or an opportunity for those who do sign, not to accept atheist indoctrination.

* * *

24. The necessity to reform church-state relations. In the last 30 years the Ministry of Cults has been a continuous source of abuses, restrictive measures, and

psychological pressure . . . ; their policy of intimidation has created a deep gulf between Christians and the State.

Our ideal is a free Church in a free State which would allow dialogue and co-operation between the two.

Source: Religion in Communist Lands, Vol. VII, No. 3 (1979), pp. 170–173.

SUGGESTIONS FOR BACKGROUND AND REFERENCE

T. Beeson, *Discretion and Valour, Religious Conditions in Russia and Eastern Europe* (Philadelphia, 1982), pp. 350–379.

J. Broun, *Conscience and Captivity. Religion in Eastern Europe* (Washington, D.C., 1988), pp. 199–244.

N. C. Nielsen, *Revolutions in Eastern Europe. The Religious Roots* (Maryknoll, N.Y., 1991), pp. 103–115.

A. Scarfe, "A Call for Truth: An Appraisal of Rumanian Baptist Church-State Relations," *Journal of Church and State*, Vol. 21, No. 3 (Autumn 1979), pp. 431–449.

———, "Dismantling a Human Rights Movement: a Romanian Solution," *Religion in Communist Lands*, Vol. VII, No. 3 (1979), pp. 166–169.

P. Walters (ed.), *World Christianity: Eastern Europe* (Eastbourne, England, 1988), pp. 247–270.

183 Dissident Catholicism in Hungary: "Marton Hartai's" Open Letter and Bulányi's Letter to Cardinal Lékai (Extracts)

September 1980 and March 7, 1982

State management of churches in Communist East Europe frequently led to bitter division in the religious community. Through control of seminaries, ordinations, and parish and episcopal appointments, governments often gained ascendancy over official church structures. Domination was further enhanced by espionage, censorship, use of informers, and imprisonment or forced emigration of objectors. Most states also sponsored collaborating clerical bodies, such as "Pacem in Terris" in Czechoslovakia and the "Peace Priests" elsewhere. Many church leaders defended conciliation as a policy of realism, a price to be paid for survival. Yet some religious people, clerical and lay, viewed such accommodation as subservience to the enemies of Christianity and betrayal of the faithful. The result was a tendency to see church hierarchy and government bureaucracy as confederated foes of true religion.

In Hungarian Catholicism the Mindszenty tradition of intransigeance was abandoned after the cardinal's deposition (1974) by the Vatican and

From *Religion in Communist Lands*, XI, No. 1 (1983), XII, No. 1 (1984). Copyright, 1983, 1984 by Keston College, publisher. Reprinted by permission of the publisher.

the development of Paul VI's *Ostpolitik*. László Lékai, cardinal arch-bishop from 1977 to 1986, believed confrontation would be disastrous and favored patient negotiation with the state by which progressive improvements might be secured. The bishops were primarily of the same temper—cautious administrators, traditional and conservative, convinced that submission was unavoidable. Consequently, they tended to regard religious protest both as an invitation to intensified state inter-ference and a challenge to their own authority. Furthermore, the state depended on the bishops to bring dissidents under ecclesiastical disci-pline. Disruption, distrust, and embitterment within the churches inev-itably followed. Reproduced below (A) is the pseudonymous "Open Letter," written by "Marton Hartai," which describes the situation in 1980.

Sometimes hostility to authority flourished in base groups, small informal associations of lay people led by popular priests, where wor-ship, prayer, and Bible study occurred. Such meetings often nurtured an ardent piety and deep personal commitment. Not all base groups were in protest. Yet they tended to stir state suspicion and some episcopal dis-trust. The base group, "The Bush," organized in about 150 societies with about five thousand participants, fostered a radical ethical absolutism—opposition to divorce, abortion, command authority, violence, and ma-terialism. Its pacifism, resulting in failure to report for army duty, alarmed the state. During the 1980s its views were warmly defended by the Piarist priest, György Bulányi (1919–   ). Imprisoned in the 1950s, Bulányi was later unable to secure a parish appointment and worked as a laborer by day and ministered to his flock in the evenings. State Church Office pressure moved Cardinal Lékai to a controversy with Bulányi, marked by charges of heresy, and suspension in 1982. Below (B) parts of Bulányi's letter to the primate (March 7, 1982), defending his base community, are reprinted.

A. From "An Open Letter to Hungarian Catholic Dissidents":

The cunning of worldly leaders is truly admirable: they can lay down the rules of the game in ecclesiastical terms. For instance, they recognised that . . . the education and training of priests can be entrusted to people who are alien to the crying needs of the faith, who will teach a distorted view of the world to their pupils.

The fierce "peace-priests," the army of those tarred with a left-wing brush, are gradually fading into the background—they were too openly and blatantly the mouthpiece of state direction and interventionism. The style of state policies has become more refined: the leadership of the Church will gradually be handed over to people who are honest and sincere . . . ; the only snag is that they are rigid traditionalists who have not learnt from their own past. . . . Unfortunately, with their principles, their value system, their educational methods, they simply cannot rise to the challenge of the present; thereby they are hindering those entrusted to their care. The novices therefore cannot find their bearings in the world. . . . Once they become priests, they cannot properly assess their true tasks in pastoral care, they do not really understand other people. It is to be feared that the education of priests may become the "opium for the people." Certainly, it is opium for the priests themselves: a distorted personality and attitude induces a kind of stupor that paralyses the will for action, prevents the recognition of, and resistance to, disguised oppression. Is this not what we may call alienation?

* * *

The State has complete control over all churches and governs ecclesiastical life by indirect methods. We have lost every means for legally valid defence. The priest would turn in vain to his bishop, the novice to his superior, a parish member with a grievance to his priest. In actual practice, every single institution or office that ought to protect the freedom of the Church acts against such protesters. Initiatives by individuals are suppressed, hopes of a community are dissipated, flocks are dispersed—all in all, the foundations of the Catholic Church are in danger. . . .

There are some amongst us who do believe that the State is willing to enter into an honest dialogue with us, if only we were ready for it. The two-faced policy of the "peace-priests" has seduced many a priest of good will. These people do not realise that every new agreement between State and Church, trumpeted around the world as a great new achievement, only gives back ridiculous crumbs of the rights originally due to the Church of Christ and to all human beings. In exchange for these "concessions," they become the tools of totalitarian state power; a power that has never given up its aim to gag every kind of dissident. . . .

* * *

What is the use of a flood of marvellously courageous articles, when it can happen—as it has recently—that a bishop reports a priest of another diocese because he holds catechism classes at his presbytery? When policemen surround the pupils and take their names, in order to intimidate them and their parents? When the State Office for Religious Affairs holds dozens of snapshots taken at religious gatherings as material exhibits against the participants? What about those ecclesiastical office-holders who are using similar underhand ways to remove "awkward" people? What should we believe? The rousing declarations about the freedom of the Church, or the statement by an official at the Ministry of Home Affairs: "Everything concerns us, including whether you are a churchgoer or not. Everything is in our hands, everything depends on us."

Another, even more dangerous, aspect of the opting-out process is that of becoming an informer. Some people may be kept on a string, as a result of some moral peccadillo; they are forced to "grass" for the files of the Office for Religious Affairs. Others turn informer simply because they cannot bear the constant tension. These "supergrass" priests are perhaps the most dangerous, as they are inside the Church. They are to be pitied most, too, as they are degrading both their own moral being and their vocation. . . .

There is also the army of the inert, that of "loyalist" church members. They are realists too: they may reject the tragi-comic kowtowing of others, but they also avoid anything that may throw doubt upon their reliability.

* * *

There are questions galore to be answered. . . . We should throw ourselves into the work of answering them, lest we, too, become adapted to the organic distortions of the system. "He who was born lame learns to live with his lameness." The Church has always been the repository of the noblest principles. Our Catholic Church, however—burdened by a long and often dubious history—seems to accept the surrender to Caesar, the identification with the interest of the rulers of the day. It considers that its situation cannot be changed, therefore it is not worth trying to change it. . . .

Viewing the present state of the Catholic Church, one has the impression that the Hungarian State is pioneering new methods of persecuting religion. Hungary may have succeeded in acquiring a certain respect abroad, rare among so-called socialist states; our standard of living is relatively high, there is freedom of religion, dissidents are not always thrown into prison. It is certainly true that the religious policies of our State are less crude than those of Czechoslovakia or Romania. Unfortunately, the essence remains hidden from the eyes of the innocent bystander. Maybe the Party is attempting to shape a new, national Church—a new historical phenomenon? In addition, it strives to gain the blessing of the Vatican on its actions; the execution of its moves is usually entrusted to our religious notables. This is doubly dangerous: not only may this shake the faith of many believers—it may also undermine our trust in Rome. The Hungarian method of refined religious persecution may become the paradigm for the next decade . . . or even for the next century.

B. From György Bulányi to Cardinal László Lékai, March 7, 1982:

I respectfully request Your Eminence to consider our aims as summarised below. These aims are our motivation, in spite of our weakness and our modest achievements.

1. Mindful of God and the Church, we consider it our constant duty, given to us by Jesus, that our little communities should become more and more acquainted with God, who wants to communicate with us, and bear witness in words and deeds to what we know of Him. We cannot be deterred from fulfilling our obligations, even if we are threatened with the harshest punishments, even if our lives are in peril, and with God's help we want to stand fast in the future, too.

2. We stick unflinchingly to our duties as human beings and as God's children. We try to see clearly, as the Second Vatican Council requires of us, by observing the signs of the times (Matt. 16, 4) what the Kingdom of God means here and now. In order to serve the Kingdom of God, we will continue committing our thoughts on the subject to paper, so that by reading, criticising and adding to each others' manuscripts, and by mutual encouragement, we shall do what we are able in this respect. If our Church has—thanks be to God—unequivocally supported freedom of thought in the Second Vatican Council, then it is our sacred duty to make this freedom an unquestionable reality within the Church. . . .

3. On the strength of what we have seen so far, we try to serve life, so that it should become more abundant (John 10, 10).

a) In the service of life, we face the death of our nation. Last year the population declined by two thousand, and according to forecasts it will decline further in the near future by hundreds of thousands. In our communities we consider it quite normal for families to have four, five, six or even more children; we think a mother should stay at home to rear the children; and we think a family should be able to manage on one person's income. Since the Second World War the nation has condemned five million lives to death by abortion. The losses in the tragic battles of Mohacs [1526] and of the Don [1943] were negligible compared with those due to abortion. Atheists have already raised their voices courageously. The families of our small communities protest with their lives against this gross immorality of our society, which eats up its own children in the interest of raising material living standards.

b) . . . we reject all other forms of killing people. . . . We do not promise the destruction of our enemies, because everybody is our neighbour. We are not pre-pared to become patriotic mass murderers, war criminals. . . . We believe . . . that without the Fifth Commandment the Kingdom of Heaven and the classless society are unattainable, violence will not cease, and the State will not wither away. Fighting will stop only when there are no more fighters. Whatever punishments or suffering we have to face, we are not going to give up our faith. We pray that Your Eminence's Catholic heart, formed like that of Jesus, should be filled with pride and joy at the knowledge that since September 1979 eight Hungarian Catholics have made a heroic confession of faith, and that at present there are still four imprisoned for their witness [in refusing military conscription.]

c) . . . we endeavour to direct our consciences in such a way as not to increase our standard of living. We want not to increase it from two to three but to reduce it from three to two, so far as purchasable goods are concerned. We do this so that the superfluity can be given to the hungry. . . .

d) . . . we exclude from our little communities all governing, commanding and subordination of others to ourselves, all forms of compelling obedience, remember-ing the words of Jesus: "All ye are brethren" (Matt. 23, 8). We place our hopes in revelation and in human conscience. We obey Jesus' commandments and we obey the Spirit, which reminds us of His words. . . . In the Church we all have to obey God (Acts 5, 29).

* * *

5. The number of our priests is diminishing alarmingly. Our churches, deprived of priests, are empty, yet we trust in the authority of Jesus (Mark 1, 22). We trust implicitly in the power of the Word and its teaching to bring society, irrespective of religion or non-religion, to the realisation that the unadulterated (Matt. 10, 16) words of Jesus speak for the life of society as a whole. . . . For this very reason we would think it natural if the chief Hungarian shepherd of Jesus' poor, meek, un-protected Catholic Church, which defies the powerful of this world, were to em-brace us with all the love of his heart, moved by our Jesus-like ideals, our optimistic efforts to reverse the population decline and our pastoral conceptions based on small communities—since, as Pope Paul VI said, the small communities are "the hope of the Church."

6. . . . I have the honour to inform Your Eminence of the following:

a) It must be evident to you from my consistent statements at the two [former] meetings and my "Answers" that . . . we adhere to the unerring teachings of our Church. . . .

b) If in any words of ours, spoken or written, you should find anything that you judge contrary to the teachings of our Church, we shall respectfully and conscientiously think over your corrections. . . .

c) I am ready and willing to take part in further dialogues, if I receive a guarantee that at the meetings not a single participant will revile us or our aims. . . . It is very sad for me to think that in 1952 under the Rakosi regime, the atheist major who interrogated me at the secret police headquarters . . . for sixty days showed more respect for my person and my activities than was my lot at the above-mentioned meetings. . . .

It may seem superfluous, but to avoid any misunderstanding I must mention that my frequent use in this letter of the first person plural means unequivocally that I do not state these things alone, but together with all my brethren of the same persuasion.

Source: Religion in Communist Lands, Vol. XI, No. 1 (1983), pp. 105–108; Vol. XII, No. 1 (1984), pp. 38–41.

SUGGESTIONS FOR BACKGROUND AND REFERENCE

J. Broun, *Conscience and Captivity. Religion in Eastern Europe* (Washington, D.C., 1988), pp. 127–162.

F. Hainbuch, *Kirche und Staat in Ungarn nach dem Zweiten Weltkrieg* (Munich, 1982).

J. K. Hoensch, *A History of Modern Hungary, 1867–1983* (London, 1988).

P. Michel, *Politics and Religion in Eastern Europe* (Oxford, 1991), pp. 116–122.

N. C. Nielsen, *Revolutions in Eastern Europe. The Religious Roots* (Maryknoll, N.Y., 1991), pp. 49–64.

184   Hungarian Diakonia Theology: Dóka's Letter to the Lutheran World Federation and "A Brotherly Word" of the Lutheran Reform Group (Extracts)

July 10, 1984, and March 1986

Protestant minorities in Eastern Europe, seeking to adjust to the ascendant communism, often developed theological themes emphasizing the gospel duty of service to a reconstructed and more beneficent social order and of cooperation with political authority in building such an order. These themes were found in both Lutheran and Reformed churches and, with forceful state endorsement, often became official and obligatory doctrine, intolerant of any difference or criticism. In the West and (more dangerously) at home, opponents charged that the trend prostituted Christianity to political and secular ends in a manner reminiscent of the "German Christians" in the Nazi era, a judgment angrily rejected by the accused theologians.

From *Religion in Communist Lands*, XIII, No. 1 (1985), XIV, No. 3 (1986). Copyright, 1985, 1986 by Keston College, publisher. Reprinted by permission of the publisher.

In Hungarian Lutheranism, Zoltán Káldy was the most prominent exponent of such a theological trend, which under the name of *Diakonia* claimed to interpret Protestant service theology. In 1958 he was the government's choice to replace a defiant and imprisoned predecessor, Lajos Ordass, and from 1967 until his death in 1986 he was Presiding Bishop. In 1984 the Lutheran World Federation, meeting in Budapest, elected him its president, though only after controversy and protest. Much of that controversy was generated by a letter from Hungarian pastor and theologian, Zoltán Dóka, condemning *Diakonia* theology as a distortion of the gospel tyrannically imposed on pastors and people by both church officials and the state. Portions of the letter are reproduced below (A).

Dóka was suspended without salary, and the official church response was to condemn his views as "treason with a theological veneer." Yet by 1986 political-ecclesiastical control in Hungary had become more relaxed; some criticism was permitted and the possibility of alternative theological interpretations admitted. A Lutheran Reform Group of pastors and laymen prepared an open letter to the government, partly reprinted below (B), protesting mandatory adherence to *Diakonia* and demanding reforms—theological pluralism, fair election of church leaders, decentralization of ecclesiastical authority, a right to Lutheran education, more lay participation, and unfettered dialogue.

A. From Zoltán Dóka's "Open Letter to the Lutheran World Federation," July 10, 1984:

Up to the present day the leadership of the Hungarian Lutheran Church (hereafter HLC) has misled the world Lutheran community by stating that its pastors and congregations uniformly confess the so-called Diakonia Theology (hereafter DT). The truth is that the concept of DT has not yet reached the consciousness of the congregations, and only a minority of pastors approve of it. Most of those who approve do so only out of personal interest or fear, and only in a public capacity. In confidential circles, however, they criticise and reject the concept. This rift is one of the most characteristic and saddest aspects of the spiritual and theological situation of the HLC.

* * *

To the question of what the task of the church in the world is DT gives the following answer: The task of the church is the proclamation of the gospel, together with the distribution of sacraments, and the practice of diakonia. With regard to the latter, it is specially emphasised that it is not enough for diakonia to deal only with individuals, and that it must extend to the burning questions both of one's own society and of the whole of humanity. In itself this can only provoke approval. But given this definition, it immediately appears puzzling—especially to Lutheran ears—that one has to make special mention of diakonia, when it is simply a result, an ethical consequence, in the life of those who answer "Yes" in faith to the gospel.

DT, however, again and again emphasises that diakonia is not merely the fruit of a faith awakened through the gospel, but is also independent from the gospel, ranked equally with the gospel as the peculiar task of the church. Such differentiation is justified by saying that in the synoptic gospels Jesus sent out his disciples not only to proclaim the approach of the Kingdom of God, but also to exorcise demons and cure the sick. . . .

On the basis of the above-mentioned definition, the thesis of the Augsburg Confession "about the church" has often been criticised as one which must be filled out with the task of practising diakonia. It is said that neither Melanchthon nor Luther gave a complete answer to the question of what the task of the church should be, because both held the proclamation of the word as the sole treasure and task of the church. But I am convinced that the "amplified gospel" is the fundamental error of DT and . . . an erroneous teaching of church history. This false theology makes no distinction between the acts of God and the acts of men, but mixes them and makes them appear equal. When Bishop Káldy repeatedly stresses: "that church which only proclaims the gospel is not a church," it is apparent that DT subordinates the gospel to diakonia, or to a socio-ethical concept. This ethical-ideological construction, however, robs the gospel of the final gracious Word of God for sinners, of its independent freedom from every human activity, and thus weakens it.

Simultaneously, the free Christian act is deprived of its well-spring and is deformed into justice through works and piety through service. This false theological basis of DT makes the theological thinking and preaching of the clergy uncertain. . . .

The socio-ethical manipulation of the gospel is shown in practice particularly when DT is applied by the church leadership. To be sure, only a few people within the member-churches of the LWF know that there is no religious freedom in the HLC. I repeat: in the HLC there is no religious freedom. The state's church policy, surprising though it may seem, demonstrates more concern for the interest of the pastors and congregations than does the church leadership. It is all the more scandalous and unendurable that the church leadership has declared DT to be the official and obligatory theology of the HLC. Everyone who resists this pressure, even in the smallest way, exposes himself to existential danger, as Bishop Káldy continually emphasises in a manner intended to intimidate the pastors.

Dear brothers, you must know this and you ought not to pass over in silence the fact that theological terror reigns in the HLC. This is the truth, which members and representatives of the church leadership try to hide from foreign churches in every possible way. The church leadership maintains this terror by telling the civil authorities that those who dare criticise DT are enemies of the state. In this way they skilfully make theological debate impossible. This is a real and perilous slander.

Together with many of my colleagues, I must admit . . . that it is no easy task for the state to develop a church policy which will remain faithful to its fundamental ideological position, and at the same time allow ideas of humanity rooted in universal human rights to prosper. During my 32 years of church service, however, I have recognised more clearly that the church leadership, which manifests loyalty to the state, has not offered true and genuine help in the development of its church policy. A few years ago Bishop Káldy frequently stressed verbally and in writing that it is not enough for a pastor to be an obedient citizen who maintains good relations with the local and state authorities, nor is it enough if a pastor of the HLC merely fulfills his calling correctly and in an up-to-date manner by accepting socialism—with the exception of atheism—and by actively and directly supporting the socialist aims of the state. Such statements, however, only appear in the Hungarian Church press, never in foreign languages!

* * *

The most serious consequence of the theological terror and the cult of personality, however, is that the standard of theological work in the HLC falls ever lower. Scholarly work is impossible where freedom of research is absent and where researchers must confirm already-established answers. The chief task of professors is the justification of DT. This also means that theological work in the HLC has no scholarly world perspective, because it cannot keep pace with foreign research. Bishop Káldy upholds this situation when he says that DT is the world's best theological concept and so we have no need of foreign, especially "western" theology. This conceited theology will do incalculable harm to the spiritual and intellectual life of the church. The damage is already great and it is vastly important that there should be a complete rethinking in total freedom and openness of the HLC's theology, church law and church politics, before suitable pastors have run out of energy for the rethinking, before the congregations are dispersed or absorbed by the sects, or before the inner life of the HLC finally collapses.

B. From "A Brotherly Word," March 1986:

We thank God that he is still working amongst us today. Nevertheless, we are conscious of our responsibility towards our church, and this inspires us to raise our voices, because we see signs of crisis in its life. . . .

1. We confess that

The greatest treasure of the church is the Gospel of Jesus Christ and if this is proclaimed purely, it is still the power of God (Romans 1:16). It effectively brings about man's reconciliation with God, and so achieves new life in the context of human existence in today's world.

The Gospel is the church's sole foundation and its guiding purpose. The church exists because the Holy Spirit, through the Gospel, awakens faith in human hearts, and through faith binds and shapes them into a congregation, the body of Christ, a brotherly communion. Equally, the church exists as the instrument of the Holy Spirit to make the Gospel known to all men.

Only the Gospel can give correct norms and direction to the inner structure of the church and to its service in the world. All other bases for the church's existence obscure its divine origin and real mission.

We consider to be mistaken those who, in considering the question of the church's mission, regard the theology of diaconia as being equivalent to the proclamation of the Gospel, making it possible, *ipso facto*, to separate diaconia from its source, the Gospel. This kind of interpretation of diaconia distorts and weakens the Gospel. Furthermore, the forcible turning of diaconia into an absolute truth curtails, even destroys, the internal freedom of church life. The breakdown of theological pluralism leads to intellectual infantilism, makes free theological discussion impossible, and poisons the atmosphere of brotherly love.

Yet diaconia, which emerges from the Gospel, represents a vital sign of church life in the healing of physical and mental debility, and also in the sense that, in church life, no one rules the other, but everyone lives and serves with self-denying love for the benefit of others.

2. We confess that the life of the church is rooted in the congregations. It follows from this that:

all general church activities must be examined and developed from the viewpoint of congregational activity;

there must be a search for a way out of the disintegrating, traditional church structure towards a new form of life;

there must be a reconsideration of the structural organisation of our church. We consider it necessary to simplify and decentralise the judicial structure, and that the election of leaders at every level should be carried out without outside influence, within a prescribed time, and with the possibility of recall.

3. We consider it extremely important, from the point of view of the present and the future of our church, to examine the theoretical and practical implications of secularisation. We have to face this world-wide phenomenon, which in our country is combined with ideological atheism, so that we can give the people of our church the help so far denied them.

* * *

4. We confess that the church carries within it a responsibility for the whole created world, and for that nation within whose political boundaries it lives. The Church practises its political responsibility by proclaiming God's word and through the activities of its institutions, as well as through the service of individual Christians within the community. We consider it offensive to the identity of the church anywhere in the world, that the church and its official representatives should be forced into active political life and the exercise of direct power, political decision-making, and the taking up of particular political standpoints. Participation in political life is the individual freedom and responsibility of every Christian—including those holding office in the church—as citizens of the state.

5. We suggest that as soon as possible national conferences should be organised in which—by voluntary application—any member of our church may take part, and where, in a responsible manner and in an atmosphere of brotherhood and freedom, we can deal with the above-mentioned and other questions concerning the church.

Source: Religion in Communist Lands, Vol. XIII, No. 1 (1985), pp. 98–102; Vol. XIV, No. 3 (1986), pp. 330–331.

SUGGESTIONS FOR BACKGROUND AND REFERENCE

J. Broun, *Conscience and Captivity. Religion in Eastern Europe* (Washington, D.C., 1988), pp. 127–160.

J. Eibner, "Pressure for Reform in the Hungarian Lutheran Church," *Religion in Communist Lands*, Vol. XIV, No. 3 (1986), pp. 323–326.

N. C. Nielsen, *Revolutions in Eastern Europe. The Religious Roots* (Maryknoll, N.Y., 1991), pp. 49–64.

185   Czech Petition for Religious Freedom

January 1988

After the 1968 Russian invasion and the collapse of the "Prague Spring" reforms of Alexander Dubcek, Czechoslovakia experienced renewed religious persecution. A rigorous censorship was imposed, seminaries and schools were closed, and some clergy were sent to prisons or labor camps. During the 1970s all religious activity, Catholic and Protestant, was carefully controlled by the State Office for Religious Affairs, which also promoted the subservient *Pacem in Terris* organization (to which at one time about one-third of the Catholic priests belonged). Less cooperative clergy and bishops were generally unable to secure government approval of church appointment, and consequently many parishes and dioceses remained vacant for long periods. In 1977 public frustration and indignation led to an unusual assertion of human rights, Charter 77, signed by numerous prominent Czech intellectuals, professionals, and churchmen. The state punished signatories with loss of employment, prison, and forced emigration, and church leaders and publications were required to denounce the document. Nonetheless, resistance became bolder in the 1980s, led in part by Cardinal Frantisek Tomasek. A growing *samizdat* religious literature escaped the censor, and a small but committed underground church expanded. After the ascendancy of Mikhail Gorbachev in 1985 and the gradual introduction of *glasnost* and *perestroika* in Russia, pressure on Czech Communists became more intense.

In early 1988 this petition for religious freedom began circulating in Bohemia/Moravia for endorsements. It received the blessing of Cardinal Tomasek, and ultimately it was signed by over a half million Czechs of various religious persuasions. It marked the beginning of erosion of the Communist religious apparatus and regime. The Marxist state fell in 1990.

1. We demand separation of Church and State. All other demands follow from this.

2. We demand that State organisations do not prevent the appointment of new bishops in Czechoslovakia.

3. We demand that State organisations do not interfere with the appointment of priests.

4. We demand that State organisations do not interfere with the selection of students, nor the number of students enrolled at theological faculties. Also that they do not interfere with the choice of teachers.

5. We demand that the theological faculty in Olomouc be re-opened.

6. We demand the introduction of a permanent body of deacons.

7. We demand that the religious orders be rehabilitated, and permitted to accept new members as in neighbouring GDR and Poland.

8. We demand that the right of believers to form lay religious associations be recognised.

9. We demand that religious instruction take place outside school, either in church, a priest's home or in another building. Parents should apply direct to the parish for religious instruction for their children (not to the school authorities).

10. We demand that priests be allowed to visit prisons and hospitals whenever prisoners, patients or their relatives request it.

11. We demand the right to hold retreats and training programmes for the laity.

12. We demand that every congregation be headed by a parish council, to assist priests in tackling parish problems.

13. We demand the right to establish contacts with Christian organisations worldwide.

14. We demand the right to organise and participate in pilgrimages, either individually or collectively.

15. We demand that believers be provided with the religious literature they need, that a religious publishing house under church control be set up and that religious libraries and reading rooms be opened.

16. We demand that the production and distribution of religious texts be no longer considered a criminal offence.

17. We demand the right to import freely religious literature from abroad.

18. We demand the right to TV and radio programmes covering religious events.

19. We demand an end to jamming of Vatican radio programmes and Sunday masses from Radio Free Europe.

20. We demand that priests and laity be permitted to spread Christian teaching.

21. We demand that confiscated church buildings, retreat centres, theological faculty buildings and buildings belonging to religious orders be returned.

22. We demand that new churches be built where they are needed.

23. We demand an end to the indiscriminate removal of crosses, sculptures and small chapels from our towns and roadways.

24. We demand that the Secretary for Church Affairs be prevented from interfering in the appointment, transfer and activity of priests.

25. We demand the immediate and complete rehabilitation of illegally sentenced priests, members of orders and active members of the laity.

26. We demand an end to discrimination against believers in employment, particularly in education.

27. We demand that believers be allowed to address particular problems which concern them, i.e. the right of petition.

28. We demand that laws which regard religious activity as criminal be dropped.

29. We demand that certain legal articles be amended.

30. We demand that all existing laws be brought into line with international pacts on human rights.

31. We demand that a committee composed of State and Church representatives be formed to discuss and make appropriate decisions.

Source: Religion in Communist Lands, Vol. XVII, No. 2 (1989), pp. 165–166.

SUGGESTIONS FOR BACKGROUND AND REFERENCE

J. Broun, *Conscience and Captivity. Religion in Eastern Europe* (Washington, D.C., 1988), pp. 67–102.

P. Michel, *Politics and Religion in Eastern Europe* (Oxford, 1991).

N. C. Nielsen, *Revolutions in Eastern Europe. The Religious Roots* (Maryknoll, N.Y., 1991), pp. 85–102.

P. Walters (ed.), *World Christianity: Eastern Europe* (Eastbourne, England, 1988), pp. 175–197.

✦ ✦ ✦

186   Soviet Law on Freedom of Conscience and Religion (Extracts)

October 1, 1990

The revolutionary "new order" of *glasnost* and *perestroika* released after 1985 by the reformer, Mikhail Gorbachev, resulted in a radical improvement in the prospects of religion. Not only was official harassment largely abandoned, but a new interest in religious tradition and practice was manifested in a population disenchanted with Marxian ideology and hungry for the recovery of continuity with pre-1917 history and culture. Like other leaders of Russian society, Orthodox churchmen joined the national debate, making proposals and criticisms of unprecedented boldness. By 1990 they were demanding the return of some 18,000 churches—buildings that for decades had been converted to secular purposes as museums, offices, shops, sports facilities, and the like. And in the same year Patriarch Pimen's death permitted his replacement by the more assertive Aleksy of Leningrad. But the new freedom brought problems as well as opportunities. Religious edifices were often in structural decay. The shortage of priests was critical.

From *Religion in Communist Lands,* XIX, No. 1 (1991). Copyright, 1991, by Keston College, publisher. Reprinted by permission of the publisher.

Even when well disposed, laity were often ignorant of religious culture by reason of education and indoctrination. Moreover, dissension within religion created new crises: Ukrainians sought an autonomous patriarchate free of Moscow, Uniates reestablished ties with Rome and demanded return of their churches, and Jews complained that the new freedom was reviving traditional anti-Semitism. Within Orthodoxy sharp controversy arose over the submission of previous hierarchs to Communist domination, resulting in refusal by some dissidents to acknowledge bishops' authority and an attempt to set up a competing worship and organization.

Throughout these changes the antireligious constitutional and legal structure of the Communist regime remained substantially intact, though it was understood after 1988 that a new law on religious freedom would eventually emerge from the Supreme Soviet. The draft law was laid before that body in May 1990 and received final approval on September 26 by a vote of 341 to 1. Though the law conferred unprecedented freedom on religion, it also reserved important oversight to the state and withheld some privileges sought by the churches. Local authorities were not required to return confiscated church properties, conscientious objection to military service was excluded, and no allowance was made for optional religious education in the schools. The last issue was particularly divisive, causing debate among entrenched atheists, proponents of historic Russian Orthodoxy, and advocates of merely private "confessional" education. (Dissolution of the Soviet Union in 1991 to 1992 left the entire corpus of Soviet law in disarray, but the Russian government continued in practice the exercise of benevolent policies toward religious organizations.)

I. General Provision

1. The Purpose of the Law

This law guarantees the rights of citizens to decide and express their attitude towards religion, to convictions corresponding to this and to the unhindered confession of a religion and the exercise of religious rites, and also to equality and protection of the rights and interests of citizens regardless of their attitude towards religion, and regulates the relations pertaining to the activity of religious organisations.

* * *

3. The Right to Freedom of Conscience

. . . each citizen independently decides his own attitude towards religion and enjoys the right of confessing any religion either alone or jointly with others, or not to confess any religion, and to express and spread convictions. . . .

Parents and persons acting in loco parentis have the right . . . to rear their own children [according to] their personal attitudes towards religion.

No compulsion of any kind is permitted when a citizen decides his own attitude towards religion or to the confession or non-confession of a religion, or to participation or non-participation in divine service . . . and in religious instruction.

The exercise of freedom of conscience, religion or conviction is subject only to the limitations necessary to maintain public safety and order, life, well-being, and morals and also the rights and freedoms of other citizens as established by law and compatible with the international obligations of the USSR.

4. Equality of Citizens Regardless of Their Attitude Towards Religion

Citizens of the USSR are equal under the law in all fields of civic, political, economic, social and cultural life regardless of their attitude towards religion. No indication of the attitude of a citizen towards religion is permitted in official documents except in cases where the citizen himself so desires.

Any . . . limitation on the rights of a citizen or the establishment of any advantages for citizens depending on their attitude towards religion, and equally incitement of enmity or hostility associated with this, or insult against the sentiments of citizens, are subject to criminal liability. . . .

No one may by reason of his own religious persuasions avoid observance of obligations established by law. Replacement of one obligation with another for reasons of religious persuasion is permitted only . . . by USSR legislation.

5. Separation of Church (Religious Organisations) and State

All religions and denominations are equal under the law. The establishment of any advantages or restrictions with respect to one religion or denomination over others is not permitted.

The state does not assign to religious organisations the discharge of any state function and it does not intervene in the activity of religious organisations if that activity does not contravene legislation. The state does not fund religious organisations or activity associated with the propaganda of atheism.

No restrictions are permitted on the conducting of scientific research, including research funded by the state, or propaganda of its results or inclusion of those results in any general programme of education on the grounds that they are in accordance with or not in accordance with the tenets of any religion or of atheism.

Religious organisations do not carry out state functions.

[They] enjoy the right to participate in public life and also to make use of the mass media on an equal footing with public associations.

[They] do not participate in the activity of political parties [or] provide [them with] financial assistance. Ministers of religious organisations have the right to participate in political life on an equal footing with all citizens.

Religious organisations are obliged to observe . . . existing legislation and law and order.

The state promotes . . . mutual tolerance and respect between citizens who confess a religion and citizens who do not, and between religious organisations and also between their followers.

6. Separation of School and State (Religious Organisations)

The state system of education in the USSR is separate from the church and is secular. . . . Access to the various kinds and levels of education is granted to citizens regardless of their attitude towards religion.

Citizens may be instructed in a religious doctrine and obtain a religious education in the language of their choice. . . .

Religious organisations that have charters (or statutes) registered in accordance with the established procedure have the right . . . to set up educational establishments and groups for the religious education of children and adults and also to engage in teaching in other forms. . . .

II. Religious Organisations in the USSR

7. Religious Organisations

Religious organisations in the USSR are religious societies, boards and centres, monasteries, religious brotherhoods, missionary societies (missions) and spiritual training institutions, and also associations made up of religious organisations. . . . they operate in accordance with their own structure and select, appoint and change their own personnel in accordance with their own charters (or rules).

8. The Religious Society

A religious society is formed by citizens for the purpose of jointly professing a faith and satisfying other religious needs, and operates on a voluntary basis.

It is not mandatory to inform the state bodies that a religious society has been set up.

9. Religious Boards, Centres and Associations

Religious boards, centres and associations operate on the basis of their own charters (or rules) insofar as they do not contravene existing legislation.

Religious organisations in the USSR that have leading centres abroad may be guided in their activity by their own charters (or rules) if . . . it does not violate Soviet legislation.

Relations between the state and religious boards . . . including those abroad, are not regulated by law and are determined in accordance with agreement between them and state bodies.

10. Monasteries, Brotherhoods and Missions

Religious boards and centres may . . . establish monasteries, religious brotherhoods and missionary organisations (missions), which operate on the basis of their own charters . . . registered in . . . the procedure established by law.

* * *

11. Spiritual Training Establishments

Religious boards and centres have the right . . . to set up religious training establishments to train clergymen and other ministers. . . . Spiritual training establishments operate on the basis of their own charter (or rules). . . .

Citizens engaged in full-time studies at higher and secondary religious training establishments enjoy the same rights . . . as laid down for students at state educational establishments as far as deferment of military service and taxation and inclusion of time spent in study at the work-place are concerned.

12. Charters of Religious Organisations

The charter (or rules) . . . must in accordance with civil law defining its legal capacity be registered under the procedure established by law. This charter contains information on the kind and location of the religious organisation, its denominational affiliation, its place within the organisational structure of a religious association, its position with respect to property, its rights to set up enterprises and means of mass information, to found other religious organisations, and to set up training establishments, on other powers and on the procedure for resolving property and other matters in the event that its activity is terminated, and also other provisions connected with the special features of the activity of that organisation.

The charter . . . or other documents defining the regulation, training aspects of activity and resolving other internal matters of a religious organisation need not be registered with state bodies. The state takes into consideration and respects the internal enactments of religious organisations if they are submitted to appropriate state bodies and insofar as they do not contravene existing legislation.

13. Religious Organisations as Legal Entities

Religious organisations are recognised as legal entities. . . .

As legal entities, [they] enjoy rights and bear obligations in accordance with legislation and their own charter (or statutes).

14. Registration of the Charters of Religious Organisations

In order for a religious organisation to obtain legal capacity . . . at least 10 persons must make an application with the charter (or rules) to the executive committee of the raion (or town) soviet of people's deputies at the place of the proposed activity of the society. In the event that a religious society belongs to some religious organisation, this is indicated in the charter and confirmed by the appropriate religious board. . . . The executive committee considers the statement within one month and makes an appropriate decision.

If the confirmation . . . is not provided, the executive committee . . . has the right to ask for additional materials and to seek the opinion of specialists. In this event the decision is made within a three-month period.

Religious associations, and also centres, boards, monasteries, religious brotherhoods, missions and spiritual training centres . . . submit the charter . . . adopted by these organisations for registration with the executive committee of the . . . soviet . . . of their location. The executive committee makes a decision . . . within one month. . . .

15. Refusal To Register the Charter of a Religious Organisation

A decision to refuse to register . . . is sent in written form, indicating the reasons for refusal. This decision, or delay beyond the period laid down by this law for reaching decisions, may be appealed in the courts. . . .

16. Discontinuance of the Activity of a Religious Organisation

The activity of religious organisations may be discontinued only when they are liquidated in accordance with their own enactments or if there is violation . . . of this law or other laws. . . .

III. The Position of Religious Organisations with Respect to Property

17. The Use of Property That Is Owned by the State, Public Organisations, or Citizens

Religious organisations have the right to use . . . buildings and property made available to them on a contractual basis by state and public organisations or citizens.

Local soviets . . . may transfer to religious organisations as property or for use gratis cultural buildings and other property belonging to the state.

Religious organisations have a preferential right to have cult buildings with their adjacent territory transferred to them.

Decisions . . . relating to the transfer . . . should be made no later than one month after . . . application is made. . . .

The transfer to . . . religious organisations of objects and articles that are of historical and cultural significance is carried out in accordance with legislation.

Religious organisations establish ownership and use of land according to the procedure laid down by law.

18. Property of Religious Organisations

Religious organisations may own buildings, cult objects, facilities for production, social work and charitable purposes, monetary assets, and other property essential for their activity.

[They may] own property acquired or created by them using their own assets donated by citizens and organisations or transferred by the state. . . .

[They] may also own property abroad.

[They may] appeal for voluntary financial and other donations. . . .

Financial and property donations and . . . incomes of religious organisations are tax exempt. . . .

19. Production and Economic Activity of Religious Organisations

Religious organisations have the right . . . to maintain publishing, printing, production, restoration and construction, agricultural, and other enterprises and also charitable institutions (shelters, boarding schools, hospitals and so forth). . . .

Profit and . . . income from enterprises belonging to religious organisations are subject to tax . . . at the rates laid down for enterprises belonging to public organisations.

20. Disposition of the Property of Religious Organisations That Discontinue Their Activity

When religious organisations discontinue their activity the disposition of property that they own is carried out in accordance with the charter . . . and existing legislation.

No penalty can be imposed or claim made by creditors against cult property. . . .
[If] no successor is found, property is transferred to state ownership.

IV. Rights of Religious Organisations and Citizens Pertaining to Freedom of Worship

21. Religious Rites and Ceremonies

Religious organisations have the right to found and maintain freely accessible places revered by a particular religion (places of pilgrimage).

Divine service [is] . . . conducted without hindrance in prayer buildings and on the territory belonging to them, at places of pilgrimage, in the establishments of religious organisations, at cemeteries and crematoria and in citizens' flats and houses.

Command authorities in military units do not hinder participation in divine services . . . by servicemen during their free time.

Divine service . . . in hospitals, military hospitals, homes for the aged and disabled, and in places of preliminary detention and places where sentences are served are conducted at the request of the citizens in them. . . . these establishments provide assistance in inviting clergymen, and . . . participate in determining the time and other conditions for holding divine service. . .

In other cases, public divine service and religious rites . . . are conducted in accordance with the procedure established for holding gatherings, meetings, demonstrations and processions.

Religious organisations have the right to submit proposals to conduct divine service . . . in hospitals, military hospitals, homes for the aged and disabled and places of detention.

22. Religious Literature and Religious Objects

Citizens and religious organisations have the right to acquire and make use of religious literature in the language of their choice. . . .

Religious organisations have the right to produce, export, import, and disseminate religious articles, religious literature, and other informational materials that are religious in content.

[They] enjoy an exclusive right to establish enterprises to publish religious literature and produce religious articles.

23. Charitable and Cultural Enlightenment Activities of Religious Organisations

Societies, brotherhoods, . . . associations . . . may be set up by religious organisations for the purpose of charitable activities and to study and disseminate religious literature and for other cultural-enlightenment activity. They may have their own charters. . . .

Religious organisations have the right to engage in charitable and philanthropic activity. . . .

Donations and payments for this purpose are not . . . liable for taxation.

24. International Links and Contacts by Believers and Religious Organisations

Citizens and religious organisations have the right to establish . . . international links and direct personal contacts, including trips abroad for pilgrimage or participation in meetings and other religious events.

Religious organisations may send citizens abroad to study. . . .

* * *

VI. State Bodies and Religious Organisations

29. State Bodies for Religious Affairs

The USSR state body for religious affairs is an informational, consultative and expert centre. In this capacity it does the following:

- maintains contacts and co-ordinating ties with similar establishments in the union and autonomous republics and abroad;
- creates a data bank on religious organisations in the USSR . . . ;
- sets up an expert council of religious experts, representatives of religious organisations and experts on . . . human rights . . . to conduct . . . assessments and . . . provide an official expert conclusion with regard to requests from bodies of state management and the courts;
- at the request of religious organisations provides assistance in reaching agreements with state bodies and all necessary help in matters requiring a decision by state bodies;
- promotes . . . mutual understanding and tolerance between . . . different denominations within the country and abroad.

The USSR state body for religious affairs is formed by the USSR Council of Ministers.

State bodies for religious affairs are set up in the union and autonomous republics. . . .

Source: Religion in Communist Lands, Vol. XIX, No. 1 (1991), pp. 119–129. Russian text in *Pravda*, October 9, 1990.

SUGGESTIONS FOR BACKGROUND AND REFERENCE

M. Bourdeaux, *Gorbachev, Glasnost and the Gospel* (London, 1990), pp. 65–86.

G. Buss, *the Bear's Hug: Religious Belief and the Soviet State* (London, 1987).

G. Codevilla, "Commentary on the New Soviet Law on Freedom of Conscience and Religious Organisations," *Religion in Communist Lands*, Vol. XIX, No. 1 (1991), pp. 130–143.

J. H. Forest, *Religion in the New Russia: the Impact of Perestroika on the Varieties of Religious Life in the Soviet Union* (New York, 1990).

K. H. Hill, *The Puzzle of the Soviet Church: an Inside Look at Christianity and Glasnost* (Portland, Oreg., 1989), pp. 217–390.

P. Mojzes, *Religious Liberty in Eastern Europe and the USSR Before and After the Great Transformation* (Boulder, Colo., 1992), pp. 101–114.

N. C. Nielsen, *Revolutions in Eastern Europe. The Religious Roots* (Maryknoll, N.Y., 1991), pp. 128–148.

N. Petro (ed.), *Christianity and Russian Culture in Soviet Society* (Boulder, Colo., 1990).

G. Yakunin, "The Orthodox Church and Politics" [Interview with Gleb Yakunin], *Uncaptive Minds*, Vol. V, No. 2 (Summer 1992), pp. 33–37.

Selected Readings

The following list is a brief selection of works dealing with broad areas of modern religious history or the history of church-state relations. References to more specialized studies are provided at the end of each document.

G. Adriányi, *The Church in the Modern Age* (New York, 1981).

S. E. Ahlstrom, *A Religious History of the American People* (New Haven, 1972).

K. Aland, *A History of Christianity* (Philadelphia, 1985).

R. Aubert et al., *The Church between Revolution and Restoration* (New York, 1981).

_____, *The Church in the Age of Liberalism* (New York, 1981).

_____, *The Church in the Industrial Age* (New York, 1981).

Cambridge Modern History (New York, 1903–12).

S. C. Carpenter, *Church and People, 1789–1889* (London, 1933).

O. Chadwick, *The Christian Church in the Cold War* (London, 1992).

R. Corrigan, *The Church and the Nineteenth Century* (Milwaukee, 1938).

G. R. Cragg, *The Church and the Age of Reason, 1648–1789* (London, 1961).

T. J. Curry, *The First Freedoms. Church and State in America to the Passage of the First Amendment* (New York, 1986).

A. Dansette, *Religious History of Modern France* (London, 1961).

A. Debidour, *Histoire des rapports de l'église et de l'état en France de 1789 à 1870* (Paris, 1898).

A. L. Drummond, *German Protestantism since Luther* (London, 1951).

J. Ellis, *The Russian Orthodox Church* (Bloomington, Ind., 1986).

C. F. Garbett, *Church and State in England* (London, 1950).

E. S. Gaustad, *Faith of Our Fathers: Religion and the New Nation* (San Francisco, 1987).

F. H. Geffcken, *Church and State* (London, 1877).

E. B. Greene, *Religion and the State* (New York, 1941).

V. Gsovski (ed.), *Church and State behind the Iron Curtain* (New York, 1955).

E. E. Y. Hales, *The Catholic Church in the Modern World* (New York, 1958).

_____, *Pio Nono. A Study in European Politics and Religion in the Nineteenth Century* (New York, 1954).

W. S. Hudson, *The Great Tradition of the American Churches* (New York, 1953).

_____, *Religion in America* (New York, 1973).

A. W. Johnson and F. H. Yost, *Separation of Church and State in the United States* (Minneapolis, 1948).

P. Kurland, *Church and State: The Supreme Court and the First Amendment* (Chicago, 1975).

H. Laski, *Authority in the Modern State* (New Haven, 1919).

_____, *Studies in the Problem of Sovereignty* (New Haven, 1917).

K. S. Latourette, *Christianity in a Revolutionary Age* (New York, 1958–1962).

E. G. Leonard, *A History of Protestantism* (London, 1961).

J. McManners, *Church and State in France 1870–1914* (New York, 1972).

K. D. Macmillan, *Protestantism in Germany* (Princeton, 1917).

J. E. Mecham, *Church and State in Latin America: A History of Politico-Ecclesiastical Relations* (Chapel Hill, N.C., 1969).

J. S. Moir, *The Church in the British Era. From the British Conquest to Confederation* (Toronto, 1972).

W. Müller et al., *The Church in the Age of Absolutism and Enlightenment* (New York, 1981).

The New Cambridge Modern History (Cambridge, 1957–1970).

J. H. Nichols, *A History of Christianity, 1650–1950* (New York, 1956).

F. Nielsen, *The History of the Papacy in the Nineteenth Century* (London, 1906).

N. C. Nielsen, *Revolutions in Eastern Europe. The Religious Roots* (Maryknoll, N.Y., 1991).

E. R. Norman, *Church and Society in England, 1770–1970* (Oxford, 1976).

————, *Roman Catholicism in England: From the Elizabethan Settlement to the Second Vatican Council* (New York, 1986).

L. von Pastor, *The History of the Popes from the Close of the Middle Ages* (London, 1941–1953).

L. Pfeffer, *Church, State, and Freedom* (Boston, 1953).

————, *God, Caesar, and the Constitution* (Boston, 1975).

C. S. Phillips, *The Church in France, 1789–1848* (London, 1929).

————, *The Church in France, 1848–1907* (London, 1956).

J. Schmidlin, *Papstgeschichte der neuesten Zeit* (Munich, 1933–1936).

A. P. Stokes, *Church and State in the United States* (New York, 1950).

A. R. Vidler, *The Church in an Age of Revolution: 1789–Present* (London, 1962).

P. Walters (ed.), *World Christianity: Eastern Europe* (Eastbourne, England, 1988).

Lightning Source UK Ltd.
Milton Keynes UK
UKOW02n1403240816

281409UK00001B/21/P